MEANING, LIFE AND CULTURE
IN CONVERSATION WITH
ANNA WIERZBICKA

MEANING, LIFE AND CULTURE

IN CONVERSATION WITH ANNA WIERZBICKA

EDITED BY HELEN BROMHEAD AND ZHENGDAO YE

PRESS

Published by ANU Press
The Australian National University
Acton ACT 2601, Australia
Email: anupress@anu.edu.au

Available to download for free at press.anu.edu.au

ISBN (print): 9781760463922
ISBN (online): 9781760463939

WorldCat (print): 1225157761
WorldCat (online): 1224950342

DOI: 10.22459/MLC.2020

This title is published under a Creative Commons Attribution-NonCommercial-NoDerivatives 4.0 International (CC BY-NC-ND 4.0).

The full licence terms are available at
creativecommons.org/licenses/by-nc-nd/4.0/legalcode

Cover design and layout by ANU Press.
Cover artwork: *Conversation* (c. 1960) by Benode Behari Mukherjee. Photo © Tate.

This edition © 2020 ANU Press

Contents

Acknowledgements vii
List of abbreviations ix
Contributors xiii
Introduction 1
Zhengdao Ye and Helen Bromhead

Part I: Meaning, life and culture: The Natural Semantic Metalanguage approach. 11

1. Prototypes, polysemy and constructional semantics: The lexicogrammar of the English verb *climb* 13
   Cliff Goddard
2. The comparative semantics of verbs of 'opening': West Africa vs Oceania. 33
   Felix K. Ameka and Deborah Hill
3. *Gezellig*: A Dutch cultural keyword unpacked 61
   Bert Peeters
4. Royal semantics: Linguacultural reflections on the Danish address pronoun *De*. 85
   Carsten Levisen
5. The Singlish interjection *bojio* 99
   Jock Onn Wong
6. The semantics of *bushfire* in Australian English. 115
   Helen Bromhead
7. The semantics of *migrant* in Australian English 135
   Zhengdao Ye
8. The semantics of verbs of visual aesthetic appreciation in Russian. 155
   Anna Gladkova
9. Christian values embedded in the Italian language: A semantic analysis of *carità*. 173
   Gian Marco Farese

10. The semantics of two loanwords in Navarrese Spanish. 193
    Mónica Aznárez-Mauleón
11. Time in Portuguese *saudade* and other words of longing. 211
    Zuzanna Bułat Silva
12. Lost in translation: A semantic analysis of *no da* in Japanese 229
    Yuko Asano-Cavanagh

Part II: Meaning, life and culture: Perspectives 247

13. Locating 'mind' (and 'soul') cross-culturally 249
    Frances Morphy and Howard Morphy
14. Teknocentric kin terms in Australian languages. 273
    Harold Koch
15. Showing and not telling in a sign language 291
    John Haiman
16. Games that people play: Capitalism as a game 303
    Annabelle Mooney
17. Our ordinary lives: Pathways to a more human-oriented
    linguistics 319
    John Newman
18. On defining parts of speech with Generative Grammar
    and NSM 333
    Avery D. Andrews
19. Cut-verbs of the Oceanic language Teop: A critical study
    of collecting and analysing data in a language documentation
    project 355
    Ulrike Mosel
20. The depiction of sensing events in English and Kalam 381
    Andrew Pawley
21. Russian language-specific words in the light of parallel corpora . .403
    Alexei Shmelev
22. 'Sense of privacy' and 'sense of elbow': English vs Russian
    values and communicative styles 421
    Tatiana Larina
23. On the semantics of *cup* 441
    Keith Allan
24. Where we part from NSM: Understanding Warlpiri *yangka*
    and the Warlpiri expression of part-hood 461
    David Nash and David P. Wilkins

Envoi. 491
Anna Wierzbicka's life. 493
    Kevin Windle and Mary Besemeres
Index 501

Acknowledgements

We are indebted to all the reviewers, both of the individual chapters and the volume as a whole, for their valuable comments. We want to express our thanks to Beth Battrick for her meticulous and efficient copyediting. We also wish to thank Christine Huber and the rest of the Humanities and Creative Arts Board of ANU Press for their guidance, and Emily Tinker of ANU Press for managing the final production process.

The publication of the book is partially supported by an ANU Publication Subsidy grant. The ANU Emeritus Faculty has also partially supported the indexing of the volume with a grant.

List of abbreviations

ABC	Australian Broadcasting Corporation
ABS	Australian Bureau of Statistics
AIATSIS	Australian Institute of Aboriginal and Torres Strait Islander Studies
AND	*The Australian National Dictionary*
ANU	The Australian National University
ASL	American Sign Language
AWARE	Association of Women for Action and Research
BSL	British Sign Language
CAP	cumulative average point
CBOT	Chicago Board of Trade
DCT	Discourse-Completion Task
DS	direct speech
EA	Euro-American
ERP	event-related potential
FOMO	fear of missing out
IDP	internally displaced persons
IOM	International Organization for Migration
IS	indirect speech
LAAL	Living Archive of Aboriginal Languages
LFG	Lexical Functional Grammar
MIT	Massachusetts Institute of Technology
NP	noun phrase
NSM	Natural Semantic Metalanguage

NSW	New South Wales
NUS	National University of Singapore
OED	*Oxford English Dictionary*
OSV	object–subject–verb
PP	prepositional phrase
RNC	Russian National Corpus
SL	sign language
SOV	subject–object–verb
SVAdj	subject–verb–adjective
SV/AVO	subject–verb/transitive subject–subject–object
SVC	serial verb constructions
SVO	subject–verb–object
TAM	tense–aspect–mood
TESOL	Teaching English to Speakers of Other Languages
TG	Transformational Grammar
VP	verb phrase
VS/VOA	verb–subject/verb–object–transitive subject

Glossing abbreviations

1, 2, 3	First/second/third person
12	First person inclusive
4	Fourth person; used in non-topical object function instead of a third person pronoun when the subject of the clause is the topic and a third person
ACC	Accusative
ALL	Allative
ART	Article
AUX	Auxiliary
CL:ANIMAL	Animal classifier
CL:MAN	Man classifier
COMP, COMPL	Complementiser

LIST OF ABBREVIATIONS

CONSEC	Consecutive marker *re* indicating that the situation denoted by the verb complex directly follows the preceding situation
DAT	Dative
DEF	Definite
DIM	Diminutive
DL, DU	Dual
DS	Different subject from the next verb
ERG	Ergative
EVOC	Evocative
EX, EXCL	Exclusive
FUT	Future
GEN	Genitive
IMP	Imperative
IN, INCL	Inclusive
INF	Infinitive
IO	Indirect object
IPFV	Imperfective aspect marker inflecting for person and number
LNK	Linker: links prepositional attributes and adverbials to the head of NPs and VCs, respectively
LOC	Locative
NOMIC	Nomic
NONPAST, NPST	Non-past
OBJ	Object
OBJM	Object marker
PF	Perfective (today's past or present habitual)
PL	Plural
PLM	Plural marker
POSS	Possessive marker inflecting for person and number and linking possessor pronouns or NPs to the possessed noun in inalienable constructions
PRED	Predicate marker

PREP	Preposition; specifically, the multipurpose preposition *te*
PRES, PRS	Present
PRIOR	Prior to the next verb
PROG	Present progressive
PRON	Pronoun
PST	Past
Q	Question particle/marker
RDP	Reduplicative
RED	Reduplication
REFL	Reflexive
REL	Relative pronoun, not inflecting, but syntactically holding the position of a topical NP
RP	Recent past
SBJ, SUB	Subject
SG	Singular
SIM	Simultaneous with the next verb
SS	Same subject as the next verb
TAM	Tense/aspect/mood marker
TOP	Topic
TRS	Transitive

Contributors

Keith Allan (MLitt, PhD (Edinburgh)) FAHA, Emeritus Professor, Monash University and Honorary Associate Professor at University of Queensland. Selected books: *Linguistic Meaning* (Routledge, 1986; 2014); *Euphemism and Dysphemism: Language Used as Shield and Weapon* (with Kate Burridge, Oxford University Press, 1991); *Natural Language Semantics* (Blackwell, 2001); *Forbidden Words: Taboo and the Censoring of Language* (with Kate Burridge, Cambridge University Press, 2006); *Concise Encyclopaedia of Semantics* (Elsevier, 2009); *The Western Classical Tradition in Linguistics Second Expanded Edition* (Equinox, 2010); *Cambridge Handbook of Pragmatics* (with Kasia Jaszczolt, Cambridge University Press, 2012); *Oxford Handbook of the History of Linguistics* (Oxford University Press, 2013); *Routledge Handbook of Linguistics* (Routledge, 2016) and *Oxford Handbook of Taboo Words and Language* (Oxford University Press, 2018).

Felix K. Ameka (PhD, The Australian National University (ANU) 1991), FGA FAHA, works at the Leiden University Centre for Linguistics and was an Associate Researcher, Language and Cognition Group, Max Planck Institute for Psycholinguistics, Nijmegen. His interests are language documentation and description, cross-cultural semantics, pragmatics, and the sociocultural and cognitive motivations of grammar, anthropological and contact linguistics. He has conducted field-based research and published on these topics on West African languages like Ewe Akan and Likpe.

Avery D. Andrews received his PhD in linguistics from Massachusetts Institute of Technology (MIT) in 1975, and began working in 1976 as a Lecturer at ANU, writing on topics including case-marking and grammatical relations, relative clauses, complex predicates and, more recently, the syntax–semantics interface and the possible relations between Natural Semantic Metalanguage (NSM) and Formal Semantics. Although officially retired in 2014, he remains active in the field.

Yuko Asano-Cavanagh is a Senior Lecturer at Curtin University, Perth. Her research focuses on the semantics and pragmatics of Japanese. She is the author of several semantic analyses of Japanese cultural keywords using the NSM approach. Her most recent publications include '*Inochi* and *tamashii*: Incursion into Japanese ethnopsychology' (2019), and 'In staunch pursuit: Revealing the semantics of the Japanese terms *shūkatsu* "job-hunting" and *konkatsu* "marriage partner hunting"' (2019).

Mónica Aznárez-Mauleón is a Lecturer at the Public University of Navarre in Spain. She holds a PhD in Spanish linguistics, specialising in Spanish phraseology. Her research interests include language teaching at the primary and secondary levels as well as Spanish semantics and pragmatics. In previous works, she has applied the NSM approach to the study of Spanish sincerity expressions and of a number of routine formulae.

Mary Besemeres is the author of *Translating One's Self: Language and Selfhood in Cross-Cultural Autobiography* (Peter Lang, 2002) and refereed articles and book chapters on translingual and cross-cultural autobiography. With Anna Wierzbicka, she co-edited *Translating Lives: Living with Two Languages and Cultures* (University of Queensland Press, 2007). She was founding co-editor, with Maureen Perkins, of the Routledge journal *Life Writing*, and now serves on its editorial board. An Honorary Lecturer in the ANU School of Literature, Languages and Linguistics, Mary is one of Anna Wierzbicka's two daughters.

Helen Bromhead is a Postdoctoral Research Fellow in the Griffith Centre for Social and Cultural Research, looking at discourse around climate and extreme weather in Australian English. She is also an Honorary Lecturer in School of Literature, Languages and Linguistics, ANU. She is the author of *Landscape and Culture – Cross-linguistic perspectives* (John Benjamins, 2018) and *The Reign of Truth and Faith: Epistemic Expressions in 16th and 17th Century English* (Mouton de Gruyter, 2009).

Zuzanna Bułat Silva works at the University of Wrocław, Poland. Her main research interests are lexical semantics, cross-cultural pragmatics and endangered languages. She published a book on Portuguese cultural key words (2008, in Polish), and several articles on emotion words in Spanish and Portuguese. Her current research project is on 'place concepts' in

Portuguese. She is a founding member of the Scales of Home in Today's Europe Group, and a member of the CLCM (Cognition, Language and Multimodal Communication) Group at the NOVA University in Lisbon.

Gian Marco Farese is a Research Associate in linguistics at Chapman University and an Honorary Lecturer in the School of Literature, Languages and Linguistics at ANU. His research interests include the relationship between language, culture and cognition, cultural semantics, cross-linguistic semantics, linguistic anthropology, translation studies, cross-cultural communication, Italian, English and Japanese linguistics. He is the author of *The Cultural Semantics of Address Practices* (Lexington Books, 2018), *Italian Discourse* (Lexington Books, 2019) and of various papers on the interface between linguistics and other social sciences, including psychology, law, musicology and economics.

Anna Gladkova is an Adjunct Lecturer in English as an International Language at Monash University and an Honorary Lecturer in linguistics at ANU. Her research interests include semantics, pragmatics, language and culture interface, and NSM. She has taught linguistics and applied linguistics at ANU, Monash University, University of New England, University of Sussex, University of Brighton and Nizhny Novgorod State Linguistic University.

Cliff Goddard is Professor in linguistics at Griffith University and a Fellow of the Australian Academy of the Humanities. A leading practitioner of the NSM approach, he is one of Anna Wierzbicka's closest collaborators and research partners. His recent books are books are *Ten Lectures on Natural Semantic Metalanguage: Exploring Language, Thought and Culture using Simple, Translatable Words* (Brill, 2018), and the edited collection *Minimal English For a Global World: Improved Communication Using Fewer Words* (Palgrave, 2018).

John Haiman's first academic position was in the linguistics department at ANU from 1971 to 1975. During this time, he engaged in fieldwork in New Guinea, and learned about semantic primitives from Anna Wierzbicka.

Deborah Hill (PhD ANU 1992) works at the University of Canberra and is a member of the Centre for Sustainable Communities. She teaches in the TESOL (Teaching English to Speakers of Other Languages) program in the Faculty of Education. Her research interests include language documentation and description, cultural semantics, Oceanic linguistics and language and development in the Pacific. Her primary linguistic fieldwork has been with the Longgu community of north-east Guadalcanal, Solomon Islands.

Harold Koch is an Honorary Senior Lecturer in the School of Literature, Language and Linguistics, ANU, where he has long been employed in the research and teaching of linguistics. His main interests are in Australian Indigenous languages, morphology and historical linguistics, including etymology.

Tatiana Larina is full professor at RUDN University, Moscow, as well as the editor-in-chief of the *Russian Journal of Linguistics*. Her research interests embrace language, culture and communication, cross-cultural pragmatics, intercultural communication, communicative ethnostyles and (im)politeness theory with the focus on English and Russian languages. She has authored and co-authored over 200 publications in Russian and English including monographs, course books and book chapters as well as numerous articles.

Carsten Levisen is an Associate Professor at Roskilde University, Denmark, and a member of the Young Academy of the Royal Danish Academy of Sciences and Letters. His research interests are in semantics, pragmatics and linguistic anthropology. His publications include *Cultural Semantics and Social Cognition* (De Gruyter, 2012), *Creole Studies* (ed. with Peter Bakker, Finn Borchsenius and Eeva Sippola; John Benjamins, 2017), and *Cultural Keywords in Discourse* (ed. with Sophia Waters; John Benjamins, 2017).

Annabelle Mooney is Professor of Language and Society at the University of Roehampton. Her most recent work deals with the language of money.

Frances Morphy is Honorary Associate Professor at the Centre for Aboriginal Economic Policy Research, ANU. An anthropologist and linguist (MA, ANU 1977), she counts herself fortunate to have been taught semantics by Anna Wierzbicka. Her first major publication (in 1983) was a grammar of Djapu, a Yolngu Matha dialect.

Howard Morphy is Emeritus Professor at the Research School of Humanities and the Arts, ANU, and heads the ANU Centre for Digital Humanities Research. He has worked with Yolngu people since the early 1970s and is the author of numerous publications on the anthropology of art and of religion, including *Becoming Art: Exploring Cross-Cultural Categories* (Bloomsbury, 2007).

Ulrike Mosel is Professor Emerita of general linguistics at the University of Kiel, Germany, and has worked on Arabic and the Oceanic languages Tolai, Samoan and Teop. Her publications include *Tolai Syntax and its Historical Development* (Pacific Linguistics, 1984), *Samoan Reference Grammar* (together with Even Hovhaugen; Scandinavian University Press, 1992), and the corpus-based, digital *Multifunctional Teop-English Dictionary* (2019, dictionaria.clld.org/contributions/teop). The present research focuses on corpus-based digital lexicography and grammaticography of under-researched languages.

David Nash studied linguistics at ANU then MIT (1980 PhD *Topics in Warlpiri grammar*). He has published on Australian languages over the last four decades, including co-editing *Forty Years On: Ken Hale and Australian Languages* (Pacific Linguistics, 2001) and *Language in Native Title* (Aboriginal Studies Press, 2002). He has an honorary appointment in linguistics, School of Literature, Languages and Linguistics, ANU.

John Newman is Professor Emeritus in the Department of Linguistics at the University of Alberta, and an adjunct research fellow in the School of Languages, Literatures, Cultures and Linguistics at Monash University. His research interests include cognitive linguistics, corpus linguistics and quantitative methods in linguistics, and he has published research on Germanic, Sinitic, Austronesian and Papuan languages. He was formerly Editor-in-Chief of the journal *Cognitive Linguistics*.

Andrew Pawley is Emeritus Professor in the School of Culture, History and Language, ANU. His research interests include Austronesian and Papuan languages and cultures, the prehistory of Pacific Island peoples, folk taxonomies and ethnobiology, lexicography, phraseology and idiomaticity. He is compiler of a dictionary of Kalam (Papuan New Guinea) and author of numerous other publications.

Bert Peeters is an Honorary Associate Professor at ANU and a 'Guest Professor' at the University of Antwerp. He previously held appointments at the University of Tasmania (1989–2006) and Macquarie University, Sydney (2007–13), and is the (co-)editor of 10 books and journal issues, more than 70 book chapters and journal articles, and close to 100 reviews and review articles. His research interests are in French linguistics, intercultural communication, and language and cultural values.

Alexei Shmelev is the Head of the Department of Linguistic Standards of Russian at the Russian Language Institute of the Russian Academy of Sciences and a Professor of Russian linguistics at Moscow Pedagogical State University. His work spans a number of disciplines including cultural studies and linguistics. He is the author of numerous books, most recently, *Russkaja aspektologija: v zashchitu vidovoj pary* [*Russian Aspectology: In Defense of the Aspectual Pair*] (co-authored with Anna Zalizniak and Irina Mikaelian, 2015).

David P. Wilkins, PhD. David is an anthropological linguist whose main interest is the human capacity for meaning-making, no matter what the modalities may be. He is currently a Research Fellow in linguistics in the ARC Centre of Excellence for the Dynamics of Language at ANU (via the School of Literature, Languages and Linguistics).

Kevin Windle is an Emeritus Fellow at ANU. His publications include a biography of Alexander Zuzenko (Australian Scholarly Publishing, 2012), the *Oxford Handbook of Translation Studies* (Oxford University Press, 2011), and numerous articles on Russian themes. Awards for his translations from various languages include the Fédération Internationale des Traducteurs Aurora Borealis prize.

Jock Onn Wong is a Lecturer in the Centre for English Language Communication, National University of Singapore. His research interests include semantics, pragmatics, intercultural communication and English-language teaching. He subscribes to the NSM school and has published a number of papers on Singlish, English, Mandarin and Cantonese using that approach. He considers himself fortunate to be bicultural because it puts him in a better position to understand ethnocentrism and intercultural communication.

Zhengdao Ye completed her Master's and PhD theses under Anna Wierzbicka's supervision. Her research interests encompass semantics, pragmatics, Chinese linguistics, language of emotion, and translatability. She is the editor of the book *The Semantics of Nouns* (Oxford University Press, 2017) and the co-editor of *'Happiness' and 'Pain' across Languages and Cultures* (with Cliff Goddard; John Benjamins, 2016). Zhengdao is currently a Senior Lecturer at the School of Literature, Languages and Linguistics, ANU.

Introduction

Zhengdao Ye and Helen Bromhead

This collective volume is dedicated to Anna Wierzbicka, one of the most influential and innovative linguists of her generation, and one of the most prolific scholars in humanities and social sciences.[1] Throughout her six-decade career, Anna has pursued a meaning-based approach to linguistics. Building on Leibniz's idea of 'the alphabet of human thoughts', she has identified basic shared human concepts and words (see Table A1, Semantic primes, in Appendix). This research has formed the foundations of the internationally recognised Natural Semantic Metalanguage (NSM) approach to meaning—a versatile tool for exploring 'big questions' concerning the diversity and universals of people's experience in the world. Her work spans a number of disciplines, including anthropology, psychology, cognitive science, philosophy and religious studies, as well as her home base of linguistics. This research has inspired generations of scholars to explore the nexus between language, culture and cognition.

In this volume, Anna Wierzbicka's former students, old and current colleagues and 'kindred spirits' engage with her ideas. They continue their engagement (including argument) with diverse aspects of Wierzbicka's work, from ethnosyntax to cross-cultural pragmatics, and from social categories to reported speech. The deep humanistic perspective, wide-ranking themes and interdisciplinary nature of Wierzbicka's research are fully reflected in the contributions.

---

1   As of April 2019, Google Scholar tells us that Wierzbicka has 35,182 citations, and that her h-index is 76 and her i10-index 260. Anna Wierzbicka is a Fellow of the Australian Academy of Humanities and a Fellow of the Australian Academy of Social Sciences. She is also a Fellow of the Russian Academy of Sciences, and a Fellow of the Polish Academy of Arts and Sciences.

The volume is divided into two parts. Part I focuses on the NSM approach. The contributors are either Anna Wierzbicka's former PhD students, grand-students or those that have been mentored by Anna. They are currently working in universities across Australia, Europe and Asia.

The first two chapters of Part I focus on lexicogrammatical meaning: in Chapter 1, Cliff Goddard illustrates NSM's approach to verb semantics by offering a detailed case analysis of the English verb *climb*; in Chapter 2, Felix Ameka and Deborah Hill compare the meanings of verbs describing 'opening' events in two languages—Ewe, a Kwa language of Western Africa, and Longgu, an Oceanic language of Solomon Islands. The next three chapters illustrate the enduring interests of NSM scholars in cultural keywords and cross-cultural pragmatics. Bert Peeters unpacks the meaning of the Dutch cultural keyword *gezellig*, roughly translated as 'convivial, cosy, fun' (Chapter 3); Carsten Levisen takes on 'royal semantics' by offering an original analysis of 'the Danish *De*' (Chapter 4). His analysis shows how the NSM approach offers a tool for high-resolution semantic and discursive analysis of address terms and for understanding 'relational grammars'; and in Chapter 5, Jock Wong extends his work on cultural keywords in the colloquial variety of Singaporean English (commonly known as Singlish) to a new expression that has become popular among young Singaporean, the interjection *bojio* (literally meaning 'why am I not invited'). Chapters 6 and 7 are both concerned with the semantics of nouns in Australian English: while Helen Bromhead focuses on extreme weather and climate event words, in particular, *bushfire*, Zhengdao Ye undertakes a detailed, corpus-assisted analysis of the distinctive meaning of *migrant* in Australian English. Both of these chapters adopt a corpus-assisted approach to meaning analysis. Chapter 8 by Anna Gladkova investigates the meanings of two Russian verbs expressing visual aesthetic appreciation—*nagljadet'sja* 'to look at someone/something to complete satisfaction/feast one's eyes on' and *ljubovat'sja*, as a means to explore the Russian folk conceptions of aesthetics. The ensuing trio of chapters all concern Romance languages: in Chapter 9, Gian Marco Farese presents a semantic analysis of the Italian *carità*, roughly translated as 'charity/act of love', arguing for the influence of Christian values on Italian language and culture; in Chapter 10, Mónica Aznárez-Mauleón focuses on the semantics of two loanwords in Navarrese Spanish, the noun *chirrinta* and the verb *ciriquiar*, which possibly have their roots in the Basque language and which are specific to the Spanish variety spoken in Navarre and generally not included in dictionaries of the Spanish language; in Chapter 11, Zuzanna

Bułat Silva investigates how the category of TIME relates to the domain of emotion by exploring the meaning of the Portuguese culture-specific *saudade*, a rough equivalent of English longing, and comparing it with the meanings of their counterparts in Spanish, Polish and Chinese. In the final Chapter of Part I (Chapter 12), Yuko Asano-Cavanagh re-evaluates previous studies of the Japanese discourse particle *no da*, and offers new analysis to capture its meanings, which are often thought to be too elusive to pin down. Together with Jock Wong's chapter on Singlish interjection, it not only attests to NSM researchers' interest in lesser-studied word classes, but also demonstrates the effectiveness of NSM in elucidating the meanings of particles.

Anna Wierzbicka's contributions to scholarship are also appreciated by those who work with diverse frameworks. Part II contains chapters by some of Wierzbicka's former and present colleagues at The Australian National University, and selected scholars who have engaged (and argued) with Anna's work continuously. The contributors explore diverse topics relating to meaning, life and culture, and directly connect with her work from their own intellectual perspectives. These perspectives include anthropological linguistics, syntax, cognitive linguistics, sociolinguistics, intercultural pragmatics and translation studies, as well as other approaches to semantics.

Part II opens with two chapters on Australian Indigenous languages. They engage with Wierzbicka's work on personhood constructs, such as 'mind', and on kinship, respectively: while Frances Morphy and Howard Morphy's chapter (Chapter 13) focuses on personhood terms in Yolngu Matha, Harold Koch, in Chapter 14, examines a largely unnoticed aspect of kinship terminology consistently appearing in widely separated regions of Indigenous Australia. In Chapter 15, John Haiman uses Wierzbicka's work on direct and indirect speech as a springboard for a discussion of the iconicity of eye contact in sign languages. In Chapter 16, Annabelle Mooney examines semantic accounts of 'game' by comparing some of its uses in representations and discussions of economic and financial activity with Wierzbicka's account of games. While pointing out the commonalities of Cognitive Linguistics and the NSM approach in their humanistic endeavour, John Newman, in Chapter 17, further argues for the individual to be more visible in linguistic analysis. In Chapter 18, Avery Andrews proposes NSM-based definitions of parts of speech (specifically, nouns, verbs and adjectives), and discusses their advantages and problems encountered. Both Chapters 19 and 20 are concerned with verb semantics: Ulrike Mosel's chapter deals with CUT-verbs of the Oceanic language Teop, spoken in Papua New Guinea's Bougainville, treating it to a critical study of collecting and analysing study of a language documentation project; Andrew Pawley's chapter compares the way sensing events are depicted in English and in Kalam, a language of the Trans New Guinea family. The next two chapters engage with Anna's work on meaning, culture and intercultural communication in Russian. In Chapter 21, Alexei Shmelev investigates language-specific words in Russian by using parallel corpora. Tatiana Larina's chapter in Chapter 22 demonstrates how the values of a culture and its communicative styles are closely related, by contrasting the idea of 'sense of privacy' reflected in English and that of 'sense of elbow' reflected in Russian.

In the Acknowledgements of her book *Imprisoned in English: The Hazards of English as a Default Language*, Wierzbicka writes:

> I am also indebted to some more distant interlocutors who over the years have engaged in controversy with me and thus pushed and provoked me to sharpen my ideas and arguments ... We do need intellectual friends, but we also need our opponents, detractors, and bêtes noires. They can all fuel the fire of what philosopher Peter Goldie (editor of the Oxford Handbook on Philosophy of Emotions) calls 'affect in intellectual activity', and consequently increase our passion and motivation. (Wierzbicka 2014: ix–x)

The final two chapters engage with Wierzbicka's work in that 'controversial' spirit which she values. In Chapter 23, the semanticist Keith Allan offers a detailed critique of her (1984) semantics for *cup*; and in Chapter 24, two anthropological linguists David Nash and David Wilkins critically respond to Wierzbicka and Goddard's (2018) paper on 'Talking about our bodies and their parts in Warlpiri'.

The topics of the volume are indeed diverse, from linguistics and anthropology to psychology. So are the languages covered. The common thread running through all the chapters in the volume is the primacy of meaning to the understanding of language and culture, and the diversity and universality in language and culture, the underlying themes that have informed Wierzbicka's lifelong work. Her productivity is astonishing. Rather than offering a full list of her 400 or so publications, we list below a selection of the work that the contributors to this volume discuss.

Selection of Wierzbicka texts discussed

Goddard, Cliff and Anna Wierzbicka (eds) (1994). *Semantic and Lexical Universals: Theory and Empirical Findings.* Amsterdam: John Benjamins.

Goddard, Cliff and Anna Wierzbicka (eds) (2002). *Meaning and Universal Grammar: Theory and Empirical Findings* (2 vol.). Amsterdam: John Benjamins.

Goddard, Cliff and Anna Wierzbicka (2009). Contrastive semantics of physical activity verbs: 'Cutting' and 'chopping' in English, Polish, and Japanese. *Language Sciences* 31: 60–96. doi.org/10.1016/j.langsci.2007.10.002.

Goddard, Cliff and Anna Wierzbicka (2014a). *Words and Meanings: Lexical Semantics Across Domains, Languages and Cultures.* Oxford: Oxford University Press. doi.org/10.1093/acprof:oso/9780199668434.001.0001.

Goddard, Cliff and Anna Wierzbicka (2014b). Semantic fieldwork and lexical universals. *Studies in Language* 38 (1): 80–126. doi.org/10.1075/sl.38.1.03god.

Goddard, Cliff and Anna Wierzbicka (2016). Explicating the English lexicon of 'doing and happening'. *Functions of Language* 23 (2): 214–56. doi.org/10.1075/fol.23.2.03god.

Goddard, Cliff, Anna Wierzbicka and Jock Wong (2016). 'Walking' and 'running' in English and German: The conceptual semantics of verbs of human locomotion. *Review of Cognitive Linguistics* 14 (2): 303–36. doi.org/10.1075/rcl.14.2.03god.

Wierzbicka, Anna (1972). *Semantic Primitives.* Frankfurt: Athenäum.

Wierzbicka, Anna (1974). The semantics of direct and indirect discourse. *Paper in Linguistics* 7 (3): 267–307. doi.org/10.1080/08351817409370375.

Wierzbicka, Anna (1979). Ethno-syntax and the philosophy of grammar. *Studies in Language* 3 (3): 313–83. doi.org/10.1075/sl.3.3.03wie.

Wierzbicka, Anna (1980). *Lingua Mentalis: The Semantics of Natural Language.* Sydney: Academic Press.

Wierzbicka, Anna (1982). Why can you *have a drink* when you can't **have an eat*? *Language* 58 (4): 753–99. doi.org/10.2307/413956.

Wierzbicka, Anna (1984). Cups and mugs: Lexicography and conceptual analysis. *Australian Journal of Linguistics* 4: 257–81. doi.org/10.1080/07268608408599326.

Wierzbicka, Anna (1985a). *Lexicography and Conceptual Analysis*. Ann Arbor: Karoma.

Wierzbicka, Anna (1985b). Different cultures, different languages, different speech acts: Polish vs. English. *Journal of Pragmatics* 9 (2–3): 145–78. doi.org/10.1016/0378-2166(85)90023-2.

Wierzbicka, Anna (1986). What's in a noun? (Or: How do nouns differ in meaning from adjectives?). *Studies in Language* 10 (2): 353–89. doi.org/10.1075/sl.10.2.05wie.

Wierzbicka, Anna (1988). *The Semantics of Grammar*. Amsterdam: John Benjamins.

Wierzbicka, Anna (1989a). Soul and mind: Linguistic evidence for ethnopsychology and cultural history. *American Anthropologist* 91 (1): 41–58. doi.org/10.1525/aa.1989.91.1.02a00030.

Wierzbicka, Anna (1989b). Baudouin de Courtenay and the theory of linguistic relativity. In Janusz Rieger, Mieczyslaw Szymczak and Stanislaw Urbanczyk (eds), *Jan Niecisław Baudouin de Courtenay a lingwistyka światowa*. Ossolineum: Wroclaw, 51–58.

Wierzbicka, Anna (1990). The semantics of color terms: Semantics, culture, and cognition. *Cognitive Linguistics* 1: 99–150. doi.org/10.1515/cogl.1990.1.1.99.

Wierzbicka, Anna (1991). *Cross-Cultural Pragmatics: The Semantics of Human Interaction*. Berlin: Mouton de Gruyter.

Wierzbicka, Anna (1992a). *Semantics, Culture, and Cognition: Universal Human Concepts in Culture-Specific Configurations*. New York: Oxford University Press.

Wierzbicka, Anna (1992b). Defining emotion concepts. *Cognitive Science* 16 (4): 539–81.

Wierzbicka, Anna (1992c). Personal names and expressive derivation. In *Semantics, Culture, and Cognition: Universal Human Concepts in Culture-Specific Configurations*. New York: Oxford University Press, 225–307.

Wierzbicka, Anna (1992d). Semantic primitives and semantic fields. In Eva Kittay and Adrienne Lehrer (eds), *Frames, Fields, and Contrasts*. Norwood, NJ: Lawrence Erlbaum, 209–27.

Wierzbicka, Anna (1992e). The semantics of interjection. *Journal of Pragmatics* 18 (2–3): 159–92.

Wierzbicka, Anna (1995). Everyday conceptions of emotion: A semantic perspective. In James A. Russell, José-Miguel Fernández-Dols, Antony S.R. Manstead and J.C. Wellenkamp (eds), *Everyday Conceptions of Emotion. An Introduction to the Psychology, Anthropology, and Linguistics of Emotion*. Dordrecht: Kluwer Academic Publishers, 17–47. doi.org/10.1007/978-94-015-8484-5_2.

Wierzbicka, Anna (1996). *Semantics: Primes and Universals*. Oxford: Oxford University Press.

Wierzbicka, Anna (1997). *Understanding Cultures through their Key Words: English, Russian, Polish, German, and Japanese*. New York: Oxford University Press.

Wierzbicka, Anna (1999a). *Emotions across Languages and Cultures: Diversity and Universals*. Cambridge: Cambridge University Press. doi.org/10.1017/cbo9780511521256.

Wierzbicka, Anna (1999b). *Semanticheskiye universalii I opisaniye yazykov* [*Semantic Universals and Description of Languages*]. Translated from English by A. Shmelev. Moscow: Yazyki russskoi kul'tury [in Russian].

Wierzbicka, Anna (2002a). Russian cultural scripts: The theory of cultural scripts and its applications. *Ethos* 30 (4): 401–32. doi.org/10.1525/eth.2002.30.4.401.

Wierzbicka, Anna (2002b). Russkie kul'turnye skripty i ix otraženie v jazyke [Russian cultural scripts and their reflection in language]. *Russkij Jazyk v Naučnom Osveščenii* [*Russian Language and Linguistic Theory*] 2 (4): 6–34.

Wierzbicka, Anna (2002c). Australian cultural scripts—*bloody* revisited. *Journal of Pragmatics* 34 (9): 1167–209. doi.org/10.1016/s0378-2166(01)00023-6.

Wierzbicka, Anna (2003a [1991]). *Cross-Cultural Pragmatics: The Semantics of Human Interaction* (2nd edn). Berlin: Mouton de Gruyter.

Wierzbicka, Anna (2003b). Singapore English: A semantic and cultural perspective. *Multilingua* 22: 327–66. doi.org/10.1515/mult.2003.018.

Wierzbicka, Anna (2006a). *English: Meaning and Culture*. New York: Oxford University Press.

Wierzbicka, Anna (2006b). Anglo scripts against 'putting pressure' on other people and their linguistic manifestations. In Cliff Goddard (ed.), *Ethnopragmatics: Understanding Discourse in Cultural Context*. Berlin: Mouton de Gruyter, 31–63. doi.org/10.1515/9783110911114.31.

Wierzbicka, Anna (2006c). Preface. In Bert Peeters (ed.) *Semantic Primes and Universal Grammar: Empirical Evidence from Romance Languages*. Amsterdam: John Benjamins, 1–6. doi.org/10.1075/slcs.81.05wie.

Wierzbicka, Anna (2006d). A conceptual basis for intercultural pragmatics and world-wide understanding. Paper presented at The 31st International LAUD Symposium, Landau, Germany.

Wierzbicka, Anna (2008). Why there are no 'colour universals' in language and thought. *Journal of the Royal Anthropological Institute* 14 (2): 407–25. doi.org/10.1111/j.1467-9655.2008.00509.x.

Wierzbicka, Anna (2009). Language and metalanguage: Key issues in emotion research. *Emotion Review* 1 (1): 3–14. doi.org/10.1177/1754073908097175.

Wierzbicka, Anna (2010). *Experience, Evidence, and Sense: The Hidden Cultural Legacy of English*. New York: Oxford University Press. doi.org/10.1093/acprof:oso/9780195368000.001.0001.

Wierzbicka, Anna (2013). Kinship and social cognition in Australian languages: Kayardild and Pitjantjatjara. Special Issue, 'Semantics and/in social cognition'. *Australian Journal of Linguistics* 33 (3): 302–21. doi.org/10.1080/07268602.2013.846458.

Wierzbicka, Anna (2014). *Imprisoned in English: The Hazards of English as a Default Language*. New York: Oxford University Press.

Wierzbicka, Anna (2015). A whole cloud of culture condensed into a drop of semantics: The meaning of the German word 'Herr' as a term of address. *International Journal of Language and Culture* 2 (1). 1–37. doi.org/10.1075/ijolc.2.1.01wie.

Wierzbicka, Anna (2016a). Making sense of terms of address in European languages through the natural semantic metalanguage (NSM). *Intercultural Pragmatics* 13 (4): 499–527

Wierzbicka, Anna (2016b). Terms of address in European languages: A study in cross-linguistic semantics and pragmatics. In Keith Allan, Alessandro Capone, Istvan Kecskes and Jacob Mey (eds), *Pragmemes and Theories of Language Use*. Springer, 209–38. doi.org/10.1007/978-3-319-43491-9_12.

Wierzbicka, Anna (2016c). Terms of address as keys to culture and society: German *Herr* vs. Polish *Pan*. *Acta Philologica* 49: 29–44.

Wierzbicka, Anna (2016d). Two levels of verbal communication, universal and culture-specific. In Andrea Rocci and Louis de Saussure (eds), *Verbal Communication*. Berlin: De Gruyter Mouton, 447–81. doi.org/10.1515/9783110255478-024.

Wierzbicka, Anna (2017). The meaning of kinship terms: A developmental and cross linguistic perspective. In Zhengdao Ye (ed.), *The Semantics of Nouns*. Oxford: Oxford University Press, 19–62.

Wierzbicka, Anna (2019). *What Christians Believe: The Story of God and People*. New York: Oxford University Press.

Appendix

Table A1. Semantic primes (English exponents).

I, YOU, SOMEONE, SOMETHING~THING, PEOPLE, BODY	substantives
KINDS, PARTS	relational substantives
THIS, THE SAME, OTHER~ELSE	determiners
ONE, TWO, SOME, ALL, MUCH~MANY, LITTLE~FEW	quantifiers
GOOD, BAD	evaluators
BIG, SMALL	descriptors
KNOW, THINK, WANT, DON'T WANT, FEEL, SEE, HEAR	mental predicates
SAY, WORDS, TRUE	speech
DO, HAPPEN, MOVE	actions, events, movement
BE (SOMEWHERE), THERE IS, BE (SOMEONE/SOMETHING)	location, existence, specification
(IS) MINE	possession
LIVE, DIE	life and death
WHEN~TIME, NOW, BEFORE, AFTER, A LONG TIME, A SHORT TIME, FOR SOME TIME, MOMENT	time
WHERE~PLACE, HERE, ABOVE, BELOW, FAR, NEAR, SIDE, INSIDE, TOUCH	place
NOT, MAYBE, CAN, BECAUSE, IF	logical concepts
VERY, MORE	augmentor, intensifier
LIKE	similarity

Notes: Exponents of primes can be polysemous; that is, they can have other, additional meanings.
Exponents of primes may be words, bound morphemes, or phrasemes.
They can be formally, that is, morphologically, complex.
They can have combinatorial variants or allolexes (indicated with ~).
Each prime has well-specified syntactic (combinatorial) properties.
Source: Goddard and Wierzbicka (2014a).

PART I

Meaning, life and culture:
The Natural Semantic
Metalanguage approach

1

Prototypes, polysemy and constructional semantics: The lexicogrammar of the English verb *climb*

Cliff Goddard

1. Anna Wierzbicka on prototypes, polysemy and constructional semantics

Three themes in the work of Anna Wierzbicka inform the present study and the predecessor work upon which it rests. The first is her long-term engagement with prototypes in semantics. Rejecting the conventional dichotomy between prototypes and semantic invariants, she has long insisted that a prototype can be 'part of the semantic invariant itself' (Wierzbicka 1996: 167).

Second, Wierzbicka has always recognised that lexical polysemy is normal, indeed ubiquitous, in everyday language and that it is impossible to reach valid generalisations about words, meaning and grammar without taking polysemy seriously. This means not only adopting a rigorous methodology whereby one can reliably distinguish genuine polysemy from generality or vagueness of meaning, but being prepared to put in weeks or months of painstaking effort to disentangle complex polysemic networks of intertwined lexical, phraseological and grammatical meanings.

Third, far from being narrowly focused on lexical meaning, Wierzbicka was one of the pioneers of what is now discussed under rubrics such as constructional semantics and lexicogrammar. In her seminal 1982 article 'Why can you *have a drink* when you can't **have an eat*?' in the journal *Language*, she proposed a set of interrelated semantic schemas for 'have a VP [verb phrase]' constructions. Although the slots in these schemas were filled by items from specific semantic–lexical subclasses, each schema as a whole expressed a larger meaning that was not a simple compositional function of its individual parts.

Thirty years ago, in *The Semantics of Grammar* (1988), she wrote:

> There is no such thing as 'grammatical meaning' or 'lexical meaning'. There are only grammatical and lexical MEANS of conveying meaning—and even here no sharp line can be drawn between them. (Wierzbicka 1988: 8)

Underpinning Wierzbicka's decades of semantic description and theoretical innovation, one goal has remained constant: the 'sustained effort to establish, and verify, the basic stock of human concepts—universal semantic primitives—out of which thoughts and complex concepts are constructed' (1996: 169). Though valuable in themselves, the hundreds of empirical studies conducted in the Natural Semantic Metalanguage (NSM) approach collectively bear on this overarching task. In 2020, NSM researchers believe that this task has essentially been accomplished.[1]

In past decade or so, there has been intensive NSM research on physical activity verbs (Sibly 2010; Ye 2010; Goddard 2012; Goddard and Wierzbicka 2016; Goddard, Wierzbicka and Wong 2016; Goddard 2018: Ch 5). In the present study, I draw on this body of work to explore the semantics and lexicogrammar of a single English verb: *climb*.

2. The puzzle of English '*climb*'

Charles Fillmore (1982) influentially used English *climb* as an example of a verb whose meaning could not be described using a set of necessary and sufficient conditions. According to Fillmore, *climb* normally or

---

[1] Goddard (2018: Ch 3) gives a brief history of the NSM approach. Though certain aspects of the metalanguage syntax remain to be worked out fully, the last amendment to the inventory of primes itself—replacing HAVE (SOMETHING) with (IS) MINE—was implemented in 2016.

prototypically signals two semantic components, roughly (i) moving upward, (ii) using a 'clambering' manner, but in extended uses either condition (but not both) can be set aside. For example, a person or a monkey can readily be said to *climb down* a tree (i.e. without the upwards direction component), while a snail or a snake can be said *climb (up) a tree* (i.e. without the 'clambering' component). The same snail or snake, however, could not be said to *climb down*.

This is indeed a striking observation. However, as noted in Wierzbicka (1996) and in earlier works, if moving upwards is merely part of a prototype and not part of the invariant meaning, why can a sentence like *The monkey climbed the flagpole* not be interpreted as meaning that the monkey *climbed down*. How can we be so sure that, unless otherwise specified, the direction of movement is upwards? Wierzbicka also noted that there is more to it than just the two components mentioned by Fillmore. For example, an extended use of another kind, in the sentence *The train climbed the mountain*, implies more than simply upwards direction. Without any qualification to the contrary, this sentence would not be a good description if the train had sped quickly up the mountain.

Over the following years and decades, English *climb* continued to be revisited by linguists of different persuasions. Ray Jackendoff (1983, 1985, 1990) formalised Fillmore's observations using a 'preference rule system', and in a series of papers Beth Levin and Malka Rappaport Hovav (e.g. Rappaport Hovav and Levin 2010; Levin and Rappaport Hovav 2013) puzzled over *climb* as they sought to develop a simple schematics for verbs, according to which Manner and Result are (or ought to be) in a complementary relationship; that is, verbs or uses of verbs ought to be Manner-oriented or Result-oriented but not both. Verbs like *climb* (and *cut*) seemed to challenge this idea and the debate shows little sign of reaching a conclusion, even after 30 years (cf. e.g. Chen and Husband 2019).

In my view, the reasons for the slow rate of progress come down to problems of method and approach. The lexical semantics of *climb* (and *cut*) in fact intertwine Manner and Result components. They also interact with grammatical aspect. It is all very semantically complex, very intricate; but conventional approaches are not greatly interested in semantic complexity (= accuracy) for its own sake. Many linguists are concerned first and foremost with formal syntax and so the effort is always to schematise the semantics, to keep the fine semantic details to a minimum. In the experience of NSM linguists, it is a false economy and a self-defeating strategy to stave off detailed work on semantics in the hope of reaching the big picture first. Deciding not to focus one's lens is a formula for seeing a fuzzy picture.

I have two further observations about verb semantics in the mainstream 'syntax and semantics' literature. First, there has been remarkably little interest in the details of Manner specifications. For decades there was no progress beyond Fillmore's descriptor 'clambering' (itself a complex and highly English-specific term). Jackendoff (1990) mentioned 'effortful grasping motions' but went straight back to using 'clambering' as an abbreviation. Not until the new century did Geuder and Weisgerber (2006) contribute a new idea, namely, 'force exertion against gravity', and although this formulation can no doubt be improved, it conveys the idea that *climbing* involves effort, and hints, perhaps, at the possibility of falling.

My second observation concerns the stubborn persistence of the idea that so-called 'syntactic alternations' can be revealingly described with minimal reference to semantics. Already in 2000, David Dowty challenged this view, from within the generative fold, in an article whose title contains the phrase 'the fallacy of argument alternation'. He wrote:[2]

> [C]ontrary to the usual view … good reasons can be given to view it as a lexical derivation analogous to rules of WORD FORMATION on the one hand, and to processes of LEXICAL SEMANTIC EXTENSION … and METAPHOR on the other. (Dowty 2000: 121; emphasis in original)

The 'main linguistic phenomenon that ought to be of interest', Dowty said, is that alternate constructions 'serve to convey significantly different meanings' (2000: 110). To make good on this insight, however, depends on being able to capture meanings and meaning differences in a rigorous and cognitively plausible fashion.

---

2 Dowty was speaking of the so-called locative-subject construction; for example, *The garden is swarming with bees*, but his comments were intended to have broader implications.

3. Verb semantics, aspect and constructional semantics: The view from 2020

This is a thumbnail sketch of current NSM work with verb semantics, aspectual transposition and constructional semantics. To explicate verbs, one must first decide on a basic grammatical frame for the verb in question, which will include its core arguments and its inherent aspect. For English physical activity verbs like *walk*, *run*, *cut*, *chop* and *grind*, the basic frame is 'activity-in-progress', expressed with the present progressive. To anticipate, for *climb* we will start with the basic frame: *Someone X is climbing something* (e.g. a tree, a ladder, garden wall).

Verbs of a given semantic class are expected to follow the same semantic template, sometimes with minor variations. In their basic activity-in-progress meanings, English physical activity verbs have a four-part semantic template. The section headings and some key points about each of them are given in Table 1.1.

Table 1.1. Semantic template for activity-in-progress, with key points.

LEXICOSYNTACTIC FRAME. Very general. Hinged around primes DO, HAPPEN and MOVE. Identifies the main participants and other grammatically salient things such as inherent aspect (e.g. 'for some time' (durational)), and whether the activity is necessarily localised (i.e. done 'in a place').
PROTOTYPICAL SCENARIO. Introduced by 'often when someone does this, it is like this: …'. Includes the intention or mental state of the prototypical actor, which is always a pivotal component.[3]
HOW IT HAPPENS (MANNER). Introduced by 'often when someone does this, it happens like this', plus, if iterative: 'it happens like this many times'. May include an incremental effect.
POTENTIAL OUTCOME. Specifies that if done 'for some time', the activity can be effective in bringing about the desired result.

Source: Author's summary.

As for the individual semantic components in NSM explications, they are chiefly written in semantic primes. Explications can also include complex lexical meanings, either as semantic molecules or as derivational bases.

---

[3] The explications in this chapter use 'often' as a portmanteau for 'at many times', as is now standard in recent NSM work.

Both are relevant to the present study. Semantic molecules, marked as [m], are complex meanings that function as recurring units in the structure of many concepts across many domains (Goddard 2011: 375–84; Goddard and Wierzbicka 2014: Chs 2–4). The explications for *climb* will require the semantic molecules 'hands [m]', 'legs [m]', 'ground [m]', 'at the top [m]' and 'at the bottom [m]'. Derivational bases, marked as [d], are complex lexical meanings that enter into explications in a much more limited and localised fashion; that is, in derivational processes, in quasi-derivational extensions from a basic lexical meaning to a more elaborated one, and in specialised lexicogrammatical constructions (Goddard 2018: 235–64).

The concept of [d] elements was originally developed to deal with 'visible' derivational relationships, e.g. between the words *ill* and *illness*, or between the noun *knife* and the verb *to knife (someone)*. The idea was that the simpler of the two meanings could appear inside the explication of the more complex one; for example, the explication of the noun *illness* could include 'ill [d]'; the explication for the verb *to knife* could include 'knife [d]'. As will be shown in the present study, however, the idea of [d] elements has turned out to have far broader applications.

One of these applications is to allow a quasi-derivational treatment of grammatical aspect. This is relevant to the present study because many semantically specialised constructions, including for the verb *climb*, are found preferentially in perfective contexts; for example, in the English simple past. Briefly, the idea is that verbs like *climb* and *cut* can also appear in a perfective (e.g. simple past) template with three sections:

(i) LEXICOSYNTACTIC FRAME: 'someone X did something (to something) at this time', that is, a temporally localised act without reference to its duration.

(ii) HOW IT HAPPENED (MANNER): described using the activity-in-progress meaning as a [d] element; for example, 'someone ate something' includes 'this someone was eating [d] it for some time'.

(iii) OUTCOME: the achievement of a particular goal envisaged by the actor.

This approach corresponds closely to standard descriptions of the perfective as viewing an event in its totality without attention to its internal temporal constituency (Comrie 1993).

4. Extended meanings and uses of English 'climb'

We begin our exploration of *climb* not by explicating its semantically basic meaning, but from the other direction, as it were: by showing how various non-basic uses of *climb* can be accounted for, assuming that we have an explication for 'is climbing' and can use it as a [d] element. Consider the simple past of *climb*. It is explicated in [A].

[A] She *climbed*₁ a tree (tree, ladder, wall) [i.e. simple past]

she (= this someone) did something in a place at this time	LEXICOSYNTACTIC FRAME
it happened like this:	HOW IT HAPPENED (MANNER)
a short time before, she thought like this about something in this place (a tree, ladder, wall):	
'I want to be at the top [m] of this something'	
because of this, she was climbing [d] this tree (ladder, wall) for some time	
because of this, after this, she was not in the place where she was before	OUTCOME
she was at the top [m] of this tree (ladder, wall) as she wanted	

Explication [A] involves literal 'climbing [d]', and as we will see when it is explicated (in section 5), 'climbing [d]' includes a semantic component of upwards motion. What about *climb down* then, or *climb onto something*?

Climb down is quite a high-frequency expression in the Collins Wordbanks Online corpus (hereafter: Wordbanks). It is explicated in [B]. Although the How It Happened section still uses 'climbing [d]', it is positioned inside in an 'analogy of manner' component: 'he did something for some time like someone does when this someone is climbing [d] something'.

[B] He *climbed*₂ down the tree (ladder, wall)

he did something in a place at this time	LEXICOSYNTACTIC FRAME
it happened like this:	HOW IT HAPPENED (MANNER)
a short time before, he thought like this about something in this place (a tree, ladder, wall):	
'I want to be at the bottom [m] of this something'	
because of this, he did something for some time <u>like someone does when this someone is climbing [d] something</u>	
because of this, after this, he was not in the place where he was before	OUTCOME
he was at the bottom [m] of this tree (ladder, wall) as he wanted	

Now let us consider examples when *climb* appears with other adverbial modifiers, especially prepositional phrases with *into, off, onto, out onto, out from, out from under*, etc. Such expressions are extremely common in English, helping to put *climb* into the 350 most frequent verbs in the English language, and, possibly, into the top 20 physical activity verbs.[4]

(1)   a.   *He climbed into bed, into the passenger seat, etc.*
       b.   *She climbed onto the roof of the car.*
       c.   *He climbed out of the car (cabin, backseat, etc.)*[5]

(2)   a.   *He opened the window and climbed out onto the windowsill.*
       b.   *They climbed out from under the table.*

---

4   These statements are based on word frequency figures taken from COCA (Corpus of Contemporary American English): www.wordfrequency.info/free.asp?s=y. 'Climb' appears in rank 334 of verbs. Rather strikingly, however, a manual count shows that physical activity verbs constitute only about 10–15% of the top 350. Restricting ourselves only to physical activity verbs, *climb* comes after the following, given in order of frequency: *go, come, play, run, hold, sit, stand, walk, build, cut, carry, eat, fight, laugh, sing, drink, cry, cook*.

5   It seems worth noting that *climbed out of* has a very high frequency in Wordbanks, more than 1,300 instances, nearly three times as many as *climbed down*.

c. *The 22-year-old New Zealand-born pilot actually climbed out onto the wing of his plane while it was at 13,000 feet …*

d. *a one-year-old boy who apparently was looking for his mother climbed out onto a window ledge …*

Explication [C] is for sentences like He climbed onto the roof of the car or He climbed into bed.

[C] He *climbed₂* onto the roof of the car

he did something at this time in a place	LEXICOSYNTACTIC FRAME
it happened like this:	HOW IT HAPPENED (MANNER)
a short time before, he thought like this about something in this place (a car):	
'I want to be on the roof of this car'	
because of this, he did something for some time <u>like someone does when this someone is climbing [d] something</u>	
because of this, after this, he was not in the place where he was before	OUTCOME
he was on the roof of the car as he wanted	

I will now sketch how other extended uses of English *climb* can be accounted for in similar fashion, beginning with instances in which non-human creatures are said to *climb*. In the case of monkeys, who, as already mentioned, can be said to *climb down* as well as *up*, explication [B] will be appropriate with only minor adjustments, given that one thinks of monkeys as having similar bodies and mental capacities to humans. For creatures like *snails* and *snakes*, on the other hand, a version of the analogy mechanism shown in [C] will be needed. Sentences like the following (garnered from the internet) are not uncommon.

(3) a. *Why do snails climb up walls when it rains?*
    b. *Can snakes climb stairs?*
    c. *I was staring at it for a while as it climbed up my shelving before it registered for me that it was a snake.*

In another phraseological cluster, *prices, wages, temperatures, sales figures, ratings, population numbers* and the like, which all involve numbers (numerical values), can be said to *climb*, implying that they move steadily upwards. For example:

(4) a. *Facebook's stock price continued to climb with few massive jumps in either direction, negative or positive.*
 b. *The Australian Bureau of Statistics says wages climbed just 2.2 per cent …*
 c. *These data show that temperatures have climbed to more than 1.8°F (1°C) above pre-industrial levels …*

To explicate these uses, a third kind of [d]-mechanism is needed. It can be termed 'analogy of effect' (cf. Goddard 2015). Roughly and loosely, the idea is that 'something happens to this number [m] like something happens to someone when this someone is climbing [d] something'—that is, it moves steadily upwards. A similar approach can be used for the place-based phraseological cluster in which a *road, trail, railway line* or the like is said to *climb through the mountains*, etc.

5. *Climbing₁ a tree (ladder, wall)*

It is time now to address the semantically basic meaning of *climb*, that is, the meaning found in its 'activity-in-progress' frame, as in sentences such as the following.

(5) a. *She was climbing a tree in the backyard.*
 b. *He was climbing a ladder when he fell.*

A note is in order here about English grammar. English puts the thing/place being climbed in the direct object/accusative role, but quite a number of languages do otherwise, expressing it in a locational phrase marked by a locative (or other oblique) adposition or case: for example, Yankunytjatjara *punu-ngka kalpanyi* 'climbing (on) a tree'. From an 'objective' point of view, this would seem very natural, insofar as a tree (ladder, wall, etc.) is not particularly affected by the climbing. After all, when one climbs a tree or ladder, one can hardly be said to be 'doing something to it'.[6]

An explication for English *climbing* (a tree, ladder) is given in [D] below. Here are brief comments on each of its four main sections. The Lexicosyntactic Frame is the same as used for other verbs of locomotion (Goddard, Wierzbicka and Wong 2016).[7] In the Prototypical Scenario, note the prior intention or a preparatory thought ('a short time before, this someone thought about it like this: …').[8] This makes sense because *climbing* is not a routine everyday activity like *walking*: it requires an effort, and it requires something like a 'commitment'. When someone sets out to *climb something*, they are aware of the possibility of physical harm to their bodies, associated with the possibility of falling. There is more discussion of the prototypical scenario after the explication. I would only add at this point that the actor's cognitive focus on the thing being climbed may help explain why it appears (in English) in the direct object position.

The How it Happens (Manner) section includes an iterative structure—that is, brief repeated episodes involving coordinated moving and touching with the hands and parts of the legs—followed by a whole-body action which brings about an incremental effect—that is, 'this someone's body is above the place where it was before'. If this iterated process carries on for long enough, the Potential Outcome is that the person 'can be at the top [m] of this big thing as they wanted'.

Note that explication [D] uses the English-specific *they* (singular) as a 'portmanteau of convenience' for 'this someone'.

---

[6] Of the 36 languages surveyed in the ValPal project on valency frames (valpal.info/meanings/climb), about 10 appear either to follow or to prefer the oblique pattern with *climb*: Ainu, Eastern Armenian, Evenki, Korean, Mandinka, Yucatek Maya, Zenzontepec Chatino, Sri Lanka Malay, Ojibwe and Japanese (Hartmann, Haspelmath and Taylor 2013).

[7] *Climb* can be used intransitively, e.g. *He was climbing,* and, in this frame, it looks parallel on the surface to the verb *crawl*, whose Manner also involves coordinated movements and contact by hands and legs. There are also other intransitive motion verbs, like *swim* and *fly*, which have special Manners adapted to the challenges presented by bodily motion in places of different kinds. I experimented with using 'intransitive *climb*' as the basic frame, but my eventual conclusion was that it is a case of omitted object construction, with the 'expected' object being place-like.

[8] A similar component appears in the explications for transitive physical activity verbs such as *cut*, *chop* and *grind* (Goddard and Wierzbicka 2016).

[D] Someone is *climbing*₁ something Y (e.g. a tree, a ladder, a wall)

someone is doing something for some time in a place
because of this, they are moving in this place during this time as they want

LEXICOSYNTACTIC FRAME

often when someone does this, it is like this:

PROTOTYPICAL SCENARIO

    there is something big (of one kind) in the place where there this someone is

    a short time before they thought about it like this:

        'I am far from the top [m] of this big thing now, I want to be at the top [m] of this big thing after some time

        I can't be there if I don't do some things with my body for some time

        I know that it is like this:

            when I am doing it, I will be far above the ground [m] for some time

            because of this, it can be bad for me if something happens not as I want

            something bad can happen to my body'

when someone does this, their hands [m] touch this big thing in many places, parts of their legs [m] touch this big thing in many places

HOW IT HAPPENS (MANNER) INCL. INCREMENTAL EFFECT

it often happens like this:

    for a short time they do something with one hand [m]

    because of this, this hand [m] touches this something somewhere above where it touched it before

    after this, they do something with one leg [m]

    because of this, part of this leg [m] touches this something somewhere above where it touched it before

    after this, they do something with the body

    because of this, after this, the body is above the place where it was before

it happens like this many times

| if this someone does this for some time, after this they can | POTENTIAL |
| be not in the place where they were before | OUTCOME |

they can be at the top [m] of this big thing as they wanted

The most notable aspects of explication [D] are in its prototypical scenario section,[9] so I will comment further on this. Most of the proposed prototypical scenario relates to the prior intention of the actor, including their awareness that to achieve the goal 'to be at the top of this big thing after some time' necessarily involves 'doing some things with my body', and being aware at the same time that there is an element of risk involved in being 'far above the ground'; that is, 'it can be bad for me if something happens not as I want, something bad can happen to my body'. This kind of mindset, I would argue, is intuitively plausible for *climbing$_1$*, such as in 'climbing a tree'.

The actor's initial construal that 'I am far from the top of this big thing' helps explain why expressions like *climb the ladder* can sound appropriate even about a small stepladder, provided that the actor is a toddler or young child. It is the subjective point of view that matters, not whether the distance to the top is or isn't 'far' from the point of view of a disinterested observer. Notice also that the prospect of bodily harm does not hinge entirely on the climber making a mistake, such as slipping from a handhold or foothold. It could come about from other (unspecified) mishaps, such as a weaker-than-expected branch giving way or something falling from above.

These various elements of the prototypical actor's mental state (the construal of a far distance to be covered and implied need for caution and concentration) help explain extended uses of *climb* in expressions like *climb the stairs*. *Climb the stairs* is a high-frequency expression, but it does not mean the same, nor is it used in the same range of contexts, as alternatives such as *take the stairs* or *go upstairs*. The expression *climb the stairs* implies effort, and for a physically fit person, this might imply (say) three or four flights of stairs. On the other hand, for a person who is weak from illness, injury or frailty, even going up a single flight of stairs can be described as *climbing the stairs*.

---

9   The Manner section may seem rather detailed in its 'motor pattern', but it is roughly comparable to the Manner sections of the explications for *crawl* and *run* (Goddard and Wierzbicka 2016; Goddard, Wierzbicka and Wong 2016).

The same applies (even more so) to *climb down the stairs*. Given that going downwards is usually less physically demanding than ascending, it makes sense that the range of use of *climb down the stairs* is even more restricted. *Climbing down the stairs* only feels appropriate when speaking of someone who is weak or unsteady on their feet, or, alternatively, in situations where the stairs are perceived to be steep and dangerous.

The physical demands of *climbing something*, together with the need for caution, help explain why the default assumption is that *climbing* is normally done slowly and steadily, and this implication carries over when 'climbing' is used as a [d] element in analogy of manner or analogy of effect components, such as we saw in section 4. (In Wordbanks, the most typical manner adverbs to collocate with *climb* are *steadily*, *slowly*, *cautiously*, *laboriously* and *unsteadily*.)

6. *Climbing$_3$ a mountain (cliff face, hill)*

Object noun phrases such as *mountain*, *cliff face* and *hill* are not fully compatible with *climb$_1$* as explicated in [D] above: first, because mountains and the like are 'places (of one kind)', rather than things (in a place) (Bromhead 2018); and second, because the physical aspects and time frame of *climbing a mountain, cliff face,* etc. are significantly different—for example, it takes much longer and special equipment is often involved.

(6) a. *Many people want to climb Mt Everest, Mt Cook, Mt Fuji, Mt Warning*, etc.
 b. *Who has climbed the Dawn Wall [a famous cliff face]?*

For these sentences, it is necessary to posit a third, polysemic meaning *climb$_3$*. It is explicated in [E] below. The main differences are, first, that in the prototypical scenario the nature of the place is described: 'this place is a big place (of one kind)'; second, that the preparatory thought is depicted as taking place 'some time before', rather than 'a short time before', as with *climb$_1$* (this is connected with the fact that *climbing a mountain, hill, cliff,* etc. is a more substantial undertaking); and third, that in the How it Happens (Manner) section, the person is depicted as doing 'some things in this place for some time like someone does when this someone is climbing [d] something'.

[E] Someone is *climbing₃* a mountain (hill, cliff face)

someone is doing something for some time in a place	LEXICOSYNTACTIC FRAME
because of this, they are moving in this place during this time as they want	
often when someone does this in a place, it is like this:	PROTOTYPICAL SCENARIO
this place is a big place of one kind	
some time before, this someone thought like this about this place:	
'I am far from the top [m] of this big place now	
I want to be at the top [m] of this big place after some time	
I can't be there if I don't do some things with my body for some time	
I know that it is like this:	
when I am doing it, it can be bad for me if something happens not as I want	
something bad can happen to my body because of it'	
when someone does this, it happens like this:	HOW IT HAPPENS (MANNER)
this someone does some things in this place for some time <u>like someone does when they are climbing [d] something</u>	
if this someone does this for some time, after this, they can be at the top [m] of this big place, as they wanted	POTENTIAL OUTCOME

In connection with *climb₃*, one should note the existence of a slew of specialised terms and phrases for *mountain climbing* and *rock climbing*.

(7) a. *mountain climber, climbers*
    b. *climbing gear, climbing ropes, climbing routes, the summit climb*
    c. *mountain climbing, rock climbing, sports climbing, free climbing, indoor climbing*

There are collocational facts to be mined as well; for example, the possibility of these meanings appearing in coordinate constructions with words such as *hiking*, *trekking* and *canoeing*.

7. *She climbed₄ the fence (gate)*: A covert alternation with '*climb*'

First, a bit of additional background is necessary. In the literature on syntactic alternations, a specialised 'crossing an obstacle' construction has been identified with intransitive English verbs of motion such as *swim* or *jump*, which imply significant bodily effort. In this specialised construction, the verb appears in a transitive frame; however, as shown in (8) and (9), the transitive versions are roughly synonymous with intransitive sentences that include a prepositional phrase with *across* or *over*.

(8) *He swam the river.*
 ≈ *He swam across the river.*

(9) *She jumped the puddle.*
 ≈ *She jumped over the puddle.*

To the best of my knowledge, the 'crossing an obstacle' construction has not previously been recognised in the literature on the verb *climb*, because, English *climb* being already transitive in appearance, the construction does not show itself via a change in surface argument structure. But consider:

(10) a. *He climbed the ladder/mountain.*
 ≠ *He climbed over the ladder/mountain.*
 b. *He climbed the fence (gate, garden wall).*
 ≈ *He climbed over the fence (gate, garden wall).*
 c. **He climbed up/down the fence (gate, garden wall).*

The examples in (10a) show that with canonical objects such as *ladder* and *mountain*, sentences with *climb* are not near-synonyms of agnate sentences with prepositional phrases using *over*—that is, *to climb a ladder* and *to climb over a ladder* mean something quite different to one another. However, when the object is something like a *fence*, a *gate* or a *(garden) wall*—a barrier that can be crossed—the equation goes through, as shown by the examples in (10b): *to climb a fence* and *to climb over a fence* do mean much the same.

Another indication that we are dealing here with a separate construction is that, as shown by the examples in (10c), adverbs like *up* and *down* cannot normally be added to 'crossing an obstacle' sentences with *climb*. It may also be noted that 'crossing an obstacle' sentences with *climb* (like comparable sentences with *swim* and *jump*) usually sound much better in the simple past than in the progressive.

For these reasons, it is necessary to recognise an additional constructional schema, with a distinctive motivation ('I want to be on the other side of this thing here'), as shown in [F].

[F] He *climbed*$_4$ the fence (gate)

he did something in a place at this time	LEXICOSYNTACTIC FRAME
it happened like this:	HOW IT HAPPENED (MANNER)
a short time before, he thought like this about something in this place (a fence, gate):	
'I want to be on the other side of this thing here'	
because of this, for a short time he did something in this place like someone does when this someone is climbing [d] something	
because of this, after this, he was not in the place where he was before	OUTCOME
he was on the other side of this thing as he wanted	

This concludes the present study of the lexicogrammar of English *climb*.

8. Concluding remarks

Given the complexity of the explications and wide range of uses I have endeavoured to cover in this short study, many improvements are no doubt possible. There is certainly scope for more detailed corpus-analytical work. It would also be extremely valuable to bring comparisons with other languages into the picture. There are sure to be many subtle but significant differences between 'climb words' in different languages. Pinpointing these differences would help firm up the optimal phrasing of various components. It is entirely possible that some cross-linguistic differences will turn out to be related to different geographic environments and lifestyles of the speakers concerned. One would also expect that cross-linguistic differences in the basic meanings will have downstream effects so far as extended meanings are concerned.

It should be emphasised that much of the present study has been concerned not with the semantically basic meaning of English *climb*, but with how this core or basic meaning can be extended and enriched by being embedded into different constructional frames. In English, the favourite mechanisms for doing this are syntactic in character, principally involving alternative prepositional phrases. In other languages, comparable meanings may be expressed by devices such as derivational morphology, verb compounding or serial verb constructions.

To conclude on a general note, it should be clear that the verb *climb* provides a perfect example of lexis, morphology, phraseology and syntax all working together to express varied and subtle meanings.

References

Bromhead, Helen (2018). *Landscape and Culture – Cross-linguistic Perspectives*. Amsterdam: John Benjamins.

Chen, Sherry Yong and E. Matthew Husband (2019). Event (de)composition. In Chris Cummins and Napoleon Katsos (eds), *Oxford Handbook of Experimental Semantics and Pragmatics*. Oxford: Oxford University Press, 62–82. doi.org/10.1093/oxfordhb/9780198791768.013.10.

Comrie, Bernard (1993). *Aspect*. Cambridge, UK: Cambridge University Press.

Dowty, David (2000). 'The garden swarms with bees' and the fallacy of 'argument alternation'. In Yael Ravin and Claudia Leacock (eds), *Polysemy: Theoretical and Computational Approaches*. Oxford: Oxford University Press, 111–28.

Fillmore, Charles J. (1982). Towards a descriptive framework for spatial deixis. In R. J. Jarvell and W. Klein (eds), *Speech, Place and Action: Studies in Deixis and Related Topics*. London: Wiley, 31–59.

Geuder, Wilhelm and Matthias Weisgerber (2006). Manner and causation in movement verbs. In Christian Ebert and Cornelia Endriss (eds), *Proceedings of 'Sinn & Bedeutung 10'* (vol. 1). Berlin, ZAS Papers in Linguistics 44, 1. Available online via: www.leibniz-zas.de/en/research/publications/details/publications/4234-proceedings-of-the-sinn-und-bedeutu/.

Goddard, Cliff (2011). *Semantic Analysis: A Practical Introduction* (2nd edn). Oxford: Oxford University Press.

Goddard, Cliff (2012). Semantic primes, semantic molecules, semantic templates: Key concepts in the NSM approach to lexical typology. *Linguistics* 50 (3): 711–43. doi.org/10.1515/ling-2012-0022.

Goddard, Cliff (2015). Verb classes and valency alternations (NSM approach), with special reference to English physical activity verbs. In Andrej Malchukov and Bernard Comrie (eds), *Valency Classes in the World's Languages*. Berlin: Mouton de Gruyter, 1649–80. doi.org/10.1515/9783110429343-020.

Goddard, Cliff (2018). *Ten Lectures on Natural Semantic Metalanguage: Exploring Language, Thought and Culture Using Simple, Translatable Words*. Leiden: Brill.

Goddard, Cliff and Anna Wierzbicka (2014). *Words and Meanings: Lexical Semantics Across Domains, Languages and Cultures*. Oxford: Oxford University Press. doi.org/10.1093/acprof:oso/9780199668434.001.0001.

Goddard, Cliff and Anna Wierzbicka (2016). Explicating the English lexicon of 'doing and happening'. *Functions of Language* 23 (2): 214–56. doi.org/10.1075/fol.23.2.03god.

Goddard, Cliff, Anna Wierzbicka and Jock Wong (2016). 'Walking' and 'running' in English and German: The conceptual semantics of verbs of human locomotion. *Review of Cognitive Linguistics* 14 (2): 303–36. doi.org/10.1075/rcl.14.2.03god.

Hartmann, Iren, Martin Haspelmath and Bradley Taylor (eds) (2013). *Valency Patterns Leipzig*. Leipzig: Max Planck Institute for Evolutionary Anthropology.

Jackendoff, Ray (1983). *Semantics and Cognition*. Cambridge, MA: MIT Press.

Jackendoff, Ray (1985). Multiple subcategorization and the θ-criterion: The case of *climb*. *Natural Language & Linguistic Theory*, 3 (3): 271–95. doi.org/10.1007/bf00154264.

Jackendoff, Ray (1990). *Semantic Structures*. Cambridge, MA: MIT Press.

Levin, Beth and Malka Rappaport Hovav (2013). Lexicalized meaning and Manner/Result complementarity. In Boban Arsenijević, Berit Gehrke and Rafael Marín (eds), *Studies in the Composition and Decomposition of Event Predicates*. Springer, 49–70. doi.org/10.1007/978-94-007-5983-1_3.

Rappaport Hovav, Malka and Beth Levin (2010). Reflections on Manner/Result Complementarity. In Malka Rappaport Hovav, Edit Doran and Ivy Sichel (eds), *Lexical Semantics, Syntax, and Event Structure*. Oxford: Oxford University Press, 21–38. doi.org/10.1093/acprof:oso/9780199544325.003.0002.

Sibly, Anne (2010). Harry slapped Hugo, Tracey smacked Ritchie: The semantics of *slap* and *smack*. *Australian Journal of Linguistics* 30 (3): 323–48. doi.org/10.1080/07268602.2010.498804.

Wierzbicka, Anna (1982). Why can you *have a drink* when you can't **have an eat*? *Language* 58 (4): 753–99. doi.org/10.2307/413956.

Wierzbicka, Anna (1988). *The Semantics of Grammar*. Amsterdam: John Benjamins.

Wierzbicka, Anna (1996). *Semantics: Primes and Universals*. Oxford: Oxford University Press.

Ye, Zhengdao (2010). Eating and drinking in Mandarin and Shanghainese: A lexical-conceptual analysis. In Wayne Christensen, Elizabeth Schier and John Sutton (eds), *ASCS09: Proceedings of the 9th Conference of the Australasian Society for Cognitive Science*. Sydney: Macquarie Centre for Cognitive Science, 375–83.

2
The comparative semantics of verbs of 'opening': West Africa vs Oceania

Felix K. Ameka and Deborah Hill

1. Introduction

Separating things into parts or constituents using different means is an everyday activity that humans everywhere undertake. The way in which humans categorise such events and label them in verbs varies considerably across languages and cultures. In a cross-linguistic study of the categorisation of separation events, Majid et al. (2007: 147) note that separation events such as opening, taking apart and peeling, which involve minimal destruction of the affected object and are mostly reversible, were distinguished from those involving cutting and breaking, which involve significant material destruction accompanied by non-reversible change in the integrity of the object.

'Opening' events are thus a subspecies of separation events. Many languages partition the 'opening' events in English among a number of different verbs, but the criteria used for this differ strikingly from one language to another. An English-like category of opening events does not seem to be inevitable to human cognition (Bowerman 2005: 229). For instance, Korean has about six verbs that cover the semantic range of opening events in English. As Bowerman put it:

> The conceptual glue that unifies for example 'opening the mouth', 'opening an envelope', and 'opening a book' for speakers of English seems to be missing [in Korean FKA & DH] and the domain is parceled out among a number of crosscutting categories that emphasise different aspects of events. (Bowerman 2005: 228)

This chapter compares the way two languages, Ewe, a Kwa language of West Africa, and Longgu, an Oceanic language of Solomon Islands, carve up the semantic space of 'opening' and provides semantic explications for a small number of verbs in each language.[1]

In morpho-syntactic terms, Ewe and Longgu share some similarities and they both deploy serial verb constructions (SVCs). They both also use reduplication to express various meanings. There are some differences too. Longgu is a head marking language where arguments are marked on the verb following an SVO (subject–verb–object) pattern. However, constituent order in the clause is typically VS/VOA (verb–subject/verb–object–transitive subject, Hill 2016a). The basic constituent order in Ewe by contrast is SV/AVO (subject–verb/transitive subject–verb–object). In addition, Longgu has verb transitivising suffixes, as we shall see. Ewe, on the other hand, is an isolating language with agglutinative features. It does not use verb derivational morphology to express transitivity and other valency changing processes. Rather, the verbs participate in multiple argument alternations. Ewe is also a tone language.

The lexicon of complex physical activities in different languages reveals differences related to culture, as well as similarities between cultures (Goddard and Wierzbicka 2009). This is reflected in verbs in the domain of 'carrying' (Hill 2016b; Ameka 2017) as well as in separation events of cutting and breaking (Ameka and Essegbey 2007; Goddard and Wierzbicka 2009). We shall demonstrate that the verbs of opening also

---

[1] Indulging in this comparative semantics of two languages spoken on continents apart allows us to reflect on and engage with the teaching and mentorship and friendship we have experienced with Anna for about three and a half decades. The authors first met in one of Anna's classes in March 1984 and have been on the quest for meaning with her since. We have enjoyed many debates with Anna not only in class but also during the first Semantics workshop in Adelaide in 1986 and subsequently. We are delighted to honour Anna on the occasion of her anniversary comparing verbs of opening in Ewe, the native language of the first author, and the first African language to have been studied within the Natural Semantic Metalanguage (NSM) framework, and Longgu, the field language specialisation of the second author who is a first-generation practitioner of NSM.

For us, the power of NSM semantic representations is the way in which it helps the analyst to allow the language to speak. Moreover, the semantic explications of signs in different languages can be easily compared and the similarities and differences become transparent even to the casual reader.

show this diversity and cultural embeddedness. Examples of culturally relevant verbs of opening in Longgu are the verbs *suvulia* 'open the eye of a coconut with an instrument (e.g. a stick or knife)'; and *tuaa* 'open the side of a bamboo by putting a hole in it (with a knife)'. Objects that are opened with instruments tend to be lexically specific in Longgu (i.e. the verb refers to opening one object in a particular way). Where Longgu has at least 10 verbs that express opening events, Ewe has three. Opening events such as 'peel something' are expressed by a specific verb in Longgu (*pagea* 'peel something (e.g. banana)'), whereas in Ewe one of three verbs expressing opening (*klé*), is also used to describe peeling.

While Ewe and Longgu carve up the semantic space of opening events differently, there are also shared properties of objects of physical actions of opening. These common properties reflect some of the properties of objects for physical action of opening events in English identified by Bowerman (2005) and include the six senses of English 'open' proposed by Levison (1993). Bowerman suggested that for English, 'openable' objects can be described as: (a) a unitary object, although it may have parts such as a pot with a lid; (b) an object that separates along predetermined lines not unpredictably (hence actions of opening are usually reversible; objects that can be opened can also be closed); and (c) separation affords access to something (e.g. a content, an interior space or a previously concealed part of the object with which you can do something). These characteristics suggest, prototypically, a container (as exemplified by the pot referred to). Levison (1993) also includes 'containers' (e.g. open the can/bottle/soda; open the house) and 'conduits' (channels and paths) as two of six suggested senses of English 'open'. Both Ewe and Longgu have verbs (*vu* and *tavangia*) to refer to opening containers and conduits. However, when these verbs are used to describe the opening of 'channels' or 'paths', the languages differ in the range of objects that can be referred to; for example, while Ewe *vu* and Longgu *tavangia* can be used to refer to opening or turning on a radio, only Longgu *tavangia* is used to refer to turning on or opening a lamp or light.

For the interpretation of linguistic signs and utterances, we assume following Wilkins and Hill (1995) that there are three levels of meaning (see also e.g. Kecskes 2008; Levinson 2000). The first level, Semantics 1, concerns the stable, context-independent meaning values of signs. These are the structured ideas about signs (lexical items, constructions, gestures, prosodic patterns etc.) that speakers share which are stored in the mind. It is these stable, intersubjective structured ideas about the verbs in the two languages that we strive to represent in the semantic explications proposed. Combinatorial rules generate an output, the literal meaning. This feeds into level 2, which is a kind of fill-in, or a filter box (Pragmatics). At this level, the literal meaning of an utterance interacts with neo-Gricean generalised Conversational Implicatures (Levinson 2000), cultural scripts (e.g. Goddard and Wierzbicka 2004), semantic frames (e.g. Fillmore and Atkins 1992) and all kinds of world and encyclopedic knowledge. These processes of enrichment and filtering lead to the online contextual interpretation of utterances (for both speaker and hearer), the third level (Semantics 2) (Wilkins and Hill 1995). These contextual interpretations may be cycled back into Semantics 1, where they become more stable meaning values of signs. This is the way in which meaning change takes place.

The organisation of the chapter is as follows: we first introduce verbs of opening in Ewe (Section 2). Section 3 presents an overview of the Longgu verbs and discusses two that share semantic similarities with the Ewe verbs. In Section 4, we draw out parallels and differences between the two languages and discuss them in the context of the key characteristics of openable objects in English, suggested by Bowerman (2005), and propose explications for them based on the Natural Semantic Metalangauge (NSM) principles following the semantic template for verbs proposed by Goddard and Wierzbicka (2016). The explications couched in semantic primes allow for easy comparison of the meanings across the two languages.

2. Opening events in Ewe

The verbs in Ewe are *ke* 'open, end, spread out, etc.', *klẽ* 'open, peel, remove outer covering; shine', and *vu* 'open'. The three verbs in Ewe that carve up the space of opening events have distinct semantics. Nevertheless, they may apply to the same entities revealing different construals of the opening events. Thus each of the verbs can take the body parts with two parts such as *ŋkú* 'eye', *nu* 'mouth', *glã* 'jaw' as object with different nuances of interpretation. Thus *ke nu* 'open mouth' implies that the two lips move apart because someone wants it; *klẽ nu* 'open mouth wide' implies that the lips come apart as someone wants it, because of this one can see inside the mouth' and *vu nu* 'open mouth' describes a situation where someone consciously and purposefully opens the mouth (e.g. to talk). It entails that it was done purposefully. In the next subsection we summarise the uses and interpretations of *ke* 'open' as presented in Ameka (2019). We then turn attention to the other Ewe verb *vu* 'open'.

2.1. The Ewe verb *ke*

Ameka (2019) provides a detailed analysis of the uses and meaning of the verb *ke* 'open, open up, spread; stop, end, be finished'. For the sake of completeness and to allow for comparison with the Longgu data, we summarise that analysis here. As the glosses of the verb suggest, the verb at first sight may look to be polysemous. And, in fact, this is the stance taken by lexicographers like Westermann (1928) and Rongier (2015). However, Ameka argues for a monosemic account, and demonstrates how the various contextual interpretations can be generated from the interaction of the verb semantics with the semantics of the argument structure constructions in which it occurs as well as the semantics of the types of entities involved in the event.

The verb is primarily monovalent but has both transitive and intransitive uses. In its intransitive use, the event is construed as being internally caused. That is, the 'opening' happened not because someone did it. The verb is predicated of different classes of nominals. They can all be viewed as unitary objects which have parts. These parts could come apart along predetermined lines but without causing the disintegration of the entity into different entities. It is thus predicated of things that open naturally like *séƒoƒo* 'flower' as when in full bloom; or *ɖetí* 'cotton (boll)'. When a *gli* 'wall' or similar entity splits open by itself, the occurrence is described with the verb *ke*. The verb also collocates with the psychologised body part *ŋu* 'eye' to express 'day break'.[2] When the verb occurs with event nominals that denote situations which have a negative effect on people, such as *tsi* 'water, rain', *dɔ* 'hunger, famine' and *ava* 'war', it is interpreted as the situation coming to an end. Adopting a three levels of semantics approach (Wilkins and Hill 1995), Ameka (2019) explains that when the verb *ke* is predicated of these event nominals with negative impact on people such as *dzre* 'quarrel' or *dzo* 'fire' to mean 'The quarrel has ended.' or 'The fire

---

2   Body part terms can either refer to a physical body part, such as the physical eye, or they may refer to parts of the body where things happen because of which one feels something (inside the body). The latter are termed psychologised body parts (Ameka 2002). The same linguistic form may refer to the physical and the psychologised part: for example, Ewe *dzi* refers to both the physical and psychologised heart. However, in some cases different words refer to the different aspects of the same part. In Ewe, for instance, the physical eye is *ŋkú* and the psychologised eye is *ŋu*.

has subsided.', the same semantics represented in [A] applies. The event nominals are seen as having parts and something happens at a point in time and these parts come apart, are scattered, leading to the situation being no more. All the situations characterised by the intransitive use of the verb are irreversible. Based on the discussion so far, we propose the explication in [A] for the Ewe verb *ke* 'open', which is a revised version of the one proposed in Ameka (2019).

[A] *Something X ke* (X = flower, nut, cotton etc.)

a. something happened to X (at this time) — LEXICOSYNTACTIC FRAME

b. because of this, something happened in X in one moment, not because someone did something to it (X)

c. often when things like this happen, — PROTOTYPICAL SCENARIO

it happens like this:

    before it happened:

        this thing was like one thing

        this thing has parts (inside it)

    after it happened:

        some parts move apart in places

        some parts are in the same place as they were before

        this thing is like one thing

        it is not two things

d. because of this, after this, — EFFECT

    some parts are on one side,

    the other parts are on the other side

e. because of this, after this, — (POTENTIAL) OUTCOME

    people can see things inside this thing

    [people can do something with things inside this thing, if they want]

Furthermore, Ameka (2019) argues that the same meaning of the verb is at play when it is used transitively. In such cases, the two-place construction licenses an Effector, thus the component of 'not because someone wants it/did it' is cancelled out and the constructional meaning component of 'someone did something to something else' combines with the other components to generate the online interpretations.

In its transitive use also, there are different categories of objects that *ke* 'open' can occur with. First are body parts that have two parts, such as *ŋkú* 'eye', *nu* 'mouth', *atá* 'thigh', *así* '(folded) hands', *glã* 'jaw' and *tó* 'ear'. These situations can be reversed and the antonym of *ke* that describes it is *miá* 'tighten'.³ A second group is tools with parts that can be stretched out such as *xéxí/sowuia* 'umbrella'. The spreading of other artefacts that are flexible and flat—for example, *asabu* 'fishing net', *eɖo* 'cloth' or *tsítse* 'sleeping mat' are also described with the verb *ke* 'open'. The reversal of this action is described by the verb *ŋlɔ́* 'fold'. Thus the opening events presented transitively with the verb *ke* 'open' are reversible. It will be shown in the next section that the opening events described by the verb *vu* 'open' are also reversible or their closed state can be restored by covering the opening. A further difference between the two verbs lies partly in their force dynamics (cf. Talmy 2000).

2.2. The Ewe verb *vu*

Ewe lexicographers present the verb *vu* 'open, be open' as a polysemic word with at least five senses. Westermann (1928) gives 'open, be open' as the first sense. The verb is primarily bivalent and, in this sense, it participates in the causative/inchoative alternation as illustrated in (1), taken from Westermann (interlinear glosses added).

(1) a. *vu*   *vɔtrú*   *lá*
       open door   DEF
       'Open the door!'
   b. *vɔtrú*   *lá*   *vu*
       door   DEF   open
       'The door opened.'

---

3   The reversal of the opening of the body part *tó* 'ear' is expressed by the verb *kú* 'die': *kú tó* [die ear] 'turn a deaf ear', which refers to the ear losing its function.

Westermann provides a further illustration of this sense with the collocation in (1c) involving an abstract object:

(1) c.   ʋu   nya   me
        open   word   containing.region
        'explain, admit, confess'

The focus in this chapter will be on this first sense. The other readings provided by Westermann are (ii) to move (house), leave a place, migrate, emigrate; (iii) to reach as far as, go up to/into, open on/in to; and (iv) to rise whirling, swirl up; shine; and burn. All these readings of the verb, we argue, can be motivated from the 'physical opening of entities' sense of the verb.

The verb *ʋu* 'open' occurs with different types of openable objects. The first group are the containers. Containers such as *aɖáká* 'hinged box' typically have a top that when opened remains attached to the whole. Other containers have removable parts that can be lifted from the objects in order to open them. Such containers are *ze* 'pot', *atukpá* 'bottle' or *núgoe* 'tin'. In talking about the opening of such containers, one can either focus on the whole, as in (2a), or on the lid, (2c). One can use a dedicated construction involving a postpositional phrase where the thing that is covering the container that has to be taken apart is the dependent in such a phrase, as in (2b). In all these cases for the physical opening to occur, one does something to a part of the whole using one's hands.

(2) a.   ʋu   ze-ɛ
        open   pot-DEF
        'Open the pot!'

     b.   ʋu   nú   le   ze-ɛ   nǔ
        open   thing   LOC   pot-DEF   mouth
        'Open the lid from the pot!'

     c.   ʋu   ze-ɛ   wó   nu-tú-nú
        open   pot-DEF   POSS   mouth-close-thing
        'Open the pot's lid!'

One can also refer to the content of the container when talking about the physical opening of the container. Typically this involves applying an instrument such as a tin opener or it may just involve the twisting of the openable part of the container. Such content can be *aha* 'drink', *bisketi* 'biscuit' or *miliki* 'milk', or *timati* 'tomato puree'. The metonymic principle here is one wants the container whose content is X to be opened and the container is referred to by the content. A similar metonymy is involved in talking about releasing domestic animals from their enclosed spaces such as chicken coops or sheep or goat pens. In these cases, the object of the verb can be the whole or it can refer to the content, namely, the animals.

As shown in example (1a), the verb also applies to conduits that are like parts of a whole such as *vɔ(trú)/hɔ* 'door', *agbŏ* 'gate'. The verb can also be applied to the whole entity to which the conduit gives access. For example, where one opens the door of the kitchen to gain access, one can just talk of opening the kitchen.

Similarly, the verb can be applied to the opening of institutions such as *sukûu* 'school' and *stɔɔ* 'store'. In fact, with these nouns as object of the verb, the interpretation is vague including the physical opening of the entity (i.e. the doors) and the commencement of activities of the institution. To unambiguously express the start of an activity, a dedicated construction is employed (see example 3).

(3) wo-ne-woe   wó-á-ʋu   stɔ-ɔ
    time-Q-time   3PL-FUT-open   store-DEF
    'When will the store be opened?'

The verb can also be used to characterise the undoing of things, especially zips, buttons and hems. One can also talk about expanding or loosening a garment or a shirt by undoing the sewing using the verb. In this case, the nominal is dependent on the postposition *me* 'containing region'.

(4) ʋu   awu-ɔ   me
    open   garment-DEF   containing region
    'Open up (i.e. undo the hem of) the garment (to make it bigger)!'

The verb is also used to describe actions involving the opening of valves, pipes and taps, as well as switching on some appliances (perhaps by turning a knob) like radios and TV sets. While on a general level this use of the transitive 'open' verb in Ewe is similar to that of Longgu, in Ewe the verb is not used to talk about the turning on of lights and lamps, nor is it used to describe the turning on of audio recorders. It appears that Ewe categorises the turning on of appliances (radio, TV) involving turning or twisting of a knob as separate from switching on other appliances such as fans or lights that involve pressing on a button. The former is described by *vu* 'open' while the latter are described by *si* 'switch on, cut (on the body)'. Actually, radios and TVs that are switched on by pressing buttons can also be described by the verb *si*. This further suggests that the manner in which one's hands are used to effect the change of state is a critical ingredient in the semantics of the verbs. When the verb *vu* is used to talk about the opening of valves and taps, the object of the verb can refer to the valve or tap or to the content that is released when the valve is turned, such as water.

As noted above, the spontaneous opening of body parts is described by *ke* 'open'. The opening of the same parts can also be described with the verb *vu* 'open', and in this case, the opening event is conceptualised as being purposeful and conscious. Consider the expressions in (5):

(5) vu   ŋkú/   nu/   atá/   así
    open   eye/   mouth/   thigh/   hand
    'Open your eyes/mouth/thighs/hand!'

Some components of the meaning of the verb *vu* can be gleaned from the company it keeps as demonstrated in the preceding discussion: the objects it occurs with have parts and one does things to one of these parts leading to the part coming apart which allows one to gain access to the other parts of the entity. It was also indicated that the physical action of opening described by the verb entails the movement of the hands to bring about the change of state. We have also shown that the internal arguments can be expressed either as noun phrases (most examples) or as postpositional phrases.

When the verb enters in construction with a postpositional phrase object headed by *nu* 'mouth' the expression gets a specialised reading, namely, 'to start or begin something'.

(6) **vu**   dɔ   /   stɔ   **nu**
    open   stomach   store   mouth
    'open the womb; start child birth, i.e. have first child'/
    'open the shop for the first time (cut the sod to open business)'

The beginning of temporal periods can also be expressed using the same structure as in (7):

(7) ʋu   ƒe-ɛ   /   ŋkeke-ɛ   nu
    open year-DEF   day-DEF   mouth
    'start the year / the day'

Furthermore, the verb participates in the causative/inchoative alternation as illustrated in (1). The verb *ʋu* also participates in various kinds of SVCs (8b) and in a resultative construction, as in (8a).

(8) a. ehɔ-ɔ-wó   pétéé   le   ʋu-ʋu ...
        door-DEF-PL   all   be.at:PRS   RED-open
        'All the doors are opened (but there is nobody in the house) ...'
    b. ɖeví-ɛ́   kɔ́   hɛ̃   ʋu   miliki-ɛ
        child-DEF   take   knife   open   milk-DEF
        'The child used a knife to open the milk.'

The resultative construction involves the nominalisation of the action verb by reduplication and it is the complement of the locative verb *le* 'be.at:PRES'. Litivinov and Agbodjo (1988) note that the construction is not very robust in colloquial Ewe; however, an utterance such as (8a) involving the verb *ʋu* is very frequent. The construction signifies a state resulting from a prior action. This result is visible. This suggests that the verb *ʋu* entails a realisation of the result of the entity being opened. Based on the discussion, we propose the explication in [B] to account for the meaning of the Ewe verb *ʋu*.

[B] Someone *ʋu* 'opened' something

a. someone (X) did something to something (Y)   LEXICOSYNTACTIC FRAME
    (at a time before now)
b. because of this, something happened to this
    something (Y) as this someone (X) wanted it

c. often, when someone does something like this to   PROTOTYPICAL
something, it is like this: SCENARIO

    this something is near this someone's body

    this someone thinks about this something like this:

    it is (like) one thing, it has parts

someone can do something to one of these parts

when someone does this, this part can move (a little)

d. when this someone (X) does this to this something (Y),   EFFECT
it happens like this:

    this someone (X) does something with the hands

        to one part of this something (Y)

    because of this, this someone's hand moves

        for a short time as this someone wants

    because of this, one part of this something

        moves as this someone wants

    after this, this part is no longer in the same place
as before

e. because of this, after this, people can see   (POTENTIAL)
    what is inside this something   OUTCOME

To sum up, the three verbs in Ewe that carve up the sematic space of opening events have distinct semantics. Nevertheless, they may apply to the same entities, revealing different construals of the opening events, as noted for body parts. Pairs of the verbs can also occur with the same referential objects and provide different perspectives on the opening event. Thus *ke* and *vu* can take *agbalẽ* 'book' as complement, suggesting flipping through a book versus purposeful and targeted opening. Similarly, *ke* and *klẽ* can take *sowuia* 'umbrella'. For *ke* it focuses on the coming apart of the blades of the umbrella while *klẽ* describes the opening wide of the umbrella.

3. Opening events in Longgu

Longgu has at least 10 verbs to refer to opening events. Within this group, one verb *tavangia* 'open something' is semantically very similar to Ewe *vu*. It is used to refer to opening containers (e.g. a pot, a house), and is used to describe the opening of channels and conduits (Levison 1993) such as the action of turning on a tap or a radio. Like Ewe *vu*, Longgu *tavangia* is used when something is opened with the hands and can describe opening the whole (e.g. a house) or opening a part (e.g. door of the house). A second verb, the stative verb *avure* 'be open' is very similar to Ewe *ke*. *Avure* is used to refer to something that has opened naturally (e.g. flower), as well as something that is open as a result of someone doing something (e.g. an open hand, an open book). This section discusses these two verbs in detail. The discussion of *avure* 'be open' includes a discussion of its transitive counterpart *vuresia* 'open something'.

Before discussing the two verbs that are semantically similar to two of the Ewe verbs, we present an overview of the domain of 'opening' in Longgu. In addition to the verbs *tavangia*, *avure* and *vuresia*, Longgu has specific verbs referring to opening events in relation to body parts, such as *rara'i* 'open eyes'. Lexically specific verbs refer to opening events that include use of an instrument (e.g. knife, stick). While the only 'instrument' that is lexicalised in the Ewe verbs is the hands, Longgu has specialised verbs with specific instruments co-lexicalised with it. This reflects a wider pattern of lexicalisation in Longgu, where manner is encoded in many lexically specific verbs (e.g. verbs of 'carrying' (Hill 2016b; see also Heath and McPherson 2009 for a discussion of Dogon)). An example is the verb *vorasia* 'open out the mat/umbrella/hand', which reflects the manner of opening.

3.1. The Longgu verbs *avure* 'be open' and *vuresia* 'open something'

The first two verbs to be discussed are morphologically related: *avure* 'be open', and *vuresia* 'open something'. The intransitive verb *avure* 'be open' is formed by a stative prefix *a-* and the verb root *vure-*. In Longgu the stative prefix *ma-*, of which *a-* is a variant, is not productive.

The verb *avure* 'be open' is used for things made of leaf or cloth, as well as an open hand, and an open book. It is used to describe the open bud in a flower, which occurs naturally, and to opened food parcels, which are wrapped in leaves. It is notable that *avure* is used to describe an open hand as the transitive counterpart is *vorasia* 'open out, unfold' and not *vuresia* 'open something'.

Longgu *avure* refers to the result of a person's action (e.g. opening the hand or opening a book) as well as a naturally occurring action, such as the opening of a flower. In this respect, Longgu *avure* is similar to Ewe *ke* and the English verb 'open', which can refer to something independently open, i.e. in the condition of being open (e.g. the hand is open), it can open on its own, or it can be opened by someone (Talmy 2000: 85). Longgu differs from English in that it distinguishes the kind of object that is being opened (e.g. the intransitive form *tavatavangi* 'be open' refers to an open door, while *avure* refers to an open flower or food parcel). (See section 3.2 for a discussion of *tavangia* 'open something'.)

The transitive form *vuresia* 'open something' is used to describe the same opening events that have been discussed for *avure* (with the exception of opening the hands). The action of opening is done with the hands. What seems to be essential here is that it is used with an object that 'separates along predictable lines' (Bowerman 2005) (as opposed to being used with an object that has visible parts). Longgu consultants noted that this verb is used when you want to see something inside. Whether to see something or do something with what is inside, this opening action 'affords access to something' (Bowerman 2005).

The verb *vuresia* 'open something' can describe the opening event involved in opening a food parcel—the cooked food within the parcel covered in leaves is opened by removing the outer covering (the leaves), giving access to the food inside. Longgu *vuresia* allows the object to be the container (the food parcel) or the food within it.

(9) a. *ami*   *vure-si-i*   *buta-gi*
       1PL.EXCL.SBJ   open-TRS-3PL.INAN   food parcel-PL
       'We opened the food parcels.'

   b. *ami*   *vure-si-i*   *vaŋa-gi*
       1PL.EXCL.SBJ   open-TRS-3PL.INAN   food-PL
       'We opened the food (i.e. removed the leaves from the cooked food).'

The stative verb *avure* 'be open' is similar to Ewe *ke* (in its intransitive use) in that it can refer to something that opens naturally, such as a flower, but different from it in that it can refer to something that has been opened by someone (e.g. a food parcel, book or hand). Like the Ewe *ke*, it is not used for objects such as doors, and pots, which have parts that can be separated and where the action can be reversed. Longgu *avure* 'be open' is vaguer than Ewe *ke* in delineating the kind of object that can 'be open', but it does not refer to opening objects that have clearly identifiable parts that can be removed from the whole object. While we can identify, for example, the outer part of a food parcel, the pages of a book and the fingers or palm of a hand, the object is perceived as a whole object rather than an 'object with parts' although there are predictable ways in which the object opens (see explication of *avure* in [C] below). A difference between intransitive Ewe *ke* and Longgu *avure* is in the other objects which it can be predicated of. Thus, Ewe *ke*, as noted, occurs with 'eye' to express 'day break' and with other entities as subject to yield a reading of 'stop, finish'.

[C] Something X *avure* (X = flower, food parcel, book, hand)

a. something happened to X (at this time) — LEXICOSYNTACTIC FRAME

b. because of this, something happened in X in one moment

c. often when things like this happen, — PROTOTYPICAL SCENARIO

    it happens like this:

        before it happened:

            this thing was like one thing

        after it happened:

            some parts are not in the same place as they were before

            some parts are in the same place as they were before

        this thing is like one thing

            it is not like two things

e. because of this, after this, — EFFECT

    people can see all sides of this thing

f. because of this, after this, (POTENTIAL)
   people can see things inside this thing OUTCOME
   [people can do something with things inside this
   thing, if they want]

The transitive verb *vuresia* 'open something' is similar to the transitive use of Ewe *ke* in the objects that it can apply to: body parts, tools such as books and umbrellas, and it can also be used with soft and flexible objects such as cloth or leaves. A crucial difference between the two is that for *vuresia* opening events are done with the hands while for the transitive *ke* opening events need not involve the hands. The other Ewe verbs *vu* and *klẽ* do entail the use of the hands just as *vuresia* and *tavangia* do.

3.2. The Longgu verb *tavangia* 'open something'

Among Longgu verbs of 'opening', the transitive verb *tavangia* occurs most frequently in texts and combines productively with other verb forms as a serial verb or compound form. *Tavangia* is used to refer to opening containers, channels and paths (Levison 1993). *Tavangia* consists of the root *tava*, the transitive suffix (in this case *-ngi*; other consonants are also found in the transitive suffix e.g. the *si* of *vuresia*) and a pronominal object suffix *-a* (third person singular object suffix).

Tavangia 'open something' is used when the action of opening involves the hands (or body) and when the object being opened is one that can be described as having parts. It is used to describe the opening of 'containers', such as a house or a pot. *Tavangia* can refer to opening the whole container (e.g. the house) or part of the container (e.g. door of the house), as exemplified below.

(10) *Takule*　　*e*　　　　　　*tali*　　**tava-ngi-a**　　　*maluma-na*
　　　Takule　　3SG.SBJ　　want　　open-TRS-3SG.OBJ　　door-3SG.POSS

　　　pilu-i　　　　*buri-na*　　　　　*ara*　　　*poso*　　　　　　*soko*
　　　fence-SG　　after-3SG.POSS　　3PL.SBJ　　caught.fish　　finish

'Takule wants to open the door of the fence [gate] after they have caught fish.'

(11) La   mai   m-e   ***tava-ngi-a***   luma   girua-i
     go   hither   CONJ-3SG.SBJ   open-TRS-3SG.   house   3DU.POSS-SG
                                                                  OBJ

'[He] came and he opened their (two) house.'

The verb can form part of an SVC, as shown in example (12), where the verb *oli* 'do again, return' precedes the object pronoun (*-a* '3SG.OBJ').

(12) *Christopher Kaimali*   *e*   ***tava-ngi-oli-a***   *dingidingi.*
     Christopher Kaimali   3SG.SBJ   open-TRS-again-3SG.OBJ   door.

'Christopher Kaimali opened the door again.'

An intransitive verb is formed by reduplicating the root. The object suffix is omitted, *tavatavangi*:

(13) *tapwi*   *e*   *tavatavangi*
     tap   3SG.SBJ   open

'The tap is on/open.'

Note that there are two possible antonyms for *tavatavangi* 'be open/on'. The first is *dingidingi* 'be closed' (a reduplication of *dingia* 'close something'), which also has a nominal meaning of 'door' (see example (12)).

(14) *tapwi*   *e*   *dingidingi*
     tap   3SG.SBJ   closed

'The tap is off.'

The alternative antonym is *bono* 'be blocked', which, if used in the context of the tap, could only mean the tap is blocked, not 'off'. Similarly, if the door is closed it is *dingidingi* 'be closed', and if it is blocked it is *bono* 'blocked'. The use of the antonym *bono* reflects the meaning of *tavangia* to express open channels and paths (i.e. a path can be blocked).

Tavangia 'open something' is also used to refer to turning on audio recorders and lights or lamps, expressing that the object is a conduit or channel for something, such as sound or light. The notion of 'path' or 'channel' as senses expressed by *tavangia* 'open something' is also found in compound verbs formed with *tava*.

(15) a. *bou-tava*
head-open
'enter; go through; e.g. bush, cloud, village'

b. *isi-tava*
bound morpheme-open
'to go outside from inside' (e.g. to out from the house)

c. *ave-tava*
bound morpheme (flood)-open
'to be at low tide; ebb'

The semantic explication of *tavangia* 'open something' is given in [D]:

[D] Someone *tavangia* 'opened' something

a.	someone (X) did something to something (Y) (at a time before now)	LEXICOSYNTACTIC FRAME
b.	because of this, something happened to this something (Y) as this someone wanted it	
c.	often, when someone does something like this to something,	PROTOTYPICAL SCENARIO
	it is like this:	
	this something is near this someone's body	
	this someone thinks about this something like this:	
	it is (like) one thing, it has parts	
	someone can do something to one of these parts	
	when someone does this, this part can move (a little)	
d.	when this someone (X) does this to this something (Y), it happens like this:	EFFECT
	this someone (X) does something with the hands to one part of this something (Y)	
	because of this, this someone's hand moves for a short time as this someone wants	

	because of this, one part of this something moves as this someone wants	
	after this, this part is no longer in the same place as before	
e.	because of this, after this, people can see what is inside this something	(POTENTIAL) OUTCOME
	something/someone can move from one place to another after this	

4. Explications and discussion of *ʋu* and *tavangia*, and *ke* and *avure*

The discussion so far has shown that while Ewe and Longgu differ in the lexical density in the domain of verbs of opening events, there are several verbs in each language that express similar meanings. At the same time, the languages vary in the range of openable objects that are used with these verbs. In this section we propose shared explications for Ewe *ke* and Longgu *avure* (in [E]) and for Ewe *ʋu* and Longgu *tavangia* (in [F]). The explications proposed for *ke* and *avure* is an improved version of the one presented in Ameka (2019) for *ke*. We highlight where the differences between the languages lie in specific components.

[E] Something X *ke* (X = flower, nut, cotton etc.), something X *avure* (X = flower, food parcel, book, hand)

Ewe	Longgu	Semantic template
something happened to X (at this time)	something happened to X (at this time)	LEXICOSYNTACTIC FRAME
because of this, something happened in X in one moment	because of this, something happened in X in one moment	
not because someone did something to it (X)		

often when things like this happen,	often when things like this happen,	PROTOTYPICAL SCENARIO
it happens like this:	it happens like this:	
before it happened:	before it happened:	
this thing was like one thing	this thing was like one thing	
this thing has parts (inside it)		
after it happened:	after it happened:	
some parts move apart in places	some parts are not in the same place as they were before	
some parts are in the same place as they were before	some parts are in the same place as they were before	
this thing is like one thing	this thing is like one thing	
it is not two things	it is not like two things	
because of this, after this,	because of this, after this,	EFFECT
some parts are on one side, the other parts are on the other side	people can see all sides of this thing	
because of this, after this,	because of this, after this,	(POTENTIAL) OUTCOME
people can see things inside this thing	people can see things inside this thing	
[people can do something with things inside this thing, if they want]	[people can do something with things inside this thing, if they want]	

The explication in [E] shows that the lexicosyntactic frame for *ke* and *avure* is shared, except that in Longgu something can be *avure* 'be open' both naturally and because someone did something, whereas intransitive *ke* is only used when the opening event happened naturally. For this reason, only Ewe includes the component 'not because someone did something to it (X)'. A key difference between the two languages lies in the prototypical scenario. Ewe views the openable object as having parts (this thing was like one thing, this thing has parts (inside it)), whereas for Longgu it is important that 'this thing was like one thing', but there is no mention of 'parts'. For both Ewe and Longgu the Effect and (Potential) Outcome are the same, or may be the same. That is, *ke* and *avure* are both verbs that express opening events (effect and outcome) but they differ in terms of which openable objects these verbs are used with.

Based on the discussion of the verbs so far, we propose explication [F] for the verbs *vu* and *tavangia* to account for all the uses related to the physical action of opening an entity. The explication in [F] shows that Ewe and Longgu share almost all of the semantic components, with the exception of the (Potential) Outcome.

The difference in the potential outcome accounts for the use of *tavangia* in Longgu to express 'paths and channels' (e.g. see the compound verbs listed in example (15)), and the discussion of *tavangia* as a verb to describe the 'opening' or turning on of lamps, lights, audio recorders, as well as opening a container (e.g. a door of a house). By contrast, Ewe *vu* is used with containers, and is more limited in its use to express paths and channels. The close semantic similarity between these two verbs suggests that the sense of 'opening' a container is cross-linguistically common. Not surprisingly, the use of verbs of 'opening' to express opening a meeting or opening a channel (e.g. sound, light) is more specific to a particular language.

[F] Someone *vu* 'opened' something, someone *tavangia* 'opened' something

Someone (X) did something to something (Y)

Ewe	Longgu	Semantic template
someone (X) did something to something (Y) (at a time before now)	someone (X) did something to something (Y) (at a time before now)	LEXICOSYNTACTIC FRAME
because of this, something happened to this something (Y) as this someone (X) wanted it	because of this, something happened to this something (Y) as this someone wanted it	

often, when someone does something like this to something, it is like this:	often, when someone does something like this to something, it is like this:	PROTOTYPICAL SCENARIO
this something is near this someone's body	this something is near this someone's body	
this someone thinks about this something like this:	this someone thinks about this something like this:	
it is (like) one thing, it has parts	it is (like) one thing, it has parts	
someone can do something to one of these parts	someone can do something to one of these parts	
when someone does this, this part can move (a little)	when someone does this, this part can move (a little)	
when this someone (X) does this to this something (Y), it happens like this:	when this someone (X) does this to this something (Y), it happens like this:	EFFECT
this someone (X) does something with the hands to one part of this something (Y)	this someone (X) does something with the hands to one part of this something (Y)	
because of this, this someone's hand moves for a short time as this someone wants	because of this, this someone's hand moves for a short time as this someone wants	
because of this, one part of this something moves as this someone wants	because of this, one part of this something moves as this someone wants	
after this, this part is no longer in the same place as before	after this, this part is no longer in the same place as before	
because of this, after this, people can see what is inside this something	because of this, after this, people can see what is inside this something	POTENTIAL OUTCOME
	something/someone can move from one place to another after this	

4.1. Summary of the semantics of 'opening' events in Ewe and Longgu

A comparison of the semantics of verbs of 'opening' in Ewe and Longgu has provided further examples of languages that carve up the semantic space of 'opening' events differently. Where Ewe has three verbs, Longgu has over 10. Longgu has specific verbs to refer to opening of body parts, and specific verbs that refer to opening specific objects with instruments. At the same time, both Ewe and Longgu have verbs whose major senses involve the characteristics suggested for opening events in English: (a) a unitary object, although it may have parts such as a pot with a lid; (b) an object that separates along predetermined lines not unpredictably (hence actions of opening are usually reversible; objects that can be opened can also be closed); and (c) separation affords access to something (e.g. a content, an interior space or a previously concealed part of the object with which you can do something). In Longgu, opening events involve separation that affords access to something but it distinguishes opening events that involve objects that have clear parts (i.e. *tavangia* 'open' e.g. the door), and opening events that involve objects that can be separated along predetermined lines, but which do not necessarily have clearly identifiable parts (i.e. *vuresia* 'open' e.g. the food parcel/food). Associated with this is the outcome of opening the openable object— for the objects that have parts, this typically allows something to move through the object (e.g. a person through a door, water through a pipe, sound through a radio), whereas for the objects that do not clearly have parts, the action may simply allow someone to see something inside or do something with part of the object (e.g. food in the parcel).

One cultural object of Longgu that consists, in part, of leaves and can also be viewed as having parts is an *umu* 'stone oven'. An *umu* is a place to cook food in the ground. The food is cooked by placing it on hot stones and covering the food with more hot stones, old leaves and cloth such as old hessian bags. The *umu* 'stone oven' can be partially opened, i.e. to check the food, or it can be completely uncovered to remove the food. Both verbs (*tavangia* and *vuresia*) can be used to refer to opening a stone oven. The use of the verbs depends on whether the speaker is perceiving the oven as having 'parts' and doing something with the food (e.g. removing it from the oven), in which case the verb *tavangia* 'open something' is used, or whether the speaker is checking the food, in which case the top leaves and hessian may be removed and the verb *vuresia* 'open something' is used. Speakers describe the purpose of opening the oven, like opening the food parcels made of leaf, to see what is inside and to do something (e.g. eat the food from the food parcel, check when the food in the oven is ready). This analysis is supported by the antonym of *vuresia*, referring to opening an oven, which is *kuvia* 'cover it'.

The key difference between *tavangia* and *vuresia*, we suggest, is that while *tavangia* is used when the object has visible 'parts', and these parts show where the object can be separated (e.g. the lid of a pot, the door of a house), *vuresia* is used when the object can be separated along predictable lines (e.g. the leaves of a book, the cooked leaves covering food) but the object does not need to be perceived as having separate parts. For example, a woven basket can be 'undone' using the verb *vuresia* 'open something'. Note Ewe uses the verb *vu* for undoing buttons, hems and zips. The basket is made of leaves, and in addition it is not perceived of as having clearly separate parts. This analysis may also explain why 'moving through' something isn't part of the meaning of *vuresia*.

Ewe distinguishes opening events according to whether the opening event is natural or caused (*ke* and *vu*) and according to whether the opened object has an 'inside part and outside part' (*klẽ*), and according to whether the action is reversible or irreversible (the natural opening events of, for example, flowers or nuts are irreversible). Longgu does not pay attention to whether the opening event is natural or caused, but does pay attention to whether the action is reversible or irreversible (underlying this seems to be whether the object is made up of clear 'parts' or whether there is separation along predictable lines) and does pay attention to the kind of object being opened (and therefore the manner). In both languages, more than one verb can be used for the same opening event, but the perception is different. For example, in Ewe a different verb is used depending on whether something is perceived as opening naturally or is caused to be open (e.g. body parts), and in Longgu a different verb is used depending on whether something is perceived as having clear parts or just predictable lines of opening (e.g. a stone oven). We have shown that the Ewe verbs have some interpretations that are extensions of the physical action of opening something. Thus, *ke* in its internally caused and intransitive use is extended to talking about the ending of negative impact events. On the other hand, the verb *vu*, in specialised construction with postposition *nu* 'mouth', is used to talk about the commencement of situations or of temporal periods. In the latter case, Ewe is similar to English where the English open is also used to talk about the start of events—for example, to open the meeting (see Levison 1993).

The comparison between verbs of opening in Ewe and Longgu has highlighted the complexity of verbs of opening cross-linguistically, using NSM to show where meaning differences between the two languages lie in a small number of semantically similar verbs.

The human experience of opening objects is both a universal experience and one that may reflect a specific culture, as both material culture and different ways of perceiving and construing objects are involved.

References

Ameka, Felix K. (2002). Cultural scripting of body parts for emotions: On 'jealousy' and related emotions in Ewe. *Pragmatics & Cognition* 10 (1): 27–55.

Ameka, Felix K. (2017). Meaning between algebra and culture: Auto-antonyms in the Ewe verb lexicon. In Lisa L.S. Cheng, Maarten Hijzelendoorn, Hilke Reckman and Rint Sybesma (eds), *Crossroads Semantics: Computation, Experiment and Grammar*, Amsterdam: John Benjamins, 227–48. doi.org/10.1075/z.210.14ame.

Ameka, Felix K. (2019). "The Nut opens" and "Hunger ends": Verb constructions at the syntax-semantics interface. In James Essegbey, Dalina Kallulli and Adams Bodomo (eds), *The Grammar of Verbs and their Arguments: A Cross-Linguistic Perspective*. Cologne: Rüdiger Köppe, 59–84.

Ameka, Felix K. and James Essegbey (2007). 'CUT and BREAK' verbs and the causative/inchoative alternation in Ewe. *Cognitive Linguistics* 18 (2): 241–50. doi.org/10.1515/cog.2007.012.

Bowerman, Melissa (2005). Why can't you 'open' a nut, or 'break' a cooked noodle? Learning covert object categories in action word meanings. In Lisa Gershkoff-Stowe and David H. Rakison (eds), *Building object categories in developmental time*. Mahwah, NJ and London: Lawrence Erhlbaum Associates, 209–43.

Fillmore, Charles J. and Beryl T. Atkins (1992). Toward a frame-based lexicon: The semantics of RISK and its neighbors. In Adrienne Lehrer, Eva Feder Kittay and Richard Lehrer (eds), *Frames, Fields, and Contrasts: New Essays in Semantic and Lexical Organization*, Albany: Lawrence Earlbaum and Associates, 75–102.

Goddard, Cliff and Anna Wierzbicka (2004). Cultural scripts: What are they and what are they good for? *Intercultural Pragmatics* 1 (2): 153–66. doi.org/10.1515/iprg.2004.1.2.153.

Goddard, Cliff and Anna Wierzbicka (2009). Contrastive semantics of physical *activity* verbs: 'Cutting' and 'chopping' in English, Polish, and Japanese. *Language Sciences* 31: 60–96. doi.org/10.1016/j.langsci.2007.10.002.

Goddard, Cliff and Anna Wierzbicka (2016). Explicating the English lexicon of 'doing' and 'happening'. *Functions of Language* 23 (2): 214–56. doi.org/10.1075/fol.23.2.03god.

Heath, Jeffrey and Laura MacPherson (2009). Cognitive set and lexicalization strategy in Dogon action verbs. *Anthropological Linguistics* 51 (1): 38–63. doi.org/10.1353/anl.0.0001.

Hill, Deborah (2016a). Narrative texts and clause order: Changes over time. *Australian Journal of Linguistics* 36 (3): 1–19. doi.org/10.1080/07268602.2015.1134299.

Hill, Deborah (2016b). Bride-price, baskets, and the semantic domain of 'carrying' in a matrilineal society. *Oceanic Linguistics* 55 (2): 500–52. doi.org/10.1353/ol.2016.0023.

Kecskes, Istvan (2008). Dueling contexts: A dynamic model of meaning. *Journal of Pragmatics* 40 (3): 385–406. doi.org/10.1016/j.pragma.2007.12.004.

Levinson, Stephen C. (2000). *Presumptive Meanings: The Theory of Generalized Conversational Implicature*. Cambridge, MA, and London: MIT Press. doi.org/10.7551/mitpress/5526.001.0001.

Levison, Libby (1993). The topic is open. Working paper presented at the University of Pennsylvania Linguistics Forum 1993. Available at: repository.upenn.edu/hms/98.

Litvinov, Victor, and Kofi Agbodjo (1988 [1983]). Resultative in Ewe. In Vladimir P. Nedjalkov (ed.), *Typology of Resultative Constructions: Translated from the Original Russian Edition,* Amsterdam: John Benjamins, 231–37. doi.org/10.1075/tsl.12.19lit.

Majid, Asifa, Melissa Bowerman, Miriam Van Staden and James S. Boster (2007). The semantic categories of cutting and breaking events: A crosslinguistic perspective. *Cognitive Linguistics* 18 (2): 133–52. doi.org/10.1515/cog.2007.005.

Rongier, Jacques (2015). *Dictionnaire éwé—français*. Paris: L'Harmattan.

Talmy, Leonard (2000). Lexicalization patterns. In *Toward a Cognitive Semantics. Volume II: Typology and Process in Concept Structuring*. Chapter 1. Cambridge, MA: Massachusetts Institute of Technology. doi.org/10.7551/mitpress/6848.003.0003.

Westermann, Diedrich (1928). *Evefiala: Ewe-English Dictionary*. Berlin: Dietrich Reimer.

Wilkins, David and Deborah Hill (1995). When GO means COME: Questioning the basicness of basic motion verbs. *Cognitive Linguistics* 6 (2–3): 209–59. doi.org/10.1515/cogl.1995.6.2-3.209.

3

Gezellig: A Dutch cultural keyword unpacked

Bert Peeters

1. Introduction[1]

The term *keyword* (or *key word*), used with or without the adjective *cultural* (which is always understood to be there), has been a staple of Natural Semantic Metalanguage (NSM) semantics for the last 20-odd years; it figures prominently in the title of Wierzbicka's trailblazing book *Understanding Cultures through their Key Words* (1997), and in that of Levisen and Waters' collective volume *Cultural Keywords in Discourse* (2017). Cultural keywords are 'highly salient and deeply culture-laden words' (Goddard and Wierzbicka 1995: 57) or, in a more recent definition, 'culture-rich and translation-resistant words that occupy focal points in cultural ways of thinking, acting, feeling, and speaking' (Goddard 2017: 9; see also Goddard 2015: 386). Cultural keywords exist in all languages but are rarely studied in a way that combines total transparency (for cultural insiders and outsiders alike) with the absence of any cultural bias. Transparency and bias avoidance can only be achieved with a sophisticated methodology such as the NSM approach, which relies on decades of empirical research into the true universals of meaning.

---

[1] This chapter is dedicated to a mentor, colleague and friend I can't thank enough for all she has meant and continues to mean to me. This is for you, Anna. Enjoy! The text has undergone a substantial rewrite, especially after the first peer review. I am grateful for all feedback received and am solely responsible for any inaccuracies remaining.

Among the North and West Germanic languages, Dutch is, to the best of my knowledge, together with Faroese, the only one never to have been subjected to properly informed NSM analysis. The table of Dutch exponents of NSM primes in Appendix 3.1 is new: no such table has ever appeared in print. One Dutch cultural keyword that has been occasionally mentioned in the NSM literature is the adjective/adverb *gezellig*. Section 2 of this chapter provides some initial information on this elusive concept. Section 3 unpacks it in an intuitively intelligible and universally accessible way using NSM primes and syntax. Dutch versions of the various explications may be found in Appendix 3.2. Importantly, explications are experiments; none of them are final. Wierzbicka (1992: 551) and Levisen and Waters (2017: 241) have described explications as 'hypotheses'. The explications in this chapter are no exception.

2. *Gezellig*, a cultural keyword

The meaning of *gezellig* is anything but straightforward, as American philosophy professor Hilde Lindemann found out shortly after arriving from the USA on a European study trip:

> Over dinner on my first night in the Netherlands, my hosts nodded when I told them how much I liked the restaurant. 'Ja,' they said, 'it's *gezellig*, isn't it?' Aha, thought I, my first lesson in Dutch.
>
> 'What's *gezellig*?' I asked.
>
> 'It means—well, sociable,' Enne explained.
>
> 'But not exactly,' Menno added. 'More like cozy.'
>
> 'Sort of like the German *gemütlich*?'
>
> 'No, not really,' said Marian. 'A place could be *gemütlich* even when you're the only person in it, but it wouldn't be *gezellig*.' The others agreed. *Gezellig* didn't go with solitude. (Lindemann 2009: 40)

Or does it? Housing ads referring to *gezellige éénpersoonskamers* '*gezellig* single rooms' are not semantically incoherent, and yet such rooms are not meant to be occupied by more than a single occupant, who will spend most of his/her time in them alone. Likewise, people who prefer to spend an evening *gezellig alleen* '*gezellig* alone' at home do make sense. Phrases such as *gezellige éénpersoonskamer* and *gezellig alleen* demonstrate that, in contemporary Dutch, the adjective *gezellig* has meanings it didn't have in centuries past. Etymologically, *gezellig* is related to *gezel*, a noun that has had several meanings over time, all implying membership of a team or a group, and that now means 'companion' or 'mate'. Another noun that derives from *gezel* is *gezelschap* 'company' (as in the phrase 'be in good company'). Nowadays, the link between *gezellig* and *gezelschap* is more keenly felt than that between *gezellig* and *gezel*, which in its everyday use has lost some currency (except in compounds such as *levensgezel* 'life companion' and *vrijgezel* 'bachelor [unmarried male]'). However, neither link is strong enough to make phrases such as *gezellige éénpersoonskamer* and *gezellig alleen* ungrammatical.

According to van Baalen (2003: 16), references to the 'untranslatability' of the word *gezellig* have become so much of a cliché that nobody goes to the trouble anymore of putting the claim to the test. The same author goes on to say that other languages don't appear to have a word that covers its entire range of use—but this, she adds, holds true for many words in many languages. One source describes *gezellig* as covering 'everything from cozy to friendly, from comfortable to relaxing, and from enjoyable to gregarious'.[2] The noun *gezelligheid* '*gezellig*-ness', on the other hand, derived from the adjective by adding the suffix *-heid*, 'may be variously translated as sociability, conviviality, companionableness or snugness and cosiness' (Pradhan 1990: 56). Instead of bringing clarity, statements such as these tend to muddy the waters; they may explain why a common strategy to clarify the meaning of the keyword *gezellig* involves exemplification, as illustrated in the same passage, which includes references to:

> *een gezellige man* (a sociable man), *een gezellig glaasje* (a cheerful or sociable glass of wine or beer), *een gezellige avond* (pleasant evening), *een gezellig avondje* (social evening), *een gezellig hoekje of café* (a cozy corner or cafe), *gezellig weer* (pleasant weather), etc. (Pradhan 1990: 56)

In his *99 Tips for Dealing with the Dutch*, cross-cultural trainer Hans Kaldenbach comes up with a list of his own:

> Drinking coffee can be *gezellig*. Visiting a friend can be *gezellig*. So can an open fire. A neighborhood can have a *gezellig* feel to it; a painting depicting a rustic setting can also be *gezellig*. If someone refers to you as *gezellig*, take this as a compliment. (Kaldenbach 1995: 22)

---

2 Available at: www.dutchamsterdam.nl/155-gezellig (published 20 April, 2007).

Goddard (2017: 9) mentions *gezellig*, which he glosses as 'convivial, cosy, fun', as a prime example of a cultural keyword that has 'rise[n] to the attention of a speech community and attain[ed] an iconic and often contested status', something many other keywords don't.[3] The iconic status of *gezellig* is beyond dispute: it is recognised at all levels of society (for some impressions, see Dronkers 2013: 99) *and* it was further enhanced by former US president Barack Obama at the end of his 2014 visit to the Netherlands, when he addressed a packed press conference in the following terms: 'I'm told there's a Dutch word that captures the spirit, which doesn't translate exactly in English, but let me say that my first visit to the Netherlands has been truly *gezellig*'.[4] Its status as a cultural keyword and an indicator of a cultural value (*gezelligheid* '*gezellig*-ness')[5] has often been noted (see e.g. Gaston Durnez quoted in Driessen 1997: 49–50; van Baalen 2003: 16, 19; Lindemann 2009: 40; Goddard 2017: 9), even though there are dissenting voices—which is normal in debates about cultural values. As it turns out, the word *gezellig* is more (perhaps even much more) salient north of the border. Native speakers of Belgian Dutch (e.g. the Belgian writer Gaston Durnez, quoted in Driessen 1997: 49–50) have been known to single out *gezelligheid* as something that typifies speakers of Netherlands Dutch much more than it does them. The internet corpus on which this chapter is based provides spectacular proof of this point: most of the examples it includes come from domain names ending in *.nl* or contain other indications that give them away as belonging to Netherlands Dutch. Even so, I would like to argue that *gezellig* is a cultural keyword of Belgian Dutch as well. There may be some minute differences in meaning, and Flemish people may not use the word as much, but they still attach a lot of importance to *gezelligheid*.[6]

---

3   Goddard (2015: 386) is a little more precise: he opposes keywords that 'rise to the attention of a speech community (usually by way of contrast with outsiders) and attain an iconic, and therefore frequently contested status, in national identity discourses' to those that for most speakers 'stay below the horizon of consciousness'.
4   Available at: www.youtube.com/watch?v=rSClTFZ6xa8 (uploaded 25 March 2014).
5   Cultural keywords are by definition indicators of cultural values (Levisen and Waters 2017: 6, 240).
6   A separate paper and a more targeted corpus of Flemish or Belgian Dutch data would be needed to prolong the current investigation and reach a more definitive view.

3. *Gezellig* unpacked

To get a better feel for the meaning(s) of the Dutch cultural keyword *gezellig*, I had a closer look at the first 250 occurrences of the corresponding lemma identified in a Sketch Engine (www.sketchengine.eu/) search carried out on 11 September 2018.[7] The sheer number of place-oriented examples in the sample suggests that *gezellig* is first and foremost a quality attributed to places. Other examples show that periods of time, activities, events and features of a place, such as its atmosphere and bustle, are often called *gezellig* as well. Humans and other living beings like animals and plants can be *gezellig*, too, and so can inanimate objects. To account for this variety of uses, several NSM explications are required. The most important are presented in the subsections that follow.[8]

3.1. *Gezellig* + N$_{PLACE}$

Just over half of *gezellig* + N combinations in the Sketch Engine sample refer to a place (an individual room, the family home, an eatery, an open-air market, an entire village or town, a hotel, etc.). A few examples are reproduced in (1) to (3).

(1) Kortom, 'Huize Pruimtabak' is hét meest **gezellige bejaardentehuis** van het land.

'In short, "Huize Pruimtabak" is *the* most *gezellig* retirement home in the country.'

(2) Wie kan me een **gezellige kroeg** aanbevelen waar het Nederlands volk in New York onze jongens kan aanmoedigen?

'Who can recommend a *gezellig* pub where Dutch people in New York can cheer on our boys?'

---

7   My thanks go to Patrick Dendale (Universiteit Antwerpen), who executed the search for me.
8   The use of *gezellig* with animals (*een gezellige poes* 'a *gezellig* cat'), plants (*een gezellige anemoon* 'a *gezellig* anemone') and inanimate objects (*een gezellige borrel* 'a *gezellig* snifter') had to be left out due to limitations of space. Search results were occasionally complemented with hits returned by more targeted Google searches and identified by means of a bracketed (G).

(3) Het **gezellige** en kleinschalige **complex** bestaat uit 3 appartementen en 3 studio's.

'The *gezellig* and small-scale complex comprises 3 flats and 3 studios.'

Use of the adjective *gezellig* often goes hand in hand with diminutive suffixation on the place name, as in (4) to (6):

(4) Mocht u echter wel een keer uit eten willen in één van de vele **gezellige restaurantjes** die Harderwijk rijk is, dan zijn onze medewerkers u vanzelfsprekend graag van dienst.

'If ever you fancied dining out for once in one of the many *gezellige* restaurants$_{DIM}$ Harderwijk is rich in, our team members will obviously be happy to be of service.'

(5) Wat te denken van Alassio, dat vele oude kerken, groene parken met palmbomen, kleurrijke planten en **gezellige pleintjes** herbergt.

'What to think of Alassio, which has plenty of old churches, green parks with palm trees, colourful plants and *gezellig* squares$_{DIM}$.'

(6) De kustlijn is maar liefst 960 km lang en er zijn heel wat **gezellige vakantieplaatsjes** met hotels van uitstekende kwaliteit.

'The coast line is a whopping 960 km long and there are plenty of *gezellig* holiday spots$_{DIM}$ with hotels of outstanding quality.'

Impersonal constructions relying on an indefinite pronoun (*het* 'it') and a copular verb (e.g. *zijn* 'to be') are common as well. They involve a place name embedded in a prepositional phrase, as in (7), or a locational adverb (*hier* 'here', *daar* 'there', *er* 'there [unstressed]') recalling a place that was mentioned before, as in (8), where *daar* refers to the stands, and (9), where *er* refers to a previously described English town:

(7) **In** Pipodorp **is het** altijd **gezellig**.

'In Pipodorp it is always *gezellig*.'

(8) Gelukkig was de tribune groot genoeg om de ruim 750 supporters te herbergen en **was het daar** best **gezellig**.

'Fortunately the stands were big enough to host the 750-odd supporters and it was really *gezellig* there.'

(9) Het is een typisch Engels plaatsje met een groot marktplein in het midden waaraan meerdere pubs, hotels en vakwerkhuisjes zijn gevestigd. **Het** lijkt **er** altijd **gezellig te zijn**.

'It is a typical English town with a big market place in the centre where several pubs, hotels and workshops are located. It always looks *gezellig* there.'

For a *place* to qualify as *gezellig*, several conditions must be met. Most crucially, there must be at least a potential for the presence of humans. A place where no humans ever dwell can't be called *gezellig*. A *gezellig* place is one that makes people feel good, even when they are not in it and nobody else is in it either. People can see themselves spending time in such a place, alone or (space permitting) together with others. They can see themselves doing things in it, once again alone or with others. In the case of bigger places that allow for a larger human presence, *gezellig* implies at least the possibility, and often the reality, of collective enjoyment. There is a perception that nothing can go wrong.

Summarising the above in NSM terms, a *gezellig* place may be described as in [A]:

[A] *een gezellige plaats* 'a *gezellig* place'

a. a place
b. when people think about this place, they feel something good
c. they want to be in this place
d. they want to do some things in this place
e. when people are in this place, they can feel something good
f. bad things can't happen to people in this place

As an attribute of places, *gezelligheid* has often been compared to the Danish concept of *hygge*, subjected to detailed NSM analysis in Levisen (2012: 80–114). To describe a place where there is *hygge*, the adjective *hyggelig* is used. Both are no doubt cultural keywords, but the noun is the base form. It is the other way around in Dutch, where *gezellig* (the adjective) is the base form, and the noun *gezelligheid* is derived (and much less commonly used).

3.2. *Gezellig* + N referring to atmosphere

Uses of *gezellig* that relate to atmosphere or ambience can be viewed as extensions of uses related to place. There can be no atmosphere, in the relevant meaning, unless there is a place where that atmosphere 'reigns'. A semantically similar verb, *heersen*, is used in Dutch; I will rely on it in the header of the NSM explication below. The place itself may be explicitly mentioned, as in (10) and (11):

(10) Onze polyvalente, sierlijke **tenten** in combinatie met hun verfijnde inrichting zorgen steeds voor een **gezellige sfeer** waarin uw feest van succes is verzekerd!

'Our versatile and graceful marquees, combined with their refined equipment, always provide a *gezellig* atmosphere in which the success of your party is guaranteed!'

(11) Deze **zaal** heeft een **gezellige uitstraling** door de informele sfeer die hier hangt.

'This hall has a *gezellig* vibe thanks to the informal atmosphere that reigns here.'

However, location is often implicit, as in (12) and (13):

(12) En dat allemaal in een **gezellige ambiance** met een hapje en een drankje.

'And all of that in a *gezellig* ambience with a snack and a drink.'

(13) **Met zijn tweeën** een avond heerlijk getafeld in een **gezellige, knusse sfeer** met goede wijn en heerlijk eten.

'The two of us spent the evening deliciously dining in a *gezellig*, cosy atmosphere with good wine and delicious food.'

Examples (14) and (15) rely on an indefinite pronoun and a copular verb, as did examples (7) to (9).

(14) De **opkomst** was **groot** en **het** was reuze **gezellig**.

'The attendance was great and it was mightily *gezellig*.'

(15) Het was heel **gezellig** met **een menigte mensen** met kleedjes en stoeltjes en een podium met koortjes, solisten, bands etc.

'It was very *gezellig*, with a crowd of people with rugs$_{DIM}$ and chairs$_{DIM}$ and a stage with choirs$_{DIM}$, soloists, bands etc.'

Examples (13) to (15) show that atmosphere is tied up with human presence. There can be no *gezellig* atmosphere (or any other kind of atmosphere for that matter) without it. In addition, there is a time factor at work as well. In this respect, atmosphere differs from place, in that a place can be *gezellig* even when there is no one around for at least a brief period of time. Obviously, though, human presence is not a guarantee for a *gezellig* atmosphere. Dentists' waiting rooms are often singled out as places that are notoriously *ongezellig* (the prefix *on-* turns a word into its opposite). How could it be otherwise, since most people, when they visit dentists, are painfully aware of the discomfort that awaits them and not in the mood to socialise?[9]

Explication [B] sums up these observations in NSM:

[B] *er heerst hier een gezellige sfeer* 'there reigns a *gezellig* atmosphere here'

a.   it is like this:
b.   there are people in this place
c.   these people want to be in this place
d.   they feel something good when they are in this place
e.   they are doing some things when they are in this place
f.   they want to do these things for some time

Related to the use of *gezellig* with nouns conjuring up an atmosphere are the commonly heard cultural imperatives *Hou het gezellig!* 'Keep it *gezellig*' (Driessen 1997: 58) and *Maak het gezellig!* 'Make it *gezellig*':

(16) **Hou het gezellig**, warm en stijlvol in de achtertuin met deze Stahl X Vuurkorf! (G)

'Keep it *gezellig*, warm and stylish in the backyard with this Stahl X Fire pit!'

---

9   McNeil and Jomeen (2010), on the other hand, have proposed to use *gezellig* as a concept for managing labour pain, the idea being that creating a *gezellig* atmosphere in the birthing place will somehow ease the discomfort of childbirth.

(17) Dus **maak het gezellig**, mensen, want het gaat een lang weekend worden. (G)

'So make it *gezellig*, people, because it is going to be a long weekend.'

The corresponding verb phrases *het gezellig houden* 'to keep it *gezellig*' and *het gezellig maken* 'to make it *gezellig*' are illustrated in (18) and (19):

(18) Burgemeester Berend Hoekstra van Leek doet een dringende oproep aan jong en oud om **het** met de jaarwisseling **gezellig** te **houden**. (G)[10]

'Leek's Lord Mayor Berend Hoekstra makes an urgent call to young and old to keep it *gezellig* on New Year's Eve.'

(19) De eigenaar zal er alles aan doen om **het gezellig** te **maken**.

'The owner will do everything to make it *gezellig*.'

Het gezellig hebben 'to have it *gezellig*' is the outcome of *het gezellig maken*:

(20) Wat zeker is is dat ook zij **het gezellig** zullen **hebben** en genieten van muziek en alle andere nieuwe kunstvormen.

'What is certain is that they, too, will have it *gezellig* and enjoy music and all other new art forms.'

Two more phrases worth singling out are *gezellig alleen* '*gezellig* alone' (cf. section 2) and *gezellig samen* '*gezellig* together'. The former is often met with incomprehension, the latter is related to the phrase *gezellig samenzijn*:

(21) Ik vier Kerstmis **gezellig alleen** met een zelfgemaakt driegangenmenu en een lekkere fles cava erbij. (G)

'I celebrate Christmas *gezellig* alone with a self-cooked three course dinner and a nice bottle of cava to boot.'

(22) Ook staat er voor iedereen een hapje en een drankje klaar om **gezellig samen** na te praten.

'In addition we have a bite$_{DIM}$ and a drink$_{DIM}$ ready for everyone for an after-chat *gezellig* together.'

---

10 Example (18) agrees with the intuition of an anonymous reviewer who believes that the phrase *Hou het gezellig!* is 'almost synonymous' with the injunction not to drink too much and that, 'in the historically Protestant influenced Netherlands alcohol is less associated with *"gezellig"-ness* (a cup of cocoa is *"gezellig"*, a glass of whiskey less likely so)'.

3.3. *Gezellig* + N/Adj referring to bustle or buzz

Places can bustle or buzz with people, and that bustle or buzz, too, can be *gezellig*:

(23) Uiteraard is het altijd een **gezellige drukte** in onze hout en parket showroom.

'Obviously there is always a *gezellig* bustle in our wood-and-parquet showroom.'

(24) Op de boulevard langs de haven was het ook **gezellig druk**.

'On the boulevard along the harbour, too, it was *gezellig* busy.'

(25) Na het officiële gedeelte van de receptie ontstond al gauw een **gezellige rumoerigheid**, die zelfs voortduurde nadat het personeel de bar had gesloten.

'After the official part of the reception there soon arose a *gezellig* buzz, which lasted even after the staff had closed the bar.'

Explication [C] accounts for the use of *gezellig* with a *noun* meaning 'bustle' or 'buzz':

[C] *er heerst hier een gezellige drukte* 'there reigns a *gezellig* bustle here'

a. it is like this:
b. there are many people in this place
c. these people want to be in this place
d. they feel something good when they are in this place
e. they are doing some things when they are in this place
f. they want to do these things for some time

There appears to be much less of a difference between explications [B] (*gezellige sfeer*) and [C] (*gezellige drukte*) than one might expect. Unlike the former, the latter relies on the prime MUCH~MANY, but only in component (b), which refers to a large human presence. The prime is not needed in the explication of *gezellige sfeer*, which does not necessarily presuppose large numbers of people, as shown in example (13). On the other hand, there is *potential* for more diverse activity in a *gezellige drukte*, but this is not a requirement. Different people may be doing different things, with each individual or subgroup contributing to a collective sense of *gezelligheid*.

3.4. Gezellig + N/V$_{Activity}$

Example (26) illustrates the use of the keyword *gezellig* with the noun *activiteit* 'activity':

(26) Vrienden of familie die op zoek zijn naar een **gezellige activiteit** zijn van harte welkom.

'Friends or family who are on the lookout for a *gezellig* activity are most welcome.'

Activities are usually expressed by means of verbs. Example (27) has a noun and a verb; example (28) has two infinitives:

(27) Dan volgt nog een **gezellig samenzijn** met muziek van onze eigen DJ Anton en kunt u **gezellig meezingen** met onze karaoke.

'Then follows a *gezellig* get-together with music by our own DJ Anton and you can *gezellig* sing along with our karaoke.'

(28) **Turnen** is niet alleen goed voor de ontwikkeling, motoriek en kracht van kinderen, maar ook nog eens heel **gezellig**. Vrienden, vriendinnen, ouders, kom **gezellig meedoen**, iedereen is welkom!

'Gymnastics is not only good for the development, motor skills and strength of children, it is in addition very *gezellig*. Friends, parents, join in the fun [lit. come *gezellig* participate], everyone is welcome!'

Examples (29) to (31) illustrate the very common association between *gezelligheid* and talking. The latter is often coupled with other activities, as in the latter two examples:

(29) Wil je meer weten, met veel plezier lichten we onze methodiek en wat het voor jullie kan betekenen toe tijdens een **gezellige babbel**.

'If you want to find out more, we will be delighted to shed further light on our methods and what they can mean for you during a *gezellig* chat.'

(30) En toen werd het zo te zien heel **gezellig** en zaten ze nog een hele tijd met elkaar te **drinken**, te **praten** en te **lachen**.

'And then things apparently got very *gezellig* and they spent quite some time drinking, talking and laughing together.'

(31) Vandaag hebben we **gezellig** op een terras in het zonnetje zitten **beppen en kleppen**, uiteraard ook **gedronken** en **gegeten**.

'Today we spent our time *gezellig* in the sun$_{DIM}$ at a table in front of a café, chit-chatting; obviously we also had drinks and food.'

Some of our examples oppose solitude or isolation to activities described as *gezellig*:

(32) Af en toe miste hij het gevoel van een goede vriendschap wel—vooral als hij zijn zus zo **gezellig met haar vriendinnen** zag **rondlopen**.

'From time to time he did miss the feeling of good friendship— especially whenever he saw his sister walk around so *gezellig* with her friends.'

(33) Waar de rest **gezellig bij ons zit** in de woonkamer, zit zij 99 per cent van de tijd het liefst beneden in de woonkeuken.

'Whereas the others *gezellig* sit down with us in the lounge, she prefers spending 99 per cent of the time downstairs in the kitchen.'

The activity envisaged is usually intrinsically social or collective, and entirely voluntary. There is no coercion, no obligation to engage in the activity if people don't want to involve themselves. Explication [D] is an attempt at spelling this out:

[D] *een gezellige activiteit* 'a *gezellig* activity'

a. something people do[11]
b. they want to do it for some time
c. they do it with other people
d. all these people feel something good when they do it

---

11   The first component of explications [D] and [E] is potentially controversial since it includes a relative clause. The role and place of relative clauses in NSM syntax remains to be further elucidated.

No reference is made to the place where the activity occurs, since there is nothing to prevent *gezellig* activities from occurring in *ongezellig* 'un-*gezellig*' places. The same is true in the case of events (section 3.5). In terms of *gezelligheid*, the link between an activity and the place where it occurs is more tenuous than that between a place and its atmosphere (section 3.2) or a place and its bustle (section 3.3).

3.5. *Gezellig* + N$_{Event}$

Examples (34) to (36) provide illustration of the use of *gezellig* with nouns referring to events:

(34) Overal in de Provence vindt u **gezellige markten** met vaten vol ronde olijven, bergen geurende kruiden en dikke schijven geitenkaas.

'All over Provence you can find *gezellig* markets with barrels full of round olives, stacks of aromatic herbs and thick slices of goat cheese.'

(35) In het zomerseizoen kunnen we elk (buiten)evenement combineren met een **gezellige BBQ**.

'In the summer season, we can combine each (outside) event with a *gezellig* BBQ.'

(36) Al jaren organiseert de bank deze **gezellige familiefietsdag** voor haar werkgebied.

'For years the bank has been organising this *gezellig* family cycling day for its work sector.'

Relying on diminutives for increased effect, examples (37) and (38) are to some extent reminiscent of examples (4) to (6):

(37) Thuis heeft zijn vrouw alles in gereedheid gebracht voor een **gezellig verjaardagsfeestje**.

'*At home* his wife took care of all the preparations for a *gezellig* birthday party$_{DIM}$.'

(38) Ik ben altijd wel voor een **avondje gezellig uit**.

'I am always in favour of an evening$_{DIM}$ *gezellig* out.'

The diminutive in (38) favours an event interpretation: the example refers to an outing rather than to a period of time.[12] The adverb *gezellig* qualifies the adverb *uit* 'out'. It would have been equally possible to talk about *een gezellig avondje uit*, in which case *gezellig* is an adjective qualifying the noun *avondje*. The two phrases are very similar in meaning.

Example (39) shows that a *gezellig* event, like a *gezellig* activity, can occur in an *ongezellig* place:

(39) De dag wordt afgesloten met een **gezellige maaltijd** bij de **ongezellige Chinees** in de haven en een borrel in de lokale bar. (G)

'The day ends with a *gezellig* meal at the *ongezellig* Chinese restaurant in the harbour quarter and a snifter in the local bar.'

Explication [E] is fairly close in its formulation to explication [D], which is of course to be expected since events and activities are related categories:

[E] *een gezellig evenement* 'a *gezellig* event'

a. something that happens
b. it happens for some time
c. it happens when people do something with other people
d. all these people feel something good when they do it

3.6. *Gezellig* + N$_{Period}$

Time spent together can be *gezellig*, too. It is usually relatively short, and filled with collective activity that makes all those present feel good:

(40) Met een volle buik en een kerstpresent werd deze **gezellige middag** afgesloten.

'We concluded this *gezellig* midday with a full tummy and a Christmas present.'

(41) Al met al toch weer een **gezellige avond** met racen, pinballen en vooral veel gein!

---

12   The phrase *een gezellige avond* 'a *gezellig* evening' (no diminutive) favours the latter interpretation. See section 3.6.

'All in all yet again a *gezellig* evening with racing and pinball machines and above all lots of fun!'

(42) Jij was bij ons de **gezelligste week** van het jaar, de kerst.

'You were with us during the most *gezellig* week of the year, Christmas.'

I propose the NSM explication in [F]:

[F] *een gezellige tijd* 'a *gezellig* time'

a. some time, not a long time
b. at this time, it is like this:
c. people are with other people in the same place for some time
d. they feel something good when they are in the same place with these other people
e. they do some things with these other people

The infinitive phrase *er een gezellig(e)* N_{Period} *van maken* 'make it into a *gezellig* N_{Period}' is related to the cultural imperative *Maak het gezellig!* 'Make it *gezellig*', discussed in section 3.2. It is illustrated in (43):

(43) Alle leden zijn welkom om **er** weer **een gezellige avond van te maken**.

'All members are welcome to help make it into a *gezellig* evening.'

3.7. *Gezellig* + N_{Hum}

'If someone refers to you as *gezellig*, take this as a compliment', wrote Kaldenbach (1995), quoted in section 2. To describe someone as *gezellig* amounts to saying that they are good company, they are fun to be with and at the same time they seek out the company of others. They try hard not to antagonise, but to socialise. Examples of *gezellig* + N_{Hum} in the Sketch Engine sample include the following:

(44) Ik ben een meid van 18 jaar en ga binnenkort bij een bureau werken. Ben tot dan nog op zoek naar **gezellige klanten** die zin hebben in een leuke, jonge meid.

'I am an 18-year old lass and will be joining an escort agency shortly. Until then, am looking for *gezellig* customers who fancy a nice young lass.'

(45) Kinderen worden gelukkiger, **gezelliger** en beter ontwikkelde **mensen** als ze de gelegenheid krijgen om met elkaar te spelen.

'Children become happier, *more gezellig* and better developed individuals if they get the chance to play with one another.'

In NSM, *een gezellig iemand* can be explicated as in [G]:

[G] *een gezellig iemand* 'someone *gezellig*'

a. someone
b. other people want to be with this someone
c. this someone wants to be with other people
d. when this someone is with other people,
 these other people can feel something good because of it
e. this someone doesn't want other people to feel something bad
 when this someone does something
g. this is good

[G] is in many ways similar to Waters' (2017: 42) explication of *nice* as a human attribute (e.g. *a nice person*). The most important difference lies in components (b) and (c), absent from the explication of *nice*.

Related to the above is the use of *gezellig* in the phrases *gezellig zijn* 'to behave *gezellig*' and *gezellig doen* 'to act *gezellig*', which denote desirable behaviours of people (as opposed to permanent properties). *Als je niet gezellig kan doen, ga je maar naar je kamer* 'If you can't do *gezellig*, you might as well go to your room' is, according to van Baalen (2003: 16), an often-heard parental threat to recalcitrant children. *Gij zult gezellig zijn* 'Thou shalt be *gezellig*', on the other hand, is according to the same author 'just about the eleventh commandment in Dutch society' (ibid.; my translation).

4. Conclusion

In May 2003, during a visit to Leiden University, Anna Wierzbicka and Cliff Goddard taught a masterclass on 'Empirical universals in semantics: lexicon, grammar, discourse'. Cultural keywords were among the topics addressed, prompting the class to try its hand at explicating a striking specimen of the category, the adjective *gezellig*. Appendix 3.3 contains English and Dutch versions of the masterclass explication, which didn't relate to the keyword per se, but to an exclamation (*Gezellig hier!* 'Gezellig here!') featuring the arguably most common use of the word *gezellig* in today's language: its use as an attribute of a place.

By contrast, the explications in this chapter rely on lexico-grammatical frames of a different nature. Use of *gezellig* with nouns shows the true versatility of a word that goes equally well with nouns of places, nouns referring to atmosphere, nouns (and adjectives) referring to a bustle or buzz, nouns (and verbs) referring to activities, nouns referring to events, nouns referring to periods, and nouns referring to humans. The list is not complete, but it accounts for the most important and indeed most salient uses of a cultural keyword that has exercised the minds of several scholars yet remains far from having yielded all its secrets.

Exploring *gezellig* through the prism of NSM, with its fine-grained reductive paraphrases, has led me on a fascinating journey into Dutch linguaculture. I hope to have shed new light on a language-specific concept in a way that makes sense to cultural insiders and outsiders alike. Unlike my predecessors, I have tried to take nothing for granted: neither Dutch linguaculture itself, as is done by those who, like anthropologist Henk Driessen (1997) and theologian Pieter Dronkers (2013), write in their own language (Dutch) for an audience that is obviously aware of what it means to live in and be part of the Dutch linguaculture; nor the cultural baggage that is inevitably embedded (but hardly ever detected) in English scholarly writing, such as that of philosopher Hilde Lindemann (2009), psychologist Alexander McNeil and maternity care specialist Julie Jomeen (2010), or ethnographer Rajendra Pradhan (1990). It should never be forgotten that English is anything but the culture-free medium it is often assumed to be. We can either remain 'imprisoned' in it, to use Wierzbicka's (2014) beautiful metaphor, or take the key that, for years, she has invited us to put to good use.

References

Driessen, Henk (1997). Over de grenzen van gezelligheid. In Huub de Jonge (ed.), *Ons Soort Mensen: Levensstijlen in Nederland*. Nijmegen: Sun, 48–75.

Dronkers, Pieter (2013). Spelbrekers: Hoe gezellig is het nieuwe wij? In Manuela Kalsky (ed.), *Alsof Ik Thuis Ben: Samenleven in een Land Vol Verschillen*. Almere: Parthenon, 99–114.

Goddard, Cliff (2015). Words as carriers of cultural meaning. In John R. Taylor (ed.), *The Oxford Handbook of the Word*. Oxford: Oxford University Press, 380–98. doi.org/10.1093/oxfordhb/9780199641604.013.027.

Goddard, Cliff (2017). Natural Semantic Metalanguage and lexicography. In Patrick Hanks and Gilles-Maurice de Schryver (eds), *International Handbook of Modern Lexis and Lexicography* (online). Berlin: Springer. doi.org/10.1007/978-3-642-45369-4_14-1.

Goddard, Cliff and Anna Wierzbicka (1995). Key words, culture and cognition. *Philosophica* 55 (1): 37–67.

Kaldenbach, Hans (1995). *Act Normal! 99 Tips for Dealing with the Dutch*. Amsterdam: Prometheus.

Levisen, Carsten (2012). *Cultural Semantics and Social Cognition: A Case Study on the Danish Universe of Meaning*. Berlin: De Gruyter Mouton. doi.org/10.1515/9783110294651.

Levisen, Carsten and Sophia Waters (eds) (2017). *Cultural Keywords in Discourse*. Amsterdam: John Benjamins.

Lindemann, Hilde (2009). Autonomy, beneficence, and *gezelligheid*: Lessons in moral theory from the Dutch. *The Hastings Center Report* 39 (5): 39–45. doi.org/10.1353/hcr.0.0188.

McNeil, Alexander and Julie Jomeen (2010). 'Gezellig': A concept for managing pain during labour and childbirth. *British Journal of Midwifery* 18 (8): 515–20. doi.org/10.12968/bjom.2010.18.8.49317.

Pradhan, Rajendra (1990). Much ado about food and drinks: Notes towards an ethnography of social exchange in the Netherlands. *Etnofoor* 3 (2): 48–68.

van Baalen, Christine (2003). Neerlandistiek zonder grenzen: Over het nut van crossculturele taalanalyses. *Colloquium Neerlandicum 15*, 13–22.

Waters, Sophia (2017). *Nice* as a cultural keyword: The semantics behind Australian discourses of sociality. In Carsten Levisen and Sophia Waters (eds), *Cultural Keywords in Discourse*. Amsterdam: John Benjamins, 25–54.

Wierzbicka, Anna (1992). Defining emotion concepts. *Cognitive Science* 16 (4): 539–81.

Wierzbicka, Anna (1997). *Understanding Cultures through their Key Words: English, Russian, Polish, German, and Japanese.* New York: Oxford University Press.

Wierzbicka, Anna (2014). *Imprisoned in English: The Hazards of English as a Default Language.* New York: Oxford University Press.

Appendix 3.1

Table A3.1. Dutch exponents of the NSM primes.

IK, JIJ, IEMAND, IETS~DING, MENSEN, LICHAAM	substantives
I, YOU, SOMEONE, SOMETHING~THING, PEOPLE, BODY	
SOORT, DEEL	relational substantives
KIND, PART	
DIT, HETZELFDE, ANDERE~ANDERS	determiners
THIS, THE SAME, OTHER~ELSE	
ÉÉN, TWEE, SOMMIGE~WAT, ALLE, VEEL, WEINIG	quantifiers
ONE, TWO, SOME, ALL, MUCH~MANY, LITTLE~FEW	
GOED, SLECHT	evaluators
GOOD, BAD	
GROOT, KLEIN	descriptors
BIG, SMALL	
WETEN, DENKEN, WILLEN, NIET WILLEN, VOELEN, ZIEN, HOREN	mental predicates
KNOW, THINK, WANT, DON'T WANT, FEEL, SEE, HEAR	
ZEGGEN, WOORDEN, WAAR	speech
SAY, WORDS, TRUE	
DOEN, GEBEUREN, BEWEGEN	actions, events, movement
DO, HAPPEN, MOVE	

(ERGENS) ZIJN, ER IS, (IEMAND/IETS) ZIJN	location, existence, specification
BE (SOMEWHERE), THERE IS, BE (SOMEONE/ SOMETHING)	
VAN MIJ (ZIJN)	possession
(IS) MINE	
LEVEN, STERVEN	life and death
LIVE, DIE	
WANNEER~MOMENT~KEER, NU, VOOR~ERVOOR, NA~ERNA, EEN LANGE TIJD, EEN KORTE TIJD, VOOR EEN TIJDJE, OGENBLIK	time
WHEN~TIME, NOW, BEFORE, AFTER, A LONG TIME, A SHORT TIME, FOR SOME TIME, MOMENT	
WAAR~PLAATS, HIER, BOVEN, ONDER, VER, DICHTBIJ, ZIJDE, IN, AANRAKEN	place
WHERE~PLACE, HERE, ABOVE, BELOW, FAR, NEAR, SIDE, INSIDE, TOUCH	
NIET, MISSCHIEN, KUNNEN, OMDAT, ALS	logical concepts
NOT, MAYBE, CAN, BECAUSE, IF	
ZEER, MEER	intensifier, augmentor
VERY, MORE	
ZOALS	similarity
LIKE~AS	

Notes: Exponents of primes can be polysemous, that is, they can have other, additional meanings.

Exponents of primes may be words, bound morphemes or phrasemes.

They can be formally complex.

They can have language-specific combinatorial variants (allolexes, indicated with ~).

Each prime has well-specified syntactic (combinatorial) properties.

Source: Author's summary.

Appendix 3.2: Dutch versions of the NSM explications proposed in this chapter

[A'] *een gezellige plaats*

a. een plaats
b. wanneer mensen aan deze plaats denken, voelen ze iets goeds

c. ze willen in deze plaats zijn

d. ze willen in deze plaats wat doen[13]

e. wanneer mensen in deze plaats zijn, kunnen ze iets goeds voelen

f. er kunnen in deze plaats met mensen géén slechte dingen gebeuren

[B'] *er heerst hier een gezellige sfeer*

a. het is zó:[14]

b. er zijn mensen in deze plaats

c. deze mensen willen in deze plaats zijn

d. ze voelen iets goeds wanneer ze in deze plaats zijn

e. ze doen wat wanneer ze in deze plaats zijn

f. ze willen het voor een tijdje doen

[C'] *er heerst hier een gezellige drukte*

a. het is zó:

b. er zijn vele mensen in deze plaats

c. deze mensen willen in deze plaats zijn

d. ze voelen iets goeds wanneer ze in deze plaats zijn

e. ze doen wat wanneer ze in deze plaats zijn

f. ze willen het voor een tijdje doen

[D'] *een gezellige activiteit*

a. iets dat mensen doen

b. ze willen het voor een tijdje doen

c. ze doen het met andere mensen

d. al deze mensen voelen iets goeds wanneer ze het doen

---

13 This very tentative proposal hinges on the realisation of the combination SOMMIGE-WAT + IETS-DING + DOEN as WAT DOEN, whereas in the English NSM DO + SOME + SOMETHING-THING = DO SOME THINGS. Unlike IETS, which is inherently singular, WAT is unmarked for number.

14 *zó* is a portmanteau for the combination *als dit* ('like this'), comparable to German *so*, French *ainsi*, Italian *così*, Spanish *así*, etc.

[E'] *een gezellig evenement*

a. iets dat gebeurt
b. het gebeurt voor een tijdje
c. het gebeurt wanneer mensen iets doen met andere mensen
d. al deze mensen voelen iets goeds wanneer ze het doen

[F'] *een gezellige tijd*

a. wat tijd, geen lange tijd[15]
b. in deze tijd is het zó:
c. er zijn voor een tijdje mensen in dezelfde plaats met andere mensen
d. ze voelen iets goeds wanneer ze in dezelfde plaats zijn met deze mensen
e. ze doen wat met deze andere mensen

[G'] *een gezellig iemand*

a. iemand
b. andere mensen willen bij[16] dit iemand zijn
c. dit iemand wil bij andere mensen zijn
d. wanneer dit iemand bij andere mensen is,
    kunnen deze mensen daarom[17] iets goeds voelen
e. dit iemand wil niet dat andere mensen iets slechts voelen wanneer dit iemand iets doet
f. dit is goed

---

15 *niet* 'not' + *een lange tijd* 'a long time' = *geen lange tijd*.
16 A quirk (?) of Dutch NSM syntax: *bij* 'with' needs to be used here instead of *met*.
17 'daarom' is a portmanteau matching the English NSM sequence 'because of this'.

Appendix 3.3: English and Dutch versions of the 2003 masterclass explication of the adjective *gezellig*

The only record of explication [H] I know of[18] is incomplete: component (g) is missing. It must have been there, though, since it is part of the Dutch translation [H'] proposed by van Baalen (2003: 21). In line with current NSM practice, components (b) to (h) have been indented to clarify they contribute to spelling out the thought referred to in component (a). Component (d) is indented even further to highlight that it is a subordinate clause depending on component (c).

[H] *Gezellig hier*! 'gezellig here'

a. everyone here can think like this:
b.   I am here now with some other people
c.   these people are all doing some things at the same time
d.   because they want to feel something good
e.   they don't want anyone here to feel something bad
f.   they all feel something good
g.   this is good
h.   I want to be here with these people

[H'] *Gezellig hier*!

a. iedereen hier kan iets denken als dit:
b.   ik ben nu hier met andere mensen
c.   deze mensen doen allen iets op hetzelfde moment
d.   omdat ze iets goeds willen voelen
e.   ze willen niet dat iemand hier iets slechts voelt
f.   ze voelen allemaal iets goeds
g.   dit is goed
h.   ik wil hier zijn met deze mensen

---

18 Available at: waij.com/gezelligheid/primitieven.html.

4

Royal semantics: Linguacultural reflections on the Danish address pronoun *De*

Carsten Levisen[1]

1. Address studies

Anna Wierzbicka's recent work on the cross-European semantics of address has reopened and invigorated 'address studies' (Wierzbicka 2015, 2016a, 2016b, 2016c). This is a remarkable achievement, given that the field of address for a long time has been considered 'old hat'—a well-studied, almost trivial area of cross-European linguistics, from which very little innovation emerged. For decades, address was popular in both sociolinguistics and pragmatics. Typologies based on the so-called T-V pronouns (such as French *tu/vous* and German *du/Sie*) emerged out of sociolinguistic research, and in pragmatics the once flourishing paradigm of 'politeness theory' analysed address as a component of 'polite' verbal behaviour. Somewhere along the line, the interest in the *meaning* of address

---

[1] I would like to acknowledge Anna Wierzbicka's profound influence and inspiration on my work, including the present work on the semantics of address. The first time I discussed address with Anna was in 2008 at the Australian Linguistics Institute. Drawing her attention to the special case of Danish address, Anna said: 'you should write about it!'. And so I did—with 10 years of delay. I would also like to thank Sophia Waters, Hartmut Haberland and the two anonymous reviewers of my chapter for engaging with my ideas, and helping me to improve on my analysis.

was lost, and Wierzbicka's work allows us to reconsider this question: what do address words mean to speakers? In this chapter, I want to contribute to the meaning-based turn in address research following Wierzbicka's lead, and the emerging semantically driven address studies (see in particular Wierzbicka 2016a, 2016b, and the important contributions of Wong 2014: 57–93; Farese 2018).

A central part of Wierzbicka's (2016a) reopening of the field has to do with her search for a more fine-grained metalanguage as a tool for description. She says:

> Simplistic distinctions such as that between 'familiar' and 'polite' forms of address, or between 'T' and 'V', are still widely relied on, and the focus of attention is often on collecting more data rather than on finding a framework within which the amassed data can be made sense of. (2016a: 523).

One has to agree with Wierzbicka that 'more data' cannot be the solution to the study of European address. We already know very well *what* the European address words are, and also great deal about *how* these words work in social interaction. The widest gap in our current knowledge is meaning, and Wierzbicka's 'meaning challenge' has consequences not only for address but also for 'relational grammars' in general—that is, the variety of ways in which different linguacultures construe the connection between the 'you' and the 'me' in conversational rituals.[2]

Another key point in Wierzbicka's criticism (2016b) is the way in which comparative studies have been wedded to Anglocentric terminology:

> conventional labels like 'informal', 'intimate', 'familiar', 'formal', and 'respectful', are all drawn from the conceptual vocabulary of English (2016b: 212)

A third problem identified by Wierzbicka (2016a) is the tendency to elevate the micro-diversity of usage above the macro-diversity of semantics, and to favour use over meaning. She says:

> Yes, the use of terms of address changes over time and varies across the social spectrum, but differences in their use do not necessarily indicate differences in meaning (2016a: 506)

---

2   The study of relational grammars belongs the more general field of ethnosyntax (Wierzbicka 1979).

I believe that all these points are important, and if I were to develop an analytical action plan based on these insights, I would propose the following:

Above all, we must insist on the retirement of the T-V system that was invented in the early '60s (Brown and Gilman 1960). While the T-V approach has taken us some distance, this simple system is too crude for meaning-based analysis, even if used critically and competently (see e.g. Braun 1988; Clyne et al. 2009; Hajek et al. 2013). The main problem is that T and V gloss over address diversity in European languages and lump together words and meanings based on superficial similarities, rather than on a deep meaning analysis. Moreover, T and V have also introduced a highly problematic dualistic thinking, as though there are only ever just two competing address terms, and as though the so-called 'Vs' are identical across Europe's languages. The dullness of analysis is partly due to the metalinguistic biases introduced by the T-V paradigm, and the solution is to adopt a metalanguage that allows for a more high-resolution analysis, and which does not impose a simplistic duality like T and V. The Natural Semantic Metalanguage (NSM) offers itself as a metalinguistic tool for doing such analysis (Goddard and Wierzbicka 2014; Goddard 2018), and in my view, NSM analysis can fully replace the T-V system.

Second, the Anglocentric bias needs to be addressed head-on. By comparing Europe's languages through English words such as *polite*, *formal*, *familiar*, etc., we run the risk of viewing all these English words as neutral words, rather than value words with an Anglo cultural take on sociality and culture (for a criticism, see Wierzbicka 2010, on the problem of Anglocentrism, see also Levisen 2019; Ye 2019). Even if some of the traditional terminologies in address studies have quasi-counterparts in (some) European languages, there is a considerable 'cryptodiversity' at play in the terminology of values (Levisen and Jogie 2015). Precision in analysis cannot be reached unless we have a *tertium comparationis*, a common yardstick. This means that none of the explanatory keywords in English, not even *solidarity* or *politeness*, should be relied on when we analyse European address words and practices (on keywords, see also Levisen and Waters 2017).

Third, address words and practices are among the most important evidence for relational grammars in and across linguacultures. Address rituals play an important part in the everyday life of speakers. They model different ideas and ideals of kinship and family relations, patterns of friendship and colleagueship, and other kinds of social cognition that constitute social and relational knowledge. Address words are never just linguistic devices; they are always manifestations of cultural meaning. They are always 'linguacultural', and they profoundly link ways of speaking with ways of thinking about others (and ways of feeling towards other people). They deserve to be studied from a macro-diversity perspective,[3] and from the perspective of cross-cultural semantics.

The chapter is structured as follows. In section 2, I will briefly introduce Danish linguaculture in relation to address words and practices. In section 3, I will present some 'rich points' on how *De* enables cultural discourse. In section 4, I will provide an explication for the Danish *De*, and contrast and compare this with Wierzbicka's explication for German *Sie*. This is followed by some concluding remarks.

2. 'Danish address' in the European context

It seems clear that Danish address does not fit neatly into any of the two main camps of European address—neither the 'Anglo' nor the 'continental European'. The difference between 'Anglo' and 'Continental' can be summarised as follows:

> One of the deepest differences between English-based human interaction and the interaction based on the languages of continental Europe has to do with terms of address. For speakers of languages like French, Italian, or German it goes without saying that 'polite' words such as *vous*, *Lei* and *Sie* are indispensable in daily exchanges with others. (Wierzbicka 2016b: 209)

At a first glance, Danish address seems to be both English-like and Continental-like. Anglo relational grammar is known for its extensive discourses of '*you*', and in terms of cultural values, *you* has been called a 'great social equaliser' (Wierzbicka 2003: 47). The same can be said about the Danish *du*. '*Du* discourse' is linked with an egalitarian ethos, in much the same way as the Anglo inclusive '*you* discourse'. But this is not

---

3   By macro-diversity, I refer to semantic differences in address words across different languages, and to *intercultural* analysis. By micro-diversity, I refer to differences in registers, genres, styles and dialects within the same linguaculture, and to *intracultural* analysis.

the full story. After all, Danish does have an address word *De*, which on the surface looks similar to German *Sie*, French *vous*, etc. An initial conclusion would be to say that discursive evidence points towards the 'Anglo' system, but that structural evidence points towards the 'Continental' systems.

Let's now take a closer look at *De*. Unlike the words *Sie* and *vous* that are ubiquitous in everyday German and French interaction, *De* is not a part of the daily exchange of words in Danish. The *De*, it would seem, has almost fallen out of use. To illustrate, I have myself, in my life as a Danish speaker, never used *De* in any 'normal' exchange of words. In fact, I have never used the word seriously at all—only for humorous or other rhetorical purposes. To the Danish mind, the 'fall of the *De*' forms part of the narrative of a Danish egalitarian ethos that grew out of the popular enlightenment and social democracy, and which was consolidated through the anti-authoritarian and anti-hierarchy discourses of the 1960s (see Hansen 1980: 89; Levisen 2012). Even the conservative newspaper *Jyllands Posten*, whose renowned slogan used to be *hvis De vil vide mere* 'if *De* want to know more' has given up on *De*. To avoid ridicule, the paper has recently changed its slogan to *hvis du vil vide mere* 'if you [*du*] want to know more'.

While the Danish *De* might be marginal in discourse, studies show that speakers are very much aware of the word (Kretzenbacher et al. 2018). *De* may have fallen, but the fall has mainly happened at the interactive level; the word is still alive and kicking in speakers' linguistic consciousness. The reason for this seems to be that *De* provides speakers with meaning potentials and indexical affordances. One of these indexical affordances is to create voices from the past: if you want to make, say, a historical Danish film, just insert *De* in the dialogue, and the Danes will be convinced that 'it feels old'. No other historically based lexicogrammatical and sociophonetic features of older stages of Danish seem to have same seductive power: *De* is recreating a sense of 'the old days' before the victory of social democracy, and the rise of an egalitarian ethos. Even the spelling of the word, with the old-fashioned capitalised D, contributes to invoking relational norms of the past.

In serious interaction, the Danish *De* is intricately linked with the Danish royal family. Almost akin to the 'royal registers' known from (for example) African linguistics (Storch 2011: 23–26), Danish '*De* discourse' seems to have a royal ring. Using myself as an example again, the only situation in which I would feel obliged to use the word *De* seriously would be if I were to have a conversation with a member of the Danish royal family. This has not happened yet.

But claiming '*De* discourse' as a royal-only register might be going too far. Perhaps it would be more apt to categorise *De* as a feature of 'residual conservatism', and with a royal prototype. There are pockets of *De* use and *De* users not only in the Danish royal court, but also in certain business cultures (such as Maersk), in certain connoisseur shops (such as Perch's tea shop), towards old elite-looking Copenhageners, but the fact of the matter is that for most speakers of Danish, *De* is a nice-to-have word, not a need-to-have word. And the reason why it is nice-to-have is that *De* can be used to humorously elevate people to a royal-like status, akin to saying *Your Majesty!* sarcastically in English. *De*, then, has something interesting to offer in terms of sarcasm, and humorous subversion, and the Danes are generally into sarcasm and humorous subversion (Goddard and Levisen forthcoming; Levisen 2018).

At a more general level, 'Danish address' stands out in a European context for its 'minimalism' and 'exceptionalism' (cf. Levisen 2017). It is 'minimalist' in the sense that address words in general seem marginal in Danish linguaculture, and it is 'exceptionalist' in the sense that the majority of the few existing address words are the stylistically marked choice. Several address words that exist in Danish are actively discouraged, and have been actively discouraged for decades. This is true for the German-based address words that index 'old style', words such as *De, Hr.* and *Fru,* (cp. German *Sie, Herr* and *Frau*) as exemplified in (1) but also socially stigmatised address words such as *ven* 'friend', *makker* 'mate', and *do* '(jovial Jutlandic address variant of) *du*', as in (2). The English translations fail to capture the stigma, but in Danish such words index marginalised social or socio-regional speech.

(1) *Vil De være så venlig?*
    'Would *De* be so kind?'
    Om forladelse, Hr. Mortensen
    'I beg your pardon, Hr. Mortensen'
    Tak, Fru Nielsen
    'Thank you, Fru Nielsen'

(2) *Ved du hvad, ven?*
'You know what, *ven?*'
Hva' så makker?
'What's up, *makker*'
Tak for hjælpen, do!
Thanks for the help, *do!*

Besides the 'old' and 'stigmatised' indexicalities, more recent influxes of English address words in slang registers such as *boss, roomie, dude, cutie* and *pal* have also found their way into Danish, where they index a 'global' street style, and often impart a humorous tone. So to recap, Danish address is marginal as such, and the address term *De* is likely to index something like 'old and noble' because of its royal-like meaning.

3. The Queen, the Swiss, the train: Encounters with *De*

To further explore the meaning of *De*, I will now discuss three 'rich points' in order to come to a clearer understanding of what *De* means.

The first rich point goes back to my childhood in a Jutlandic town. As a 10-year-old pupil, I remember having the first '*De* awareness' moment in my life. Rumours had it that the Queen was coming to visit my town and that her procession would pass the town hall square where I happened to wait for the bus every day. Anxiously, I asked my mother what I should do if the Queen wanted to talk to me when she was passing the town square. I had heard in the schoolyard that I couldn't say *du* to her, and that there was another word *De* that was used to address royals. I had never heard about this word before and asked my mother if it was true. She said that it was highly unlikely that the Queen's visit would coincide with my bus ride. My mother was right, of course. The Queen's procession didn't pass during the 20 minutes that I happened to wait for my bus. Also, my mother reassured me that the Queen couldn't get mad at me if I forgot to say *De*. Since I missed the Queen that day, I never got the chance to test my new word *De*, and still to this day, this was the closest I ever got to using a serious *De* in my life.

A second rich point in my life with *De* happened a couple of months ago, when I was travelling by train from Aarhus to Copenhagen. I was in a train carriage full of people, some standing, some sitting on the floor, and I was trying to write emails on my laptop in a very small personal space in the middle of a crowded car. There were elderly people who found it difficult to keep their balance as the train was rocking along, and it was truly uncomfortable for all of us. I decided to explore the train to see if there was better seating elsewhere, and to my surprise I found two completely empty carriages. This annoyed me. I was thinking of all the people in the other carriage, and I complained to the conductor. I asked her why she hadn't informed the passengers via the loudspeaker system that there were empty carriages when she knew that passengers were struggling in the overcrowded carriage. She responded that it wasn't her problem and that it was the passengers' own responsibility to find a place to sit. I disagreed with her publicly. Then she started addressing me with *De*. For the rest of our slightly heated conversation, she called me both *Hr.* and *De*, which upset me further. It felt like she was saying 'mind your own business, Your Majesty'. I felt that she talked down to me in a passive-aggressive way, and that what she really communicated was that I had dared to think of myself as someone 'above her'. The *De*, then, was clearly in the service of 'cutting me down', and also ridiculing me for my alleged hubris.

The third rich point happened a few years ago, when the Swiss-based multinational coffee chain Nespresso opened their business in the Jutlandic town of Aarhus. I went to the shop one day, and to my surprise I was greeted with a *De*. As a matter of fact, all employees used the address pronoun *De* when interacting with their Danish customers, and this was so unusual for me that I decided to do fieldwork in the store for a while. I listened to the *De*-based conversations, and I soon found out that most customers were bewildered by the *De*. In fact most customers were annoyed by it, and some even angry. I interviewed an employee about the *De* use, and I was told that they were simply following company policy. The 'Swiss logic' seemed to be that the German *Sie* or the French *vous* needed a counterpart in Danish, and since this counterpart existed in the form of *De*, all employees had been instructed to use it. I was further told in the store that the *De* was meant to express *høflighed* 'politeness'. When I queried it further, the employee admitted that a large number of customers found it incredibly *uhøfligt* 'impolite'. A couple of months later, I returned to the store and the *De* had gone. I interviewed the employees again and they confirmed that the *De* policy had been reconsidered, and that they had found new ways of expressing *høflighed* 'politeness' that were more in line with Danish customers' preferences.

4. The Danish *De* and the German *Sie*

The German *Sie* serves as a historical model for the Danish *De* (see e.g. Kretzenbacher et al. 2018), and the same is true for other address terms that index 'old' style in contemporary Danish such as *Hr.* (Herr), and *Fru* (Frau). In Denmark, German language is no longer an important model for the borrowing of words and concepts, and general knowledge of the German language is no longer strong among Danish speakers. But the German *Sie* is one of the German words 'known' by the Danes—and the German *Sie* is largely reinterpreted and misunderstood. The Danish stereotype of German conversation as 'hierarchical' and 'stiff' to the point of being 'comical' is to a large degree finding its symbolic rationale in the notion of 'address'[4]—and with a basis in '*Sie*-for-*De*' transference. Let us take a look at the German *Sie*, as explicated by Wierzbicka (2016b: 229):

[A] The German *Sie*

a. when I say this, I don't think about you like I can think about children

 at the same time, I don't think about you like I can think about some other people

b. I don't think about you like this: 'I know this someone well'

c. I think like this:

 'people can know some good things about this someone,

 like they can think some good things about many other people'

In Wierzbicka's analysis, German *Sie* differs in meaning from other European address pronouns such as the French *vous*, and the Italian *Lei* and *Voi*. The explication reflects these differences (for an extensive semantic analysis of the two Italian words *Lei* and *Voi*, see Farese 2018). One of the key elements in *Sie* is that 'people can know some good things about this someone, like they can think some good things about many other people'. This 'positive', and 'pro-social' meaning is not conveyed by the *De*. In fact, the Danish *De* seems quite far removed from *Sie*, *vous*, *Lei* and *Voi*, and based on my analysis so far, I will propose the following explication for *De*:

---

4   Ørsness (2016) provides an interesting case study on the *De*–*Sie* complex, by exploring address practices in the teaching of German in Denmark. He proposes that a cultural cognitive dissonance analysis can explain the complex.

[B] The Danish *De* (in its rare, serious sense)

a. when I say this, I don't think about you like I can think about other people
b. I don't think about you like this: 'this someone is someone like me'
c. I think like this:

    'people can know that this someone is above other people,

    like a king [m] is above other people, like a queen [m] is above other people

First, the theme about adults and children, which is present in German *Sie* (component (a)) as well in *vous*, *Lei* and *Voi*, does not seem to be a part of the meaning of *De*. This reflects the fact that neither adult Danish, nor children's Danish, nor adult–children interactions in general have any age-based construal of address, and a shift from *du* to *De* does not seem to activate 'age' either. The main idea conveyed in *De* is 'specialness'—'I don't think about you like I can think about other people', and 'difference'—'I don't think about you like this: "this someone is someone like me"'. Also, and importantly, the idea is to convey 'hierarchy' modelled on 'royalty'. I have used the two molecules king [m] and queen [m]—in Danish, *konge* 'king' and *dronning* 'queen'—to convey the royal prototype of the hierarchical cognition embedded in *De*. This final component should account for an '*aboveness* of a royal-like kind'; that is, it should account for both the use in real interaction with royals (such as between journalists and the Queen), and the occasional shop in certain neighbourhoods in Copenhagen that uses *De* to enact a *fornem* 'posh, distinguished, noble' style.

The third component also provides us with a hook for explaining the humorous and sarcastic scripts associated with *De*. With *De* one can mock another person's alleged special, outstanding and royal-like attitude or perceived status, and thereby police the cultural value of *lighed* 'equality, similarity'. For instance, the sarcastic *De* could be interpreted through a general Danish *sarkasme* script (see Goddard and Levisen forthcoming), but the master script that undergirds the aversion towards *De* discourse is a script against 'hierarchical social cognition':

[C] A high-level Danish script against 'hierarchical social cognition'

many people think like this:
    it is bad if someone thinks like this:
        'I am not like other people, I am above other people'
    it is good if someone can think like this:
        'no one is above other people, no one is below other people'

The script in [C] spells out the socio-cognitive norm for thinking about good and bad thoughts in relation to being below and above others. The exception to script [C] is the Danish royal family. They are allowed to be 'above others', they can live by other scripts and follow other grammars of relationality. But even the royal family can go too far if they too demonstratively verbalise their exceptional status. In a much-discussed televised episode, Prince Joachim, the younger son of the Danish queen, once snapped at a journalist who failed to use *De* address, and insisted that the journalist changed his pronouns to fit the royal *De* code. The Danish public reacted very negatively towards the prince, and these reactions can be viewed as strong evidence in support for the cultural ethos reflected in script [C].

The script can also explain in part why Danish speakers, through a *De-for-Sie* transfer, largely misunderstand (or, to be more descriptive, reinterpret) the German *Sie*. The master script in [C] governs several lower-level scripts that remain to be articulated, including the scripts for 'royal registers', and scripts for humorous, sarcastic and subversive uses, and the indexical scripts for invoking 'old style', 'German style', and so on.

5. Concluding remarks

This chapter offered a first NSM-based analysis of Danish address, focusing on the Danish address pronoun *De*. It was found that *De* is different from European words that have been compared to *De*, such as German *Sie* and French *vous*. It would seem that Danish linguaculture has its own cultural logics, based on Danish words and scripts, and that it is not just a copy of the German or the Anglo system. Close in spirit to the Anglo system of address, and close in form to Continental address culture, it seems that

Danish, with its normalisation of 'zero address', with its focus on royal registers and humorous usages, constitutes a special case to the study of address that can help to explore the diverse ways in which Europeans do relational grammar in their daily lives. In order to study this diversity in depth, we need new approaches and new visions for address, and most of all we need to relinquish the strangleholds that prevent us from achieving this progress. I will conclude by sharing Wierzbicka's (2016a) vision, a vision that I also hold. It is a vision that can truly transform the study of address in Europe and the world:

> we need to let go of technical terms (such as 'polite', 'familiar', 'distance', 'formality', and so on) and look for semantic components intelligible to native speakers and testable in context; and if we want to do so without ethnocentrism, we need to formulate our hypotheses (that is, the hypothesized semantic components) in cross-translatable words, put together into cross-translatable phrases and sentences (2016a: 523)

References

Braun, Friederike (1988). *Terms of Address: Problems of Patterns and Usage in Various Languages and Cultures*. Berlin: Mouton De Gruyter.

Brown, Roger and Albert Gilman (1960). The pronouns of power and solidarity. In T.A. Sebeok (ed.), *Style in Language*. Boston: MIT Press, 253–276.

Clyne, Michael, Catrin Norrby and Jane Warren (2009). *Language and Human Relations*. Cambridge: Cambridge University Press.

Farese, Gian Marco (2018). *The Cultural Semantics of Address Practices: A Contrastive Study between English and Italian*. Lanham, Maryland: Lexington Books.

Goddard, Cliff (2018). *Ten Lectures on Natural Semantic Metalanguage: Exploring Language, Thought and Culture Using Simple, Translatable Words*. Leiden: Brill.

Goddard, Cliff and Anna Wierzbicka (2014). *Words and Meanings: Lexical Semantics Across Domains, Languages and Cultures*. Oxford: Oxford University Press. doi.org/10.1093/acprof:oso/9780199668434.001.0001.

Goddard, Cliff and Carsten Levisen (forthcoming). The semantics of 'sarcasm' in Danish and English.

Hajek, John, Heinz L. Kretzenbacher and Robert Lagerberg (2013). Towards a linguistic typology of address pronouns in Europe—past and present. *Proceedings of the 2012 Conference of the Australian Linguistic Society*, 1–15.

Hansen, Judith F. (1980). *We are a Little Land: Cultural Assumptions in Danish Everyday Life*. New York: Arno Press.

Kretzenbacher, Heinz L., John Hajek and Anne H. Fabricius (2018). 'Lånt men ikke kopiereret': The Danish 3pl address pronoun *De* as a historic calque from German *Sie* and its present use amongst Danish university students. Presentation at The fourth meeting of the International Network of Address Research, Helsinki University.

Levisen, Carsten (2012). *Cultural Semantics and Social Cognition: A Case Study on the Danish Universe of Meaning*. Berlin: Mouton de Gruyter. doi.org/10.1515/9783110294651.

Levisen, Carsten (2017). Danish—Communication Modes. In *International Encyclopedia of Intercultural Communication*. John Wiley & Sons.

Levisen, Carsten (2018). Dark, but Danish: Ethnopragmatic perspectives on black humor. Special issue, 'Conversational humor: Forms, functions, and practices across cultures', ed. by Kerry Mullan and Christine Béal. *Intercultural Pragmatics*, 15 (4): 515–531. doi.org/10.1515/ip-2018-0018.

Levisen, Carsten (2019). Biases we live by: Anglocentrism in linguistics and cognitive sciences. Special issue, 'Biases in Linguistics', ed. by Simon Borchmann, Carsten Levisen and Britta Schneider. *Language Sciences* 76: 101173, doi.org/10.1016/j.langsci.2018.05.010.

Levisen, Carsten and Melissa Reshma Jogie (2015). The Trinidadian 'Theory of Mind': Personhood and postcolonial semantics. *International Journal of Language and Culture* 2(2): 169–93. doi.org/10.1075/ijolc.2.2.02lev.

Levisen, Carsten and Sophia Waters (eds) (2017). *Cultural Keywords in Discourse*. Amsterdam: John Benjamins.

Ørsness, Bjarne (2016). Forms of address as cross-cultural code-switching: The case of German and Danish in higher education, *Linguistik Online* 79 (5).

Storch, Anne (2011). *Secret Manipulations: Language and Context in Africa*. Oxford: Oxford University Press.

Wierzbicka, Anna (1979). Ethno-syntax and the philosophy of grammar. *Studies in Language* 3 (3): 313–83. doi.org/10.1075/sl.3.3.03wie.

Wierzbicka, Anna (2003 [1991]). *Cross-Cultural Pragmatics: The Semantics of Human Interaction* (2nd edn). Berlin: Mouton de Gruyter.

Wierzbicka, Anna (2010). *Experience, Evidence, and Sense: The Hidden Cultural Legacy of English*. New York: Oxford University Press. doi.org/10.1093/acprof:oso/9780195368000.001.0001.

Wierzbicka, Anna (2015). A whole cloud of culture condensed into a drop of semantics: The meaning of the German word *Herr* as a term of address. *International Journal of Language and Culture* 2 (1): 1–37. doi.org/10.1075/ijolc.2.1.01wie.

Wierzbicka, Anna (2016a). Making sense of terms of address in European languages through the Natural Semantic Metalanguage (NSM). *Intercultural Pragmatics* 13 (4): 499–527.

Wierzbicka, Anna (2016b). Terms of address in European languages: A study in cross-linguistic semantics and pragmatics. In Keith Allan, Alessandro Capone, Istvan Kecskes and Jacob Mey (eds), *Pragmemes and Theories of Language Use*. Springer, 209–38. doi.org/10.1007/978-3-319-43491-9_12.

Wierzbicka, Anna (2016c). Terms of address as keys to culture and society: German *Herr* vs. Polish *Pan. Acta Philologica* 49: 29–44.

Wong, Jock Onn (2014). *The Culture of Singapore English*. Cambridge: Cambridge University Press.

Ye, Zhengdao (2019). The politeness bias and the society of strangers. Special issue, 'Biases in Linguistics', ed. by Simon Borchmann, Carsten Levisen and Britta Schneider. *Language Sciences* 76: 101183, doi.org/10.1016/j.langsci.2018.06.009.

5

The Singlish interjection *bojio*

Jock Onn Wong

1. The evolving nature of Singapore English

One of the most important publications by Wierzbicka for me as a Singaporean is the paper entitled 'Singapore English: A semantic and cultural perspective' (Wierzbicka 2003). In my opinion, this was the first paper incisively written on the meaning and culture of Singapore English. In the paper, Wierzbicka pioneered the argument that there is a 'Singapore culture' (2003: 328) over and above the various cultures (Chinese, Malay and Indian) that thrive in the country. By studying a number of Singaporean cultural keywords, she showed that while Singaporeans are said to speak English, their English is culturally distinct from what was traditionally known as native varieties of English or what some might now call Anglo English (Wong 2008; Goddard 2012). Cultural keywords are 'special, culture-specific meanings' that 'reflect and pass on not only ways of living characteristic of a given society but also ways of thinking' (Wierzbicka 1997: 5) and studying Singapore English cultural keywords can help us understand and appreciate Singaporean ways of thinking. Regrettably, there seems to be little scholarly interest in the studying of the Singapore English with a view to understanding the ways of thinking it embodies. This chapter tries to fill this gap.

One of the ideas that stood out for me in Wierzbicka's paper is that Singapore culture is 'evolving' (2003: 328) and that is the theme that I want to broach in this chapter. That Singapore culture is evolving is reflected in Singlish, the main variety of Singapore English used among Singaporeans in all but the most formal settings. It may be seen in how Singlish cultural keywords or phrases can emerge or disappear, often in a short period. Examples of Singlish phrases that went out of use or are no longer relevant might be *Marina kids*, *graduate mothers* and *dangerous dogs*, phrases documented in Ho's book chapter (1992: 212). Marina kids were younger teenagers who spent their leisure time socialising in Marina Square, a shopping mall, during the early years of the mall (late '80s/early '90s) when it was not yet popular with shoppers. The Marina kids socialised in groups and were seen as a public nuisance. They disappeared when the mall became popular. Graduate mothers were the beneficiaries of the controversial 'Graduate Mothers Priority Scheme' introduced by the government in 1984, which saw the government using 'financial and social incentives to encourage graduate women to marry and procreate'.[1] The discriminatory scheme understandably antagonised many women, which led to the formation of AWARE (Association of Women for Action and Research), whose mission is to 'To remove all gender-based barriers so as to allow individuals in Singapore to develop their potential to the fullest and realise their personal visions and hopes', the following year.[2] Apparently, the discriminatory nature and unpopularity of the Graduate Mothers Priority Scheme led to its demise less than a year later. Subsequently, the phrase *graduate mothers* began to lose its cultural salience. The phrase *dangerous dogs* was used to refer to kinds of pet dogs that 'must be muzzled when outside their owners' premises' (Ho 1992: 212). However, a search for the phrase on the AVS (Animal & Veterinary Service) homepage now does not yield any result, except for the clause, 'Such potentially dangerous dog breeds are listed under the Second Schedule of the Animals and Birds (Dog Licensing and Control) Rules ("**Specified Dogs**").'[3] Presumably, this is because the owning of such dogs in Singapore is now regulated. This in turn suggests that there have been fewer and fewer 'dangerous dogs' in Singapore, which might explain why the phrase has lost its cultural importance and dropped out of use.

---

1 Available at: www.aware.org.sg/2010/11/the-birth-of-awarepart-one/.
2 Available at: www.aware.org.sg/about/.
3 Available at: www.nparks.gov.sg/avs/pets/owning-a-pet/licensing-a-pet/dog-licensing.

New words in Singlish have emerged, including those culturally associated with the word *kiasu*, which literally means 'afraid to lose' or, according to the Oxford English Dictionary, 'a selfish, grasping attitude arising from a fear of missing out on something'. Wierzbicka (2003: 333) in 2003 correctly described it as 'the most salient cultural keyword in Singaporean English'. She proposed that the meaning may be represented in Natural Semantic Metalanguage (NSM) in this way (with added punctuation marks and a more reader-friendly layout for ease of reading):

[A] *kiasu*

a. Some people often think like this:

'Many people can do something now.

If someone does it, something good will happen to this person.

If I do it, this good thing will happen to me.

If I don't do it, this good thing will not happen to me.

If it doesn't happen to me, I will have to think:

'This good thing happened to other people, it didn't happen to me.'

I don't want to have to think like this.

Because of this I have to do something now.

I want to do it.'

b. Because these people think like this, they do many things.

c. I think: it is bad if people think like this. (Wierzbicka 2003: 335–336)

As a Singaporean, I think that Wierzbicka's explication has a high degree of descriptive adequacy. The part 'If it doesn't happen to me, I will have to think: This good thing happened to other people, it didn't happen to me' seems to capture rather nicely the essence of *kiasu* or the 'fear of losing out', so to speak.

While some Singlish words dropped out of use, the word *kiasu* or at least the value it embodies is still relevant in Singapore culture today. The National Values Assessment survey of 2,000 people, conducted by local business consultancy aAdvantage Consulting Group and Barrett Values Centre in 2018, suggests that Singapore citizens perceive the

Singapore society to be first and foremost *kiasu*.[4] Also, an article written for the *Los Angeles Times* by David Pierson says that 'Singapore's "kiasu" culture makes FOMO look like child's play' (Pierson 2019). In the same article, Pierson states: 'Long before Americans discovered FOMO—the fear of missing out—Singaporeans were fixated with its more excessive forebear, kiasu.' At this point, one might ask how *kiasu* is 'more excessive' than FOMO. The Cambridge Dictionary defines FOMO in this way, with an example:

> a worried feeling that you may miss exciting events that other people are going to, especially caused by things you see on social media: *Don't get FOMO. Get a ticket now!*[5]

In other words, FOMO is about the 'fear' of 'missing' 'exciting events' in the context of 'social media'. By contrast, *kiasu* seems to be culturally more primal and contextually far more pervasive. It could be about something from as minor as piling up one's plate in a buffet (thus maximising the dollar) to as major as enrolling one's primary school child in a host of extracurricular activities (thus giving the child a good head start in life). The cultural salience and importance of the word *kiasu* in Singapore culture thus cannot be overemphasised. The difference is that, since 2003, a number of Singlish words that reflect values or behaviour associated with the word *kiasu* have emerged or gained cultural salience. If Singaporeans were considered *kiasu* then, they may be even more so now.

2. The Singaporean interjection *bojio*

An example of a Singlish word that reflects the *kiasu* value might be *bojio*, which very roughly means 'no invite', literally, or 'you didn't invite me'. It is usually used as a response to someone who did not invite the speaker to join them in an activity, which means that the speaker feels that they are missing out on something. While it can be used as a verb, *bojio* is more often used as an interjection. In fact, as we shall see, it may be considered an 'emotive interjection', which has in its meaning the component 'I feel something' (Wierzbicka 1991: 291; 1992: 165). More specifically, an emotive interjection is one 'whose primary burden is to express feelings

---

4 Available at: www.slideshare.net/aAdvantageConsulting/2018-singapore-national-values-assessment.
5 Available at: dictionary.cambridge.org/dictionary/english/fomo?q=FOMO.

in the emotional sense' (Goddard 2014: 54); an emotion refers to a feeling that follows a thought ('someone X thought something' and 'because of this, this someone X felt something') (Goddard 2018: 72). This means that the meaning of *bojio* has the components 'I think like this …' and 'because of this, I feel something …'.

It is difficult to say but the word probably only entered Singlish in the last five or six years; some of my current undergraduate students said that they first used it in high school. It is not documented in *The Coxford Singlish Dictionary* (Goh and Woo 2009), which is a dictionary written and produced by laypeople (i.e. not professional lexicographers) published in 2009. This probably implies that *bojio* was not commonly used in Singlish then. Moreover, it is observed that the word is mainly used among younger Singaporeans who are in their teens and early 20s. Limited evidence at this stage thus suggests that it is a relatively new Singlish word. To the best of my knowledge, it has not received much scholarly attention, if any.

Interestingly, although I argue that *bojio* is a culturally important Singlish word, I concede that it may not be a particularly salient one to some people. For example, it is not documented in the tongue-in-cheek *A Companion to How Singaporeans Communicate* (Gwee 2018), published in 2018. Nevertheless, its importance can be seen in the fact that the word or its meaning is discussed in various websites; a Google search yields a number of results. The word is also exploited for commercial purposes in Singapore. There was a 'Bojio Café' (although it did not seem to survive beyond one or two years). The Singapore Zoo used a phrase with the word 'Don't say *bojio*' in a publicity poster for its 45th anniversary in 2018.[6] In fact, a Google search suggests that the phrase 'Don't say *bojio*' is used by some bloggers exclamatorily as a tagline to tell Singaporeans about eating places that give customers value for money. Additionally, the word *bojio* has a positive counterpart *jio*, a verb which roughly means 'invite' and which is not infrequently used. The Singlish word *bojio* thus deserves attention and the interjection is the object of study in this chapter. The objective of this chapter is thus to study the meaning of *bojio* and what it could possibly tell us about how younger Singaporeans think. For data collection, a survey was administered to my last batch of students (August–November 2018) at the National University of Singapore (NUS).

---

6   Available at: www.straitstimes.com/singapore/dont-say-bojio-all-are-invited-to-singapore-zoos-45th-birthday-celebrations.

The survey mainly asked students for authentic examples of use and the context for each example. Data were also collected with the help of a student assistant and from internet sources.

I hasten to add that this chapter is particularly important in part because it focuses on an aspect of Singapore English that is regrettably seldom discussed: interjections. Generally speaking, interjections are said to be 'among the most characteristic peculiarities of individual cultures' (Wierzbicka 1992: 160) and 'they express the personal intentions, attitudes, assumptions, and the feelings of the speaker' (Goddard 2011: 163). Interjections can thus reveal certain ways of thinking associated with a culture. As we shall see, this is exactly what the Singlish interjection *bojio* does; it speaks about intentions, attitudes, assumptions and the feelings of its Singaporean speakers. This study could thus be seen as an attempt to understand an aspect of contemporary Singapore culture, an aspect that has evolved rather recently in the last few years.

The word *bojio* comes from Hokkien, a southern Chinese language from the Min family originally spoken in Fujian province. It is a transliteration of the characters 没 and 招, which very roughly means '(did) not invite'. However, *jio* in Singlish refers to a verbal 'invitation'. As an exclamation, *bojio* is used by someone to accost, often teasingly, the addressee for not inviting them to participate in an activity or event. Of course, the implication is that the addressee would know that the activity or event was one that the speaker would have wanted to participate in. One might translate the exclamation into something like this in English: 'you didn't ask me to join you'. Here are some examples of use:[7]

(1) A: Yesterday we went out to eat supper.
B: *Bojio!*[*]

(2) A: I went to the IT fair last night.
B: You went without telling me? *Bojio!*[*]

(3) Someone finds out that their friend went out for a movie, and says to that friend,
'Why *bojio*? Go watch movie never ask me.'[*]

---

7   Examples marked with an asterisk in brackets are collected by student assistant Michelle Hoe, to whom I am grateful.

(4) Someone sees an Instagram story of his friends on an outing together and comments: *Bojio!*(*)

(5) Someone A indicates on Facebook that he is in Kuala Lumpur. A friend B comments on the post using a meme with the interjection 'Boh jio!!!', a spelling variation of *bojio*. This is followed by a brief exchange as presented below (unedited for spelling and punctuation, but with some information omitted).

    A: *Boh jio*!!!

    B: Halo, u so busy going gym (…) Jio u will go meh [particle]?

    A: you didn't ask lor [particle], how you know I won't go????

Usually, such an exchange happens after the outing to which the speaker was not invited. The formula is straightforward. An individual or a group of friends went out somewhere or did something together. A friend who was not invited found out about it afterwards. This friend then says to the individual or one of the group, '*Bojio!*' Examples collected from the survey show that events that are referred to when the speaker says '*bojio*' include a birthday party, a gathering of friends, a movie, a lunch, a dinner, a trip to buy bubble tea, a soccer game, a tempura-making session in the college's pantry and a mah-jong game. All these activities seem to be fun things that the speaker might like to do with the addressee. Thus, the speaker feels excluded and can think something like someone who feels *kiasu* thinks: 'Something good happened to other people, it didn't happen to me.' It is argued here that this is how *bojio* reflects the Singaporean *kiasu* attitude; its meaning embodies a similar way of thinking.

It is noted that in most of the examples studied, the event has happened at the time of speaking. However, the time of speaking could happen before the event, as example (6) illustrates.

(6) Several friends are getting ready to go to a club. Someone, upon seeing them dressed up, asks them where they are going. The following exchange ensues.

    A: Wa, dress until so nice! Where are you all going?

    B: We are going to the club tonight.

    A: Wa! *Bojio!*

    B: You can come man!

    A: Nah, just kidding.

MEANING, LIFE AND CULTURE

This means that the statement of meaning should take into account both situations.

Example (6) is particularly interesting, because it shows that the interjection, when taken literally, can make the addressee feel bad (and immediately issue a verbal 'invitation'). This seems obvious; if someone approached one to say that they were not invited by one, one would naturally tend to feel bad. The speaker cannot not know it. Thus, it might be said that the speaker has, at least on the surface, the intention to make the addressee feel bad.

As mentioned, *bojio* can also be used as a verb, as the following examples of exchanges between friends show.

(7) A: I went to buy new running shoes last night.
    B: Why you *bojio* me?(*)

(8) A: I had dinner with Lucy yesterday.
    B: What? So exclusive? Why *bojio*?(*)

Speaker comments that the addressee did not invite someone (Jenny) to dinner:

(9) You *bojio* Jenny for today's dinner.

As mentioned also, *bojio* has a 'positive' counterpart, *jio*, which is not infrequently used as a verb, as in *jio someone* (roughly, 'invite someone [to do something with one]'), but sometimes a noun (roughly, 'invitation'). A few examples of *jio* might help us appreciate the cultural significance of *bojio*. The verb *jio* suggests that some form of inclusiveness among friends is an important value and the use of *bojio* may be seen as a 'protest' when the value is not upheld, as when the speaker is excluded from an activity.

(10) Some friends are talking about their holiday activities.
     A: What did y'all do?
     B: Mike and myself went to play soccer!
     A: Wah! Next time *jio leh* [particle]

(11) A friend asks the speaker why they did not invite someone to an event, saying:
     Why you never *jio* her for KBBQ [Korean barbeque].

(12) Some friends decided to ask someone to join them: Let's *jio* her for dinner.

Although it is tempting to think that *jio* means 'invite' and *bojio* 'didn't invite', one should not make that association. The English counterparts can sound polite and formal. After all, an invitation could come with a card, as in a wedding invitation. As the online Oxforddictionaries.com phrases it, in English, *to invite* is to make 'a polite, formal, or friendly request to (someone) to go somewhere or to do something'.[8] By contrast, the Singlish *jio* cannot be considered polite or formal, nor can it be considered a request.

Let us now try to state the meaning of the exclamation *bojio* from the inside. In simple English, when someone exclaims *bojio*, they are in a way complaining that the addressee did not tell them about an event and tell them to join in. Similar to swear words (Goddard 2015), its meaning thus embodies a cognitive trigger and a reaction. The cognitive trigger is that the speaker now knows that the addressee has planned to do something without including them. It is something that the speaker would have liked to do with the addressee. As a result, the speaker thinks that they have missed out on something, which is indicative of a *kiasu* attitude, and feels bad, rendering the interjection an emotive one. The speaker wants the addressee to know how they feel (the reaction) and consequently feel bad (if the interjection is taken literally). I propose that the meaning may be stated in NSM in this way:

[B] *Bojio*!

a. I now know you wanted to do something at some time before now.
b. You didn't say to me at that time:
    'I will do this something, I want you to do it with me.'
c. You knew that if you said it to me at that time,
    I would say to you something like 'I will do it with you',
    I would feel something good because of this.
d. Because you didn't say it to me, I now think like this:
    'Something good happened to other people, it didn't happen to me.'

---

8   Available at: en.oxforddictionaries.com/definition/invite.

e. Because of this, I feel something bad,
> like people can feel something bad when they think like this.
g. I want you to know it.
h. I want you to feel something bad because of this.

It thus follows that the meaning of the verb *jio* could be stated in this way, which suggests inclusivity:

[C] He *jio*[9] her

a. He said something like this to her:
> 'I will do something. I want you to do it with me.'
b. When he said it to her, he thought like this: 'She will want to do it with me.'
c. He wanted her to feel something good because of this.
d. He knew at that time that if he didn't say it to her,
> she could think like this if she knew about what he did afterwards:
>> 'Something good happened to other people, it didn't happen to me.'
e. She would feel something bad because of this.
f. He didn't want her to think like this.
g. He didn't want her to feel something bad because of this.

The examples also suggest that one would only exclaim *bojio* to someone whom one is familiar with; there is a degree of familiarity between the speaker and the addressee. At this point, one may be reminded of the idea of a *shúrén* (roughly, 'insider') in Chinese culture. However, the Chinese word *shúrén*, the meaning of which is described by Ye (2017: 76), is not used in Singlish and the word would thus not be part of any Singlish cultural script. However, some components of the meaning proposed by Ye may seem relevant for the purposes of formulating a script to reflect the attitude of a Singlish speaker who says *bojio* to someone:

---

9   Singlish verbs are not always inflected for tense.

[D] Cultural script: Who one can say *bojio* to

a. I think about this someone (i.e. the addressee) like this:

> 'I said some things to this someone many times before.
>
> This someone said some things to me many times before.
>
> Because of this, this someone is like someone I have known for some time.'

b. Because I think about this someone like this, I can say things to this someone

> like I say things to people I know well.

c. I can say '*bojio*' to this someone.

From an Anglo perspective, the presence of an exclamation like *bojio* might appear odd because such an exclamation does not respect what the addressee wants, and thus a semantically similar exclamation is not found in Anglo English. Studies have shown that Anglo culture values personal autonomy and Anglo people have a deep-rooted respect for what one wants (Wierzbicka 1991). Also, according to an Anglo-British informant, asking someone why one is not invited is 'demeaning' because it is like 'begging to be asked'. Similarly, the speech act associated with *jio* is uncommonly used in Anglo English because it embodies an imperative, and we know that Anglo culture restricts the use of the imperative (Wierzbicka 1991).

By contrast, it seems easy to see why the exclamation is commonly used in Singapore culture, a culture that does not seem to place much emphasis on personal autonomy and space, as my own studies show (Wong 2014). What Wierzbicka noted some years ago is still descriptive of Singapore culture today:

> When one watches, for example, the interaction of Singaporeans in the squeeze and the bustle of a hawker centre (with people's elbows touching, and loud conversations criss-crossing the dense network of tables and food stalls), one can well imagine the functionality of interactive Singaporean particles (as well as expressive interjections); and the contemporary Anglo notions of 'privacy', 'personal space', 'autonomy', and 'non-imposing on other people' seem scarcely germane. (Wierzbicka 2003: 346)

However, this does not fully explain the emergence and popularity of *bojio*. As discussed, the *kiasu* attitude is also responsible but, again, it does not fully explain why either. After all, older Singaporeans (perhaps forties and above) tend not to use the exclamation even if many of them may be considered group-oriented and *kiasu*; if they do, it is probably because they picked up the word from the youngsters. Presumably, there is an additional reason which has to do with face or more specifically, *mianzi*, an important value in Chinese culture (Ming and Zhang 2011; Zhou and Zhang 2017). *Mianzi* has to do with one's 'public self-image' (Zhou and Zhang 2017: 165), and accosting a friend for not asking oneself to an event, even in jest, risks embarrassing that friend, causing them to lose face or *mianzi*. This is not what many older Singaporeans are prepared to do. The speaker might also embarrass themselves; the speaker might be seen as trying to inflate their own social importance, and older Singaporeans tend to be careful not to display any sense of self-importance.

3. Changing Singapore values

This leaves us with the question of why younger Singaporeans in their teenage years and early 20s uninhibitedly use the exclamation *bojio* to accost their friends, teasingly or otherwise. I propose here that *bojio* reflects a cultural change happening, in that some values that parents in their 40s and 50s uphold are giving way to competing values. I argue here that *mianzi* has diminished in value in the face of rising *kiasuness* among Singaporeans in general and younger Singaporeans in particular. As Pierson (2019) noted:

> It's a survival instinct born out of Singapore's dominant Chinese culture and deep-rooted insecurity as a blip on the map, one that's only slightly bigger than the San Fernando Valley.
>
> Letting opportunity pass is tantamount to failure, the thinking goes. And if you do, you have no one to blame but yourself.

It would appear that many Singaporeans, Chinese or otherwise, have an incessant worry about missing opportunities. This probably comes from how Singaporeans perceive Singapore as a fiercely competitive society, and increasingly so, where every opportunity is to be taken advantage of. This *kiasu* attitude or emotion can be quite overbearing and contagious. As a white American undergraduate studying in NUS noted in a newspaper article:

> Most of my classmates are very concerned with academic achievement, success and economic security.
>
> Not long after arriving in Singapore, my own values began to shift.
>
> I constantly heard people talking about elite education institutions and prestigious entry-level jobs, and for the first time in my life, I too decided that those were what I needed. (Linder 2019)

In NUS, where this study was undertaken, many students are unduly concerned about their 'cumulative average point' (CAP), which affects a student's chance of graduating with a good honours degree. Students may thus avoid reading modules in which they are not confident in securing a good grade, which may be considered a *kiasu* behaviour. In response, the university introduced a few years ago the 'satisfactory/unsatisfactory' (S/U) option to replace the grades of a given number of modules.[10] The S/U option, if used, means that the grade of the module does not contribute to the CAP. As stated in the NUS website:[11]

> The S/U option is also intended to encourage students to pursue their intellectual interests, without undue concern that exploring a new subject area may adversely affect their CAP.

However, this S/U option has ironically become an advantage to be exploited by some students seeking to maximise their CAP. These students exercise the option for every grade that is below the A range (A-, A and A+), which in turn maximises their CAP. This means that the intended purpose of the S/U option may now be largely irrelevant to students. The *kiasu* attitude prevails and it may thus be said that some members of the younger generation (in NUS at least) carry the *kiasu* attitude to new heights. What was once an attitude has now become a way of life that expresses itself in relation not just to things that matter (e.g. one's CAP) but the less relevant things as well (e.g. an outing with friends).

Over the years, words have emerged or gained salience (in terms of frequency of use) to reflect what I might call the augmentation of the *kiasu* value across generations. Such words include *bojio*, *chope* (very roughly, 'putting one's mark on something to reserve it for later use') and the NUS cultural keyword *S/U*. In this respect, it might even be

---

10 Available at: www.nus.edu.sg/registrar/academic-activities/satisfactory-unsatisfactory-(s-u)-option.
11 Available at: www.nus.edu.sg/nusbulletin/yong-siew-toh-conservatory-of-music/undergraduate-education/degree-requirements/satisfactory-unsatisfactory-option/.

tempting to think that Grab, 'Southeast Asia's largest ride-hailing app operator', a 'Singapore-based company' (Iwamoto 2018), which entered the Singapore market in 2014 (Lin and Dula 2016), owes its huge success in recent years in Singapore in part to its name. Although it has received little or no scholarly scrutiny, the word *grab* as used in Singlish could be considered a cultural keyword that reflects the value of *kiasu*. The word *grab* and the value it symbolises are things many Singaporeans can identify with; Singlish-speaking Singaporeans are all too familiar with the phrase 'everything also must grab', which is not uncommonly used as a tagline or punchline for commercial purposes. The title of a comic book published in Singapore, *Mr Kiasu: Everything Also Must Grab* (Lau and Lim 2018) sums it all up. Wierzbicka (2003) recognised the evolving nature of Singapore culture in 2003 and provided us with a methodology to examine this linguistic evolution.

This present study on the evolving nature of Singlish has allowed me, a native Singaporean, to reach a deeper understanding of my own culture. It has helped me appreciate some of the values and behaviours associated with the younger generation in Singapore, such as my university students. This in turn helps me, an educator, to appreciate their challenges, sympathise with them and connect with them.

Acknowledgements

This chapter benefited from comments by Zhengdao Ye, Brian Poole, Kit Mun Lee, Helen Bromhead and an anonymous reviewer. Ye and the anonymous reviewer gave me very helpful suggestions on the formulation of the semantic explication for *bojio*.

References

Goddard, Cliff (2011). *Semantic Analysis: A Practical Introduction* (2nd edn). Oxford: Oxford University Press.

Goddard, Cliff (2012). 'Early interactions' in Australian English, American English, and English English: Cultural differences and cultural scripts. *Journal of Pragmatics* 44 (9): 1038–50. doi.org/10.1016/j.pragma.2012.04.010.

Goddard, Cliff (2014). Interjections and emotion (with special reference to 'surprise' and 'disgust'). *Emotion Review* 1: 53–63. doi.org/10.1177/1754073913491843.

Goddard, Cliff (2015). 'Swear words' and 'curse words' in Australian (and American) English: At the crossroads of pragmatics, semantics and sociolinguistics. *Intercultural Pragmatics* 12 (2): 189–218. doi.org/10.1515/ip-2015-0010.

Goddard, Cliff (2018). *Ten Lectures on Natural Semantic Metalanguage: Exploring Language, Thought and Culture Using Simple, Translatable Words.* Leiden: Brill.

Goh, Colin and Woo, Yen Yen (eds) (2009). *The Coxford Singlish Dictionary.* Singapore: Flame of the Forest Publishing.

Gwee, Li Sui (2018). *Spiaking Singlish: A Companion to How Singaporeans Communicate.* Singapore: Marshall Cavendish Editions.

Ho, Chee Lick (1992). Words in a cultural context: Term selection. In Anne Pakir (ed.), *Words in a Cultural Context: Proceedings of the Lexicography Workshop.* Singapore: UniPress, 202–14.

Iwamoto, Kentaro (2018). Grab to tackle ASEAN's traffic tangles amid antitrust pressure. *Nikkei Asian Review.* 19 July. Available at: asia.nikkei.com/Spotlight/Sharing-Economy/Grab-to-tackle-ASEAN-s-traffic-tangles-amid-antitrust-pressure.

Lau, Johnny and Lim, Yu Cheng (2018). *Mr Kiasu: Everything Also Must Grab.* Singapore: Shogakukan Asia.

Lin, Mei, and Dula, Christopher William (2016). Grab Taxi: Navigating new frontiers. *Asian Management Insights* 3 (2): 40–45. Available at: ink.library.smu.edu.sg/cgi/viewcontent.cgi?article=4434&context=sis_research.

Linder, Harrison (2019). Gen Y speaks: How living in Singapore almost changed my attitude towards my studies. *Today.* 6 January. Available at: www.todayonline.com/commentary/gen-y-speaks-how-living-singapore-almost-changed-my-attitude-towards-studies.

Ming, He and Zhang, Shao-jie (2011). How face as a system of value-constructs operates through the interplay of *mianzi* and *lian* in Chinese: A corpus-based study. *Journal of Pragmatics* 43: 2360–72. doi.org/10.1016/j.langsci.2017.08.001.

Pierson, David (2019). Singapore's 'kiasu' culture makes FOMO look like child's play. *Los Angeles Times.* 18 January. Available at: www.latimes.com/world/asia/la-fg-singapore-kiasu-fomo-20190118-story.html.

Wierzbicka, Anna (1991). *Cross-Cultural Pragmatics: The Semantics of Human Interaction.* Berlin: Mouton de Gruyter.

Wierzbicka, Anna (1992). The semantics of interjection. *Journal of Pragmatics* 18 (2–3): 159–92.

Wierzbicka, Anna (1997). *Understanding Cultures through their Key Words: English, Russian, Polish, German, and Japanese.* New York: Oxford University Press.

Wierzbicka, Anna (2003). Singapore English: A semantic and cultural perspective. *Multilingua* 22: 327–66. doi.org/10.1515/mult.2003.018.

Wong, Jock (2008). Anglo English and Singapore English tags: Their meanings and cultural significance. *Pragmatics and Cognition* 16 (1): 88–117.

Wong, Jock Onn (2014). *The Culture of Singapore English.* Cambridge: Cambridge University Press.

Ye, Zhengdao (2017). The semantics of social relation nouns in Chinese. In Zhengdao Ye (ed.), *The Semantics of Nouns: A Cross-Linguistic and Cross-Domain Perspective.* Oxford: Oxford University Press, 63–88. doi.org/10.1093/oso/9780198736721.003.0003.

Zhou, Ling, and Zhang, Shao-jie (2017). How face as a system of value-constructs operates through the interplay of *mianzi* and *lian* in Chinese: A corpus-based study. *Language Sciences* 64: 152–66. doi.org/10.1016/j.langsci.2017.08.001.

6

The semantics of *bushfire* in Australian English

Helen Bromhead

1. Introduction

Australian English can act as a mirror of conceptualisations of and attitudes towards extreme weather and climate events in the country, such as bushfires, drought, cyclones and floods.[1] This variety of English encodes specific local meanings; for example, in the domain of landscape, words like *creek* and *bush* have particular senses in Australian English (Arthur 2003; Bromhead 2018). *Bushfire* is an Australian word for an uncontrolled fire in dry trees and shrubs, an event that can threaten homes and people, as well as vegetation and wildlife. The word could be seen as analogous to *wildfire* as used in North American English for forest fires.[2] However, this would be to misunderstand the semantic content brought by the component *bush*. This chapter provides a rigorous

---

1   Many thanks to Zhengdao Ye, James Grieve and two anonymous reviewers for helpful comments on this chapter. I am grateful to Anna Wierzbicka and Jock Wong for workshopping of the semantic explication of *bushfire*. Participants at the Workshop on NSM Semantics and Mimimal English, The Australian National University, 15–16 April 2019, provided useful feedback.
2   *Wildfire* is not nearly as common in Australian English as *bushfire*. While there are 249 occurrences of the lemma *bushfire*, *bush fire* and *bush fires* in the Australian material of the Collins Wordbanks corpus, there are 35 of the lemma *wildfire*, *wild fire* and *wild fires*. Of these only 15 refer to events in Australia.

semantic analysis of *bushfire*, discusses the term's status as a cultural keyword in Australian English and offers a cultural script of Australian practices surrounding bushfires.

Employing the Natural Semantic Metalanguage (NSM) approach to semantic and conceptual analysis (Wierzbicka 1985, 1996; Goddard and Wierzbicka 2014; Ye 2017), the cultural scripts approach to the analysis of cultural practices and values (Wierzbicka 2003; Goddard 2006) and drawing on literature on cultural keywords (Wierzbicka 1997; Levisen and Waters 2017a), the study is assisted by corpus-based collocational analysis. Discussion draws on environmental communication, environmental history, community bushfire information, news reports and survivor accounts, which are referred to in the chapter. The chapter provides a starting point for showing how semantic analysis and cultural scripts can help to capture the varying, conflicting and evolving assumptions about climate and extreme weather, influenced by factors such as climate change and increased understanding of Indigenous knowledge in Australia.

The chapter begins with an overview of extreme weather and climate event vocabulary as a domain, and the possible status of *bushfire* as a cultural keyword in Australian English. It then moves to provide an analysis of *bushfire*, discussing the examples used and meaning components, then providing a semantic explication and a *bushfire*-related cultural script. The chapter concludes with a discussion of the prospects for semantic analysis of extreme weather and climate event words, including *bushfire*, and the writing of cultural scripts pertaining to these events.

2. The semantic domain and cultural keywords

Extreme weather and climate events have played a role in the shaping of settler Australian history and national identity since Australia was colonised by Britain (e.g. West 2000; Sherratt et al. 2005). Non-Indigenous Australians have had to deal with a climate prone to events such as droughts, floods and bushfires, different from that in lands from which they, or their ancestors, came, and try to come to terms with what Indigenous people already knew about the Australian environment (e.g. Gammage 2011; Barton and Bennett 2013; Pascoe 2014). Battling nature's elements and helping affected communities are seen as central to an Australian cultural ethos, which is both valorised and contested. The climate emergency increases the likelihood of extreme weather events in Australia, such as heatwaves and, the focus of the chapter, bushfires (CSIRO-BOM 2018). Australian English discourse in mainstream and social media often draws a connection between these kinds of events and the need for political action to address climate change (e.g. Hackett et al. 2017; Flanagan 2019).

Extreme weather and climate events in Australia have been studied from the point of view of disciplines including meteorology, history, sociology, public health, community safety and environmental communication (e.g. Webb 1997; Morrissey and Reser 2007; Handmer and Haynes 2008; Leitch and Bohensky 2014), yet consideration of the semantics of terms like *bushfire* and *cyclone*, and their possible status as Australian cultural keywords, remains unexplored. Australians have a number of options as to what to call a period without rain, such as *drought*, *dry season* and *El Niño event*.[3] When they either select a term to use, or encounter the word in discourse, different ideas about the Australian climate are revealed. *Drought* evokes a natural disaster, *dry season* an expected happening, and *El Niño event* a circumstance that comes about due to global factors. Pinning down the precise senses of words of these kinds and their associated cultural scripts sheds light on conceptualisations of the Australian environment. This chapter uses the case of the word *bushfire* as a way to begin exploring the semantic domain.

A brief word on the cultural and geographic context of bushfires in Australia is in order. Bushfires are more likely during the hotter, drier months of summer in many regions of Australia, and spread more easily in winds. They burn in 'bush', a mass noun denoting vegetation, dominated by eucalypts, as an undifferentiated mass (Bromhead 2011, 2018). Fire is a natural part of some Australian ecosystems; a majority of Australia's plant species either need or tolerate fire (Gammage 2011). Aboriginal people used fire as a tool, in part, to manage vegetation growth and prevent severe uncontrolled fires, practices that continue in some places today (AWNRMB-DEWNR 2014). Somewhat similar burning regimes have been adopted by Australian government bodies as part of

---

3   Swings in rainfall in Australia are associated with an atmospheric event involving the Southern Oscillation, part of a global system of ocean–atmosphere interaction. Also involved are temperature variations in the eastern Pacific Ocean known as El Niño (Whetton 1997: 189).

bushfire prevention (Pyne 2006). Although fire may be a natural part of the Australian environment, uncontrolled fires in bush constitute natural hazards that threaten vegetation, wildlife, homes and people's lives, and are therefore culturally significant and have affordances in discourse (see Enfield 2008).

Bushfire could be considered an Australian cultural keyword. Drawing on Anna Wierzbicka's pioneering *Understanding Cultures through their Key Words* (1997), Levisen and Waters (2017b) write that cultural keywords 'govern the shared cognitive outlook of speakers and encode certain culture-specific logics, and impose on their speakers a certain interpretative grid through which they make sense of the world' (2017b: 3). In Bromhead (2011, 2018), I presented *the bush* as a cultural keyword in Australian English and touched on its productivity in the formation of compounds, one of which is *bushfire*. This word, also, has an amount of associated phraseology too vast to detail in any depth (see also Arthur 2003: 147–50). *Bushfire*-related vocabulary can range from scientific concepts, such as *fuel load*, to community safety terms, such as *bushfire survival plan*, to Aboriginal land management practices, as in *caring for country with fire*, to informal language, such as *firies* for firefighters, or even *vollie firies* for volunteer firefighters (see Wierzbicka 1986, 1992 on colloquial 'depreciatives').

The meaning of *bushfire* brings with it the meaning of the Australian word for an undifferentiated mass of dry vegetation, *bush* (Bromhead 2011, 2018). A crucial point of that meaning is 'dry'—Australians expect that *bush* is likely to burn. This local Australian English meaning of the word *bushfire* can help explain why people feel especially confronted by fires burning in rainforest, which is not the canonical Australian bush.

The significance of bushfires to the psyche of Australians can be seen by the attribution of names for some major bushfires, such as Ash Wednesday (Victoria and South Australia, 1983). The fact that many Australians know the names of the American water-bombing aircraft used to fight bushfires in the Australian summer, such as Elvis, is indicative (Caruana 2012). Further, native animals that have survived bushfires become symbols of community resilience, such as Lucky the koala, found severely injured after the 2003 Canberra bushfires (Doherty 2008). Keyword status can also be seen in semiotic phenomena other than language (Levisen and Waters 2017b: 7–8). The multicoloured, adjustable fire danger rating signs that appear along many Australian roads (Campbell 2017), and other bushfire awareness signs, constitute examples of visual discourse about bushfires in place, experienced by many Australians as they drive (see Scollon and Scollon 2003 on discourses in place, also Jaworski and Thurlow 2010). In what follows, I explore the semantics of this cultural keyword and give a cultural script of Australian practices concerning bushfires.

3. *Bushfire* examples used

My study of *the bush* (Bromhead 2011, 2018) was assisted by corpus analysis of the Australian English Oznews subcorpus of Collins Wordbanks of English,[4] a relatively small corpus of Australian English, but one of the most suitable (see Ye, this volume). As part of this corpus assistance, a word sketch, a summary of a word's collocational behaviour sorted via grammatical relations and based on statistical significance, was used to find representative examples and indicative collocates. Such analysis is trickier for *bushfire*. The examples of *bush* in the corpus are far more numerous than those of *bushfire* and *bush fire*. In the Australian material of Wordbanks, 235 instances of the lemma *bushfire* appear (a frequency of 6.44 per million words), and 14 of *bush fire* or *bush fires* (a frequency of 0.38 per million).

The word sketch of the lemma *bushfire* reveals collocational behaviour, yet some data may not be sufficiently robust. For example, the most statistically significant collocate of which *bushfire* is a subject is *ravage*; however, this is based on only one token in the corpus. By contrast, *claim* is the fourth most significant subject collocate, and this is based on a more robust five tokens. The chapter uses significant collocations as evidence of the semantics of *bushfire* (see Andrews 2016: 98 and *n*11 on the use of collocations in NSM analysis). One token with statistical significance can tell us something. All collocations taken from the word sketch based on token counts smaller than five have been checked in an ABC (Australian Broadcasting Corporation) news search to ensure that they in fact do occur more widely.[5] For example, a search of *bushfire* with the verb *ravage* yields many results, so this collocate is taken as indicative. On the other hand, *afternoon* is a significant collocate based on two tokens, but it is not attested on ABC news, so it is not mentioned. Unless otherwise indicated,

---

4   Searched at: wordbanks.harpercollins.co.uk.
5   Searched at: www.abc.net.au/news.

all examples used in the chapter are taken from Australian material in Wordbanks. The analysis of *bushfire* in this chapter can be seen as assisted by a corpus as opposed to corpus-driven (McEnery and Hardie 2011).

4. Evidence from use

Bushfires are events situated in particular kinds of places. These must be places that span some distance, and in which a certain vegetation type grows, what can be described in Australian English as bush. Not all fires that take place in the natural environment can be classed as bushfires. There is also the category of a grass fire, often a less serious event, which takes place over a smaller area and has a different fuel source. An example of use of *bushfire* adduced by *The Australian National Dictionary* (*AND*) reads:

(1) 'You ever seen a **bush fire**?' 'Not a real one … just **grass fires** in a paddock.' (John Cleary, *The Sundowners*, 1952, in *AND* 2016)

While a particular type of vegetation is present, places in which bushfires occur are not necessary counted as being 'the bush'. *The bush* is a polysemous term, and two of its senses particularly pertinent to this discussion I delineated in Bromhead (2011, 2018). One meaning of *this bush* is a kind of Australian folk biological zone. This meaning of *the bush* conveys not just that the vegetation type, 'bush', grows there, but also the presence of uniquely Australian wildlife, the nature of it as a place where not many people live and the fact that one may not see many people there. Another relevant meaning is *the bush* is zone where people can live—these places are outside major cities and near 'the bush' as a biological zone. A Queensland state government extreme weather events safety website 'Get Ready Queensland' writes the following about bushfires in (2):

(2) You don't have to live in **the bush** to be threatened by **bushfire**— you just have to be close enough to be affected by burning material, embers and smoke. (Get Ready Queensland n.d.)

For example, the western suburbs of Canberra affected by a bushfire in 2003 could not be described as being part of *the bush*, either as *the bush* as a biological zone (the first *the bush* sense mentioned above), or *the bush* as a place in Australia opposed to the city (the second *the bush* sense mentioned above).

Bushfires occur at hot, dry times of year. *Bushfire* collocates with *season*, the most numerous of all the significant collocates of which *bushfire* is a modifier, as in (3).

(3) The Queensland **bushfire season** lasts from August to December …

A bushfire is unwanted. Burning undertaken by people as a way of reducing fire fuel can be described as *burning off*, *controlled burns* and *prescribed burns*, which are part of the associated phraseology (see (4)). Yet no matter how big these fires, they could not be called *bushfires*, unless they were to move beyond the control of those undertaking them.

(4) What would you do to prevent fires like the one that devastated Canberra? You need deliberate **prescribed burns** …

In the main, bushfires are caused by lightning strikes or, unfortunately, deliberately lit (Muller and Bryant 2008). *Arson* and *arsonist* appear as significant collocates modified by *bushfire* in a word sketch (as in (5)), and *light* also appears as a significant verb collocate in examples that refer to arson.

(5) … as a Government we have doubled the penalties for **bushfire arson** …

Many collocates of *bushfire* pertain to the nature of fire, such as *flare* (see (6)), *rage*, *burning* and *smoke*. The movement of bushfires can be described by saying that bushfires *rip* and *sweep* across areas (see (7)), and a bushfire can have a *path*.

(6) Hundreds of people … were evacuated after the **bushfire flared** at lunchtime.

(7) More than 400ha have been burnt, with the **bushfire sweeping** from the residential hills fringe suburb … to the Cleland Conservation Park …

Bushfires are significant because of the destruction they wreak on bushland, animals, people's houses and the person. Numerous collocates reflect this destructive nature, such as the verbs *claim* and *ravage* (see (8)), the adjectives *deadly*, *devastating* and *bad* (see (9)), and the nouns *emergency*, *horror*, *catastrophe*, *hazard*, *danger*, *disaster*, *casualty*, *destruction* and *victim* as in (10).

(8) When **bushfire has ravaged** a farm …

(9) South Australia's **worst bushfire** in 22 years was simply impossible to control.

(10) Governor Marjorie Jackson-Nelson was on the Eyre Peninsula …, visiting **bushfire victims**.

Looking at a selection of Australian television news reports of bushfires in videos uploaded to YouTube, one sees that the effects of bushfires are measured by their impact on people, houses and land, as in (11).

(11) Thirty-six homes have been destroyed and over 30,000 hectares of national park have gone up in smoke as massive fires roar through the territory. News just at hand of unconfirmed reports of at least one fatality and several burns victims being flown to the Canberra hospital. ('Canberra firestorm news coverage' 2019: 2:03–2:12)

However, a bushfire need not necessarily destroy homes and threaten people's lives. Example (12) gives a definition of a bushfire from Australia law.

(12) The Criminal Law Consolidation Act 1935 … defines a **bushfire** as 'a fire that burns, or threatens to burn, out of control causing damage to vegetation (whether or not other property is also damaged or threatened)'.

A bushfire leaves a characteristic burnt, black landscape in its wake. The documentary *Rising From The Ashes*, in part, depicts the devastated Victorian landscape after the Black Saturday bushfires of 2009. In (13), a bushfire survivor tells of the visual experience after the fire on his property.

(13) Immediately after the fire, you couldn't see any green at all. All of that was just black. (*Rising From The Ashes* (2018): 2:37–2:43)

The evidence from collocations and examples discussed in this section can be used to capture the meaning of *bushfire* in a semantic explication.

5. A semantic explication of *bushfire*

As is the case for all NSM conceptual analysis, this study employs a human-centred perspective (see especially Wierzbicka 1989; for reflection, see Newman, this volume, Allan, this volume). Like geographic concepts, such as *mountain* and *the bush* (Bromhead 2018), there are human interests in extreme weather and climate events, such as *bushfire*. Sherratt (2005: 2) cites the American historian of weather, David Laskin (1996: 3–4), writing 'weather "doesn't just happen … it happens to us"'. These human interests make their way into analysis of *bushfire* not only via the effect of bushfires on people and the places where they live, but also by way of concepts such as 'bush' and 'fire', which contain human elements in their semantics. The following explication [A] presents the sense of *bushfire*. Its components are structured as follows: places, what happens, very bad things can happen and what a place is like after it happens.

[A] semantic explication of *bushfire* (Australian English)

[PLACES]

a. something bad can happen in places of some kinds

    places of these kinds are very big, they have many parts

    there is a lot of bush$_1$ [m] in these places

    at some times, there can be very little water [m] in some parts of these places

[WHAT HAPPENS]

b. when it happens in a place, it is like this:

    there is a big fire [m] in this place not because people want it

    something bad is happening to the bush [m] in this place for some time because of this

    it is burning [m], it happens like this:

        fire [m] moves quickly [m] in this place because the wind [m] is moving quickly [m] in this place

        if it is in one part of this place at one moment, a short time after this it can be in another part

    there is a lot of smoke [m] in this place

MEANING, LIFE AND CULTURE

[VERY BAD THINGS CAN HAPPEN]

c. when something like this happens in a place, it can be like this:

   very bad things can happen to many parts of this place

   very bad things can happen to the bush [m] in this place

   very bad things can happen to the creatures [m] in this place, they can die

   very bad things can happen to people in this place, they can die

   very bad things can happen to the places where people live in this place

[WHAT A PLACE IS LIKE AFTER IT HAPPENS]

d. after something like this happens in a place, this place is not like it was before

   when someone sees this place, they can think like this:

   'something bad happened to the bush [m] in this place

   as happens to wood [m] if fire [m] touches it for some time.'

Section (a) of the explication of *bushfire* presents the places in which a bushfire happens. They are very big, composed of many parts, and there is a lot of bush in these places. The semantic molecule 'bush', as in *bush* as a vegetation type, not as a kind of place (*the bush*), appears. This molecule brings with it the sense of dry vegetation as a mass, indigenous to Australia and in its natural state (see Bromhead 2011, 2018, for a semantic explication). The fact that bushfire occurs in places where at times there is little water in a place is also conveyed.

Section (b) depicts what happens—a bushfire is an event. The molecule 'fire', naturally, is used (see Wierzbicka 1996: 223; Goddard 2010: 141–42). This fire is big and unwanted by people. Bushfires caused by arson were mentioned previously. The component 'not because people want it' still holds in such cases; an arsonist, 'someone', may desire the fire, but 'people' in general do not. The destruction of bush is portrayed. The movement of the fire as a result of wind, and the presence of smoke, is also treated.

Components in section (c) address the very bad things that happen as a result of bushfire. Damage to parts of places, to the vegetation (the bush), to creatures (even to death), to people (even to death) and to places where people live are covered.

Section (d) portrays the characteristic burnt landscape following a bushfire. This is represented through human vision and the thought that fire has occurred.

6. Human responses to bushfire in Australian English: A cultural script

The response of humans to bushfires is a significant part of the discourse around the word. Extensive efforts go to fighting bushfires and, as previously touched on, these efforts are seen as shaping the nation's psyche. Significant verb collocates of *bushfire* are *fight* and *battle* (see (14)). Professional fire brigades are supplemented by a large number of volunteer firefighters. The word sketch attests the significant collocations *volunteer bushfire fighters* (see (15)) and *bushfire brigade*.

(14) Fire crews are still **battling a bushfire** at Bicheno …

(15) … **volunteer bushfire fighters**, a national resource too easily taken for granted …

Furthermore, battling bushfires is too large a matter to be solely dealt with by dedicated fire brigades, who often focus on attacking the fires in a systematic way and protecting government assets, leaving the defence of individual houses to their occupants. Householders are urged to prepare for bushfires by drafting a bushfire survival plan, and by reducing hazards, such as by clearing gutters of leaves (see e.g. 'Get Ready Queensland' website). At a government level, the aforementioned prescribed burns are carried out in preparation for bushfire season.

Australians pride themselves on helping one another after a disaster, as seen in folk belief and in political discourse following disastrous extreme weather events, and this ties in with a national ethos of solidarity (e.g. West 2000; Rudd 2009; Rowan 2017: 76–77, *n*12). The idea that Australians have a particular distinction in providing community assistance after disaster has been disputed; it has also been pointed out that this assistance can be subject to racial and class inequities (e.g. Fisher 2011). This community assistance is reflected in the corpus, in which *bushfire appeal* is a significant collocation, as in (16).

(16) Real estate agents ... will have a monster auction ... to raise money for the **bushfire appeal**.

Bushfires are events from which people often try to get away. A significant collocate of *bushfire* is *flee* (see (17)). In Australia, there has been a policy, often called 'stay or go', whereby those whose houses are threatened by bushfire are advised to either stay and defend their property, or leave early, before it becomes too dangerous to do so (Griffiths 2012). Fleeing is not a safe thing to do; people are advised to leave in an orderly manner in accordance with their bushfire survival plan.

(17) ... killed as they tried to **flee the bushfire** were Judy Griffith and her grandchildren ...

Some human responses to bushfires can be captured in a cultural script, a simply phrased script composed in NSM conveying a culture's practices and values, as following in [B].

[B] a cultural script of Australians' response to bushfires

a. in Australia, many people think like this:
b. people don't want a bushfire to happen in a place

    because of this, it is good if some people do some things because of this

c. they do some things in this place when a bushfire is not happening because they don't want it to happen
d. when a bushfire happens, they do some other things because they don't want fire to be in this place

    they know that they can die when they do these things

    they don't want to not do it because of this

e. some people don't want to be in a place where there is a bushfire when it is happening

    they want to be in other places, not near places where there is fire, they do some things because of this

    when it is like this, it is good if they do these things before the fire is very near the place where they are

f.   after the bushfire happens, some people can do some other things
     because they want to do something good for the people living in this place
   this is good

Component (a) contains the header, similar to those in most cultural scripts. The script is particular to Australia and is widely shared, but not necessarily by all people in the country, so the wording 'many people' is used. Component (b) portrays the desire for a bushfire not to happen in a place, and the cultural evaluation that it is good if some people respond to combat it. These responses follow in components (c) and (d).

In component (c), some people are portrayed as taking steps to prevent bushfire. Component (d) addresses people doing things to combat the fire while it is happening. These actions are with risk (they know they can die when they do these things); however, they still want to do them.

Component (e) depicts people's leaving of areas in which there is a bushfire. It is good if they do this early, before the fire is very near. Component (f) conveys the idea of people doing good things for people affected by fire after it has taken place. This action by people is evaluated as good.

7. Concluding remarks and prospects for further research

The chapter has shown that the semantics of *bushfire* in Australian English encode certain environmental attitudes. The event is conceptualised as bad and destructive to land, creatures, people and the places in which people live. There is same recognition in the sense of *bushfire* that the vegetation can be expected to burn—semantic content contained within the component 'bush'. In 2003, Arthur outlined how *wildfire* may replace *bushfire* for problematic fires in Australian English due to a greater understanding of the necessity of fire for Australian vegetation. This may have happened in a scientific register, but has not come to pass in wider Australian English, as *bushfire* is still used for problematic fires in the 2010s. The cultural script portraying Australians' responses to bushfire details how Australians value people acting to prevent and combat bushfires, leaving their residences early and helping the affected after the event.

The cultural script given above is a very general one encompassing a variety of Australians' responses to bushfires. Prospects for continuing research into *bushfire* and other extreme weather and climate event words include identifying more specific cultural scripts associated with the event. For example, as covered in this script, Australians place value on helping others after natural disasters. A cultural script could be written that details all the surrounding beliefs around this practice. The values elucidated by such a script would be related to the Australian emphasis on mateship and associated ideals, such as the injunction: 'don't abandon a mate' (see Wierzbicka 1997: 101–18, 2002: 1171–72). Australian mateship is the relationship of someone with people thought of as 'like me'. This could help to explain why a critic like Fisher (2011), mentioned previously, sees the practice as excluding racial minorities and the economically disadvantaged.

Australians banding together to fight bushfires and other natural forces has often been connected to the nation uniting to fight a common enemy at war. The official Australian historian of the First World War, C.E.W. Bean, argued that the experience of battling natural forces shaped Australians as soldiers (Sherratt 2005: 3–4). A recruitment poster from 1917 depicts a farmer walking away from a scene in which other men are trying to fight back a fire. The poster asks: 'Would you stand by while a bushfire raged?' and urges 'Get busy and drive the Germans back!' (Weston 1917). This fighting is conceived of as gendered; men have traditionally been responsible for the fighting of both opposing countries and nature. A specific cultural script could be formulated based on notions of many men doing things together in a place because they want something bad not to happen. They know that they could die when they are doing these things, but, despite this, they don't want to not do them. People can think of these men as part of one thing, and they think it is very good if men do these things. In drafting such a script, I would seek not to devalue the contribution women have made to this activity, but capture the still prevailing notion of fighting bushfires as 'men's business' (Eriksen et al. 2010).

Some of the beliefs Australians hold about climate and weather may be culturally ingrained but not necessarily serve them well. Explicitly stating the beliefs and values around extreme weather and the Australian climate allows us to examine them for what they are and, possibly, re-evaluate them. For example, the use of military discourse around individuals battling bushfires has been criticised for contributing to loss of life during the 2009 Black Saturday Victorian bushfires. Some people, who may otherwise have left for safety, were led to believe they could stay and defend their houses against what turned out to be unprecedentedly severe bushfires (Griffiths 2012: 163–64). Griffiths writes, 'military metaphors make us believe that we can and must *beat* fire, somehow. Yet our challenging task as Australians is to learn to live with it' (Griffiths 2012: 164). Griffiths sees such metaphors as a comfort to people because they imply that measures can be taken to stem a powerful natural force.

Metaphors concerned with violence in cancer discourse (such as, 'fought a long battle with leukemia'), too, have been criticised for misleading patients. Yet, they have been found to help sufferers deal with negative emotions, and they are seen as psychologically useful for those with whom they resonate (Semino et al. 2017). Military metaphors may have their drawbacks but may be helpful if used judiciously, as in discourse such as the title of a newspaper article: 'Science fights bushfires on a number of fronts' (Spinks 2014). The article, in part, details how mitigating climate change can reduce the likelihood of bushfire-prone weather.

Further research prospects include examining the idea that some Australian extreme weather event words can be thought of as local cultural keywords rather than Australian cultural keywords. Communities hold high levels of local knowledge about their immediate environments (Foxwell-Norton 2017). *Bushfire* is built on the Australian English *bush*, so it may be easier to accept as an Australian cultural keyword than, for example, *flood*, common to all varieties of English. The word *bushfire* has a higher degree of salience in the discourse of Victorians than in that of Northern Queenslanders in which *cyclone* is a more relevant term. The matter requires more investigation and analysis of the senses other words of this kind.

Another fruitful area to explore is the discourse about the relationship between climate change and bushfires. This relationship is becoming more of a part of the Australian consciousness. Yet there is also a discourse opposing this view (Hackett et al. 2017). An entire separate cultural script could be written covering the cultural beliefs behind these conflicting positions.

The linguistics of extreme weather and climate remains open to exploration. This chapter has shown that detailed semantic analysis of one extreme weather event word *bushfire* can reveal the cultural and environmental attitudes of Australians.

References

The Australian National Dictionary (AND) (2016). *The Australian National Dictionary: Australian Words and their Origins* (2nd edn) (Bruce Moore, Mark Gwynn, Amanda Laugesen and Julia Robinson, eds). Melbourne: Oxford University Press.

Andrews, Avery (2016). Reconciling NSM and formal semantics. *Australian Journal of Linguistics* 36 (1): 79–111. doi.org/10.1080/07268602.2016.11 09431.

Arthur, Jay (2003). *The Default Country: A Lexical Cartography of Twentieth-Century Australia*. Sydney: University of New South Wales Press.

AWNRMB-DEWNR (Alinytjara Wilurara Natural Resources Management Board and Department of Environment, Water and Natural Resources) (2014). *Alinytjarar Wilurara Fire Management Strategy 2014*. Adelaide: Government of South Australia. Available at: www.environment.sa.gov.au/files/sharedassets/public/fire_management/fire-management-strategy-alinytjara-wiluara-gen.pdf.

Barton, Gregory and Brett Bennett (2013). Environment. In Alison Bashford and Stuart Macintyre (eds), *The Cambridge History of Australia*. Port Melbourne: Cambridge University Press, 452–71.

Bromhead, Helen (2011). *The bush* in Australian English. *Australian Journal of Linguistics* 31 (4): 445–71.

Bromhead, Helen (2018). *Landscape and Culture – Cross-linguistic Perspectives*. Amsterdam: John Benjamins.

Campbell, Ian (2017). Fire danger signs—Who changes them? What do they mean? *about regional*. 10 September. Available at: aboutregional.com.au/fire-danger-signs-who-changes-them-what-do-they-mean.

Canberra firestorm news coverage [video] (2019). Uploaded 5 August, 2007. Available at: www.youtube.com/watch?v=7Upzya1yUH0.

Caruana, Patrick (2012). Elvis back in town for hot Vic weekend. *Herald Sun*. 7 December. Available at: www.heraldsun.com.au/news/breaking-news/elvis-to-battle-vic-bushfires-again/news-story/99a7080980a0d4e7a312719cf14c9aac.

CSIRO-BOM (Commonwealth Scientific and Industrial Research Organisation and Bureau of Meteorology) (2018). *State of the Climate 2018*. Report. Available at: www.csiro.au/~/media/OnA/Files/State-of-the-Climate-2018-CSIRO-BOM-Dec2018.pdf.

Doherty, Megan (2008). Lucky charmed city to the end. *The Canberra Times*. 17 July. Accessed via Factiva. Available at: global-factiva-com.virtual.anu.edu.au/redir/default.aspx?P=sa&an=CANBTZ0020080716e47h0001n&cat=a&ep=ASE.

Enfield, N.J. (2008). Linguistic categories and their utilities: The case of Lao landscape terms. *Language Sciences* 30 (2–3): 227–55. doi.org/10.1016/j.langsci.2006.12.030.

Eriksen, Christine, Nicholas Gill and Lesley Head (2010). The gendered dimensions of bushfire in changing rural landscapes in Australia. *Journal of Rural Studies* 26: 332–42. doi.org/10.1016/j.jrurstud.2010.06.001.

Fisher, Naomi (2011). Nationalism and identity in a disaster. *ABC News*. 20 January. Available at: www.abc.net.au/news/2011-01-20/nationalism_and_identity_in_a_disaster/43148.

Flanagan, Richard (2019). Tasmania is burning. The climate disaster future has arrived while those in power laugh at us. *The Guardian*. 5 February. Available at: www.theguardian.com/environment/2019/feb/05/tasmania-is-burning-the-climate-disaster-future-has-arrived-while-those-in-power-laugh-at-us.

Foxwell-Norton, Kerrie (2017). *Environmental Communication and Critical Coastal Policy: Communities, Culture and Nature*. Abingdon, Oxfordshire: Routledge. doi.org/10.4324/9781315757056.

Gammage, Bill (2011). *The Biggest Estate on Earth: How Aborigines Made Australia*. Sydney: Allen & Unwin.

Get Ready Queensland (n.d.). Bushfire. Available at: getready.qld.gov.au/natural-disasters/bushfire (site discontinued).

Goddard, Cliff (ed.) (2006). *Ethnopragmatics: Understanding Discourse in Cultural Context*. Berlin: Mouton de Gruyter.

Goddard, Cliff (2010). Semantic molecules and semantic complexity (with special reference to 'environmental' molecules). *Review of Cognitive Linguistics* 8 (1): 123–55. doi.org/10.1075/ml.8.1.05god.

Goddard, Cliff and Anna Wierzbicka (2014). *Words and Meanings: Lexical Semantics Across Domains, Languages and Cultures.* Oxford: Oxford University Press. doi.org/10.1093/acprof:oso/9780199668434.001.0001.

Griffiths, Tom (2012). Remembering. In Christine Hansen and Tom Griffiths (eds), *Living with Fire: People, Nature and History in Steels Creek.* Collingwood, Victoria: CSIRO Publishing, 159–85. doi.org/10.1071/9780643104808.

Hackett, Robert A., Susan Forde, Shane Gunster and Kerrie Foxwell-Norton (2017). Journalism(s) for climate crisis. In Robert A. Hackett, Susan Forde, Shane Gunster and Kerrie Foxwell-Norton (eds), *Journalism and Climate Crisis: Public Engagement, Media Alternatives.* Abingdon, Oxon: Routledge. doi.org/10.4324/9781315668734.

Handmer, John and Katharine Haynes (2008). *Community Bushfire Safety.* Collingwood, Victoria: CSIRO Publishing.

Jaworski, Adam and Crispin Thurlow (2010). *Semiotic Landscapes: Language, Image, Space.* London: Continuum.

Laskin, David (1996). *Braving the Elements: The Stormy History of American Weather.* New York: Doubleday.

Leitch, Anne M. and Erin L. Bohensky (2014). Return to 'a new normal': Discourses of resilience to natural disasters in Australian newspapers 2006–2010. *Global Environmental Change* 26: 14–26. doi.org/10.1016/j.gloenvcha.2014.03.006.

Levisen, Carsten and Sophia Waters (eds) (2017a). *Cultural Keywords in Discourse.* Amsterdam: John Benjamins.

Levisen, Carsten and Sophia Waters (2017b). How words do things with people. In Carsten Levisen and Sophia Waters (eds), *Cultural Keywords in Discourse.* Amsterdam: John Benjamins, 1–23.

McEnery, Tony and Andrew Hardie (2011). *Corpus Linguistics: Method, Theory and Practice.* Cambridge: Cambridge University Press.

Morrissey, Shirley A. and Joseph P. Reser (2007). Natural disasters, climate change and mental health considerations for rural Australia. *Australian Journal of Rural Health* 15: 120–25. doi.org/10.1111/j.1440-1584.2007.00865.x.

Muller, Damon and Colleen Bryant (2008). Understanding and preventing bushfire arson. In John Handmer and Katharine Haynes (eds), *Community Bushfire Safety.* Collingwood, Victoria: CSIRO Publishing, 99–106. doi.org/10.1071/9780643095618.

Pascoe, Bruce (2014). *Dark Emu, Black Seeds: Agriculture or Accident?* Broome, Western Australia: Magabala.

Pyne, Stephen J. (2006). *The Still-Burning Bush.* Melbourne: Scribe.

Rising From The Ashes [film] (2018). Produced by Orsino Images. Indimax Films. Uploaded 12 June 2018. Available at: www.youtube.com/watch?v=FOYR_SwZ3d4.

Rowan, Roz (2017). Bogan as a keyword of contemporary Australia: Sociality and national discourse in Australian English. In Carsten Levisen and Sophia Waters (eds), *Cultural Keywords in Discourse.* Amsterdam: John Benjamins, 55–82.

Rudd, Kevin (2009). Nation shows its courage and compassion. *The Sydney Morning Herald.* 23 February. Available at: www.smh.com.au/national/nation-shows-its-courage-and-compassion-20090222-8eq0.html.

Scollon, Ronald and Suzie Wong Scollon (2003). *Discourses in Place: Language in the Material World.* London: Routledge. doi.org/10.4324/9780203422724.

Semino, Elena, Zsófia Demjén, Andrew Hardie, Sheila Payne and Paul Rayson (2017). *Metaphor, Cancer and the End of Life: A Corpus-Based Study.* New York: Routledge. doi.org/10.4324/9781315629834-11.

Sherratt, Tim (2005). Human elements. In Tim Sherratt, Tom Griffiths and Libby Robin (eds), *A Change in the Weather: Climate and Culture in Australia.* Canberra: National Museum of Australia Press, 1–17.

Sherratt, Tim, Tom Griffiths and Libby Robin (eds) (2005). *A Change in the Weather: Climate and Culture in Australia.* Canberra: National Museum of Australia Press.

Spinks, Peter (2014). Science fights bushfires on a number of fronts. *The Age.* 1 December. Available at: www.theage.com.au/education/science-fights-bushfires-on-a-multitude-of-fronts-20141201-11xudb.html.

Webb, Eric K. (ed.) (1997). *Windows on Meteorology: Australian Perspective.* Collingwood, Victoria: CSIRO Publishing.

West, Brad (2000). Mythologising a natural disaster in post-industrial Australia: The incorporation of Cyclone Tracy within Australian national identity. *Journal of Australian Studies* 24 (66): 197–204. doi.org/10.1080/14443050009387625.

Weston, Harry J. (1917). [Poster.] NSW Recruiting Committee and Win the War League. Item held at Australian War Memorial, Canberra: item number ARTV00148. Available at: www.awm.gov.au/collection/ARTV00148.

Whetton, Peter (1997). Floods, droughts and the Southern Oscillation connection. In Eric K. Webb (ed.), *Windows on Meteorology: Australian Perspective*. Collingwood, Victoria: CSIRO Publishing, 180–99.

Wierzbicka, Anna (1985). *Lexicography and Conceptual Analysis*. Ann Arbor: Karoma.

Wierzbicka, Anna (1986). Does language reflect culture? Evidence from Australian English. *Language in Society* 15 (3): 349–73. doi.org/10.1017/s0047404500011805.

Wierzbicka, Anna (1989). Baudouin de Courtenay and the theory of linguistic relativity. In Janusz Rieger, Mieczyslaw Szymczak and Stanislaw Urbanczyk (eds), *Jan Niecisław Baudouin de Courtenay a lingwistyka światowa*. Ossolineum: Wrocław, 51–58.

Wierzbicka, Anna (1992). *Semantics, Culture, and Cognition: Universal Human Concepts in Culture-Specific Configurations*. New York: Oxford University Press.

Wierzbicka, Anna (1996). *Semantics: Primes and Universals*. Oxford: Oxford University Press.

Wierzbicka, Anna (1997). *Understanding Cultures through their Key Words: English, Russian, Polish, German, and Japanese*. New York: Oxford University Press.

Wierzbicka, Anna (2002). Australian cultural scripts—*bloody* revisited. *Journal of Pragmatics* 34 (9): 1167–209. doi.org/10.1016/s0378-2166(01)00023-6.

Wierzbicka, Anna (2003 [1991]). *Cross-Cultural Pragmatics: The Semantics of Human Interaction* (2nd edn). Berlin: Mouton de Gruyter.

Ye, Zhengdao (ed.) (2017). *The Semantics of Nouns*. Oxford: Oxford University Press. doi.org/10.1093/oso/9780198736721.003.0001.

7

The semantics of *migrant* in Australian English[1]

Zhengdao Ye

1. Introduction

According to the report entitled *Trends in International Migrant Stock: The 2019 Revision* (UNDESA 2019), Australia has one of the highest rates of foreign-born people as a percentage of its total population, far exceeding other English-speaking countries such as Canada, the United Kingdom and the United States. Indeed, according to the 2016 Census data released by the Australian Bureau of Statistics (ABS 2016), 29 per cent of the estimated residents population in Australia were born overseas.

The ABS refers to overseas-born persons generally as 'migrants'. As an example, in its media release of 27 July 2018 entitled 'Australia's dynamic population', it reports that 'in 2016–17, 377,000 people moved interstate, 276,000 moved overseas, and 539,000 people arrived as migrants'; of the latter, '315,000 arrived on a temporary visa, including just over 150,000 international students, just over 50,000 working holidaymakers, and 32,000 workers on temporary skill visas'. It further elaborates that

---

[1] I dedicate this chapter to Anna Wierzbicka, an exemplary migrant. Extraordinary scholarly achievements aside, Anna has built a new life in a new country. Together with her husband John, she raised two multilingual daughters; and she is the doting *babcia* of Liz (Clem), Nick, Catherine, Therese, Benedict and John (for the meaning of the Polish term *babcia*, see Wierzbicka 1992: 282; cf. Wierzbicka 2017: 45–49).

'106,000 migrants arrived on permanent visas including 45,800 on skill visas, 29,800 on family visas and 23,900 on humanitarian visas' (ABS 2018).

For speakers of Australian English, however, perhaps only those who 'arrived on permanent visas' would be referred to as *migrants*;[2] international students, backpackers and working holidaymakers would hardly be assigned such a label. Equally, it is hard to imagine that these people would refer to themselves as *migrants*. Nor is it conceivable that, when referring to themselves, migrants would prefer the description 'those who arrived on permanent visas' to the label *migrants*. So what does the word *migrant* mean in everyday Australian English? How is it used?

This chapter attempts to provide some answers to these questions. Its chief objective is to conduct a detailed semantic analysis of the word *migrant* as used in Australian English and in non-institutional contexts, and to offer a semantic explication in Natural Semantic Metalanguage (NSM). I first discuss the importance of studying nouns that denote social categories, drawing on Anna Wierzbicka's seminal work on nouns and conceptual analysis (e.g. Wierzbicka 1985, 1986). I then explain the corpus I use for the semantic analysis conducted in this study, and the limitation of the data set. The main part of the chapter is an in-depth, corpus-assisted meaning analysis, which entails examining patterns of usage and using NSM as a tool for meaning description. In this process, I also compare and contrast the meaning and usage of *migrant* with those of *immigrant*. This is followed by a brief discussion of the use of *migrant* in government and international contexts.[3]

2. Nouns for people

To categorise people is a human penchant. Salient categories of people are more often than not assigned labels, such as *migrant*, *digger* and *battler* in Australian English. Therefore, studying the meanings of the nouns that people use to label themselves and others can help pinpoint the priorities

---

2   Australian English refers to the Standard Australian English, a regional variety of English. It is a common language of Australia, largely taking its present form since the Second World War and codified in publications such as *The Cambridge Australian English Style Guide* (Peters 1995; see also Delbridge 1999).
3   Due to limitations of space, the chapter will not compare the meaning and usage of *migrant* in Australian English and those in American and British English; for such a study, see Ye (2018).

underlying social categorisation and social groupings within a speech community, and reveal the kind of generalisations that people make about themselves and others in general.

The importance of studying nouns for people is intrinsically related to the role and function of nouns as a universal word class. In her paper entitled 'What's in a noun? (Or: How do nouns differ in meaning from adjectives?)', Anna Wierzbicka stresses the categorisation role of nouns as opposed to the description role of adjectives:

> A description implies the presence of a number of characteristics, all on the same level of importance. Thus, one might describe a person as tall, thin, blond, freckled, and so on. But if one categorizes a person as a hunchback, a cripple, a leper, a virgin, or a teenager, one is not mentioning one characteristic among many; rather, one is putting that person into a certain category, seen at the moment as 'unique'. One is putting a label on that person, as one might put a label on a jar of preserves. One might say that a noun is comparable to an identifying construction: 'that's the kind of person that this person is'. An adjective, on the other hand, is comparable to a simple predicate compatible with many other such predicates: 'this person is X, Y, Z'. (Wierzbicka 1986: 358)

Recognising the dual functions of nouns—referring and categorising—Wierzbicka questions the feature approach to the meanings of nouns:

> I submit that what most nouns (prototypical nouns) do is to identify a certain kind of person, a kind of thing, a kind of animal. These kinds are identified in language in positive terms, not in terms of their mutual differences. For examples, the words *man*, *woman* and *child* identify certain kinds of people, each of them with a certain positive image. I think that popular descriptions which suggest that the word *man* means HUMAN + MALE + ADULT or that child means – ADULT + HUMAN (cf. e.g. Bierwisch 1970), miss a crucial point about the semantics of human categorization, embodied in natural language. The meaning of a noun cannot be represented as a set of 'features', because the basic function of a noun is to single out a certain KIND, a kind which may be partly described in terms of features but which cannot be reduced to a set of features. (Wierzbicka 1986: 360)

What this means for semantic analysis is that NSM-based definitions should include how people *think about* the referent in question and not simply the referent itself.

Wierzbicka's insistence on understanding the meanings of (prototypical) nouns based on the semantic prime of KIND has influenced the NSM approach to the semantics of nouns (e.g. Ye 2017a); rather than identifying features, it attempts to elucidate and articulate what makes a category a certain KIND.[4] This chapter deals with the semantics of KINDS of people; particularly, the kind of people who are referred to as *migrants* in Australian English.

3. A word on the semantic primes and semantic molecules

The chapter employs the methods of reductive paraphrasing (that is, to say the same things but in simpler words) to explain the meaning of words concerned, and uses NSM as a descriptive language to represent paraphrased meaning. Research in NSM has shown that, despite their obvious referents, the semantic structure of nouns is complex, which often includes layers of embedded semantic molecules, in addition to the 65 atomic-level semantic primes (e.g. Wierzbicka 1985, 1996; Ye 2017b; see Goddard 2018a for the list of semantic molecules). To explicate the meaning of *migrant* and related words, the semantic molecules 'be born' and 'country', which belong to the 'biosocial' domain and the domain of 'place where one lives', are necessary in order to paraphrase the more complex idea of 'country of birth'. This idea can be paraphrased as 'they were not born in this country/here; they were born in another country/ in another place'. The presence of the semantic prime 'here' and the combination of primes 'in another place' ('another' being a variant of 'other') indicate that the terms containing a reference to changing places are in fact deictic in nature.

---

4 Obviously, kinship terms are not KIND-based but specify relations between two persons. The relational nature of kinship terms means that they do not have to select the word class of nouns exclusively; they can, in fact, be verbs (see e.g. Evans 2000).

4. Corpus-based contrastive semantic analysis

4.1. The corpus

This study analyses the meaning of *migrant* as it is used in Australian English. For this purpose, I draw on examples from the Oznews subcorpus of Collins Wordbanks Online (hereafter Wordbanks).[5] There are two advantages of using Wordbanks. One is that the inclusion of diverse varieties of English in this corpus—such as American English, British English, Canadian English, South African English—makes it possible to compare, within one site, the usage of concerned terms in Australian English and other varieties of English. The other is that the many existing functions of the database allow quantitative analysis of usage and collocational data.[6] However, there are also serious limitations in relying on Oznews as the main source of data for semantic analysis. First, Oznews, being the only subcorpus representing Australian English usages in Wordbanks, comprises examples chiefly drawn from newspapers.[7] Notwithstanding that discourse about *migrants* often takes place in public, the reader should keep in mind that the data presented in this chapter are drawn from one genre only. The second limitation is the relatively small size of the Oznews corpus, which contains about 35 million tokens, accounting for 6.33 per cent of the total tokens in Wordbanks. The third limitation concerns the age of Wordbanks, which spans 1960 to 2005, the bulk of the corpus deriving from the period 2001–05. Given that many people change places due to social, political and economic events, be they local or global, the semantics of *migrant*, as discussed in this chapter and based on Oznews, is inevitably marked by the time period in which the term is used. Although the phrase 'Australian English' is used sparingly in the chapter, its referential range is largely limited, owing to the data set used in the study.[8]

---

5   Collins Wordbanks Online: wordbanks.harpercollins.co.uk.
6   For these two reasons, Wordbanks is preferred to the Australian National Corpus: www.ausnc.org.au/.
7   This is different from the subcorpora of both American English and British English, which contain diverse genres, ranging from newspapers to spoken language.
8   The earliest example of *migrant* included in the Oznews subcorpus is from 1995, and the majority of the examples date from 2000–05. The age of Wordbanks, and the more recent examples of *migrant* in Oznews, also mean that this study is unable to comment on the usage of *migrant* between the late 1940s and early 1960s, a crucial period during which a large number of what are referred to today as migrants arrived and settled in Australia.

Table 7.1. Frequencies of the lemmas MIGRANT and IMMIGRANT in Wordbanks.

Lemma	All varieties of English	Australian English	Other varieties of English by country					
			America	Great Britain	Canada	India	Ireland	New Zealand	South Africa
MIGRANT	3,693	443	1,683	1,133	111	88	21	236	21
IMMIGRANT	13,892	379	9,379	2,603	1,023	136	86	250	104

Source: Wordbanks.

Table 7.2. Frequencies of MIGRANT and IMMIGRANT in news.

Lemma	Oznews	Brnews	Cannews	Indnews	USnews
MIGRANT	443	24	111	88	226
IMMIGRANT	379	97	1,023	136	2,558

Source: Wordbanks.

4.2. Frequency data

Table 7.1 shows the tokens of MIGRANT as a lemma, in contrast to those of IMMIGRANT across all varieties of English included in Wordbanks.[9]

A striking feature of the pair of words concerned here is that the frequency of MIGRANT is higher than that of IMMIGRANT, in reverse trend to all other varieties of English. This suggests that *migrant* is perhaps used more frequently than *immigrant* in Australian English. The frequency data are consistent with the observation offered by *The Australian National Dictionary* (*AND* 2016), which specifically includes the term *migrant* and says that it is 'of special significance to the history of Australia' and 'now more usual than *immigrant*' (*AND* 2016: 951; see also Peters 1995: 483).

What is also interesting is that roughly one-third of the 443 tokens of MIGRANT are used as a modifier of a following noun, such as *workers*, *doctors*, *service* and *waves*. In contrast, all the 379 tokens of IMMIGRANT are of nominal usage.[10]

The distinctiveness of *migrant* in Australian English is brought out further when compared with other varieties of English against the same genre of news, as reflected in Table 7.2.

4.3. Semantic analysis

The frequency data presented in Tables 7.1 and 7.2 point to the fact that, of the two terms, *migrant* and *immigrant*, the former could be seen as being more salient than the latter in Australian English.

In its nominal usage, the word *migrant* has two distinctive senses. *Migrant$_1$* has a country-specific meaning, 'people who have migrated to Australia', and *migrant$_2$* refers to interstate migrants. These two senses will be discussed in turn.

The country-specific characteristic of *migrant$_1$* is clearly reflected in the following examples:

---

9   In Table 7.1, the Part of Speech of the two lemmas is not specified.
10 In Oznews, the phrase 'migrant workers' typically refers to those based in countries other than Australia.

(1) Jan Bassett's collection draws the distinction between visitors who came to Australia and **migrants** who intended to stay.

(2) Like many new **migrants**, she felt lonely and isolated, unable to speak English and communicate with her new neighbours.

(3) Many of the thousands of **migrants** who came to this country after the Second World War thrived despite not being able to speak English …

(4) They are some of South Australia's greatest imports—the **migrants** who brought their hopes, skills …

The collocational patterns of *migrant* in Oznews reveal many interesting points about the concept. They relate to its group-oriented nature, its references to countries of origin, age, language ability, the society's attitudes and a high level of government planning.

In many cases, *migrant$_1$* is used in a plural sense and collocated with a collective noun, as shown in examples (5–6):

(5) **a new generation of migrants** from continental Europe

(6) **waves of migrants**

The majority of the corpus examples convey a group sense. The suggestion that *migrant$_1$* is normally evoked in a collective sense does not mean that it cannot refer to an individual. There are many such examples in Oznews, such as (7–8):

(7) The year was 1998 and **the migrant** who came to Australia for a better life had found it.

(8) Yet, **a migrant** from Beijing such as Guan Wei, who has settled in Sydney with his wife and small daughter, is a latecomer in the short history of European Australia.

The data in Oznews also show that migrants' ethnicities are frequently mentioned. They include British, Danish, English, German, Greek, Italian, Lithuanian, Macedonian, Maltese and Slovenian. These descriptors simultaneously indicate migrants' countries of origin. Expressions such as 'a Fijian-born migrant' explicitly mention the place of birth.

The range of countries alluded to in Oznews undoubtedly reflects the make-up of the migrant population and the history of migration in Australia.[11] This is clearly shown when the frequency data of *migrant$_1$* in Australian English are compared with that of *migrant* across all varieties of English. Wordbanks' Word Sketch shows that, across all varieties of English, the most frequently used modifiers for *migrant* are actually Albanian, Haitian, Bangladeshi, Mexican, North Korean, Burmese and Cuban. None of these appear in the examples of *migrant* in the Oznews corpus, however.

Apart from country of origin, global modifiers such as African, Asian and European are also commonly collocated with *migrant$_1$*, indicating the larger continents the migrants come from.

It is interesting to note that although expressions such as 'the daughter of Slovenian migrants' and 'her father a German migrant' exist in the corpus, there is no reference of migrants being children.[12] This makes sense when we think of the typical motivations attributed to migrants, a point to be discussed later. However, we do find examples of *migrant$_1$* where age is implied, such as 'young migrants living in Australia' (in this example, 'young migrants' refers to teenage) and 'elderly Asian migrants'. When such descriptions are given, they often stress the vulnerability of being a migrant.

In general, the data show that migrants are portrayed positively, and seen as representing a disadvantaged social group because of their very limited language ability and of the fact that they are new to the country, as reflected in examples (2–3) and (9–10):

(9) Textile unions are concerned the tariff cuts between 2010 and 2015 will force mainly older **non-English speaking migrants** out of work.

(10) **Early migrants** faced confusion, fears and frustrations settling into **a foreign land**.

---

11 For a succinct account of Australia's migration history, see www.migrationheritage.nsw.gov.au/belongings-home/about-belongings/australias-migration-history/index.html.
12 Another example of migrants, implying adults, comes from the same website mentioned in Footnote 11. In this article, entitled 'Australia's migration story', the opening paragraph states that 'In New South Wales, four out of every 10 people are either migrants or the children of migrants'.

Other indications that migrants are thought of as being socially disadvantaged include the frequent mention of the word *migrants* along with *refugees, women* and *Aboriginal people* in Oznews.[13]

The corpus data indicate that Australian society shows an overwhelmingly sympathetic attitude towards migrants, recognising the difficulties they face and providing various services to assist them. Some of the corpus examples are given in example (11) (see also example (3)):

(11) a. **welcoming** refugees and new migrants
 b. Migrant Resource Centres/Migrants and Refugee Settlement Services **assist** new migrants
 c. (the women's and children's hospital) to **help** migrants and refugee women
 d. **create** a migrant friendly community
 e. voluntary work **teaching English** to Vietnamese migrants and illiterate adults

The institution name Migrant Resource Centre is especially worth mentioning because it has become a fixed phrase in Australian English. The word 'resource' itself suggests that the society recognises that migrants need support.[14]

The verbs that go with $migrant_1$, as shown in (11a–e), look markedly different from those that go with *migrant* in Word Sketch: when used as the object of a verb, the latter are most likely to collocate with *repatriate, deport, intercept* and *detain*. This difference in collocation affirms that $migrant_1$ in Australian English has its distinctive usage, and that it has a positive connotation.

One also observes marked differences in the kind of modifiers the word *migrant* selects in Oznews and in Word Sketch, which confirm the dominantly positive sense of $migrant_1$ in Australian English. Whereas Word Sketch reveals that the top three modifiers most likely to be combined with *migrant* are *illegal* (168 tokens/T-score 8.46), *undocumented* (15 tokens/T-score 8.24) and *skilled* (42 tokens/T-score 8.09), in the Oznews subcorpus, the phrase *illegal migrants* only occurs

---

13 And in government websites as well: see Footnote 17.
14 Peters (1995: 483) particularly mentions that 'the word [migrant] is enshrined in institutions such as the Adult Migrant English Service (AMES)'.

nine times (compared with the 134 instances of *illegal immigrant/s* in the same subcorpus); the phrase *undocumented migrant* simply does not exist; and the collocation *skilled migrant* occurs 39 times, accounting for almost all the examples contained in Wordbanks.

Upon a close examination of the nine occurrences of the phrase *illegal migrant/s*, it becomes clear that half of these refer to a foreign context. When referring to the Australian context, the situations described are actually positive, as is the case of example (12):

(12) Prime Minister John Howard and Immigration Minister Senator Amanda Vanstone are refusing to say sorry to the mentally ill woman, who was **mistaken for an illegal migrant** and forced to spend 10 months in detention.

Overall, the examples in Oznews show that the word *migrant*, when used in the Australian context, has a positive sense.

Words and expressions, such as 'settle' and 'call Australia home', also suggest the societal expectations of migrants in Australia, where there is a high degree of government planning in matters relating to migrants, as reflected in the frequent mention of 'Government's plan for migrant intakes', 'intake of skilled migrants' and 'to attract skilled migrants' in Oznews. Example (13) suggests that the uniqueness of the skill-based migration policy initiated by the Australian government is recognised overseas.

(13) The British Labour Party in turn has attempted to steal the thunder of the Conservative party, announcing the introduction of an 'Australian-style' migration system which will give preference to **skilled migrants** over the unskilled.

Using NSM, the full explication of *migrant*$_1$ is presented in [A]:

[A] *migrant₁* (Australian usage)

a.	someone of one kind	CATEGORY
b.	people can know that it is like this:	KNOWLEDGE
	people of this kind were not born in Australia, they were born in another country	STATUS
	after they lived for some time in that country where they were born, they wanted to live in Australia	
	because of this, sometime after this, they lived in Australia, not in that country where they were born	CHANGING PLACES
c.	people in Australia can think about people of this kind like this:	PERCEPTION
	'they wanted to live here, because at some time they thought like this:	
	'if we live in Australia, very good things can happen to us, we want this'	MOTIVATION
	because they thought like this, they did many things	ACTION
	after this, they could live in Australia because Australian government said so'	PERMISSION
d.	many people in Australia think about people of this kind like this:	ATTITUDES
	'many people of this kind can't speak English well, many people of this kind can't do much	
	it is good if other people do many good things for them'	

Explication [A] is framed around a semantic template encompassing CATEGORY, KNOWLEDGE, PERCEPTION, MOTIVATION and ATTITUDE. Component (a) reflects that *migrant₁* refers to an individual belonging to a category. The components in (b) describe people's general knowledge about migrants. They suggest that there are certain facts about migrants that are public knowledge. For example, they are not born in Australia, they come from another country, and it is their voluntary decision to take up residency in Australia ('they wanted to live in Australia'). This mature way of thinking, as well as the geographic knowledge of Australia itself as the intended destination, explain why the referential range of the word *migrant₁* does not extend to children. Components under (c) describe societal perception of migrants as reflected in Australian English, including their seeking a better life in

Australia and that they have the Australian government's permission to reside in Australia. This sense of 'for a better life' is pervasive in the data (e.g. examples (4) and (7)), and the idea of their having a legal status adds to the positive meaning of the term.

In addition to semantic primitives and semantic molecules, the reductive paraphrases in [A], written in the English version of NSM, also include words belonging to Minimal English, such as *Australia* and *government*.[15]

The name of the country *Australia* is built into the explication to reflect the use of the term *migrant* in Australian English and the fact that the meaning being explicated is confined to the Australian language context.

The word *government* is included to reflect the idea that 'they can live in this country because the government of this country says so'. It seems that, for ordinary speakers, the idea of people entering a country legally has much to do with what the government of that country says, whereas that of unlawful entry into a country is associated with not complying with the law.

4.4. *Migrant$_1$* vs *immigrant* in Australian English

To further appreciate the positive sense of the word *migrant$_1$* in Australian English, it is instructive to look at the general usage of the word *immigrant*. As already shown in Tables 7.1 and 7.2, the frequency data associated with this pair of words look very different from that in other varieties of English. A close look at the collocations of *immigrant* confirms that it is largely used in negative contexts. Further evidence comes from the fact that of the 379 total occurrences of *immigrant/s*, 134 actually are *illegal immigrant/s*, with references mostly to contexts outside Australia (e.g. 'illegal Thai immigrants in NY'; 'illegal Mexican immigrants in US'); and the related examples depict the means of people entering a specific country (e.g. 'boat', 'truck' and 'smuggling … into'), and the actions taken by the government (e.g. 'send back'; 'interviewed by customs officers'). In Oznews, there are no collocations of *immigrant* with positive verbs, such as *settle* and *help*, or with nouns such as *community*. Nor does the word *immigrant* have a deictic reference to Australia.

---

15   For the notion of Minimal English, see Wierzbicka (2014: 185–96) and Goddard (2018b).

For reasons of space, the full explication of *immigrant* is not offered here. However, the differences in the explications between the two words can be summarised. First, the explication of *immigrant* does not contain the specific reference to 'they want to live in Australia'; rather, the component 'they want to live in another country' can refer to any country. Second, the meaning of *immigrant* does not include reference to activities under the PERCEPTION component; it only has the reference to motivation 'if we live in another country, very good things can happen to us, we want this'. This 'thinner' semantic content of *immigrant* is consistent with the fact that it has become a marginal word in Australian English. The third difference is that the word *immigrant* is associated with a negative attitude: 'often, people in Australia think bad things about people of this kind'.

4.5. *Migrant$_2$* in Australian English

The second nominal usage of *migrant* (i.e. *migrant$_2$*) in Australian English refers to interstate migrants, who change places for reasons of retirement, employment opportunities or lifestyle, as illustrated in examples (14–15):

(14) The biggest proportion were **interstate migrants**, overwhelmingly from Sydney fleeing soaring housing prices for southeast Queensland's relative affordability and better lifestyle.

(15) No longer is Queensland attracting mainly elderly people escaping the bustling capital cities of NSW [New South Wales] and Victoria, but Queensland's **migrants** are likely to be young and from regional areas.

This second sense of the word *migrant* is spelt out in [B].

[B] *migrant$_2$* (Australian usage, as in 'Queensland's migrants')

a.	someone of one kind	CATEGORY
b.	people in Australia can know that it is like this:	KNOWLEDGE
	people of this kind live now in one part of Australia,	
	before, they lived in another part of Australia	CHANGING PLACES

c. people in Australian can think about people of this kind   PERCEPTION
   like this:

   'they wanted to live in another place in Australia,
   because at some time they thought like this:

   'this other place is not the same as where I live   MOTIVATION
   now in Australia,

   very good things can happen to me if I live in this
   other place,

   these things can't happen to me when I live here'

   because they thought like this, they did many things   ACTION

   after this, they did not live any more where they lived
   before, they lived in this other place in Australia

Obviously, the notion of 'country' is absent in the meaning of *migrant₂*. It follows that people do not think about interstate migrants in terms of 'being lawful' or 'unlawful'. Explication [B] focuses on changing place and motivation. The corpus data do not suggest any particular attitudes that people have towards interstate migrants.

5. The meaning of *migrant* in institutional contexts

In either of the two meanings discussed above, the use of *migrant* in media and the public space in Australia conveys the sense that the people being referred to intend to stay and settle. This folk understanding of the word *migrant* is different from its institutional meaning. The quotations taken from the ABS at the beginning of the chapter illustrate one institutional context where *migrants* refers to people who live in another country temporarily, such as international students, who typically spend a few years studying and living in Australia. Some may wish to settle in Australia; others may not. But they come to Australia mostly voluntarily. In fact, the ABS Glossary for the Migrant Data Matrices indicate that 'being born overseas' and 'residing in Australia for a period of 12 months or more' are integral to ABS's definition of 'migrant' (ABS 2011).[16]

---

16   However, it is also interesting to note that on the Department of Human Services website, the everyday sense of *migrants* is used. For example, in talking about the kind of services available to different clients, the social categories of 'migrants', 'refugees' and 'visitors' are distinguished (e.g. www.humanservices.gov.au/individuals/information-in-your-language).

The 12-month residence element is also key to the definition of migrant in international contexts. For example, the International Organization for Migration (IOM) states that it follows the United Nations' definition of 'migrant' as 'an individual who has resided in a foreign country for more than one year irrespective of the causes, voluntary or involuntary, and the means, regular or irregular, used to migrate' (IOM 2011).[17] This is a broad definition which includes references to 'migrant workers, refugees, asylum seekers and IDPs [internally displaced persons], as well as of remittances', as is evident in the IOM's *World Migration Report 2018*:

> Current estimates are that there are 244 million international migrants globally (or 3.3 per cent of the world's population). While the vast majority of people in the world continue to live in the country in which they were born, more people are migrating to other countries, especially those within their region. … migrant workers constitute a large majority of the world's international migrants … Global displacement is at a record high, with the number of internally displaced at over 40 million and the number of refugees more than 22 million. (IOM 2018)

6. Coda

Back to the Australian context. The Heritage Museum of the Bonegilla Migrant Experience provides information relevant to the meaning of migrant analysed in this chapter. Bonegilla, once a military barracks, was converted to a migrant reception and training centre in 1947. According to the information provided at the site, migrants stayed at Bonegilla for a few days or several weeks, depending on their level of English, before being dispatched to other places. And from 1958, it became the only centre of this type, until its closure in 1971. As stated on the website of the Bonegilla Migrant Experience, 'more than 300,000 migrants passed [through] its doors between 1947 and 1971, most of those originating from non–English speaking European countries' (Bonegilla n.d.a).[18]

---

17 According to the UN definition, the term 'migrant' can be understood as 'any person who lives temporarily or permanently in a country where he or she was not born, and has acquired some significant social ties to this country' (UNESCO 2017). See: www.unesco.org/new/en/social-and-human-sciences/themes/international-migration/glossary/migrant/.

18 A brochure about the place states: 'Today the centre touches the lives of millions of Australians. One in 20 Australians have had either a parent, brother, sister, uncle, aunty or grandparent who spent time at Bonegilla before work allocations dispersed them Australia wide' (Bonegilla n.d.b).

The Bonegilla camp serves as a reminder of the scale of postwar migration, early migrants' experiences and their living conditions, as well as the enormous contributions they made to building Australian society. For example, the timeline on display shows that in 1951, the year when the Displaced Persons Scheme ended and Assisted Migrant Scheme began in Australia, 10,000 migrants arrived at Bonegilla. The same year saw the first Australian naturalisation ceremony. Between 1949 and 1974, the Snowy Mountains Hydro-Electric Scheme was completed, largely with migrant labour (100,000 migrants from over 30 countries). In 1973, the Multicultural policy speech, 'Strength in diversity', delivered by Al Grassby (the then Minister for Immigration), marked a new era in Australian government policy.

But what is perhaps most striking in Bonegilla is that migrants received there were from non–English speaking countries, and that a great deal of their training was about learning English. Signs displayed at the Bonegilla site, such as 'no English, no Jobs', remind people of such reality. The site has kept the name 'Tudor Hall'. It is so named 'because it contained pictures of the Tudor monarchs and the British coat-of-arms to help migrants identify with the British heritage of Australia' (Bonegilla n.d.b).

At the time when the Bonegilla camp was operating, migrants to Australia also included many from Great Britain, but they came under a different scheme, according to the information provided at the camp site: from 1946 onwards, the Commonwealth could act as their nominee. They were free to choose their own type of work and live in work hostels with their families, usually located in capital cities.[19] Later, under pressure of numbers, some also came to Bonegilla, but not before the camp was readied and considerably improved.

---

19   In fact, they could also vote after six months!

Thus, in reality, it seems to me that there were, and continue to be, two kinds of migrants: the marked and the unmarked. The latter come from English-speaking countries (particularly England),[20] which are typically developed countries; and the former non–English speaking countries. Explication [A] offered in this chapter indicates that typical conceptions of migrants are that they are non–English speaking. This point, which is ubiquitously observed in the Oznews subcorpus, is also reinforced by the enormous emphasis placed on learning and speaking English for migrants' social advancement.

Thus, it seems that in the public image and perception, migrants are simultaneously 'accented'. This marks their position as a socially disadvantaged group. A typical migrant to Australia is, therefore, one who comes from a non–English speaking country.[21]

References

ABS (Australian Bureau of Statistics) (2011). *3415.0—Migrant Data Matrices, Nov 2011*. Canberra: ABS. Available at: www.abs.gov.au/AUSSTATS/abs@.nsf/Lookup/3415.0Glossary1Nov+2011.

ABS (2016). *Special Article: The 2016 Census of Population and Housing*. Canberra: ABS. Available at: www.abs.gov.au/ausstats/abs@.nsf/Lookup/by%20Subject/1001.0~2016-17~Main%20Features~The%202016%20Census%20of%20Population%20and%20Housing~10009.

---

20 British-born migrants to Australia make up the largest overseas-born migrants in Australia. The Records of British migrants held at the National Archives of Australia states that 'Since European settlement to Australia began in 1788 more migrants have come from Great Britain to settle in Australia than from any other country' (National Archives of Australia 2019: Fact Sheet 123). And according to the article entitled 'Australia's migration history' (NSW Migration Heritage Centre 2010), 'In 1996, for the first time in Australia's migration history, the number of British migrants arriving fell to second place behind New Zealand'. In Australian English, to say 'New Zealand migrants' or 'American migrants', 'Irish migrants' or 'Canadian migrants' sounds unnatural. Although 'British migrants' is a fixed expression, it primarily refers to the origins of those who settled in Australia. The Oznews subcorpus records four occurrences of *British migrants*: one in the context of New Zealand, one about the new waves of British migrants heading to South Australia, one about a Parliamentarian's renunciation of dual citizenship and one about British migrants outnumbering the Aboriginal inhabitants. These are quite different contexts from those discussed in this chapter.

21 It is clear that a close examination of the meaning and usage of the word *migrant* during the postwar period is needed in order to better understand whether it replaces the word *immigrant*, and when, how and why this change took place. Foremost, this will require scrutinising media and government documents of that period.

ABS (2018). *Media Release: Australia's Dynamic Population*. Canberra: ABS. Available at: www.abs.gov.au/ausstats/abs@.nsf/lookup/3412.0Media%20 Release12016-17.

The Australian National Dictionary (AND) (2016). *The Australian National Dictionary: Australian Words and their Origins* (2nd edn) (Bruce Moore, Mark Gwynn, Amanda Laugesen and Julia Robinson, eds). Melbourne: Oxford University Press.

Bonegilla (n.d.a). About Bonegilla Migrant Experience. *Bonegilla Migrant Experience*. Available at: www.bonegilla.org.au/about-us/about-bonegilla-migrant-experience.

Bonegilla (n.d.b). Bonegilla Migrant Experience site guide [brochure]. *Bonegilla Migrant Experience*. Available at: www.bonegilla.org.au/Portals/2/Downloads/Site_Guide_October_2019.pdf?ver=2020-01-13-134513-500.

Delbridge, Arthur (1999). Standard Australian English. *World Englishes* 18 (2): 259–70.

Evans, Nicholas (2000). Kinship verbs. In Patra M. Vogel and Bernard Comrie (eds), *Approaches to the Typology of Word Classes*. Berlin: Mouton de Gruyter, 103–72.

Goddard, Cliff (2018a). *Ten Lectures on Natural Semantic Metalanguage: Exploring Language, Thought and Culture Using Simple, Translatable Words*. Leiden: Brill.

Goddard, Cliff (ed.) (2018b). *Minimal English for a Global World: Improved Communication Using Fewer Words*. London: Palgrave.

IOM (International Organization for Migration) (2011). *Glossary on Migration* (2nd edn). International Migration Law No. 25. Geneva: International Organization for Migration. Available at: publications.iom.int/system/files/pdf/iml25_1.pdf.

IOM (2018). Chapter 02: Migration and migrants: A global overview [website introductory text]. *World Migration Report 2018*. Geneva: International Organization for Migration. doi.org/10.18356/2aede4d9-en.

National Archives of Australia (2019). *Records of British Migrants Held in Canberra*. Fact sheet 123. Available at: www.naa.gov.au/sites/default/files/2020-05/fs-123-records-of-british-migrants-held-in-canberra.pdf.

NSW Migration Heritage Centre (2010). Australia's migration history. *Migration Heritage Centre*. Available at: www.migrationheritage.nsw.gov.au/belongings-home/about-belongings/australias-migration-history/index.html.

Peters, Pam (1995). *The Cambridge Australian English Style Guide* (1st edn). Melbourne: Cambridge University Press.

UNESCO (United Nations Educational, Scientific and Cultural Organisation) (2017). Migrant/Migration. Available at: www.unesco.org/new/en/social-and-human-sciences/themes/international-migration/glossary/migrant/ (site discontinued).

UNDESA (United Nations Department of Economics and Social Affairs) (2019). *Trends in International Migrant Stock: The 2019 Revision*. Geneva: United Nations.

Wierzbicka, Anna (1985). *Lexicography and Conceptual Analysis*. Ann Arbor: Karoma.

Wierzbicka, Anna (1986). What's in a noun? (Or: How do nouns differ in meaning from adjectives?). *Studies in Language* 10 (2): 353–89. doi.org/10.1075/sl.10.2.05wie.

Wierzbicka, Anna (1992). *Semantics, Culture, and Cognition: Universal Human Concepts in Culture-Specific Configurations*. New York: Oxford University Press.

Wierzbicka, Anna (1996). *Semantics: Primes and Universals*. Oxford: Oxford University Press.

Wierzbicka, Anna (2014). *Imprisoned in English: The Hazards of English as a Default Language*. New York: Oxford University Press.

Wierzbicka, Anna (2017). The meaning of kinship terms: A developmental and cross linguistic perspective. In Zhengdao Ye (ed.), *The Semantics of Nouns*. Oxford: Oxford University Press, 19–62.

Ye, Zhengdao (ed.) (2017a). *The Semantics of Nouns*. Oxford: Oxford University Press. doi.org/10.1093/oso/9780198736721.003.0001.

Ye, Zhengdao (2017b). The semantics of nouns: A cross-linguistic and cross-domain perspective. In Ye Zhengdao (ed.), *The Semantics of Nouns*. Oxford: Oxford University Press, 1–18.

Ye, Zhengdao (2018). The semantics of 'migrant', 'immigrant', and 'refugee': A cross-linguistic perspective. Invited Keynote Address, presented at the *International Conference on Nommer L'Humain: Description, Categorisation, Enjeux: Multidisciplinary Approaches*, Strasbourg University.

8
The semantics of verbs of visual aesthetic appreciation in Russian

Anna Gladkova

Ty postoj, postoj, krasavica moja,
Daj mne nagljadet'sja, radost' na tebja.
'Wait, wait, my beauty,
Let me feast my eyes on you, my joy!'
Russian folk song

1. Introduction

The lines of the Russian folk song chosen as an epigraph for this article contain an interesting Russian verb *nagljadet'sja*, which defies translation into English due to its language and culture specificity. Here, I chose to translate this verb as 'to feast one's eyes on' but true translational equivalence is not achieved. The chapter is devoted to the analysis of two Russian verbs expressing visual aesthetic appreciation: *nagljadet'sja* 'to look at someone/something to complete satisfaction/feast one's eyes on' and *ljubovat'sja* 'to admire/feast one's eyes on', both defying translation into English. These verbs provide a key to understanding folk aesthetics (Gladkova and Romero-Trillo 2014, forthcoming(a), forthcoming(b)) because they capture the desire and longing for something through looking—the primary sense of appreciation of what is considered 'beautiful'. This study also contributes to the area of 'visual semantics' (e.g. Wierzbicka 2005; Apresjan 2018; Levisen 2019) where linguistic and cultural variation is at an early stage of exploration.

The study will use data from the Russian National Corpus and will aim to provide semantic explications of these words in semantic primes as they are represented in the Natural Semantic Metalanguage (NSM) developed by Anna Wierzbicka and Cliff Goddard (Goddard and Wierzbicka 2002, 2014). Anna Wierzbicka has applied NSM to the study of Russian language and culture in her numerous publications (Wierzbicka 1972, 1990, 1992, 1997, 1998, 2002, 2009, 2011, 2012, among others). This chapter to a significant extent builds on Wierzbicka's research in this area.

2. The semantics of *nagljadet'sja*

Nagljadet'sja belongs to a group of Russian verbs that share structural similarity (prefix *na-* and reflexive suffix *-sja*) as well as the meaning 'to do something to the degree of complete satisfaction' (Švedova 1980). Some examples of other verbs belonging to this group are: *napit'sja* 'to drink enough', *naest'sja* 'to eat enough', *naslušat'sja* 'to listen enough', *naguljat'sja* 'to walk enough', *nakatat'sja* 'to ride enough', *naradovat'sja* 'to rejoice enough', *načitat'sja* 'to read enough', *naplakat'sja* 'to cry/whip enough', *nasmejat'sja* 'to laugh enough', as well as others.

For *nagljadet'sja*, as well as other verbs in this group, it is difficult to identify equivalent verbs with exact meanings in English, which express completeness of an action as well as a degree of satisfaction on the part of the actor. *Nagljadet'sja* expresses satisfaction from looking at something.[1] In this regard, it is notable that the verbs expressing 'seeing' or 'looking' fall within the same group of verbs as 'eating', 'drinking', 'walking', 'crying', 'laughing' and 'reading'. These verbs present activities that a person might want to do for existential need or pleasure and might want to do it for some time and achieve a degree of satisfaction from doing them. This fact emphasises the role of 'seeing' in human perception. Analysing it through

---

1   Along with *nagljadet'sja* there is another verb with similar meaning—*nasmotret'sja*. They share morphological structure (prefix *na-* and suffix *-sja*), but differ slightly stylistically due to the difference of root verbs they derive from: *gljadet'* and *smotret'*, both translating into English as 'to look/see'. While the analysis of *nasmotret'sja* can be equally enlightening in terms of linguistic and cultural specificity of the semantics of visual aesthetics, we will ignore the analysis of *nasmotret'sja* due to space limit and focus on the meaning of *nagljadet'sja*.

the prism of language-based 'folk aesthetics', one might get important insights and understandings relevant to this salient human function (cf. Itier and Batty 2009; Hansen and Ji 2010).

Nagljadet'sja, as suggested by the Russian Grammar (Švedova 1980), has the meaning 'to look at someone/something to the degree of complete satisfaction'. Interestingly, in actual use, the verb might have a slight variation in meaning depending on the structure and the context. Observations over corpus data suggest that when used in the past, the verb mainly refers to a negative experience and involves one looking at something to the degree that one does not want to do it anymore. Some contexts contain direct reference to some negative experience. In others, there is a hint of negativity that might be arising from the component of meaning implying satisfaction and not wanting to do it anymore. In this use, *nagljadet'sja* frequently collocates with adverbs expressing a high level of satisfaction: *vvolju*, *vdostal'*, *vdovol'*, all translating into English as (approximately) *enough*, *in full* or *in plenty*.

In certain contexts, the object or objects of observation and the associated emotions are clearly negative:

(1) Ljudi **nagljadelis'** na vsevozmožnye akty žestokosti, svireposti …

 'People **have seen enough** acts of cruelty and ferocity …'

(2) **Nagljadelis'** v gorode vsjakoj grjazi, načitalis' knižek, vse uprostili i prišli, estestvenno, k vyvodu, čto nadobno stroit' novyj mir.

 '[They] **have seen** all sorts of filth in the city, read books, simplified everything and consequently concluded that [they] need to build a new world.'

In numerous contexts the objects are not mentioned straightforwardly and involve words like *mnogoe* 'a lot', *raznoe* 'different things' and *vse* 'everything', thus indicating a great degree of experience, including both positive and negative, but mainly negative:

(3) Poživ v Moskve, ona, pravda, na mnogoe **nagljadelas** …

 'Having lived in Moscow she **has seen** a lot …'

(4) Oni oba dolgie gody proveli v stalinskix lagerjax i **nagljadelis'** mnogogo.

'They both spent many years in Stalin's camps and **had seen** a lot.'

(5) My ne sumasšedšie. My prosto vsego **nagljadelis'**.

'We are not mad. We simply **have seen** all sorts of things.'

(6) Vsego **nagljadelas'**, ko vsemu privykla, daže k prestupnikam!

'[I] **have seen** everything, got used to everything, even to criminals!'

Certain contexts do not necessarily involve an evaluation, but there is a possible interpretation of the situation as negative:

(7) … on otslužil v armii, a zaodno i vdovol' **nagljadelsja** na kraski russkogo severa, poskol'ku načalas' ego služba v Komi, a zakončilas' pod Arxangel'skom …

'… he had served in the army and had seen the colours of the Russian North a lot as his service started in Komi and ended near Arkhangelsk …'

The use that interests us most is the use of *nagljadet'sja* expressing a high degree of visual aesthetic appreciation. In this use, *nagljadet'sja* is used in constructions expressing modality:

dat' nagljadet'sja:	'let (someone) *nagljadet'sja*' (as in the song quoted in the epigraph)
ne moč' nagljadet'sja:	'can not *nagljadet'sja*'
ne nagljadet'sja:	'not *nagljadet'sja*' 'not be able to *nagljadet'sja*'
nevozmožno nagljadet'sja:	'impossible to *nagljadet'sja*'

Let us consider some examples of such use from the corpus:

(8) … pjat'desjat let ja každyj den' gljažu na Volgu i vse **nagljadet'sja ne mogu**.

'… I have been looking at the Volga for fifty years and **cannot see enough** of it.'

(9) Skol'ko ja ni smotrju na ètot pejzaž – **ne mogu nagljadet'sja**.

'No matter how much I look at this landscape, I **can't see enough** of it.'

(10) Potrjasennyj, ja **ne mog nagljadet'sja** na otkryvšujusja vzoru krasoty.

'Stunned, I **could not see enough** of the beauty in front of my eyes.'

(11) Ona ljubit smotret' na nizkie oblaka – **ne nagljadet'sja**.

'She likes to look at low clouds; one **can't see enough** of them.'

(12) Ne toropis', vse budet. **Daj** xot' **nagljadet'sja** na tebja …

'Don't be in a hurry, everything will happen. **Let** me at least **look** at you enough …'

In the second use in modal frames, the verb tends to be used with people and landscape or creations of nature as objects. It can also be used with objects created by people. In all cases, these objects are characterised by some special beauty or they are of particular value to the observer. For example, as in example (12), the object of admiration is someone's dear relative or friend they haven't seen for a long time.

A close link between the action *nagljadet'sja* and one's close and dear people is well illustrated by its derivative *nenagljadnyj* (literally, 'someone that one cannot look enough at'). It is an adjectival form which means 'one's dear/beloved person'. It is commonly used as an endearment form of address—*moj/moja nenagljadnyj(-aja)* 'my dear/beloved'. This form fits well the value of warmth in interactions with close and dear people (Gladkova 2013a).

It is debatable whether there is enough justification to posit polysemy for *nagljadet'sja*. We would argue that despite the observed difference in use, it is unlikely that this difference is the case of polysemy (cf. Goddard 2009; Polguère 2018). Rather, we observe some different resonance due to the context and the tendency to occur in different structures. However, we will tentatively propose two different explications: one for the use in the past (as the invariant of meaning) and one in modal constructions.

The following explication[2] can represent the invariant meaning of *nagljadet'sja*:[3]

---

2   Presumably, this explication, with the change of the prototype verb can be extended to other Russian verbs expressing an action performed to the degree of complete satisfaction.

3   The explications proposed in this chapter use the semantic universal SEE. It is also possible that in certain contexts it would be preferable to use *to look* as a semantics molecule to reflect the intentional element of the seeing process. The relationship between SEE and *to look* is complex and requires further investigation (see Padučeva (2004) on the relationship between the Russian equivalents of *to see* and *to look*).

[A] *X nagljadelsja na Y* 'X has seen enough of Y'

a. someone X saw someone/something Y for a long time
b. someone X saw someone/something Y many times
c. because of this, after this, X didn't want to see someone/something Y anymore

When referring to events in the past, *nagljadet'sja* emphasises the idea of sufficiency of the action of 'seeing'; it happens to the degree that one does not want to do it anymore. In many contexts, there is a shade of meaning of this action being unavoidable. However, it is unlikely that this component could be posited as part of meaning of the word; rather, it comes from the context.

For the use of *nagljadet'sja* in a modal frame we would propose the following explication:

[B] *X ne mog nagljadet'sja na Y* 'X couldn't look enough at Y'

a. someone X saw someone/something Y for a long time
b. someone X saw someone/something Y many times
c. someone X wanted to see someone/something Y more

　　because when someone X sees someone/something Y,

　　someone X feels something very good

d. someone X felt something very good when someone X was doing it

This frame of use involves a prolonged process of looking at something or someone and also a desire to do it more. This desire is associated with inherent pleasure acquired from this process.

It might be illuminating to mention again morphological and structural similarity of *nagljadet'sja* with other Russian verbs, such as *napit'sja* 'to drink till satisfaction', *naest'sja* 'to eat till satisfaction', among others, which express actions that one wants to do till complete satisfaction. In this regard, seeing someone or something (usually for the sake of pleasure or satisfaction) is conceptualised as a kind of basic need along with eating or drinking.

3. The semantics of *ljubovat'sja*

We will now turn to the analysis of another Russian verb expressing aesthetic admiration and appreciation: *ljubovat'sja* 'to admire/feast one's eyes on'. Etymologically it relates to the verb *ljubit'* 'to like/love', therefore one can interpret its meaning as 'to like something by looking at it'. Jurij Apresjan describes *ljubovat'sja* as:

> a controlled prolonged action, in the process of which the gaze can be gliding from one detail of the object to the other; this movement of the eyes can be accompanied by bending of the head, mimics, etc. (2004: 527)

Importantly, this process brings pleasure to the observer.

As it is the case with *nagljadet'sja*, *ljubovat'sja* defies translation into English. The English verb *to admire*, its closest equivalent, is broader in use. The expressions like *I admire your sense of humour* or *I admire your strength* would be more suitable to translate with the verb *vosxiščat'sja*. Also, *to admire* can extend to hearing and smell, while *ljubovat'sja* is strictly limited to seeing. Another possible translation of *ljubovat'sja*—'to feast one's eyes on'—is a metaphoric expression and has more limited use in English than *ljubovat'sja* does in Russian. The suggested difference in conceptualisation between the two languages emphasises the role of linguistic influence in the conceptualisation of senses and their relationship to aesthetic appreciation (Iordanskaja 1979; Wierzbicka 2010; Gladkova and Romero-Trillo 2014; see also Ye 2007). While this point requires further investigation, it is possible to hypothesise that Russian suggests a sharper distinction between 'senses' than English does and 'seeing' occupies a clearly 'leading' role among other ways of perception.

Ljubovat'sja is a process taking place over some time, it cannot be momentary. Looking at something or someone brings satisfaction to the person. The objects of *ljubovat'sja* can be quite diverse—people and parts of their bodies, elements of nature and landscapes, objects produced by people as well as people's actions. I will provide examples from the corpus to illustrate each of the uses:

Nature and landscape:

(13) Egor stal **ljubovat'sja** pejzažem.

'Egor **was admiring** the landscape.'

(14) Paroxod otxodil tol'ko noč'ju, a ja, vzjav bilet, sel, ožidaja pribytija paroxoda, na vysokom beregu, **ljubovalsja** Volgoj, zaxodjaščim solncem, večernim nebom.

'The ship was leaving only in the evening; after buying the ticket I sat on the bank **admiring** the Volga, the sunset and the evening sky while waiting for the ship.'

(15) Ej vsego-to i hotelos' – **ljubovat'sja** krasivymi rastenijami, uxaživat' za nimi, trogat' inogda rukami i vdyxat' ix zapaxi …

'All she wanted was to **admire** beautiful plants, look after them, sometimes touch them and inhale their smell …'

People and parts of their body:

(16) I moej babuške bylo prijatno, vsjakoj materi prijatno, kogda **ljubujutsja** ee rebenkom.

'It was pleasing to my grandmother, like to any mother, when her child **is being admired**.'

(17) Stoja na beregu ruč'ja, ja **ljubovalsja** djadej i ego lošad'ju.

'Standing on the bank of the creek I was **admiring** my uncle and his horse.'

(18) Ja dolgo **ljubovalsja** ego licom, krotkim i jasnym, kak večernee nebo.

'I **was admiring** his face for a long time, meek and clear like evening sky.'

(19) Každyj raz, kogda on prixodil, ja **ljubovalsja** na ego ruki.

'Every time he came I was admiring his hands.'

People's actions:

(20) Kogda byval v nastroenii i delal čto-to putnoe, na nego nel'zja bylo ne **ljubovat'sja**.

'When he was in good mood and did something worthwhile, it was impossible not to **admire** him.'

(21) **Ljubujas'** dočer'ju, on smejalsja, gljadja, kak ona lovko laviruet meždu poklonnikami, ne podozrevajuščimi o suščestvovanii drug druga.

'**Admiring** his daughter he laughed seeing how skilfully she was manoeuvring between her admirers who did not suspect about the existence of each other.'

Objects:

(22) I posle obeda my **ljubovalis'** kovrami.

'After lunch we **admired** the carpets.'

(23) Takie 3D-kartiny pritjagivajut vzgljad, xočetsja postojanno **ljubovat'sja** imi, čtoby obresti duševnoe ravnovesie i spokojstvie.

'Such 3D pictures attract the eye; one want to constantly **admire** them in order to achieve spiritual balance and calm.'

Šmelev (2005a: 454) argues that *ljubovat'sja* occupies a special place in the Russian value system because, overall, the Russian language encodes a negative attitude to gaining and experiencing pleasure. However, *ljubovat'sja* is an exceptional type of pleasure that is encouraged by public opinion because it is a 'selfless' aesthetic pleasure. In this regard, Zalizniak and Šmelev (2004: 210) also note that *ljubovat'sja* would not be applicable to a person gaining pleasure from looking through a pornographic magazine.

Undoubtedly, *ljubovat'sja* is associated with positive value. It indicates pleasure derived from looking at something and implies beauty of the object. As a general cultural rule, *ljubovat'sja* is an accepted action. However, in the situation of gender relations, one might want to not demonstrate it openly because it signals one's admiration. Some contexts from the corpus point to that:

(24) Valentina Ivanovna daže slegka ustranilas' ot del i **ljubovalas'** so storony Ėdikom-Siloj.

'Valentina Ivanovna even briefly put aside her job to admire Edik from the side.'

(25) Ljudmila, otkrovenno **ljubujas'** nežnym rumjancem, prisuščim vsem ryžim ljudjam, ne otpuskala ego podborodka …

'Ludmilla openly admiring the tender blush characteristic of all red-haired people, did not leave his chin …'

We will attempt the following explication of *ljubovat'sja*:

[C] *X ljubovalsja Y* 'person X was admiring Y'

a. someone X saw someone/something Y for some time, not a short time
b. someone X wanted to do it
c. when someone X was doing it,
   someone X wanted to see many parts of someone/something Y
   someone X wanted to see someone/something Y well
d. when someone X was doing it, someone X couldn't not feel something very good
   like people can't not feel something very good at some times
   when they see some things
e. someone X thought something very good about someone/something Y

This explication captures that *ljubovat'sja* is a prolonged and intentional process (components a and b) which involves looking at the object in detail (component c). This process brings pleasure to the observer (component d) that is akin to 'aesthetic' admiration and involves a positive evaluation of the object (component e).

In the semantics of both verbs it is interesting to observe an overlap with the meaning of *krasivyj* 'beautiful' (Gladkova and Romero-Trillo 2014; Gladkova forthcoming). *Krasivyj* implies an absolute characteristic. This quality is absolute in the sense that looking at the object should bring pleasure regardless of personal preferences of the observer. In Gladkova and Romero-Trillo (2014) the relevant component is formulated as 'this someone can't not feel something very good because of this, like people can't not feel something very good at some times when they see some things'. This component is explicit in the meaning of *ljubovat'sja*, thus making it a verb of aesthetic appreciation. This difference is blurred in the case of *nagljadet'sja* in the sense that this word denotes primarily personal pleasure derived from looking at someone or something that might or might not be 'beautiful'.

4. Discussion and conclusions

This work presented the analysis of two Russian verbs of visual aesthetic appreciation—*nagljadet'sja* and *ljubovat'sja*. It demonstrated that *nagljadet'sja* involves looking at someone or something to the degree of complete satisfaction. We observe some difference in the use of the verb. In the past use, it mainly refers to a negative or neutral experience. Its use in the frame expressing modality is of particular interest to us, where it conveys a high degree of pleasure derived from looking at someone or something and the desire to continue doing it longer. *Ljubovat'sja* expresses a desired, controlled and concentrated action, which involves looking attentively at someone or something for some time. This process also brings pleasure and involves a positive evaluation of the object.

While there is no scope in this chapter for a full-fledged cross-cultural and cross-linguistic analysis that could bring light on cultural characteristics and diversity in this area, it is possible to make some observations about specificity of the lexicon in question and set a possible agenda for future research in the domain of aesthetics-related visual semantics.

To start with, it is possible to consider the semantics of the verbs in question against several Russian 'cultural themes', which have mainly been described by Wierzbicka.

First, the verbs of 'aesthetic appreciation' discussed in this chapter relate to the general theme of 'open' and 'sincere' expression of emotion. Wierzbicka (2002) formulates relevant scripts as follows:

[people think like this:]
it is good if a person wants to say to other people what this person thinks (feels)
it is bad if a person says to other people that this person thinks (feels) something if it is not true
it is good if a person wants other people to know what this person thinks (feels)

In some regard, the verbs in question denote a desire to look at someone/something as a demonstration of a genuine and spontaneous positive attitude and this desire is openly shown as the conducted analysis suggests.

Second, the role of 'desire' to look at someone or something for aesthetic pleasure is quite prominent in the semantics of the verbs in question. These elements of meaning can be associated with the theme of a 'strong' desire, discussed by Wierzbicka in relation to the role of *gorjačij* 'hot' in Russian conceptualisation of feelings and desires (Wierzbicka 2009). She formulates a relevant cultural script as follows (Wierzbicka 2009: 430):

[people think like this:]

it is good if someone can think like this about some things:

    'something very good can happen

    I want it to happen

    I want it very much'

it is good if this someone feels something because of this

    like people feel when they want something very much

Third, the analysis of these verbs makes it possible to relate their meanings to other Russian cultural themes. Primarily, it is a special role of human relations and warmth in interactions with close and dear people (Wierzbicka 1997, 2002; Gladkova 2010, 2013a, 2013b; Larina 2015; Larina et al. 2017). As it has been observed, the words under analysis might have close people as objects; that is, someone whom one wants to see for a long time. At the same time, the verb *nagljadet'sja* is an interesting example of encoding an action performed 'to the full' that correlates with the cultural theme of 'doing things to the full or extreme' (Šmelev 2005b).

Fourth, the Russian verbs can also be discussed in the light of the tendency of openly telling another person what would be good or not to do (Wierzbicka 2011, 2012). This could be interpreted as 'putting pressure' from the point of view of Anglo culture, but it does not have this implication in Russian. A request *daj mne nagljadet'sja na tebja* ('let me look enough at you') might sound imposing from an Anglo perspective. However, from the point of view of Russian culture, it does not have such implication because it is primarily interpreted in view of expressing positive feelings among close people.

It is also notable that the Russian verbs in question defy translation into English. This might suggest that aesthetic admiration and appreciation is an important cultural theme in Russian. It testifies itself in the fact that such kind of admiration can be expressed and is encouraged to be expressed.

When it comes to exploring cultural diversity, it would be interesting to consider what standards of 'beauty' in terms of human body and clothes are, as well as nature (e.g. Bromhead 2011, 2018; Romero-Trillo and Espigares 2012; Lišaev 2015). This can lead us to the issue of cultural difference in the arena of non-verbal communication and different attitudes to gazing at someone or something for a prolonged time.

With a brief reference to possible English translational equivalents of the verbs in question, we could observe difference in the role of senses in aesthetic appreciation. The Russian verbs under analysis have a distinct reference to vision as a primary source of aesthetic pleasure. The difference in distinction and separation of senses for Russian and English has been observed earlier (Iordanskaja 1979; Wierzbicka 2010) and in particular in relation to aesthetic appreciation (Gladkova and Romero-Trillo 2014; Gladkova forthcoming). Russian seems to differentiate more distinctly than English does the role of senses in aesthetic appreciation, assigning 'seeing' a particularly prominent role. To put it differently, Russian associates aesthetic pleasure mainly with seeing and hearing, while in English this type of pleasure more easily extends to all senses. This indicates a further need of exploration of the field of aesthetics in relation to different senses.

Overall, the study supports the need for further investigation in the field of folk aesthetics and understanding how different languages conceptualise human aesthetic experience. The study of visual semantics and in particular aesthetics of visual semantics cannot be exhausted by the study of words as such, but it would require a development of cultural scripts and rules associated with appreciation of 'beautiful' and attitudes to 'ugly'. Tentatively, the data analysed in this chapter support the ideas expressed earlier in the literature (Levontina 2004; Zalizniak and Šmelev 2004; Šmelev 2005a) that aesthetic appreciation occupies a special role in the Russian linguistic world view and might suggest the existence of the following cultural script in Russian culture:

[many people think like this:]

it can be good if someone can't not feel something very good when this someone sees someone/something

    like people can't not feel something very good when they see something

it can be good if someone wants to see this someone/something for some time

References

Apresjan, Jurij (2004). Ljubovat'sja, zagljadet'sja. In Jurji Apresjan, (ed.), *Novyj ob"jasnitel'nyj slovar' sinonimov russkogo jazyka* [*The New Explanatory Dictionary of Russian Synonyms*]. Moskva-Wien: Jazyki slavjanskoj kul'tury-Wiener Slawistischer Almanach, 526–29.

Apresjan, Valentina (2018). Russian constructions with syntactic reduplication of color terms: A corpus study. *Russian Journal of Linguistics* 22 (3): 653–74. doi.org/10.22363/2312-9182-2018-22-3-653-674.

Bromhead, Helen (2011). *The bush* in Australian English. *Australian Journal of Linguistics* 31 (4): 445–71.

Bromhead, Helen (2018). *Landscape and Culture – Cross-linguistic Perspectives*. Amsterdam: John Benjamins.

Gladkova, Anna (2010). *Russkaja kul'turnaja semantika: èmocii, cennosti, žiznennye ustanovki* [*Russian Cultural Semantics: Emotions, Values, Attitudes*]. Moscow: Languages of Slavonic Cultures [in Russian].

Gladkova, Anna (2013a). 'Intimate' talk in Russian: Human relationships and folk psychotherapy. *Australian Journal of Linguistics* 33 (3): 322–43. doi.org/10.1080/07268602.2013.846453.

Gladkova, Anna (2013b). 'Is he one of ours?' The cultural semantics and ethnopragmatics of social categories in Russian. *Journal of Pragmatics* 55: 180–94. doi.org/10.1016/j.pragma.2013.06.010.

Gladkova, Anna (forthcoming). What is beauty? Cultural semantics of the Russian folk aesthetics. *International Journal of Language and Culture*.

Gladkova, Anna and Jesus Romero-Trillo (2014). Ain't it beautiful? The conceptualization of beauty from an ethnopragmatic perspective. *Journal of Pragmatics* 60: 140–59. doi.org/10.1016/j.pragma.2013.11.005.

Gladkova, Anna and Jesus Romero-Trillo (forthcoming(a)). The linguistic conceptualization in folk aesthetics. *International Journal of Language and Culture*.

Gladkova, Anna and Jesus Romero-Trillo (eds) (forthcoming(b)). Special issue, '"Beautiful" and "ugly" across languages and cultures'. *International Journal of Language and Culture*.

Goddard, Cliff (2009). Polysemy. A problem of definition. In Yael Ravil and Claudia Leacock (eds), *Polysemy: Theoretical and Computational Approaches*. Oxford: Oxford University Press, 129–51.

Goddard, Cliff and Anna Wierzbicka (eds) (2002). *Meaning and Universal Grammar: Theory and Empirical Findings* (2 vol.). Amsterdam: John Benjamins.

Goddard, Cliff and Anna Wierzbicka (2014). *Words and Meanings: Lexical Semantics Across Domains, Languages and Cultures*. Oxford: Oxford University Press. doi.org/10.1093/acprof:oso/9780199668434.001.0001.

Hansen, Dan Witzer and Qiang Ji (2010). In the eye of the beholder: A survey of models for eyes and gaze. *IEEE Transactions on Pattern Analysis and Machine Intelligence* 32 (3): 478–500. doi.org/10.1109/TPAMI.2009.30.

Iordanskaja, Lidia (1979). O semantike russkix glagolov: *vosprinimat', oščuščat' i čuvstvovat'* [On the semantics of the Russian verbs *vosprinimat', oščuščat'* and *čuvstvovat'*]. *Wiener Slawistischer Almanach* 3: 207–17.

Itier, Roxane and Magali Batty (2009). Neural bases of eye and gaze processing: The core of social cognition. *Neuroscience & Biobehavioral Reviews* 33 (6): 843–63. doi.org/10.1016/j.neubiorev.2009.02.004.

Larina, Tatiana (2015). Culture-specific communicative styles as a framework for interpreting linguistic and cultural idiosyncrasies. *International Review of Pragmatics* 7 (5): 195–215. doi.org/10.1163/18773109-00702003.

Larina, Tatiana, Arto Mustajoki and Ekaterina Protassova (2017). Dimensions of Russian culture and mind. In Katja Lehtisaari and Arto Mustajoki (eds), *Philosophical and Cultural Interpretations of Russian Modernisation*. London/New York: Routledge, 7–19.

Levisen, Carsten (2019). 'Brightness' in color linguistics: New light from Danish visual semantics. In Ida Raffaelli, Daniela Katunar and Barbara Kerovec (eds), *Lexicalization Patterns in Color Naming: A Cross-Linguistic Perspective*. Amsterdam: John Benjamins, 83–105. doi.org/10.1075/sfsl.78.05lev.

Levontina, Irina (2004). Ostorožno, pošlost'! [Beware of vulgarity]. In Nina D. Arutjunova (ed.), *Logičeskij analiz jazyka. Jazyki èstetiki. Konceptual'nye polja prekrasnogo i bezobraznogo* [*Logical Analysis of Language. Languages of Aesthetics. Conceptual Fields of Beautiful and Ugly*]. Moscow: Indrik, 231–50 [in Russian].

Lišaev, Sergej (2015). *Aestetika prostranstva* [*The Aesthetics of Space*]. St Petersburg: Aleteya.

Padučeva, Elena. (2004). *Dinamičeskie modeli v semantike leksiki* [*Dynamic Models in the Semantics of Lexicon*]. Moscow: Jazyki slavjanskoj kul'tury [in Russian].

Polguère, Alain (2018). A lexicographic approach to the study of copolysemy relations. *Russian Journal of Linguistics* 22 (4): 788–820. doi.org/10.22363/2312-9182-2018-22-4-788-820.

Romero-Trillo, Jesus and Tescar Espigares (2012). The cognitive representation of natural landscapes in language. *Pragmatics and Cognition* 20: 168–85. doi.org/10.1075/pc.20.1.07rom.

Šmelev, Alexey (2004). Vidy aestetičeskoj ocenki v predstavlenii russkogo jazyka [Types of aesthetic evaluation in Russian]. In Nina D. Arutjunova (ed.), *Logičeskij analiz jazyka. Jazyki ėstetiki. Konceptual'nye polja prekrasnogo i bezobraznogo* [*Logical Analysis of Language. Languages of Aesthetics. Conceptual Fields of Beautiful and Ugly*]. Moscow: Indrik, 303–11 [in Russian].

Šmelev, Alexey (2005a). Skvoznye motivy russkoj jazykovoj kartiny mira [Central motifs of the Russian linguistic world view]. In A. Zalizniak, I. Levontina and A. Šmelev (eds), *Ključevye idei russkoj jazykovoj kartiny mira* [*Key Ideas of the Russian Linguistic World View*]. Moskow: Jazyki slavjanskoj kul'tury, 452–64 [in Russian].

Šmelev, Alexey (2005b). Širota russkoj duši [The breadth of the Russian soul]. In A. Zalizniak, I. Levontina and A. Šmelev (eds), *Ključevye idei russkoj jazykovoj kartiny mira* [*Key Ideas of the Russian Linguistic World View*]. Moskow: Jazyki slavjanskoj kul'tury, 51–63 [in Russian].

Švedova, N. (ed.) (1980). *Russkaja grammatika* [*Russian Grammar*] (2 vols). Moscow: Nauka [in Russian].

Wierzbicka, Anna (1972). *Semantic Primitives*. Frankfurt: Athenäum.

Wierzbicka, Anna (1990). Duša ('soul'), toska ('yearning'), sud'ba ('fate'): Three key concepts in Russian language and Russian culture. In Zygmunt Saloni (ed.), *Metody formalne w opisie języków słowiańskich* [*Formal Methods in the Description of Slavic Languages*]. Bialystok University Press, 13–36.

Wierzbicka, Anna (1992). *Semantics, Culture, and Cognition: Universal Human Concepts in Culture-Specific Configurations*. New York: Oxford University Press.

Wierzbicka, Anna (1997). *Understanding Cultures through their Key Words: English, Russian, Polish, German, and Japanese*. New York: Oxford University Press.

Wierzbicka, Anna (1998). Russian emotional expression. *Ethos* 26 (4): 456–83.

Wierzbicka, Anna (2002). Russian cultural scripts: The theory of cultural scripts and its applications. *Ethos* 30 (4): 401–32. doi.org/10.1525/eth.2002.30.4.401.

Wierzbicka, Anna (2005). There are no 'color universals' but there are universals of visual semantics. *Anthropological Linguistics* 47 (2): 217–44.

Wierzbicka, Anna (2009). Pragmatics and cultural values: The hot centre of Russian discourse. In Bruce Fraser and Ken Turner (eds), *Language in Life, and a Life in Language: Jacob Mey—A Festschrift*. Bingley: Emerald, 423–34. doi.org/10.1163/9789004253209_055.

Wierzbicka, Anna (2010). *Experience, Evidence, and Sense: The Hidden Cultural Legacy of English*. New York: Oxford University Press. doi.org/10.1093/acprof:oso/9780195368000.001.0001.

Wierzbicka, Anna (2011). Arguing in Russian: Why Solzhenitsyn's fictional arguments defy translation. *Russian Journal of Communication* 4 (1/2): 8–37. doi.org/10.1080/19409419.2011.10756788.

Wierzbicka, Anna (2012). 'Advice' in English and in Russian: A contrastive and cross-cultural perspective. In Holger Limberg and Miriam A. Locher (eds), *Advice in Discourse*. Amsterdam: John Benjamins, 309–32.

Ye, Zhengdao (2007). Taste as a gateway to Chinese cognition. In Andrea C. Schalley and Drew Khlentzos (eds), *Mental States: Volume 2: Language and Cognitive Structure*. Amsterdam: John Benjamins, 109–32.

Zalizniak, Anna A. and Alexey D. Šmelev (2004). Ėstetičeskoe izmerenie v russkoj jazykovoj kartine mira: *byt, pošlost', vran'e* [Aesthetic dimension in the Russian linguistic worldview: *byt, pošlost', vran'e*]. In Nina D. Arutjunova (ed.), *Logičeskij analiz jazyka. Jazyki ėstetiki. Konceptual'nye polja prekrasnogo i bezobraznogo* [*Logical Analysis of Language. Languages of Aesthetics. Conceptual Fields of Beautiful and Ugly*]. Moscow: Indrik, 209–30 [in Russian].

9
Christian values embedded in the Italian language: A semantic analysis of *carità*

Gian Marco Farese

1. Christianity in Italian language

In an essay titled '*Perché non possiamo non dirci cristiani*' ('Why we cannot help calling ourselves Christians', 1942), the Italian philosopher and linguist Benedetto Croce contended that it is impossible to deny the Christian roots of Italian society and the influence of what he called 'the Christian revolution' on Italian history and culture:

> The Christian revolution worked upon the very centre of the soul, upon the moral consciousness, and by emphasizing the inner essence of that consciousness, almost seemed to confer on it a new power, a new spiritual quality, which had hitherto been lacking in humanity. ... We must hold that those men most effectively carried on the advances both in thought and life. And, in spite of some superficial anti-Christianity, these were in fact the humanists of the Renaissance. (Croce 1949: 37)

One may or may not agree with Croce on the idea that Italian society and culture have inherently Christian roots. However, at least from a strictly linguistic point of view, Croce is no doubt right: the influence of Christianity on the Italian language is undeniable. Italian is rich in words, fixed phrases and idiomatic expressions which reflect Christian values and are frequently used by speakers in discourse. Even the most fervent upholders of the secular nature of Italian society must have said *che peccato!* ('what a sin', meaning 'what a pity!'), *beato te!/beati voi!* ('blessed you', meaning 'lucky you!'), *misericordia!* ('mercy!'), *Madonna mia!* ('my Madonna!') and *per carità!* ('for charity's sake') at least once in their lives.

The peculiarity of various Italian words and phrases expressing Christian values is that they are polysemous: in discourse, they are used both in their Christian meaning and in a phraseological meaning which may or may not be related to the Christian one. A glaring example of this kind of polysemy is the word *carità* (/kari'ta/, roughly 'charity', 'act of love'), which expresses both a Christian meaning and a series of distinct phraseological meanings which are only partly related or completely unrelated to the Christian one. The different meanings of *carità* coexist, but do not compete in the same contexts; therefore, it is possible to identify and distinguish these meanings clearly and precisely by analysing how *carità* is used in different contexts and by looking at specific collocations. Both the Christian and the phraseological meanings of *carità* are represented by prototypical collocations: *atto di carità* ('act of *carità*') for the Christian meaning and *per carità* (literally, 'for *carità*'s sake') for the phraseological meanings.

This chapter presents an analysis of the different meanings expressed by the word *carità* in different contexts and discusses the conceptual and semantic relation between these meanings. The analysis is made by adopting the methodology of the Natural Semantic Metalanguage (NSM) (Wierzbicka 1992a, 1996, 1997, 2001; Goddard 2011, 2018; Goddard and Wierzbicka 2014) from an exclusively synchronic perspective and is in line with Wierzbicka's (2001, 2019) semantic analysis of the core principles of Christianity as expressed in language. Separate semantic explications are presented for each meaning of *carità*. The body of data includes examples from the CORIS/CODIS corpus of contemporary written Italian, from contemporary novels and online material.[1] The chapter concludes with a brief discussion of the relation between the polysemy of Italian words reflecting Christian values and the double-sided (Christian and secular) nature of Italian society.

---

1   CORIS/CODIS (n.d.) Corpus of Written Italian. Available at: corpora.dslo.unibo.it/TCORIS/.

2. The Christian meaning of *carità*

As Wierzbicka has demonstrated in her works on the semantics of Christianity (most notably 2001, 2019), it is impossible to elucidate the key principles of Christianity without analysing Christian keywords and their meanings. Language, Wierzbicka writes, has the ability 'to express what Christians believe, and to do so clearly, intelligibly and truthfully' (2019: 28). At the same time, Wierzbicka has often pointed out that the language of Christianity is not easy to analyse, both for reasons of style (e.g. the ubiquitous use of metaphors) and because of linguistic differences and translation inaccuracies characterising different versions of Christian texts (e.g. the Bible). For these reasons, a semantic analysis of words that are carriers of Christian values like *carità* needs to be scrupulously grounded in discourse and in texts. In *What Christians Believe* (2019), Wierzbicka has stressed the importance of sticking as close as possible to the texts not only for the sake of semantic accuracy, but also for the correct interpretation of the Christian values encapsulated in the meanings of Christian keywords like *carità*.[2] This can be done only by simplifying the often-abstruse language of metaphors and by identifying any translation inaccuracies. Following Wierzbicka's analytical approach, in my analysis of the Christian meaning of the Italian word *carità* presented in this section I have kept the New Testament and other key texts of Christian thinking under close scrutiny.

The noun *carità* is conceptually, etymologically and semantically related to the adjective *caro* ('dear'), which denotes an expression of good feelings towards someone (Farese 2018a). More precisely, *carità* has always been used in the Christian tradition to talk about a specific form of 'love': God's love of people above all things, the love which unites people with God. It was Jesus who preached this form of love in his commandment '*ama il prossimo tuo come te stesso*' ('love your neighbour as yourself'). In doing so, Jesus referred to God's feelings for people, and this raises the much-debated question of whether or not 'mental actions' and anthropomorphic features like feeling

---

[2] One glaring example of semantic misinterpretation discussed by Wierzbicka is that of the English word *almighty* and of the Latin *omnipotens* in contrast to the original Greek *pantokrator* used in relation to God in the Old Testament. Wierzbicka argues that the English *almighty* and the Latin *omnipotens* give a distorted idea of God as someone who can basically do whatever he wants. This, in her view, is very different from the actual idea of God reflected in the meaning of the Ancient Greek *pantokrator*, which is semantically much more focused on 'happening' than 'wanting'. For Wierzbicka, the main component of the meaning of *pantokrator* is 'if God wants some things to happen, after some time they will all happen, as God wants'.

(and wanting) are at all ascribable to God. Discussing this point in detail, Wierzbicka (2019) has shown that there is compelling evidence in Christian texts unambiguously proving that God 'feels', and more precisely that 'God feels something very good towards people'. It is Jesus himself who speaks about God's love ('God so loved the world that he gave his only son …') in the New Testament. Moreover, Wierzbicka emphasises the fact that several times God himself speaks about Jesus in terms of his 'beloved son'. Although there is no semantic equivalent for the Greek *agapao* used in the Bible to talk about God's feelings towards Jesus and people, Wierzbicka contends that it is possible to capture these feelings in universal terms and proposes to do so by positing the components 'God feels something very good towards people' and 'people feel something very good towards God'. This mutual expression of very good feelings between God and people constitutes the conceptual and semantic base of the Christian meaning of the Italian *carità*. Crucially, Wierzbicka contends that if all words (including *feel*) could not be attributed to God there could be no dialogue between God and people, and this would conflict with the very foundations of Christianity (2019: 36). Although the meaning of *carità* includes an expression of good feelings towards someone, this word is not an emotion term like, for example, *pietà* ('pity'); in discourse, one does not say **provare/sentire carità per qualcuno* ('to feel *carità* towards someone') as one can say *provare/sentire pietà per qualcuno*. Italian speakers talk about *un atto/un gesto/un'opera di carità* ('an act/a show/a work of *carità*') and about actions inspired by a *spirito di carità* ('spirit of *carità*'). In verb phrases, *carità* collocates with *domandare/chiedere* ('ask'), *accettare* ('accept'), *rifiutare* ('refuse') and especially *fare* ('do/make/perform'). The constructions *fare la carità a qualcuno* ('to perform an act of *carità* for someone') and *fare la carità di* + N_{ph}/V_{ph} ('to make the *carità* of') are by far the most frequent collocations in the body of collected data:

(1) Papa Francesco ai ragazzi ambrosiani: 'Testimoniate la vostra fede con **gesti di carità**'.[3]

Pope Francis to the Milanese teens: 'Testify your faith through **acts of *carità*.**'

(2) Mi domando: quanto si può chiedere a un uomo? A un essere di carne e sangue? Gli si può chiedere di non rubare, di lavorare con il sudore della fronte, di **fare la carità** ai poveri.

---

3   Available at: www.chiesadimilano.it/news/chiesa-diocesi/papa-francesco-ai-ragazzi-ambrosiani-testimoniate-la-vostra-fede-con-gesti-di-carita-212987.html.

I wonder: how much can one ask of a man? To a being of flesh and blood? One can ask him not to steal, to work with the sweat of his brow, to **make the *carità*** to the poor. (CORIS/CODIS corpus, narrativa)

(3) Dovrei ringraziarti in ginocchio? Per **avermi fatto la carità** della tua attenzione?

Am I supposed to go down on my knees and thank you? For **having made me the *carità*** of your attention? (CORIS/CODIS corpus, narrativa)

The discourse on *carità* clearly indicates that conceptually and semantically this word is related to 'doing' before being related to 'feeling'; the word does express the idea of feeling something good towards someone, but these good feelings are manifested through actions. An act of *carità* consists in doing something good for someone who needs help and suffers, and is inspired by the good feelings that the helper expresses towards the sufferer. The characteristic of these good feelings and their associated way of thinking is that they are instilled in people as a value. Christians are taught that it is good to feel something good and to do good things for people who suffer as they would feel and would do for their brothers and sisters, the underlying assumption being that all people are sons and daughters of God. The idea of 'brotherly love' and of belonging to the same family of God is reflected in the collocation *carità fraterna* ('brotherly *carità*') used in Italian discourse. Like other words expressing Christian values, the semantics of *carità* does not just encapsulate a particular way of thinking about other people, but also serves as a moral and ethical code for people's conduct. *Carità* denotes a way of thinking that has implications both for people's feelings towards other people and for people's actions: more precisely what people do to other people. Its semantics synthesises thinking, feeling and doing, and ultimately relates to 'how people can live well with other people' and 'how people can live well with God', to use Wierzbicka's words (2019).

There are significant semantic differences between acts of *carità* and acts of *gentilezza* ('kindness') or *solidarietà* ('solidarity'), which also consist in doing something good for someone. Differently from acts of *carità*, acts of *kindness* are not triggered by someone's suffering. As pointed out by Travis (1997), the *kind* person does something good for someone because he/she does not want this person to feel something bad, but not because this person is suffering or because he/she cares for this person. An act of *solidarietà* is performed towards people to whom something bad has happened recently and who suffer because of this (Farese 2018b), whereas disgraces or calamities are not triggers of *carità*.

The performer of an act of *carità* does something good for someone whose current life conditions do not permit him/her to live well and who suffers because of this. The helper witnesses this person's suffering and decides to offer his/her help, both because he/she was taught to feel and to do something good for people in need and because he/she does not want this person to suffer. The helper knows that what he/she can do won't permit the sufferer to live well and that he/she can only alleviate the suffering momentarily. However, the helper can at least satisfy an immediate necessity of the sufferer and can bring momentary relief from sorrow, as stated in Benedict XVI's encyclical *Deus Caritas Est*:

> Following the example given in the parable of the Good Samaritan, Christian charity is first of all the simple response to immediate needs and specific situations: feeding the hungry, clothing the naked, caring for and healing the sick, visiting those in prison, etc. (Benedict XVI 2005)

An act of *carità* can be defined as such if it satisfies four conditions related to the helper's attitude: (i) the helper does not expect to receive anything in return for his/her good actions; (ii) the helper does not expect that something good will happen to him/her because he/she offered his/her help; (iii) the act is not performed to attract people's respect and admiration; (iv) the helper does not consider the person in need 'someone below me'. The fourth condition is related to the fact that sometimes an act of *carità* can be refused because it can be perceived as a way of highlighting the social differences (in power, life conditions and opportunities) between the people involved in the act:

(4) Il fabbro appoggia le due nocche sul tavolo e mi dice a voce diversa, ora bassa come un ringhio: '**Non ci serve la tua carità**. Ci serve che scendi dall'altare'.

The locksmith puts his two knuckles on the table and with a different tone of voice, now low as a growl, says to me: '**We don't need your *carità***. We need you to get down the altar.' (CORIS/CODIS corpus, MON2014_16)

Essentially, an act of *carità* is inspired by a genuine expression of good feelings towards someone with no ulterior motives or personal interests in mind, as stated by St Paul in the First Letter to the Corinthians (13: 4–7):

> *La carità è magnanima, benevola è la carità; non è invidiosa, non si vanta, non si gonfia d'orgoglio, non manca di rispetto, non cerca il proprio interesse, non si adira, non tiene conto del male ricevuto, non gode dell'ingiustizia ma si rallegra della verità. Tutto scusa, tutto crede, tutto spera, tutto sopporta.*

> Charity suffereth long, and is kind; charity envieth not; charity vaunteth not itself, is not puffed up, doth not behave itself unseemly, seeketh not her own, is not easily provoked, thinketh no evil; rejoiceth not in iniquity, but rejoiceth in the truth; beareth all things, believeth all things, hopeth all things, endureth all things.

The Christian meaning of *carità* used in Italian discourse is captured in the following explication. It is divided in two big cognitive scenarios: the first captures how the helper thinks, whereas the second captures how the helper does not think. The explication captures the conceptual relation between living, feeling and doing, the idea of 'brotherly love', the immediacy and momentariness of the helping act and the idea 'I know that I can do it'. Wanting to help is only one aspect of the act of *carità*; the helper also needs to be able to help and most of all, he/she acts following his/her conscience. Knowing that one can help excludes any hesitations and emphasises the awareness that *carità* is a matter of moral duty. The final component captures the fact that *carità* is a value:

[A] *la carità verso il prossimo* (*carità* towards the neighbour)

a. it can be like this:
b. someone thinks like this about someone else:

> 'this someone can't live well now if someone else doesn't do something good for this someone
>
> because of this, this someone feels something bad
>
> when I think about this, I feel something good towards this someone like I can feel towards some people if it is like this:
>
> > these people are part of something, I am part of the same something

I don't want this someone to feel something bad

because of this, I want to do something good for this someone in this moment, I know that I can do it'

c. because this someone thinks like this, this someone does something good for this other someone

d. when this someone does it, this someone doesn't think like this about this other someone:

'this someone is someone below me

I want to do it because if I do it people will think something good about me

I want to do it because if I do it something good will happen to me

if I do something good for this someone now,

this someone can't not-do something good for me after this'

e. it is good if it is like this

3. The meanings of *per carità*

The phraseological meanings of *carità* emerge in the idiomatic prepositional phrase *per carità*, which is highly polysemous. Only in the construction *fare qualcosa per carità* ('to do something for *carità*') *carità* retains its Christian meaning. In this construction, the preposition *per* performs the function of 'purpose' and the phrase expresses the idea of an action inspired by the Christian spirit of *carità* and performed to help someone who suffers:

(5) 'Ebbene, si tratta di questo. Ieri mi trovavo nei paraggi, vicino alla riva del mare. Un uomo **mi aveva offerto per carità** un tozzo di pane, e io lo gustavo lentamente.'

'Well, it is about this. Yesterday I was around here, near the seashore. A man **had offered me a crust of bread for *carità*** and I was enjoying it slowly.' (CORIS/CODIS corpus, narrativa)

In various other contexts, *per carità* is used as an additional, indented fixed phrase in different positions in an utterance. The insertion of *per carità* does not add content to the utterance, which already makes sense without this phrase. Its semantic contribution consists either in emphasising the speaker's feelings or in clarifying the speaker's position on a statement, an intention or an opinion. The fixed phrase *per carità* is no longer a simple prepositional phrase, but an interjection expressing a series of distinct meanings (cf. Ameka 1992; Wierzbicka 1992b); for this reason, it seems plausible to consider *per carità* used in specific contexts as the result of a process of grammaticalisation.

Various dictionaries of Italian (including Treccani, Nuovo De Mauro and Zanichelli) ascribe a generic meaning 'rejection/refusal' to *per carità*, as well as the more specific meanings 'scorn/disdain' and 'of course/surely'. However, the contexts in which this fixed phrase is used as an interjection in Italian discourse are too different to posit an invariant meaning 'not'. This 'not' means different things in different contexts—in NSM terms, 'I don't say', 'I don't want' or 'it can't be like this'. It is impossible to produce a single explication which would be valid for all the contexts in which *per carità* is used. Therefore, it is necessary to produce separate semantic explications for the different phraseological meanings of *per carità* expressed in different contexts, not only for the sake of semantic accuracy and clarity, but also for the sake of accurate language teaching and translation. In addition to the Christian meaning, *per carità* expresses six different phraseological meanings; their numbering in the present analysis is based on their similarity to the Christian meaning, *per carità*$_6$ being the least similar. The main semantic difference between the Christian and the phraseological meanings of *per carità* is the shift in perspective from 'someone else' ('doing something good for someone else') to 'I' ('I don't say/'I don't want'). The Christian and the six phraseological meanings of *per carità* cannot overlap because they are expressed in different contexts; however, it is also possible to express different meanings of *per carità* in the same turn.

The first meaning of *per carità* as an interjection is expressed when the speaker asks the interlocutor to do something good for him/her as people would do for someone they care for.

This can mean either doing or not doing something to save the speaker from feeling something bad. The speaker's bad feelings are associated with a specific thought and are intentionally emphasised by uttering *per carità*. The speaker rejects these bad feelings and 'begs' the interlocutor to help him/her. In (6) the speaker asks the interlocutor to do something, whereas in (7a) and (7b) not to do something (e.g. not to kill him):

(6) Adesso il piccolo Ambrogio, svegliato dal rumore e dal caldo, gridava come un'aquila attaccato alle sbarre del lettino. Sua madre, che faceva la cassiera nella pasticceria di fronte, era arrivata di corsa e adesso gridava: '**Fate qualcosa, per carità! Qualcuno vada a salvare il mio bambino!**'

By now the little Ambrogio, who had been woken up by the noise and the heat, was shouting like an eagle hanging on the bars of his tiny bed. His mother, who worked as a cashier in the patisserie on the other side of the road, had run back home and now was screaming: '**Do something, *per carità*! Somebody go save my child!**' (CORIS/CODIS corpus, narrativa)

(7) a. Fazio si fece vivo che erano le dieci passate. 'Come mai avete fatto così tardo?' '**Dottore, per carità, non me ne parlasse!** Prima abbiamo dovuto aspettare il sostituto del Sostituto!'

Fazio didn't turn up until after 10. 'Why so late, Fazio?' '**Please, Chief, I don't want to hear about it.** First we had to wait for the assistant prosecutor's assistant.'

b. Il professore si era susuto addritta e Montalbano, lento lento, isò la pistola e gliela puntò all'altezza della testa. Allora capitò. Come se gli avessero tranciato l'invisibile cavo che lo reggeva, l'omo cadì in ginocchio. Mise le mani a preghiera. '**Per carità! Per carità!**'

The doctor was now standing up, and Montalbano ever so slowly raised the gun and pointed it at his head. Then it happened, as if someone had cut the invisible rope holding him up, the man fell to his knees. He folded his hands in prayer. '**Have pity! Have pity!**' (Andrea Camilleri, *La Gita a Tindari*, 2000)

The meaning *per carità*$_1$ can be explicated as follows. It is the idea of someone doing something good for someone else and of this good action being inspired by good feelings towards a sufferer that makes this first phraseological meaning of *per carità* the closest to the original Christian meaning. The component 'I can't not say it' captures the idea that the speaker cannot refrain from expressing his/her bad feelings in discourse:

[B] *per carità₁*

a. I say: 'when I think about this, I feel something bad
    I can't not say it
    I don't want to feel something bad
    because of this, I want you to do something good for me now, like people can do something good for someone if they feel something good towards this someone'

As an interjection, *per carità* can also be used to express the meaning 'I don't want to do this'. In this case, too, the refusal is caused by the thought of something that generates bad feelings. This is the kind of bad feelings prototypically associated with the thought 'something bad can happen to me if I do this'. Thus, by uttering *per carità* it is as if the speaker 'protected' themselves from potential dangers by stating clearly that he/she is not going to do something. In this case, not only does *per carità* emphasise the speaker's feelings, but also what the speaker does not want to do. Sometimes, the refusal can be emphasised even more by raising one's arms and hands in the air to make a sort of 'not me' or 'send-away' gesture. The meaning *per carità₂* can be explicated as follows:

[C] *per carità₂*

a. I say: 'I don't want to do this, I want you to know it
    when I think about it, I feel something bad'

A good example of *per carità₂* can be found in the dialogue between the Neapolitan brothers Capone and their friend Mezzacapa in the famous comical film *Totò, Peppino e la Malafemmina* (1956).[4] The brothers need to go to Milan for the first time and ask their friend, who has been there before, for advice. Mezzacapa scares the two brothers and warns them against the dangers of a big city like Milan with a lot of dangerous traffic and fog. By uttering *per carità*, each of the brothers makes clear that he is not going to do something:

---

4   Available at: www.youtube.com/watch?v=F2V0av8ypY4, uploaded 28 October, 2006.

(8) Mezzacapa: 'Ma c'è un traffico enorme. Anzi, vi dovete stare accorti, eh? Là attraversare una strada è una cosa pericolosa assai.'

Antonio: '**E chi attraversa? E chi si muove, per carità**.'

Mezzacapa: 'There's a huge traffic there. In fact, you've got to be careful, okay? Crossing the road is very dangerous there.'

Antonio: '**Not me … I'm not crossing, I'm not moving, *per carità*.**'

Mezzacapa: 'A Milano, quando c'è la nebbia non si vede …'

Antonio: 'Ma dico se i milanesi a Milano quando c'è la nebbia non vedono, come si fa a vedere che c'è la nebbia a Milano?'

Mezzacapa: 'No, ma per carità, ma quella non è una cosa … che si può toccare …'

Peppino: 'Aaah, ecco.'

Antonio (al fratello): 'Non si tocca.'

Peppino: 'Io adesso … a parte questa nebbia, **non la tocco, per carità** …'

Mezzacapa: 'In Milan, people can't see when there is fog …'

Antonio: 'But I mean, if the Milanese in Milan can't see when there is fog how can one see that there is fog in Milan?'

Mezzacapa: 'No, but *per carità*, that's not something … one can touch.'

Peppino: 'Right, I see.'

Antonio (to his brother): 'Don't touch it.'

Peppino: 'What I'm wondering now … apart from this fog, **I won't touch it, *per carità* …**'

Another prototypical context of *per carità$_2$* is when someone refuses to have more food or drinks. The speaker fears that he/she will feel bad if he/she eats or drinks more and utters *per carità* to express a clear refusal:

(9) *Vuoi ancora un po' di pasta?*

Per carità!

Would you like some more pasta?

Per carità! ('No way!')

In the dialogue in (8) there is another instance of *per carità* uttered by Mezzacapa when he states that fog is not something one can touch. In this case, *per carità* expresses the meaning 'it can't be like this, I know it well, I want you to know it well now'. The context of this meaning of *per carità* is when a speaker considers a specific scenario emerged from the discussion with the interlocutor and totally excludes that it can be the case. The speaker sounds extremely confident and convincing by talking with the didactic tone typical of the '*sapientone*' ('the know-it-all, clever-clogs', Farese 2019), the omniscient narrator who knows or claims to know the facts in question well thanks to first-hand or reported experience. At the same time, the speaker emphasises the statement with an expression of feelings. This specific meaning, labelled here *per carità₃*, can be explicated as follows:

[D] *per carità₃*

a. I say: 'it can't be like this, I know it well, I want you to know it now
    when I think about it, I can't not feel something'

Per carità₃ can be easily identified and distinguished from the other meanings of this phrase because only in this context *per carità* can be preceded by *ma* ('but'), which emphasises the speaker's statement and feelings even more:

(10) 'Mia moglie non mi capisce …' 'Tra noi non c'è dialogo.' 'Tra noi non c'è nessun afflato spirituale.' 'Tra noi non ci sono più rapporti sessuali …' 'Con altri? Mia moglie? **Per carità, è pazza di me …**'

'My wife doesn't understand me …' 'There's no dialogue between us.' 'There's no spiritual impulse.' 'We don't have sexual intercourses anymore …' 'Sleeping with someone else? My wife? ***Per carità*, she's crazy about me …**' (CORIS/CODIS corpus, narrativa)

(11) L'esercito per le strade di Napoli? **Ma per carità.** Non credo che la semi-militarizzazione della città sia la soluzione del drammatico problema criminalità.

The army around the streets of Naples? **But *per carità*.** I don't think that the semi-militarization of the city is the solution to the dramatic problem of criminality. (CORIS/CODIS corpus, MON2005_07)

A similar context is when a speaker does not exclude that something can be the case, but at the same time cannot say that it can be the case either. In this context, *per carità* is typically followed by *ma* or *però* ('but/though'), which express a contrast between the first and the second part of the statement. In the first part, the speaker makes clear that he/she does not exclude something; in the second part, the speaker adds that something cannot be the case unless the circumstances change or anyway, not *a priori*:

(12) Berlusconi torna alla carica con il documento politico. Quello, almeno, Follini potrebbe sottoscriverlo. **Per carità, nessun problema**, risponde il segretario dell'Udc, **però** … la mia priorità riguarda la necessità che questo governo sia più attento al suo profilo istituzionale.

Berlusconi insists on the political document. Follini could sign that, at least. ***Per carità*, no problem at all**, replies the UDC [Unione di Centro: the Union of the Centre political party] secretary, **but** … my priority is the necessity that this government pays more attention to its institutional profile. (CORIS/CODIS corpus, MON2001_04)

(13) 'Contro la Danimarca, vi basta perdere per 1-0.' 'Non ci passa per la testa. **Si può anche perdere, per carità. Ma non certo per principio**. Vogliamo vincere e vincere bene.'

'Against Denmark, it is sufficient for you to lose 1-0.' 'That's out of the question. **Losing is possible, *per carità*. But certainly not in principle**. We want to win and win well.' (CORIS/CODIS corpus, stampa)

Per carità$_4$ is added to let the interlocutor know well what the speaker's position is. This specific meaning can be explicated as follows:

[E] *per carità*$_4$

a. I don't say: 'it can't be like this'
b. at the same time, I don't say: 'it can be like this'
c. I want you to know it

Per carità as a fixed phrase can also express the speaker's way of thinking about something. Like the context of *per carità₄*, *per carità₅* is followed by *ma* in a statement which contains two contrasting ways of thinking: in the first part of the statement, the speaker denies that something is bad, whereas in the second part the speaker states that it is not good either:

(14) **Per carità, il film è bellissimo**, Ferrara è bravissimo, un grande regista che fa commuovere, **ma** in Sicilia donne come Teresa non esistono.

Per carità, **the film is great**, and Ferrara is excellent, a great director that makes people cry, **but** there are no women like Teresa in Sicily. (CORIS/CODIS corpus, ephemera)

(15) Segno evidente che l'imputato si interessò per le due pratiche. **Nulla di illecito, per carità: ma,** allora, perché hanno mentito dicendo di aver avuto frequentazioni superficiali?

This is the unmistakable sign that the accused dealt with the two cases. **Nothing illicit,** *per carità***: but,** then, why did they lie saying they only knew each other superficially? (CORIS/CODIS corpus, miscellanea)

Stating first that something is not bad before stating that it is not good is a specific discursive strategy on the part of the speaker not to sound hypercritical of something and to 'mitigate' the criticism expressed in the second part of the statement. *Per carità₅* expresses the speaker's evaluations and its meaning is clearly distinct from the other ones because it is based on the primitive concepts GOOD and BAD, which are not inherent in the other meanings of this phrase. *Per carità₅* is explicated as follows:

[F] *per carità₅*

a. I don't say: 'I think about it like this: "this is bad"'
b. at the same time, I can't say: 'I think about it like this: "this is good"'
c. I want you to know it

Finally, the interjection *per carità* is also used to protect oneself from the risk of passing for someone who does not know the facts well, which is countercultural and potentially dangerous for one's public image in Italy (Farese 2019). In this context, *per carità* expresses the meaning 'I don't say: it is not like this, I want you to know it'. By clarifying that he/she is not denying something, the speaker demonstrates that he/she knows the facts well and, in this way, saves him/herself from making statements which could be perceived as superficial or potentially offensive:

(16) Caro signor Manganaro, per quel che riguarda i documenti d'archivio stranieri, tutte le carte dei servizi segreti americani e sovietici venute alla luce quarant'anni dopo quell'estate del 1964 (**da prendere con le molle, per carità**) ci dicono che—diversamente da quel che all'epoca si suppose—la Cia non solo non favorì ma, anzi, si preoccupò moltissimo del possibile deragliamento del nostro convoglio democratico.

Dear Mr. Manganaro, as far as the foreign archive documents are concerned, all the documents about the American and Soviet secret services which came to light forty years after that summer of 1964 (**to be taken with a pinch of salt,** *per carità*) tell us that—differently from what was believed at that time—not only did the CIA encourage, but it was also deeply concerned about the derailment of our democratic train. (CORIS/CODIS corpus, MON2001_04)

(17) Solo l'Argentina ora come ora mi sembra abbia qualcosa in più di tutti, anche di noi. La Francia no. **Per carità, è forte, affidabile**, ma con loro voglio giocarci …

Right now, it seems to me that only Argentina have something more than the other teams. Not France. ***Per carità*, France are strong and reliable**, but I don't want to play against them … (CORIS/CODIS corpus, MON2001_04)

The speaker's self-defence is complemented by the idea that the interlocutor does not think well if he/she thinks that the speaker does not know the facts well. This sixth meaning of *per carità* can be explicated as follows:

[G] *per carità*$_6$

a. I don't say: 'it is not like this', I want you to know it
b. if you think about me like this: 'this someone doesn't know well how it is', you don't think well

4. Concluding remarks

The semantic analysis of *carità* presented in this chapter has highlighted one of the most striking cases of polysemy which characterises Italian words expressing Christian values. The parallel shift in function and context of use (from a word expressing a Christian value to an interjection expressing the speaker's feelings and way of thinking in discourse) and in semantic perspective (from 'someone else' to 'I') reflects a significant semantic change of *carità* which should be investigated in diachronic perspective. Unfortunately, this kind of analysis could not be made here for reasons of space. One of the main aims of the present analysis was to emphasise the unparalleled benefits and contributions that the Wierzbickian NSM methodology has brought to the understanding of the foundations and principles of Christianity and its undisputed influence on everyday discourse in many European languages, including Italian. Adopting the NSM framework, it is possible to

> convey the essentials of Christian faith accurately, making every word count and be justifiable from a theological and historical, as well as linguistic point of view … An explication couched in simple and universal words can help us to identify that intended meaning and to articulate … faith more accurately and more authentically, as well as more cross-translatably, for a global world. (Wierzbicka 2019: xiv)

The copresence of Christian and phraseological meanings of Italian words expressing Christian values is relevant to the analysis of the influence of Christianity on Italian language and culture and, at the broader level, to the relationship between meaning, culture and society. A parallel could be drawn between the polysemy of Italian words expressing Christian values and the dual nature of the Italian society, which is traditionally characterised by a constant tension between Christianity and secularism. Article 7 of the Italian Constitution sanctions the secular nature of the Italian State and the juridical separation from the Vatican. Yet, in Article 8, the Catholic religion is given a privileged position over the other faiths because it is the only religion that is recognised at constitutional level (Farese 2018b). One of the most significant and controversial events in contemporary Italian history was the so-called *compromesso storico* ('the historical compromise'), the political alliance between the Christian Democratic Party and the Communist Party. The tension between Christianity and secularism is not a contradiction, but a well-known and accepted fact in Italy; they are two sides of the same coin. The huge popularity of the TV series *Don Camillo e Peppone* (1952) and later *Don Matteo* (2000–present), where priests are in constant conflict with politicians and with the police, confirms that the Italians like this tension, as they somehow recognise themselves and their society in those fictional characters. The Italian society is both Christian and secular and the language needs to have words that express both Christian and phraseological meanings. As in the case of *carità*, if a word originally expresses a Christian meaning, it is very likely that over time it will be shaped and changed by speakers so that new, phraseological meanings develop and become regularly used in discourse.

References

Ameka, Felix (1992). Interjections: The universal yet neglected part of speech. *Journal of Pragmatics* 18: 101–118. doi.org/10.1016/0378-2166(92)90048-g.

Benedict XVI (2005). Encyclical letter: *Deus Caritas Est*. Given 25 December. Available at: w2.vatican.va/content/benedict-xvi/en/encyclicals/documents/hf_ben-xvi_enc_20051225_deus-caritas-est.html. doi.org/10.18290/rt.2017.64.3-1en.

Camilleri, Andrea (2000). *La Gita a Tindari*. Palermo: Sellerio. [English translation available: Camilleri, Andrea (2005). *Excursion to Tindari*. Translated by Stephen Sartarelli. London/New York: Penguin.]

Croce, Benedetto (1942). Perché non possiamo non dirci cristiani. *La Critica* 40: 289–97.

Croce, Benedetto (1949). Why we cannot help calling ourselves Christians. In *My Philosophy*, translated by Edgar F. Carritt. London: Allen and Unwin.

Farese, Gian Marco (2018a). *The Cultural Semantics of Address Practices: A Contrastive Study between English and Italian*. Lanham, Maryland: Lexington Books.

Farese, Gian Marco (2018b). The fundamental principles of the Italian Constitution: A semantic analysis. Special issues, 'Perspectives on semantics'. *Quaderni di Semantica*, 3–4: 664–746.

Farese, Gian Marco (2019). *Italian Discourse. A Cultural Semantic Analysis*. Lanham/London: Lexington.

Goddard, Cliff (2011). *Semantic Analysis: A Practical Introduction* (2nd edn). Oxford: Oxford University Press.

Goddard, Cliff (2018). *Ten Lectures on Natural Semantic Metalanguage: Exploring Language, Thought and Culture Using Simple, Translatable Words.* Leiden: Brill.

Goddard, Cliff and Anna Wierzbicka (2014). *Words and Meanings: Lexical Semantics Across Domains, Languages and Cultures.* Oxford: Oxford University Press. doi.org/10.1093/acprof:oso/9780199668434.001.0001.

Travis, Catherine (1997). Kind, considerate, thoughtful: A semantic analysis. *Lexikos* 7: 130–52. doi.org/10.5788/7-1-976.

Wierzbicka, Anna (1992a). *Semantics, Culture, and Cognition: Universal Human Concepts in Culture-Specific Configurations.* New York: Oxford University Press.

Wierzbicka, Anna (1992b). The semantics of interjection. *Journal of Pragmatics* 18 (2–3): 159–92.

Wierzbicka, Anna (1996). *Semantics: Primes and Universals.* Oxford: Oxford University Press.

Wierzbicka, Anna (1997). *Understanding Cultures through their Key Words: English, Russian, Polish, German, and Japanese.* New York: Oxford University Press.

Wierzbicka, Anna (2001). *What Did Jesus Mean?* New York: Oxford University Press.

Wierzbicka, Anna (2019). *What Christians Believe: The Story of God and People.* New York: Oxford University Press.

10

The semantics of two loanwords in Navarrese Spanish

Mónica Aznárez-Mauleón

1. Introduction

This study focuses on the semantics of two words used in the variety of Peninsular Spanish spoken in Navarre, one of the regions in northern Spain where Spanish and Basque have been in intense contact for centuries. Although their real origin still needs to be proven, the two words studied have been traditionally identified as borrowings from Basque—that is, words that at some point came into the Spanish spoken in the area by transfer from that language.

The existence of borrowings in languages can be explained by the need of speakers to refer to culturally specific objects, traditions and, most importantly, ways of thinking that cannot be found in their language. As Wierzbicka explains, there are language-specific names for special kinds of 'things', for customs and social institutions, as well as for people's values, ideals, attitudes and ways of thinking about the world (1997: 2).

In this case, I am going to study words that are not language-specific but varietal-specific, since they only exist at present in the variety of Peninsular Spanish spoken in some areas of Navarre. The particularity of the two words chosen is that they convey special meanings, non-existent in general Spanish and definitely different from the ones encoded in other Spanish words that are usually identified as their equivalents. I believe that an appropriate semantic analysis of these borrowings will reveal the specific way of thinking about certain human experiences of Navarrese speakers of Spanish—that is, some of the 'ethnopsychological constructs' (Goddard 2007a: 29) that characterise this regional variety.

Analysing and explaining the meaning of such words, especially to people from other cultures, is not an easy task. The theory of the Natural Semantic Metalanguage (NSM) developed by Wierzbicka and Goddard (see Goddard and Wierzbicka 2002, 2014) has provided semanticists with the appropriate tool to tackle the analysis of meanings. As Wierzbicka and her colleagues have demonstrated over the last four decades, NSM is the most appropriate analytical framework to accomplish this task, since it allows the researcher to explain meanings through a self-explanatory mini-language, constituted by a set of semantic primitives, which are universal, innate and language-independent (Gladkova 2010; Wong 2014; Wierzbicka 2015; Ye 2017; among others).

Since the words I am going to study do not generally appear in Spanish corpora due to their limited use and testimonies of their use are scarce, I based my analysis mainly on the information gathered from a few lexicographic sources and, especially, from the interviews I carried out with 20 Spanish monolingual speakers from the region.[1] This information, together with my own insights as a Spanish speaker from Navarre, allowed me to accurately describe and provide the NSM explications of the meanings of these words.

Before presenting the semantic analysis, and in order to contextualise the words studied, I will provide first an overview of the nature of lexical borrowings between these two languages in contact.

---

[1] Interviewees were men and women, between 35 and 70 years old, who were born and still live in the capital city (Pamplona) or in neighbouring villages. They answered the following questions in written form: Do you use this word?; Can you provide some examples of phrases in which you would use this word?; How would you explain its meaning to someone who does not know this word? A few days later, and after an analysis of this information, oral interviews were carried out in which the researcher asked further questions on specific aspects of the meaning of each word.

2. Basque and Spanish in contact: Loanwords

In spite of being genetically unrelated, Spanish and Basque have influenced each other along the centuries of intense contact between them. Although evidence exists at different linguistic levels, mutual influence between these two languages is especially salient at the lexical domain, since lexical items are the elements most easily transferred from one language to another (Thomason and Kaufman 1988; Haspelmath 2008). Importantly, lexical transfer occurs primarily from Spanish, the dominant language, into Basque. Thus, Basque has borrowed words from Spanish like *kamioi* (from *camión* 'truck'), *ligatu* (from *ligar* 'flirt'), *saltsa* (from *salsa* 'sauce') and many others, adapting them to its phonological particularities (Cid-Abasolo 2010).

Although there are more instances of borrowings from Spanish into Basque, there is evidence of lexical transfer in the opposite direction as well. The Basque word *ezker* 'left', for example, has been borrowed not only by Spanish (*izquierda*) but also by other Romance languages like Catalan (*esquerra*) and Gascon (*querr* and *esquerr*) among others (Echenique 2016). In the Spanish spoken in Navarre, quite a few words have been claimed as borrowings from the Basque spoken in the area such as *sarde* 'pitchfork', *zartaco* (from *zartako* 'bump, slap, spank'), etc. (Ciérvide 1979). These words have been labelled 'léxico residual' ('residual lexicon') to indicate they are remains of the Basque once spoken in the area. However, as Santazilia and Zuloaga (2018) point out, lexicographers should be cautious, since there is not always enough evidence to support this kind of claim.

Among the words registered as borrowings from Basque in Navarrese Spanish, we find nouns referring to objects (farming and domestic tools, musical instruments, food, games, shows' characters …), adjectives referring to personal qualities (physical appearance, personality traits …) and verbs referring to various human actions or experiences. Some of the lexical transfers from Basque into Spanish probably took place decades or centuries ago, through bilingual speakers who used a word from one language when speaking the other language. Others have occurred more recently, accelerated by cultural globalisation, mobility and new technologies. As Tabernero (2008, 2012) explains, this is the case of cultural loanwords which are known and used not only in the whole region of Navarre and the Basque Country, but also in other areas of Spain as well: *trikitixa* (a musical instrument similar to a small accordion), *pelotari* 'pelota player' and *chacolí* (from *txakoli* (a kind of wine))—the last two already registered in the *Dictionary of the Spanish Language* by the Real Academia Española (2014).[2]

One of the reasons these borrowings came into Navarrese Spanish and got easily adopted over time by Navarrese Spanish monolinguals is the fact that they name things that do not exist in other places (certain objects, games etc.) or concepts that are culture-specific, like the words I am going to study here. Basque–Spanish bilinguals who started using these words when speaking Spanish most probably felt the need to express something that could not be conveyed with other Spanish words at their disposal. As Wierzbicka explains when talking about the lexicon of bilinguals, there are certain concepts that are never substituted by the other language counterparts:

> For example, I think that in my own mental lexicon the concept linked with the Polish color word *niebieski* (from *niebo* 'sky') has never been replaced with the English concept 'blue' (much wider than that of *niebieski*). (2011a: 203)

The cases studied here, which have reached the other language as borrowings, correspond to these kinds of words: 'those deeply rooted in perception and those which are linked with a given lingua-culture's cultural key words' (Wierzbicka 2011a: 203).[3]

At present, Navarrese Spanish monolinguals keep using these borrowings for the same reason, since they need to refer to the same things and to the same concepts that are culturally specific to the region.

---

2   It should be highlighted that all these loanwords have become part of the recipient language (Navarrese Spanish or, in a few cases, general Peninsular Spanish); that is, they are used, transmitted and modified according to Spanish rules and patterns.
3   The words *chirrinta* and *ciriquiar* have been chosen for this study among other existent Basque loanwords in Navarrese Spanish because, in my view, they constitute the most clear examples of how human experiences and actions have been culturally shaped by this community.

3. *Txirrinta/Txirrintxa, Chirrinta/Chirrintas/ Chirrincha/Chirlinta*: Sources and testimonies

The word *chirrinta* and its variant *chirrincha* was registered by Iribarren in his lexicographic work *Vocabulario Navarro* (*Navarrese Vocabulary*) (1984). He reports its use in the north, in Pamplona and in the Améscoa region (69 km west from Pamplona); that is, within the areas now established as 'Basque-speaking' (north) and 'mixed' (centre).[4] Although other sources report its use in other areas of Navarre and in a few villages of neighbouring regions (Goicoechea 1961; De Cruchaga y Purroy 1970; Andolz 1992; Marín Royo 2006), judging by the testimonies found, it seems that, at present, the word is more generally used in northern and central Navarre.

The origin attributed to this word is the Basque *txirrinta* (Ciérvide 1979; Rebolé del Castillo 2003), which appears in different varieties of Basque spoken in Navarre and is defined by the *General Dictionary of Basque* (Michelena and Sarasola 1987–2013) as *deseo, ansia* 'desire, want'. In my interviews with Spanish monolinguals, many speakers associated the word with the Basque language, since they chose the Basque graphemes ('tx-') instead of the Spanish ones ('ch-') when writing it. The hypothesis of the Basque origin of this word is reasonable, since it exists in this language with a similar meaning and it is nowadays mainly used by Spanish speakers from the 'Basque-speaking' and from the 'mixed' areas. However, as I explained above, more evidence, which has not yet been found, would be needed to confirm it.

In Iribarren's dictionary (1984, s.v. *chirrinta*), this word appears with two different meanings: one meaning is described as *deseo vehemente, capricho, anhelo, antojo* 'strong desire, caprice, wish, craving' and the other as *dentera, envidia, rabia, tirria* 'envy, jealousy, grudge, ill will'. The examples he provides for the first meaning are the following:

---

4   The regional government established in 1986, for administrative purposes, three linguistic areas: the *Basque-speaking* area in the north, the *mixed* area in the north and centre, and the *non–Basque speaking* area in the south. If we look at the number of speakers in each of these areas, we find that the biggest percentage of Basque speakers lives in the north, where 61.1 per cent of the population speak the language. By contrast, in the mixed area, the percentage of Basque speakers is 11.3 per cent and in the south is 2.7 per cent (Gobierno de Navarra et al. 2017).

(1) ¡Tengo una **chirrinta** de ver Madrid!
'I have such a **chirrinta** of seeing Madrid!'

(2) Me quedé con la **chirrinta** de comer churros.
'I was left with the **chirrinta** of eating churros.'

For the second meaning, the example provided is:

(3) Le ha tomado **chirrinta** a su hermanica
'He/She has taken **a dislike** to his/her little sister.'

In her sociolinguistic study of the lexicon of Pamplona, Aragüés (2003) finds that 60 per cent of the informants use this word, instead of other similar Spanish words, with the meaning of 'strong desire for something'. More specifically, the context for which the informants used the word *chirrinta* is that of eating and food, in response to the following item in the questionnaire: 'We all sometimes feel like eating special things: sometimes strawberries, some other times chocolate, some other salty things, etc. In that case, we say we have …?'. Regarding the second meaning of this word, only one informant used it to refer to envy or jealousy.

In my interviews, all users of this word and its variants give examples and explanations related to the first meaning; none of them recognises its use with the second. The information found in Aragüés (2003) and in my interviews makes it possible to presume that the second meaning is in the process of disappearing. Because of this, and provided the scarce evidences of the use of this word in its second meaning, I have decided to focus on the analysis of the first one.

4. The prototypical scenario of *chirrinta*

Iribarren's account (1984, s.v. *chirrinta*) seems to consider that this word refers to a strong desire to do something, and that this something could be equally visiting a place or eating something, that is, any activity. In the examples provided by the informants in my study, *chirrinta* and its graphic and phonological variants are primarily used in reference to the desire of eating some food (see examples (4) to (6)), although in a few of them the word appears in other contexts as well (see examples (7) and (8)):

(4) Tengo **txirrinta** de txistorra
'I have **txirrinta** of txistorra (a kind of chorizo).'

(5) Me he quedado con la **chirrinta** de unos churros
'I have been left with the **chirrinta** for churros.'

(6) ¡Qué **chirrinta** de comer fresas!
'What a **chirrinta** of eating strawberries!'

(7) Tengo **chirrinta** de ir a una sidrería
'I have **chirrinta** of going to a cider house.'

(8) Tengo **chirrintas** de visitar ese pueblo
'I have **chirrintas** of visiting that village.'

When asked about its possible use in other contexts, many of the speakers who used the word to refer to the desire of eating something considered examples like (7) and (8) acceptable, but reported that they would never use it in those contexts. Speakers who provided examples like (7) and (8), in turn, recognised examples like (4)–(6) as equally used by them. Hence, based on this evidence and on my own intuition as a native speaker, I think that feeling *chirrinta* is prototypically associated to some kind of desire to eat some food in particular.

The association of *chirrinta* with the desire to eat a particular food explains why, when trying to explain its meaning, many speakers mentioned the word *antojo*, used in general Spanish to refer to cravings. However, they made it clear that the Spanish word *antojo*, although close in meaning, corresponds to a very different concept, as we will discuss below.

The following example from an article about a gluten-intolerant boy that appeared in the regional newspaper *Diario de Navarra* illustrates the kind of feeling that *chirrinta* conveys. Also, although I will not go into this matter here, it is interesting to observe how this meaning of *chirrinta* is related to that second meaning of 'envy and jealousy' registered by Iribarren, which may have developed from the first (seeing somebody eating something makes you feel *chirrinta* of that something but it also may make you feel envious of that person).

(9) Desde entonces, Jesús no ha tenido ningún problema de salud y una vez al año acude a una revisión. Pero no puede evitar pasar un poco de '**chirrinta**'. 'La dieta la llevo muy bien, pero me da un poco de envidia no poder comer las mismas cosas que mis amigos, como bollos o palmeras. Y en los cumpleaños, cuando voy a sus casas, tampoco puedo comer todas las cosas. Ahora ya lo saben todos mis amigos y sus madres, pero antes me aburría de tener que contarle a todo el mundo que soy celíaco'.

'Since then, Jesús has not had any health problem, and once a year he goes for a check-up. But he cannot help feeling a bit of '**chirrinta**'. 'I am dealing well with the diet, but it makes me feel jealous not being able to eat the same things as my friends, like a bun or a puff pastry. And at birthday parties, when I go to their homes, I can't eat those things either. Now all my friends and their mothers know it, but in the past I was bored of having to tell everybody I was gluten intolerant'. (Lamariano, A dieta desde los dos años y medio, *Diario de Navarra*, 18 April 2009)

In the following lines I will analyse the prototypical scenario of *chirrinta*, based on this example, on my own insights as a native speaker and user of the word, and on the information gathered in the interviews.

First, as this example shows, *chirrinta* refers to a feeling of desire for some particular food, in this case, sweet buns and pastries. Although most examples provided include sweets or some kind of special food that one does not eat every day, speakers agreed that what is relevant is not the kind of food, but one's feelings associated to past experiences of eating it. Thus, a person can feel *chirrinta* of something as common as fried eggs, as long as this person felt good when he/she ate them in the past. Some speakers highlighted this component, explaining that they feel *chirrinta* for things they ate in the past in pleasant situations and with their loved ones, for example, when their grandparents took them to a café to have chocolate with churros. Hence, unlike the Spanish word *antojo*, *chirrinta* involves thinking about that food in a particular way (recalling previous experiences) and includes an emotional component.

Second, the feeling of *chirrinta* seems to be triggered by one's sensory perception of that food: the boy in example 9 feels *chirrinta* when seeing his friends eating buns and pastries. In my interviews, a general insight among speakers is that, though not necessarily simultaneous, there is usually something that triggers the feeling of *chirrinta*, most prototypically seeing that food, although smelling it could also produce the same effect. Again, the word *antojo* does not imply any sensory perception of the desired food; feeling *antojo* is not prototypically linked to the presence of that food in the situational context.

Third, feeling *chirrinta* also seems to imply that the speaker has not been eating that food lately. Definitely, a person cannot say that he/she feels *chirrinta* for something he/she ate the day before, or for something that he/she eats usually. As I explained earlier, this feeling is associated with past pleasant situations, not everyday or very recent ones.

So, the prototypical scenario implied by *chirrinta* is that of a desire to eat some food that the speaker has just seen or is seeing, that he/she associates to past pleasant situations and that he/she has not eaten for some time.

5. An NSM explication of *chirrinta*

Since *chirrinta* is an abstract noun, the frame proposed by Goddard and Wierzbicka (2014) for this kind of word has been used in the explication. On the other hand, the molecule eat [m] is needed in the explication. Semantic molecules are complex lexical meanings which, although could be further decomposed, function as 'chunks' in the semantic structure of more complex concepts (see Goddard 2007b, 2012). Among the different categories from which molecules are drawn, eat [m] belongs to the category of physical activities (Goddard 2007b, 2012).

[A] *Chirrinta* (e.g. Someone has *chirrinta* of something)

a. something

b. people can say what this something is with the word *chirrinta*

c. when someone says something with this word, this someone can think like this:

d. 'It can be like this:

e. someone wants to eat [m] something at some time when this someone sees this something

f. because this someone thinks like this':

g. 'I have eaten [m] this thing before now a few times
h. I felt something very good when I ate [m] this thing at these times
i. I haven't eaten [m] this thing for some time
j. Because of this, I want to eat [m] this thing now'

Components (a) to (d) correspond to the frame used for the explications of abstract nouns, as proposed by Goddard and Wierzbicka (2014). Component (e) makes clear that *chirrinta* conveys the desire of someone to eat something and that this experience is triggered when this someone sees this particular food. Component (f) introduces the prototypical thought content of the experiencer of *chirrinta*, which is spelled out in the four components of the cognitive scenario: (g) and (h) referred to the pleasant experience of eating this thing in the past; (i) referred to the time since the person last ate that thing; and finally (j) referred to the resulting desire to eat this thing.

6. *Ziriquiar/Ciriquiar*: Sources and testimonies

The second word used in Navarrese Spanish that I am going to analyse is the verb *ziriquiar/ciriquiar*. This word, like the previous one, is also registered by Iribarren's dictionary of Navarrese lexicon (1984) together with the variant *ciricar*. It appears with two orthographic variants: *ziriquiar*, which combines Basque (using the initial 'z') and Spanish (using 'qu' instead of the Basque 'k') spelling, and *ciriquiar*, which uses Spanish spelling. The phonetic variant *ciriquear* has been also found in some examples.

Iribarren registers its use in central and northern Navarre and, like Ciérvide (1979) and Rebolé del Castillo (2003), attributes its origin to the Basque *zirikatu*, which, according to the *General Dictionary of Basque* (Michelena and Sarasola 1987–2013), has different meanings such as: 1. *hurgar (con un palo*, etc.) 'to rummage (with a stick, etc.)', 2. '*inchar, punzar* 'to poke, to prick', 3. *tentar, provocar, incitar, hostigar* 'to tempt, to provoke, to incite, to annoy'.

There is no doubt that *ciriquiar* is semantically related to the Basque word *zirikatu*. Iribarren's dictionary includes three meanings for *ciriquiar*. The first one is *hurgar con un palo u otro objeto en un orificio* 'to rummage in a hole with a stick or another object'. The second, considered an extension of the previous, is described as *toquitear, manosear, enredar* 'to handle, to finger, to fiddle with'. The third one is *molestar, importunar* 'to annoy, to pester'.

Due to the space limit of this contribution, I am going to focus on only one of the three meanings: *ciriquiar$_3$*. This meaning is the most abstract and it seems to be a figurative development from the other two. It is the meaning that appears first in my interviews with Navarrese speakers and the only one registered by Ciérvide (1979) and Rebolé del Castillo (2003), who explain it as *fastidiar, enredar* 'to annoy, to fidget with' and *importunar* 'to pester somebody'.

As the information given so far shows, *ciriquiar$_3$* is a complex concept that is not clearly defined by lexicographic sources, which only provide a very general and approximate idea of what this verb conveys. The cultural specificity of *ciriquiar$_3$* is mentioned in this text written by an English speaker living in Pamplona:

> There is a word that I learnt thanks to reading one of the books written by that great Pamplonican doctor, writer and historian, Jose Joaquin Arazuri, that apparently is typically Navarran. The word is 'ciriquiar.' To make mischief. Well, Pamplona is full of mischief makers, jokers and comedians. I don't know if the Catholic Church has a saint for that little trio of fun-folksters, but I think they should have. (heartofpamplona.com/sf-2018-escalera-2 (site discontinued))

However, the cultural specificity of this word is overlooked by the author of this text when he offers the translation 'to make mischief' as an equivalent to it. As many NSM studies have shown, it is not possible to explain the meaning of a word by translation means (Wierzbicka 2011b, 2013; Goddard and Ye 2014; Wong 2018; among other works).

7. The prototypical scenario of *ciriquiar$_3$*

In this section I will try to explain the meaning of this verb on the basis of the testimonies found in written texts and the examples provided by the informants in the interviews.

The prototypical context in which *ciriquiar$_3$* appears is 'A person *ciriquia* another person'—that is, it is a verb referring to an action that someone does to another person. Interestingly, when native speakers think about the person who *ciriquia*, they immediately think of a child. In fact, although the word can be used in other contexts, when asked to provide examples of their use of this word, most interviewees provided contexts referring to children's behaviour:

(10) ¡Deja de **ciriquear** a tu hermano!
 'Stop **ciriquear**-ing your brother!'

(11) Le encanta **ciriquear**, hasta que no le deja llorando a su hermano, no puede parar.
 'He loves **ciriquear**-ing, he does not stop until he leaves his brother crying.'

(12) Está todo el rato **ciriqueando**, y luego le sacuden. ¡Normal!
 'He is **ciriquear**-ing all the time and then he gets hit. What else does he expect?'

If these are the kind of examples that first come to mind to native speakers, it is reasonable to think that the kind of action that *ciriquiar$_3$* depicts is one usually carried out by children, even though adults can perform it too.

The second semantic component that can be drawn from these examples is that the action performed can be annoying—that is, it can make the other person feel something bad. In example (10), the speaker tells the child to stop doing it since he/she is considering the negative feelings that this action can produce in the child's brother. In example (11), this component can clearly be seen since the action makes the boy cry. In example (12), this negative feeling produces a violent reaction against the person who *ciriquea*, which is judged by the speaker as a totally normal reaction. To this respect, it should be noted that *ciriquiar$_3$* seems to involve a physical action, more specifically, it seems to involve touching the other person. This component of physical contact is consistent with the other two meanings of this verb (*ciriquiar$_1$* and *ciriquiar$_2$*), both referring to touching something with the hands or with a stick.

Another aspect that should be pointed out is that this verb is always used in a non-perfective tense, like in these three examples. This means that when someone *ciriquia* another person, he/she does not do so in one moment, but rather, he/she does so for some time or repeatedly.

Finally, *ciriquiar$_3$* seems to include an expectation on the part of the agent: when children act like this, they are expecting some kind of reaction from the other person.

The use of *ciriquiar$_3$* in the following testimony confirms these first insights about its meaning. In this case, the subject is not a child but a *kiliki*, a character with oversized head who comes out during festivals to tease children with a sponge tied with a thread to a stick:

(13) Toda la Comparsa sería menos alegre sin la presencia de los kilikis, que van **ciriquiando** a todos los críos, produciendo carreras y tonadillas jocosas a cada uno de los personajes por toda la chiquillería.

'The whole troupe would be less lively without the presence of the kilikis, who go **ciriquiar**-ing all the children, producing runs and ditties by all the kids to each of the characters.' (Ilargi, Vienen los gigantes, *El tut*o 14, 1989)

However, some testimonies have also been found where this verb is not used either in the context of children or to refer to an action involving physical contact. The following example illustrates such case:

(14) Los poetas de Umbría eran muy suyos. Eso sí, tenían, como todos los del mundo, la manía de no dejarse en paz ni a sol ni a sombra y de formar tribu y tener acólitos, cómplices, aliados, allegados, etc., etc., etc. … Había uno que disfrutaba enormemente haciendo daño al prójimo, confundiéndolo, mortificándolo, humillándolo, que luego se hizo psicoanalista para poder hacer lo mismo que antes pero con patente de corso, que le **ciriquiaba** a Eguren con que si sus versos no tenían pathos.

'The poets from Umbría were very special. They had, like all poets in the world, a fixation with not giving each other a moment's peace and with making tribes and having acolytes, accomplices, allies, intimates, etc., etc., etc. … There was one who enjoyed enormously doing harm to neighbours, confusing them, tormenting them, humiliating them; who later on became a psychoanalyst so that he could do the same thing he used to do but with a carte blanche, who used to **ciriquiar** Eguren saying that his verses didn't have pathos.' (Sánchez-Ostiz, *Un infierno en el jardín*, 1995; in Real Academia Española (n.d.))

This kind of testimony shows that, although the prototypical situation that this verb evokes is a child touching another child repeatedly and for some time, *ciriquiar₃* can also be used to refer to adults doing things that don't imply physical contact but can be equally annoying and conform to the features of that kind of behaviour discussed above.

8. An NSM explication of *ciriquiar₃*

Based on the information on the meaning of this word explained in the previous section, I propose below an NSM explication of *ciriquiar₃*. For this explication, two molecules are needed: child [m], which belongs to the category of basic social groups, and hand [m], which is included in the category of body parts (Goddard 2007b, 2012).

[B] *Ciriquiar₃* (e.g. Someone X was *ciriquiar*-ing someone Y)

a. someone X was doing something of one kind to someone else Y for some time
b. like a child [m] can do something of this kind when this child [m] thinks like this:
c. 'I want this someone to feel something bad now
d. because of this, I will do something with my hand [m] now
e. if I do this, my hand [m] will be touching this someone's part of the body many times for some time
f. I want this someone to do something because of this'
g. because someone X was doing it to someone Y for some time, someone Y felt something bad

Since *ciriquiar₃* is prototypically a physical action, the first component corresponds to the lexicosyntactic frame of physical activity verbs (Goddard 2012, among others). The second component introduces the prototypical motivational scenario, which includes the reference to children as the prototypical agents of this kind of action. This prototypical motivational scenario is spelled out in components (c) to (f), expressing the intention to annoy the other person by touching this person repeatedly and the expectation of a reaction from him/her. Finally, component (g) expresses the negative feelings that this action produces in the other person.

9. Conclusion

This contribution has sought to explain the meaning of *chirrinta* and *ciriquiar$_3$*, two loanwords of cultural relevance used by Navarrese Spanish speakers, which are unknown to speakers from other areas of Spain. As has been discussed, the few regional dictionaries that offer information about these words fail to spell their meaning out, probably because of their cultural specificity and the absence of equivalents in general Spanish. The present study has shown that, in spite of their complexity, these two culture-specific words can be fully understood by non-native speakers through NSM explications based on simple universal concepts. As Anna Wierzbicka has argued in her numerous publications, it is only through this self-explanatory set of semantic primes that complex meanings can be explained and compared in an intelligible way. Although they constitute a first approach and they may be subject to future revisions, the explications provided here will definitely help Spanish speakers as well as speakers of other languages to understand these two culture-specific concepts.

Acknowledgements

First, I would like to thank the editors for giving me the opportunity to contribute to this Festschrift with this chapter. I am also very grateful to Anna Gladkova for her helpful insights and to the anonymous reviewers for their valuable comments. And last but not least, I would like to express my gratitude to Anna Wierzbicka for her extremely inspiring work and her great kindness.

References

Andolz, Rafael (1992 [1977]). *Diccionario aragonés* [*Aragonese Dictionary*] (4th edn). Zaragoza: Mira.

Aragüés, Itziar (2003). *Y tú ¿cómo dices …? Vocabulario actual de Pamplona* [*And You, How Do You Say…? Present-day Vocabulary of Pamplona*]. Pamplona: Ayuntamiento de Pamplona.

Cid-Abasolo, Karlos (2010). La lexicografía vasca a lo largo de la historia [Basque lexicography throughout its history]. *Revista de Filología Románica [Journal of Romance Philology]*, 27, 163–78.

Ciérvide, Ricardo (1979). Léxico vasco en la Navarra romance: Análisis puntual de un problema de léxico en una zona de marca o límite lingüístico [Basque lexicon in romance Navarre: a detailed analysis of a lexical problem in a linguistic boundary or limit area]. *Fontes Linguae Vasconum* 11 (33): 515–28.

De Cruchaga y Purroy, José (1970). Un estudio etnográfico del Romanzado y Urraúl Bajo [An ethnographic study of the Romanzado and Urraúl Bajo]. *Cuadernos de etnografía y etnología de Navarra* [*Journal of Ethnography and Ethnology of Navarre*] 2: 143–265.

Echenique, Maria Teresa (2016). Lengua española y lengua vasca: una trayectoria histórica sin fronteras [Spanish Language and Basque Language: a trajectory with no boundaries]. *Revista de Filología de La Universidad de La Laguna* [*Journal of Philology of the University of La Laguna*] 34: 235–52.

Gladkova, Anna (2010). *Russkaja kul'turnaja semantika: èmocii, cennosti, žiznennye ustanovki* [*Russian Cultural Semantics: Emotions, Values, Attitudes*]. Moscow: Languages of Slavonic Cultures [in Russian].

Gobierno de Navarra, Gobierno Vasco and Euskararen Erakunde Publikoa (2017). *VI Encuesta Sociolingüística de Navarra* [*6th Sociolinguistic Survey of Navarre*]. Pamplona.

Goddard, Cliff (2007a). A culture-neutral metalanguage for mental state concepts. In Andrea C. Schalley and Drew Khlentzos (eds), *Mental States. Vol. 2: Language and Cognitive Structure*. Amsterdam: John Benjamins, 11–35. doi.org/10.1075/slcs.93.04god.

Goddard, Cliff (2007b). Semantic molecules. In Ilana Mushin and Mary Laughren (eds), *Selected Papers of the 2006 Annual Meeting of the Australian Linguistic Society*. Brisbane: Australian Linguistic Society, Available at: research-repository.griffith.edu.au/bitstream/handle/10072/92413/GoddardPUB4.pdf?sequence=1.

Goddard, Cliff (2012). Semantic primes, semantic molecules, semantic templates: Key concepts in the NSM approach to lexical typology. *Linguistics* 50 (3): 711–43. doi.org/10.1515/ling-2012-0022.

Goddard, Cliff and Anna Wierzbicka (2002). Semantic primes and universal grammar. In Cliff Goddard and Anna Wierzbicka (eds), *Meaning and Universal Grammar: Theory and Empirical Findings Vol. I*. Amsterdam: John Benjamins, 41–85. doi.org/10.1075/slcs.60.08god.

Goddard, Cliff and Anna Wierzbicka (2014). *Words and Meanings: Lexical Semantics Across Domains, Languages and Cultures*. Oxford: Oxford University Press. doi.org/10.1093/acprof:oso/9780199668434.001.0001.

Goddard, Cliff and Zhengdao Ye (2014). Exploring 'happiness' and 'pain' across languages and cultures. *International Journal of Language and Culture* 1 (2): 131–48.

Goicoechea, Cesáreo (1961). *Vocabulario riojano [Riojan Vocabulary]*. Madrid: Anejos del BRAE.

Haspelmath, Martin (2008). Loanword typology: Steps toward a systematic cross-linguistic study of lexical borrowability. In Thomas Stolz, Dik Bakker and Rosa Salas Palomo (eds), *Aspects of Language Contact: New Theoretical, Methodological and Empirical Findings with Special Focus on Romancisation Processes*. Berlin: Mouton de Gruyter, 43–62.

Ilargi (1989). Vienen los gigantes [The giants are coming]. *El Tuto*, 14, 57. Available at: tutoberri.info/aleak/014a.pdf.

Iribarren, José María (1984 [1952, 1958]). *Vocabulario Navarro [Navarrese Vocabulary]*. Segunda edición preparada y ampliada por Ricardo Ollaquindia. Pamplona: Comunidad Foral de Navarra – Institución Príncipe de Viana.

Lamariano, Goizeder (2009). A dieta desde los dos años y medio [On a diet since being two years-old]. *Diario de Navarra*, 18 April.

Marín Royo, Luis María (2006). *El habla en la Ribera de Navarra [The speech in Ribera de Navarra]*. Pamplona: Gobierno de Navarra.

Michelena, Luis and Ibon Sarasola (1987–2013). *Orotariko Euskal Hiztegia – Diccionario General Vasco [General Dictionary of Basque]*. Bilbao: Euskaltzaindia.

Real Academia Española (n.d.). Banco de datos (CREA). *Corpus de referencia del español actual [Present-day Spanish Reference Corpus]* [online]. Available at: www.rae.es.

Real Academia Española (2014). *Diccionario de la Lengua Española [Dictionary of the Spanish Language]* (23rd edn) [online]. Available at: dle.rae.es.

Rebolé del Castillo, Eusebio (2003). Toponimia y léxico vascos en Irunberri/Lumbier [Basque toponymy and lexicon in Irunberri/Lumbier]. *Euskera: Euskaltzaindiaren lan eta agiriak [Basque: Works and Proceedings of the Academy of the Basque Language]* 48: 795–822.

Sánchez-Ostiz, Miguel (1995). *Un infierno en el jardín [Hell in the Garden]*. Barcelona: Anagrama.

Santazilia, Ekaitz and Eneko Zuloaga (2018). Zer (ez) dakigun Iruñean egiten zen euskarari buruz [What we do (not) know about the Basque that was spoken in Iruña]. In Iñaki Azkona and Roldán Jimeno (eds), *Iruñeko historia: Hiriaren ibilbidea historian barna* [*History of Iruña: the Path of the City throughout History*]. Iruñea: Iruñeko Udala and Pamiela, 475–505.

Tabernero, Cristina (2008). Disponibilidad léxica y contacto de lenguas [Lexical availability and language contact]. *Oihenart: Cuadernos de Lengua y Literatura* [*Oihenart: Journal of Language and Literature*] 23: 545–65.

Tabernero, Cristina (2012). Tradición y actualidad en los estudios lingüísticos sobre Navarra [Tradition and current state of affairs in linguistic studies about Navarre]. *Archivo de Filología Aragonesa* [*Archives of Aragonese Philology*] 68: 185–212.

Thomason, Sara Grey and Terrence Kaufman (1988). *Language Contact, Creolization, and Genetic Linguistics*. Berkeley and Los Angeles: University of California Press.

Wierzbicka, Anna (1997). *Understanding Cultures through their Key Words: English, Russian, Polish, German, and Japanese*. New York: Oxford University Press.

Wierzbicka, Anna (2011a). Bilingualism and cognition: The perspective from semantics. In Vivian Cook and Benedetta Bassetti (eds), *Language and Bilingual Cognition*. Hove, UK: Routledge, 191–218.

Wierzbicka, Anna (2011b). Arguing in Russian: Why Solzhenitsyn's fictional arguments defy translation. *Russian Journal of Communication* 4 (1/2): 8–37. doi.org/10.1080/19409419.2011.10756788.

Wierzbicka, Anna (2013). Translatability and the scripting of other people's souls. *The Australian Journal of Anthropology* 24 (1): 1–22. doi.org/10.1111/taja.12018.

Wierzbicka, Anna (2015). Innate conceptual primitives manifested in the languages of the world and in infant cognition. In Stephen Laurence and Eric Margolis (eds), *The Conceptual Mind: New Directions in the Study of Concepts*. Cambridge, MA: MIT Press, 379–412. doi.org/10.7551/mitpress/9383.003.0023.

Wong, Jock Onn (2014). *The Culture of Singapore English*. Cambridge: Cambridge University Press.

Wong, Jock Onn (2018). The semantics of logical connectors: *therefore, moreover* and *in fact*. *Russian Journal of Linguistics* 22 (3): 581–604.

Ye, Zhengdao (ed.) (2017). *The Semantics of Nouns*. Oxford: Oxford University Press. doi.org/10.1093/oso/9780198736721.003.0001.

11

Time in Portuguese *saudade* and other words of longing

Zuzanna Bułat Silva

1. Introduction

The basic aim of this article is to see how the category of TIME relates to the domain of EMOTIONS. I believe that the dimension of TIME is important while defining emotion concepts and that the recognition of this fact can have profound consequences for cross-cultural psychology.[1] Drawing on some Natural Semantic Metalanguage (NSM) explications of emotions[2] referring to 'pain caused by distance' in different languages, I am going to show the differences between various cultural conceptualisations of that 'intersection' of emotional spectrum. Comparing the Portuguese word *saudade*, roughly 'longing', with its Polish (*tęsknota*), Spanish (*morriña*), and Chinese (*chou*) counterparts, I am going to look at how the domain of TIME is captured in their meaning and how TIME relates to the intensity of emotions described by these terms. To be able to express myself from a culturally neutral perspective, I will rely here on the NSM approach (Wierzbicka 1996; Goddard and Wierzbicka 2002). Thanks to NSM,

---

[1] The previous versions of this article were presented at the STALDAC conference, held at the University of Cambridge, UK, in April 2010 and at the talk given at the School of Language Studies, ANU, Canberra, in August 2013.
[2] When I refer to *emotions* in this article, in most cases I mean 'emotion concepts embedded in words'.

we are able, as Wierzbicka (2009: 4) notes, to 'explore human emotions from a universal point of view, independent of any particular languages and cultures'.

The present article will be organised as follows. First, in section 2, the NSM primes referring to TIME will be examined. Then, in section 3 different ways in which emotions may relate to TIME will be discussed. Section 4 will consist of the presentation of a key Portuguese emotion, *saudade*, together with its metalinguistic explication. And finally, in section 5, the explication of *saudade* will be contrasted with the explications of *tęsknota*, *morriña* and *chou* in order to show the different role TIME plays in each of these emotions.

2. Semantic primes referring to the domain of TIME

NSM is a theory of semantic analysis that has been developed over the period of more than 40 years. There are eight TIME primes in the most recent version of NSM: WHEN~TIME,[3] NOW, BEFORE, AFTER, A LONG TIME, A SHORT TIME, FOR SOME TIME and MOMENT. As with all the NSM primes, it is assumed that they exist in all languages in the world. Interestingly, in the earliest versions of NSM (Wierzbicka 1972), there were no TIME primes at all; temporal phenomena were defined via 'worlds becoming worlds' (Goddard 1998: 325).

Basic TIME primes proposed in Goddard and Wierzbicka (1994) were WHEN, BEFORE and AFTER. The authors argued that in every language one may ask simple questions, such as: '*When* did it happen?' or '*When* will you do it?', and also 'This someone died *before* this other someone' or 'This other someone died *after* this someone' (see Wierzbicka 1996: 57). Thanks to the categorical element WHEN~TIME, it is easy to explicate different time adverbs. *Then* can be explained as 'at that time'; *often*—'at many times'; *always*—'at all times'; *sometimes*—'at some times'; and *ago*—'some time before'. WHEN~TIME can be used with all the predicates as a 'temporal adjunct', as in '*at that time* you did something bad' or '*some time before* these people were doing something else' (Wierzbicka 1996: 132; Goddard

---

3   WHEN and TIME are two English allolexes (contextual variants) of the same prime.

and Wierzbicka 2002: 66).[4] These temporal adjuncts are best identified with reference to the prime NOW, introduced in 1996; in other words, if one can substitute the temporal phrase with NOW (or *at this time*), it is well-formed (Goddard and Wierzbicka 2002: 67).

As for AFTER and BEFORE, at first sight, one may contend that they are converses, so there is no need to postulate them both as primes. But as the authors of the NSM approach state (Wierzbicka 1996: 57; Goddard 1998: 326; Goddard and Wierzbicka 2002: 15–16), there is a difference in perspective, a different configuration of *trajector* and *landmark*, if we were to use Langackerean terms (see Langacker 2009). 'Y happened *after* X' cannot be paraphrased without loss of meaning as 'X happened *before* Y'; it is a matter of a different viewpoint. Reducing the two to something as 'temporal sequence' also seems counterintuitive, because it is much easier to find terms such as AFTER and BEFORE across languages of the world, than the very abstract term of 'temporal sequence'.

In the classic NSM work, *Semantics: Primes and Universals* (Wierzbicka 1996), the TIME set was expanded. Four new primes were added—two duration (or time period) antonyms A LONG TIME and A SHORT TIME, accounting for the 'passage of time', a deictic NOW and a 'vague' duration term FOR SOME TIME, which was posited only tentatively. As for NOW, it was earlier believed that it could be explicated as 'when I say this', but then it was discovered that the range of application of NOW is much wider (Wierzbicka 1996: 100; Goddard 1998: 328). NOW, being the basic deictic time marker, is used with all NSM predicates, especially the mental ones: '*now* I know/feel/see … something'. The duration primes A LONG TIME and A SHORT TIME combine not only with predicates such as DO, HAPPEN, MOVE, LIVE, but also with mental predicates FEEL and THINK: 'I felt something bad *for a long time*'. What is less obvious is that they both collocate well with BEFORE and AFTER, and hence can appear within temporal adjuncts, as in 'it happened *a long time before*' (see also Goddard and Wierzbicka 2002: 70). And they can function on their own, as can be seen from the previous examples, as 'durational adjuncts'. What is important to note though, is that the range of contexts in which they

---

4   WHEN can also be used in a bi-clausal construction, such as: 'when I did these things, I felt something bad' (see Wierzbicka 1996: 132).

can occur depends on the lexical aspect of the predicate (one may say 'this someone lived for a long time', but not *'this someone died for a long time', see Goddard and Wierzbicka 2002: 71).[5]

The most recent TIME prime is MOMENT, added in 2002 (Goddard 2002: 301). This prime accounts for the immediacy of some actions and reactions, and expresses the idea of suddenness (Goddard 2018: 75). It is, so to say, punctual, it is time with almost no duration: such as in 'it happened a *moment* before'. And, as we can see from this example, MOMENT, just as the duration primes, can be used with BEFORE and AFTER.[6]

Interestingly, in many languages of the world (e.g. Polish, Hopi, Kayardild) the exponents of BEFORE and AFTER are polysemous and mean also 'in front of' or 'going ahead of' and 'behind' or 'following', respectively (see also Goddard 2001: 46; Goddard and Wierzbicka 2002: 68). It is worth noting here that there is a strict correspondence between the NSM primes of TIME and SPACE. As Goddard and Wierzbicka put it:

> There is a certain degree of parallelism in the inventory of proposed primes of time and space ... we can see that both domains have a 'categorical' or substantive-like element [correspondingly WHEN~TIME and WHERE~PLACE], that both have a deictic element [NOW and HERE], that both have a pair of relational antonyms [AFTER, BEFORE and ABOVE, BELOW], and also a pair of 'scalar' antonyms [A LONG TIME, A SHORT TIME and FAR, NEAR]. In view of these facts, it is not surprising that there are numerous parallels in the combinatorial characteristics of temporal expressions and spatial expressions. (2002: 66)

3. Emotions and TIME

As Averill (1994: 384, 385) points out, our emotional experience 'is not static, but [it] extends in time' and 'emotions differ greatly in their temporal course'. Many researchers view emotions as *scripts*, *narratives* or *scenarios*

---

5   One may think that these durational elements, A LONG TIME and A SHORT TIME, are based on the prime TIME, and hence are too complicated to be considered primitive. We must remember though that in many languages their exponents are simple, unanalysable words—e.g. in Polish, DŁUGO and KRÓTKO—that have nothing to do with the lexical exponent of the prime WHEN~TIME (see Goddard and Wierzbicka 2002: 67).
6   The introduction of the prime MOMENT is also related to the fact that the combination 'a very short time' is not available cross-linguistically (Goddard 2002: 301–03).

(see e.g. Shweder 1994; Kövecses 1995; Apresjan and Apresjan 2000). If emotions are narratives, they extend over time, hence the importance of temporal primes in their explications.

Within the NSM framework, emotions are normally defined through a *prototypical cognitive scenario* (Goddard 1998: 95; Goddard 2018: 70). Usually there is someone who 'is thinking about something' that he *did* or about something that *happened* or *can happen* to him. As a result, this person is feeling 'something good' or 'something bad' *for some time*. Hence, the prototypical scenario gives us a clue how a person experiencing the given emotion may feel. These thoughts and feelings are considered a prototype of the emotion in question: 'like people often feel when they think like this'. As Páez and Vergara (1995: 415) note, the prototypical emotional scenarios 'are embedded in, and dependent on, culture'. That is why emotion terms are so different in every linguaculture. And they can be seen as 'a record of how earlier generations of speakers of a given language thought about their feelings' (Besemeres and Wierzbicka 2010: 20). In a sense, names of emotions are linguistic artefacts in which past experiences of a given community are crystallised. As such, they are dependent on the geographical and historical conditions that community lives in (for interesting examples, see Briggs 1971 on Inuit emotions). By analysing emotion names, we gain an insight into the history of that community. It is not surprising that in Portuguese we find a word *saudade*, an emotion term basic to the Portuguese identity, that relates to the centuries-long history of Portuguese colonisation of the world and to the separation of families caused by that maritime expansion.

Emotions may also differ as far as time perspective is concerned. Some of them relate to past experiences, others are about things happening now and 'have distinctly present perspective' (Goddard 1998: 92 on *happy* and *joy*; see also Goddard 2018: 77 on *pleased* and *contented*). Emotions differ in their intensity as well. 'Some emotions are more like sneezes, others more like crimes', as Dixon (2003: 246) notes, wittily. And, as Clore (1994: 391) suggests, emotional intensity is a function of amplitude multiplied by duration, rather than merely amplitude. So there must be some correlation between the duration and the intensity of an emotion. Expressions like *for some time* and *in one moment* help us to distinguish between prolonged feelings (e.g. *saudade*) and momentary ones (e.g. *surprise*; see also Goddard 2018: 71).

According to some psychologists (Davidson 1994: 51; Ekman 1994: 16), emotions do not last longer than a few minutes, and if they do, they are dysfunctional (Ekman and Davidson 1994: 419; see also Ekman 1994: 16: '[h]ere is not the place to argue about just how long an emotion typically lasts, but certainly it is not hours or days, but more in the realm of minutes and seconds'). Watson and Clark (1994: 90) claim along similar lines that 'emotions ... are typically quite short-lived in their full form, lasting only a few seconds or perhaps minutes'. Ekman (1994: 56) goes even further, stating that the emotional state that lasts several weeks should be classified as an affective disorder. As I will try to demonstrate later, this is a very Anglocentric point of view.[7] In many cultures of the world, people are used to feelings that go on for hours, or even days, and consider long-lasting and intense emotional states as a sign of mental health, not an affective disorder (see e.g. Wierzbicka 1995: 22 on how absence of emotions is perceived as an indicator of 'a deadening of a person's *duša* ('heart/soul')' in Russian culture).

There is one more question we should touch upon in speaking of the relations between emotions and time. Time perception is a very subjective phenomenon, there is no unique sense of time, but there are multiple experiences of time. And, most importantly, our judgement of time depends on how we feel. When we are happy, 'time flies'.[8] On the contrary, when we are in deep sorrow, time may almost stop (see Droit-Vallet and Gil 2009: 1947, on how sadness induces a general slowing down). As Geoffard and Luchini (2010: 271) say, 'time is not exogenous to the individual, it is elastic, and this will be influenced by the emotion the person experiences'.

As we can see, investigating the relations between time and emotions is a fascinating field of study, and there certainly is a 'critical need for research on the temporal dynamics of emotional processing' (Ekman and Davidson 1994: 419). Exploring the topic in more depth is beyond the scope of the present chapter though, so let us proceed to see how four emotion concepts referring to 'longing' differ in their time perspective.

---

7   As one of the anonymous reviewers of this chapter rightly noticed, it may be more a question of what English-speaking psychologists and not ordinary speakers of English have in mind when they talk about emotions.
8   At the same time, when we are happy, we often feel we have plenty of time, even though it passes by quickly; in fact, research shows that experiencing awe leads to expanding one's perceptions of time availability (see Rudd et al. 2012).

4. Portuguese *saudade*

Saudade is a key emotion term in Portuguese, usually translated into English as *longing, missing, homesickness* or *nostalgia*. Its uniqueness resides in the fact that for a long time the Portuguese have seen it as a national identity marker. It is said to have emerged during the times of Great Portuguese Discoveries (*Época dos Descobrimentos*), when many left their families and departed to the unknown. Those left behind, suffering from the absence of their loved ones and longing for their return, thought of them with a mixture of melancholy and pride (see Bułat Silva 2012).

The *Great Dictionary of the Portuguese Language* (Machado 1981: 13) states that *saudade* is 'a word that probably doesn't have equivalents in other languages, and that expresses a lot of feelings, especially melancholy, caused by recalling something good that one was deprived of'.[9] In the *Dictionary of Contemporary Portuguese Language* (Casteleiro 2001), *saudade* is defined as 'a memory of something that was pleasant but is distant in terms of time or space'.[10] In my opinion, it refers more to the domain of TIME than to the domain of SPACE, and not simply to distance in TIME, but rather, I believe, it is the PAST that constitutes the prototypical object of *saudade* (Bułat Silva 2012: 207). One may say that *saudade* is a feeling about times gone by. But, interestingly enough, it can also refer to the future (one may have *saudades do futuro*, '*saudades* of the future'). It is typically an overwhelming and long-lasting feeling. The element of 'thinking', recalling the past, is inherent to its meaning (*saudades* in plural can also mean 'memories', see Casteleiro 2001). As I have written earlier (Bułat Silva 2012), equally important is the positive evaluation it has in the Portuguese culture—'*não ha nada mais triste que a saudade de saudade*', 'there's nothing sadder than *saudade* of *saudade*' (Barreto 1959: 22). When we have a look at the verbs that collocate most frequently with *saudade*, the impression of its intensity is even stronger. One may *morrer de saudade*, 'die of *saudade*', and one can also *matar saudade*, 'kill *saudade*' (by seeing people he missed so badly), just as one can *morrer de fome*, 'die out of hunger', and *matar a fome*, 'kill the hunger' (by eating something). These parallels in metaphorical expressions show that psychological reaction to *saudade* may be similar to the body's reaction to hunger (see Apresjan and

---

9 *Vocábulo considerado sem equivalente noutras línguas e que exprime multiplicidade de sentimentos, sobretudo a melancolia causada pela lembrança do bem do qual se está privado.*
10 *Recordação de alguma coisa que foi agradável mas que está distante no tempo ou no espaço.*

Apresjan 2000: 205: 'emotion is hardly ever expressed directly, but always compared to something'). And just as hunger, *saudade* is perceived as an emotion that doesn't leave much space for other thoughts or feelings.

Now let us try to summarise what have just been said about *saudade*, using the simple and cross-translatable words of NSM:

[A] *Tenho saudades de …*

a. I think like this:
b. <u>some time before</u> something very good was happening to me <u>for some time</u>
c. I felt something very good because of this
d. it is not happening <u>now</u>
e. I very much want this to be happening <u>now</u>
f. I know it can't happen anymore
g. this is bad
h. I can't not think about it
i. <u>at the same time</u> I think like this:
j. <u>some time before</u> something very good was happening to me <u>for some time</u>
k. I felt something very good because of this
l. I can think about it <u>now</u>
m. this is good
n. <u>when</u> I think like this, I feel something like people feel <u>at many times</u> <u>when</u> they think like this <u>for a</u> <u>long time</u>
o. it is good if someone can feel something like this

Source: Bułat Silva (2012: 207).

The explication in [A] starts with 'I think' to capture the element of nostalgic thoughts that constitute the base for the feeling (a). *Saudade* is paradoxical—its cognitive scenario is that of having ambiguous thoughts about the past. Therefore someone thinks: '*some time before* something very good was happening to me for some time' (b) and because of that 'I felt something very good' (c). But it is not happening anymore (d), even though this person would very much like it to be happening (e). It is a very acute feeling. And that fact is stressed by the use of the deictic *now* twice. First, in line (d) when the person experiences some kind of loss or emptiness and then, in line (e) when this somebody desires to revive the past. There is also some kind of Portuguese fatalistic resignation *towards the future* embedded in (f), 'I know it can't happen anymore', and a negative appraisal, 'this is bad', in (g). The pervasiveness of *saudade* is captured in line (h): 'I can't not think about it'. At the same time the person appreciates having good past experiences (j) and feelings (k). Those memories are a reason for a positive appraisal *now* (l, m). All this makes this person feel 'something like people often feel when they think like this *for a long time*'. In that component the long-lasting quality of *saudade* is substantiated. The very last component (o) shows that *saudade* is positively valued in the Portuguese culture.

5. *Saudade* and other emotions of longing

5.1. *Saudade* vs *tęsknota*

Patrick Farell, in his article 'Portuguese saudade and other emotions of absence and longing' (2006: 336), suggested that of all the languages known to him, the closest counterpart of Portuguese *saudade* is the Polish word *tęsknota*. I must disagree with him though. In spite of being a very salient Polish emotion word, *tęsknota* has a different focus than that of *saudade*. Having a quick look at the explications of the two ([A] and [B] respectively), we may easily see that *tęsknota* is much more SPACE-oriented. As Wierzbicka (1992: 125) argues, it has *ojczyzna*, 'patria', as its prototypical stimulus. *Tęsknota* is said to have gained its status of a Polish key concept during the so-called Great Emigration in the nineteenth century. In 1795, Polish lands were divided and seized (for the third time) by three neighbouring powers, Austria, Prussia and Russia, and that caused a great exile of the political, literary and artistic elite. One of the dominant themes (and the driving force) of their work was *tęsknota*, the pain of being away from their homeland (cf. Goddard and Wierzbicka 2008: 205–07). Today *tęsknota* is often felt towards a person, as in the explication quoted below, but even then it implies absence or separation in SPACE rather than in TIME. One feels something very bad, because one thinks about someone who is *very far from the place* that person is. In NSM simple terms, the verb *tęsknić*, 'to have *tęsknota* towards someone' is explicated as follows:

[B] *ktoś* (X) *tęskni do kogoś* (Y)

a. this someone (X) thinks about someone else (Y)
b. <u>when</u> X thinks about Y, X feels something very bad
c. like someone can feel <u>when</u> they think like this about someone:
d.   this someone is very far from the place where I am <u>now</u>
e.   because of this I can't be with this someone <u>now</u>
f.   when I was with this someone <u>before</u>, I felt something good
g.   I want to be with this someone <u>now</u>

Source: Goddard and Wierzbicka (2008: 206).[11]

As we can see, there are less temporal primes featuring in the above definition, and it is due to the fact that prototypical stimulus of *tęsknota* is distance in SPACE, not in TIME[12] (although *tęsknota* is also a very acute feeling: the deictic *now* is used three times in its explication). It is important to distinguish two syntactic frames of the verb *tęsknić*: *tęsknić do* and *tęsknić za*.[13] According to Grzegorczykowa (1999), the former is future-oriented, while the latter is past-oriented and somewhat fatalistic, but both refer to *cierpienie wywołane rozłąką z bliskimi ludźmi (miejscami)*, 'pain caused by separation from a beloved person (or place)' (Grzegorczykowa 1999: 203). *Saudade*, as it was said before, is TIME-oriented, it is about something good one had in the past, and it can also refer to something good that can happen in the future, but it most likely won't—as in *saudades do futuro*, 'nostalgia of the future', or *saudades do que ainda não aconteceu*, 'saudades of something that hasn't come to being yet'.

5.2. *Saudade* vs *morriña*

Interestingly, *saudade* doesn't have a cognate in Spanish. Maybe the closest Spanish counterpart of *saudade* would be *añoranza*, 'longing' (from *añorar*, '*recordar con pena la ausencia, privación o pérdida de alguien*

---

11 For the explication of *tęsknić do miejsca*, 'to feel *tęsknota* towards a place', see Goddard (2018: 80).
12 One of the anonymous reviewers of this chapter suggested that the prototypical stimulus of *tęsknota* is *nieobecność* 'absence' rather spatial distance. I think being separated from one another implies distance in SPACE, whatever the reason for that separation is (emigration, work travel, end of the relationship).
13 *Do* is roughly 'to' in English, and *za* could be translated as 'for'. Actually, there is one more syntactic frame *tęsknić po*, roughly 'after', but as it is an archaic expression (which can be found e.g. in Adam Mickiewicz's works), it lies beyond the scope of the present chapter.

o algo muy querido' 'to recall with sorrow the absence or loss of someone or something we love', see RAE 2014). Often *saudade* is translated into Spanish as *nostalgia*. And there is one more Spanish word of Galician origin that can be considered equivalent to *saudade*, that is *morriña*, defined by the *Dictionary of Spanish Language* as '*tristeza o melancolía, especialmente la nostalgia de la tierra natal*', 'sadness or melancholy, especially nostalgia for one's homeland' (RAE 2014). *Morriña* is said to emerge as a result of the emigration of people from rural Spain to Argentina in the second half of the nineteenth century, so it is strongly SPACE-oriented, very much like Polish *tęsknota* (Goddard and Wierzbicka 2008). Unlike *tęsknota* though, *morriña* has also a very clear reference to the past, specifically to the times of one's childhood. As the explication in [C] says:

[C] *morriña*

a. someone (X) thinks about this place (Y)
b. <u>when</u> X thinks about place Y, X feels something bad
c. like someone can feel <u>when</u> they think like this about a place:
d. 'I am like a part of this small place
e. I did many things with people there <u>when I was a child</u> [m]
f. I felt many good things <u>at many times</u> <u>when</u> I was there
g. I want to be in this place <u>now</u>
h. I know that I can't be in this place <u>now</u> because it is far from here'

Source: Goddard and Wierzbicka (2008: 12).

Morriña has one's *tierra natal*, 'homeland' or 'land of one's birth' (*Heimat* in German), as a prototypical target (*small place* in line (d)). One is far away from that place and cannot easily come back (g–h). *Morriña* is accompanied by memories of one's childhood (e) and of happiness resulting from being a part of a community and sharing joys and troubles with it (f).[14] *Morriña* is similar to *saudade* in that memory-based element. Comparing to *saudade* though, it is more focused on SPACE, but they both share the component of a desire that cannot be fulfilled (line (f) in [A] and (h) in [C]) that Polish *tęsknota* lacks.

---

14 In the most recent explication of *morriña* in Goddard (2018: 83), there is a stronger reference to *community*. Line (d) in [C] is rewritten as 'some people are like a part of this small place, I am one of these people'.

5.3. *Saudade* and *chou*

Having compared *saudade* with two 'nostalgic emotions' relating to SPACE, *tęsknota* and *morriña*, let us look now at a Chinese nostalgia, *chou*, that is, just like *saudade*, TIME-oriented. Unlike *saudade* though, it refers more to the *present* than to the *past*. *Chou* is a very salient Chinese emotion usually translated into English as 'sadness', 'homesickness' or 'profound melancholy' (Ye 2001: 378–91). Comparing to other SADNESS words in Chinese, *bei* (roughly 'sorrow', 'sadness') and *ai* ('sorrow', 'grief'), *chou* is strikingly ego-oriented. When describing *chou*, Ye (2001: 379) gives the following glosses 'sadness at leaving a friend; the loneliness of setting out on a journey in a tiny boat on the vast sea; … emptiness …; yearning …; depression and dissatisfaction caused by the inability to achieve what one yearns for; confusion in not knowing what to do …; the inability to put an end to one's *chou*'.

[D] *chou*

a. X felt something because X thought something
b. <u>sometimes</u> a person thinks:
c. 'something very bad is happening to me
d. <u>before</u> this, I did not think this would happen
e. I don't want things like this to happen to me
f. because of this, I want to do something if I can
g. I don't know what to do
h. I cannot not think about this <u>all the time</u>'
i. <u>when</u> this person thinks this, this person feels something bad <u>for a long time</u>
j. X felt something like this
k. because X thought something like this

Source: Ye (2001: 383).

When we look at the NSM definition in [D] proposed by Ye (2001: 383), we may see that *chou* is experienced in difficult, stressful and unpredictable situations ('something very bad is happening to me/before this I did not think this would happen', (c)–(f)). The experiencer is confused and doesn't know what to do (g). The feeling of *chou* is overwhelming and persistent and this person cannot stop thinking about bad things that are happening to them (h). The component (i) conveys the long duration of *chou*, 'this person feels something bad *for a long time*'. If we compare *saudade* to *chou*, we can see immediately that both of them are long-lasting emotions.[15] They are both overwhelming, pervasive feelings—one cannot stop thinking about what is happening. We may notice that in the definition of *chou* this pervasiveness is even more *intense*—it is stressed by the expression *all the time* in line (h). While *saudade* is a bipolar, paradoxical feeling based on both positive and negative thoughts towards the past, *chou* is negative and refers in a more straightforward manner to 'feeling something bad'.

6. Concluding remarks

The present comparison of 'nostalgia' terms in Portuguese, Polish, Spanish and Chinese seems to confirm the fact already pointed out by Geertz (1973: 81) that emotions are cultural artefacts. We cannot translate emotion names easily, because of rich semantic content such words possess. Nostalgia-like emotion terms have a special relation to the past, and a great deal of what happened to a given community can be seen when we unpack their meaning. *Saudade* recalls the epoch of Great Portuguese Discoveries (*Época dos Descobrimentos*), when the Portuguese were one of the most powerful nations in the world. *Tęsknota* speaks about the three partitions of Poland, and the great pain of those who had to leave the country. *Morriña* brings into one's mind millions of *gallegos* who emigrated to Argentina and Chile in the nineteenth century. As Apresjan and Apresjan (2000: 203) note, 'language contains the experience of millennia of psychological and cultural introspection and its data are every bit as reliable as those provided by experimental research'. By studying semantics we may learn a lot about history.

Emotions are not punctual, but they are more like stories or scenarios that extend in time. And, as we have seen, in some cultures emotions that we refer to as 'longing' simply last longer than in others. *Saudade* and *chou* seem to be more pervasive, more overwhelming emotions than *morriña* and *tęsknota*. Why is that so? My hypothesis would be that what makes *saudade* such a long-lasting feeling is the CHANGE between all the good

---

15   Note that also *toska*, a Russian word for 'longing' or 'ennui' shares the same component of lasting for hours or even days, see Wierzbicka (1992).

memories of the past and the present feelings of emptiness and absence that are experienced by the subject. It is this constant change between *feeling something good* and *feeling something bad* that allows *saudade* to persist for such long periods of time. It does not focus on something bad happening to a person, but rather submerges in the past and then comes back to the present. And it is that swinging motion between good and bad feelings that allows the TIME pendulum to go on for so long. Further studies on *chou* are needed in order to explain its long-lasting quality.

We can also note that the emotions we feel change our subjective sense of time. When we feel nostalgic, or sad, time is most likely to slow down and we may experience it differently. Portuguese identity is said to be based on experiencing *saudade*—maybe this is why Portuguese people are perceived as passive by their more energetic Spanish neighbours?

Summing up, we may say that emotions relate to time in three different ways—as cultural artefacts of the past (1), as scenarios taking place within a specific amount of time (2) and as psychological processes that can change our subjective sense of time, adjusting our internal clock to the kind of emotion we feel (3).

Acknowledgements

The author of this article would like to thank two anonymous reviewers whose insightful comments helped improve the final draft.

References

Apresjan, Jurij and Valentina Apresjan (2000). Metaphor in the semantic representation of emotions. *Systematic Lexicography:* 203–14.

Averill, James R. (1994). I feel, therefore I am—I think. In Paul Ekman and Richard J. Davidson (eds), *The Nature of Emotions: Fundamental Questions.* Oxford: Oxford University Press, 379–85.

Barreto, Mascarenhas (1959). *Fado: A canção portuguesa.* Lisboa.

Besemeres, Mary and Anna Wierzbicka (2010). Emotion terms as a window on culture, social psychology and subjective experience. In S.V. Ionov (ed.), *Jazyk i emociia.* Volgograd: Volgogradskoe Nauchnoe Izdatel'stvo, 14–32.

Briggs, Jean L. (1971). *Never in Anger.* Harvard: Harvard University Press.

Bułat Silva, Zuzanna (2012). *Saudade* – A key Portuguese emotion. *Emotion Review* 4 (2): 203–11. doi.org/10.1177/1754073911430727.

Casteleiro, João Malaca (2001). *Dicionário da Língua Portuguesa Contemporânea* [*Dictionary of the Contemporary Portuguese Language*]. Lisboa: Verbo.

Clore, Gerald L. (1994). Why emotions vary in intensity. In Paul Ekman and Richard J. Davidson, *The Nature of Emotions: Fundamental Questions*. Oxford: Oxford University Press, 386–93.

Davidson, Richard J. (1994). On emotion, mood and related affective constructs. In Paul Ekman and Richard J. Davidson (eds), *The Nature of Emotions: Fundamental Questions*. Oxford: Oxford University Press, 51–55.

Dixon, Thomas (2003). *From Passions to Emotions: The Creation of a Secular Psychological Category*. Cambridge: Cambridge University Press.

Droit-Volet, Slyvie and Sandrine Gil (2009). The time–emotion paradox. *Philosophical Transactions of the Royal Society* 364: 1943–53. doi.org/10.1098/rstb.2009.0013.

Ekman, Paul (1994). All emotions are basic. In Paul Ekman and Richard J. Davidson (eds), *The Nature of Emotions: Fundamental Questions*. Oxford: Oxford University Press, 15–19.

Ekman, Paul and Richard J. Davidson (eds) (1994). *The Nature of Emotions: Fundamental Questions*. Oxford: Oxford University Press.

Farrell, Patrick (2006). Portuguese saudade and other emotions of absence and longing. In Bert Peeters (ed.), *Semantic Primes and Universal Grammar: Empirical Evidence from the Romance Languages*. Amsterdam: John Benjamins, 235–58. doi.org/10.1075/slcs.81.16far.

Geertz, Clifford (1973). *The Interpretation of Cultures*. New York: Basic Books.

Geoffard, Pierre Yves and Stéphane Luchini (2010). Changing time and emotions. *Philosophical Transactions of the Royal Society* 365: 271–80. doi.org/10.1098/rstb.2009.0178.

Goddard, Cliff (1998). *Semantic Analysis: A Practical Introduction*. Oxford: Oxford University Press.

Goddard, Cliff (2001). Lexico-semantic universals: A critical overview. *Linguistic Typology* 5: 1–65. doi.org/10.1515/lity.5.1.1.

Goddard, Cliff (2002). The ongoing development of the NSM research program. In Cliff Goddard and Anna Wierzbicka (eds), *Meaning and Universal Grammar: Theory and Empirical Findings* (Vol. 2). Amsterdam: John Benjamins, 301–21. doi.org/10.1075/slcs.61.11god.

Goddard, Cliff (2018). *Ten Lectures on Natural Semantic Metalanguage: Exploring Language, Thought and Culture Using Simple, Translatable Words*. Leiden: Brill.

Goddard, Cliff and Anna Wierzbicka (eds) (1994). *Semantic and Lexical Universals: Theory and Empirical Findings*. Amsterdam: John Benjamins.

Goddard, Cliff and Anna Wierzbicka (eds) (2002). *Meaning and Universal Grammar: Theory and Empirical Findings* (2 vol.). Amsterdam: John Benjamins.

Goddard, Cliff and Anna Wierzbicka (2008). Universal human concepts as a basis for contrastive linguistic semantics. In María de los Ángeles Gómez-Gonzáles, J. Lachlan Mackenzie, Anne-Marie Simon-Vandenbergen and Elsa Gonzáles Álvarez (eds), *Current Trends in Contrastive Linguistics: Functional and Cognitive Perspectives*. Amsterdam: John Benjamins, 205–26. doi.org/10.1075/sfsl.60.13god.

Grzegorczykowa, Renata (1999). Z badań nad porównawczą semantyką leksykalną: nazwy 'tęsknoty' w różnych językach [From the research on comparative lexical semantics: names for 'longing' in different languages]. In Zbigniew Greń and Violetta Koseska-Toszewa (eds), *Semantyka a konfrontacja językowa* [*Semantics and Linguistic Confrontation*]. Warszawa: 199–204.

Kövecses, Zoltan (1995). Language and emotion concepts. In James A. Russell, José-Miguel Fernández-Dols, Antony S.R. Manstead and J.C. Wellenkamp (eds), *Everyday Conceptions of Emotion: An Introduction to the Psychology, Anthropology, and Linguistics of Emotion*. Dordrecht: Kluwer Academic Publishers, 3–15. doi.org/10.1007/978-94-015-8484-5.

Langacker, Ronald W. (2009). *Gramatyka kognitywna. Wprowadzenie*. Kraków: Universitas. [Original title: Langacker, Ronald W. (2008). *Cognitive Grammar: A Basic Introduction*. Oxford: Oxford University Press.]

Machado José Pedro (ed.) (1981). *Grande Dicionário da Língua Portuguesa* [*Great Dictionary of the Portuguese Language*]. Lisboa: Amigos do Livro Editores.

Páez, D. and A.I. Vergara (1995). Culture differences in emotional knowledge. In James A. Russell, José-Miguel Fernández-Dols, Antony S.R. Manstead and J.C. Wellenkamp (eds), *Everyday Conceptions of Emotion: An Introduction to the Psychology, Anthropology, and Linguistics of Emotion*. Dordrecht: Kluwer Academic Publishers, 415–34. doi.org/10.1007/978-94-015-8484-5_24.

RAE (Real Academia Española) (2014). *Diccionario de la Lengua Española* [*Dictionary of the Spanish Language*] (23rd edn) [online]. Available at: dle.rae.es.

Rudd, Melanie, Kathleen D. Vohs and Jennifer Aaker (2012). Awe expands people's perception of time, alters decision making, and enhances well-being. *Psychological Science* 23 (10): 1130–36. doi.org/10.1177/0956797612438731.

Shweder, Richard (1994). 'You're not sick, you're just in love': Emotion as an interpretive system. In Paul Ekman and Richard J. Davidson, *The Nature of Emotions: Fundamental Questions*. Oxford: Oxford University Press, 32–44.

Watson, David and Lee Anna Clark (1994). Emotions, moods, traits, and temperaments: Conceptual distinctions and empirical findings. In Paul Ekman and Richard J. Davidson, *The Nature of Emotions: Fundamental Questions*. Oxford: Oxford University Press, 89–93.

Wierzbicka, Anna (1972). *Semantic Primitives*. Frankfurt: Athenäum.

Wierzbicka, Anna (1992). *Semantics, Culture, and Cognition: Universal Human Concepts in Culture-Specific Configurations*. New York: Oxford University Press.

Wierzbicka, Anna (1995). Everyday conceptions of emotion: A semantic perspective. In James A. Russell, José-Miguel Fernández-Dols, Antony S.R. Manstead and J.C. Wellenkamp (eds), *Everyday Conceptions of Emotion: An Introduction to the Psychology, Anthropology, and Linguistics of Emotion*. Dordrecht: Kluwer Academic Publishers, 17–47. doi.org/10.1007/978-94-015-8484-5_2.

Wierzbicka, Anna (1996). *Semantics: Primes and Universals*. Oxford: Oxford University Press.

Wierzbicka, Anna (2009). Language and metalanguage: Key issues in emotion research. *Emotion Review* 1 (1): 3–14. doi.org/10.1177/1754073908097175.

Ye, Zhengdao (2001). An inquiry into 'sadness' in Chinese. In Jean Harkins and Anna Wierzbicka (eds), *Emotions in Crosslinguistic Perspective*, Berlin/New York: Mouton de Gruyter, 359–404.

12

Lost in translation: A semantic analysis of *no da* in Japanese

Yuko Asano-Cavanagh

1. Introduction

The Japanese expression *no da* (のだ, as well as its variants *n da* んだ and *no* の) is frequently used at the end of a sentence and it adds a nuance to the statement (Alfonso 1966). Syntactically, *no da* consists of the nominalising particle *no* and the copulative *da*, and *no da* roughly corresponds to *it is a fact that* (Aoki 1986), or *it is that* in English (Kuno 1973a; Noda 1997). A translation of *no da* is commonly considered untranslatable or unnecessary when converting text from Japanese into English. For example (Yoshimoto 1988: 180; translated by Backus 1993: 121):

(1) いつか冬の日、等が言った。「弟がいるんだけどさ、柊っていうんだ。」

'One winter day Hitoshi had said, "I have a younger brother. His name is Hiiragi."'

In (1), a man is stating the fact that he has a younger brother and his name is Hiiragi. *N da* (んだ) appears twice in the original Japanese; however, the meaning is not expressed at all in the English translation of the text. Although *n da* is lost in translation, these utterances in Japanese without *n da* would indisputably sound unnatural. As a consequence, it can be assumed that *n da* in Japanese has a significant, definable meaning and relevance. The following example is also worthy of consideration and supports this idea. In this example, the speaker is attempting to motivate or encourage someone:[1]

(2) しっかりするんだ！
 'Pull yourself together!'

N da is used in giving a command to the listener, and without *n da*, the utterance in (2) would not convey the same meaning. As Wierzbicka (2003) and Wong (2004) state, the meaning of particles is crucial to the interaction between interlocutors. Particles 'express the speaker's attitude towards the addressee, or towards the situation spoken about, his assumptions, his intentions, his emotions' (Wierzbicka 2003: 341). The meaning of a particle can be so subtle that the intended proposition would not significantly differ, in a practical sense, with or without the particle being used. Notwithstanding this, however, mastering the meaning and function of particles significantly enhances a speaker's ability to communicate.[2] In fact, in the field of teaching Japanese, several error analyses have been carried out regarding *no da*, indicating that the expression is a difficult but crucial form to understand and master for learners of Japanese (McGloin 1984; Koganemaru 1990).

There are a considerable number of studies dedicated to clarifying the meaning of *no da* (e.g. Alfonso 1966; Kuno 1973a, 1973b; McGloin 1984; Koganemaru 1990; Tanomura 1990; Maynard 1992; Noda 1993, 1997; Najima 2007). The research here mentioned has helped to define the function of *no da*. However, from a semantic point of view, the definitions are inadequate. They do not comprehensively articulate the exact meanings of *no da*, as they equally apply to other particles. This study uses the Natural Semantic Metalanguage (NSM) approach (Wierzbicka 1986, 2003, 2006, 2010; Goddard and Wierzbicka 1994, 2002; Goddard 1998; Peeters 2006) to examine the semantics of *no da*, using examples found in newspaper articles, tweets, blogs and translated texts. As a full study of *no da* including its variants lies outside the scope of this study, this chapter will focus on the semantics of *no da*, which are considered to represent an 'explanation' (Alfonso 1966; Kuno 1973a, 1973b), or to indicate the

---

1 seiga.nicovideo.jp/seiga/im5830462 (2016).
2 It has been pointed out that the misuse of particles could be considered a reflection of the speaker's lack of communicative skills rather than as a grammatical mistake (Wong 2004; Saigo 2011).

speaker's mood (Koganemaru 1990; Noda 1993, 1997). The following section includes an examination of studies that have elaborated on the use of *no da* in a variety of contexts, shedding light on the above mentioned uses of *no da*. This is followed by a practical application of the NSM framework, which will clarify two distinct meanings expressed by *no da*.

2. Previous research on *no da*

2.1. Arguments in previous research

Among the previous analyses on the meanings of *no da*, Kuno (1973a, 1973b), Noda (1993, 1997) and Najima's studies (2007) are particularly noteworthy as they were detailed investigations that greatly helped in clarifying the functions and meanings of *no da*. First, Kuno (1973a, 1973b) states that *no da* is used to offer an 'explanation' for something the speaker has said or done, or for a state or condition (1973b: 144):

(3) 風邪を引きました。雨に濡れたんです。

 'I have caught a cold. I got wet in the rain.'

(4) 体重が１０ポンド減りました。病気なのです。

 'I have lost 10 pounds. I am sick.'

No da in (3) indicates that 'the explanation for catching a cold is that I got wet in the rain'. In (4) *no da* means that 'the explanation for losing 10 pounds is that I am sick'. In both examples, the explanation is also the cause or reason for the preceding situation, and the meaning is almost the same as 'I have caught a cold. It is because I got wet in the rain', or 'I have lost 10 pounds. It is because I am sick'. However, Kuno also states that there is another usage of *no da,* which cannot be paraphrased with 'it is because'. Kuno instead, uses the term 'evidence', as demonstrated in the following example (1973a: 226):

(5) 病気です。体重が１０ポンド減ったのです。

 'I am sick. The evidence for my being sick is that I have lost 10 pounds.'

(6) 僕は馬鹿です。いくら勉強してもダメなのです。

'I am a fool. <u>The evidence for</u> my being a fool is that I am no good however hard I may study.'

Kuno argues that 'losing 10 pounds' is presented as evidence for 'being sick'; and 'being no good however hard I may study' is given as evidence for 'being a fool'.

Next, Noda (1993, 1997) points out that *no da* should be classified into two categories, depending on the existence of a listener. In examples (7) and (8) below, *no da* indicates that one has just grasped or come to understand an aspect of a situation. In these examples the speakers are speaking inwardly; therefore, it does not matter if a listener is or is not present to hear or witness the utterances (Noda 1997: 67):

(7) 山田さんが来ないなあ。きっと用事があるんだ。

'Mr. Yamada has not come. <u>Surely he must have something to do</u>.'

(8) そうか、このスイッチを押すんだ。

'Oh, I see. <u>I just need to press this switch</u>.'

In (7), *no da* relates a preceding context and the resultant situation. Thus, *no da* in this context is called 'relating *no da*' (1997: 71). Here *no da* implies that the speaker has understood the situation that 'Mr Yamada has something to do', as the reason or explanation for the preceding context that 'Mr Yamada has not come'. In contrast, in example (8), *no da* is used but does not connect two separate situations or contexts. Thus, (8) is considered an example of 'unrelating *no da*' (1997: 71). Rather, *no da* here indicates that one has just grasped or come to understand that 'one should press the switch' as a newly perceived, stand-alone fact.

According to Noda, another function of *no da* is to present a listener, someone at whom or for whom the utterance is expressed, with information that the speaker had previously known but is now sharing so that the listener is also made aware. Therefore, when *no da* is used in this way, by definition, the existence of a listener becomes obligatory (1997: 67):

(9) 僕、明日は来ないよ。用事があるんだ。

'I will not come tomorrow. <u>I have something to do</u>.'

(10) このスイッチを押すんだ！
'Press this switch!'

No da in (9) directly associates one idea with another and therefore it is regarded as 'relating *no da*'. It expresses the speaker's wish to inform the listener of a situation Q (e.g. 'I have something to do'), of which the speaker presumes the listener was not aware. By providing information to the listener about a situation Q, *no da* facilitates the listener's understanding of the situation P (e.g. 'I will not come tomorrow'). In contrast, *no da* in (10) does not make a connection between two concepts and it is therefore an example of 'unrelating *no da*'. *No da* here indicates the speaker's desire that the listener perceives whatever it is that, in the speaker's mind, is an established fact. This usage can often be observed when someone is giving an order or confession and it adds emphasis to the phrase being spoken.

Finally, it is worth considering Najima's detailed analysis of *no da* from the perspective of Relevance Theory (Sperber and Wilson 1986). Najima (2007) says that the interpretation of *no da* depends primarily on the speaker's intention. Najima argues that *no da* has only one basic function: one intentionally and explicitly presents a listener with a proposition—a proposition interpreted from the listener's point of view. This point is illustrated well by the example below, where *no da* is a crucial component of the utterance, without which the sentence in Japanese would be nonsensical. Suppose that a student, who has arrived late for class, makes the following utterance to their teacher (Najima 2007: 61):

(11) a. 犬のポチがご飯を食べなかったんです。
'My dog Pochi didn't eat his food.'
b. ?犬のポチがご飯を食べませんでした。
'My dog Pochi didn't eat his food.'

The utterance (11b) without *no da* is, as a result, not appropriate, natural or sensical in the aforementioned context. This is because, 'being late for class' and 'the fact that the dog did not eat his food' are not concepts that have an obvious cause and effect relationship. By using *no da*, the utterance can imply the speaker's intention to convey a proposition to the listener and can therefore be interpreted as a reason for the situation; that is, being late. *No da,* in this context, indicates that the speaker is inferring that there is a connection between the proposition and the context wherein the utterance is being made. Najima argues that the various functions, such as 'explanation', 'recognition', 'order', or 'emphasis', are the derivatives of this basic function of *no da*.

2.2. Inadequacies of previous research

Previous attempts to provide definitions of *no da* offer some general explanations for its usage. However, these definitions are inaccurate as they do not clarify the subtle semantic differences between *no da* and other particles in Japanese (especially in situations where the translations into English would be the same).

First, *no da* is considered to possess the function of giving an 'explanation' (Kuno 1973a, 1973b). As argued by many (e.g. Tanomura 1990), the term 'explanation' is problematic, since there are various cases where it does not apply, such as when the speaker is giving an order or instruction. Second, Noda (1997) argues that a function of *no da* is to indicate that one has newly ascertained a concept or situation. However, this claim is also flawed, as this function is not only expressed by *no da,* but also communicated by other particles in Japanese. Consider the following utterance where someone has just experienced an earthquake:[3]

(12) うわ！地震だわ。。

'Oh my! An earthquake …'

It is well recognised (e.g. Hattori 1993; Washi 1997) that the sentence-final particle *wa* (わ) is often used with a falling intonation, by both male and female speakers, when the speaker has come to newly appreciate or perceive something. Likewise, the sentence-final particle *ka* (か) has a similar function (Moriyama 1992). See the following example, where a woman has just realised that Christmas is coming very soon:[4]

(13) 郵便局に行ったら、今回もまたオススメされた。サンタクロースからの手紙の申込書。ええ！もうクリスマスですか！？

'When I went to the post office, they gave me the application form for a letter from Santa Claus. Wow! <u>Is it Christmas already</u>!?'

---

3 ameblo.jp/mimizuku-cafe/entry-12252046129.html (2017).
4 ameblo.jp/moji-moji-tsushinkyoku/entry-12312648949.html (2017).

In this way, the sentence-final particle *ka* (か) is used when the speaker has come to appreciate something new.

According to Noda (1997), another function of *no da* is to present the listeners with information of which they were not previously aware. However, the sentence-final particle *yo* (よ) has a similar function, as demonstrated by the following example:[5]

(14) 明日香レンタサイクル 観光に便利ですよ。

'Asuka bicycle hiring service. <u>It's convenient for sightseeing</u>.'

In (14), a traveller who hired a bicycle for sightseeing is informing other tourists that it is convenient. *Yo* (よ) is used to inform readers who may be looking for information or a recommendation. In (14), *no da* could also be used. One may therefore ask what the difference would be between using *no da* and *yo* in this context. This point will be discussed in section 3.1.1. Finally, there is a point that contradicts the claim that the function of *no da* is to intentionally and explicitly present the listener/s with a proposition (Najima 2007). In the following example an office worker has just learned about business etiquette:[6]

(15) へ〜そうなんだ！社会人になって初めて知ったビジネスマナー

'<u>Oh, that's how it is</u>! Business etiquette which I have only come to know after starting work.'

In (15), the office worker is talking inwardly to herself. *No da,* in this context, is not being used by the speaker to convey information to someone else. The meaning of *no da* in this case does not include one's intention to convey information to the listener/s. Thus, it is not reasonable to claim that the main function of *no da* is to present the listener/s with a proposition intentionally and explicitly. In summary, the definitions provided by previous research are descriptively inconclusive and inaccurate. Although there have been detailed investigations into the functions of *no da*, the explanations can apply to the usage of sentence-final particles such as *wa*, *ka* and *yo*, and therefore ambiguity remains. In order to define the subtle

---

5   www.jalan.net/kankou/spt_29402ee4590068726/kuchikomi/0003875770/ (2016).
6   woman.mynavi.jp/article/150406-10/ (2018).

meanings of *no da*, this study utilises the NSM method and proposes two definitions for *no da*. The proposed explications apply exclusively to *no da* and explain the core usages of *no da*.[7]

3. Analysis of *no da*

3.1. Two meanings of *no da*

As Noda (1997) points out, there is considerable value in making a distinction between two uses of *no da*: where *no da* is directed to the listener/s (*no da$_1$*); and where *no da* can be used with or without a listener or listeners (*no da$_2$*). The distinction is an important component of the analysis, since the meaning of *no da* is slightly different depending on whether the existence of a listener is required. Therefore, two explications of *no da* will be proposed here using semantic primes.

3.1.1. *No da* as used when directed towards a listener: *no da$_1$*

First, *no da* is used when the speaker addresses a listener or listeners (*no da$_1$*). Its function is considered to be to provide an 'explanation' (e.g. Kuno 1973a, 1973b). In the following example, *no da$_1$* gives background information by connecting two contexts (Yoshimoto 1990: 203; translated by Sherif 1994: 177):

(16) 咲いないよ。旅行に行ったんだ。

'Saki's not here. <u>She went on a trip</u>.'

---

7   See below for examples of NSM explications defining the sentence-final particles *wa*, *ka* and *yo* (Asano 2004):

wa
a.   I know this
b.   I want to say this now
c.   I didn't know before that I would know this

ka
a.   you know this
b.   I can know the same now
c.   I didn't know this before you said it

yo
a.   I know this
b.   I want you to know this

By using *n da*, the speaker is stating that 'Saki went on a trip', which led to the present condition that 'she is not here now' (Noda 1997: 91–95). *N da* is necessary, as it links two separate pieces of information. In short, the speaker is attempting to help the listener understand the situation by adding supplementary information. Note that the existence of a listener or listeners is obligatory for this usage. Without the listener, the use of *no da*$_1$ would sound awkward. Maynard (1992) also suggests that *no da* functions as a 'marker of conscious mention'. It is therefore possible to deduce that *no da*$_1$ in this situation expresses the speaker's desire to convey information to the listener by linking two pieces of information, indicating 'I want to say something X about something Y to you; I say: it is like this; I can say it because I know it'.

Noda (1997: 71) classifies *no da*$_1$ into two categories: 'relating *no da*' and 'unrelating *no da*'. Example (16) is a typical example of 'relating *no da*'. However, the difference between 'relating *no da*' and 'unrelating *no da*' is simply whether or not there is a preceding context, and there does not seem to be any observable semantic difference between them. Consider the following example of *no da*$_1$, which is used when the speaker addresses a listener, but does not connect two contexts (unrelating *no da*$_1$). In (17), a young man is making a phone call to his friend at midnight (Yoshimoto 1988: 70; translated by Backus 1993: 45):

(17) 「あいつはちゃんと、戦って死んだんだよ。」雄一はいきなりそう言った。

'"<u>She died fighting</u>." Yuichi said without preamble.'

In (17), a young man is talking to his friend on the phone and bluntly states that his mother had died. By using *no da*$_1$, the speaker attempts to convey the information to the listener, indicating 'I want to say something X about something Y to you; I say: it is like this; I can say it because I know it'. *No da*$_1$ represents the speaker's wish to give a piece of information to the listener, and it does not matter whether there is any preceding context. The following example also demonstrates this definition. In (18), someone who previously studied in New Zealand is recommending the country as the ideal destination for study abroad to readers of the website:[8]

---

8   schoolwith.me/columns/31800 (2016).

(18) ニュージーランド、留学するなら断然オススメの国なんです！！

'New Zealand is highly recommended for study abroad!'

In (18) also, *no da*₁ indicates the speaker's desire to give readers information, which can be paraphrased as 'I want to say something X about something Y to you; I say: it is like this; I can say it because I know it'. There is no significant semantic difference between relating *no da*₁ and unrelating *no da*₁. Now recall that *no da*₁ is often used in relaying the speaker's decision or when giving an order to a listener. For instance:[9]

(19) 今度　東京へ行くんですが　東京駅から月島まで一番簡単なルート教えてもらえませんか

'<u>I am going to Tokyo</u>. Could anyone tell me the easiest way to get from Tokyo to Tsukishima station?'

(20) 頑張るんだよ！応援しているからね！

'<u>Do your best</u>! I am rooting for you!'

In (19), a man is seeking advice on how to get from Tokyo to Tsukishima station. Although this is not an established fact in the speaker's mind, the man declares his decision, indicating 'I can say it because I know it'. Similarly, in (20), someone is encouraging a sports team to do their best. Here *no da*₁ is indicating that, by presenting an action that the speaker believes the listener should perform, the speaker wants to urge the listener to do something.[10] That is, the speaker is declaring that she knows the action will be done in the future, stating that 'I can say it because I know it'. This is how *no da*₁ qualifies as a command.

Noda (1997) claims that the speaker gives the information that the listener has not previously recognised. It is true that the *no da*₁ may connote that the information is new to the listener. In fact, the use of *no da*₁ becomes somewhat inappropriate in situations where the listener shares the same information.[11] However, it is questionable whether *no da*₁ includes the

---

9 (19): oshiete.goo.ne.jp/qa/6211711.html (2010); (20): twitter.com/hashtag/%E9%A0%91%E5%BC%B5%E3%82%8B%E3%82%93%E3%81%A0%E3%82%88 (2018).
10 Note that *no da* used in giving an order is different from an imperative form (頑張れ！) which signifies 'I want you to do it'.
11 As commonly noted (e.g. Maynard 1992), the sentence-final particle *ne* is usually used to signal that the information is equally shared between the speaker and the listener.

speaker's assumption regarding the listener's stance or previous knowledge. Recall example (1) (Yoshimoto 1988: 180; translated by Backus 1993: 121):

(1) いつか冬の日、等が言った。「弟がいるんだけどさ、柊っていうんだ。」

'One winter day Hitoshi had said, "I have a younger brother. His name is Hiiragi."'

In (1), a man is stating the fact that he has a younger brother and his name is Hiiragi. So, does *n da* (*no da*₁) here signify that the speaker has made a presumption about the listener's previous knowledge, indicating 'I think: you don't know this', or 'I want you to know this'? Actually, it does not. Although the presence of a listener is obligatory, *no da*₁ does not infer or make any suggestion regarding the listener's epistemic stance. Using *no da*₁, Hitoshi is simply stating what he knows to be a fact, focusing on his own knowledge, while disregarding the listener's stance. This is the reason why the utterance can infer that the information is being presented to the listener as new information. On the other hand, the sentence-final particle *yo* implies the speaker's wish to convey new information to the listener, indicating 'I want you to know this'. As Martin (1975: 918) points out, '*yo* is often used in asserting a claim, advocating a course of action or emphasising a warning'. For instance, suppose that an adult sees a child playing on a busy street and cautions the child about the dangers of the traffic. *Yo* is thus the natural choice instead of *no da*₁ in (21):

(21) a. 危ないよ。
 '(Look out—) it's dangerous!'
 b. ?危ないんだ。
 'It's dangerous.'

Yo (よ) clearly functions as a warning about the traffic, while *n da* does not, because in (21a) the particle *yo* insinuates the speaker is giving new information to the listener. *Yo* is used to give the listener information perceived to be necessary, indicating 'I know this; I want you to know this' (Asano 2004). On the other hand, *no da*₁ merely conveys the information ('I want to say something X about something Y to you'), and therefore the utterance does not qualify as a warning. To further illustrate this point, recall example (14) where *yo* is used:

(14) 明日香レンタサイクル 観光に便利ですよ。

    'Asuka bicycle hiring service. It's convenient for sightseeing.'

In (14), a traveller who hired a bicycle for sightseeing is informing other tourists that it is convenient. *Yo* signifies the speaker's intention to tell the listener/s what the speaker knows, indicating 'I want you to know this'. This is the reason why the utterance is for the benefit of those who did not previously possess the information. It is possible to use *no da*$_1$ instead of *yo* in (14), however the particle will merely connote that a fact is being stated:

(14)' 明日香レンタサイクル 観光に便利なんです。

    'Asuka bicycle hiring service. It's convenient for sightseeing.'

By using *no da*$_1$, the writer is simply connecting two pieces of information; Asuka bicycle service exists and it is convenient for sightseeing. Therefore, if the writer had intended to deliberately infer she was conveying new information to the viewers, she may have combined *no da*$_1$ with *yo*, as in (14) below:

(14)" 明日香レンタサイクル 観光に便利なんですよ。

    'Asuka bicycle hiring service. It's convenient for sightseeing.'

N desu yo (んですよ or *n da yo* んだよ) is often used in daily conversation. The combination of *no da*$_1$ and *yo* signifies 'I want to say something X about something Y to you; I say: it is like this; I can say it because I know it; I want you to know it'.

Based on these observations, *no da*$_1$, which is directed to a listener, can be defined using semantic primes as follows:

[A] *no da*$_1$

a.   I want to say something X about something Y to you
b.   I say: it is like this
c.   I can say it because I know it

Component (a) expresses the speaker's desire to portray information to the listener/s. Components (b) and (c) mean that the speaker claims that the information is factual.

3.1.2. *No da* as used with or without a listener: *no da*$_2$

The second meaning of *no da*, referred to here as *no da*$_2$, can be used with or without the existence of a listener/s. In short, the existence of a listener is optional. There are two significant differences between *no da*$_1$ and *no da*$_2$. First unlike *no da*$_1$, semantically *no da*$_2$ does not include the component 'to you'. Second, as Noda (1997) suggests, *no da*$_2$ signifies that the speaker has perceived something or become aware of a situation of which they (the speaker) had not previously been aware. Therefore, *no da*$_2$ can express a speaker's new understanding or realisation. See the following:[12]

(22) 冷蔵庫に行こうとしたら、トイレに入ってた。疲れているんだなと思った瞬間。

'When aiming to go to the fridge I realised I'd entered the toilet room. That was the moment <u>I realised how tired I am</u>.'

In (22), *no da*$_2$ indicates that the writer, of this comment on twitter, has just realised she is tired, evidenced by the fact that she went to the toilet when intending to go to the fridge. Here, *no da*$_2$ connotes that the speaker has just recognised something new. This can be explicated as follows: 'I know something now; because of this, I want to say something about it now; I say: it is like this'.

Noda (1997) divides *no da*$_2$ into 'relating *no da*$_2$' and 'unrelating *no da*$_2$'. It is true that *no da*$_2$ can be used to connect two separate concepts (relating them to each other), as shown in (22). However, the distinction does not seem to affect the core meaning of *no da*$_2$. Consider the following example, where *no da*$_2$ is used without linking two separate concepts or situations:[13]

(23) 今日って祝日だったんだ。

'I just realised that today is a public holiday.'

In (23), the speaker just became conscious of the fact that it is a public holiday. *No da*$_2$ is often used when one suddenly registers something; that is, suddenly becomes conscious of it. Thus, in such situations it would not

---

12 twitter.com/hashtag/%E7%96%B2%E3%82%8C%E3%81%A6%E3%82%8B%E3%82%93%E3%81%AA%E3%81%AA%E3%81%A8%E6%80%9D%E3%81%A3%E3%81%9F%E7%9E%AC%E9%96%93 (2017).
13 ameblo.jp/lapi-slomaga/entry-12410469115.html (2018).

matter whether or not there is a related statement before the utterance. In example (23), *no da₂* is used to express surprise, indicating 'I know something now; because of this, I want to say something about it now; I say it is like this'.

Similarly, *no da₂* is also used when one recollects information that had been forgotten:[14]

(24) 結婚記念日って今日だったんだ。

'Today is our wedding anniversary.'

In (24), a woman has suddenly remembered that it is her wedding anniversary. *No da₂*, in this context, connotes that the speaker has recollected something in that moment but is not making a connection between the realisation and any other idea or concept. Here, *no da₂* does signify that one has just become aware, indicating 'I know something now; because of this, I want to say something about it now; I say: it is like this'. It is reasonable to surmise that linking two unrelated contexts is not a factor in the fundamental meaning of *no da₂*. Judging by the analysis discussed above, the meaning of *no da₂* can therefore be explicated as follows:

[B] *no da₂*

a. I know something now
b. because of this, I want to say something about it now
c. I say: it is like this

Components (a), (b) and (c) show one's desire to convey that one has just grasped a situation, of which one was not previously consciously aware.[15] As demonstrated in the explication, *no da₂* does not involve listeners 'to you', and therefore it can be used when speaking inwardly to oneself.

---

14 3594-chika.jugem.jp/?eid=462599 (2018).
15 One may argue that *no da₂* represents thoughts rather than tangible knowledge. However, this perspective lacks plausibility because *no da₂* is usually used when stating facts. In instances where the speaker shows understanding, *no da₂* can be combined with *omou* 'think': *no da to omou* (which would signify 'I say: I think like this; I can say it because I know something now').

4. Conclusion

This chapter examined the meanings of *no da* and proposed new definitions using semantic primes. This study has clarified the meaning of *no da* when the existence of a listener is obligatory, and when the existence of a listener is not a compulsory component. The difference between the two can subsequently be explained based on whether or not *no da* includes the components 'to you' and 'now':

[A] *no da*$_1$

a. I want to say something X about something Y to you
b. I say: it is like this
c. I can say it because I know it

[B] *no da*$_2$

a. I know something now
b. because of this, I want to say something about it now
c. I say: it is like this

One may argue that the difference between *no da*$_1$ and *no da*$_2$ is contextual. However, the use of *no da*$_1$ is not natural or sensical without a listener and in contrast, *no da*$_2$ can be used when speaking to oneself. Furthermore, the component 'now' does not apply to examples of utterances wherein *no da*$_1$ has been used. The proposed definitions are consistently applicable to a range of usages and in a range of contexts.

This research is an example of the applicability of the NSM approach to reveal the subtleties and nuances of Japanese particles that are often lost in translation. Wierzbicka states that particles 'are what distinguishes human language from the languages of robots' (1986: 519). Wierzbicka asserts that particles 'reflect the culture of a given speech community' better than other aspects of language (2003: 341). Her statements are directly applicable to the Japanese language, as it would be nearly impossible to hold a natural conversation without particles in Japanese (Saigo 2011). If *no da* is absent, the utterance would indicate that the speaker is simply presenting the information mechanically, with no emotional involvement.

Acknowledgements

I would like to express my gratitude to Zhengdao Ye and the anonymous reviewers for their comments. In addition, I would like to thank Elizabeth Miller for her assistance in editing the text.

References

Alfonso, Anthony (1966). *Japanese Language Patterns Volume 1*. Tokyo: Sophia University.

Aoki, Haruo (1986). Evidentials in Japanese. In Wallace. L. Chafe and Johanna Nichols (eds), *Evidentiality: The Linguistic Coding of Epistemology*. Norwood: Ablex Publishing Corporation, 223–38.

Asano, Yuko (2004). Semantic Analysis of Epistemic Modality in Japanese. Unpublished PhD dissertation, The Australian National University, Canberra.

Goddard, Cliff (1998). *Semantic Analysis: A Practical Introduction*. Oxford: Oxford University Press.

Goddard, Cliff and Anna Wierzbicka (eds) (1994). *Semantic and Lexical Universals: Theory and Empirical Findings*. Amsterdam: John Benjamins.

Goddard, Cliff and Anna Wierzbicka (eds) (2002). *Meaning and Universal Grammar: Theory and Empirical Findings* (2 vol.). Amsterdam: John Benjamins.

Hattori, Tadashi (1993). Hanseigo no shūjoshi wa ni tsuite [On the function of the general sentence-final particle *wa*]. *Dōshisha Joshi Daigaku Gakujutsu-Kenkyū Nenpō* [Annual Reports of Studies, Dōshisha Women's College of Liberal Arts] 43 (4): 1–15.

Koganemaru, Harumi (1990). Sakubun ni okeru 'no da' no goyōrei-bunseki [Error analysis of *no da* in compositions]. *Nihongo Kyōiku* [Journal of Japanese Language Teaching] 71: 182–96.

Kuno, Susumu (1973a). *The Structure of the Japanese Language*. Cambridge, MA: MIT Press.

Kuno, Susumu (1973b). *Nihon bunpō kenkyū* [Studies in Japanese Grammar]. Tokyo: Taishūkan Shoten.

Martin, Samuel E. (1975). *A Reference Grammar of Japanese*. New Haven and London: Yale University Press.

Maynard, K. Senko (1992). Cognitive and pragmatic messages of a syntactic choice: The case of the Japanese commentary predicate *n(o) da*. *Text* 12 (4): 563–613. doi.org/10.1515/text.1.1992.12.4.563.

McGloin, Naomi Hanaoka (1984). Danwa bunshō ni okeru 'no desu' no kinō [Function of *no desu* in discourse]. *Gengo* [*Language*] 13 (1): 254–60.

Moriyama, Takuro (1992). Gimon-gata-jōhō-juyō-bun o megutte [On question-type Information acceptance sentences]. *Osaka Daigaku Gobun* [*Gobun, University of Osaka*] 59: 35–44.

Najima, Yoshinao (2007). *No da no imi kinō* [*The Meaning and Function of No Da*]. Tokyo: Kuroshio Shuppan.

Noda, Harumi (1993). 'No da' to shūjoshi 'no' no kyōkai o megutte [The boundary between *no da* and the sentence-final particle *no*]. *Nihongogaku* [*Japanese Linguistics*] 12 (10): 43–50.

Noda, Harumi (1997). *'No (da)' no kinō* [*Functions of No Da*]. Tokyo: Kuroshio Shuppan.

Peeters, Bert (ed.) (2006). *Semantic Primes and Universal Grammar: Empirical Evidence from the Romance Languages*. Amsterdam: John Benjamins. doi.org/10.1075/slcs.81.

Saigo, Hideki (2011). *The Japanese Sentence-Final Particles in Talk-in-Interaction*. Amsterdam: John Benjamins.

Sperber, Dan and Deirdre Wilson (1986). *Relevance: Communication and Cognition*. Oxford: Blackwell.

Tanomura, Tadaharu (1990). *Gendai nihongo no bunpō I—'no da' no imi to yōhō* [*Modern Japanese Grammar I—The Use and Meaning of No Da*]. Osaka: Izumi Shoin.

Washi, Rumi (1997). Shūjoshi to hatsuwa-ruikei—tōkyō-go shūjoshi 'wa' to 'na' no danwa ni okeru hataraki [Sentence-final particles and utterance types—the function of *wa* and *na* in Tokyo dialect]. *Osaka Gaikokugo Daigaku, Nihongo Nihon Bunka Kenkyū* [*Studies in Japanese Language and Culture, Osaka University of Foreign Languages*] 7: 65–79.

Wierzbicka, Anna (1986). Introduction. Special issue, 'Particles'. *Journal of Pragmatics* 10: 519–34.

Wierzbicka, Anna (2003 [1991]). *Cross-Cultural Pragmatics: The Semantics of Human Interaction* (2nd edn). Berlin: Mouton de Gruyter.

Wierzbicka, Anna (2006). *English: Meaning and Culture*. New York: Oxford University Press.

Wierzbicka, Anna (2010). *Experience, Evidence, and Sense: The Hidden Cultural Legacy of English*. New York: Oxford University Press. doi.org/10.1093/acprof:oso/9780195368000.001.0001.

Wong, Jock (2004). The particles of Singapore English: A semantic and cultural interpretation. *Journal of Pragmatics* 36 (4): 739–93. doi.org/10.1016/s0378-2166(03)00070-5.

Yoshimoto, Banana (1988). *Kicchin*. Tokyo: Fukutake Shoten. [English translation: Yoshimoto, Banana (1993). *Kitchen*. Translated by Megan Backus. London: Faber and Faber.]

Yoshimoto, Banana (1990). *N.P.* Tokyo: Kadokawa Bunko. [English translation: Yoshimoto, Banana (1994). *N.P.* Translated by Ann Sherif. London: Faber and Faber.]

PART II

Meaning, life and culture:
Perspectives

13

Locating 'mind' (and 'soul') cross-culturally

Frances Morphy and Howard Morphy

1. Introduction

In 2016 Anna Wierzbicka extended her 1989 analysis of words akin to 'mind' and 'soul' in European languages to include discussion of Australian Aboriginal languages, and offered a critique of our treatment of Yolngu conceptualisations of mind and, particularly, soul.[1] She was responding to a seminar paper that we gave at The Australian National University (H. Morphy and F. Morphy 2013). That paper was never published, and this chapter presents us with a welcome opportunity to continue the conversation.

We are in agreement with Wierzbicka that mind is not a 'thing', but a culturally embedded, language-specific way of conceptualising mental states and processes. From our perspective—and this is where we begin to differ from her—the semantic overlap that she discerns between

---

1 The Yolngu, numbering between 6,000 and 7,000 and speaking closely related languages known collectively as Yolngu Matha (*matha* is 'tongue, language'), are the people of north-east Arnhem Land in the Top End of Australia's Northern Territory. They were colonised relatively late, with arrival of the first Methodist Overseas Mission at Milingimbi in the western part of the Yolngu region in the mid-1920s. They live at the hub settlements of Milingimbi, Galiwin'ku and Yirrkala, all former mission settlements; at Gapuwiyak, originally established as an outstation from Galiwin'ku; and at numerous small 'homeland' settlements on their clan estates established during a period of decentralisation in the early 1970s. The vast majority of Yolngu speak one or more varieties of Yolngu Matha as their first languages.

meanings of 'mind-like' words in different languages suggests a family resemblance; there are both similarities and differences between them, and it is productive to set up a potential cross-cultural metacategory—let us call it MIND to differentiate it from the English word—for use in cross-cultural analysis. Wierzbicka describes 'words that are cognate and may share some semantic components but differ significantly in their over-all meaning and cultural significance' as 'false friends' (2016: 451). Our approach is to consider them instead as particular instantiations of a polythetic metacategory that can fruitfully be compared with one another to reveal both similarity and difference. Wierzbicka herself comes close to taking such an approach in saying that, with reference to the articulation between mind-like and soul-like concepts, 'one could even arrange European languages on a scale, with Russian and English at opposite ends and with French and German between' (1989: 41).

In this chapter, our major focus is on what Wierzbicka refers to as the 'modern Anglo concept of mind' and our comparator is an analogous Yolngu concept which is not realised as a single lexeme.[2] But while Yolngu do not have a word that can be directly translated as 'mind', they do have words for 'know', 'think', and so on, and they locate those processes in the top and front parts of the head.[3] Our analysis will reveal an overlap between Anglo and Yolngu conceptualisations that suggest they share much in common, as well as differing, and that they can be encompassed within a cross-cultural metacategory MIND.

2. Body, mind and soul

In post-Enlightenment Anglo (and arguably European) thought, mind is seen as part of a person. 'I think therefore I am' gives mind a central place in the existence of the individual. But can it be located in the body, and if so, where? In recent European theory of mind, and in everyday understanding, mind is associated with the brain and located in the head. It is possibly, then, also a part of the body.

---

2   And here we cannot resist pointing out that if semantic primes are not universally realised as lexemes (Wierzbicka 2016: 448), the same might be true for concepts.
3   The Yolngu Matha online dictionary does in fact give 'mind' as one of the meanings of *buku* ('front of the head and upper face'). For reasons that will become clear, we think this is an oversimplification and does not represent its core meaning. Rather it is a locational referent for a lexically unmarked concept (Available at: yolngudictionary.cdu.edu.au) (*Yolngu Matha Dictionary* 2015).

The body can be viewed as an assemblage of anatomical parts and physiological processes. Parts can be seen, MRI-ed, revealed through dissection and felt. Processes can be observed or theorised—limbs move, breath is inhaled and exhaled from the lungs, the heart beats. Body parts are theorised in Western systems of knowledge on an underlying premise that they are connected to the functioning of the organism. Theory has made the function of the heart easy to understand; the heart pumps blood around the body. The heart stops beating, life ends. Of course, this is only part of the story but it is one most people understand—the heart is a pump. The relationship between mind, as our capacity to think and know, and the brain seems more complex—very much under exploration, poorly understood.

In this chapter, we look at the location of thought and knowledge in Yolngu conceptions of the body. We do so to see if the Yolngu can be said to have a concept of mind that links the process of thinking and the transmission of knowledge to the body in a way that has anything in common with the Anglo concept of mind or English-speakers' use of the word mind. Since Yolngu do not have a word that easily translates as mind,[4] what we posit is, in analytical terms, a cross-cultural metacategory MIND, that is shared but differently elaborated in each case, and differently articulated with other metacategories. To signpost the direction of our thinking, two factors will prove salient. Yolngu associate mental processes and mental states with the front and top of the head; and in talking about their world to English-speakers, in English, they frequently use 'mind'.[5]

Wierzbicka's 1989 definition of 'modern English' mind (as cited in Wierzbicka 2016: 458) is as follows:

> one of the two parts of a person
> one cannot see it
> because of this part, a person can think and know

---

4 Wierzbicka (1989) argues that that is the case with most languages, including other European languages.

5 Yolngu, like many other people who inhabit a contact zone, have an explicit theory of biculturalism—of different but coexisting systems of knowledge and ways of thinking about and acting in the world—that individuals can productively apply both when acting and communicating among themselves and in articulating their position to outsiders. We would argue that those systems of thought are only relatively autonomous because people are always in a context of cross-cultural communication. Analytically minded Yolngu are able to recognise the relative autonomy of their 'own' concepts and also think about areas of overlap just as the culturally Anglo person/anthropologist can.

This explication has an implied association with the discourse on mind–body dualism—the other part of the person, in this case, is the body.[6] A later version of the explication (Wierzbicka 2016: 458) spells this out more explicitly, while simultaneously removing the (absolute) dualism:

> *someone's mind (2014)*
> something
> this something is part of this someone
> people can't see this something
> this something is not part of this someone's body
> when this someone is thinking about something
> something happens in this part
> because this someone has this part, it is like this:
> this someone can think many things about many things
> this someone can know many things about many things

The Yolngu concepts that will emerge from our discussion differ in some ways from the one captured in these explications.[7] But a family resemblance will remain. A full comparative analysis would involve an exploration of the history of the mind in English-language usage and conceptual thinking from prehistory to the present. That history would reveal many changes over time as both understanding of thinking and understanding of the brain have evolved. The history of Yolngu concepts is even harder to research, but there is no reason to think it has not also been a history of change.

Wierzbicka acknowledges that the sense of the English word mind has changed over time—and this change has crystallised in the post-Enlightenment era. An earlier concept of mind that was associated with the soul and goodness has become 'morally neutral'.

> The older mind had spiritual and psychological dimensions, but it did not have the predominantly intellectual orientation which it has now, with thinking and knowing dominating over any other nonbodily aspects of a person's inner life. (Wierzbicka 1989: 49)

---

6   Lillard's summary of research into Euro-American (EA) folk conceptions of mind is compatible with Wierzbicka's in that the 'major functions of the mind in the EA view … are housing mental states and generating mental processes' (Lillard 1998:10).
7   A topic that we will not cover here for reasons of space is the problem of 'part' in Yolngu Matha and many other Australian languages (for a summary see Nash 2014: 84).

Lillard similarly concludes that 'the EA [Euro-American] mind has become a unitary concept, has lost much of its spiritual connotation, and has come to have an especially strong (although not exclusively) rational connotation' (1998: 13). We will argue, perhaps surprisingly, that Yolngu ideas about mind are similarly focused on thinking and knowing—but that they are also entangled with *birrimbirr* (the Yolngu Matha instantiation of SOUL) in the more general Yolngu theory of personhood, in ways that are very unlike the English mind's relationship to the English soul today. We suggest that cross-culturally and cross-temporally it may be meaningful to talk about a MIND–SOUL complex in which the two metacategories are deeply entangled—indeed, that much of Western theological discourse has concerned their entanglement or separation.

The emergence of the 'rationalist' concept of mind is clearly linked to the history of religion in Western Europe, including Britain. In the Yolngu case we will be investigating:

- whether we can identify Yolngu concepts that are analogous to Anglo 'mind' and 'soul' and whether they are entangled in similar or in different ways. We are not looking for precisely bounded equivalences and indeed will argue that the role given to 'goodness' in Wierzbicka's explication of soul does not have a central place in the Yolngu case. The absence of goodness in the Yolngu soul and the entanglement of soul in the Yolngu mind makes for an interesting contrast to both Wierzbicka's 'modern' Anglo mind and to its antecedents in Anglo thought.
- whether Yolngu conceptions of the corporeal location of thinking and knowing share a family resemblance with what Wierzbicka refers to as the 'modern' concept of mind. We will argue that, in the Yolngu case, the location of the capacity for thinking and knowing, as in the case with much Christian belief and theology (see Bieniak 2010), is seen as partly of the body and partly external to it.

3. Cross-cultural metacategories

The development of cross-cultural metacategories has explicitly or implicitly been integral to the history of anthropology. The challenge to evolutionary paradigms of progress—for example, from 'magic' though 'religion' to 'science'—has involved a continuing discourse over religion.[8]

---

8   For a relevant discussion with reference to the categories of art and aesthetics see H. Morphy (2007).

Anthropology has searched, through definitional discourse, for a cross-cultural definition of religion, which has, over time, encompassed greater diversity and, we might argue, framed a cross-cultural metacategory RELIGION. There have been similar discourses over art, the person, politics and so on. Such discourse has often involved shifting the meaning of English words away from a temporally based Anglo- or Euro-centric focus and working towards comparators from the vocabulary of other languages. Words such as habitus are redefined, and words such as taboo are appropriated to become part of the categorical vocabulary of anthropology. The vocabulary of anthropology may have an Anglo bias, but it is not the language of the everyday. While similar changes occur in the conceptual vocabularies of other disciplines, the creation of agreed epistemologies for communicating across languages and cultures, the openness to revision and to encompassing different ways of thinking, are integral to anthropology's methodology.

The categorising exercise is very different from the process of word for word translation. There are differences and similarities that cannot be grasped at the level of the word. The absence of a word that can be easily translated into a direct equivalent in another language, in particular English, is not evidence that the culture's conceptual and cognitive systems do not overlap with those of English-speakers in a particular domain—that there is not a family resemblance that can be grasped though categorical analysis. Anthropology does not reduce one ontological system or world view to another. Rather, it sets them in conversation, just as communication and contact across borders and boundaries has done throughout human history more generally. Indeed, many of the shifts in meaning of English words have been in response to a widening of understanding of difference in the world.

Those changes are also reflected relatively independently in the ways in which people in postcolonial contexts map their own concepts onto English vocabulary and use English terms in explaining the particularities of their own society. Yolngu, for example, use words such as 'law', 'parliament', 'embassy', to indicate to outsiders the family resemblance between their own political and religious institutions and those of their colonisers—in effect, they create analogies based on their intuitions about overlapping categories, as a means of cultural translation (see F. Morphy 2009).

Such processes are not neutral—in Australia, neither the Yolngu world nor the Anglo world remains the same. However, we would argue that their deployment allows the relative autonomy of cultural systems to be maintained, while changing (see F. Morphy and H. Morphy 2013, 2017). By explaining aspects of their own way of life to non-Yolngu through creating a shared vocabulary, Yolngu hope to facilitate understanding and mutual adjustment. Yolngu can explain aspects of their own sociocultural world to non-Yolngu by using emergent categories that they sense are helpful in conveying aspects of their world to non–Yolngu speakers: 'We have our own laws just as you do, let us work them together.' We use the word emergent deliberately, in that the adoption of English words in their particular Yolngu sense is a process that takes place over time according to the relevance of the concept and the development of cross-cultural ('two-way' in Yolngu parlance) learning. Yolngu use of the word 'mind' is indeed more recent than their incorporation of the word 'law'. It overlaps with but is not subsumed by the contemporary Anglo use of the term. And, interestingly, their sense of 'mind' points towards earlier senses that the word had in English usage.

By arguing for a cross-cultural metacategory of MIND or ART or RELIGION, we are not arguing that people across cultures or times share the same concept as is conveyed by the English words; rather, we are enabling a discourse over difference in an area of family resemblance. We make explicit that the comparative analytic statement of the kind 'Yolngu locate mind in the head whereas Illongot locate mind in the heart' makes sense, while requiring deep explication.[9]

People who take on board Wierzbicka's explication of the modern Anglo mind respond by using terms such as 'counterparts' and 'approximations', in effect creating an implicit cross-cultural metacategory. Toril Swan, for example, writes that 'English uses the term mind very differently than its *seeming counterparts* are used in the other Germanic languages (as well as in French, Polish, etc.)' (2009: 462, emphasis added; see also Low 2001: 11).

---

9 The sentence references Rosaldo's rich ethnography of the Illongot (1980, 1984) and Lillard's (1998: 12ff) discussion.

MEANING, LIFE AND CULTURE

4. On the Yolngu head be it

Yolngu Matha (Yolngu language) has a rich vocabulary of verbs for things that we, as English-speakers, think of as things the mind does (*marrngi* 'know', *guyangirri* 'think', *guyanga* 'think of/about, remember', *moma* 'forget', *dharangan* 'understand', and so on), and a rich vocabulary of metaphorical forms (both verbal and nominal) for what we, as English-speakers, might describe as 'states of mind', 'characteristics of mind' and 'processes of mind'. These take the form of compounds in which the first word is *buku* or one of its near-synonyms *dämbu*, *mulkurr* and *liya*. All refer to the top and front parts of the head: *mulkurr* is the top part of the head in a general sense, including the temples, *liya* is more precisely the crown, and the close synonyms *buku* and *dämbu* refer to the forehead, and to the upper part of the face more generally. A final term, *wanda*, which does not participate in these kinds of compounds, references the skull. But, as we shall see, it has a role to play as a container.

A word that does not figure at all in such compounds is *mamburungburung* 'brain', or any of its synonyms. Thus Yolngu do not suffer from 'brain fade', and there are no 'brainy' or 'brainless' Yolngu. Mental operations and states are located, it seems at first sight, rather precisely on the top and frontal regions of the head rather than inside it.

This is not the place for a detailed analysis of Yolngu Matha semantics; rather, our aim is to give a flavour of how the vocabulary of mental states and processes works, with a few examples.[10]

4.1. 'Minimal pairs'

The addition of the privative suffix ('lacking/without') to the words for parts of the head yields the following idioms that might be seen as analogous to the minimal pairs of phonology:

mulkurr-miriw	'muddleheaded'
liya-miriw	'stupid'
dämbu-miriw	'senseless, idiotic' (*buku-miriw* is not attested)

There seems to be a cline of severity here that we will return to below.

---

10   For a general grammar of a Yolngu Matha language, see F. Morphy (1983).

4.2. *Djambatj* idioms

The adjective *djambatj* on its own summarises the distributed qualities of a good hunter: alertness, quick reactions, sharp eyesight, skill with weapons. When this occurs as the second part of a compound we get:

mulkurr-djambatj or liya-djambatj   'intelligent, clever, able'

focusing thus on the mental aspects of being *djambatj* (cf. *mel-djambatj* 'keen of eye, marksman', which focuses on aspects related to vision).

Idioms that predominantly involve one part of the head help us to refine the aspects of mental states or attributes that each seems to reference.

4.3. *Mulkurr* idioms

Mulkurr-gulku, literally 'top of head-many', translates as 'indecisive' (a property of a group or individual) as opposed to *mulkurr-wanggany* 'top-of-head-one', 'of one mind' (property of a group). Compounds with *mulkurr* seem to reference general states of mind that in their negative versions are related to lack of clear purpose (recall *mulkurr-miriw*). *Mulkurr-wanggany* contrasts with *wanda-wanggany* (skull-one), which refers to people who are spiritually linked to the same ancestral being—a point we will return to later.

4.4. *Liya* idioms

Recall that *liya-miriw* 'lacking the crown of the head' was glossed roughly as 'stupid'. There are two further *liya* compounds that allow us to refine the import of *liya* constructions further: *liya-yalnggi*, literally 'crown-weak': 'impressionable, lacking in understanding, intellectually challenged'; and *liya-gulinybuma*, literally 'crown-criticise': 'reject (someone else's) ideas, disagree'. It would seem that *liya* is associated with the notion of 'idea' in a rather intellectual, perhaps almost context-free sense. To be without *liya* is to be lacking in ideas and therefore 'stupid', to be weak in the *liya* is to be too susceptible to the ideas of others.

4.5. *Buku* idioms

Buku metaphors are all about mind in its social context. We will leave aside the many compounds that reference particular kinds of speech acts and mental operations, and focus on those that seem to reveal aspects of the Yolngu conceptualisation of the nature of mind in context.

First, *buku* can be used as an alternative to *dämbu* or *liya* in combination with the adjective *dhumuk*, which means 'closed, blocked, impenetrable or blunt', in the expression *buku-dhumuk* 'forgetful, stupid'. And it contrasts with *liya* in one telling 'minimal pair': whereas *liya-marrtji*, '*liya*-go', means (roughly) 'feel homesick' (or more precisely 'go to the idea (of home)'), *buku-marrtji* means 'to go with one thing or purpose in mind'.[11] Purpose or intent is the metaphorical core of *buku* compounds, so we will start there, with the following examples (all of which are *buku*-specific):

buku-däl	(+ strong, hard, steady, firm, difficult) 'persistent, hard-headed, can't be deflected'
buku-duwat	(+ upwards) 'persistent, insistent'
buku-duwatthun	(+ go up) ' persist, keep trying'
buku-dhuwalyun	(+ say 'this') 'nag, keep asking for something'

As in all but the last of these examples it can be an admirable (or perhaps neutral) quality. But this quality can veer into obsession, for example:

buku-dhayka	(+ woman) 'woman-crazy'
buku-guya	(+ fish) 'always thinking about fish' (to hunt and eat)
buku-dharpa	(+ tree) 'always climbing trees' (e.g. of a child)
buku-mari	(+ trouble) 'troublemaker who wants to keep feuds alive'
buku-dhirr'yun	(+ disturb) 'incite by reminding of past injury'
buku-man.guma	(+ collect) 'accumulate possessions, hoard'

And so on. This is a very productive construction.

---

11 We will see later in the analysis why the idea 'of home' in particular is invoked by *liya*.

A second theme might be characterised as 'thinking together', for example:

buku-mala	(+ set, group) 'crowd, flock, school of fish' (i.e. a group that acts as if it has one mind/purpose)
buku-lukthun/luŋ'thun	(+ come together, collect) 'come together, gather together for one purpose' (used e.g. for a memorial ceremony)

also:

buku-lupthun(marama)	(+ wash, bathe) 'perform cleansing ceremony following an illness or death and burial (also baptise)'

and:

buku-manapan	(+ join, link, mix, combine) 'gather together'

as opposed to:

buku-gänang'-thirri	(+ alone, separate, distinct + become) 'wander off alone'

and:

buku-lalawukthun	(+ peel off, shed (snakeskin)) 'refuse to become involved in quarrels between one's kin'

Whereas the first of these suggests 'group mind' in some instinctive sense, and the last two suggest the rejection of group mind, the three metaphors in the middle are the core of this theme. And they link to the first theme through the idea of purpose. This leads us to a third metaphorical theme concerning what happens to the mind at death. For example:

buku-mulka	(+ hold, touch, reach, feel, arrive at) 'end of a person's life'
buku-y-moma	(+ INSTR case-forget) 'leave others behind at death' (as opposed to *buku-moma* (+ forget) which means to 'forget, lose or misunderstand')

and lastly:

buku-bu̱t(marama)   (+ fly away (cause))

which is the descriptive name for a ceremony in which a person's bones are brought back to their own country, to their final resting place.

In this series of metaphors the aspect of mind that is the socialised (sometimes group), purposeful mind is conceptualised as being realised to its full potential in an individual as they near death, and then it leaves the living behind on death. Freed from the weight of embodiment, it returns with the *birrimbirr* (soul) to the ancestral realm.

5. The Yolngu mind as process

In surveying the sets of metaphors associated with regions of the head our focus has been on the individual, human mind. But understanding of the semantics requires us to step outside the head and place knowledge and understanding in a wider cultural context. The Yolngu mind is both inside and outside the body. In talking about knowledge Yolngu give priority to the Wangarr—the ancestral determinants of the present (H. Morphy 1991).[12] Narratives of the journeys of Wangarr beings centre on them as a source both of knowledge and of human existence. Wangarr beings think their way through the world and externalise their thoughts and actions in the form of objects and features of the landscape. These objects are referred to as *ma̱dayin rom* which can be translated into English as ancestral/sacred law/knowledge.

Yolngu society is based on a division into two moieties, Dhuwa and Yirritja, and Wangarr beings belong to one or other moiety. Wangarr beings travelled cross-country transforming features of the landscape and creating sacred objects, songs and dances that commemorate their actions. Certain places in each clan's estate are centres of their spirituality. These are referred to as *djalkiri* (footprints or foundations) of the clans that succeeded the Wangarr in place. They are locations of spiritual power, restricted of access and adjacent to sites of major ceremonial performance.

---

12   Wangarr is very similar to concepts such as Tjukurrpa and Altyerre (in desert languages) that are translated into English as Dreamtime or Dreaming. However, the Yolngu point out that Wangarr is not related either etymologically or semantically to the notion of 'dream' in Yolngu Matha, and do not like the connotation of 'unreality' that dream conveys. Both they and we avoid using the term.

Each place is associated with a *mangutji*—a sacred well (literally 'eye') that is the source of and emanates Wangarr power (*märr*).[13] The songs, paintings, dances, objects and sacred names that provide the substance of ceremonies re-enacting the founding ancestral events are manifestations of the Wangarr and are centred on the *mangutji*.

There are many different narratives centred on this knowledge. For example, the Dhuwa moiety ancestors known as the Djan'kawu sisters carried their knowledge with them in their sacred dilly bags and also gave birth to the ancestors of clan members beside the *mangutji*.[14]

Clan members are deeply connected to their Wangarr; in Munn's phrase they are consubstantial with the Wangarr domain (1970: 141). Life is initiated by a conception spirit emanating from one of the clan's Wangarr entering the mother's womb. The person's relationship with the Wangarr dimension is cumulative. Experience of the Wangarr dimension through participating in ceremonies and living in the ancestrally created landscape adds to a person's spiritual identity—knowledge and spirituality are intertwined. On a person's death both *buku* and *birrimbirr* leave the body and become reincorporated within the ancestral domain. The return takes place over a number of years and is associated with a ritual process that transforms the individual's identity into an ancestral one. There is a process of remembering and forgetting that moves the focus of ritual from the sense of loss that follows death to the positive presence of the Wangarr domain and the strength of the foundation (*djalkiri*) that continues across the generations.

We can see now how this complex process of the entanglement of knowledge with the spiritual dimension of Wangarr is reflected in the ways in which the metaphors associated with different parts of the head are structured. *Liya* is the locus of the initial connection between Wangarr mind and knowledge and the individual mind. When an infant's fontanelle is still open and pulsating, they may be described as *liya gapu-mirr* or *liya mänha-mirri* '*liya*-water-having'. This water, occurring in a depression in the skull (*wanda*), is thought to be water from the place where the baby's conception spirit originated, that is the *manutji* where the Wangarr knowledge that flows in the waters beneath the land wells to the surface through the *wanda* of the Wangarr ancestor (see also Blake

---

13   For a general discussion of Yolngu religion see H. Morphy (1991).
14   For more on the Djan'kawu sisters see Berndt (1952) and West (2008).

2012: 54 and Stubbs 2012: 39). The human *wanda* is consubstantial with the ancestral *wanda*. Head wounds sustained as a result of conflict are considered much more serious than other wounds, because, as someone explained to us, 'you are also hitting the *wanda* of the Wangarr when you hit that person's head'.

Yolngu metaphors and their referents are framed by Yolngu ontology and enacted through ritual processes. It is significant that following a person's death, in the past, the *liya* (of the skull) was painted with *likan'puy miny'tji*—the painting that represents the *mangutji* associated with the person's clan, the *wanda* from which the conception spirit came.[15]

Liya, then, is the locus of the connection between the Wangarr and human mind. In the infant's fontanelle it is just a potential, as yet not fully realised. *Buku*, on the other hand, is the locus of the socialised, individuated, often purposefully developed mind. It is telling that a number of the *buku* metaphors centre on the process of the mind leaving the body and with the process of forgetting the identity of the individual person. Consciousness goes, and so too, gradually, does the memory of the individual person among those who remain behind.

6. Yolngu mind and the use of English 'mind'

In May 2017 we attended an event at the Australian Consulate in Los Angeles. Yinimala Gumana, a young Yolngu ceremonial leader and artist raised and educated at his clan's homeland settlement of Gängän, had just concluded the event with a powerful rendition of a sacred song (*manikay*). The audience was moved, and so clearly was he. He said to us: 'The *rirrakay* ('sound, voice') was here in Los Angeles but my mind was in Gängän.'

Gängän is not just a homeland. It is a *djalkiri* place associated with Barama, a major Yirritja moiety Wangarr. Yinimala sees his *rirrakay* as an aspect of the emplaced Wangarr knowledge. The *rirrakay* carries *manikay*, an expression of that emplaced knowledge. When Yolngu use the English word 'mind' they 'have in mind' the Wangarr body of knowledge and

---

15   In the past Yolngu performed several ceremonies to effect the transfer of the dead person's *birrimbirr* back to the Wangarr realm. The body was first buried or exposed on a raised platform. When the flesh was gone the bones were retrieved and cleaned, then carried by relatives for several years before final disposal. It was at this point that the skull was painted with *likan'puy miny'tji*.

sources of power invoked in songs, performances and the sacra—the dilly bags and sacred objects. Yinimala's mind is, in a profound sense, always in Gäṉgäṉ, wherever he happens to be himself. Like all clan members he is *rirrakay dhawalwu* 'the voice of the land'—this is the duty of Yolngu towards the Wangarr.

Song equally connects the singer emotionally to other people associated with the place in a way readily accessible to European audiences. Referring to a performance of the Yolngu *manikay*-jazz improvisation 'Crossing Roper Bar' Daniel Wilfred explained:

> In my mind when I sing I cry. You listen to me when I changed my voice, I am crying ... Always singing this song, always thinking about my brothers, sisters, all my nieces, nephews. When I sing this song, it's always in my mind, making me cry. Maybe you listen and hear my voice changing: that's me crying. (cited in Curkpatrick 2019: 90)

In our experience the association between thought and painting is routine in Yolngu accounts of the production of paintings. In the 1970s, Narritjin Maymuru stressed to Howard Morphy the connection of the *marwat* (brush made from human hair) with the head and the connection of hair to the fontanelle as a source of knowledge. He 'thought with' or 'through' his *marwat* (*marwat-thu*). Narritjin's daughter Galuma, 20 years after his death, sat before a plain sheet of bark and said that she had to 'think hard' before she began a painting.

About 15 years on, in April 2011, the late Joe Gumbula, speaking to an audience in Geneva in the lecture theatre where Ferdinand de Saussure taught, stated unequivocally, 'we paint in our mind'. And, more recently, Gunybi Ganambarr is quoted in a catalogue essay for the Annandale Gallery in Sydney in 2012: 'I try and bring the Yolngu law into reality. That is what is in my mind. To show what is already there.' His use of the word 'law' translates Yolngu Matha *maḏayin rom*, which refers to the body of knowledge that people inherit from the Wangarr who pre-exist them in their country, and pass to one another in life.

It is interesting that in these statements in English, Narritjin and Galuma speak in terms of thinking, whereas both Joe and Gunybi, speaking more recently, use the word 'mind', as did Yinimala in 2017. We did not hear Yolngu routinely use the word 'mind' until about 15 years ago. This suggests a process. In earlier Yolngu English, people used English words that map more closely onto Yolngu translation equivalents when they spoke in the 'art frame'. They spoke in terms of 'thinking' (*guyanginyara*) and 'meaning' (*mayali*). But more recently they have adopted 'mind', and their use of it makes perfect sense to their English-speaking audiences.

It is important to note at this stage in our argument that Yolngu would not substitute the English word 'spirit' or 'soul' in any of these uses of the word 'mind'. Yolngu do also use 'spirit' when speaking in English. For example, we were once sitting in clearing in the bush working on the Blue Mud Bay native title claim, drinking tea. A hint of breeze touched our skin. Ralwurranydji said: 'That was the spirit of X', referring to a woman who had died at Yirrkala the previous week. We must have looked sceptical, though we did not say anything. Ralwurranydji elaborated: 'Couldn't you smell it? She was a drinker, you could smell the alcohol in the air.' We postulate that when using English, Yolngu are likely to choose 'spirit' when they are referring to external manifestations or expressions of the ineffable part of a person (the 'soul' *birrimbirr*, or in this case the 'ghost' *mokuy*), and 'mind' when they are referencing the Wangarr generator of knowledge located in a *mangutji*.

Since Wangarr are also the source of animating conception spirits, there is no absolute boundary division in the Yolngu conceptual universe between mind and spirit. But when speaking in English, Yolngu distinguish the two—they do not conflate them.

7. Yolngu mind and English mind as instances of MIND

Our analysis so far suggests that Yolngu have a complex set of concepts about the location, nature and processes of thinking and knowledge that can be placed in the same cross-cultural metacategory MIND as the set of lexemes from different European languages that Wierzbicka places in her comparative frame. We will now suggest areas in which the Yolngu mind differs from and overlaps with the Anglo concept. While we cannot complete a full comparison of all of the languages encompassed in Wierzbicka's argument, it will be apparent that in some cases the Yolngu concept shows more in common with non-Anglo concepts and in other cases less. We will centre on the dialogue that Wierzbicka sets up between spirit and mind in European ontology and theory and suggest ways in which, as cross-cultural metacategories, MIND and SOUL relate to Yolngu concepts.

If we accept Lillard's conclusion that the EA (Euro-American) concept of mind can be summarised as the 'housing [of] mental states and generating mental processes' (1998: 10), it provides evidence for an overlap between EA and Yolngu conceptual schema. Although Yolngu do not have a word for mind, we have seen that they do have an elaborate vocabulary associated with the head that makes it the locus for knowledge and processes of thought. When Yolngu use the word mind in English, they are referencing cognitive capacities that enable them to act in the world, as it is construed by them. It is significant that Yolngu do not associate mind with a specific organ such as the brain, but with (external) parts of the head. There is also an association between the water pulsing under the newborn's fontanelle and the waters of the clan *mangutji*, the source of Wangarr knowledge, with the entire skull (*wanda*) of the infant conceptualised as consubstantial with the skull of the Wangarr being.

The metaphors associated with parts of the head and the Yolngu use of mind when speaking English suggest areas of overlap with the Anglo concept of mind. However, Yolngu have a theory of the origin and acquisition of knowledge that posits Wangarr origin and an initial entry point into the human body through the fontanelle. The Wangarr source of *madayin rom* and also of *birrimbirr* means that mind and soul are more closely linked than in modern Anglo usage. However, the fact that Yolngu, when speaking in English, distinguish between mind and spirit, and do not conflate them, suggests that Yolngu knowledge-in-mind is substantively different from the individual's *birrimbirr*. There are no compounds or phrases that link *birrimbirr* to knowledge, in marked contrast to *buku* and *liya*. The distinction captures different processual aspects of Yolngu ontology, which involve the separation and reintegration of the sentient human body and the sentient ancestral body.

A person's accumulation of knowledge is conceived of as a transferral—a passage of knowledge from the Wangarr domain into the human domain where it is for a while manifest in the actions of human beings in the world. Yolngu praxis centres on processes that ensure that the knowledge that pre-exists the individual is acquired incrementally through their lifespan. And it grows through exposure to Wangarr knowledge in the form of sacred objects, paintings and songs. These externalised manifestations of the Wangarr beings are the substance of ceremonies—the major context in which people develop the expertise to live under *maḏayin rom*.

The person who becomes knowledgeable also becomes closer to the Wangarr. Yolngu mortuary rituals can be seen as a process for returning both the mind and the *birrimbirr* to the Wangarr dimension—a process through which they ultimately forget or leave behind the person of which they were for a time a part. The *birrimbirr* does not carry with it the characteristics of the living person beyond the Wangarr essence itself. The *birrimbirr* does not come back to haunt the living or express anger towards relatives left behind. That role is left to the *mokuy* (ghost). The *buku* metaphors discussed above suggest that the accumulated mind—knowledge purposefully acquired during life—also becomes disembodied and returns to the Wangarr domain at death (H. Morphy 1997).

8. *Birrimbirr*, soul and SOUL

In Yolngu Matha, as we have seen, something very similar to Anglo 'soul' is lexicalised as *birrimbirr*; in our terms both belong to the cross-cultural metacategory SOUL. But *birrimbirr* seems not to share certain essential characteristics with the 'European' concept of soul. Wierzbicka writes of the soul that:

> We can begin with what seems reasonably clear: the word soul can only refer to persons, not to things; it doesn't normally refer to a person as a whole, but only to one part of person; the part to which it refers is not a part of the body; and it cannot be seen. (1989: 43)

Wierzbicka writes further of the soul's 'moral character, that is, to its links with the idea of "good."' (ibid: 43) and 'to a person's capacity to be good' (ibid: 44).

In 2016, Wierzbicka sets out her explication of *birrimbirr* (2016: 472). Here we want to respond briefly to some details of that explication in the light of the discussion in this chapter.

Our first and perhaps most substantive comment is that *birrimbirr* does not carry the connotation of 'goodness' that Wierzbicka's detailed explication of both soul and *birrimbirr* entails. Whereas Wierzbicka notes people can be referred to as 'good souls' in English, in Yolngu we have never heard an equivalent reference to *birrimbirr*. In the Yolngu case people have a responsibility to follow the ancestral law (*maḏayin rom*), and to do so is to be *dhunupa* 'straight'. But morality is not involved; *maḏayin rom* is not inherently good or bad, it just *is*. If anything it is inherently dangerous, and transgression potentially invites catastrophic consequences.

We also think that Yolngu would find the absence of any reference to the Wangarr very strange, and unsatisfactory. Wierzbicka's explication attempts to capture the, perhaps unique, emplaced nature of Yolngu (and by extension other Indigenous Australian) belief systems in the following way in part [D] of her explication (2016: 44):

> [D] [WHAT PEOPLE CAN KNOW ABOUT THIS PART OF SOMEONE]
> people can know that it is like this:
>> some time before this someone was born/this part of someone was part of a place
>> where some people lived before
>> after this someone dies, this part of this someone can be part of the same place

The Yolngu *birrimbirr* is the ancestral identity of the person, something that is consubstantial with and a manifestation of the Wangarr. *Djalkiri* places, and the *mangutji* from whence the *birrimbirr* comes, is not just *any* place where 'people have lived before'—that would be true of many places in Yolngu country. It is a special kind of place imbued with Wangarr *märr*, and any explication would have to account for that in some way if it were to ring true to a Yolngu person. *Birrimbirr* is an expression of an ancestral (Wangarr) process that connects a spiritual domain with the lived and living world through a transformational process that includes spirit conception, the growth of the *birrimbirr* in the living person and the return of the spiritual dimension on death. The human cycle is one manifestation of the Wangarr that can also appear in material form and in the forces of nature—winds, tides, lightning, trees. But certain places are focal pints of the spiritual essence (*märr*) of particular Wangarr. The body (perhaps particularly the skull) is the container of both the MIND and SOUL, which are arguably different aspects of the same *märr*, but conceptually distinct. The *birrimbirr* is the SOUL of the individual, consubstantial with the Wangarr, and *maḏayin rom* is the socially shared and transmitted product of the associated Wangarr MIND.

Both *birrimbirr* and *maḏayin rom* differ in another significant way from the Anglo concepts as analysed by Wierzbicka, in that arguably both are intimately associated with material objects. In Wierzbicka's (1989) explication of both mind and soul 'one cannot see it'. In the Yolngu case, paintings, sacred objects, elements of the environment, properties of the ecosystem are all in different ways externalised manifestations of the Wangarr. The connection with the person is emphasised in metaphor and ritual. On a person's death in the past the skull—the *wanḏa*—was painted with a design that comes from the *mangutji*—the source of Wangarr knowledge. A sand sculpture in a mortuary ritual originates from the same place, and the grave has the name of the *mangutji* sung into it. In each of these cases, from a Yolngu perspective, the material objects and the images and sounds they convey carry the agency of the Wangarr. As Daniel Wilfred puts it when referring to sound and rhythm of the clap sticks in song: 'The clapping sticks, they lead everything. You think they are just sticks but they have a song. Everything comes out of the clapping sticks' (Curkpatrick 2019: 24–25).

In our terms, and as Wierzbicka's detailed (2016) analysis of soul-like concepts including *birrimbirr* shows very clearly, the cross-cultural metacategory SOUL needs to encompass the diversity of *birrimbirr* and other soul-like concepts. If it is to encompass the English soul and *birrimbirr* it needs to encompass a polythetic set of attributes, and 'goodness' is not a necessary attribute of every instantiation of the category.

9. Conclusion: The nature of cross-cultural metacategories

In her comparative analyses of soul and mind across a wide set of languages, Wierzbicka uses the difficulty of translation of key terms from one language to another as part of the evidence for cultural difference. Yet at the same time what she chooses to translate is evidence of an intuition that the concepts compared have something in common. Translation from one language to another involves a double articulation, which is why it can seldom be 'literal'. On either side of the divide is an enculturated language, such that the categorisations salient to each culture are encoded in its language in complex ways. The task of anthropology is in part to focus on the commonalities that exist within trajectories and discourses of difference that intuitively make comparison possible. A long view of contact between human societies suggests a history of interaction across boundaries, histories of translation and comparison, in which categories are continually emerging and boundaries shifting. Methodologically, we believe it is important to make explicit the categories of comparison and frame them in such a way that they encompass difference and change while reflecting intuitions of similitude. Often communication reveals difference at moments of profound misunderstanding, when people find themselves using apparently the same word with very different senses (see e.g. F. Morphy 2007). A cross-cultural metacategory should facilitate discourse by holding certain things in common while anticipating difference. Not all concepts are going to be amenable to a cross-cultural analysis; the widening of a metacategory may result in a change to its definition, but too much widening may make it meaningless.

Implicit in our cross-cultural metacategory MIND is that the family resemblance which defines the polythetic set of culturally embedded concepts centres on the cognitive capacities of thinking and knowing. The boundaries around a concept may be fuzzy and may change through time; the modern Anglo mind is continuous with early and more morally or spiritually entangled variants, but all are instances of MIND. Discourses that occur across boundaries of language, culture, religion and discipline may also cause boundary shifts. The category MIND can thus be compared across cultures and/or time on the basis of factors such as its location, or its relationship to SOUL, or the degree to which it can be distributed among persons, supernatural forces and things. Our comparison of Wierzbicka's 'modern Anglo' mind with 'our' Yolngu concept is highly productive in that it sets both within their own local cultural trajectories. The Yolngu mind complex, though historically distant from the concepts belonging to the set of European languages and cultures that Wierzbicka compares, is not categorically discontinuous. Which is to say, the concepts are not incommensurable, but may be meaningfully compared because they are members of the polythetic MIND.

References

Berndt, Ronald M. (1952). *Djanggawul: An Aboriginal Religious Cult of North-Eastern Arnhem Land*. London: Routledge and Keegan Paul. doi.org/10.4324/ 9781315017587.

Bieniak, Magdalena (2010). *The Soul-Body Problem at Paris, ca. 1200–250*. Leuven: Leuven University Press.

Blake, Andrew (2012). Of hollowness and substance. In Anne Marie Brody (ed.), *Larrakitj: The Kerry Stokes Collection*. Perth: Australian Capital Equity, 51–57.

Curkpatrick, Samuel (2019). *Singing Bones —Ancestral Creativity and Collaboration*. Sydney: Sydney University Press.

Lillard, Angeline (1998). Ethnopsychologies: Cultural variations in theories of mind. *Psychological Bulletin* 123 (1): 3–32. doi.org/10.1037/0033-2909.123.1.3.

Low, Soon-Ai (2001). Approaches to Old English vocabulary for 'mind'. *Studia Neophilologica* 73: 11–22. doi.org/10.1080/713789805.

Morphy, Frances (1983). Djapu, a Yolngu dialect. In Robert M.W. Dixon and Barry J. Blake (eds), *Handbook of Australian Languages* (vol. 3). Amsterdam: John Benjamins, 1–188.

Morphy, Frances (2007). The language of governance in a cross-cultural context: What can and can't be translated. *Ngiya: Talk the Law* 1: 93–102.

Morphy, Frances (2009). Enacting sovereignty in a colonized space: The Yolngu of Blue Mud Bay meet the native title process. In Derek Fay and Deborah James (eds), *The Rights and Wrongs of Land Restitution: 'Restoring What Was Ours'*. Abingdon: Routledge-Cavendish, 99–122. doi.org/10.4324/9780203895498.

Morphy, Frances and Morphy, Howard (2013). Anthropological theory and government policy in Australia's Northern Territory: The hegemony of the 'mainstream'. *American Anthropologist* 115 (2): 174–87. doi.org/10.1111/aman.12002.

Morphy, Frances and Morphy, Howard (2017). Relative autonomy, sociocultural trajectories and the emergence of something new. *Insight* 10 (9): 1–11. Available at: www.dur.ac.uk/ias/insights/volume10/article9/.

Morphy, Howard (1991). *Ancestral Connections: Art and an Aboriginal System of Knowledge*. Chicago: University of Chicago Press.

Morphy, Howard (1997). Death, exchange and the reproduction of Yolngu society. In Francesca Merlan, John Morton and Alan Rumsey (eds), *Scholar and Sceptic: Australian Aboriginal Studies in Honour of L.R. Hiatt*. Canberra: Aboriginal Studies Press, 123–50.

Morphy, Howard (2007). *Becoming Art: Exploring Cross-Cultural Categories*. Oxford: Berg.

Morphy, Howard and Morphy, Frances (2013). We think through our *marwat* (paintbrush)—conceptualising mind cross-culturally. Paper presented at the Anthropology Seminar Series, The Australian National University, Canberra, 29 May 2013.

Munn, Nancy (1970). The transformations of subjects into objects in Walbiri and Pitjantjatjara myth. In Ronald Berndt (ed.), *Australian Aboriginal Anthropology*. Nedlands: University of Western Australia Press, 141–63.

Nash, David (2014). Alternating generations again again: A response to Wierzbicka on generation moieties. In Lauren Gawne and Jill Vaughan (eds), *Selected Papers from the 44th Conference of the Australian Linguistic Society (2013)*. Melbourne: University of Melbourne, 77–101. Available at: hdl.handle.net/11343/40958.

Rosaldo, Michelle (1980). *Knowledge and Passion: Illongot Notions of Self and Social Life*. Cambridge: Cambridge University Press.

Rosaldo, Michelle (1984). Toward an anthropology of self and feeling. In Richard A. Shweder and Robert A. LeVine (eds), *Culture Theory: Essays on Mind, Self, and Emotion*. Cambridge: Cambridge University Press, 137–57.

Stubbs, Will (2012). Water, kinship and the cycle of life. In Anne Marie Brody (ed.), *Larrakitj: The Kerry Stokes Collection*. Perth: Australian Capital Equity, 39–42.

Swan, Toril (2009). Metaphors of body and mind in the history of English. *English Studies* 90 (4): 460–75. doi.org/10.1080/00138380902796292.

West, Margaret (ed.) (2008). *Yalangbara: The Art of the Djang'kawu*. Darwin: Charles Darwin University Press.

Wierzbicka, Anna (1989). Soul and mind: Linguistic evidence for ethnopsychology and cultural history. *American Anthropologist* 91 (1): 41–58. doi.org/10.1525/aa.1989.91.1.02a00030.

Wierzbicka, Anna (2016). Two levels of verbal communication, universal and culture-specific. In Andrea Rocci and Louis de Saussure (eds), *Verbal Communication*. Berlin: De Gruyter Mouton, 447–81. doi.org/10.1515/9783110255478-024.

Yolngu Matha Dictionary (2015). Published online by Charles Darwin University. Available at: yolngudictionary.cdu.edu.au.

14

Teknocentric kin terms in Australian languages

Harold Koch

1. Introduction and overview[1]

Australian Indigenous languages have long been known to have systems of kinship terminology that are shared across much of the continent and differ widely from those of well-known European languages.[2] For instance, they typically distinguish between elder and younger siblings, between a mother's and a father's child, between maternal and paternal 'uncles' and 'aunts' (MB vs FB and MZ vs FZ: see note 3 for clarification of abbreviations), between maternal and paternal grandparents (MM vs FM, MF vs FF).[3] On the other hand, some relations are not distinguished terminologically; for example a parent and their same-sex siblings (so F = FB and M = MZ); or siblings and parallel cousins (so FBS or MZS = B, etc.). Another characteristic of Australian kin terminologies is

---

1   It is with pleasure that I present this study in honour of my long-term colleague Anna Wierzbicka. I thank the editors and two reviewers for useful feedback.
2   Further discussion and exemplification of Australian kinship systems can be found in standard works on Australian anthropology, e.g. Elkin (1964) and Berndt and Berndt (1977).
3   For the description of kin relations I here use a version of the kind of abbreviations widely used in kinship studies; all kin relations are reduced to strings of these symbols. Kinship symbols used, following the practice of the AustKin project (see below), are: B = brother, C = child, D = daughter, e = elder, f = female's, F = father, H = husband, m = male's, M = mother, S = son, Sb = sibling, Sp = spouse, W = wife, y = younger, Z = sister. For a critique of this style of definition from the Natural Semantic Metalanguage (NSM) perspective see Wierzbicka (2013). See section 5.3 and note 24 for further comments relating the findings of this study to the NSM approach.

the reciprocal use of some terms.[4] The same term may denote a grandparent and grandchild: for example, FF = mSC, MM = fDC.[5] Likewise for affinal (in-law) terms: for example, WM = fDH, HB = mBW. Abbreviations for the main kin relations discussed here are set out in Table 14.1, arranged according C(onsanguineal) vs A(ffinal) relation and to generation (G) relative to the propositus.

Table 14.1. Kin abbreviations.

C G+2	**MM** mother's mother	**MF** mother's father	**FM** father's mother	**FF** father's father
C G−2	**fDC** female's daughter's child	**mDC** male's daughter's child	**fSC** female's son's child	**mSC** male's son's child
C G+1	**M** mother	**MB** mother's brother	**F** father	**FZ** father's sister
C G−1	**fC** female's child	**mZC** male's sister's child	**fBC** female's brother's child	**mC** male's child
C G0	**Z** sister	**MBC** mother's brother's child	**FZC** father's sister's child	**B** brother
A G0	**W** wife	**WSb** wife's sibling	**H** husband	**HSb** husband's sibling
A G+1	**WM** wife's mother	**WF** wife's father	**HM** husband's mother	**HF** husband's father
A G−1	**fDH** female's daughter's husband	**mDH** male's daughter's husband	**fSW** female's son's wife	**mSW** male's son's wife

Source: Author's summary.

Two further characteristics of Australian kin terminology should be mentioned. First, kin terms may be extended beyond the immediate family. There are widely recurrent principles by which kin terms that describe genealogically close relations are extended to more distantly related relatives; these have been explored especially by Scheffler (1978). Second, affinal (in-law) relatives typically belong to particular classes of consanguineal relatives (depending on the marriage rules applying in each society); for example, a spouse is often a kind of cross-cousin (i.e. child of FZ or MB), WM a kind of FZ, WF a kind of MB, etc. There may

---

4   *Cousin* is a reciprocal term in English.
5   In some cases, the terms are not identical but are derivationally related: either the senior or the junior term may involve an affix added to the shared stem.

be alternative ways of referring to someone depending on whether they are (potentially) related by marriage in addition to their (classificatory) consanguineal relation.

The subject of this chapter is a further kind of terminological relation that has come to light in connection with the compilation of kinship terminology for the AustKin project (see Dousset et al. 2010; www.austkin.net). A puzzling systematic formal relation exists between terms denoting one's spouse's parents (and reciprocally one's child's spouse) and grandkin terms. This was first noted in Dharumba data (from around Ulladulla, NSW), then observed in Ngarrindjeri from South Australia, and finally found, with more of an explanation, in languages of Cape York Peninsula. The respective data sets are discussed in sections 2, 3 and 4 respectively. This unavoidably involves some discussion of the morphology of the forms. Then in section 5, I provide an explanation in terms of pragmatics, the altercentric usage of consanguineal terms to denote affinal relatives, for which I propose the term 'teknocentric', and explore some of the implications of these results for semantic description, semantic change and the etymological study of Australian kin terms.

2. Dharumba

The Dharumba kinship data were collected as one of the 'schedules' prepared at the behest of Fison and Howitt.[6] The Fison and Howitt schedule F.15, said to be from the Búrgural tribe in the Jervis Bay district, was recorded on 28 September 1874 by Andrew Mackenzie of Moelly, Wandandian (near Ulladulla).[7] This is the same Andrew Mackenzie whose documentation of Dharumba (and Dharrawal) is analysed in Besold's (2012) study of historic documentation of the Yuin languages of the New South Wales South Coast. Mackenzie's kinship data are presented as a family tree with 22 named individuals, followed by 10 lists detailing the terms used by 10 of the individuals for the other persons on the table. This yields 44 kin terms, many of which have several senses. The use of the genealogical method of elicitation has yielded not only a greater

---

6   For Fison and Howitt's kinship studies, including the 'schedules' they solicited, see McConvell and Gardner (2016).
7   The manuscript containing the Australian kinship schedules is in the Lorimer Fison papers within the Tippett Collection in the library of St Marks National Theological Centre, Canberra.

number of kin terms,[8] but increased precision in the reference of terms usually translated as 'grandmother', 'father-in-law', etc. Mackenzie's data, however, also present us with a puzzle; the terms reveal an intriguing set of formal relations between grandkin terms and parent/child-in-law terms, which cries out for an explanation.

Table 14.2 sets out the relevant terms, with spellings normalised and rendered into a standard orthography.[9] Note that the grandkin terms occur both with and without a final syllable *-nga*, whose significance is not known. For *pawu(nga)* the longer form occurs only with reference to the junior member (i.e. fDC). For *kupa(nga)*, both the longer and the shorter forms occur in both senior and junior reference. For *ka(ty)panga* (forms with and without *ty* occur) there is no short form. *Ngapupu*, which appears to be a partially reduplicated form of *ngapu*, occurs only as a senior term, and the corresponding junior term involves a suffix *-ara*, with elision of the stem-final *u*.

Table 14.2. Dharumba terms for grandkin and affines.

Grandkin gloss	Grandkin form	Affine form	Affine gloss
MM/fDC	*pawu(nga)*	*pawiri*	WM/fDH
FF/mSC	*kupa(nga)*	*kupanthiri*	HF/mSW
FM/fSC	*ka(ty)panga*	*ka(ty)panthiri*	HM/fSW
MF/mDC	*ngapupu/ngapara*	*ngaparama*	WF/mDH

Source: Adapted from Mackenzie (1874) [see note 7, this chapter].

Affinal terms for parent-in-law and child-in-law appear to be based on the stem of the grandkin terms—although there are irregularities. Thus *pawiri* involves *-iri* added to *pawu*, with vowel elision. Two other terms, *ka(ty)panthiri* and *kupanthiri*, appear to contain a suffix *-nthiri*. The fourth affinal term, *ngaparama*, appears to suffix *-ma* to the junior grandkin term *ngapara*. Although the suffixes differ somewhat, there is a clear pattern of deriving terms for parent/child-in-law from terms for grandparent/grandchild. Specifically, the term for spouse's parent (and its reciprocal) is consistently related to that for the parent of one's own parent of the same sex as the spouse: compare WM with MM, WF with MF, HM with FM, and HF with FF. Why should this be so? Is a similar pattern found elsewhere?

---

8   The traditional stories he recorded yielded only eight kin terms.
9   It is impossible to know whether *r* represents a tap/trill or an approximant; the two rhotics typically contrast in Australian languages.

3. Lower Murray languages

3.1. Ngarrindjeri

The language spoken—up to the mid-twentieth century—by the Narrinyeri, now called Ngarrindjeri, around the mouth of the Murray River in South Australia was described in the nineteenth century by Meyer (1843) and Taplin (1873), reproduced in an appendix to Taplin (1879). I am here concerned with a subset of the kinship terms. Some of the kin terms are extraordinarily difficult to understand, due to a plethora of prefixes, suffixes and suppletive stems. The grandkin terms to be discussed, however, lack some of these complexities. The meanings are assured due to the fact that Taplin used Fison and Howitt's genealogical method of eliciting kin terms; that is, terms were gathered with reference to the relationship of individuals known to the informant. The same kin terms are also given in later works by Radcliffe-Brown (1918) and Berndt and Berndt (1993).

The grandkin terms are presented in Table 14.3. The citation forms for the grandparental terms include the marker of first person propositus, *-ano(wi)* 'my'. The base of the lexeme is given in the next column. (For MF the form marked for third person propositus, *ngatyapali* 'his/her MF' is also known.) The junior reciprocal terms, female's daughter's child (fDCh) etc., are provided in column four. They are derived from the senior terms by means of a suffix *-ari* (or probably just *-ar*, since *-i* is singular marker). Forms without the final *-i* are found in Radcliffe-Brown (1918) and Berndt and Berndt (1993). These later sources also indicate junior forms without the suffix (i.e. *pak*, *muth* and *ngaty*), which suggests that the junior relatives need not be overtly marked with the junior suffix; that is, the unsuffixed forms have as their referent either a grandparent or the reciprocal grandchild. As in many Australian kin systems, these grandparental terms extend to the siblings of each grandparent; thus *pakanowi* MM can also refer to MMZ or MMB. The same extension applies to junior terms; thus *pakari* can refer not only to daughter's child of a woman but also to the daughter's children of the sister or brother of the grandmother. The same suffix *-ar(i)* that indicates the junior member of a grandkin relation is found with some other kin terms as well. Thus the reciprocal of FZ *ngampano(wi)*, which has a short form *(m)pano*, is *(nga)mpari*, and the reciprocal of FeB *ngopano(wi)* is *ngopari*.

Table 14.3. Grandkin terms.

Gloss	Senior	Base	Junior	Gloss
MM	*pakanowi*	*pak-*	*pakari*	fDC
FM	*muthanowi*	*muth-*	*muthari*	fSC
MF	*ngatyanowi*	*ngaty-*	*ngatyari*	mDC
FF	*mayanowi*	*may-*	*mayarari*[10]	mSC

Source: Adapted from Taplin (1879).

Now the base of two of the grandkin terms of Table 14.3, plus the FeB term *ngop-*, are found additionally in affinal (in-law) terms, shown in Table 14.4. Two separate suffixes are involved, *-antun* and *-eli*. Meyer gives three forms in *-antun*. The only similar form in the other sources is Berndt and Berndt's *mayanti*, which looks like Meyer's *mayantun* without the *-un* but with the addition of the singular suffix *-i*. I therefore analyse the derivational suffix as just *-ant*. *Mayareli*, which contains the same extra *-ar-* as *mayarari* in Table 14.3, is attested from Taplin, Radcliffe-Brown and Berndt and Berndt. *Ngopeli* is attested from Radcliffe-Brown and Berndt and Berndt, who omit the final *-i*. Hence I treat the relevant suffix as just *-el*. The function of the suffixes *-ant* and *-el* is not otherwise known. For our purposes, it is sufficient to treat the affinal terms as derivatives of the grandkin terms.

Table 14.4. Grandkin and affine terms.

Gloss	Base	Junior *-ar*	In-law *-ant*	In-law *-el*	Gloss
FF/mSC	*may(ar)-*	*mayarari*	*mayant-*	*mayarel-*	HF/mSW
FM/fSC	*muth-*	*muthari*	*muthant-*	–	[HM]/fSW
FeB/myBC	*ngop-*	*ngopari*	*ngopant-*	*ngopel-*	HB/mBW

Source: Adapted from Meyer (1843), Taplin (1879), Radcliffe-Brown (1918) and Berndt and Berndt (1993).

As for the meanings of the in-law terms, *mayant-* and *mayarel-* appear to be synonyms, although there is the possibility that they belong to different dialects. Berndt and Berndt give two senses for *mayant-*: the senior affine 'husband's father (or his brother)' as well as its junior reciprocal 'man's (or brother's) son's wife'. Meyer gives only the junior term 'daughter-in-law', which I interpret as mSW on the basis of the other

---

10 The form *mayarari* presents a difficulty in that it appears to have an extra syllable. But the expected *mayar* is attested in the forms spelled *maiyar* (Radcliffe-Brown 1918) and *maiar* and *mair* (Berndt and Berndt 1993).

sources; the expected senior sense would be HF. For *mayarel* both Taplin and Radcliffe-Brown give both the senior and junior senses, while Berndt and Berndt give only the junior meaning 'man's or brother's son's wife'. For *muthantun* as well Meyer gives only the junior sense—in fact the same undifferentiated gloss 'daughter-in-law' as for *mayantun*; I assume that it must be interpreted as fSW, and probably had the reciprocal senior sense HM as well. For *ngop(ano)* vs *ngopar-*, the senses of FeB and its reciprocal yBC are assured from Taplin, Radcliffe-Brown and Berndt and Berndt, while Meyer gives simply 'uncle' vs 'nephew'. For *ngopel* both Radcliffe-Brown and Berndt and Berndt provide glosses HB and its reciprocal mBW; for *ngopantun* Meyer gives an undifferentiated gloss 'sister-in-law', which I infer is mBW. The semantic relations between the grandkin terms and their affinal derivatives can be seen by comparing the first and last columns of Table 14.4.

3.2. Ngangaruku

Radcliffe-Brown (1918: 243–46) discusses the kinship terms of what he called the 'Ngangaruku tribe', located further up the Murray River from the Ngarrindjeri, between Mannum and Herman's Landing, whose social organisation he found to be similar in the main to that of the Ngarrindjeri.[11] Here two of the grandkin terms, *paka* and *ngatta* (in his spelling), appear to be cognate with Ngarrindjeri *pak-* and *ngaty-* respectively. The grandkin terms extend to the grandparent's siblings of both sexes (e.g. MF = MFB/Z) and the same applies to their reciprocal use (mDC = BDC). Radcliffe-Brown notes as an interesting feature the application of grandkin terms to refer to in-laws of the parents' and children's generations, discussing how this works only from a woman's viewpoint (his informant being a woman named Jenny).

> A woman applies the term *noidla* to her father's mother and to the brothers and sisters of the latter, and also to her husband's mother and to her son's wife. Her son's children are also *noidla* … A woman calls her husband's father *metsa*, that being the term she also applies to a father's father. She also calls the wife of her *napnap* (brother's son) *metsa*[12] … (Radcliffe-Brown 1918: 245)

---

11   The language is apparently in a dialect relation with Ngayawung.
12   This is the reciprocal of HFZ; hence we can assume that the usage of these terms extends to siblings. It would be expected that *metsa* would also be used by HF for mSW.

The resultant senses are set out in Table 14.5.

Table 14.5. Ngangaruku grandkin and affinal terms.

Grandkin gloss	Form	Affinal gloss
MM(Sb), f/ZDC[13]	paka	–
MF(Sb), m/BDC	ngatta	–
FM(Sb), f/ZSC	noidla	HM/fSW
FF(Sb), m/BSC	metsa	HF, [HFZ]/[mSW], fBSW

Source: Adapted from Radcliffe-Brown (1918).

3.3. Summary of Lower Murray kin terms

In both Ngangaruku and Ngarrindjeri it is only paternal grandkin terms that have been documented as being related to affinal terms, unlike Dharumba, where all four grandkin terms are involved. Note that in Ngangaruku the senior and junior terms are identical, whereas in the other languages one is usually a derivative of the other. In Ngarrindjeri the relationship between terms for parent's sibling and sibling-in-law seems to be a related phenomenon and deserving of a similar explanation. In an attempt at explanation Taplin (1879: 164) correctly noted that a man's daughter-in-law, *mayarel-* mSW, is the mother of mSC, the man's paternal grandchild, *may-*, reciprocal of FF. His further explanation in terms of patrilineal clan succession is too vague, as is Radcliffe-Brown's suggestion that the terminological equivalence represent traces of an earlier matrimoiety system.

4. Cape York Peninsula

4.1. Wik Mungkan

In some of the languages of western Cape York Peninsula we find similar phenomena. The anthropologist Donald Thomson did a considerable amount of work on kinship in the area in the 1930s. He described some patterns in the use of kin terms that provide the clue to our puzzle; I begin with his data on 'Wik Moŋkan' (Thomson 1972: 15–20). In Wik Mungkan, a Middle Paman language, only three grandparental terms are used: the same

---

13 To be read as: mother's mother or her siblings, and reciprocally the daughter's child of a female ego or of one's sister.

terms is used for cross-grandparents MF and FM. The junior reciprocals involve a suffix *-i(n)yaŋ*; see Table 14.6. A more recent linguistic source, the Wik Mungkan dictionary (Kilham et al. 1986), gives the grandkin terms shown in Table 14.7. For the older generation the basic stems are compounded with *wuut* 'old man' and *wayyow* 'old woman'. Otherwise a suffix *-(an)chin* may occur, including when used for address.

Table 14.6. Wik Mungkan grandkin terms.

Senior gloss	Senior form	Junior form	Junior gloss
FF	*pola*	*poliyaŋ*	mSC
MM	*kema*	*keminyaŋ*	fDC
MF	*ŋatja*	*ŋatjiyaŋ*	mDC
FM	*ŋatja*	*ŋatjiyaŋ*	fSC

Source: Thomson (1972).

Table 14.7. Wik Mungkan grandkin terms.

Senior gloss	Senior form	Senior address	Junior form	Junior gloss
FF(B)	*puulwuut*	*puulanchin*	*puuliyang*	mSC
MM(Z)	*kemwayyow*[14]	*kemchin*	*kemiyang*	fDC
MF(B)	*ngechwuut*[15]	*ngechanchin*	*ngechiyaŋ*	mDC
FM(Z)	*ngechwayyow*		*ngechiyaŋ*	fSC

Source: Kilham et al. (1986).

In this society, the normal marriage is between classificatory cross-cousins. A woman's preferred husband is the son of a (classificatory) *kala* MyB. A (prospective or actual) HF is distinguished as *kal amp* 'poison uncle' vs *kal kampan*, a 'friend-uncle, not for marrying'. But an alternative form of address—making reference to her children—is available.

> A woman's *kala* [MyB] may be her father-in-law. If he is she calls him *puk pol'nyin*, child's *pola* [FF], and he calls her *poliyaŋ* [reciprocal of FF] *kallin*, *poliyaŋ* carrier, or mother of (my) *poliyaŋ*. Similarly a woman calls her HM (her *pinya* [FeB]) *puk ŋat'njin*, child's *ŋatja waiyo* [FMZ] and she calls her SW *kat'n ŋatjiyaŋ*, mother of (my) *ŋatjiyaŋ*. (Thomson 1972: 20)[16]

---

14 A short form *kem* is also used.
15 An alternative form is *athiy*.
16 On the previous page Thomson says that the woman and her father-in-law 'may address' one another in these terms. So it seems there are two possibilities for addressing in-laws, both using consanguineal terms: one based on marriage practices and the other based on relations to a child.

This naming practice—using the child as a reference point—is confirmed, at least for parents-in-law, from the Wik Mungkan dictionary.[17] The kin term *puulanchin* (FF) is:

> used especially in phrases such as *puk ngath puulanchin*[18] 'my children's grandfather on father's side' and as such is the term used by a woman to address her father-in-law. (Kilham et al. 1986: 195)

A similar statement is made concerning *ngechanchin*, a term of address for FM and MF: 'A common expression is also: *puk ngathar ngechanchin*[19] "she's grandmother of my children"' (Kilham et al. 1986: 140). Although the dictionary does not give phrasal glosses for grandchildren, it goes beyond Thomson's data in providing analytical glosses of a similar type for siblings-in-law. Table 14.8 indicates the available terms for affinal relations. Husband's parents are referred to as 'my child's grandparent', spouse's senior sibling-in-law as 'my child's parent's elder sibling', and spouse's junior sibling-in-law in terms of the function of the in-law in relation to the child.

Table 14.8. Wik Mungkan in-law terms.

Cons. gloss	Consanguineal	Affinal form	Affinal gloss
FF	*puulanchin*	*puk ngath puulanchin*	HF
FM	*ngechanchin*	*puk ngathar ngechanchin*	HM
FeB/Z	*piny(chin)*	*puk ngath pinychin*	HeB/Z
MeB/Z	*muk(anchin)*	*puk ngath mukanchin*	WeZ
yZC	*mukayng*	*mukay-wunpan*[20]	yZH
FyB	?	*puk ngath emathan*[21]	HyB

Source: Kilham et al. (1986).

It becomes clear from the data of both Thomson (1972) and Kilham et al. (1986) that parents-in-law and siblings-in-law and their reciprocal relations may be described in terms of their relation to the child of the propositus. That is, the relationship is referenced from the viewpoint of the child: the propositus refers to their parent-in-law in terms of the child's grandparents, and, reciprocally, the senior affinal relatives refer to

---

17　There is an alternative strategy for describing parents-in-law as taboo or 'poison' uncles and aunties: *kaal-aamp* WF, *piny-kench* WM, the first member of the compounds being MyB and FZ respectively.
18　Literally, 'child-to.me FF-SENIOR'.
19　Literally, 'child-to.me FM-SENIOR'.
20　Literally, 'yZC begetter'.
21　Literally, 'my child raiser'.

their daughter- or son-in-law in terms of their own grandchild. Likewise a person may refer to their brother- or-sister-in-law in terms of the child's relation to their parent's sibling, and reciprocally these refer to their in-laws as the parent of their nephew or niece.

4.2. Other Cape York languages

Similar derivation of affinal terms from terms for grandkin and uncles and aunts can be found in some Northern Paman languages. Thomson (1972: 21–24) presents data from Tjungundji and Hale (1965, 1997) from Linngithigh. Here phonological changes have somewhat obscured the etymological relations and the morphological details are not fully understood. Accordingly, and for reasons of space, I will refrain from presenting the full evidence here. Regarding forms, an example of the relations can be seen in Tjungundji *thaya* MF, *thandhi* (*-ndhi* is the junior suffix) mDC but also affinal mDH, and *thanuma thandhi* WF. In Tjungundji affinal terms are based on all four grandkin terms as well as on FeB/Z and FyB/Z. (Wik Mungkan is the only language in my data that attests a terminological relation between MeSb and WeSb.) For Linngithigh Hale (1965) provides revealing glosses such as *ngom inhaghay* 'HeB, his (i.e. woman's son's) FeB' in comparison to *inhaghay* FeB and *ayom.thindhigh* 'mDH/WF, to whose child I am *thiy*' vis-à-vis *thiy* MF. Such glosses emphasise the child-centred nature of the terms.

5. Discussion

5.1. Teknocentricity

We have now found a recurrent pattern of lexical relationships in three widely separated regions of Australia: the south-east coast, the lower Murray River, and Cape York Peninsula in the far north-east. In this pattern affinal kin are referred to in terms that reflect the consanguineal relation they bear to a child: my spouse's parents in terms of my child's grandparents and my spouse's siblings in terms of my child's uncle or aunt. Furthermore, since kin terms may be reciprocal, a person's son- or daughter-in-law is referred to in terms of being the parent of a (potential) grandchild.

I propose to call this a 'teknocentric' usage of kin terms. The word teknocentric is derived from a classical Greek noun *teknon* meaning 'offspring', whether son or daughter, which is based on a root *tek-* 'bear', 'beget'. Note that this root refers to both maternal and paternal relations, which makes the term especially suitable for describing parent–child relations in Australian languages, since these typically distinguish terminologically between a woman's and a man's children.[22]

5.2. Pragmatic explanation

These equivalences are not simply a matter of semantic structure but require a pragmatic explanation. They involve a shift in propositus, the person from whose perspective the relationship is calculated. This is a kind of altercentric usage, as described by Merlan (1982: 127) for the Mangarrayi:

> A senior speaker, in talking to a junior relative (especially a young child), tends to refer to third persons in terms of the junior's relationship to them. Thus MoMo addressing DaCh may say with reference to her own husband 'Where is (your) *jabjab*?' (speaker's husband, child's MoFa) using the altercentric referential mode.

Several kinds of motivations may be hypothesised for teknocentric usage. The most obvious is accommodation to children within a family context. Parents would refer to their own in-laws using the terms that their children use. This would apply especially in speech directed to a child (e.g. 'give it to grandma'). Then a mother may, especially in the presence of her child, address her own HM with a grandparental term, used almost as a name (e.g. 'here, take it grandma'). These habits may extend to using the grandparental term in more general contexts as well. Altercentric reference also serves an instructional purpose: 'children are constantly being taught how they should refer to others by being spoken to in terms of their relationship to them' (Merlan 1982: 129).

---

22 McConvell (2018: 249) has used a similar term, filiocentricity, based on Latin *filius* 'son' and *filia* 'daughter', for a narrower sense describing a 'pattern where the term used converges on the form used to and by the child in a parent-child dyad'.

A second motivation may involve avoidance. Fêng (1937: 203) describes teknocentric usage as 'a circumlocutory way of expressing embarrassing relationships'.[23] The use of consanguineal terms for affinal relatives thus constitutes a kind of euphemism. It serves to disguise reference to the marriage relationship with its sexual connotations (cf. Garde 2013: 121). Note that all the examples we have discussed involve the replacement of a spousal term: 'husband's or wife's father, mother, brother, sister' by 'father's or mother's father, mother, brother, sister' respectively; likewise, 'son's wife' by 'son's child's mother' and 'daughter's husband' by 'daughter's child's father' (although here the reference to the child may not be explicit).

Third, teknocentric reference to affines is one of a number of strategies employed in the etiquette of Australian societies to make indirect reference to individuals. It is becoming well known that Aboriginal people use many strategies other than the use of names to indicate who they are referring to. Some of this indirect referencing requires much inferencing on the part of hearers, as is amply illustrated in Garde (2013) and Blythe (2018).

5.3. Implications for semantic description

It is clear that the shared semantic content in teknocentrically related kin terms—especially where there is pure polysemy, as in Ngangaruku between *noidla* FM and HM—would be impossible to capture in a componential analysis, such as that illustrated for the Australian language Nyamal in Burling's (1970) chapter 'Kinship terminology', where all possible senses of a term are to be captured by a combination of features such as generation, sex, seniority, etc.

Scheffler's (1978) approach is more promising. He accounts for many of the multiple senses of individual Australian kin terms (i.e. polysemies) in terms of equivalence rules, stated as expansions or extensions of a primary sense along various parameters. Thus F is extended to FB and M to MZ by a 'same-sex sibling-merging rule'. Actually the direction of his merging rules is the opposite of extension: they involve rewriting a string of relations in terms of fewer symbols: for example FBS → FS (since FB = F) = B. Scheffler (1978: 145) has a 'spouse-equation rule' that relates affinal to consanguineal

---

23   Fêng uses the term 'teknonymic' to describe this usage in Chinese. But teknonymy is not the same thing as our teknocentricity: it is a term invented by E.B. Tylor 'to describe the custom whereby a person is called the father, mother, grandfather or grandmother, etc. of one of his descendants instead of by his own name' (Lévi-Strauss 1969: 348–49). For example, Anna may be referred to as 'Mary's mother'.

relationships: Sp → Cousin, SpM → FZ, SpF → MB, etc. These relations result from marriage practices, such as intermarriage between kin who are terminologically first cross-cousins. Scheffler's equivalence formulas do not make direct reference to their motivation. Nor do any of them involve shifts of propositus of the kind we have seen here. One could however construct a rule for the equivalence HF = FF, which would substitute fCF for H, thus HF → fCFF, and for the reciprocal equivalence mSW = mSCM, one which replaces W with mCM.

The Natural Semantic Metalanguage (NSM) approach championed by Anna Wierzbicka, could, it seems, account for the kinds of relations I have described here. Her approach to the explication of kin term meanings, as outlined in Wierzbicka (2017), is anchored in the child's perspective, pays attention to who is using the term and to whom, incorporates pragmatics and could apparently incorporate the shifts in propositus of the type described above.[24]

5.4. Semantic change

The reader will have noticed that our teknocentric terms involve different degrees of explicitness with respect to the altered propositus. An expression like Wik Mungkan *puk ngath puulanchin* 'my child's FF [= my HF]' is fully explicit. A term like Linngithigh *ngom inhaghay* 'his FeB [= my HeB]' requires the hearer to infer that the perspective is the speaker's child. A form like Ngarrindjeri *mayarel* mSW, presumably derived from mSC, requires an inference concerning how the referent is related to the grandchild. Ngangaruku *metsa* FF, which is used without any modification in the sense HF, either requires a strong inference or has to be understood as a synonymous kin term. When the teknocentrically used term has become opaque—whether through the irrecoverability of the shifted propositus, the lack of transparency of the derivational morphology, or replacement of the term for the consanguineal relation—semantic change will have taken place. Even without these prerequisites, semantic change takes place when invited inferences are reanalysed as primary senses (Traugott and Dasher 2002).

---

24   I am not competent to attempt to supply NSM-style formulas explicating these kin terms. I would however welcome an NSM description of these phenomena.

5.5. Implications for etymology[25]

If the teknocentric usage of consanguineal kin terms to indicate affinal relations has been widely used and has resulted in semantic change, we can expect that more cognates between the two kinds of kin terms remain to be discovered. This applies both within and across languages. Within a given language, a form like Linngithigh *ayom.londhigh* mSW may no longer be synchronically perceived as being lexically related to *olay* FF. Interaction with other kinds of semantic extension may lead to some interesting cognate senses. For example, *kami* (or a reflex such as Wik Mungkan *kem(a)*) is MM in many Pama-Nyungan languages. Apparent derivatives are found in the sense of WM in languages that lack *kami* as MM: *kamintha* in Gathang and *kamiyan* in Wangaaybuwan. These are nevertheless plausible reflexes of an earlier **kami* MM. Furthermore, there is often polysemy between WM and FZ in Australian languages. In Wangaaybuwan *kamiyan* has both meanings—possibly by extension from WM. In some languages (e.g. Duungidjawu), *kami* has only the FZ sense—the language having unrelated terms for both WM and MM. It would be hard to account for the apparent cognacy of terms for MM and FZ without a teknocentrically based shift of the kind we have found.

6. Conclusions

Indigenous Australian societies are characterised by a multiplicity of means of referring to one's relatives, including various strategies of indirection. One such strategy is to substitute consanguineal kin terms for affinal ones, especially given the sensitivity surrounding allusions to spousal relations. Although the actual use in interaction of kin terminology has not been studied in many societies, and although the recorded kin terminology for many societies is lacking in detail, there are indications among attested kin vocabularies that a teknocentric usage of kin terms has led in a number of languages to the lexicalisation of consanguineal kin terms or derivatives therefrom as affinal kin terms. Thus the communicative practices are revealed by a careful study of the vocabulary of kinship.

---

25 I should admit that my main interest in Australian kin terminology is etymological: establishing which terms are cognates and identifying their earlier form and meaning.

References

Berndt, Ronald M. and Catherine H. Berndt (1977). *The World of the First Australians*. Sydney: Landsdowne Press.

Berndt, Ronald M. and Catherine H. Berndt (1993). *A World that Was: The Yaraldi of the Murray River and the Lakes, South Australia*. Melbourne: Melbourne University Press.

Besold, Jutta (2012). Language Recovery of the New South Wales South Coast Aboriginal Languages. Unpublished PhD dissertation, The Australian National University, Canberra.

Blythe, Joe (2018). Genesis of the Trinity: The convergent evolution of trirelational kinterms. In Patrick McConvell, Piers Kelly and Sebastien Lacrampe (eds), *Skin, Kin and Clan: The Dynamics of Social Categories in Indigenous Australia*. Canberra: ANU Press, 431–71. doi.org/10.22459/skc.04.2018.13.

Burling, Robbins (1970). *Man's Many Voices: Language in its Cultural Context*. New York: Holt, Rinehart and Winston.

Dousset, Laurent, Rachel Hendery, Claire Bowern, Harold Koch and Patrick McConvell (2010). Developing a database for Australian Indigenous kinship terminology: The AustKin project. *Australian Aboriginal Studies* 2010/1: 42–56.

Elkin, Adolphus P. (1964). *The Australian Aborigines: How to Understand Them* (4th edn). Sydney: Angus and Robertson.

Fêng, H.Y. (1937). The Chinese kinship system. *Harvard Journal of Asiatic Studies* 2 (2): 141–275.

Garde, Murray (2013). *Culture, Interaction and Person Reference in an Australian Language: An Ethnography of Bininj Gunwok Communication* (Culture and Language Use—Studies in Anthropological Linguistics 11). Amsterdam: John Benjamins. doi.org/10.1075/clu.11.

Hale, Kenneth (1965). Unpublished letter to R. Lauriston Sharp. Cornell University Archives.

Hale, Kenneth (1997). A Linngithigh vocabulary. In Darrell Tryon and Michael Walsh (eds), *Boundary Rider: Essays in Honour of Geoffrey O'Grady* (Pacific Linguistics C-136). Canberra: The Australian National University, 209–46.

Kilham, Christine, Mabel Pamulkan, Jennifer Pootchemunka and Topsy Wolmby (compilers) (1986). *Dictionary and Source Book of the Wik-Mungkan Language*. Darwin: Summer Institute of Linguistics, Australian Aborigines Branch.

Lévi-Strauss, Claude (1969). *The Elementary Structures of Kinship* (rev. edn). Translated from the French by James Harle Bell, John Richard von Sturmer and Rodney Needham, editor. Boston: Beacon Press.

McConvell, Patrick (2018). Enhancing the kinship anthropology of Scheffler with diachronic linguistics and centricity. In Warren Shapiro (ed.), *Focality and Extension in Kinship: Essays in Memory of Harold W. Scheffler*. Canberra: ANU Press, 227–260. doi.org/10.22459/FEK.04.2018.

McConvell, Patrick and Helen Gardner (2016). The unwritten Kamilaroi and Kurnai: Unpublished kinship schedules collected by Fison and Howitt. In Peter K. Austin, Harold Koch and Jane Simpson (eds), *Language, Land and Song: Studies in Honour of Luise Hercus*. London: EL Publishing, 194–208. Available at: www.elpublishing.org/PID/2014.

Merlan, Francesca (1982). 'Egocentric' and 'Altercentric' usage of kin terms in Mangarayi. In Jeffrey Heath, Francesca Merlan and Alan Rumsey (eds), *Languages of Kinship in Aboriginal Australia* (Oceania Linguistic Monographs No. 24). Sydney: University of Sydney, 125–40.

Meyer, Heinrich August Edward (1843). *Vocabulary of the Language Spoken by the Aborigines of the Southern and Eastern Portions of the Settled Districts of South Australia … Preceded by a Grammar*. Adelaide: James Allen.

Radcliffe-Brown. A.R. (1918). Notes on the social organization of Australian tribes: Part 1. *Journal of the Royal Anthropological Institute of Great Britain and Ireland* 48: 222–53. doi.org/10.2307/2843422.

Scheffler, Harold W. (1978). *Australian Kin Classification* (Cambridge Studies in Social Anthropology 23). Cambridge: Cambridge University Press. doi.org/10.1017/CBO9780511557590.

Taplin, George (1873). *The Narrinyeri*. Adelaide: Government Printer.

Taplin, George (1879). *The Folklore, Manner, Customs, and Languages of the South Australian Aborigines*. Adelaide: Government Printer.

Thomson, Donald (1972). *Kinship and Behaviour in North Queensland*. Edited by H.W. Scheffler. Canberra: Australian Institute of Aboriginal Studies.

Traugott, Elizabeth C. and Richard B. Dasher (2002). *Regularity in Semantic Change* (Cambridge Studies in Linguistics 96). Cambridge: Cambridge University Press.

Wierzbicka, Anna (2013). Kinship and social cognition in Australian languages: Kayardild and Pitjantjatjara. Special Issue, 'Semantics and/in social cognition'. *Australian Journal of Linguistics* 33 (3): 302–21. doi.org/10.1080/07268602.2013.846458.

Wierzbicka, Anna (2017). The meaning of kinship terms: A developmental and cross linguistic perspective. In Zhengdao Ye (ed.), *The Semantics of Nouns*. Oxford: Oxford University Press, 19–62.

15

Showing and not telling in a sign language

John Haiman

Anna Wierzbicka's classic article on direct and indirect speech (1974) is one of the very few that I have read in linguistics whose major insight, once seen, can never again be unseen: direct speech (DS)—or at least that recycling of other speakers' words that is meant to be recognised as such—is a dramatic mimetic performance.

Direct speech (DS) is obviously an act of impersonation, in which a speaker identifies with and inhabits a character. Indirect speech (IS), on the other hand, is a distanced descriptive act whereby the speaker talks about the speech of others, as of all things other, from their own perspective, that is to say, from the outside. DS and IS therefore contrast exactly, as do vocal *showing* what's going on (e.g. shouting with anger/crooning with pleasure; paralanguage; ideophones) and *telling* a story about it (e.g. saying 'I am angry/ecstatic' or anything else in so many words; propositional language). Minimally contrasting utterances like, for example,

She said 'you're a liar'
She said (that) I was a liar

can thus be distinguished on the basis of simple syntactic tests. One of these is the 'go …' or 'be, like …' framing test in English. As is well known, these predicates introduce a dramatic performance:

She goes _____
She's, like, _____

On the basis of this test, a dramatic performance may be any action (e.g. scratching one's ear), any posture (e.g. hunching over), any gesture (e.g. a shrug), any facial expression (e.g. a smile) or any ideophone (e.g. 'Yuk!'). It may also be any direct quote, but it can *not* be an indirect quote.

She goes/'s, like, 'You're a liar'
*She goes/'s like, that I was a liar

Comparable 'quotative frames' in other languages pick out the same roster of behaviours (cf. Güldemann 2008).

The present essay does not so much argue for the correctness of Anna's illuminating analysis (which strikes me as self-evident, now that she has pointed it out for all of us to see), as to point out another formal distinction between direct and indirect speech, this one in signed languages like ASL (American Sign Language), BSL (British Sign Language), German SL, Italian SL, Catalan SL and Quebec SL, which may be seen to follow naturally from this analysis. As such, it argues for the thesis that iconicity is unexpectedly the natural motivation for the expression of yet another conceptual distinction. And, via the circumstantial evidence afforded by this one example, it suggests, at least as an optimistic heuristic, that all signs (written, spoken or signed) may well derive from comparably natural beginnings. Laziness, convention and other factors may have rendered these iconic origins obscure over time.

One formal distinction in many if not all sign languages is this: in IS, signers maintain eye contact with their addressees, while in DS this eye contact is interrupted.

Since the scholars who originally described the phenomenon in ASL (Bellugi and Klima 1976: 521–22) and BSL (Sutton-Spence and Woll 1999: 95) provided no reason for this contrast, the distinction may seem to the outside observer to be yet another unremarkable example, among thousands, of the arbitrariness of the linguistic sign. Yet the coincidence among sign languages in this marking strategy argues that there must be some natural motivation behind it. (It should be noted that ASL and BSL, unlike American and British English, are totally distinct languages, as unlikely to trace their commonalities to common origin as Arabic and Hungarian.) Indeed, Quer (2005) and Jarque and Pascual (2015) report that the 'temporal interruption of eye contact with the interlocutor in the here and now', which they describe for DS in Catalan SL, is 'typical' in a variety of signed languages (Jarque and Pascual 2015: 429).

Suspension of eye contact is in fact only the tip of an iceberg of concomitant non-manual 'role shift' markers (Padden 1986) that signal DS. The others include change of head position, body shift and facial expression, with eye gaze change being the most frequent, most probably because it is the most compatible with the principle of least effort (Hermann and Steinbach 2012: 13; Hübl 2012).

The transparent, natural (and indeed to signers presumably self-evident) motivation for the marking of DS is immediately manifest once one correctly models the difference between Jakobson's (1965) 'Speech Stage', which is inhabited by the participants of the speech act (the speaker and the interlocutor right here and right now) and the 'Event Stage', which is inhabited by the signs they make: models of the things and events that they are talking about. It may seem from Jakobson's nomenclature that the Speech Stage (with its two inhabitants) is therefore infinitesimally small compared to the Event Stage, which may encompass the entire universe at any time; but the truth is the opposite. Consider the relationship between the two in Douglas Adams' immortal, but grammatically unexceptionable, sentence: 'Thus, the universe ended.' (Adams 1981: 146). (Spoken when, by whom, standing where?) As in the Adams example (1981), the participants of the speech act (in this case, Adams and his readers) are a part of the real world, but the Event Stage, rather than being the real world, for all its apparent size, is not 'the universe' but only a picture of it: it is merely a theatre in which they stage their linguistic productions. Not only is the Event Stage totally contained within the Speech Stage, those puppets that speakers animate are as remote from the real world inhabited by the speaker and the interlocutor as the characters of a play are supposed to be from the playwright and from their audience. As countless adages and proverbial expressions in a number of traditions make clear, all stages, like all games, are temporary bubbles of pretence, and what transpires on any stage is ideally distinct from what goes on in the real world. Thus, 'It's only a game', 'The show must go on', the notorious polysemy of the word 'play' in English and other languages for both games and dramatic representations (noted by Huizinga 1955), etc.

That the bubble may in fact be punctured is well known. There are hybrid performances that are partially acts of showing and acts of telling: exhibitions of divided empathy with the characters on stage on the part of the impresarios (as in free indirect discourse), and self-referential 'postmodern' hijinks where the characters 'step off the stage' and directly address and thereby recognise the presence of their audience—also known as mugging. For all the hipness of these playful tweaks, it is notable that the bubble has some integrity: the distinction between showing and telling is a real one that is recurrently enforced by grammatical rules. Thus, in language after language, ideophones (dramatic performances on the Event Stage) cannot be negated (negation being a metalinguistic judgement expounded from the Speech Stage) (cf. Haiman 2018: 126).

The simplest model that diagrammatically characterises this contrast is one of two concentric circles. The innermost—the Event Stage, which I am calling a theatrical bubble—is admittedly a small part of the real world, like all theatres (Goffman 1974), but through the willing suspension of disbelief, separated from the real world for the duration of the performance. The outermost or Speech Stage, for all that it seems to contain only the speaker and the listener, is the one whose limits are actually coextensive with those of the real world. The formally heterogeneous class of shifters or egocentric particulars (among them the personal pronouns and tense, as well as the conventional deictics of time and place, but also a whole slew of apparently ordinary words like '(un)natural', 'foreign', 'familiar' and, arguably, most others) serve as anchors to situate the Event Stage and its participants and props with respect to the Speech Stage and the rest of the real world outside.

The extreme thesis that *all* words ultimately depend for their meanings on who is saying them and to whom, and thus serve as such shifty anchors, is proverbial; for example, one of these words, 'beauty', is exclusively in the eye and ear of the beholder. The same point is worked out in a fable by Ivan Krylov (1848) about a noted preacher whose spellbinding eloquence leaves one of his listeners completely unmoved, because he hails from a different parish. That truth is in the mouth of the speaker is notoriously asserted by Jorge Luis Borges in his 'Pierre Menard, author of the Quixote'. He argues, with a concrete demonstration, that the exact same words written by the historical Miguel Cervantes, a Spaniard of the seventeenth century, and his 'Pierre Menard', a fictional French symbolist poet of the twentieth century, mean radically different things. A random sentence of what is mere verbal wallpaper in Cervantes, writing in the seventeenth century, becomes radically, 'brazenly pragmatic' issuing from the pen of Pierre Menard (Borges 1941).

Consider now the position of the participants of the speech act, who can be thought of as the real-world impresarios on the Speech Stage who put on the make-believe show that proceeds on the Event Stage. They are not themselves a part of the show. They and the Speech Stage that they inhabit are equally part of the real world: as far as that communal participation goes, interlocutors relate as equals to each other. They recognise each other and give each other attention; they are equally 'above the fray'. But when as mimes/impersonators they 'step into character' in the Event Stage, they leave the real world behind. For the duration of their mimicry, the play's the thing and during their display they relate only to the other puppets on the Event Stage that they have created. This means that they do not recognise or relate to their real-life interlocutors when on stage, any more than do the characters portrayed by actors to the members of their audience. As eavesdropping inhabitants of the real world, we can see them, but they are not supposed to see us, or to be addressing us.

How can speech act participants in a gestured medium most naturally signal when they are above the fray (telling their story, talking about stuff from outside) or when they go native (acting it out)? A most natural performance of these two contrasting modes of discourse is for the signer to maintain eye contact in narrative/telling mode (explicitly signalling that 'I am talking to you'), and drop eye contact in dramatic/showing mode (leaving it to be inferred that 'I am not talking to you').

Accordingly, the absence of eye contact is also a distinctive feature of all pantomimed 'constructed action' (Quinto-Pozos 2006; Lillo-Martin 2012), where the signer as mime largely abandons conventional sign language and 'becomes one with'—and thereby shows, rather than tells—what s/he depicts. Maintaining eye contact, as in the use of conventional sign language, is how one signals that s/he remains above the fray, which is what s/he does when engaged in acts of telling. Not surprisingly the same distinction is used to signal the difference between direct and indirect speech.

As Capirci notes (pers. comm.) apropos of Italian SL:

> The signer of DS takes the look of the character who speaks, so s/he usually does not look at the actual interlocutor, but in the direction of the locutor within the [staged] narration.

This is also the matter of fact observation of Hübl (2012: 7) regarding German SL:

> Non-manual markers reflect iconically the matrix signer's adoption of the role of the reported signer and his/her alignment towards the reported addressee.

Nothing could be more natural. As Dwight Bolinger sensibly observed (1975), there is probably nothing in language that is arbitrary simply because its original creators wanted it to be that way. In this case, we can see the iconicity behind apparent arbitrariness not, as we often can, by undoing the work of convention and abbreviation, but by identifying the appropriate model in terms of which signers conceive of direct and indirect speech. That natural model, as all signers and students of signed languages seem to recognise, and as Anna Wierzbicka taught the rest of us 45 years ago, is the iconic metaphor of the stage.

What is remarkable about this insight is how hard-won it is to workers in one tradition (spoken language theoreticians like me), but how self-evident it is to workers in another (sign language researchers). In a way my own recognition of this commonplace recapitulates an observation I once made about the metalinguistics of ordinary language, with particular reference to the stage model I have presented here, wherein the Speech Stage surrounds and encloses the Event Stage. The ontology of this diagram is explicit in the philology of the word 'about' in a number of spoken languages including English (Haiman 1998), and in at least one signed language, ASL, where 'about' is rendered by:

> The left hand is held at chest height, all fingers extended and touching the thumb, and all pointing to the right. *The right index finger circles about the left fingers several times.* (Sternberg 1994: 1; emphasis added)

Language is everywhere more or less arbitrary, but it was probably born iconic. In fact, all human languages may have been born from what is now regarded by grammarians, if it is considered by them at all, as paralanguage (Fonagy 2002; Haiman 2018): unsystematic, largely idiosyncratic, analogue displays or performances that now linger in the spoken language as accompaniments to the digitally coded message, and in the written language not at all.

Perhaps even now paralanguage is not quite so facultative as it is made out to be. Some authors (Nugent 2008) have suggested that the failure to attend to the paralanguage of others or to produce the required paralanguage oneself can be socially crippling, and is even a defining property of people with Asperger's syndrome, a population that, he argues, overlaps with canonical nerds.

Of course, making a distinction between language and paralanguage in signed languages is very much an unresolved issue, as is the distinction between language and gesture. I have myself suggested that gestures are those portions of the signal that are performed/shown rather than narrated/told (Haiman 2018: chapter 1). I have seen no discussion on whether 'constructed action' counts as language or paralanguage, for example, and I am unsure whether sign language theoreticians even consider the distinction a useful one. Sherman Wilcox (pers. comm.) suggests a convenient test for determining whether pantomimed 'constructed action' in signed languages is linguistic or paralinguistic: if it is linguistic, then fluent signers can identify as 'ungrammatical performances' those that they judge to be made by non-signers, while 'grammatical performances' are those that are attributed to native signers. If, however, fluent signers accept as equally grammatical all constructed action performances, whether they are produced by native signers or not, then constructed action will count as paralinguistic.

No present definition of paralanguage is entirely acceptable. One possible candidate might be the following one: what counts as paralanguage is always definable relative to an institutional code. Given such a code, paralanguage in any medium is those spontaneous dramatic performances (that is, gestures, by my definition) which co-occur with the coded signs of a message, but are so disinherited in that code that they cannot occur by themselves. They survive only as accompaniments to the coded linguistic signal. Matters are different when communicators share no common code: then paralanguage comes into its own as the only medium they've got.

Another possible definition, suggested by Wilcox's idea about grammaticality judgements of constructed action, is this: if a signal is universal (made with equal fluency and authority by both native speakers/signers and others), then it's probably motivated, and ipso facto paralinguistic. If, on the other hand, it's parochial, and properly produced only by native speakers/signers, then it is part of the grammatical code where it occurs. (I am cheerfully ignoring the ostensible charter of the whole 'generative enterprise', which is to assert hardwired externally unmotivated grammatical universals.) For example, in a small number of languages, interrogation is signalled by subject–verb inversion. This is a highly parochial fact, and part of the grammatical code wherever it happens. In many, if not most languages, interrogation is signalled by a rising intonation. This should count as paralinguistic signal, one that is so natural that it doesn't warrant a grammatical description. It becomes a grammatical fact if rising intonation is conventionalised in different ways in different languages. Thus, for example, Javanese is one of the many languages in which interrogativity can be signalled by rising intonation (as well as by conventional lexemes). But rising intonation in Javanese is not the same as rising intonation in English:

> Normally, Javanese questions have intonation like the rising-falling pattern [characteristic of statements], except that the pitch does not fall so low at the end as for statements; it ends on a suspended note, as in the 'B' speech of this sort of context:
>
> [A. I like rainy weather.]
>
> B. Well, I don't! (Horne 1961: xxvi)

Now it seems that the perfectly natural means of signalling DS that I have been describing is shared by several sign languages, and is naturally motivated. But if it is not shared by all of them, then, however natural its motivation may be, it becomes a parochial fact. So, if there is even one sign language in which gaze direction shift is not (or, possibly, cannot be) used to signal the shift into DS, then such gaze shift becomes part of the grammar, and no longer a paralinguistic natural accompaniment to the message, in those sign languages where it is so employed.

One final observation. To the extent that the degree of arbitrariness, indeed of the very systematicity, of a sign system is a consequence of conventionalisation over time, we may 'predict' a couple of present truisms: that the signs of written language, with its relatively shallow history, are more transparently or reconstructably iconic than those of spoken language (consult any history of writing), and that those of signed languages are more iconic than those of written ones (although the early history of signed language studies is replete with well-intentioned but (surely!) grotesque attempts by their promoters to assert that signed languages like ASL are by God as arbitrary—hence as worthy of respect—as spoken languages). And we may well make a 'prediction' about the future: that signed languages will continue to grow ever more arbitrary as they become canonically sanctioned through repetition by established communities of the deaf. This prediction is already borne out by the existence of separate grammars for the various signed languages that have been described.

Acknowledgements

My thanks to Sherman Wilcox and Pamela Perniss for introducing me to the ideas of constructed action and role shift in sign languages. Thanks to Pamela also for answering my questions about German SL, and directing me to the wealth of literature on the topic. I am very grateful also to Paola Pietrandrea and Olga Capirci for answering my questions about Italian SL.

Anna Wierzbicka and I were colleagues at ANU for a few years more than 40 years ago and we had some great arguments. They were fun and I still miss them, although I never won any of them.

References

Adams, Douglas (1981). *The Restaurant at the End of the Universe*. New York: Ballantine Books.

Bellugi, Ursula and D. Klima (1976). The two faces of the sign. Special issue, Stevan Harnad, Horst D. Steklis and Jane Lancaster (eds), 'Origins and evolution of language and speech'. *Annals of the New York Academy of Sciences* 280 (1): 514–38. doi.org/10.1111/j.1749-6632.1976.tb25514.x.

Bolinger, Dwight (1975). *Aspects of Language* (2nd edn). New York: Harcourt Brace Jovanovich.

Borges, Jorge Luis (1941). Pierre Menard, autor del Quixote [Pierre Menard, author of the Quixote]. In Jorge Luis Borges, *Ficciones* [*Fictions*]. Madrid: Alianza Editorial, 47–60.

Fonagy, Ivan (2002). *The Languages Within Language: An Evolutive Approach*. The Hague: De Gruyter Mouton.

Goffman, Erving (1974). *Frame Analysis*. Chicago: Northwestern University Press.

Güldemann, Tom (2008). *Quotative Expressions in African Languages*. Berlin: Mouton de Gruyter.

Haiman, John (1998). The metalinguistics of ordinary language. *Evolution of Communication* 2 (1): 117–35.

Haiman, John (2018). *Ideophones and the Evolution of Language*. Cambridge: Cambridge University Press.

Hermann, Annika and Markus Steinbach (2012). Quotation in sign languages: A visible context shift. In Isabelle Buchstaller and Ingrid van Alphen (eds), *Quotations: Cross-linguistic and Cross-disciplinary Perspectives*. Amsterdam: John Benjamins, 203–28. doi.org/10.1075/celcr.15.12her.

Horne, Elinor (1961). *Beginning Javanese*. New Haven: Yale University Press.

Hübl, Annika (2012). Role shift, indexicals and beyond: New evidence from German SL. *Texas Linguistics Forum* 13: 1–11.

Huizinga, Johan (1955). *Homo Ludens*. Boston: Beacon.

Jakobson, Roman (1965). *Shifters, Verbal Categories, and the Russian Verb*. Cambridge, MA: Harvard University Department of Slavic Languages and Literatures.

Jarque, Maria Josep and Esther Pascual (2015). Direct discourse expressing evidential values in Catalan Sign Language. Available at: www.semanticscholar.org/paper/Direct-discourse-expressing-evidential-values-in-Jarque-Pascual/dd7fd16a6be11e9ec1d3486a6bfc30446b33503b.

Krylov, I.A. (1848 [1963]). Prixozhanin [The parishioner]. In *Basni* [*Fables*]. Moskva: Izdatel'stvo Xudozhestvennoj Literatury.

Lillo-Martin, Diane (2012). Utterance reports and constructed action. In Markus Steinbach, Roland Pfau and Bencie Woll (eds), *Sign Language: An International Handbook*. Berlin: Mouton de Gruyter, 365–87. doi.org/10.1515/9783110261325.365.

Nugent, Benjamin (2008). *American Nerd*. New York: Scribner.

Padden, C. (1986). Verbs and role shifting in ASL. In C. Padden (ed.), *Proceedings of the Fourth National Symposium on Sign Language Research and Teaching*. Silver Spring, Maryland: National Association of the Deaf, 44–57.

Quer, Josep (2005). Context shift and indexical variation in sign languages. In Efthymia Georgala and Jonathan Howell (eds), *Proceedings of Semantics and Linguistic Theory XV*. Ithaca: Cornell University, 152–68. doi.org/10.3765/salt.v15i0.2923.

Quinto-Pozos, David (2006). Can constructed action be considered obligatory? *Lingua* 117: 1285–314. doi.org/10.1016/j.lingua.2005.12.003.

Sternberg, Martin (1994). *American Sign Language Concise Dictionary*. New York: Harper.

Sutton-Spence, Rachel and Bernice Woll (1999). *The Linguistics of BSL: An Introduction*. Cambridge: Cambridge University Press.

Wierzbicka, Anna (1974). The semantics of direct and indirect discourse. *Papers in Linguistics* 7 (3): 267–307. doi.org/10.1080/08351817409370375.

16

Games that people play: Capitalism as a game

Annabelle Mooney

In this chapter, I draw on Wierzbicka's explication of 'game' in order to show that it is an extremely useful tool in understanding aspects of contemporary capitalism. I begin with an overview of discussions of Wittgenstein's definition of 'game', including the difference between 'play' and 'game'. While it is tempting to think that both are inconsequential, they are not. As Huizinga writes, 'All play means something' (1949: 1). The same is true of games. I then rehearse Wierzbicka's elegant account of 'game' (1996). Building on Wierzbicka's analysis, I attempt to situate the concept of games in contemporary life, particularly in the domain of economics and finance. I draw on work that shows discussion of capitalism and its activities in terms of games and their attributes in order to show that while there is a comparison to be made between these activities and Wierzbicka's explication of 'game' there are nevertheless important differences. Specifically drawing on Zaloom's work on risk and Buchanan's work on austerity, I argue that the 'game of capitalism' does not follow the same kind of rules as those succinctly explained by Wierzbicka for 'game'. Specifically, the separation of the game world from the real world breaks down in the game of capitalism.

There is a feature of Wierzbicka's work that is both a great advantage and a 'problem'. This is the fact that there are very few places she has not turned her analytical lens. This is advantageous, especially to those of us without the analytical precision that Wierzbicka consistently brings to bear on any topic. Indeed, because of her precision and her wide-ranging research, I have always found her work extremely useful in thinking through semantic issues in the specific domains in which I am interested. As Wierzbicka is concerned with clear semantic explications in service of better understanding both language and culture, her work has been particularly useful to me in thinking about topics we *think* we understand. This chapter uses her insights in order to provide a different way of understanding aspects of contemporary capitalism. My aim is modest. I simply want to raise some questions about the consequences of thinking about capitalism as a 'game' by considering some of the consequences of the game of capitalism itself. To do so, I begin with the semantics of 'game'.

1. 'Game'

In *Philosophical Investigations* (1958), Ludwig Wittgenstein argues that at least some concepts cannot be defined in terms of semantic features; instead, they may best be approached by thinking about 'family resemblances'. As Wierzbicka notes, even though Wittgenstein did not explicitly refer to prototypes, his theory of family resemblances suggests the same kind of approach.[1] The particular passage in which Wittgenstein discusses games is a precursor to this and as Wierzbicka notes it does indeed have a 'hypnotic force' (1996: 158). Nevertheless, Wittgenstein's discussion of games does not appear to have been the subject of a great deal of philosophical scrutiny (especially when compared to work on 'family resemblances'), but there is some commentary in this field. I now provide a brief account of two works commenting on Wittgenstein's discussion of 'games'. As will become clear, they draw out the importance to games of skill, chance, reality and rules.

In the first of these, Rowe (1992) seeks to further refine Wittgenstein's account of 'games'. Rowe draws on Callois's typology of games as set out in *Man, Play and Games* (2001). Rowe initially suggests the following typology of games:

---

1 Also, see Manser (1967) for what is essentially a prototype analysis.

(1) Games with internal point
   (a) games of skill
   (b) games of pure chance
(2) Make-believe games
(3) Sequential games (Rowe 1992: 469–70).

The 'internal point' (1) refers to the goal of the game. The internal point of chess, for example, is checkmate, while the internal point of roulette is to choose the right number on the wheel. The point is 'internal' in that the goal is meaningless outside of the game itself. There are, however, differences among games with internal points. For example, a distinction between chess and roulette can be made on the basis of whether skill or chance is determinative of reaching the goal. Rowe also argues that make-believe games (2) are games. Key here is that make-believe games are quite separate from real life and reality (1992: 469). Finally, 'sequential games' develops one of Callois's categories: 'Games of physical exhilaration (twirling round and round)'. While conceding that Callois's is 'not a helpful category', Rowe nevertheless accepts that if such activity was *repeated,* he would be 'happy to describe this as a game' (1992: 468).

Perhaps the most important feature of games as Rowe defines them is their separation from real life. For games with an internal point (1), the separation from 'real life' is implicit in the point itself. As the internal point has no meaning outside of the game, there is already a disconnection. Rowe is careful to distinguish games of type (2) and (3) in particular from 'rituals, works of art, and several other activities which involve sequences of make-believe, and are all insulated from reality in ways which are difficult to define' (1992: 470). His initial typology of three kinds of game (above) is refined to fuse (2) and (3). He thus suggests two kinds of game 'those that are constituted by sequences and those that are constituted by goals' (1992: 478). He provides the following definition of 'game':

> An abstract object (either a sequence or a goal) which is designed to have no instrumental value; the realization or pursuit of which is intended to be of absorbing interest to participants and spectators. (Rowe 1992: 478)

The second account, Manser (1967), also dwells on the distinction between games and real life.² Drawing on Huizinga (1949), Manser argues that 'the area of a game is "marked off" either literally or conceptually from the normal area of human life, that of genuine 'action' to which moral predicates apply' (1967: 217). He continues 'What is done in the course of the game is not meant to have effects in the "real world"' (1967: 217). The most important feature across both accounts is the suspension of reality. As Rowe writes:

> Games are designed to be purpose*less*, and this can be done, either by giving them no point at all, or a point which is valueless or unintelligible outside the context of the game. (1992: 477, emphasis in original)

2. Wierzbicka's account

In Wierzbicka's account of 'game', we find a distillation of the themes already encountered but with important additions. In contrast to Wittgenstein, Wierzbicka argues that we can in fact define games in terms of their semantic features. In contrast to Rowe and Manser, she provides a fuller account phrased in accessible terms. She suggests the following components as central to 'games':

(1) human action (animals can play, but they don't play games);
(2) duration (a game can't be momentary);
(3) aim: pleasure;
(4) 'suspension of reality' (the participants imagine that they are in a world apart from the real world);
(5) well-defined goals (the participants know what they are trying to achieve);
(6) well-defined rules (the participants know what they can do and what they cannot do);
(7) the course of events is unpredictable (nobody can know what exactly is going to happen). (Wierzbicka 1996: 159)

---

2   In his account of games, there is also a focus on pleasure (whether for the producer or spectator) and rules of some kind.

The inclusion of goals and rules means that we are clearly talking about games rather than play. As Wierzbicka notes, the components (and the explication) do 'not apply to a situation when a child idly throws his ball at the wall and catches it again, but in English this activity would not be called a game' (1996: 159). She notes that while this may be called 'Spiel' in German, this term 'has a wider range of use' than the English 'game' (1996: 159; see also Manser 1967: 217).

The explication for 'game' that Wierzbicka proposes is as follows:

games

a. many kinds of things that people do
b. for some time
c. 'for pleasure' (i.e. because they want to feel something good)
d. when people do these things, one can say about these people:
e.   they want some things to happen
f.   if they were not doing these things, they wouldn't want these things to happen
g.   they don't know what will happen
h.   they know what they can do
i.   they know what they cannot do. (Wierzbicka 1996: 159)

This account captures extremely well the aim of games (pleasure) and their structure and outcome as discussed by both Rowe and Manser. Games have rules (elements (h) and (i)) but there is a certain degree of chance involved (element (g)). The game is played voluntarily (elements (e) and (f)) and activity is not unlimited—it has a beginning and an end (element (b)). The duration of the game and the voluntary nature of participation (element (f)) also mean that the game is set apart from ordinary life. As with other explications in Natural Semantic Metalanguage (NSM), this account has the advantage of being clear and accessible. It is translatable and, most importantly, it sets out the key elements of 'games'.

3. Games and capitalism

I want to suggest that Wierzbicka's definition of game provides an important analytical viewpoint when thinking about capitalism. This requires, of course, that a connection be made between 'game' and capitalism. I come to this presently. First, it is necessary to define what I mean by capitalism, for as Chun notes 'capitalism means many different things to different people' (2017: 141).[3] I define capitalism here as late neoliberal capitalism, which has political and economic features and consequences. At its heart, capitalism is a system that values economic growth and in which people (rather than states) hold capital, trade in a market and seek profit. Neoliberal capitalism makes further political claims, that is, it makes claims about how the relationship between the state, the market and people should be configured. As the International Monetary Fund explains, neoliberalism involves two things: increased competition 'through deregulation and the opening up of domestic markets' and 'a smaller role for the state' (Ostry et al. 2016, cited in Pettifor 2017: 125).

The connection of games to capitalism (or indeed any ordered human behaviour) can be made, at least in part, by noticing that economic activity requires rules. For markets to work, for trade to take place and for people to hold capital and property, rules are needed. Some take the form of laws, others are found in regulation, and still others operate as more or less stable conventions and norms. It is not my purpose to enter into an analysis of the myriad laws and practices that regulate the modern economy and the various activities within it. Rather, I turn to research on people engaged in activity that is clearly connected to the capitalist system in order to see whether considering capitalism as a game is either warranted or useful.

I first outline the argument that capitalism is a discourse before turning to work on the metaphors found in both news media reports on the financial crisis and in the language of foreign exchange traders. This kind of trade is sometimes construed as gambling. I then turn to a discussion of risk, relying on Zaloom's ethnographic account of the Chicago Board of Trade. I want to suggest that while capitalism is sometimes construed as a game, there is a key difference in relation to Wierzbicka's explication. The capitalist game is neither completely voluntary nor of limited duration. It is also not separate from real life. The 'game' of capitalism is, in many ways, the game of life.

---

3   For an excellent account and analysis of the different views people hold, see Chun (2017).

4. The discourse of capitalism: Human action and rules

Dahlberg (2014) argues that capitalism is a practice that combines specific elements (concepts, objects and subject identities). He therefore suggests that it may be productive to think of capitalism as a discourse and argues that this helps us understand the norms and rules of capitalism. Discourses, like games, are connected to human thought and action. Discourses have a structure as well as a relation to both language and practice. Perhaps they tend not be thought of in terms of 'rules' as they are—in the final analysis—arbitrary. Rules of all kinds, however, are also often arbitrary and insufficient to the task they are supposed to perform. This is clear at times of crisis (Dahlberg 2014: 260). At such times, either rules are not available or they do not solve the current challenge. This can be seen in the most recent financial crisis. As Cox notes, 'Former Federal Reserve Chairman Alan Greenspan, a hero for free-marketeers, famously acknowledged that the market's capacity for self-regulation had failed' (Cox 2018: 198). In this crisis, the discourse had too few rules. Economic crises may be a result of rules or gaps in the system itself: the existing rules and practices fail to deliver what they promise.

In order to fully analyse capitalism as a discourse, Dahlberg makes use of the concept of 'social logics' (from Glynos and Howarth 2007), explaining that social logics can be either general or specific. These logics can be considered on a continuum from rules (or law) to norms as they 'consist of rule following' (Laclau 2005: 117 cited in Dahlberg 2014: 264). As they may be more or less explicit, social logics may not take the form of 'concrete social codes, such as explicit work place rules … they operate at a more abstract level, characterizing practices' (2014: 263).

The connection of social logics to games is clear when Dahlberg considers whether social logics can have predictive effects. He compares their operation to chess. Once a game of chess starts:

> the rules, together with the player's knowledge of past games and their aim of winning, progress the game in particular directions that can be prognosticated before each move, as more or less likely. (2014: 265)

Along these lines, Dahlberg considers what would happen if interest rates were to rise:

> there will be a range of likely responses from a range of actors—with a variety of roles (from parent to banker), goals (from paying bills to maximizing profit) and knowledge of the system—and an associated range of consequences for actors. (2014: 265)

It seems to me that we need not even consider the predictive power of social logics in order to see the similarity with games. The responses from actors will be oriented towards certain rules: the rules and norms by which the economic system functions. These rules certainly differ from those of, for example, board games. Economic 'rules' are not always set out in a clear summary of instructions to 'players'. In a similar vein, Bjerg in his book *Poker: The Parody of Capitalism* argues that the card game poker is 'an *idealized* version of democratic capitalism where everybody has equal access to the spheres of value circulation' (2011: 242, emphasis added). Nevertheless, the point is that there are more or less predictable actions and consequences in these economic domains. In Wierzbicka's terms, 'the participants know what they can do and what they cannot do' and 'the participants know what they are trying to achieve' (1996: 159).

5. Metaphor: Rules and reality

The presence of rules and games in capitalism is also attested in the language that describes particular kinds of economic activity. A good example of this is Pühringer and Hirte's (2015) work documenting metaphors (in the tradition of Lakoff and Johnson (1980)) in texts written by economists in magazines and newspapers. In addition to finding that the 2007–08 economic crisis is described as a natural disaster, military attack and infection or disease, they also find evidence for the idea that the crisis is misfortune in an economic game. That is, the financial crisis is represented as a result of 'bad luck'. This is consistent with games in which outcomes are not determined, 'nobody can know what exactly is going to happen' (Wierzbicka 1996: 159). The presence of luck in these metaphors is also consistent with other economic and financial metaphors. Stock market trading, for example, also uses the language of gambling (for example, 'betting' on a stock or the market more generally). As Pühringer and Hirte argue, 'The game metaphor suggests that the economy follows specific rules … which have been designed by a superior authority' (2015: 618). This metaphor has a bearing not only on how we conceptualise economic events, but also how society responds to them.

> An 'extraordinary event' as the financial crisis according to an understanding of the economy as a game is then consequently interpreted either as a consequence of someone breaking the rules or simply as misfortune. (2015: 618)

In terms of Rowe's game with internal point, the crisis is thus explained in terms of bad luck (like roulette) or breaking the rules (as one might attempt to in chess, for example, moving the king more than one space). Note that attributing the crisis to a lack of skill is not prominent.

It is worth stating that the presence of the game metaphor in relation to economic activity is not simply a consequence of media representations. Oberlechner, Slunecko and Kronberger's research (2004) focuses on 'participants' subjective experience of the [foreign exchange] market and on the role of metaphors in this experience' (2004: 134) and finds ample evidence of game metaphors.[4] The markets in which traders trade are conceptualised as bazaars, machines, oceans, wars, living beings, sports and gambling spaces. Clearly sports and gambling are connected to games: both have rules and depend on skill and chance. I turn first to sport and then consider gambling.

> A sports competition … is always conducted within a defined framework. It has an agreed-upon beginning and end; it takes place on a particular playground … and it follows a set of constitutive rules. (Oberlechner et al. 2004: 141)

In examples of this metaphor in Oberlechner et al.'s research, informants refer to 'competition', 'teams' and 'goals' (2004: 143). Sometimes the comparison is directly made in the form of a surface simile, for example: 'to me trading is like sports. It's about winning. It's a competitive game that starts every morning at 7 o'clock' (informant B14, 2004: 143).[5] As it is a competition, players have the same goal (Wierzbicka 1996: 159).

---

4   Foreign exchange markets are clearly tied to contemporary economic activity, as they would not exist but for particular features of the economic world: different nations have different currencies, these can be traded, their values fluctuate in relation to each other.
5   B14 is a reference to an informant in Oberlechner et al.'s research.

While success in sports usually presupposes physical ability and skill, the other metaphor identified, gambling, relies on chance. Here, traders refer explicitly to 'casinos', 'roulette' and having 'little chips on your table'. The casino, like the sports arena, is set off from everyday life (Wierzbicka, 1996: 159). The reference to the casino substitutes for money ('little chips') may be designed to suggest such a separation. And while chance is a feature of gambling, this activity is represented as requiring skill, technique and discipline. Oberlechner et al. write:

> Besides pure gambling, the metaphorical field of gambling includes strategic games, such as professional poker or a game like chess perhaps [B17], in which the combination of chance and strategic thinking becomes manifest. These games highlight elements of discipline, skilfulness and expertise, and may thus be seen as a bridge between the metaphorical fields of gambling and of sports. (2004: 141)

The case of gambling presents an interesting example in relation to games. Gambling is connected with the real world but in mediated ways. This is clear in the convention of using 'chips' instead of everyday currency notes when gambling in a casino. Despite not being conventional money, there is a direct correlation between these chips and 'real' money. The chips can be purchased and redeemed for money. But as Wierzbicka notes, in games 'the participants imagine that they are in a world apart from the real world' (1996: 159). If one is playing with real money (albeit represented by a token), this separation from the real world is much less clear.

6. Risk

Where there is gambling there is risk. And while contemporary society has been called the 'risk society' (e.g. Beck 1992) examining individual behaviour in relation to risk provides a clearer picture of what it means and the consequences it may have. The kind of risk I discuss here is directly connected to economic activity. I draw on Zaloom's work, which focuses on risk in the Chicago Board of Trade (CBOT), 'a major global financial futures exchange' and shows the centrality of competitive game playing in this arena (2004: 365). While risk might be thought of as the absence of rules, Zaloom demonstrates that risk *requires* rules. Zaloom explains:

16. GAMES THAT PEOPLE PLAY

'The tightly regulated markets of the CBOT make speculation possible. Aggressive risk taking is established and sustained by routinization and bureaucracy; it is not an escape from it' (2004: 365).

What is striking about Zaloom's fieldwork is how it shows the connection between capitalism's games and real life. In her study, she shows how the games that are played on the trading floor have consequences outside of this domain.

> Financial calculations are always present. However, with each trade, these dealers wager much more than money. Their market engagements are significant social games, a form of 'deep play' in the heart of capitalism. Each trader displays a risk-taking self that his competitors, the market, and he himself will judge ... These games gain their significance from voluntarily placing the self under threat of annihilation. The reward is creating a newly defined self. (Zaloom 2004: 367)

There are many games present here. The trading pit itself has rules (about who buys and sells, where people can stand and so on). The market they are trading in has rules (of supply and demand, regulation, laws and so on). There are also rules about how the trader behaves in the market itself (what the trader can and cannot do while trading). These behavioural norms are collectively described as a particular kind of 'discipline'. 'Traders use discipline as a tool to shape themselves into actors who can produce appropriate and successful interactions with the risks of the market' (Zaloom 2004: 378). This requires traders not to behave as emotional individuals, but rather as finely tuned instruments.

> According to their professional norms, discipline enables traders to coast with the uncertainties of the market and judge effectively when to enter and exit the game. Speculators train themselves to become embodied instruments for reading the market and reacting to its every twitch. (Zaloom 2004: 379)

While part of the trading identity and practice is to enter into the trading game for its own sake (2004: 378), to really be successful as a trader (financially and in identity terms) one has to win more often than one loses. But as Zaloom observes, 'Traders play the game, but winning is not necessarily the first objective' (2004: 383) in that their personal identities are also at stake. This is not just a profession, it is a constant expression of self. This expression and performance of self also brings pleasure, a key aspect of games (Wierzbicka 1996: 159). But the game does not always end well. Zaloom documents the effects of 'playing' this 'game' on the real world in a particularly acute way, as this game (which already has serious identity stakes) has effects on traders' bodies even to the point of death, with instances of suicide among 'failed' traders well known among her informants (2004: 380–81).

7. Policy and individuals

Zaloom's work shows the leakage of the game of capitalism into the real lives of real people. Similar evidence can be found, however, by looking at the way particular terms are used. Here, I briefly consider 'austerity', a term and set of practices (a discourse) that became popular in the wake of the 2007–08 financial crisis.

Austerity is a set of economic and political policies aimed at reducing public spending. It can be seen as a tactic of neoliberal capitalism in this sense, as a reduction in public spending will usually mean a smaller role for the state in society. With national debt incurred because of the bailouts of the financial crisis, many nations sought to rationalise their domestic budgets through introducing austerity measures. In the face of high national debt, austerity appears to be a logical solution (see Borriello 2017). This is only the case, however, if certain economic positions and views of national economies are taken. That is, there are abundant arguments against austerity on purely economic grounds (see, for example, Krugman and Layard 2012). There are also arguments that can be made against austerity by focusing on language use.

Buchanan writes:

> Let us consider the grammar of the following: 'necessary austerity measures in health'; 'due to necessary austerity measures this service will close'; to, 'due to necessary austerity measures your surgery has been cancelled'. While using essentially the same clause 'necessary austerity measures' this one clause plays three different games. (2013: 39)

Perhaps because 'austerity' has become so familiar as a term, it is difficult to immediately see these three different games. But if we substitute another noun phrase in each instance, we might arrive at:

> 'funding cuts in health';
> 'due to lack of money this service will close';
> 'due to low staff numbers your surgery has been cancelled'.

Examining the use of 'austerity', Buchanan argues that 'austerity' functions like a metaphor that obscures the real people affected by the real harm austerity policies cause (2013: 39). That is, 'austerity' is given more representational weight than the people involved; they are simply 'the collateral damage of necessary austerity measures' (2013: 39). Paying particular attention to health care and health outcomes, he argues that:

> A sleight of hand has indeed occurred as the reality of a person's suffering due to actual cutbacks is repackaged as collateral damage (a metaphor) and the metaphor of the *game of capital* has become the more literal. (2013: 39; emphasis added)

The reason this can happen is because national economies are closely connected to the game of capital. Buchanan argues that 'The game of capital does not take place due to conceptual confusion—rather this game thrives because of conceptual confusion and the game itself actively promotes such confusion' (2013:40). He continues, observing that 'the game of capital thrives because of the threats held within its game', threats which 'force governments to the bargaining table' (Buchanan 2013: 40).

The difference between Buchanan's account of the game of capital and Wierzbicka's explication of 'game' above is clear. First, the game of capital does not have clear rules that everyone knows (even though everyone knows, or pretends to know, that it functions according to certain rules). Second, the game of capital is not set apart from real life, it is real life. To take one example, the most recent recession coincided with a rise in male suicide across Europe and appears to be caused by unemployment (Reeves et al. 2015).[6]

8. Conclusion

Games involve human action, directed by rules and goals, played for a fixed period of time, with an uncertain outcome but nevertheless involving some enjoyment in the activity. The central feature of games for Rowe and Manser is the separation of games from real life. This is also a key element in Wierzbicka's account. But this separation between the game and real life does not apply to 'capitalist games'. As research on

---

6 'Each percentage point rise in the male unemployment rate is associated with a 0.94% rise' in male suicide (Reeves et al. 2015: 405).

foreign exchange traders, traders working in the CBOT and indeed in relation to austerity itself shows, the consequences of these 'games' are not confined to the world of the game. The world of the game is the real world. The game of capitalism has effects on real people. Does it make sense, then, to describe capitalism and its attendant practices as games?

Wierzbicka provides a clear account of the semantic features of games. They begin and end, they are voluntarily entered into, they have clear rules and they are distinct from real life. While specific games in capitalism may only last for a period of time, for capitalism itself there is no final end point. There is no final winner; only periodic winners and losers. The game continues. Further, while it is possible to opt out of some of capitalism's domains and activities, given how enmeshed nation states are with global economic practices, it is difficult to escape altogether. While theoretically our participation may be voluntary, it is a kind of coerced consent. While there may be 'rules' and norms, these are not always transparent. Considering the effects of the games of capitalism on real life, and the inability to avoid the consequences of some of these games, it seems that while contemporary capitalism is often discussed and described in terms of rules and games, as it is so connected to real life, it is clearly not a 'game'.

Metaphor, as Aristotle (1991) observed, brings something before the eyes. It allows us to see something new or to appreciate the world in a new way. However, metaphors are always selective. They provide new perspectives, but they erase others. What they 'show', therefore, needs to be carefully examined. Wierzbicka's analysis of 'games' clearly shows that usually games are separate from real life. But the games of capitalism are the rules we increasingly live by. It would perhaps be more appropriate to think of these activities not in terms of games but in terms of war. Perhaps then, the very real suffering that people endure would not be forgotten.

The language choices we make are never innocent.

References

Aristotle (1991). *The Art of Rhetoric*, trans. by H.C. Lawson-Tancred. London: Penguin.

Beck, Ulrich (1992). *Risk Society: Towards a New Modernity*. London: Sage.

Bjerg, Ole (2011). *Poker: The Parody of Capitalism*. Ann Arbor: University of Michigan Press.

Borriello, Arthur (2017). 'There is no alternative': How Italian and Spanish leaders' discourse obscured the political nature of austerity. *Discourse & Society* 28 (3): 241–61. doi.org/10.1177/0957926516687419.

Buchanan, David A. (2013). The austerity bargain and the social self: Conceptual clarity surrounding health cutbacks. *Nursing Philosophy* 14 (1): 38–44. doi.org/10.1111/j.1466-769x.2012.00549.x.

Callois, Rodger (2001 [1961]). *Man, Play and Games,* trans. Meyer Barash. Urbana, Illinois: University of Illinois Press.

Chun, Christian W. (2017). *The Discourses of Capitalism: Everyday Economics and the Production of Common Sense*. London: Routledge.

Cox, Adam (2018). Reform in retreat: The media, the banks and the attack on Dodd-Frank. In Laura Basu, Steve Schifferes and Sophie Knowles (eds), *The Media and Austerity: Comparative Perspectives*. London: Routledge, 196–208. doi.org/10.4324/9781315178912-14.

Dahlberg, Lincoln (2014). Capitalism as a discursive system? *Critical Discourse Studies* 11 (3): 257–71.

Glynos, Jason, and David Howarth (2007). *Logics of Critical Explanation in Social and Political Theory*. London: Routledge.

Huizinga, Johan (1949). *Homo Ludens: A Study of the Play-Element in Culture*. London: Routledge and Kegan Paul.

Krugman, Paul and Richard Layard (2012). A manifesto for economic sense. *The Financial Times*. 27 June. Available at: www.ft.com.

Laclau, Ernesto (2005). *On Populist Reason*. London: Verso.

Lakoff, George, and Mark Johnson (1980). *Metaphors We Live By*. Chicago: University of Chicago Press.

Manser, Anthony (1967). Games and family resemblances. *Philosophy* 42 (161): 210–25. doi.org/10.1017/s0031819100001297.

Oberlechner, Thomas, Thomas Slunecko, and Nicole Kronberger (2004). Surfing the money tides: Understanding the foreign exchange market through metaphors. *British Journal of Social Psychology* 43 (1): 133–56. doi.org/10.1348/014466604322916024.

Ostry, Jonathan D., Prakash Loungani, and Davide Furceri (2016). Neoliberalism: Oversold? *Finance and Development.* June: 38–41.

Pettifor, Ann (2017). *The Production of Money: How to Break the Power of Bankers.* London: Verso.

Pühringer, Stephan, and Katrin Hirte (2015). The financial crisis as a heart attack: Discourse profiles of economists in the financial crisis. *Journal of Language and Politics* 14 (4): 599–625. doi.org/10.1075/jlp.14.4.06puh.

Reeves, Aaron et al. (2015). Economic shocks, resilience, and male suicides in the Great Recession: Cross-national analysis of 20 EU countries. *European Journal of Public Health* 15 (3): 404–09. doi.org/10.1093/eurpub/cku168.

Rowe, M.W. (1992). The definition of 'game'. *Philosophy* 67 (262): 467–79.

Wierzbicka, Anna (1996). *Semantics: Primes and Universals.* Oxford: Oxford University Press.

Wittgenstein, Ludwig (1958). *Philosophical Investigations* (2nd edn) trans. G.E.M Anscombe. Oxford: Blackwell.

Zaloom, Caitlin (2004). The productive life of risk. *Cultural Anthropology* 19 (3): 365–91.

17

Our ordinary lives: Pathways to a more human-oriented linguistics

John Newman

1. Introduction[1]

When one considers the range of data types, methods and research questions that characterise contemporary linguistics, it is clear that the field is diverse and ever expanding in ways that were hardly conceivable 100, or even 50, years ago. One shift underlying many of these developments within linguistics has been the increased attention given to the speakers and writers of language. This shift is manifest in a variety of ways: how speakers interact in conversation, the cognitive processes accompanying acts of speaking and writing, the language used by speakers and writers in the form of language corpora, the role of the human body in shaping language (i.e. the idea of 'embodiment'), etc. It is clear that the idea that linguistics is primarily concerned with a system untethered to the speakers and writers of the language no longer holds sway in the way it once did.

---

1   It is a distinct pleasure to contribute to the present volume in honour of Anna Wierzbicka, whose body of linguistic research has been so uniquely original and insightful. Also, I thank the two anonymous reviewers for their helpful and thought-provoking comments on an earlier version of this chapter.

The excerpt from Lass (1997: xviii) in (1) epitomises this earlier bias towards the language system that was dominant throughout much of the twentieth century:

(1) My main interest, and I suggest this ought to be one prime focus of the discipline, is in systems, not their users; the latter simply have to make do with what's historically presented to them, and cope with it when it changes ... This is not of course to say that the users aren't interesting; merely that they and their properties and actions belong to another subject-area, not historical (or perhaps any) linguistics proper.

Although the immediate context of the above quote is the subfield of historical linguistics, Lass here advances the opinion that 'language users' (he means human beings), their properties and their actions perhaps do not belong to 'linguistics proper'. Even by 1997, however, speakers and writers of language, their intentions and their actions had come well into focus in many subfields of linguistics and the quote above must be seen as a decidedly conservative view of linguistics on the cusp of the twenty-first century. Croft's (2011: 1) statement in (2) offers, I believe, a more accurate reflection of contemporary practice in linguistics and how linguistic structure is viewed in the twenty-first century.

(2) Language structure cannot be fully understood without situating it with respect to current theories of joint action, social cognition, conceptualization of experience, memory and learning, cultural transmission, and evolution, shared knowledge and practice in communities and demographic processes in human history.

In what follows I advocate two lines of research that reflect a more human-oriented kind of linguistics, in keeping with the larger trends in the field noted by Croft: (i) research that acknowledges the role of human experiential realities in the explication of language and (ii) a shift in research focus to the individual speaker and the agency of an individual.

2. Human experiential realities

One can identify an 'experientialist' orientation in disciplines that study human behaviour. An experientialist orientation is one that tries to understand human behaviour in terms of the human experience, as opposed to, say, understanding human behaviour in terms of abstract systems. One simple example of experientialist approaches in contemporary life would include the widespread acknowledgement that the 'user experience' is critical in evaluating and improving the delivery of modern technology. In academic fields such as anthropology and sociology, adopting the so-called 'insider's perspective', or an 'emic' perspective, may also be viewed as a type of experientialism.

An experientialist orientation in the study of human language can be seen in the writings of various linguists.[2] For Lakoff (1987: xv, 266), the experientialist approach in linguistics represents an attempt 'to characterize meaning in terms of the nature and experience of the organisms doing the thinking', to be contrasted with an 'objectivist' approach in which meaning in human language is defined independently of the experience of humans. The label 'embodiment' is also applied to this kind of approach (Lakoff and Johnson 1999: 16–44), albeit with a slightly different nuance through the presence of the 'body' morpheme in this label (see Rohrer 2005 and Bergen 2015 for further discussion of the varieties of experientialism and embodiment). The field of Cognitive Linguistics has provided a natural home for experientialist approaches like that espoused by Lakoff, though the field has developed over the years to give more weight to the larger goal of reconciling the facts of language with the study of human and social cognition more generally (cf. Dancygier 2017). The quote in (3) is taken from the writings of Anna Wierzbicka and is indicative of the Natural Semantic Metalanguage (NSM) approach to the study of language which can also be understood as a kind of experientialism, as I use that term:

(3)   In natural language, meaning consists in human interpretation of the world. It is subjective, it is anthropocentric, it reflects predominant cultural concerns and culture-specific modes of social interaction as much as any objective features of the world 'as such'. (Wierzbicka 1988: 2)

---

2   A reviewer has drawn my attention to the extensive and insightful analysis of the English word *experience* in Wierzbicka (2010: Chapter 2) in which the author elucidates the Anglocentric semantics of the word and its non-universality as a concept. The reviewer poses the question: 'Can humans across the world be meaningfully studied through an English-specific keyword, and can we base a universal theory on untranslatable words such as "experience"?' I accept that there is a vagueness associated with terms such as *human experience* and *experientialist* and that they are not necessarily easily or precisely translatable into other languages. One would need to consult the works of individual authors to gain a more precise understanding of the ways in which a particular linguistic theory or framework is 'experientialist' (cf. in particular the discussion of varieties of experientialism in Rohrer 2005).

The NSM approach undertakes semantic analysis through an analytical technique of reductive paraphrase that justifiably lays claim to 'conceptual authenticity' through its reliance on concepts that are familiar in the ordinary lives of speakers (Goddard and Wierzbicka 2014: 82). The concepts that are the building blocks of meanings in the NSM methodology are claimed to be 'simple, intelligible, and universally available words' (Wierzbicka 2010: 17) and are drawn from ordinary natural language. Relating aspects of language structure and use to culture is also very much in the spirit of an experientialist agenda and is something that Wierzbicka in particular has written about extensively (e.g. Wierzbicka 1992, 1997). In short, while Cognitive Linguistics and the NSM approach are clearly differentiated from each other and adopt quite different methods, they both see the human dimension as central to their cause and to their methods, in stark contrast to the position advocated by Lass and quoted above. While an experientialist orientation in contemporary linguistics is not confined to these two approaches, I have singled them out here since they have very explicitly acknowledged this element throughout their respective histories.

An additional way in which an experiential orientation may enter into the study of language is to seek out experientially salient aspects of human life as the object of study itself. In my own research I have chosen to make the verbs in (4), and their semantic equivalents in other languages, a focus of study and this is what I will elaborate on in what follows in this section. Clearly, these 'basic' verbs involve the human body in essential ways. The verbs are associated with a variety of body parts as elements that are salient in the semantics of the concept. Thus, we have the position of upper torso, buttocks and legs relevant to the semantics of *sit*, *stand* and *lie*; legs and even the body as a whole are relevant to *come* and *go*; eyes are relevant to *see*, just as ears are relevant to *hear*; the mouth and the digestive tract are relevant to *eat* and *drink*; hands and arms are relevant to *give* and *take*. The verbs make a linguistically satisfying set of concepts to study in the sense that they show a balance between being relatively static or dynamic in terms of their internal configuration.

(4) a. sit, stand, lie
  b. come, go
  c. see, hear
  d. eat, drink
  e. give, take

As verbs that encode quite basic aspects of our everyday lives, they can be rewarding objects of study and for a variety of reasons. For a start, the verbs can be expected to function as key sources for conceptualising other aspects of our lives. In Euchee (Amerindian isolate, possibly Siouan), for example, the morphemes *ci* 'sit, stay', *fa* 'stand' and *'e* 'lie' function as the suffixed articles occurring with singular inanimate nouns, and form the basis of what has been called a three-way 'gender' system (Watkins 1976: 35–36; Linn 2000: 364–70). This reliance on the 'sit/stand/lie' conceptual set as a classificatory basis of inanimate nouns is an indication of the cardinal role these concepts play in our lives. Another instance of how the basicness of these concepts underlies unusual linguistic phenomena is the structural basicness associated with some of these verbs. The syntax associated with 'give' in some languages would be a case in point (cf. Newman 1996: 17–21). In Amele (Papuan, Roberts 1987), for example, affixes that would normally attach to verb stems such as tense, aspect, mood, verb agreement etc., appear merely as a string of affixes without any verb root in the 'give' construction. Compare the Amele three-place predicate 'show' example in (5a) with the 'give' example in (5b):

(5) a. Jo   eu   ihac-i-ad-ig-en.
     house that show-PRED-2PL.IO-1SG.SUBJ-FUT
     'I will show that house to you (plural).' (Roberts 1987: 69)
  b. Naus Dege ho ut-en.
     Naus Dege pig 3SG.IO-3SG.SUBJ.PAST
     'Naus gave Dege the pig.' (Roberts 1987: 34)

The concepts behind the basic verbs in (4) are typically productive sources for many kinds of semantic extensions in languages. As far as semantic extensions are concerned, 'eat' is particularly remarkable in its productivity and has attracted much attention (cf. Newman 2009). Welmers' comments on the range of uses of Akan *di* 'eat' as shown in (6) point to something remarkable about this verb that even Welmers, writing as a structuralist linguist, found necessary to add to his description.

(6) I have attempted to sum up its [the Akan 'eat' verb's] uses under the general word for 'eat', but with other objects it refers among other things to using up or wasting money, taking a day off, having sexual relations with someone, accepting a bribe, inheriting goods, winning a victory, defeating an opponent, playing a game, holding an office, enduring suffering, making a bargain, living in some specified way, and so on at considerable length. *A language has not been well studied until the nature of such semantic ranges, if not an exhaustive list of all recordable collocations, has been noted.* (Welmers 1973: 477, emphasis added)

Grammaticalisation is another kind of extension that can be found among the basic verbs. Reference was already made to how 'sit', 'stand' and 'lie' can function as a three-way basis for a classificatory system in languages. These same verbs may also give rise to aspect markers. In Manam, for example, *soaʔi* 'sit' is extended to express the progressive aspect, referring to an event that is in progress at the time of the speech act or the time of another event, as in (7a) (Lichtenberk 1983: 197–98). The Manam verb *eno* 'lie' also functions as an auxiliary, but in this case to indicate persistive aspect; that is, indicating that the event is performed persistently, as in (7b).

(7) a. siresíre   di-bulabula-í-be   di-sóaʔi
       grass   3PL.REALIS-set.RDP-3SG.OBJ-and   3PL.REALIS-sit
       'They are burning grass.' (Lichtenberk 1983: 199)
    b. i-pile-lá-be   i-éno
       3SG.REALIS-speak-LIMITER-and   3SG.REALIS-lie
       'He kept talking.' (Lichtenberk 1983: 200)

The verb 'give' is a rich source of grammaticalisations in the world's languages, as illustrated in the examples in (8) (cf. Heine and Kuteva 2002: 149–55 for a more complete overview). These examples illustrate extensions to manipulative/causative uses (8a), light verbs (8b), benefactive marker (8c), existential marker (8d), presentative marker (8e) and passive auxiliary (8f).

(8) a. antaa   jonkun   korjata   jokin
       give   person.GEN   repair.INF   thing
       'to have a person repair something' (Finnish)

b. give the car a push/give it a try/give the ball a kick (English)
c. ʔoːpùk tɛɲ siəʊphɨ̀u ʔaoy khɲom.
   father buy books give me
   'Father buys books for me.' (Cambodian, Jacob 1968: 141)
d. Es gibt viele Kinder in den Schulen.
   it gives many children.ACC in the schools.DAT
   'There are many children in the schools.' (German)
e. Si se da el caso …
   if REFL gives the event
   'If the circumstance should arise …' (Spanish)
f. E gët pensionnéiert.
   he gives pensioned
   'He's going to be pensioned off.' (Luxembourgish, Schanen 1987: 38)

This has been a necessarily selective illustration of the potential value of making ordinary everyday human experiences a focus of linguistic research. Nevertheless, I believe that the data provided are sufficient to show the range and diversity of linguistic phenomena associated with basic human experiences. I contend that the basicness of the experiences encoded by the verbs in (4) is a reason for the proliferation of extensions in usage of these verbs and their counterparts in other languages. They constitute natural starting points for linguistic research.

3. Individuals

Another direction for linguistics that leads to a more complete understanding of language and its use is to shift attention to language as experienced by individuals, as opposed to focusing only on the aggregate population.[3] Linguistics has always acknowledged the shared social basis of language as essential to communication of course, as expressed by de Saussure (1959: 13–14): 'For Language [*langue*] is not complete in any speaker; it exists perfectly only within a collectivity'. A focus on the

---

3 An individual experience of language is arguably also evident in the NSM approach where both 'I' and 'you' perspectives ('I think …', 'I feel …' etc.) may occur alongside statements referring to what '(many) people' say, do, etc.

aggregate behaviour is especially common in the current digital age, where large amounts of data across many individuals (as in a typical corpus) are analysed to ascertain the typical behaviour, or central tendency, of the aggregate of language users. Without denying the importance of the collective, or aggregate, population in the study of language, I nevertheless believe that a shift of attention to individual users is a worthwhile complement to this practice (cf. Newman 2017). In the remainder of this section I offer some examples of this shift of attention within linguistics.

As a preliminary observation, we might note that a greater acknowledgement of individual linguistic realities of speakers has parallels outside of linguistics that may be helpful in approaching the linguistic equivalent. An obvious parallel is literature where it is commonplace to study the corpus of an individual's output (e.g. John Keats), as well as the corpus of a selection of writers from a particular epoch (e.g. the Romantic period of English literature). The study of history has expanded from the study of whole societies or populations or eras (e.g. history of the First World War) to allow for the study of individuals participating in these events (e.g. tracking the life of an individual who experienced the First World War). Of most relevance in the present context, we see a shift of attention to individuals in the neighbouring discipline of psychology in the research agenda pursued most conscientiously in the pages of the *Journal for Person-Oriented Research* and summarised in (9), taken from the introductory article in the first issue of the journal:[4]

(9)   It is the aim of this issue to present and discuss approaches for bringing the individual back into focus in developmental psychology, as well as other areas of psychology. As far as possible, findings should be interpretable at the level of the single individual and they should be informative of patterns of individual functioning. (Bergman and Lundh 2015: 2)

Specifically, the person-oriented focus advocated by Bergman and Lundh is characterised by three foci: a pattern focus, a focus on the individual, a process focus (Bergman and Lundh 2015: 3).

There are indeed pockets of research in linguistics where an individual corpus or subcorpus is a familiar kind of data. Where there is a serious interest in human agency, then it would seem inevitable that it must

---

4   The *Journal for Person-Oriented Research* is freely available at: www.person-research.org/page3_1.php.

be an individual, their personal circumstance and their particular personality that must be the object of study. Coupland's (2002) research on the stylistics of individual language use is an example of this kind of research. First language acquisition also comes to mind, with data on individual children readily available. Studies of individual children have certainly played their part in the research on first language acquisition, extending back to the meticulous documentation by Werner F. Leopold of his two daughters' simultaneous acquisition of German and English in the 1930s (cf. Lanza 2004: 18–23 for a summary and critical review of this work). Vihman, Ferguson and Elbert (1986: 29) offer a more contemporary opinion on the value of appreciating individual differences in language acquisition: 'In each of the areas investigated—phonetic tendencies, consonant inventory, and word selection—the prevalence of individual variation was the strongest lesson to be learned.' The extent of individual variation in language acquisition allows for, indeed points to the necessity of, thorough studies of individuals and their patterns of language acquisition (cf. the detailed case study of language acquisition in Theakston et al. 2012).

A more person-oriented agenda of research would include greater attention to documenting and attempting to explain changes over the lifespan of an individual, or at least phases of a lifespan, rather than just documenting the changes that are deemed to affect a whole community. Hinton (2015) studied the changes in a number of phonetic variables in the pronunciations over a lifetime of four public figures in British life: Her Majesty Queen Elizabeth II, Baroness Thatcher, Sir David Attenborough and David Dimbleby. Interestingly, Hinton found that the diachronic accent changes of these individuals over their lifetimes (1950s onwards) did not simply mirror sound changes that are known to have occurred in the norms of Received Pronunciation in this period of time. Changes observable in the speech of these individuals are not reducible to the overall intergenerational changes. Although public figures and celebrities are an obvious focus of interest in lifespan studies, the lives of ordinary speakers are equally revealing. To take just one example of such research, Bowie (2010) tracked changes in the realisation of post-vocalic /r/ and the aspiration of syllable-initial /ʍ/ in 10 speakers (non-celebrities) across three to four decades of their lives. The data for this study came from a corpus of recorded religious addresses to conferences of The Church of Jesus Christ of Latter-day Saints (the Mormon Church), with the earliest longitudinal data collected in the years 1940, 1950 and 1960, and the latest data collected in the years 1970, 1980, 1990 and 2000. Bowie found that all 10 individuals exhibited some variation with respect to both of the variables investigated, but did not find any consistent pattern of change across all 10 speakers or from speaker to speaker. Once again, the variation in any one individual cannot be ascribed to simply ageing or changing community norms. Bowie suggests instead that the individual variation in this data reflects the reality of intra-speaker variation that exists in all phases of the lifespan:

(10) All sociolinguistically competent adults, no matter how old, have the ability to display different facets of their linguistic identities whenever a need to do so is perceived to arise. In a very real sense, we all possess the capacity to reinvent ourselves linguistically at any time, at any age. (Bowie 2010: 66)

Alongside such lifespan accounts are more personal, autobiographical accounts of specific life changes and accompanying linguistic changes. Jhumpa Lahiri's (2015a, 2015b) writings about her experiences and feelings as she immersed herself more and more in an Italian-speaking world is a case in point. Lahiri's personal circumstances are unusual: she considers Bengali her mother tongue; she is an accomplished and celebrated author of English language novels and short stories (and winner of the 2000 Pulitzer Prize for Fiction); and she takes it upon herself to become a speaker and writer of Italian, which includes moving to Italy to live. Not surprisingly, her account of becoming a speaker and writer of Italian is an intensely personal, artistic expression rather than any kind of objective documentation, but it is no less interesting on account of its literary flavour. Arguably it is all the more interesting to a general audience precisely because of the literary nature of the writing.

Beyond simply observing individual differences in language behaviour, it is natural to inquire into the factors determining these differences beyond the usual ones of gender, age and social class. Dąbrowska (2015) provides an overview of some of these broadly 'experiential' factors and the interesting findings from this line of research. She reports on a number of studies that show the influence of education, occupational status and general reading skills on performance in carrying out linguistic tasks. This line of research points to quite different linguistic realities for individuals who fall into the 'low academic achievement' category compared with those in the 'high academic achievement' category, comparing their performance on tasks involving passive sentences, for example.

At the very least, we need to make provision for case studies of individuals within linguistics, whether synchronic or diachronic, as a way of probing the lived realities of language users, to better understand all the factors that come into play in language use. This would mean incorporating into linguistics the methodologies of case studies, as advocated for the whole field of social sciences by Gerring (2017), as well as incorporating experimental methodologies that yield dense data on individuals and their processing of language (e.g. eye-tracking and event-related potential (or ERP) methodologies).

4. Conclusion

The suggestions offered here as directions for research in linguistics are unlikely to be considered as directions that all linguists would wish to make primary goals of their research. The allure of, and the undeniable intellectual rewards of, the intense study of language as an abstract system, far removed from the world of human speakers and writers, remains undeniably attractive to some linguists. Nevertheless, for some time now, the field of linguistics has been opening itself up to incorporate the study of language users, Lass' remarks cited above notwithstanding, and the field is richer because of that. Ultimately, languages are the products of human societies and human needs, and the more we acknowledge that truth the more complete our understanding of languages and language will be.

References

Bergen, Benjamin (2015). The cognitive foundations of language. In Ewa Dąbrowska and Dagmar Divjak (eds), *Handbook of Cognitive Linguistics*. Berlin: De Gruyter Mouton, 10–30.

Bergman, Lars R. and Lars-Gunnar Lundh (2015). Introduction. The person-oriented approach: Roots and roads to the future. *Journal for Person-Oriented Research* 1 (1–2): 1–6. doi.org/10.17505/jpor.2015.01.

Bowie, David (2010). The ageing voice: Changing identity over time. In Carmen Llamas and Dominic Watt (eds), *Language and Identities*. Edinburgh: Edinburgh University Press, 55–66.

Coupland, Nikolas (2002). Language, situation, and the relational self: Theorizing dialect-style in sociolinguistics. In Penelope Eckert and John R. Rickford (eds), *Style and Sociolinguistic Variation*. Cambridge University, 185–210. doi.org/10.1017/cbo9780511613258.012.

Croft, William (2011). Language structure in its human context: New directions for the language sciences in the twenty-first century. In Patrick Colm Hogan (ed.), *The Cambridge Encyclopedia of the Language Sciences*. Cambridge: Cambridge University Press, 1–11.

Dąbrowska, Ewa (2015). Individual differences in grammatical knowledge. In Ewa Dąbrowska and Dagmar Divjak (eds), *Handbook of Cognitive Linguistics*. Berlin: De Gruyter Mouton, 649–67.

Dancygier, Barbara (2017). Introduction. In Barbara Dancygier (ed.), *The Cambridge Handbook of Cognitive Linguistics*. Cambridge: Cambridge University Press, 1–10. doi.org/10.1017/9781316339732.001.

de Saussure, Ferdinand (1959). *Course in General Linguistics*. [English Translation of *Cours de linguistique generale* [1916], edited by Charles Bally and Albert Sechehaye with Albert Reidlinger, translated by Wade Baskin.] New York: Philosophical Library.

Gerring, John (2017). *Case Study Research: Principles and Practices*. Cambridge: Cambridge University Press.

Goddard, Cliff and Anna Wierzbicka (2014). Semantic fieldwork and lexical universals. *Studies in Language* 38 (1): 80–126. doi.org/10.1075/sl.38.1.03god.

Heine, Bernd and Tania Kuteva (2002). *World Lexicon of Grammaticalization*. Oxford: Oxford University Press.

Hinton, Martin (2015). Changes in Received Pronunciation: Diachronic case studies. *Research in Language* 13 (1): 21-37. doi.org/10.1515/rela-2015-0010.

Jacob, Judith M. (1968). *Introduction to Cambodian*. London: Oxford University Press.

Lahiri, Jhumpa (trans.) (2015a). *In Other Words* [translation of *In Altre Parole* by Ann Goldstein]. Knopf Doubleday Publishing Group.

Lahiri, Jhumpa (trans.) (2015b). Teach yourself Italian [translated from Italian by Ann Goldstein]. *The New Yorker*, 7 Dec: 30–36.

Lakoff, George (1987). *Women, Fire, and Dangerous Things: What Categories Reveal About the Mind*. Chicago: University of Chicago Press.

Lakoff, George and Mark Johnson (1999). *Philosophy in the Flesh: The Embodied Mind and Its Challenge to Western Thought*. New York: Basic Books.

Lanza, Elizabeth (2004 [1997]). *Language Mixing in Infant Bilingualism: A Sociolinguistic Perspective* (corrected edition). New York: Oxford University Press.

Lass, Roger (1997). *Historical Linguistics and Language Change*. Cambridge: Cambridge University Press.

Lichtenberk, Frantisek (1983). *A Grammar of Manam*. Honolulu: University of Hawai'i Press.

Linn, Mary Sarah (2000). A Grammar of Euchee (Yuchi). Unpublished PhD dissertation, University of Kansas.

Newman, John (1996). *Give: A Cognitive Linguistic Study*. Berlin and New York: Mouton de Gruyter.

Newman, John (ed.) (2009). *The Linguistics of Eating and Drinking*. Amsterdam: John Benjamins.

Newman, John (2017). When individuals matter: Person-oriented research in contemporary linguistics. In Anastasia Makarova, Stephen M. Dickey, and Dagmar S. Divjak (eds), *Each Venture a New Beginning: Studies in Honor of Laura A. Janda*. Bloomington, Illinois: Slavica Publishers, 15–27.

Roberts, John (1987). *Amele*. Beckenham, Kent: Croom Helm.

Rohrer, Tim C. (2005). Embodiment and experientialism. In Dirk Geeraerts and Herbert Cuyckens (eds), *The Handbook of Cognitive Linguistics*. Oxford: Oxford University Press, 25–47.

Schanen, François (1987). Grundzüge einer Syntax des Lëtzebuergeschen: Die Verbalgruppe [Essentials of Luxembourgish syntax: The verbal group]. In Jean-Pierre Goudaillier (ed.), *Aspekte des Lëtzebuergeschen* [*Aspects of Luxembourgish*]. Hamburg: Helmut Buske Verlag, 3–90.

Theakston, Anna L., Robert Maslen, Elena V.M. Lieven, and Michael Tomasello (2012). The acquisition of the active transitive construction in English: A detailed case study. *Cognitive Linguistics* 23 (1): 91–128. doi.org/10.1515/cog-2012-0004.

Vihman, Marilyn M., Charles A. Ferguson, and Mary Elbert (1986). Phonological development from babbling to speech: Common tendencies and individual differences. *Applied Psycholinguistics* 7 (1): 3–40. doi.org/10.1017/s0142716400007165.

Watkins, Laurel J. (1976). Position in grammar: Sit, stand, lie. *Kansas Working Papers in Linguistics* 1: 16–41. doi.org/10.17161/kwpl.1808.702.

Welmers, William Everett (1973). *African Language Structures*. Berkeley, California: University of California Press.

Wierzbicka, Anna (1988). *The Semantics of Grammar*. Amsterdam: John Benjamins.

Wierzbicka, Anna (1992). *Semantics, Culture, and Cognition: Universal Human Concepts in Culture-Specific Configurations*. New York: Oxford University Press.

Wierzbicka, Anna (1997). *Understanding Cultures through their Key Words: English, Russian, Polish, German, and Japanese*. New York: Oxford University Press.

Wierzbicka, Anna (2010). *Experience, Evidence, and Sense: The Hidden Cultural Legacy of English*. Oxford Scholarship Online. doi.org/10.1093/acprof:oso/9780195368000.001.0001.

18

On defining parts of speech with Generative Grammar and NSM[1]

Avery D. Andrews

1. Introduction

There is a long-standing controversy as to whether it makes sense to try to define parts of speech cross-linguistically, and if so, how to do it. The generativist position, advocated by Chomsky (1970), Baker (2003), Chung (2012a, 2012b), Panagiotidis (2015) and many others, has almost always assumed that it does, focusing on noun (N), verb (V) and adjective (A), applying a combination of syntactic and semantic ideas and concepts. On the other hand, functionally oriented typologists such as Dryer (1997), Croft (2001) and Haspelmath (2010, 2012) seem to have largely come to the conclusion that it does not; while Wierzbicka (2010) argues that it can be done, using the grammatical treatment of certain Natural Semantic Metalanguage (NSM) primes as universal exemplars. Here I will propose a different NSM-based approach, intended to be complementary to Wierzbicka's, which uses NSM to define 'semantic cores', whose members are treated equivalently by certain kinds of grammatical phenomena, restricted in order to avoid the problem of 'methodological opportunism' discussed by Croft (2001). The goal is definitions that can be applied

---

[1] I would like to acknowledge the anonymous reviewers and Dominie Dessaix for helpful questions and suggestions.

universally, and also in an empirically meaningful manner, so that it is possible, in principle, for them to yield the result that the defined part of speech does not exist in a given language, whether or not this happens in fact. We will find definitions for noun and verb that apply universally and always seem to find something, whereas this is not the case for adjectives. A major difference from Wierzbicka (2010) is that the approach can be applied without working out the prime set of the language being investigated, with its attendant complexities such as identifying allolexes, since the relevant NSM specifications will take the form of NSM formulas which can be stated in the NSM of any language, including that of the investigator. The present approach can therefore be applied at a much earlier stage of work on a language.

The approach can be seen as a development of that of Lyons (1968), Schachter and Shopen (2007) and Wierzbicka (1986), aspiring to meet the criticisms by the latter of the former two, although I won't be able to go through this in detail. Since parts of speech are a complex problem, in section 2, I go through a number of preliminary issues for defining them, and then examine nouns in section 3. Then I will consider adjectives in section 4, verbs in 5 and some general conclusions in 6.

2. Preliminaries

Generative syntacticians generally believe that 'parts of speech', however ultimately defined, involve labels or features of some kind that occur in syntactic structures, which have a degree of autonomy from both sound and meaning. There are various ways of accomplishing this, but for convenience I will adopt the approach used in Lexical Functional Grammar as well as original Transformational Grammar (TG) and various other approaches, where they are labels on the nodes of trees, either all levels (TG), or only overt c-structure (LFG).

But, given the labels, there is a further issue of labels vs classes of lexical items. It is possible, for example, that there are universal labels such as N or V for syntactic positions, determining aspects of the surrounding syntactic environment (e.g. 'nominal' vs 'verbal' projections), but no restrictions on what open class lexical items can occupy them. That is, there might be just one open class of 'contentives', capable of functioning as nouns, verbs, etc. depending on their position in the structure. Such a position has in fact been argued for certain languages, including Austronesian and

Salishan languages, and also Nootka and Mundari. However, as discussed by Panagiotidis (2015: 29–37), these arguments are not convincing; see Chung (2012a, 2012b) for discussion of nouns vs verbs in Chamorro (Austronesian), arguing that in spite of the existence of many stems that can function as either nouns or verbs, these are distinct parts of speech due to unpredictable meaning shifts between the uses of putative 'noun' or 'verb' stems in the different positions. See also Evans and Osada (2005) for similar points on Mundari from a non-generative point of view, and issue 41(2) of *Studies in Language* for a number of further relevant studies (brought to my attention by an anonymous reviewer). Therefore, the current preponderance of research seems to indicate that all languages have distinct classes of lexical items associated with what are normally analysed as nominal and verbal positions, even though in some languages there are many words that can appear in both.

Assuming that we regard parts of speech as classes of items rather than kinds of syntactic positions, there are at least two approaches to trying to give them a characterisation in universal terms, one in terms of structure, the other in terms of meaning. Purely structural approaches do not appear to have been worked out to any extent, while the traditional definitions took a meaning-based approach, although with shortcomings discussed by Wierzbicka (2010) and, previously, many others. Baker (2003) takes a mixed approach, arguing that verbs are characterised structurally by the property of projecting a specifier, while for nouns he draws on a proposal by Geach (1962) and Gupta (1980) that the meanings of nouns, but not members of other parts of speech, involve 'criteria of identity'. Panagiotidis (2015) on the other hand proposes to differentiate nouns from verbs on the basis of their semantics, following Acquaviva (2009),[2] but in a much more abstract way than Wierzbicka. I won't claim that the approaches of Baker and Panagiotidis are wrong, only that they are somewhat abstract and theoretical; the present proposal aspires to more immediate applicability by people who don't have much time to delve into complex theoretical and philosophical issues, as well as providing fewer potential loopholes for saving proposals that are in difficulty. Wierzbicka's on the other hand requires working out the prime set of a language, making it difficult to apply at the early stages of work on a language.

---

2   References are to the version available through LingBuzz (ling.auf.net/lingbuzz).

Parts of speech are sometimes defined in terms of the possibilities for substitution, along roughly the following lines:[3]

(1) A word class is a set of words that can be substituted for each other without affecting grammaticality

This definition depends on the concept of 'word', whose nature is another long-term controversy in linguistics; see Goddard (2011) for discussion with respect to NSM. I will not attempt to say anything substantial here about this controversy, but will merely note that WORDS is an NSM prime (however this works out for formulating technical definitions), and, for all languages, some kind of reasonably satisfactory notion of 'word' seems to be available (even if it is coextensive with 'formative', or is somewhat arbitrary in certain respects), and that the way in which controversial issues of word-hood are resolved doesn't seem to have much substantive effect on issues of what parts of speech are taken to exist in a language, and none on what open ones are to be accepted.

But (1) encounters a problem with inflection, in that different inflected forms of the same word are frequently not inter-substitutable in all environments, and in addition, a further problem, first discussed at length by Gross (1979), is that on a rigorous application of the criterion of (1), words fall into very large numbers of very small classes, and the traditional parts of speech would only be the highest divisions in the category system, and would not be very clearly defined. Mass and collective nouns, for example, have different substitutional properties than count or plural ones, and split into further subcategories on various grounds, as discussed by Goddard (2017: 256); would they be one part of speech as traditionally assumed, or two? In the opposite direction, adjectives and adverbs have certain things in common, so perhaps they should be combined into one part of speech, and, indeed, sometimes are.

The original definition of part of speech was, however, given in terms of inflection, and we do not wish to abandon that. What I suggest is the following: in each language, each part of speech has a system of inflectional categories, such that any form that belongs to that part of speech must

---

3   Cf. the definition of 'syntactic category' in Culicover (1976: 13): 'A syntactic category is a group of words or sequences of words in a given language that can replace one another in an sentence of the language whatsoever without affecting grammaticality'. This generalises the definition in (1) to cover phrases as well as single words.

belong to at least one of the categories. For example, in English, a given noun might lack a singular or plural form, but must appear in one form or the other.

But in languages with little or no inflection, there needs to be more, which I suggest is based on word order. In English, for example, most adjectives come before the head noun in the noun phrase unless they have a prepositional complement, in which case they come after. What we do *not* want is the possibility or necessity of basing parts of speech distinctions on compatibility with certain kinds of complements or determiners, or phenomena of selection, such as the choice of unitisers with different kinds of mass nouns (Goddard 2009, 2017):

(2) I need several items of cutlery/?furniture/*water/*meat/*fork

I therefore propose a relatively 'theoretical' definition of the concept of part of speech, compatible with LFG works and other frameworks that give a relatively direct account of overt structure:

(3) A part of speech is a class of lexemes defined by:
   (a) how it is involved in the phrase structure rules or equivalent, that is, with the constraints that are responsible for the overt structure of relative ordering of words in utterances, and
   (b) the requirement that it has a system of inflectional categories such that the form of any word that is functioning as a member of that part of speech belongs to at least one of the categories (specified in all dimensions if there are multiple ones, such as gender, number and case, in German or Russian).

Observe that (3), a definition of the concept of part of speech, is a 'comparative' concept as described by Haspelmath (2010), based on formal ideas, while the definitions of specific parts of speech to come have a semantic aspect, but will still be comparative concepts in Haspelmath's sense. By limiting the criteria, we aspire to avoid, or at least reduce, methodological opportunism (Croft 2001).

With these preliminaries in hand, we can proceed to the problem of defining the part of speech 'noun'.

3. Nouns

As discussed above, our strategy, essentially derived from Lyons and Schachter, will be to define a semantic core, such that everything or almost everything that falls into it will be a noun. A problem we wish to avoid, however, is to give the appearance of assuming that nouns will already be present (although that appears to be the case). Therefore we formulate the definition in two parts, an existential statement that is empirical, and might be falsified (but hopefully is not), and the definition itself, based on the empirical assertion. We state our assertion as follows, mostly now in NSM, but using '[T]' to mark first use of technical terms which we have not and will not here attempt to explicate. The need for the 'open[T]' qualification will be discussed below:

(4) There is an open[T] part of speech[T] like this:
    A word[T] is in this part of speech if one of these things are true:
        This word says what kind of thing something is
        This word says what kind of person someone is
        This word says what kind of place some place is
        This word says what kind of living thing some living thing is

Having made our empirical claim, we can then use it to define a part of speech:

(5) People can say what this part of speech is with the word 'noun'

Although I've expressed (5) in something very close to NSM, the role of NSM is less essential here.

The empirical claim of (4) is that words that fall into the semantic core provided by (4) obey the requirement of belonging to one of the inflectional classes associated with some single part of speech, and will also not behave differently from each other under the principles determining relative order. That is, a word meaning 'dog' will not precede a definite article while one meaning 'tree' follows it. On the other hand, we can observe that this core is split in extremely random ways by grammatical gender classifications, which, however, do not appear to ever affect relative order, and so therefore do not distinguish parts of speech by our definition. A potential problem with this definition is exactly what a 'kind' is taken to be. Is a big dog a kind of dog, for example (Dominie Dessaix, pers. comm.)? I propose not, on the basis that if somebody says 'what kind of animal is that', and somebody else answers 'a (bloody) big one', they are clearly indicating that they don't know the answer to the question. But the issue of 'core' vs 'extended' uses of the primes, is nevertheless important.

A subtlety of this definition is that it does not preclude the existence of languages with only one part of speech, as discussed in the previous section. For this, we need a principle that requires the existence of at least one additional part of speech. The most obvious proposal for this is 'verb', for which we propose a definition in section 5. We do on the other hand have an effective safeguard against the problem of indefinite subdivisions of word classes; there can be subclasses of noun, such as proper names or mass nouns (not covered by (4)), but these will not be parts of speech according to the definition, since mass nouns do not obey different principles of ordering than those that fall under (4), in English or other languages known to me.

The proposal is not inconsistent with that of Wierzbicka (2010), but has somewhat different properties. She proposes that the primes THING(s) and PEOPLE provide a grammatical prototype for nouns, which implies that there are at least two nouns, but not, actually, that there are any more, although one might be able to derive some expectations on the basis of further assumptions. A somewhat peculiar point is that (4–5) do not actually imply that the exponents of THING(s) and PEOPLE are nouns, since they do not designate kinds of things and people, but rather the entire supercategories. The present proposal furthermore differs from Wierzbicka's in that it does not require that the investigator find the exponents of these primes and ascertain their syntactic properties. Both approaches appear to do something useful, and there is more to be done to fit them together.

But an issue arises with the semantic core: what should really be in it? (4) provides for four kinds, but there are others that might plausibly be included. One is proper names, which often have some special properties, but appear to be nouns nevertheless according to our criteria. Another (pointed out by Martin Haspelmath, pers. comm.) is mass nouns. Both of these raise some puzzles, but they are not critical, because although it would be good to make the semantic core as large as it can be, (4) already asserts the existence of one big enough to provide the basis of a part of speech definition.

Another problem that needs to be addressed is provided by classifiers, reviewed extensively by Aikhenvald (2000). These occur in a number of different types, sometimes together in a single language, occurring in combinations with nouns and other items, especially numerals and other quantifiers, in various environments. The classifier used with a nominal expression is normally determined by its meaning, sometimes also saying what kind of thing something is (along with other possibilities), in accordance with (4). But they are clearly different from nouns, in the languages that have them, appearing in different positions. For example, the 'noun classifiers' *naj* and *no7* in Kanjobolan (Mayan, Craig 1992: 284)[4] apply to people and animals, respectively, occurring before the noun:

(6) xil   [naj   xuwan]   [no7   lab'a]
    saw   CL:MAN   John   CL:ANIMAL   snake

'The man saw the snake.'

For this chapter, the important fact about classifiers is that there are a finite number of them, although the number can be reasonably large, up to several hundred (Aikhenvald 2000: 84). Classifiers are therefore a closed class in languages that have them, and where they are independent words.

For this reason we have included in (4) the specification that the class be open. A potential problem is presented by so-called 'repeaters', which are nouns that appear to be used as classifiers, appearing in classifier positions, often instead of the normal classifiers (Aikhenvald 2000: 361). But repeaters can be treated as nouns, since any noun can be a repeater. Classifiers are very intricate, and there may be more problems for our definition lurking within them; for example, Truquese with its 'virtually open' system of relational classifiers (which classify possessed nouns according to their properties and mode of possession; Aikhenvald 2000: 187); is this really open, or not? However, I don't think that this problem needs to be solved immediately.

---

4   Cited in Aikhenvald (2000: 82).

4. Adjectives

Adjectives are the most questionable of the three categories we are considering. Even 'traditional' adjectives (as recognised by the grammatical traditions of the languages in question) are sometimes difficult to distinguish from either nouns, verbs or both. In some languages, they arguably not distinct at all. And our conclusion will be that they are not a universal category, at least in the sense that nouns and verbs are. Familiar European languages clearly have an open 'adjectival' part of speech distinct from noun (arguably, in some cases, according to our criteria, two of them, as we shall see). In English, for example, they inflect differently from both nouns and verbs (showing neither tense nor number, but having limited comparative), and appear in a special position in the noun phrase (NP), between determiners and nouns. But 'adjective' fails as a universal category under our criteria, for a number of reasons, including lack of a reliable semantic core, failure in some languages to differentiate clearly from other categories such as noun and verb, and failure to have a consistent treatment in terms of principles of ordering.

The absence of a semantic core was in effect observed in the classic paper Dixon (1977), who discussed languages in which the apparent adjective class had as few as eight members (Igbo) or even seven (Mulluk-Mulluk) or, possibly, none at all (Samoan). Although the properties expressed by the closed adjective classes are similar (predominantly size and dimension, newness, colour, and quality), the only ones that actually appear on all the lists of supposed adjectives are 'big/large' and 'small/little'. The semantic core would have to be 'size', but this is not enough to be useful, because a semantic core needs to contain a reasonable number of things in order for unsplittability to be an interesting property.

Then there are the various languages that have been claimed to have no adjective class at all. Warlpiri has, for example, been proposed to be a language where putative adjectives are not distinct from nouns (with demonstratives also included in this category, which is sometimes called 'nominals'). One basis for this claim is that there appear to be no inflectional differences, and while there are differences in ordering tendencies between words translated into English as nouns vs adjectives, they are apparently not very strong. Some additional motivation is provided by the claimed interpretations of example (7), due ultimately to Ken Hale (Simpson 1991: 265):

(7) *kurdu-ngku*   *wita-ngku*   *ka*   *Wajilipi-nyi*
    child-ERG   small-ERG   PRES   chase-NONPAST
    'The small child is chasing it.'
    'The childish small thing is chasing it.'

In the first, more standard-looking, gloss, 'child' plays the role of noun (in Simpson's LFG analysis, supplying the PRED-value for the NP), 'small' that of the modifier (within the ADJUNCT attribute), while the second gloss has the roles reversed. But this is a rather subtle intuition due to Ken Hale (1973), and perhaps it is time to re-examine the situation. Consider for example the following two variants of (8):

(8) a. *Kurdunkgu ka wajilipinyi*
    b. *Witangku ka wajilipinyi*

Can (8a) really mean 'the childish thing' is chasing it, as well as 'the child is chasing it'? And can (8b) simply mean 'the small thing is chasing it', or 'something small is chasing it', or does it rather require a contextually determined understanding of what kind of thing is being described as small (child? dog? drone?), as would be the case for an English sentence such as 'a/the small one is chasing it'? At this point, we don't know, but a closer look seems warranted.

Stative verbs are the other category from which adjectives sometimes seem to not be distinct. As examples of this, Dixon cites Yurok and Samoan, neither refuted, and the latter supported by subsequent work (Mosel and Hovdhaugen 1992: 73–74). Baker (2003) discusses these and additional cases in some detail, concluding that the languages do have adjectives after all, but this conclusion can be challenged on the basis that he doesn't provide any criteria distinguishing the putative adjectives from stative verbs. We might consider postulating that languages can lack stative verbs, using only adjectives for this purpose, but as far as I know, whenever there is a clear distinction between adjectives and verbs, there are also some stative verbs alongside the adjectives, often with no very clear difference in meaning. For example, in Greek, we have the adjective *kurazménos* 'tired', which we can combine with the copula *íme* 'I am' to say *íme kurazménos* 'I am tired', as well as the verb *kurázome* 'I am tired'. If the verb category always spills over to include some stative verbs when it is easily distinguishable from 'adjectives', then it is probably theoretically better to say that we have stative verbs but not adjectives when such a distinction does not appear to exist.

A case that might be of this kind that has attracted substantial discussion is the Austronesian language Chamorro (Chung 2012a, 2012b). Chung argues that Chamorro has standard noun, verb and adjective categories, disagreeing with Topping (1973), who proposes that there are only two major categories, noun and verb, with 'adjectives' being (stative) verbs. Chung discusses a modification construction that putative adjectives can appear in but not verbs, but does not provide any worked out contrast between 'adjectives' on the one hand, and stative verbs on the other (although morphologically transitive but stative *tungu'* 'know' appears as a verb (Chung 2012a: 14)). Topping (1973: 231–32) also notes that intransitive 'verbs' but not 'adjectives' can take manner adverbs, while the latter but not the former can take intensifiers. But the predicates shown as taking the manner adverbs are all non-stative, and those taking intensifiers stative; therefore, a distinction between stative verbs and adjectives is not established.

On the other hand, the nature of the modification construction that Chung discusses suggests that there is a structural role of 'modifier', distinct from relative clauses, and not available to non-stative verbs. This suggests that there is something real behind the label 'adjective', even if it does not meet the requirements to be a label for a universal part of speech in the present sense.

The opposite problem for a universal adjective category is too many arguably distinct word classes that are candidates for the title of 'adjective'. The classic case is Japanese, with its 'noun-like' and 'verb-like' adjectives, but there is by now a fairly robust consensus that the differences between these are essentially a matter of morphological realisation of the same inflectional categories; furthermore, the positional criteria appear to be the same. Therefore, the two types can be regarded as the same part of speech. For further discussion, see Yamakido (2005).

But in Romance languages especially, and to a limited extent in English and Greek, the positional criteria don't fully work. As is well known, in Romance languages, adjectives usually follow the head N, but there are some that can only precede, others that only follow, and many that can appear in either position, often with differences in meaning, including restrictive (postnominal) vs non-restrictive (prenominal), and various kinds of more idiosyncratic shifts, as discussed for example by Demonte (2008):

(9) *El   hombre   pobre*
     the   man   poor
     'The poor [not rich] man.' (Demonte 2008: 80)

(10) *El   pobre   hombre*
     the   poor   man
     'The poor man.' (who evokes pity (cf. Demonte 2008: 76))

Nationality adjectives, on the other hand, appear only to follow (*empresarios americanos/*americanos empresarios* 'American businessmen'), while modal adjectives can only precede (*el presunto asesino/*el asesino presunto* 'the alleged murderer').

On the basis of positional criteria, the implication is that these two kinds of 'adjectives' are different parts of speech. This conclusion is strengthened by the fact that they differ (as in English) in the kinds of complements they can take. Postnominal adjectives can take prepositional phrase (PP) complements, while prenominal ones cannot:

(11) *las   condiciones   buenas   para   nosotros   prolongarán   nostra   vida*
     the   conditions   good   for   us   will.prolong our   life
     'Conditions good for us will prolong our lives.' (this example found online has been lost, but searching for 'condiciones buenas para' will turn up more like it)

(12) **las buenas para nosotros condiciones*

This cannot be due to some kind of universal restriction on adjective phrase structure inside NP, because in Greek, prenominal adjectives can take PP complements (and, according to my observations, do, at a rate of about 1 per 5,000 words of newspaper text[5]), and even sometimes in spoken TV news. This is possible even for modal adjectives, which, as in English, cannot be used as predicate adjectives:

---

5 Based on a bit more than 50,000 words' worth of articles from the online edition of To Βῆμα (www.tovima.gr/), selected on the basis of being the leftmost three on the banner that used to appear at the top of the webpage, or fewer if the articles were long, on multiple days chosen on no systematic basis.

(13) | i | ipotheméni | apo | ton | Iosíf | apistía | tis | Marías
     | the | suspected | by | the | Joseph | infidelity | of(GEN) | Mary(GEN)

'Mary's suspected/alleged infidelity according to Joseph.' (Available at: www.sostis.gr/blog/item/490-h-gennhsh-sta-evaggelia.)

English and Greek lack a distinction between postnominal and prenominal adjectives, but they have some comparable phenomena, concerning adjectives which occur prenominally but not as predicate adjectives, as well as, in Greek, in the 'polydefinite' construction (Alexiadou 2001: 233). On the other hand, the traditional adjectives in Greek and Spanish have the same kind of agreement morphology, marking the nominal inflectional categories.

All in all, 'adjectives' make a rather poor showing as a universal category, at least by comparison with nouns:

(14) a. No semantic core.
  b. Sometimes fall into multiple types by morphological criteria emphasising form.
  c. Sometimes fall into multiple types under position-based criteria.
  d. Sometimes putative adjectives are not clearly distinct from verbs or nouns

A property that does seem to unify different kinds of adjectives to some degree is degree modification, sometimes by specific words. In Spanish, for example, *muy* 'very' expresses extreme positive degree for both prenominal and postnominal adjectives, but not verbs, which use *mucho*. But adverbs also take *muy*, so if we want to use this as a criterion, we should be prepared to accept adverbs and adjectives as a single part of speech. This is in fact advocated by Baker (2003), but is not universally accepted, and arguably not a very useful position for people interested in the primary description of languages. Furthermore, there are many traditional adjectives that reject degree modification.

The overall conclusion is that 'adjective' is probably not best regarded as a universally present or even definable part of speech, at least by the general approach used here. On the other hand, it is plausible that there is a universal 'modification' construction, so that if there is a part of speech to which all of its fillers belong, we could call that 'adjective'. But the distinctions between different kinds of adjectives in Spanish and Greek above indicate that there might be more than one kind of 'modification' construction, with different kinds of fillers. This conclusion is supported by a great deal of additional work on adjectival constructions, going back to Siegel (1976), recently surveyed by Pfaff (2015), in the course of an extremely detailed treatment of adjectival modification in Icelandic.

5. Verbs

Perhaps surprisingly, verbs do not submit to the kind of treatment that works for nouns. Suppose we try something like (15), where '…' represents some kinds of things that happen that are only expressible by verbs:

(15) There is a part of speech into which a word falls if it says that something like this happens: …

Unfortunately, there doesn't seem to be any such part of speech. The problem is primarily presented by what are often called 'complex verb constructions', which consist of two words, one, traditionally called a so-called 'light verb', that usually give some kind of generic information about the event, but sometimes very little, and another word, sometimes called a 'coverb', often an apparent noun, adjective, which provides more detailed information about the event. Constructions similar to these occur in most languages. In English, for example, we have a choice between (16a) and (16b):

(16) a. I went to the liquor store
 b. I had/made/did a trip/run/dash to the liquor store

In (16a) we have a conventional verb that indeed says what kind of thing happens, but in (16b), the same information is conveyed by one of several possible nouns, with at least three possible choices of verb, none of which provides significant information about the nature of the event, which comes from the nouns. In some languages making extensive use of such constructions, the traditional verb often makes a more substantial contribution to saying what kind of thing happened, but the noun usually says more.

In English, this kind of construction can be regarded as a minor pattern, but in Hindi (Mohanan 1994), Urdu (Butt 1995), Japanese (Matsumoto 1996) and many other languages, they are more prominent, while in certain other languages such as Kalam (Papua New Guinea, Pawley 2006) and Jaminjung (Australia, Schultze-Berndt 2002) they are the major technique for describing events. In fact, in both of these languages, the 'verb' category is closed, containing 125 members in Kalam, 25 in Jaminjung. A further difference is that in English, the 'coverb' is clearly a noun heading an NP, while in the latter two languages, its status as a part of speech is unclear, and it is very clear that it is not head of an NP. This is because of the extremely limited possibilities for modifying or otherwise extending the coverb, which are limited to certain morphological operations that can be regarded as derivational. (17) from Jaminjung illustrates a simple coverb, (18) a reduplicated one, reduplication of the coverb being 'very frequent—almost obligatory—with coverbs representing repetitive events' (Schultze-Berndt 2002: 77):

(17) *yalumbarra*   *[V marrug   ga-jga-ny]*   *yarrajgu,*   *warnda-bina*
   King.Brown   hidden   3SG-GO-PST   afraid   grass-ALL
   'The King Brown snake went into hiding—being afraid—into the grass.' (Schultze-Berndt 2002: 120)

(18) *mang-mang*   *ganu-ngg-m*
   RDP-move.knees.outward   3SG:3SG-SAY/DO-PRS
   'She is moving her knees in and out, dancing.' (Schultze-Berndt 2002: 77)

The normal order is coverb first and then light verb, although the opposite is possible, similarly with verbs and preverbs in Warlpiri.

Wierzbicka (2010: 294–95) suggests defining verbs via the protypes provided by the exponents of DO and HAPPEN, and while this seems viable, it does not guarantee the existence of more than two verbs, and I think that it is useful to try to define an open class making a stronger claim. To enable this, I propose extending the notion of parts of speech to include what can be called 'complex words', which I will define as words that have a certain amount of internal structure, but arguably sit under a single lexical node, which we can call 'V' for combinations meeting a workable definition of 'verb'. To cover Jaminjung, this internal structure must be sufficient to allow clitics to intervene, but not major categories (Schultze-Berndt 2002: 120). Such 'semipermeable V' constructions are also found with Warlpiri preverb–verb combinations (Nash 1986: 51–52) and serial verbs in Tariana (Aikhenvald 2000), languages where the (traditional) verb category is open. I suggest they would also be plausible for languages such as Romance ones and Standard Modern Greek, where object clitics attach to the verb, but show signs of syntactic autonomy (Preminger (2019) and previous work cited there).

With this adjustment, which is intriguingly not necessary for nouns, we can get a universal open category of verbs, corresponding reasonably well to what is found in linguistic descriptions, with a two-step definition, assuming a prior definition of noun:

(19) a. There is a single open, possibly complex, part of speech, different from 'noun', into which words saying what kind of thing happened can fall.
 b. A word saying what kind of thing happened is in this part of speech if it is not in 'noun'. We can call it 'verb'.

This seems complex, but I think that the complexity is necessary, because it is clear that on the one hand nouns can provide sufficiently rich descriptions of events in order to count as 'saying what kind of thing happened', whereas other widely recognised parts of speech (adjectives, adverbs, prepositions) do not (setting aside some rather complex issues involving 'mixed categories', as discussed recently by Panagiotidis (2015)). The aspect of this where NSM is most critically relevant is 'what kind of thing happened', which includes things that people do.

Not so clear is the status of the parts of complex verbs, often 'coverbs'. These are very diverse, and sometimes regarded as a heterogeneous collection of nouns, adjectives and adverbs, and the question of what part of speech they belong to is generally regarded as difficult (e.g. Pawley 2006: 10). Schultze-Berndt (2002: 71–76) argues that they should be taken as a distinct part of speech, distinct from adverbs and nominals. Another possibility is that they might be regarded as essentially morphology rather than syntax, and have no category label at all. Adapting a somewhat similar proposal by Panagiotidis (2015: 18) within the framework of Distributed Morphology for Greek, we might propose this as the structure for 'dive' in Jaminjung (Schultze-Berndt 2002: 475):

(20) *[V buwu*   *[V irdbaj]*   *]*
       Enter.water   FALL
       'dive'

We want the second component as well as the whole thing to be a V because that is what the cross-reference and TAM (tense–aspect–mood) marking prefixes apply to, but, according to this idea, the first component has no category label at all. Regardless of the issue of what, if any, label coverbs have, it is clear that they do not project higher phrasal structure. So if they have a syntactic category label, it is a non-projecting one in the sense of Toivonen (2001).

A further complexity arises in certain languages such as the Germanic ones, whereby additional words such as idiomatically interpreted prepositions and particles may combine non-compositionally with the verb, such as in the numerous idiomatic and one compositional meaning of 'put down', or the combination 'put up with'. Unlike the components of complex verbs, these 'supplementary items' are from closed rather than open classes, and therefore can provisionally be set aside. There is also a question of what percentage of the vocabulary they constitute, both in the lexicon and in actual use.

The main empirical claim made by (19) is that if a word describes what kind of thing happens, it has two choices of part of speech, one being 'noun', the other being the additional one that we call '(possibly complex) verb'. Comparably to with nouns, we just do not seem to find words meeting the semantic criteria of (19) divided between three rather than just two parts of speech. For states, however, things are different: in many languages states can be expressed by a third part of speech, traditionally called 'adjective' (or maybe even by two or more additional parts of speech, depending on how we treat 'nominal' vs 'verbal' 'adjectives' in Japanese). Another interesting fact is that there doesn't seem to be anything corresponding to nominal gender for verbs: one could imagine a language in which verbs were divided into semi-arbitrary classes calling for different forms of adverbs, but this does not seem to happen.

This proposal is not empirically contradictory to that of Wierzbicka (2010); indeed, it seems plausible that they could be integrated along the lines that the non-complex verbs might always include exponents of DO and HAPPEN. However it can be hard to find these. In Jaminjung, the verb *yu(nggu)* 'do/say' seems plausible as an exponent for DO (Schultze-Berndt 2002: 355), but I have not yet been able to identify any exponent for HAPPEN. This of course does not mean that there isn't any, but indicates that even extensive and careful descriptive semantic work can fail to identify the exponent(s) of a prime if that task is not specifically one of the research goals.

6. Conclusion

The main conclusions are as follows:

(21) a. There are at least two universally definable and universal parts of speech, which can be called noun (or 'nominal', when there is no contrast with adjectives or demonstratives), and verb.

b. These have semantic cores that can be stated using NSM, which do not split in ways indicative of a part of speech difference (evidence for different phrase structure rules or a different inflectional system).

c. There is an asymmetry in that words in the semantic core of 'verb' can be nouns or verbs, but those in the semantic core of 'noun' can only be nouns.

d. There is a further asymmetry in that we need a notion of 'complex word' to deal with languages with (traditionally so-called) coverb + verb constructions, but no such thing is needed for nouns.

e. The universality of adjectives is not established, and indeed, seems dubious, although there is plausibly universal 'modification' construction restricted to states.

There are many areas wanting further investigation. Some of the ones closest to the topics I have discussed are:

(22) a. Can the definition of 'noun' be simplified to a single specification without lists that are essentially disjunctions (such as 'things, living things, or …'), or widened to include mass nouns and various kinds of collections, or, ideally, both?

b. Is there after all a distinction between 'adjectives' and 'stative verbs' in languages where this is not obvious from factors such as morphology and the use of copulas?

c. Given that 'adjectives' are dubious, what about 'adverbs'?

d. Is there a universal asymmetry between nouns and verbs with respect to the closed class supplements?

Although the existence of at least two universal parts of speech might be taken as evidence that there is an autonomously syntactic Universal Grammar that includes a list of categories, including required and perhaps possible ones, it also seems plausible that the apparently universal parts of speech are aspects of the interface between grammar and meaning, and are essentially cognitive and semantic rather than syntactic.[6] The difference between kinds of things (living things, etc.), on the one hand, and kinds of things that can happen, on the other, is after all very important in life (for example, the former can be returned to, and often retain traces of what has happened to them, while the latter cannot be returned to, and so cannot retain traces of their history), so it would not be a surprise if this difference injected itself rather forcefully into the structure of language.

References

Acquaviva, Paolo (2009). The roots of nominality, the nominality of roots. *LingBuzz*. Available at: ling.auf.net/lingbuzz/000824.

Aikhenvald, Alexandra Y. (2000). *Classifiers: A Typology of Noun Classification*. Oxford: Oxford University Press.

Alexiadou, Artemi (2001). Adjective syntax and noun raising: Word order asymmetries in the DP as the result of adjective distribution. *Studia Linguistica* 55: 217–248.

Baker, Mark C. (2003). *Lexical Categories: Verbs, Nouns, and Adjectives*. Cambridge: Cambridge University Press. doi.org/10.1017/cbo9780511615047.

Butt, Miriam (1995). *The Structure of Complex Predicates in Urdu*. Stanford, California: CSLI Publications.

Chomsky, Noam (1970). Remarks on nominalizations. In R. Jacobs and P. Rosenbaum (eds), *Readings in English Transformational Grammar*. Waltham, Massachusetts: Ginn, 184–221.

Chung, Sandra (2012a). Are lexical categories universal? The view from Chamorro. *Theoretical Linguistics* 38: 1–56. doi.org/10.1515/tl-2012-0001.

---

6   Note, however, that it is perfectly possible to have a universal grammar (UG) that says nothing at all about specific categories, requiring these to be stated in the actual grammars provided by the theory of UG. The Xerox Linguistic Environment (XLE) is an example of this.

Chung, Sandra (2012b). Reply to the commentaries. *Theoretical Linguistics* 38: 137–43.

Craig, Collette Grinewald (1992). *Classifiers in a Functional Perspective*. In R.E. Ascher (ed.), *The Encyclopedia of Language and Linguistics*. Oxford: Pergamon Press. 565–69.

Croft, William (2001). *Radical Construction Grammar*. Oxford: Oxford University Press.

Culicover, Peter (1976). *Syntax*. New York: Academic Press.

Demonte, Violeta (2008). Meaning–form correlations and adjective positions in Spanish. In Louise McNally and Christopher Kennedy (eds), *Adjectives and Adverbs*. Oxford: Oxford University Press, 71–100.

Dixon, R.M.W. (1977). Where have all the adjectives gone? *Studies in Language* 1: 19–80. doi.org/10.1075/sl.1.1.04dix

Dryer, Matthew S. (1997). Are grammatical relations universal? In Joan Bybee, John Haiman and Sandra Thompson (eds), *Essays on Language Function and Language Type*. Amsterdam: John Benjamins, 115–43.

Evans, Nicholas and Toshiki Osada (2005). Mundari: The myth of a language without word classes. *Linguistic Typology* 9: 351–90. doi.org/10.1515/lity.2005.9.3.351.

Geach, Peter (1962). *Reference and Generality*. Ithaca, New York: Cornell University Press.

Goddard, Cliff (2009). A piece of cheese, a grain of sand: The semantics of mass nouns and unitizers. In Francis Jeffrey Pelletier (ed.), *Kinds, Things and Stuff*. New York and Oxford: Oxford University Press, 132–65. doi.org/10.1093/acprof:oso/9780195382891.003.0008.

Goddard, Cliff (2011). The lexical semantics of 'language' (with special reference to 'words'). *Language Sciences* 33: 40–57. doi.org/10.1016/j.langsci.2010.03.003.

Goddard, Cliff (2017). Furniture, Vegetables, Weapons: Functional collective superordinates in the English lexicon. In Zhengdao Ye (ed.), *The Semantics of Nouns*. Oxford: Oxford University Press, 246–81. doi.org/10.1093/oso/9780198736721.003.0010.

Gross, Maurice (1979). On the failure of generative grammar. *Language* 55: 859–85.

Gupta, Anil (1980). *The Logic of Common Nouns*. New Haven, Connecticut: Yale University Press.

Hale, Kenneth L. (1973). Person marking in Warlpiri. In Stephen Anderson and Paul Kiparsky (eds), *A Festschrift for Morris Halle*. New York: Holt, Rinehart and Winston, 308–44.

Haspelmath, Martin (2010). Comparative concepts and descriptive categories in crosslinguistic studies. *Language* 86: 663–87. doi.org/10.1353/lan.2010.0021.

Haspelmath, Martin (2012). Escaping ethnocentrism in the study of word-class universals. *Theoretical Linguistics* 38: 91–102. doi.org/10.1515/tl-2012-0004.

Lyons, John (1968). *Introduction to Theoretical Linguistics*. Cambridge: Cambridge University Press.

Matsumoto, Yo (1996). *Complex Predicates in Japanese*. Palo Alto, California: CSLI Publications.

Mohanan, Tara (1994). *Argument Structure in Hindi*. Stanford, California: Center for the Study of Language and Information.

Mosel, Ulrike and Even Hovdhaugen (1992). *Samoan Reference Grammar*. Oslo: Scandinavian University Press.

Nash, David G. (1986). *Topics in Warlpiri Grammar*. New York: Garland Press.

Panagiotidis, Phoevos (2015). *Categorial Features*. Oxford: Oxford University Press.

Pawley, Andrew (2006). Where have all the verbs gone: Remarks on the organisation of languages with small, closed verb classes. Paper presented at *Eleventh Biennial Symposium on Intertheoretical Approaches to Complex Verb Constructions*. Houston, Texas: Rice University.

Pfaff, Alexander Peter (2015). Adjectival and Genitival Modification in Definite Noun Phrases in Icelandic. Unpublished PhD dissertation, University of Tromsø.

Preminger, Omer (2019). What the PCC tells us about 'abstract' agreement, head movement, and locality. *Glossa* 13: 1–42. doi.org/10.5334/gjgl.315.

Schachter, Paul and Timothy Shopen (2007). Parts-of-speech systems. In Timothy Shopen (ed.), *Language Typology and Syntactic Description*. Cambridge: Cambridge University Press, 1–60.

Schultze-Berndt, Eva (2000). *Simple and Complex Verbs in Jaminjung: A Study of Event Categorization in an Australian Language*. MPI Series in Psycholinguistics. Neimegen: MPI.

Siegel, Muffy (1976). Capturing the Russian adjective. In Barbara Partee (ed.), *Montague Grammar*. New York: Academic Press, 293–309. doi.org/10.1016/b978-0-12-545850-4.50016-9.

Simpson, Jane H. (1991). *Warlpiri Morpho-Syntax*. Boston: Kluwer Academic.

Toivonen, Ida (2001). The Syntax of Non-Projecting Words. Unpublished PhD dissertation, Stanford University.

Topping, Donald M. (1973). *Chamorro Reference Grammar*. Honolulu: University of Hawai'i Press.

Wierzbicka, Anna (1986). What's in a noun? (Or: How do nouns differ in meaning from adjectives?). *Studies in Language* 10 (2): 353–89. doi.org/10.1075/sl.10.2.05wie.

Wierzbicka, Anna (2010). Lexical prototypes as a universal basis for cross-linguistic identification of parts of speech. In Petra M. Vogel and Bernard Comrie (eds), *Approaches to the Typology of Parts of Speech*. Berlin/New York: Mouton de Gruyter, 285–317. doi.org/10.1515/9783110806120.285.

Yamakido, Hiroko (2005). The Nature of Adjectival Inflection in Japanese. Unpublished PhD thesis, Stony Brook University.

19

Cut-verbs of the Oceanic language Teop: A critical study of collecting and analysing data in a language documentation project

Ulrike Mosel

1. Introduction

Teop is an Oceanic language spoken in Bougainville, Papua New Guinea, and has been documented for more than two decades in close collaboration with a team of native speakers from coastal villages of the Tinputz region.[1] The present study of Teop CUT-verbs was inspired by Anna Wierzbicka when she invited me to a workshop on endangered meanings held in Canberra in 2013. Having been a tutor for her courses in the '90s, I soon realised that the English translation equivalents of Teop CUT-verbs in the Teop Language Corpus do not provide sufficient information for a semantic analysis, because the translators (including myself) have been 'imprisoned in English' (Wierzbicka 2014). To understand the meanings of CUT-verbs, we therefore need to complement the corpus data by

---

1   The Teop language documentation has been funded by the Australian Research Council in 1994, the Volkswagen Stiftung 2000–07, the Deutsche Forschungsgemeinschaft 2007–11 and the private sponsor Annemarie Dahlhaus 2011–14.

observing what people are doing when cutting things, document what we see by videos or photographs and ask native speakers for explanations in their language.

The following sections start with a brief description of the compilation and content of the Teop Language Corpus in section 2. In section 3 I discuss my method of collecting the data for the analysis of CUT-verbs and present a list of all CUT-verbs that are analysed in section 4. This analysis shows that by syntactic and semantic criteria two general and 17 specific CUT-verbs can be distinguished, none of which correspond to English types of CUT-verbs. The last section contains a summary and some thoughts about the compilation of dictionaries of endangered languages.

2. The Teop Language Corpus

The Teop Language Corpus (Mosel et al. 2007) is compiled in ELAN, and currently consists of approximately 250,000 words. ELAN[2] is a software tool that facilitates time-aligned transcriptions and further annotations such as translations on separate tiers. In ELAN, annotated corpora can be searched simultaneously on several tiers by using the query language regular expressions (see Friedl 2006; Mosel 2015, 2018: 260–61).

The corpus contains folk tales, personal histories, procedural texts of house building, canoe building, fishing and cooking, and descriptions of plants and animals. All texts are translated into English. We distinguish between three types of texts: (1) transcriptions of audio recordings, (2) edited versions of the transcriptions done by native speakers and (3) texts written by native speakers without previous recordings. The edited and written texts were checked by indigenous teachers who wanted to use them in school. In the abbreviations of the references for the examples given below these three text types are distinguished by R, E and W. In addition to these texts, the corpus contains collections of example sentences that were written by native speakers on the basis of Teop word lists.

---

2   ELAN is available through the Max Planck Institute for Psycholinguistics, The Language Archive, Nijmegen, The Netherlands. Available at: archive.mpi.nl/tla/elan.

Figure 19.1. *Koro* 'carve the inside of a canoe'; *taraha* 'carve the outside of a canoe'.

Source: Photograph by the author.

For the documentation of the material culture we often took photographs, which were used as illustrations of previously produced texts or as stimuli for eliciting new texts. For example, I watched the butchering of a chicken and of a pig and took a series of photographs that depict every single activity of these complex events. Later the photographs were used for the elicitation of texts (Mosel 2014: 148–49). To get further examples of cutting events I simply observed people, asked them what they were doing, and if they didn't mind, took photographs (Figure 19.1).

In contrast to Majid et al. (2007), I never used video clips or pictures made outside the fieldwork site for elicitation or elicited data by asking for translations from English or Tok Pisin into Teop (see Mosel 2012: 81–82), but a weakness of our corpus is that it lacks data giving negative evidence (cf. Hellwig 2010: 817–19, 824).

3. Data mining

I started my investigation of CUT-verbs by searching the corpus for the English word forms *cut, cuts, cutting* on the free translation tier (f) and their aligned Teop counterparts on the transcription tier (t). The former were searched for by the regular expression <cut(ting)?s?>, the latter by the so-called wild card <.*>. This first search found 18 different Teop words. Then, each of the 18 Teop words was searched for on the transcription tier to find more translation equivalents on the translation tier.

The search for *taraha*, for instance, not only found Teop utterances in which *taraha* was translated by 'cut', but also utterances with the translation equivalents 'carve' and 'shave'. When I then searched for *carve* and *shave*, I did not only find the expected word *taraha*, but also the word *kamuru* 'shave'.

Table 19.1 shows all CUT-verbs of the present study, including reduplicated forms, the number of tokens, meaning descriptions and the referents of the objects. The referents of the subjects are not included, because only the subject of the verb *pee* 'cut' occasionally occurs with a non-human subject referring (e.g.) to the thing that cuts.

(1) *erau   ta   kehaa   pee   vai   bona*
    so   piece   shell   cut   now   4SG.PRON

'(and) so a piece of shell cut her,' (Pur 05R 105)

Table 19.1. Teop CUT-verbs.

Teop verb	Tokens	Meaning descriptions with translation equivalents in brackets	Referents of the object in the corpus
govara, govagovara	38	1) 'cut the head off a person or animal' ('behead') 2) 'cut a person's or animal's head off' 3) 'cut the pointed ends of a canoe' ('carve')	1) person; animal 2) head 3) canoe
hape, hapehape	3	'cut off a protruding part'	branch, fin of a shark
kaku, kaakaku	27	'cut an animal into pieces' ('butcher')	pig, chicken, turtle, fish
kamuru	3	'shave a person's head'	person
kaporo, kapokaporo	28	1) 'cut something with scissors' 2) 'cut a person's hair with scissors'	1) hair, dress 2) person
kepo, kepokepo	35	1) 'cut a log into the shape of something' ('carve') 2) 'cut up (a log)' ('chop')	1) canoe 2) stem of a tree or palm
kopaa, kopakopaa	69	1) 'cut something lengthwise' 2) 'cut something from top to bottom'	1) chicken, pig, stem of a palm, bamboo; strap 2) papaya; watermelon

Teop verb	Tokens	Meaning descriptions with translation equivalents in brackets	Referents of the object in the corpus
koro	37	1) 'cut something out' ('carve out') 2) 'cut the inside of something out'	1) canoe, stem of a sago palm 2) inside of something
kosi, kookosi	28	1) 'cut leaves off a tree, branch or frond' 2) 'cut off the leaves'	1) branch, sago palm, banana plant, pandanus 2) leaves
kurusu, kurukurusu	63	1) 'cut off something long' 2) 'cut off a part of something long'	1) vines, string, dreadlocks 2) head of a pig, crown of a tree, bananas hanging from their stalk
mosi, mosimosi	217	'cut something with any kind of tool except scissors'	all kinds of things
pee, peepee	66	use a small knife or shell and 1) 'make a cut into something' 2) 'cut a part off a whole' 3) 'cut something into pieces'	1) body part 2) body part 3) chicken, cake
poana	10	'cut the upper part off a log resting horizontally when building a canoe' ('slice')	canoe
papaesi	6	'cut the sides of a canoe into shape' ('chop')	canoe
potaa	16	'cut something open'	chicken, pig, bêche-de-mer
rapisi	4	'cut something with a bush knife'	grass, belly of pig
rom, romrom	34	'cut something long crosswise into pieces' ('slice')	trunk of a pig, body of a person, stem of a tree, eggplant, greens
tagava	44	'cut a tree' ('fell')	tree, palm
taraha, tarataraha	46	1) 'cut little parts off a wooden thing to make its surface smooth' ('chop, shave') 2) 'cut something off' ('chop')	1) canoe, knots of bamboo; pestle; mortar; planting stick 2) bark
Total	**774**		

Source: Author's summary, based on Teop Language Corpus.

All CUT-words and multiword expressions containing CUT-words are documented with examples and pictures in *A Multifunctional Teop–English Dictionary* (Mosel 2019). When you search the semantic domain for *cutting*, you find 89 entries with examples and illustrations.

4. The meaning of CUT-words

4.1. Introduction

In accordance with my search methods, the term 'Teop CUT-verbs' does not denote a Teop semantic domain. Before we have analysed the data, we don't know if there is anything other than the translation equivalents that justifies grouping the words together (see Haviland (2006: 153) on 'carry' verbs in Chinese and Tsoltil). My analysis is largely based on Goddard and Wierzbicka's (2009, 2016) parameters of the lexicosyntactic frame, the effect the cutting event has on the object, the instrument and the manner of using the instrument, but for reasons of space and time it does not employ the Natural Semantic Metalanguage. With respect to the corpus-based analysis of CUT-words and their collocations and constructions my approach is influenced by Hanks' work (2012, 2013).

In the following I distinguish between 17 specific and 2 general CUT-verbs. Since the most obvious formal characteristic of the two general CUT-verbs is that they can be modified by specific CUT-verbs in serial verb constructions, the specific CUT-verbs are analysed before the general ones.

In view of these considerations, this chapter is structured as follows: I will first describe the valency patterns of CUT-verbs with a focus on verbs that encode cutting events that separate a part from its whole. In section 4.3, I identify several semantic characteristics that distinguish specific from general CUT-verbs, and then analyse the semantics of two specific CUT-verbs in section 4.4 and of the two general CUT-verbs in section 4.5 and section 4.6, and the origin of two modern CUT-verbs in section 4.7.

4.2. Valency patterns of Teop CUT-verbs

All Teop CUT-verbs are transitive verbs. Their subjects prototypically denote the person doing the action and the objects the person, animal or thing that is affected by the cutting event. With respect to their valency patterns, the verbs denoting events in which a part is cut off its whole form a special group. The object may either refer to the part that is cut off or to the whole that loses the part, which suggests that the kind of part that is cut off is implied in the meaning of the verb or the context.

In the following example the verb *kosi* 'cut leaves' is used in the second type of construction in (2a) and in the first one in (2d). Note that the serial verb construction *mosi hapehape* 'cut off branches' in (2c) also represents the second type of construction.

(2) a. *Be=an   tau   kosi   o   atovo,*
       When=2SG.PRON   TAM   cut.leaves ART   sago palm
       'When you are about to <u>cut sago palm leaves</u>,'

   b. *taba   momohu   toro   paku   an,*
       thing   first   must   do   2SG.PRON
       'the first thing you must do,'

       ean   toro   tagava roho   o   atovo.
       2SG.PRON   must   fell   before   ART   sago palm
       'you must fell a sago palm.'

   c. *Ean   re=   paa   <u>mosi   hape-hape</u>   <u>o   atovo</u>.*
       2SG.PRON   CONSEC TAM   cut   RED-cut.off.   ART   sago.
                                          protruding.part   palm
       'Then you <u>cut off the branches of the sago palm</u>.'

   d. *Ean   re=   paa   <u>kosi   a=maa   paka   atovo</u>*
       2SG.PRON   CONSEC TAM   cut.leaves ART=PLM leaf   sago
                                                              palm
       'Then you <u>cut the sago palm leaves</u>'
       kahi   bono   sinoo   vaa   tobina.
       off   ART   bone   LNK   middle
       'off the midrib.' (Sii Joy 03W 007–009)

Table 19.2 lists all verbs that are attested in both construction types, the verb *kaporo* 'cut with scissors' will be discussed in section 4.3.

Table 19.2. CUT-verbs with two kinds of object referents.

Teop verb	Meaning descriptions	1) Object referent: the whole	2) Object referent: the part
govara	'cut off a person's or an animal's head'	person; animal	head
hape	'cut off a protruding part'	palm	branch, fin of a shark
kaporo	'cut something with scissors'	person dress or skirt	hair —
kosi	'cut the leaves off something'	tree, palm, branch	leaves
koro	'cut out the inside of something'	log, canoe	the inside of something
taraha	'shave something off'	log	bark

Source: Author's summary, based on Teop Language Corpus.

4.3. The meaning of CUT-verbs in context

As illustrated by the examples (3) and (4) and summarised in Table 19.3, most cutting events encoded by the specific CUT-verbs and their constructions can be distinguished by one or more of the following characteristics:

1. a certain part that is cut off a whole; for example *kosi* 'cut leaves' (2), *koro* 'cut out the inside of a log, a canoe, a mortar' (3d)
2. the fact that something is cut off and removed from its original place; for example *tagava* 'cut, fell a tree' (2b, 3a, 3b)
3. the fact that something is cut into pieces (4)
4. the instrument used for the cutting; for example *kaporo* 'cut with scissors' (4)
5. the movement of the cutting instrument in relation to the dimensions of the thing that is cut (3b, 3c).

The citation (3) comes from a description of the sago palm, whereas (4) is said by a teacher of needlework in a personal oral narrative.

(3) a. *Na* antee *ra=* *ara* tea *tagava*,
    TAM2 can 1PL. 1PL. COMPL fell
    IN.IPFV= IN.PRON

   'We can fell (it),'

   o *atovo* *mee* *o* *manoto*.
   ART sago.palm also ART ready to be harvested

   'the sago palm is also ready to be harvested.'

   b. <u>*Tagava*</u> *vai* *ori,* *o=re* *paa* <u>*rom*</u> *bari*.
   fell now 3PL. 3PL. TAM3 cut.crosswise 4PL.
   PRON, PRON=CONSEC PRON

   'They <u>fell</u> (it), and then they <u>cut</u> it <u>crosswise into pieces</u>.'

   c. *O=re* *paa* <u>*kopaa*</u> *pete* *bari*.
   3pl.pron=consec tam3 cut. in.addition 4PL.
   lengthwise PRON

   'Then they <u>cut</u> them (the pieces) <u>lengthwise</u>.'

   d. *Matatopo* *vai* *tea* <u>*koro*</u> *bono* *koma* *atovo* ...
   ready now COMPL carve.out ART inside sago.palm

   'Now (the people) are ready to <u>carve</u> out <u>the inside</u> of the sago palm ...'

   (Sii 17W 124–126)

(4) a. *be=* *naa* <u>*kaporo*</u> *bata* *nom*
   when= 1SG.PRON cut.with.scissors for.a.while 1SG.IPFV

   '(You keep watching) while I am <u>cutting</u> (the cloth for)'

   b. *o* *koros* *te=an* *ge* *sikioti* *te=an*.
   ART dress PREP=2SG.PRON or skirt PREP=2SG.PRON

   'your dress or your skirt (into size).' (Nan 01R 099)

Table 19.3. Types of cutting events.

Cutting events	Verbs	Meanings of the verbs and their contexts
Cut-off-a-part-from-its-whole	*govara*	'cut off a person's or an animal's head'
	hape	'cut off a protruding part (branch of a tree, the fin of a shark)'
	kamuru	'shave a person's head'
	kaporo	'cut a person's hair with scissors'
	koro	'cut out the inside of a log, a canoe, a mortar'
	kosi	'cut off the leaves of a tree, palm, branch or frond'
	kurusu	1) 'cut off something long' (e.g. an animal's tail) 2) 'cut off a part of something long' (e.g. the head of a pig, the crown of a felled tree)
	poana	'cut off the upper part of a log'
	taraha	'cut little parts off the surface of a wooden thing to make it smooth'
Cut-off-something-from-its-place	*kurusu*	'cut off something long' (e.g. vines in the jungle)
	tagava	'cut a tree' ('fell')
Cut-something-into-pieces	*kaku*	'cut an animal into many different parts'
	kaporo	'cut something into pieces with scissors' (4)
	kepo	'cut up a log; cut a log into the shape of something'
	kopaa	'cut something lengthwise or from the top to the bottom' (see §4.4)
	rom	'cut something crosswise into pieces' (§4.4)
Cut-something-by-a-specified-movement of the instrument	*kopaa*	'cut something lengthwise or from top to bottom' (§4.4)
	rom	'cut something crosswise' (see §4.4)
Cut-something-with-a-specific-instrument	*kaporo*	'cut something with scissors' (4–6)
	rapisi	'cut something with a bush knife'

Source: Author's summary, based on Teop Language Corpus.

In Table 19.3, the specific CUT-verbs are sorted according to the five characteristics of cutting events listed above. Due to the interaction of the meaning of CUT-verbs and the meaning of their contexts, several verbs are listed in more than one field of the types of cutting events. A typical verb that can be used for the encoding of distinct cutting events is *kaporo* 'cut something with scissors'. While the construction of *kaporo* in (4) belongs to the type Cut-something-into-pieces, the construction of *kaporo* in (5) belongs to the type Cut-off-a-part-from-its-whole.

(5) be=an   *kaporo*   nom   a   vunuu na=e
    when=2SG.   cut.with.   2SG.IPFV   ART   hair   3SG.POSS=3SG.
    PRON   scissors   PRON

    'when you <u>cut</u> his hair' (Sia 01E(Joy) 120)

In (5) the part, *vunuu* 'hair', and the whole, *nae* 'his', are explicitly mentioned, but hair-cutting events can also be encoded by clauses in which the object of *kaporo* 'cut with scissors' does not refer to the hair, but to the person who gets a haircut as in (6).

(6) *Meve*   paa   *kaporo*   bene   *Sookara.*
    And.3SG.PRON   TAM   cut.with.scissors ART   Sookara

    'And she <u>gave</u> Sookara a <u>haircut</u>.' (Sia 01E(Joy) 123)[3]

In (6) *vunuu* 'hair' is not mentioned but nevertheless the clause refers to a hair-cutting event and does not mean 'she cut Sookara with scissors'. Since all 14 occurrences of *kaporo* with an object referring to a person mean that this person gets his or her hair cut with scissors, this construction can be regarded as a conventional phraseological pattern (Hanks 2012: 75, 2013: 95).

4.4. Cutting lengthwise and crosswise

The meanings of the two verbs *kopaa* 'cut something lengthwise or from top to bottom' and *rom* 'cut something crosswise' are not evident from their original translations in texts, because both verbs are simply translated by 'cut' or 'cut up'. Occasionally *kopaa* is translated by 'cut open' and *rom* by 'slice'.

---

3   Note that (5) and (6) refer to the same event in a personal narrative.

Figure 19.2. *Kopaa* 'cut something lengthwise'.
Source: Photograph by the author.

That the two essential distinctive semantic features of *kopaa* and *rom* are 'lengthwise or from top to bottom' and 'crosswise', respectively, only became obvious to me when I observed cutting events and asked native speakers what they were doing.

The objects of *rom* and *kopaa* typically refer to long things like a bamboo or the trunk of a pig (Figure 19.2). But I also heard people using the verb *kopaa* when they showed me how they cut up citrus fruit and watermelons. In this case, the cut starts at the stalk and runs down to the bottom (Figure 19.3), while *rom* denotes a crosswise cut (Figure 19.4). These observations and the native speakers' comments led me to the hypothesis that the distinctive feature between *kopaa* and *rom* is the movement of the cutting instrument in relation to the dimensional properties of the thing that is cut, though only very few of the original translations reflect this semantic characteristic.

Furthermore, with respect to the butchering of chickens and pigs, my interpretation is supported by the observation that in the context of butchering the cut called *kopaa* and translated by 'cut open' starts at the throat and runs down to the anus. Additional evidence is found in the descriptions of colourful fishes and the drawings by the Teop artist Neville Vitahi. Stripes that run from the head to the tail are called *rahirahi kopaa* 'horizontal stripes' and those that run crosswise *rahirahi rom* 'vertical stripes'.

Figure 19.3. *Kopaa* **'cut from top to bottom'.**
Source: Photograph by the author.

Figure 19.4. *Rom* **'cut crosswise'.**
Source: Photograph by the author.

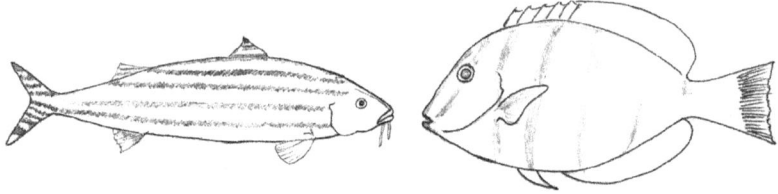

Figure 19.5. *Riivivi* (an unidentified fish), *koinia* 'Convict Surgeonfish'.
Source: Photograph by the author.

(7) *A   iana   riirivi …,*
    ART   fish   riivivi
    'The *riirivi* fish …,'
    evehee   a   sii   rahirahi kopaa   a   rom   na=e.
    but   ART   DIM   stripes   lengthwise ART   trunk   3SG.POSS=3SG.
                                                                PRON
    'but its trunk is a bit <u>striped from the head to the tail</u>.' (Sii 11W 096)

(8) *A   koinia …   a   rahirahi   rom   paru …*
    ART   Convict Surgeonfish …   ART   stripes   crosswise   black
    'The Convict Surgeonfish … has black <u>vertical stripes</u> …'
    (Vaa 09W 212)

Once I had discovered the essential semantic features 'crosswise' and 'lengthwise or from top to bottom', I started revising the translations. The following revised example illustrates how confusing the earlier version was that translated *romrom* simply by 'cut' and *kopaa* by 'cut open'.

(9) *Be=ara   rom-rom   vakavara   e,*
    When=1PL.IN   RED-cut.crosswise   finished   3SG.PRON
    'When we have finished <u>cutting</u> it <u>up crosswise</u>,' (i.e. the palm stem)
    eara   re=paa   paku pete   a   kiu   vaa   tea   kopaa.
    1PL.   CONSEC=TAM do   also   ART   work   LNK   COMPL   cut.
    IN.PRON   lengthwise
    'we also do the work of <u>cutting lengthwise</u>.'
    Eara   he   toro   kopaa   e   te=o   hum   buaku.
    1PL.   but   must   cut.lengthwise   3SG.PRON   PREP=ART piece two
    IN.PRON
    'But we must <u>cut</u> them <u>lengthwise into</u> <u>two pieces</u>.' (Eno 04W 015)

In other contexts, however, the translation of *kopaa* by 'cut open' can make sense for the reader of the English translation, as in the examples (3c) and (10):

(10) *Murinae   eara   re=paa   pee   kopaa   e   guu.*
     after.that 1PL.   CONSEC=   cut.with.   cut.   ART   pig
                 IN.PRON   TAM   knife   lengthwise

'After that we <u>cut</u> the pig <u>open</u>'. (Then we start pulling out the inside of the pig.)'
(Eno 10E(Eno) 028–029)

Events of cutting open a palm or an animal's belly are also expressed by *potaa* 'cut something open', which in contrast to *kopaa* is not attested in any other contexts or with translation equivalents:

(11) *Me=ori   paa   potaa   bene   guu, …*
     And=3PL.PRON   TAM   cut.open   ART   pig

'And they <u>cut</u> the pig <u>open</u> (and put the intestines on a raft).'
(Aro 15R 110–112)

These data suggest that the translation 'open' is not a semantic component of the word *kopaa*, but results from the word's usage in particular contexts where a lengthwise cut has the effect that something is cut open.

In conclusion, the semantic analysis of words should not exclusively rely on translation equivalents, because the source and the target languages may differ in their selection of which specific features of events, things and properties they encode (cf. Hellwig 2010), so that subtle distinctive features of the source language may not surface in translation equivalents, and vice versa: translation equivalents may encode features that are absent in the words of the source language. While in Teop the meanings 'open' and 'into pieces' are not encoded in the verb *kopaa*, the meaning 'lengthwise or from top to bottom' is not encoded in English 'cut' (cf. the explications of 'cut' in Goddard and Wierzbicka 2009: 64, 2016: 224).

4.5. The general CUT-verb *mosi* 'cut'

The verb *mosi* 'cut' encodes various kinds of cutting events that are distinguished by specific CUT-verbs, which leads to the assumption that *mosi* can be classified as a general CUT-verb or even as a hypernym of several other CUT-verbs. The actions denoted by *mosi* 'cut' can be carried out by knives and axes, but in contrast to English 'cut' not by scissors (see section 4.7).

There are three kinds of evidence for *mosi* being a general CUT-verb:

1. its high frequency (see Table 19.1)
2. its use in the very same context as specific CUT-verbs
3. its modification by specific CUT-verbs in a serial verb construction.

The verb *mosi* 'cut' is used to refer to the same kind of cutting events as *hape* 'cut off a protruding part', *koro* 'cut the inside out', *pee* 'cut with a knife or shell' and *tagava* 'fell a tree'. For example, in the legend of the origin of the coconut, *mosi* 'cut' and *pee* 'cut with a knife or shell' occur in exactly the same kind of context:

(12) *Ean   toro   mosi   a   moo-naa,* ...
     2SG.PRON   must   cut   ART   leg-1SG.PRON

   'You must cut off my leg, (and then throw it to him).' (San 01R 042)

(13) *Me   keara   teve   paa   pee   bona   moo-na=e*
     and   brother   PREP.3SG.   TAM3   cut   ART   leg-3SG.
                       PRON   POSS=3SG.PRON

   'And his brother cut his leg (and threw (it) to the spirit).'
   (San 01R 047)

Mosi may also be used in a context where someone cuts into something.

(14) *E   sumeke   paa   mosi   bona   moo-na=e   me=paa   rerevasin.*
     ART   old.man   TAM   cut   ART   leg-3SG.POSS=   and=TAM   bleed
                                             3SG.PRON

   'The old man cut his leg, and it bled.' (Jub 01W 031)

The distinction between the events of Cutting-off-something and Cutting-into-something is not lexicalised or encoded by conventional phraseological patterns, but only understood from the individual contexts of the verb *mosi* 'cut'.

Similar to the pair of *mosi* 'cut' and *pee* 'cut with a knife or shell', the two verbs *mosi* 'cut' and *koro* 'cut out the inside' are found in the very same context.

(15) ... <u>*mosi*</u>   bata   bona   <u>*koma*-*n=o*</u>   *sinivi*.
... cut   for.a.while   ART   inside-3SG.POSS=ART   canoe

'(then it is finished,) (and they) <u>cut</u> the <u>inside</u> of the canoe.'
(Tah 02R 087)

(16) ... *a=re*   *paa*   *taneo*   *tea*   <u>*koro*</u>   *a*   <u>*kom-a-n=o*</u>   *sinivi* ...
1PL.IN=CONSEC   TAM   start   COMPL   carve   ART   inside-3SG.POSS=ART   canoe

'... (and) we then start <u>carving</u> out the <u>inside</u> of the canoe, ...'
(Tah 02E(Eno).023)

The third kind of evidence, the modification of the verb *mosi* 'cut' by specific CUT-verbs in a serial verb construction suggests that the semantic features of these modifying verbs are not part of the meaning of *mosi* (see Table 19.4).

Table 19.4. *Mosi* and modifying serial verbs.

Serial verbs		Meaning descriptions of *mosi* and serial verbs	Examples
mosi govara	cut	cut the head off	22
mosi hape	cut	cut off a protruding part	17
mosi hapehape	cut	cut off protruding parts	2c
mosi kopaa	cut	cut lengthwise	18
mosi kurusu	cut	cut off something from something long cut off something long	19
mosi rom *mosimosi rom*	cut	cut something crosswise cut something into slices	Sii 41W 051, Jen 01R 073

Source: Author's summary, based on Teop Language Corpus.

(17) *Be=an rake ta   mosi hape   to peho peana, …*
　　 if=2SG. want COMPL cut cut.off.   ART some branch
　　 PRON   protruding.part
　　 'If you want to <u>cut off</u> a branch, …' (Sii 41W 037)

(18) *me=paa mosi kopaa   bene toa   te=o   buaku o   hum*
　　 and=TAM cut cut.   ART chicken PREP= two   ART part
　　 lengthwise   ART
　　 '… and he <u>cut</u> the chicken <u>lengthwise</u> into two parts.'
　　 (Pau 01E 019)

(19) *A   otei paa mosi kurusu   bono kakarusu*
　　 ART man   TAM cut   cut.something.long   ART   claw
　　 'The man is <u>cutting off</u> the claws'
　　 moo-n=e   toa.
　　 leg-3SG.POSS=ART   chicken
　　 'from the chicken's legs.' (Joy 11W 018)[4]

Further evidence for the classification of *mosi* 'cut' as a general CUT-verb is provided by the following quotation from a text about canoe building in which the author speaks of various kinds of cuts.

(20) *Me=an   antee nom   tea   mosi a=maa   kaku mosi*
　　 and=2SG. can   2SG.IPFV COMPLI   cut   ART=PLM   kind cut
　　 PRON
　　 　'And you can <u>cut</u> the <u>kinds of cutting</u>
　　 tabae   to   paku   nom=an
　　 what   REL   do   2sg.ipfv=2sg.pron
　　 　'whatever (it is) that you (want to) do' (Mor 04R 44–47)

4　The text Joy 11W are captions that Joyce Maion wrote for 54 photographs showing the butchering of a chicken, see also (22–24).

4.6. The cut-verb *pee* 'cut with a knife or shell'

Compared to *mosi* 'cut', the verb *pee* 'cut with a knife or shell' is a specific cut-verb as it only denotes cutting events that are carried out with a small instrument.

(21) ... *enam   re=   paa   gono   o   koopu,*
                                             vahabana
     1PL.   CONSEC=   get   again   ART   small.knife
     EX.PRON   TAM

'... we get the small knife again,'

   nam   paa   pee-pee   e   toa.
   1PL.EX   TAM   RED-cut.with.   ART   chicken
                          knife/shell

'we cut up the chicken.' (Hel 13R 029–030)

But similar to *mosi* 'cut', it may be modified by a specific cut-verb in a serial verb constructions (10, 22–23) and does not function itself as a modifying serial verb (see Table 19.5). Therefore I also classify it as a general cut-verb.

(22) *E   toa   paa   pee   potaa   vaevuru   a   otei.*
     ART rooster   TAM   cut.with.   cut.open   already   ART   man
                           knife/shell

     'The rooster has already been cut open by the man.'
     (Joy 11W 017)

(23) *A   otei   na   pee   kopaa   nana   bene   toa*
     ART man   TAM   cut.with.   cut.   3SG.IPFV   ART   chicken
                     knife/shell   lengthwise

'The man is cutting the rooster'

   te=o   buaku   hum
   PREP=ART   two   piece

'into two pieces.' (Joy 011W 037)

Table 19.5. Serial verb constructions headed by *pee*.

Serial verbs	Meaning descriptions of *mosi* and serial verbs		Example
pee kopaa	cut with a knife/shell	cut something lengthwise	10, 24
pee kurusu	cut with a knife/shell	cut off something long	23
pee potaa	cut with a knife/shell	cut something open	22

Source: Author's summary, based on Teop Language Corpus.

Depending on its context, *pee* 'cut with a knife or shell' may be interpreted as 'cut something into pieces' (21) or 'cut into something' (24). In the following example, the cut denoted by *pee* marks the place where later the head of the pig is cut off.

(24) ... *e-ara   re=paa   taneo   tea   pee   vakikiimana   bana*
     ... H-1PL. CONSEC=TAM start   COMPL   cut   mark   again
     IN.PRON

'... then we start to <u>cut</u> (and) <u>mark</u> again'

o   hum   to   kahi   mosi   govara   kaakoo   ra=ara
ART part   REL   TAM   cut   behead as.directed 1PL.IN.IPFV=1PL.
                                                                                    IN.PRON

'the place where we have to <u>cut off</u>'

a   kaho-na=e.
ART   head-3SG.POSS=3SG.PRON

'its head.'

4.7. Cut-verbs derived by semantic extensions

There are two CUT-verbs that are derived by semantic extensions, namely *kaporo* 'cut with scissors' and *rapisi* 'cut grass; cut with a long bush knife'. The original meaning of the verb *kaporo* is 'remove the hot stones from the fire in the earth oven with tongs', but with the introduction of scissors the meaning was obviously extended to 'cut with scissors'. The word form *kaporo* is also a noun, meaning 'tongs' from which the noun *kaporo* 'scissors' is derived. The colexification[5] of tools and the actions done with tools is a common pattern in the Teop language. Scissors and tongs have similar shapes and also the movements of their two parts are similar.

---

5   The term colexification was coined by François (2008).

Figure 19.6. *Rapisi* 'cut with a bush knife'.
Source: Photograph by the author.

The verb *rapisi* 'cut with the bush knife' originally means 'whip'. Whipping and cutting, for example, the grass with a bush knife have in common that both activities are carried out by holding the stick or the knife in one hand, raising the arm behind one's head and swinging it down. This characteristic also explains why *rapisi* does not cover the meaning of mowing the grass with a mower.

5. Summary and concluding remarks

The Teop Language Corpus was systematically searched by three successive searches:

1. the search for 'cut' and its Teop counterparts
2. the search for the Teop words found in the first search (e.g. *govara* etc.), to find more English translation equivalents than 'cut' (e.g. 'behead')
3. the search for the new English translation equivalents to discover new Teop CUT-words.

The corpus-based analysis and the observation of cutting events with subsequent explanations by native speakers show that in many aspects Teop CUT-verbs are significantly different from their English translation equivalents:

1. The verb *mosi* 'cut' is a general CUT-verb. First, it is used within the same context as more specific CUT-verbs; second, it can be modified by specific CUT-verbs; and third, the action denoted by *mosi* 'cut' can be carried out by any kind of instrument with one sharp edge. The third characteristic explains why the word *kaporo* 'cut with scissors'

was created when scissors were introduced into the Teop culture (see point 6, below). In contrast to the Teop word *mosi*, the English translation equivalent 'cut' includes the meaning 'cut with scissors' (see Goddard 2012: 713, 2015: 1692; Goddard and Wierzbicka 2016: 224[6]).

2. The number of distinct Teop CUT-verbs—19—exceeds the number of their 7 English translation equivalents 'behead, butcher, carve, chop, fell, shave, slice'.

3. The specific CUT-verbs distinguish between:
   1. different kinds of objects that are cut (section 4.3);
   2. different placements of the cut in relation to the dimensional properties of the thing or animal that is cut (section 4.4);
   3. different instruments (sections 4.6 and 4.7).

4. Although *pee* 'cut with a small knife or shell' is a specific CUT-verb, it can also be considered as a general CUT-verb because like *mosi* 'cut' it can be modified by other specific CUT-verbs (section 4.6).

5. Specific CUT-verbs meaning 'cut a part off its whole' show two alternating valency patterns that denote the same kind of cutting event. The object of these verbs may either refer to a part of the whole or to the whole; that is, a thing, a person or an animal (section 4.2).

6. The verb-object constructions of the three verbs *kopaa* 'cut lengthwise or from top to bottom', *mosi* 'cut' and *pee* 'cut with a knife or a shell' do not distinguish between 'cut something into pieces' and 'cut into something'. The effect of the cutting event can only be understood from the wider context.

7. The verbs *kaporo* 'cut with scissors' and *rapisi* 'cut something with a bush knife', which denote cutting events with recently imported instruments, are derived by semantic extensions from traditional action verbs. In both cases, the motivation for the semantic extension seems to be the movement of the cutting instrument.

The findings of our analysis suggest that lexicographers in language documentation projects should be aware of the fact that translation equivalents do not render the meanings of words and that the senses of words depend on their contexts. Consequently, if the dictionary is meant

---

6   In their explications of 'cut', Goddard and Wierzbicka give 'paper' as an example for the object of 'Someone is cutting something'. Since the cutting of paper is prototypically performed with scissors, their analysis of the English word 'cut' seems to include the cutting with scissors.

to document the semantics of the lexicon rather than serving as a tool for rapid translations, the production of the dictionary requires time-consuming semantic analyses (Haviland 2006; Mosel 2011). In any case, the dictionary entries should contain authentic translated examples that show the conventional use of the lemma (headword) and its different senses in context (Hanks 2013: 3–5; Mosel 2018: 262–63; Rehg 2018: 319–21).

References

François, Alexandre (2008). Semantic maps and the typology of colexification: Intertwining polysemous networks across languages. In Martine Vanhove (ed.), *From Polysemy to Semantic Change*. Amsterdam: John Benjamins, 163–215. doi.org/10.1075/slcs.106.09fra.

Friedl, Jeffrey E.F. (2006). *Mastering Regular Expressions*. Beijing, Cambridge: O'Reilly.

Goddard, Cliff (2012). Semantic primes, semantic molecules, semantic templates: Key concepts in the NSM approach to lexical typology. *Linguistics* 50 (3): 711–43. doi.org/10.1515/ling-2012-0022.

Goddard, Cliff (2015). Verb classes and valency alternations (NSM approach), with special reference to English physical activity verbs. In Andrej Malchukov and Bernard Comrie (eds), *Valency Classes in the World's Languages*. Berlin: Walter de Gruyter, 1649–80. doi.org/10.1515/9783110429343-020.

Goddard, Cliff and Anna Wierzbicka (2009). Contrastive semantics of physical activity verbs: 'Cutting' and 'chopping' in English, Polish, and Japanese. *Language Sciences* 31: 60–96. doi.org/10.1016/j.langsci.2007.10.002.

Goddard, Cliff and Anna Wierzbicka (2016). Explicating the English lexicon of 'doing and happening'. *Functions of Language* 23 (2): 214–56. doi.org/10.1075/fol.23.2.03god.

Hanks, Patrick (2012). Corpus evidence and electronic lexicography. In Syviane Granger and Magali Paquot (eds), *Electronic Lexicography*. Oxford: Oxford University Press, 57–82. doi.org/10.1093/acprof:oso/9780199654864.003.0004.

Hanks, Patrick (2013). *Lexical Analysis: Norms and Exploitations*. Cambridge, MA: MIT Press.

Haviland, John (2006). Documenting lexical knowledge. In Jost Gippert, Nikolaus P. Himmelmann and Ulrike Mosel (eds), *Essentials of Language Documentation*. Berlin, New York: Walter de Gruyter GmbH, 129–62.

Hellwig, Birgit (2010). Meaning and translation in linguistic fieldwork. *Studies in Language* 34 (4): 802–31.

Majid, Asifa, Melissa Bowerman, Miriam van Staden and James S. Boster (2007). The semantic categories of cutting and breaking events: A crosslinguistic perspective. *Cognitive Linguistics* 18 (2): 133–52. doi.org/10.1515/cog.2007.005.

Mosel, Ulrike (2011). Lexicography in endangered language communities. In Peter Austin and Julia Sallabank (eds), *The Handbook of Endangered Languages*. Cambridge: Cambridge University Press, 337–53. doi.org/10.1017/cbo9780511975981.017.

Mosel, Ulrike (2012). Morphosyntactic analysis in the field: A guide to the guides. In Nick Thieberger (ed.), *The Oxford Handbook of Linguistic Fieldwork*. Oxford: Oxford University Press, 72–89.

Mosel, Ulrike (2014). Corpus linguistic and documentary approaches in writing a grammar of a previously undescribed language. In Toshihide Nakayama and Karen Rice (eds), *Practical and Methodological Issues in Grammar Writing* (Language Documentation and Conversation. Special Publication No. 8). Honolulu: University of Hawai'i at Manoa, 135–57. Available at: hdl.handle.net/10125/4589.

Mosel, Ulrike (2015). *Searches with Regular Expressions in ELAN Corpora*. 13 July. Available at: tla.mpi.nl/wp-content/uploads/2011/12/Searches in ELAN with regular expressions.pdf.

Mosel, Ulrike (2018). Corpus compilation and exploitation in language documentation projects. In Kenneth Rehg and Lyle Campbell (eds), *The Oxford Handbook of Endangered Languages*. Oxford: Oxford University Press, 248–70. doi.org/10.1093/oxfordhb/9780190610029.013.14.

Mosel, Ulrike. (2019). A multifunctional Teop-English dictionary. *Dictionaria* 4: 1–6488. Available at: dictionaria.clld.org/contributions/teop. doi.org/10.5281/zenodo.3257580.

Mosel, Ulrike, Enoch Horai Magum, Jubilie Kamai, Joyce Maion, Naphtali Maion, Siimaa Ruth Rigamu, Ruth Saovana Spriggs and Yvonne Thiesen (2007). *The Teop Language Corpus*. Available at: dobes.mpi.nl/projects/teop/.

Rehg, Kenneth L. (2018). Compiling dictionaries of endangered languages. In Kenneth Rehg and Lyle Campbell (eds), *The Oxford Handbook of Endangered Languages.* Oxford, New York: Oxford University Press, 303–26. doi.org/10.1093/oxfordhb/9780190610029.013.16.

Wierzbicka, Anna (2014). *Imprisoned in English: The Hazards of English as a Default Language.* New York: Oxford University Press.

20

The depiction of sensing events in English and Kalam

Andrew Pawley

1. Introduction

Languages are designed for talking about events and situations (for brevity's sake I will use 'event' to cover both).[1] The quintessential means for constructing word-pictures of events are sentence-sized constructions in which acts, processes and states and their participants can be analytically specified—represented by words and phrases that are assigned grammatical roles, as verb, subject, direct object, etc. As the senses provide the basis of human experience of the world, it is of some interest to compare the way different languages represent sensing events and to consider explanations for the commonalities and the differences. This essay compares the way sensing events are depicted in English and in Kalam, a language of the Trans New Guinea family. Some striking differences in syntactic and semantic representations are found.

---

1   I am very pleased to dedicate this essay to Anna Wierzbicka, a great philosopher of language. Anna has written perceptively about understanding the senses, with reference to the semantic primitives of Natural Semantic Metalanguage (NSM), though she has not, as far as I know, focused squarely on the central concern of this chapter, which is cross-linguistic variation in ways of representing sensing events (but see Wierzbicka 1996:81–82 and 2010:78–82). For helpful comments on a draft, I am indebted to Andy Rogers, the editors and an anonymous referee.

Neuroscientists accept the five primary senses distinguished by Aristotle—sight, hearing, smell, taste and feeling by touch—but tell us that humans have other senses as well. Some, such as sensitivity to temperature and vibrations, and itching, are attributable to receptors in the skin, but others, such as awareness of balance/movement (where the body is in space), of various bodily needs and urges (hunger, thirst, needing to vomit, urinate, etc.) and of pain in an internal body part, occur by means of different receptors. For want of a better name I will refer to these other, non-primary senses as 'body internal' or 'visceral' senses.

All sensing events may be viewed as involving a *stimulus* or *sensation* (the thing that is sensed), an *experiencer* (a sentient being that is aware of the stimulus or sensation) and a *sensing process* or *mechanism* (the means by which the stimulus is received, e.g. by hearing, smelling, etc.). However, sensing events are otherwise quite diverse—the nature of the stimuli and the sensing mechanisms and their relation to the experiencer differ across the senses—and one might expect this diversity to be mirrored in the way different kinds of sensing events are represented linguistically.

The question arises how far the structural commonalities and differences that languages show in their representations of sensing events are predictable from common sense observations about the nature of these events. By 'common sense observations' I mean those that might be made by casual observation and reflection, without recourse to scientific study of human anatomy, physiology, perception, etc. For example, a common sense view of the mechanics of seeing is that we see things with our eyes, as opposed to the 'scientific' view that we see by using light in the visible spectrum reflected by objects in the environment, converting it into neuronal signals which travel from the retina to central ganglia in the brain.

There are many different logical possibilities for representing sensing processes linguistically. One is for each sense to be represented by a different verb, as with English *see, hear, smell, taste* and *feel (by touch)*. Given that each of the five primary senses is associated with a different sensory organ—the eyes, ears, nose, mouth and skin (or body), respectively—another possibility is for a language to employ a single general verb of sensing, gloss it *perceive* and to combine this verb with the name of each of the sensory organs, yielding a set of phrasal verbs along the lines of *perceive with the eyes, perceive with the ears*, etc.

Another way of distinguishing sensing processes might be to combine a verb meaning 'perceive' with a verb denoting an act that is preparatory to the achievement of perception, such as *look perceive, listen perceive, sniff perceive, consume perceive* and *touch perceive*. This makes sense, at least for tasting and feeling by touch, because normally before you taste something you put it in your mouth and start to consume it, and before you feel an object you come into bodily contact with it. It fits less well with seeing, hearing and smelling, because while these sensing processes may be preceded by an act of looking, listening or sniffing, this need not be the case. The act of perception may be accidental.

Wierzbicka (1996, 2010) argues for a contrast between sense concepts that are 'mental predicates' and those that are 'sensory predicates'. She regards 'see' and 'hear' as mental predicates on the grounds that we can conceive of 'seeing' and 'hearing' in a more abstract, less physical way than we can conceive of the 'sensory predicates', 'smell', 'taste' and 'touch' (Wierzbicka 1996: 82).

> The five senses are different from one another in various respects. Some of them (smell, taste, and touch) refer to what a person feels in particular parts of the body. Others (sight and hearing) do not refer to any bodily feeling but to processes (seeing and hearing) which are conceptually distinct from 'feeling'. This means that the notion of 'senses' in general cannot be reduced to what a person *feels* in particular parts of the body (as a source of knowledge about the environment). (Wierzbicka 2010: 157)

'See' and 'hear' are accorded the status of semantic primitives, which are undefinable. The notion that 'see' and 'hear' mean to know something by means of one's eyes or ears is rejected. To accept such a definition would mean that we could not define eyes and ears via 'see' and 'hear' without circularity. She observes that of all the senses only seeing and hearing are grammaticised in the category of evidentials, reflecting their special status in human cognition.

> The hypothesis that SEE is a universal semantic primitive is consistent with the view widespread across cultures that there is a special relationship between seeing and knowing, and that eyewitness evidence is more reliable than any other kind of evidence, and the hypothesized status of HEAR as universal semantic primitive tallies well with the special role of vocal speech in human communication. (Wierzbicka 1996: 81)

I am not entirely convinced that the senses of seeing and hearing are universally viewed as more mental and less physical than the others.[2] But if such a distinction is valid we might expect some languages to have distinct verbs for seeing and hearing but a single verb for smelling, tasting and feeling by touch, relying on naming the sensory organ or the stimulus to make distinctions between the latter three senses. Indeed, *The Shorter Oxford English Dictionary* (vol. 1: 736) records Middle English *feel* as meaning to perceive by smell, taste or touch.

However, various other groupings occur. Tariana, an Arawak language of Brazil, has a single verb covering both sight and hearing. The hearing sense of this verb is distinguished by taking a direct object with 'auditory' properties ('words', 'sounds', 'language', 'voice', etc.) (Aikhenvald pers. comm., cited by Wierzbicka 2010: 80). Samoan, a Polynesian language, has a single verb, *lagona* (with variant *logo*), for hearing, smelling, perceiving by taste and feeling by touch, as opposed to a verb for seeing, *va'ai* (Milner 1966). Hausa, a Chadic language, is reported to have one term for sight and another for the other four primary senses (Classen 1993, cited by Wierzbicka 1996: 81).

Representations of visual, hearing and smelling events might differ in the way the stimulus is viewed. Whereas one sees an object, one does not hear an object; one hears a sound. The occurrence of a sound requires a sound-making event (someone calling, a falling tree crashing, waves splashing on rocks). It is not the source of the sound that we hear but the sound that comes from it. We can hear a call without perceiving the caller.

Smelling something is parallel to hearing in that what we smell is not an object but, in this case, an odour. One can smell an odour without being aware of its source. In the case of hearing and smelling one might conceivably represent the relation between stimulus and experiencer not in terms of the experiencer performing a sensing act (in the grammatical role of subject) but in terms of a sound or odour *moving to* or *affecting* the experiencer (in the role of direct object or dative object).

---

2   I readily concede that English *see* and *hear* are polysemous, having 'mental' meanings such as 'know' and 'understand' in some contexts (*Do you see what I mean?*, *I hear what you're saying*), but would argue that their primary senses belong to the domain of physical perception, by means of the eyes and ears, respectively. *Smell* also has mental senses. Andy Rogers (pers. comm.) suggests that if dogs could talk, perhaps *smell* would be taken as a mental predicate, given the efficiency and accuracy of their sense of smell.

Let us now look at how sensing events are represented in English and Kalam. I will be concerned with the most routine or common ways of depicting sensing events in these languages, rather than with highly marked alternatives; for example, compare *I heard a screeching sound* with the highly marked *A screeching sound assaulted my ears*.

2. English constructions for depicting the senses

2.1. Verbs of sensing

Besides the basic sense verbs *see*, *hear*, etc. English has two other sets of verbs that refer to the senses. Let us call the three sets 'cognitive', 'active' and 'affective', after their distinct semantic functions, discussed below.[3] Each set has at least five members, representing the five primary senses, though some of the same forms occur in each of the sets. Visceral feeling is represented in the cognitive and affective sets but not the active.

Table 20.1. Verbs of sensing.

Cognitive	Active	Affective
see	look (at)	look + adj.
hear	listen (to)	sound + adj.
smell	smell	smell + adj.
taste	taste	taste + adj.
feel (by touch)	feel	feel + adj.
feel (viscerally)	–	feel + adj.

Source: Author's summary.

2.2. Constructions with cognitive verbs of sensing

The cognitive verbs of sensing are labelled 'cognitive' rather than 'active' because they depict an experiencer subject as being cognisant of the sensory data but are neutral with regard to intentionality. The experiencer notices the sensory data but may do so accidentally. Cognitive sensing

---

3   Rogers (1971), Viberg (1984) and I independently arrived at the same three-way classification of English perception verbs. I subsequently adopted two of Rogers' class labels: 'cognitive' and 'active'. I use 'affective' for the set he called 'descriptive'. Viberg's labels for the three classes are 'experience', 'activity' and 'copulative', respectively.

events associated with the five primary senses differ from each other both in the nature of the sensory data received and with respect to the body part with which the data are received. *The Macquarie Dictionary* gives the following definitions: *see* 'to perceive with the eyes', *hear* 'to perceive by the ear', *smell* 'to perceive through the nose, inhale the odour of', *taste* 'to perceive or distinguish the flavour of'. Arguably, there are two *feel* verbs: (i) 'perceive by touch' (*I felt the wind in my face*) and (ii) 'become conscious of' (*he felt the hot sun/a surge of anger*). However, a case can be made for treating (i) and (ii) as a single verb whose basic meaning is 'experience a sensation other than by sight, hearing, smell or taste'.[4]

The cognitive verbs of sensing can each be used as transitive verbs (*see something, hear something*, etc.) and as intransitives (*Can you see (clearly)?, Can you hear (well)?, I can no longer smell, taste or feel*).

Besides the primary cognitive sensing verbs, English has other simple and phrasal verbs that refer to perception by means of one of the senses with added information: for example, about manner, such as *glimpse, (take in a) view, catch sight of, watch, overhear, catch a whiff of*. There are verbs that denote awareness without specifying a particular sense, such as *notice, perceive, be conscious of*, and *sense* itself.

To depict a cognitive sensing event, English speakers commonly use an SVO (subject–verb–object) clause structure:

(1) *I saw a pig*
I heard bagpipes
I smelt petrol
I tasted garlic
I felt something soft

These SVO constructions are formally parallel to canonical transitive sentences such as *I captured/killed/sold a pig*. This is a typical example of a language economising in its range of constructions, in this case taking a construction type that prototypically depicts an actor wilfully performing an activity that affects another entity and using this construction to depict events in which an experiencer perceives a stimulus.

---

4   This last option is preferred in a number of English dictionaries but here I separate the two uses of *feel*.

The direct object of *hear* and *smell* may be a noun phrase that refers not to a sound or odour but to an object that is the source of the sound or odour. That is, one speaks as if the experiencer hears or smells the object itself, just as one sees an object. *Hear* and *smell* can, however, also take a direct object that refers to the sound or odour or to an event that creates the sound or odour.

(2) *Do you hear the sound of the bell?*
Do you smell something burning?

Visceral sensory experiences can also be expressed by an SVO construction, where the sensation is represented by a noun phrase, answering the question *What did X feel?*

(3) *She felt a dull pain/an itch/pangs of hunger/a surge of anger/jealousy/ dizziness*

However, they are often expressed by an SVAdj (subject–verb–adjective) construction, where the sensation is represented by an adjectival phrase, answering the question *How did X feel?*

(4) *She felt cold/itchy/hungry/angry/dizzy/as if she would burst*

The latter construction, with quasi-copular use of *feel*, shows some resemblance to one with an affective verb of sensing, discussed in section 2.4, the difference being that in the latter the experiencer is coded as dative object whereas in (4) the experiencer is the subject.

2.3. Constructions with active verbs of sensing

Each of the five primary cognitive verbs of sensing has an active counterpart, in which an actor-experiencer pays attention by means of a particular sense in order to perceive. *Look* and *listen* are the active counterparts of *see* and *hear*.[5] A distinction must be made between *smell*, *taste* and *feel (by touch)* as cognitive verbs, which are neutral with respect to intent, and the same forms as active verbs. Active verbs of sensing can all be used intransitively, without overt reference to a stimulus, and transitively, but to be made transitive *look* and *listen* require a following particle, as *look at*, *listen to*. Visceral *feel* does not have an active counterpart.

---

5   In colloquial usage, *see* and *hear* can also be used as active verbs in imperative constructions: *See that man there!*, *Hear what she has to say!*

To depict an active sensing event directed at a target or stimulus English speakers commonly use an SVO clause structure, in which the actor is the subject and the target-stimulus is the direct object:

(5) *We looked and looked at the photo but could not see the cat.*

2.4. Constructions with affective verbs of sensing

Affective verbs of sensing, together with a modifier, refer to the impression a particular stimulus makes on the perceiver by means of a particular sense: *look* (appear to the eye), *sound* (be heard, appear to the ear), *smell* (give off an odour), *taste* (have a certain flavour), *feel* (have a sensation induced by touch) and visceral *feel* (have a sensation felt body-internally).

Affective verbs of sensing occur in dative experiencer constructions, in which the sensing experience is depicted as happening to an experiencer. The stimulus is the grammatical subject and the experiencer is the dative object, represented by an oblique case phrase introduced by the preposition *to*. The verb cannot stand alone (**The beer tasted to me*, **The cloth felt to her*) but must be followed by a modifier, describing the effect associated with the stimulus. Reference to the experiencer may be omitted if it is recoverable from the context.

(6) *The flowers looked beautiful (to him)*
The singing sounded off key (to us)
The eggs smelled rotten (to them)
The beer tasted bitter (to me)
The cloth felt like silk (to her)
The pain felt excruciating (to me)

The affective verb serves as a quasi-copular verb, linking the subject with the adjectival predicate. Compare the use of *be* and *seem* in *The flowers were beautiful (to him)*, *The singing seemed off key (to us)*.

3. Kalam constructions for depicting sensing events

Kalam belongs to the Madang branch of the Trans New Guinea family.[6] It has upwards of 20,000 speakers, most of them living in the Simbai, Kaironk and Asai Valleys near the junction of the Bismarck and Schrader Ranges. There are two main dialects, Etp Mnm and Ti Mnm, which in morphology differ about as much as Spanish and Portuguese. Data cited here are in the Etp Mnm dialect. There is a large dictionary (Pawley and Bulmer 2011) and a fairly extensive literature on Kalam phonology, grammar, ethnobiology and social organisation.[7]

In grammatical structure, Kalam is a fairly typical Trans New Guinea language. Verbs carry suffixes marking person and number of subjects, and tense, aspect and mood. Inflected verbs may be dependent or independent. Dependent verbs carry a suffix indicating whether their subject is the same as or different from that of the following clause and marking tense (prior, simultaneous or prospective) relative to the next verb. Kalam has only about 130 verb roots but has a large stock of phrasal verbs consisting either of a series of verb roots or of verb adjunct + verb. Verb adjuncts are words with noun-like properties that always occur in partnership with a verb to form a complex predicate; for example, *si ag* (crying say) 'cry', *guglum ag* (snoring say) 'snore', *suk ag* (laughing say) 'laugh'. In canonical transitive constructions the preferred order of constituents is SOV (subject–object–verb). To depict involuntary sensations and bodily conditions much use is made of impersonal subject constructions. In these the verb is always marked for a third person singular subject, the noun phrase (NP) denoting the condition or sensation is (in at least some cases) the subject, and the experiencer is the grammatical object.

---

6   Trans New Guinea, containing between 350 and 500 languages, is by far the largest of the more than 20 non-Austronesian language families found in Melanesia (Palmer 2017; Pawley and Hammarstroem 2017). Trans New Guinea languages occupy most of the mountain chain that runs for more than 2,000 km east–west along the centre of New Guinea. They also dominate many of the lowland areas to the south of the central cordillera and patches of the lowlands to the north.

7   The Kalam orthography used here is phonemic but phonetically opaque. /b, d, j, g/ are prenasalised, occurring as [mb, nd, ɲdʒ, ŋg] word initially and medially and as [mp, nt, ɲtʃ, ŋk] word finally. /p, t, c, k/ occur as [ɸ, t, tʃ, k] word initially, as [β, r, tʃ, ɣ] medially and as [b or p, r, tʃ, k] word finally. A predictable vowel, most commonly very short [ɨ], occurs between contiguous consonant phonemes within a phonological word, e.g. /mdp/ is [mindip], /wsb/ is [wusimp], /nŋnk/ is [niɲinik].

The following abbreviations occur in interlinear glosses: DL dual, DS different subject from the next verb, IMP imperative, PF perfective (today's past or present habitual), PL plural, PRIOR prior to the next verb, PROG present progressive, RP recent past, SG singular, SIM simultaneous with the next verb, SS same subject as the next verb.

3.1. A single verb of perception: *nŋ*

Kalam has only one verb root denoting perception and cognition: *nŋ*. The dictionary treats *nŋ* as highly polysemous, listing some 22 different senses, distinguishable in context. English glosses for these senses include *perceive, sense, know, be aware, be awake, be conscious, notice, realise, understand, learn, see, look, hear, listen, smell, feel by touch, feel emotionally, try* or *test, be familiar with* or *used to, believe, think that (something is the case)*. In interlinear glosses of sentences cited below, *nŋ* will be glossed 'perceive'—a compromise rather than an ideal gloss.

In the following sentence *nŋ* can be understood either as an intransitive verb or as a transitive verb with direct object omitted.

(7) *Mñi   nŋ-sp-an?*
    now   perceive-PROG-2SG
    'Now do you notice/see/hear/smell/feel/understand (it)?'

In terms of the tripartite classification of English verbs of sensing outlined in section 2.1, *nŋ* can serve both as a cognitive verb, denoting an act of perception which may be accidental, and an active verb, where an actor pays attention in order to perceive. However, *nŋ* is not used alone as a cognitive verb meaning '(experience a) taste'. To express the experience of tasting Kalam uses a construction which depicts different kinds of taste sensations as 'acting on' the experiencer; see section 3.5). Furthermore, while *nŋ* is commonly used as an active verb meaning 'look' or 'listen', it is not by itself used for the active senses of 'smell', 'taste' or 'feel by touch'. Each of these three active senses is represented by a lexicalised series of verb roots with *nŋ* as the final verb.

Table 20.2. Kalam sensing verbs.

Cognitive	Active
nŋ 'see'	*nŋ* 'look (at)'
nŋ 'hear'	*nŋ* 'listen (to)'
nŋ 'smell'	*pug nŋ* 'smell' (lit. 'sniff perceive')
– 'taste'	*ñb nŋ* 'taste' (lit. 'consume perceive')
nŋ 'feel (by touch)'	*d nŋ* 'feel (by touch) (lit. 'touch perceive')
nŋ 'feel (viscerally)'	–

Source: Author's summary.

Although Kalam has only a single verb root for all the cognitive senses, these senses are distinguished by occurring in different syntactic constructions, which are discussed below, in sections 3.2 to 3.7.

3.2. Seeing

Seeing something is expressed by a canonical transitive clause, headed by the verb *ŋ*, with the experiencer as subject and the stimulus as object. The direct object can be a minimal NP, such as a noun or pronoun, denoting the thing seen, as in (8) or a sentential NP, denoting an event, as in the second clause of (9).

(8)   *Yad*   *kaj*   *koŋay*   *nŋ-n-k.*
      I   pig   many   perceive-1SG-PAST
      'I saw many pigs.'

(9)   *Ygen*   *tap-nonm*   *ma-nŋ-b-un,*
      wind   substance   not-perceive-PF-1PL

      pen   *ykop*   *kawn*   *a-nep*   *mon*   *d-ab*   *nŋ-b-un,*
      but   just   swaying   precisely   tree   catch-RP:3SG   perceive-PF-1PL

      wak   *ak*   *takl*   *ap*   *d-e-k*   *nŋ-b-un.*
      skin   the   cold   come   touch-DS:3SG-PAST   perceive-PF-1PL

      'We can't see the actual substance of the wind, but we can see it makes the trees sway when it catches them, and when the cold touches our skin we can feel it.'

Seeing can be distinguished from other senses by using the phrasal expressions *wdn nŋ*, literally 'eye perceive', and *wdn-magi nŋ* 'eyeball perceive'.

(10)   *Tk*   *jak-i,*   *mñi*   *nep*   *wdn*   *nŋ-sp-in.*
       start   arise-SS:PRIOR   now   only   eye   perceive-PROG-1SG
       'I've just woken up, (my) eyes are only now starting to see.'

The body part nominal *wdn* 'eye' or *wdn-magi* 'eyeball' is often accompanied by a possessive pronoun, and when combined with *nŋ* often emphasises that someone saw something with their own eyes, rather than hearing about it from others. Another conventional expression is *wdn nŋ tep g* (lit. eye perceive well do) 'have good eyesight, see well'.

3.3. Hearing

Hearing something is also expressed by a canonical transitive construction, with the experiencer as subject. However, unlike seeing, to speak of hearing something minimally requires a two-clause construction, the object being expressed by a verbal clause. In Kalam you cannot simply hear a sound (*I heard thunder/an explosion*) or an object that is the source of a sound (*I heard you/a plane*). You can only hear something make a sound. Sound-making is expressed by the verb *ag* 'make a sound, say, utter', often in combination with a noun or verb adjunct denoting a particular kind of sound (speech, calling, snoring, rattling, etc.).

(11) *Nad*　　　*ag-e-na-k*　　　　　*nŋ-n-k.*
　　　you　　　say-DS-2SG-PAST　　perceive-1SG-PAST
　　　'I heard what you said.'

(12) *Yad*　*tumuk*　　*ag-e-k*　　　　　*nŋ-n-k.*
　　　I　　thunder　　say-DS:3SG-PAST　perceive-1SG-PAST
　　　'I heard thunder.' (lit. 'I thunder sounded I heard.')

(13) *Yad*　*kaj*　*way*　　　*ag-e-k*　　　　　*nŋ-n-k.*
　　　I　　pig　　squealing　say-DS:3SG-PAST　perceive-1SG-PAST
　　　'I heard a pig squeal.' (lit. 'I pig squealed I heard')

In (12), *tumuk* 'thunder' is a noun and is the subject of *ag*. In (13) *way* 'squealing' is a verb adjunct, not a verb; it is always partnered by the verb *ag*.

A phrasal expression used to distinguish hearing from other senses is *tmud nŋ*, literally 'ear perceive'.

3.4. Smelling

In Kalam one cannot speak of smelling an object. One can only smell an odour. Two alternative constructions are available for describing the smelling of an odour. Most commonly, an impersonal subject construction is used in which an odour (the subject) is depicted as 'coming to' the perceiver. To translate 'I smelled a pig' one would usually say:

(14) *Yp*   *kaj*   *kuy*   *ow-a-k*.[8]
      me   pig   odour   come-3SG:PAST
      (lit. 'pig odour came to me.')

The act of perception is not mentioned but is implied. In this context *ap* 'come' is understood as implying 'come to the experiencer's attention'. The experiencer is represented by a pronoun or noun phrase that is grammatically an object.[9]

Constructions with impersonal subject are not canonical transitive constructions in that they usually show OSV (object–subject–verb) order, whereas the preferred order in canonical transitives is SOV. What shows that impersonal subject constructions are transitive is the choice of personal pronoun denoting the experiencer. Kalam has two sets of free-form personal pronouns: one marking the grammatical subject (and possessor of a noun which is the subject) and the other marking object (and possessor of a noun which is the object).

Table 20.3. Kalam personal pronouns.

	Subject	Object
1SG	*yad*	*yp*
2SG	*nad*	*np*
3SG	*nuk*	*nup*
1DL	*ctmay*	*ctpmay*
2DL	*ntmay*	*ntpmay*
3DL	*kikmay*	*kipmay*
1PL	*cn*	*cnp*
2PL	*nb*	*nbp*
3PL	*kik*	*kip*

Source: Author's summary.

---

8   Kalam born after about 1970 say *ki* for *kuy*. *uy* > *i* is a sound change in progress.
9   One might call this a dative object because the object is the receiver but in Kalam there is no formal distinction between direct objects and dative objects.

The second option is to use an experiencer subject construction, in which the experiencer perceives an odour, as in (15) and (16). Here the first clause describes an odour as rising towards the experiencer and the second clause describes the experiencer's act of smelling it.

(15) *Mñi   kuy   ap   tan-b   nŋ-sp-an?*
     now   odour   come   rise-PF-3SG   perceive-PROG-2SG
     'Now do you smell the odour coming up?'

(16) *Pakam   gutgut   kuy   ak   ow-pnŋ,   nŋ-b-ay.*
     bandicoot stench   odour   this   come-DS:SIM   perceive-PF-3PL
     'When this rank odour of bandicoot comes they smell it.'

A deliberate act of smelling something is expressed by a sequence of verb roots: *pug nŋ* (sniff perceive), or in the case of a dog picking up a scent and following it, *pug d am nŋ* (sniff hold go perceive). The verbs share an actor subject and take as object *kuy* 'odour'.

(17) *Kayn   sgaw   kuy   ak   pug   d   am   nŋ-sp-ay.*
     dog   wallaby   odour   the   sniff   hold   go   perceive-PROG-3PL
     'The dogs are following the scent of a wallaby'

3.5. Tasting

Experiencing a tasting sensation is depicted by an impersonal subject construction; that is, a taste happens to one. But whereas Kalam has a noun meaning 'odour, smell' it does not have a noun with the general meaning 'taste, flavour'. Instead it has a few terms for particular kinds of taste or feeling in the mouth, which serve as adjectives and, marginally, as nouns; for example, *ydk* 'tasty, delicious, tastiness', *km* 'bitter, bitterness', *slk* 'pungent, spicy, hot-tasting, itchy'. These select the verb *g* 'do, make, happen'.

(18) *Yad   kaj   ak   ñb-e-n-k,   yp   ydk   g-a-k.*
     I   pig   the   eat-DS-1SG-PAST   me   tasty   do-3SG-PAST
     'When I ate the pork, it tasted delicious to me.'

(19) Snb   ñb-e-n,   yp   joŋb   slk   g-p.
    ginger   eat-DS-1SG   me   mouth   pungent   do-PF:3SG
    'When I eat ginger, it gives my mouth a pungent sensation.'

Deliberate tasting is expressed by a sequence of two verbs that share an actor subject: *ñb ŋŋ* 'consume perceive' and an object, the thing consumed.

(20) Nad   sup   ak   ñb   ŋŋ-an!
    you   soup   the   consume   perceive-2SG:IMP
    'Taste the soup!/Try eating the soup!'

3.6. Feeling by touch

Experiencing a particular tactile sensation, like experiencing a taste or smell, is usually depicted as something that happens to one. Tactile sensations are represented by adjectives; for example, *dlob* 'slimy', *deg* 'slippery, smooth', *gac* 'dirty', *kd* 'sharp', *kls* 'firm, hard', *sayn* 'soft'. The verb that partners these is *g* 'do, make, happen'. The experiencer is the object of the verb. The construction can be analysed as having a dummy subject, represented only by the third person singular subject-marking on the verb.

(21) Yad   kaj   wak   d   ŋŋ-e-n-k,   yp   gac   g-a-k.
    I   pig   skin   touch   perceive-DS-   me   dirty   do-3SG-PAST
                                 1SG-PAST
    'When I touched the pig's skin, it felt dirty to me.'

However, feeling a sensation by touch can also be expressed by an experiencer subject construction headed by *ŋŋ* 'perceive', as in (22) (= (9), repeated here for convenience), where *ŋŋ-b-un* in the final clause can be interpreted as 'we (habitually) feel (the cold)' because the preceding clause means 'the cold comes and touches the skin':

(22) Ygen   tap-nonm   ma-ŋŋ-b-un,
    wind   substance   not-perceive-PF-1PL
    pen   ykop   kawn   a-nep   mon   d-ab   ŋŋ-b-un,
    but   just   swaying   precisely   tree   catch-   perceive-PF-
                                                   RP:3SG   1PL

wak	ak	takl	ap	d-e-k	nŋ-b-un.
skin	the	cold	come	touch-DS: 3SG-PAST	perceive-PF-1PL

'We can't see the actual substance of the wind, but we can see it makes the trees sway when it catches them, and when the cold touches our skin we can feel it.'

Deliberate touching, as opposed to experiencing a tactile sensation, is expressed by a sequence of two verbs sharing an actor subject: *d nŋ* 'touch perceive'.

(23)   *Yad*   *waknaŋ*   *ak*   *d*   *nŋ-n-k.*
      I   eel   the   touch   perceive-1SG-PAST
      'I felt the eel.'

3.7. Body internal feelings

Body internal or visceral feelings, with a few exceptions, are treated like sensations of smelling (option 1, see section 3.4), tasting and feeling by touch: they happen to one. The thing felt (bodily sensation, emotion, etc.) is encoded as a noun, serving as the subject, the experiencer is the object and the verb specifies the manner in which the stimulus acts on/relates to the experiencer. The same construction is used to denote all involuntary bodily conditions, such as shivering, shuddering, hiccupping, sweating, having boils, pimples, ringworm, scabies or warts, being numb or paralysed, or feeling angry, nauseated or sleepy.

Some sensations or conditions, such as sleepiness, salivating or wanting to laugh, 'come to' the experiencer:

(24)   *Yp*   *wsn*   *ow-p.*
      me   sleep   come-PF:3SG
      'I feel sleepy.'

(25)   *Yp*   *suk*   *ow-p.*
      me   laughter   come-PF:3SG
      'I feel like laughing.'

(26) Yp   kuñk   ow-p.
      me   saliva   come-PF:3SG
      'I feel a craving (esp. for food).'/'I am salivating.'

yap, yow 'fall' expresses a sensation in which something is felt to fall in the experiencer.

(27) Yp   ss   yow-p.
      me   urine   fall-PF:3SG
      'I feel like urinating.'

(28) Yp   sb   yow-p.
      me   faeces   fall-PF:3SG
      'I feel like defecating.'

(29) Yp   mluk   yow-p.
      me   nose   fall-PF:3SG
      'I feel upset/annoyed.' (cf. English 'his face fell', 'his nose is out of joint.')

g 'do, act, happen, make' depicts a sensation, such as shame, pain, hunger, itching, as acting on the experiencer:

(30) Yp   nabŋ   g-p.
      me   shame   do-PF:3SG
      'I feel shame/shy.'/'I am ashamed/shy.'

(31) Yp   yuwt   g-p.
      me   pain   do-PF:3SG
      'I feel pain.'/'I'm in pain.'

(32) Yp   yuan   g-p.
      me   hunger   do-PF:3SG
      'I feel hungry.'/'I'm hungry.'

(33) Yp   slk   g-p.
    me   itch   do-PF:3SG
    'I feel itchy.'/'I am itchy.'

pk 'hit, strike, contact' occurs in a construction where the subject noun denotes a body part and *pk* denotes a throbbing sensation:

(34) Yp   jun   pk-p.
    me   head   hit-3SG:PF
    'I have a headache.'

There are a very few exceptions to the generalisation that body internal sensations are depicted by impersonal subject constructions. The exceptions are cases where an internal organ (*mapn* 'liver', *sb* 'bowels') is viewed as the seat of the emotions and the experiencer is cast as the subject of the verb.

(35) Yad   nup   mapn   nŋ-b-in.
    I   him   liver   perceive-PF-1SG
    'I feel sorry/affection for him.'

3.8. 'Be like' construction

Kalam lacks a set of affective verbs of sensing, corresponding to English *look*, *sound*, etc., where the verb plus modifier describes the impression the stimulus makes on the experiencer, as in *Jane sounded elated, Jake looked as if he'd seen a ghost, Did that feel like an earthquake?*

The nearest Kalam has to a functional equivalent of such a construction is an impersonal subject construction in which a noun X modified by the clitic *tek* 'like, similar, as if, seem like' combines with a verb to describe a resemblance between X and the subject.

(36) Wak   yp   mon=tek   yn-b.
    skin   my   fire-like burn-PF:3SG
    'My skin feels like it's on fire.'

The verb is often *ay-* 'become in a certain condition or state, take the form of, form, put, stabilise'.

(37) *Sofia   jomluk   no-nm   =tek   ay-a-k.*
     Sofia   face   her-mother   like   form-3SG-PAST
     'Sofia looks like her mother.' (lit. 'Sofia face like her mother it formed.')

(38) *Yp   kum-eb   =tek   ay-p.*
     me   dying   like   form-PF:3SG
     'I feel as if I'm dying.' (lit. 'like dying forms me.')

However, this construction is sense-neutral: it does not say whether the resemblance is in look, sound, smell, etc.

4. Conclusion

It is through data provided by the senses that we perceive and construct models of the world. This applies to the linguistic modelling of sensing events themselves. We noted earlier that there are various logical possibilities for representing particular kinds of sensing events, each being compatible with common sense understandings of how these events work—of the nature of the stimuli and the sensing processes and their relation to the experiencer. One might expect this diversity to be mirrored in the syntactic and semantic representations of different kinds of sensing events across languages. This expectation is confirmed by differences in the way sensing events are depicted in English and in Kalam.

i. English has three sets of verbs of sensing with distinct semantic functions: 'cognitive', 'active' and 'affective'. Kalam distinguishes cognitive and active verbs of sensing but lacks an exact equivalent of affective verbs.

ii. English has a separate verb root for each of the five primary senses in each of the three sets. A sixth verb representing the visceral senses occurs in the cognitive and affective sets. Kalam has a single verb root, *nŋ*, which alone can refer to any of the cognitive senses with one exception: taste. To distinguish between the senses Kalam speakers specify the nature of the stimulus: one perceives (sees) a scene or object, one perceives (hears) a sound-making event, one perceives (smells) an odour and one perceives (feels) an object touched. There is no single cognitive verb of tasting. Instead, particular tasting sensations happen to the experiencer.

iii. Kalam speakers can also distinguish between seeing and hearing by placing the term for 'eye' or 'ear' before *nŋ*, although this is only done for emphasis. This analytic strategy is available to English speakers—it is reflected in English dictionary definitions of sensing verbs that use the verb 'perceive' and identify the sensory organ and/or the nature of the stimulus associated with each sense—but for English speakers it is a highly marked strategy.

iv. Kalam also provides a more analytic representation of active sensing verbs than English. Deliberate acts of smelling, tasting and feeling by touch are each represented by a sequence of two verb roots literally meaning, respectively, 'sniff perceive', 'consume perceive' and 'touch perceive'.

v. Another difference between the two languages concerns the handling of control or intentionality in sensing events. In English each of the six kinds of cognitive sensing events is normally represented by a canonical transitive construction, in which the experiencer appears as the subject of the verb and the stimulus as the object. Canonical transitive constructions treat the experiencer as if he/she exercises a measure of control over the sensing process. Such a uniform treatment of the cognitive senses masks differences in the degree of control that the experiencer typically has over the sensing experience.

Kalam treats seeing and hearing differently from the other senses. Whereas seeing and hearing are represented, as in English, by canonical transitive constructions, smelling and feeling by touch (as cognitive senses) are usually represented by impersonal subject constructions, in which the sensing experience is depicted as something that happens to the experiencer. Tasting and nearly all visceral sensations are always depicted by impersonal subject constructions.

vi. A further difference resides in the representation of what it is that we hear and smell. English allows us to say that we can hear an object such as a pig or a gun, whereas common sense tells us that what we hear is the sound made by the object. The interlocutor is expected to make the logical connection between object and a sound-making event. Kalam does not allow this sort of metaphor, in which an object stands for an event; it must specify the event. Similarly, English allows us to say that we smell an object whereas in Kalam one must speak of smelling an odour associated with or coming from an object.

References

Classen, Constance (1993). *Worlds of Sense: Exploring the Senses in History and across Cultures*. London: Routledge.

Milner, George B. (1966). *Samoan Dictionary. Samoan–English, English–Samoan*. London: Oxford University Press.

Palmer, Bill (ed.) (2017). *The Languages and Linguistics of the New Guinea Area: A Comprehensive Guide*. Berlin: de Gruyter Mouton.

Pawley, Andrew and Ralph Bulmer (2011). *A Dictionary of Kalam with Ethnographic Notes*. Canberra: Pacific Linguistics.

Pawley, Andrew and Harald Hammarstroem (2017). The Trans New Guinea family. In Palmer (ed.), *The Languages and Linguistics of the New Guinea Area: A Comprehensive Guide*. Berlin: de Gruyter Mouton, 21–195. doi.org/10.1515/9783110295252-002.

Rogers, Andy (1971). Three kinds of physical perception verbs. In *Papers from the Seventh Regional Meeting of the Chicago Linguistic Society*. Chicago: Chicago Linguistic Society, 206–22.

The Macquarie Dictionary (2nd edn) (1991). Macquarie University: Macquarie Library Pty Ltd.

The Shorter Oxford English Dictionary on Historical Principles (3rd edn) (1944). Oxford: Clarendon Press.

Viberg, Åke (1984). The verbs of perception: A typological study. In Brian Butterworth, Bernard Comrie and Oesten Dahl (eds), *Explanations for Language Universals*. Berlin: Mouton de Gruyter, 123–62. doi.org/10.1515/9783110868555.123.

Wierzbicka, Anna (1996). *Semantics: Primes and Universals*. Oxford: Oxford University Press.

Wierzbicka, Anna (2010). *Experience, Evidence, and Sense: The Hidden Cultural Legacy of English*. New York: Oxford University Press. doi.org/10.1093/acprof:oso/9780195368000.001.0001.

21

Russian language-specific words in the light of parallel corpora

Alexei Shmelev

The starting point for this chapter is the hypothesis that one may regard translation equivalents and paraphrases of a linguistic unit extracted from real translated texts as a source of information about its semantics (cf. the approach developed in Anderman and Rogers 2008). This may be especially useful for the so-called language-specific words since the great variety of possible translations is an indicator of the high language specificity of a word. The multiplicity of translations may be used as a quantitative measure of language specificity: the greater the number of different translations of a single lexical unit in existing translations, the higher its language specificity (Shmelev 2015: 562–63). As is known, language-specific linguistic expressions are often culture-specific as well and can be linked to the notion of 'cultural keywords' (Wierzbicka 1997); therefore, one may assume that culture-specific words often have several translations and their translation counterparts may emphasise different aspects of their meaning. In what follows, I will concentrate on Russian words that are language-specific with respect to English.[1] I will pay special attention to some Russian discourse markers—that is, words or

---

1   For a discussion of language specificity as a relative notion, see Shmelev (2015).

a phrases that play a role in managing the flow and structure of discourse (in particular, *ešče*, *že*, *razve*, *neuželi*, *avos'* and *nebos'*) as well as the specific 'Russian' emotion *toska*.

Russian linguists traditionally employ language data taken from original Russian texts or artificial examples specially created by native speakers (usually the linguist themselves). Examples taken from translated texts are usually viewed with distrust, and, when I cited such texts in my publications of the 1980s, some colleagues asserted that these examples were not indicative of Russian usage, as they were created under the influence of a foreign language. I believe, in contrast, that translated texts provide highly valuable material for studying the specifics of the target language (Russian in this case). When Russian is the source language, the choice of translation may depend on the translator's metalinguistic reflection, while an occurrence of a Russian language–specific expression in the target text, more often than not, reflects a 'naïve' choice of words. These translations are usually (although not invariably) produced by native target language speakers who should understand the original text; that is, they encode the semantic representation given in the original text into a text in the target language, which may be treated as a model of 'natural' linguistic activity.

Translated texts are especially useful for studying the semantics of language-specific words and expressions that have no direct equivalents in other languages. The very appearance of such words in translated texts may seem paradoxical. Indeed, if a word or expression expresses a configuration of meanings that is specific to the target language, then one may ask what aspects of the original text made the translator use this expression. The answer to this question often helps to describe the semantics of the language-specific word or expression.

The development of corpus linguistics and the appearance of electronic parallel corpora of the Russian language have made it possible to study the usage of language-specific words and expressions in translated texts in a systematic fashion. The identification of elements of original texts that incite translators to use language-specific expressions in the target language helps not only to verify the descriptions of these words obtained without the use of electronic corpora but also, in some cases, to take a new look at certain language-specific words. In this respect, translations into Russian tend to be even more revealing than translations from Russian.

However, the study of different ways of translating language-specific words in the original text may also prove interesting, and so let us begin by looking at them.

1. Language-specific expressions in the Russian original and their translations

When Russian is the original language, the translation of language-specific words poses a problem that is solved differently by different translators. One of the biggest difficulties is the translation of expressions of the original language whose 'presumptions' or 'hidden meanings' (presuppositions, connotations, background aspects of meaning, etc.) contain notions that do not lie in the 'presumptions' of the expressions of the target language (indeed, these semantic and pragmatic elements are precisely what constitutes the language specificity of a word). These elements are taken for granted by native speakers of the original language but not of the target language. Such linguistic expressions often create the impression of 'untranslatability'. Indeed, if we try to make such presumptions explicit in the target language, they will lose their 'presumptive' status; however, if we fail to do so, the underlying meaning will not be expressed. As a rule, the translator tries first and foremost to bring across the aspects of meaning that are the focus of attention. They often do not notice the background aspects at all or, if they do, are frequently ready to sacrifice them. At the same time, if they try to express such expressions in the target language, they almost always attract attention to them, shifting them from the quasi-invisible 'background' into the focus of attention, which is also a distortion of the original semantic task.

However, individual translator solutions with respect to language-specific words may be based on different considerations depending on the goals that the translator sets. Generally speaking, one can distinguish between two approaches (and, correspondingly, two strategies) of translation. One is predominantly source-oriented and tries to bring across everything that the author 'meant' ('had in mind', 'wanted to say'). To this end, a translator may insert notes, commentaries, etc. Such a translation gives the readers a more or less complete understanding of the semantic content of the original yet does not give them a direct impression of the text. The other approach is predominantly oriented towards the reader, and strives to make the translation create the same impression on the foreign-language speaker that the original has on the native speaker. The dynamic approach is used by certain translators of fiction (yet not only of fiction: also drama, verse, non-fiction and many non-literary genres).

The choice of strategy is determined by the translator's aims, and there is no universal strategy that is applicable in all cases. This is particularly true of literary translations. When a translator comes across a language-specific expression, they can try to select an equivalent that will best bring across the meaning of the original in a given context ('meaning strategy'), or they can choose a single equivalent of the expression and try to use it in all contexts ('form strategy'). In the case of the meaning strategy, there often arises a variety of different translations of a single language-specific word, as the latter has no single equivalent in the target language, and the translator must choose each time an equivalent that best expresses, in their opinion, the aspects of meaning that are the most significant in the given context.

For example, the Russian language-specific word *avos'*[2] has a considerable variation of translation in the principal European languages. The range of translations of *avos'* in those languages shows its high language specificity with respect to the target languages and helps to verify its semantic analysis. The inevitable loss of meaning during the translation of this word leads to the emphasis of specific aspects of meaning. The fact that this word is usually translated by a word with the meaning 'maybe, possibly' indicates that *avos'* marks a hypothesis that is made without sufficient grounds (with the exception of the speaker's desire for it to be true). The use of words and expressions with the meaning 'hope' in some cases reflects the relation of utterances with the word *avos'* to the future, the desire for the corresponding situation to occur, and the lack of guarantees that it will indeed do so. The addition of words with the meaning 'luck' emphasises the aspect 'X wants the situation to occur yet cannot influence it in any way'; the lack of guarantees that the desirable will occur is emphasised by the addition of expressions with the meaning 'no one knows ahead of time whether the situation will occur'.

Wierzbicka (1992: 169–74) has also made a subtle analysis of the Russian language–specific word *toska*. As expected, translations of this word into the principal European languages also vary greatly—often within a single

---

2   Anna Wierzbicka (1992: 435) has proposed an explication of this word, which was subsequently made more precise in Shmelev (1996).

translation. This shows that translators follow the meaning strategy, and provides additional evidence for the high language specificity of the word *toska*. Let us take a look at English translations in the Russian National Corpus (RNC); in particular, Constance Garnett's translations of Dostoyevsky's works.[3] Her translation of *White Nights* contains the equivalents 'despondency', 'anguish', 'misery', 'depression'. Her translation of *Crime and Punishment* (a novel in which the motif of *toska* plays a major role) also makes use of different equivalents. The most common equivalent in this translation (used 5 times out of the 22 occurrences of the word *toska* in the original) is 'misery'; at other times, 'wretchedness' is used. Another equivalent used by Garnett is 'anguish'. However, she also employs other equivalents in this translation: 'dismay', 'depression', 'dejection', 'distress', 'agony', 'restlessness', 'misgivings'. The novel *Demons* is also represented in the RNC by Garnett's translation (under the title *The Possessed* or *The Devils*), which contains a similar variety of translations. The words 'yearning' and, most often, 'distress' are repeatedly used as translations, yet other equivalents also occur: 'trouble', 'anguish', 'misery'. It should be said that in the novel *The Possessed* the word *toska* is sometimes used with the non-standard meaning 'grief, suffering' (as in the phrase *v ètu nesčastnuju nedelju ja vynes mnogo toski*, which Garnett translates as 'I suffered a great deal during that unhappy week'). This leads to such translations as 'grief' and 'woe'. For the collocation *bajronovskaja toska*, which occurs in *The Possessed*, the translation is 'Byronic spleen', as expected.

Let us consider how Wierzbicka defines the word *toska*. In a nutshell, *toska* means that a person wants something without knowing exactly what. At the same time, s/he has a feeling that it cannot be attained and feels something (bad) as a result.[4] In different cases, one of these aspects may predominate: the desire for something ('yearning'), the lack of a precise idea of what it is (this aspect is absent in Constance Garnett's

---

3 The Russian National Corpus is available at: www.ruscorpora.ru/en/.
4 Consider the explication in the Natural Semantic Metalanguage (NSM):
toska
X thinks something like this
   I want something good to happen
   I don't know what
   I know: it cannot happen
Because of this, X feels something (Wierzbicka 1992: 172).

translations, as a rule), the impossibility of attaining it, and the ensuing feeling that something bad has happened or is happening now[5] (this aspect predominates in most translation equivalents used by Garnett).

The Brothers Karamazov is also represented in the RNC by Constance Garnett's translation. Just as in *The Possessed*, the word *toska* in *The Brothers Karamazov* sometimes has the predominant connotation of grief or suffering, and Garnett uses precisely these words (in addition to other equivalents such as 'anguish' that we already know from her translations of *Crime and Punishment* and *The Possessed*). However, the most common translation of *toska* in this work is the word 'depression'. One sometimes even gets the impression that Garnett overuses it in her translation. The following example shows a clear predominance of the aspect 'the subject wants something very much yet does not know what exactly' (as can be seen from the context):

(1) *Toska do tošnoty, a opredelit' ne v silax, čego xoču.*
    I feel sick with depression and yet I can't tell what I want.

Garnett's use of the word 'depression' in her translation is not entirely equivalent to the meaning of *toska* here: the latter points to a strong desire, while 'depression', as Anna Wierzbicka (1999: 309) notes, presupposes that all desires have already waned ('one is already past wanting', as she puts it). The translation of the word *toska* by 'depression' in the following example, in which Ivan Karamazov wants to embark on a new and totally unknown path, experiencing a great feeling of hope without knowing where precisely he is heading, subsequently leads Garnett to translate the word *toska* in the expression *toska novogo i nevedomogo* by the word 'apprehension', replacing the original meaning by almost its opposite: Dostoyevsky speaks of Ivan's strong desire for something new and unknown to occur, while the word 'apprehension' points to a fear or presentiment of something dangerous; hence the translation may be confusing:[6]

---

5   Some English words with the aspect 'something bad occurred' ('sadness', 'unhappiness', 'distress', 'sorrow', 'grief,' 'despair') were analysed and interpreted in (Wierzbicka 1999: 60–70).
6   The English word 'apprehension' is described in (Wierzbicka 1999: 86–87). As one of the reviewers of this chapter pointed out, older senses of this word don't necessarily imply fear or danger.

(2) *No strannoe delo, na nego napala vdrug <u>toska</u> nesterpimaja i, glavnoe, s každym šagom, po mere priblizenija k domu, vsë bolee i bolee narastavšaja. Ne v <u>toske</u> byla strannost', a v tom, čto Ivan Fedorovič nikak ne mog opredelit', v čem <u>toska</u> sostojala. <u>Toskovat'</u> emu slučalos' často i prežde ... I vse-taki v ètu minutu, xotja <u>toska novogo i nevedomogo</u> dejstvitel'no byla v duše ego, mučilo ego vovse ne to.*

But, strange to say, he was overcome by insufferable <u>depression</u>, which grew greater at every step he took towards the house. There was nothing strange in his being <u>depressed</u>; what was strange was that Ivan could not have said what was the cause of it. He had often been <u>depressed</u> before ... Yet at that moment, though <u>the apprehension of the new and unknown</u> certainly found place in his heart, what was worrying him was something quite different.

However, when the word *toska* unambiguously signifies a striving or strong desire for contentment, Garnett translates it as 'craving' (rather than even 'yearning').

The translation 'depression' is also clearly impossible with regard to the following words of the Elder addressed to the visiting lady: *Ja vpolne veruju v iskrennost' vašej toski.* Here the key parameter is *iskrennost'*, which is poorly compatible with 'depression'. Garnett translates this expression as 'the sincerity of your suffering'.[7]

Of course, one may say that Garnett's translations are far from perfect and even contain numerous misleading literalisms. However, this does not contradict the thesis that the variety of translations serves as an indicator of language specificity. Indeed, the presence of calques may show that the translator is taking the formal equivalence approach,[8] at least in part. If one and the same linguistic expression is, nevertheless, translated in different ways, one can conclude that there is no clear equivalent to the original expression in the target language and thus that it is language-specific at least with respect to the target language.

A study of translations of other Russian texts made by different translators shows an even greater variety of equivalents: 'sadness', 'yearning', 'depression', 'restlessness', 'wretchedness', 'despondency', 'anguish', 'misery', 'distress', 'dismay', 'dejection', etc.

---

7 The Russian word *iskrennost'* and the English word 'sincerit'y do not have the same meaning either (Wierzbicka 2002: 25–27).

8 Formal equivalence approach, a term coined by Eugene Nida, tends to emphasise fidelity to the lexical details and grammatical structure of the original language (Nida and Taber 1969: 200).

Let us also note that translators often change parts of speech and the sentence structure, as the following translation by Constance Garnett of an excerpt from *The Possessed* shows: *v ètu nesčastnuju nedelju ja vynes mnogo toski*—'I suffered a great deal during that unhappy week'. When making such changes, they can use words such as 'sadly', 'depressed', 'dejectedly', 'worried', 'miserable', etc.

A case apart is special types of usage (possibly, special lexical meanings) of the word *toska* in such expressions as *toska po rodine* or *toska po ušedšim godam molodosti* and also in cases when the connotation of *skuka*[9] comes to the fore. The expression *toska po rodine* is usually translated by 'homesickness', while the word *skuka* is rendered with the word 'boredom' or the verb 'to bore'.

At the same time, some translators choose unusual equivalents, and this may be considered their individual stylistic trait. For example, Franklin Abbott in his translation of Ivan Turgenev's short story *Asya* renders the expression *toska po rodine* as 'enthusiasm towards my country', where the connotation of strong desire comes to the fore (such a translation may seem odd to some speakers of English though).

Richard Pevear and Larissa Volokhonsky's translation of Mikhail Bulgakov's *The Master and Margarita* (also included in the RNC) is particularly interesting in this context. The word *toska* is one of the key words of this novel (with 17 occurrences). The translators, sticking to the formal equivalence approach, and as hardliners of this approach, consistently render it as 'anguish', although its meaning clearly shifts in some cases. The word 'anguish' is a fairly imprecise equivalent of *toska*. It is no coincidence that in the English–Russian subcorpus of the RNC, Russian translators seldom translate 'anguish' by *toska*, preferring words with the connotation 'pain, torment, suffering'.[10]

---

9   Note that *toska* may be directly opposed to *skuka*. As a character in Dostoyevsky's *The Possessed* said, *Toska ne skuka* (in Constance Garnett's translation, 'Sadness is not dullness').
10   Note that, in one of her translations, Garnett renders the word *toska* by the same word throughout. I am referring to Chekhov's short story *Toska* (included in the RNC). Here, this emotion is at the centre of attention (in this short work, the word occurs six times, not counting the title), and a variation of translations would have disrupted the author's intentions. Garnett translated the story's title as *Misery*, and this is also the translation that she gives in five cases out of six. In the remaining case, she slightly changes the syntactic structure and uses the related adjective 'miserable'.

It should be said that small shifts also occur when translators take the meaning approach. In each individual case, they have to decide (assuming that they correctly understand the original text) what implicit aspects of meaning can be sacrificed and what aspects are important for the meaning of the phrase or the text as a whole. These shifts help us to see where the specificity of the language-specific expression lies.

2. Language-specific expressions in translations into Russian

The appearance of language-specific expressions in translations may seem paradoxical. After all, if a text is translated, then it should express only the meanings that were present in the original text, whereas language-specific expressions, as we know, express a configuration of meanings that are specific to a given language (in our case, the target language, that is, Russian). Language-specific expressions used in translated texts may be separated into two classes: discourse markers, for which there are usually no immediate equivalents in the original text and which seem to arise 'out of nowhere'; and autosemantic units that usually formally correspond to some expressions in the original text yet contain additional meaning components that are implicitly present in the original text. Let us examine these cases separately.

2.1. Discourse markers in the target text

Speaking of discourse markers that can be used in the target text, it is useful to distinguish between cases in which the discourse marker has to be employed in the Russian translation of a foreign text and cases in which the use of the discourse marker in the Russian translation is at the translator's discretion. In the former case, one must identify the characteristics that make it necessary to use a given discourse marker; in the latter, one should examine the characteristics that incited the translator to use a given discourse marker, although it was possible to do without it.

In Levontina and Shmelev (2005), we introduced the notion of the 'pragmatic necessity' of a particle. We are referring to a situation in which the absence of a certain discourse expression engenders a false implicature or violates the coherence of the text without leading to grammatical error. For example, the particle *ešče* that is described in the aforementioned article is pragmatically obligatory in one of its meanings that is implemented in the future context: *Ja ešče vernus'* (this—and not simply *Ja vernus'*—would be the most natural translation into Russian of the Terminator's phrase 'I'll be back'). Depending on the context, this meaning may be implemented as a threat or, conversely, as a consolation.

Here are a few conditions for the use of the particle *ešče* in this sense:

1. There exists a different hypothesis about how things will turn out; in many cases, the phrase containing the particle *ešče* begins with the conjunction 'no'.
2. The event that one is speaking about will not occur immediately after the moment of speech (the phrase *My ešče pogovorim ob ètom* is often used to cut short a conversation on a given subject).
3. At the time of speaking, the situation is developing in such a fashion that it does not suggest the predicted outcome in any way.

The use of the particle *ešče* is necessary if a person is obliged to refrain from doing something at the present time (or if they were unable to do what they wanted) and consoles themselves by the fact that this is not definitive and that the situation may change some time in the (possibly distant) future.

On the other hand, the use of *ešče* is impossible if the utterance specifies a condition for a situation to occur, as this contradicts the meaning implied by *ešče* that 'at the present time, nothing indicates that this situation will occur': *Stučite, i (*ešče) otvorjat vam* 'Knock, and it shall be opened unto you'.

When the conditions for the use of the particle *ešče* with the meaning considered here are fulfilled, it almost inevitably appears in Russian translation, although it has no equivalent in the original text (some examples are given in Shmelev and Zalizniak (2017)).

Another example of a pragmatically necessary particle that is quasi-automatically (and, most likely, unconsciously) used by translators is the 'emphatic' particle *že*. Examples of the usage of *že* in Russian translation are quite numerous (I should emphasise that I am not speaking here of the particle *že* in an 'identifying' sense, i.e. in such collocations as *tot že, takoj že, tam že*, etc.).

The interrogative particles *razve* and *neuželi* are also close to being pragmatically necessary; they have been examined by numerous linguists (e.g. Apresjan 1980: 51–52; Bulygina and Shmelev 1982, 1987; Baranov 1986). Bulygina and Shmelev (1982, 1987) described the particles *razve* and *neuželi* as follows:

Razve p?

I previously thought that not p
Now I see or hear something that could not be true if not p
I want you to tell me whether p or not p

Neuželi p?

I thought that p is impossible
Something makes me think that perhaps p
I'm telling you that I have trouble believing that p
I want you to tell me whether p or not p

The material of the English subcorpus of the RNC confirms this description on the whole: the particles in question are used with a high degree of likelihood in Russian translations of questions in which the aforementioned conditions are met, although the original texts contain only general questions without particles of any kind (some examples are cited in Shmelev 2015).

An example of discourse markers that are used in Russian translations at the translator's discretion is the aforementioned particle *avos'* (and also *nebos'*). With regard to *avos'*, one should say that it seldom occurs in translation, which is undoubtedly linked to the fact that it is gradually disappearing from the Russian language and that most native speakers disapprove of the attitude that it conveys. Nevertheless, certain translators use it occasionally. In particular, it is sometimes used when the original contains a word that indicates hope (this word itself may be omitted in the translation).

The word *nebos'* occurs a lot more frequently in Russian translation. However, the use of *nebos'* is never the only possible solution: one can always use a different modal marker, even if it is not entirely identical stylistically: *naverno, dolžno byt', dumaju, verojatno*, etc. All the occurrences of the discourse word *nebos'* in translation pertain to informal speech. In literary translations, the word *nebos'* occurs almost exclusively in direct or free indirect speech. However, informal speech is a necessary yet not a sufficient incentive for using *nebos'*. The parallel subcorpora of the RNC show that *nebos'* is used in contemporary Russian in situations when a speaker voices a confident assumption (usually with a note of familiarity or contempt) based on their experience that allows them to pass a judgement on things about which they have no direct information. The word *nebos'* also has a parallel usage in which the speaker mentions reliably known facts that show that someone's behaviour was silly, inconsistent or hypocritical. On the whole, these data make it possible to formulate a more precise description of the conditions that allow the appearance of the word *nebos'* in contemporary Russian discourse.[11]

An example of an autosemantic language-specific expression used in Russian translations is the word *toska*, which was examined in the first part of this chapter. It turns out that this word is not all that rare in translations into Russian. This naturally leads us to ask about the factors responsible for the appearance of the word *toska* in Russian translations, as we know that the English language has no word or expression for which this word would be a precise equivalent.

The list of words and expressions that are translated as *toska* partially coincides with the list of English translations of this Russian word: 'distress', 'depression', 'despair', 'anguish', 'grief', 'agony', etc., as well as 'sadness'; however, the word *toska* often corresponds to other words as well.[12] For example, some translators regularly use it to translate the word 'melancholy' (which also occurs in English translations of Russian texts, yet more often as the equivalent of *grust'*, *pečal'* or even *melanxolija*). In some cases, *toska* corresponds to 'nostalgia' although the Russian word *nostagia* is a more common equivalent.

The study of the incentives that lead Russian translators to use the word *toska* often reveals important aspects of the semantics of this word; indeed, the most important aspect is often the overall context in which one speaks about this emotion.

---

11 For a further discussion of the words *avos'* and *nebos'* in the parallel subcorpora of the NRC, see Shmelev (2017).
12 In a few (rare) cases, the word *toska* is used to translate the word *boredom*.

The word *toska* often appears when the original speaks about a strong desire for something. It can be used as an equivalent not only of the word 'yearning' but also (no surprise) of the word 'longing', for example:

(3) the world of <u>longing</u> and baffled common-sense

mir nastojčivoj <u>toski</u> i nedoumevajuščego rassudka

The object of desire is sometimes well defined, yet this is not the most typical context of the usage of the word *toska* in translation:

(4) I don't think I ever in my life, before or since, felt I <u>wanted</u> mustard as badly as I felt I wanted it then.

Nikogda v žizni, ni prežde, ni potom, ja ne ispytyval takoj <u>toski</u> po gorčice, kak v tu minutu.

The word *toska* is most often used when the desire is vague and poorly defined (the subject has trouble saying exactly what they want). This is the most common context of the use of the word *toska* in translation:

(5) A sort of <u>undefined longing</u> crept upon them.

Kakaja-to <u>smutnaja toska</u> napala na nix.

(6) It caused him to feel a vague, sweet gladness, and he was aware of wild <u>yearnings</u> and <u>stirrings for he knew not what</u>.

Bèk ispytyval kakuju-to smutnuju radost', i bespokojstvo, i bujnuju <u>tosku nevedomo o čem</u>.

In certain cases, the object of desire turns out to be variable, while the feeling of *toska* stays constant:

(7) She <u>longed</u> and <u>longed</u> and <u>longed</u>. It was now for the old cottage room in Columbia City, now the mansion upon the Shore Drive, now the fine dress of some lady, now the elegance of some scene.

Ee snedala <u>toska</u>, <u>toska</u>, <u>toska</u>. Ona <u>toskovala</u> to po staromu domiku v Kolumbii-siti, to po osobnjakam na naberežnoj, to po izyskannomu plat'ju, zamečennomu na kakoj-to dame, to po krasivomu pejzažu, brosivšemusja ej v glaza dnem.

In addition, the word *toska* often corresponds to a vague and ill-defined emotion that can be designated by such words as *languor*.

Toska frequently implies that the subject feels lonely:

(8) I felt so <u>lonesome</u> I most wished I was dead.

Takaja napala <u>toska</u>, xot' pomiraj.

(9) ... Dorothy built a splendid fire that warmed her and made her feel less <u>lonely</u>.

... Doroti razožgla bol'šoj koster, vozle kotorogo bystro sogrelas' i zabyla uže podstupivšuju k serdcu <u>tosku</u>.

(10) He wanted to be alone—to be <u>lonely</u>.

Emu xotelos' byt' odnomu, otdat'sja svoej <u>toske</u>.

(11) During these days he got immensely <u>lonely</u>.

V èti dni ego gryzla <u>toska</u>.

(12) But he felt <u>lonely</u>.

No na duše u nego byla <u>toska</u>.

(13) fear and <u>loneliness</u> goaded him.

podstreknuli strax i <u>toska</u>.

This emotion is sometimes not even explicitly designated in the English original, which uses descriptive constructions such as *broken heart, sinking heart* or *sinking of heart*:

(14) Jane will die of a <u>broken heart</u>

Džejn umret ot <u>toski</u>

(15) ... I felt a <u>sinking</u> in my heart.

... <u>toska</u> snova sžimala mne serdce.

When the original speaks of a morose or despondent state of mind (e.g. it uses such words as *gloom, mope* or simply *excruciating feelings*), translators tend to describe this state with the word *toska*:

(16) The <u>gloom</u> which had oppressed him on the previous night had disappeared ...

<u>Toska</u>, ugnetavšaja ego noč'ju, rassejalas' ...

(17) I gazed on it with <u>gloom and pain.</u>

Ja smotrela na nego s <u>nevyrazimoj toskoj</u>.

In general, when the original describes some bad feelings, Russian translators often use the word *toska*. The latter often appears when the original speaks of a subject's unsatisfied desire. This desire may be vague and not well understood and, in any case, it usually cannot be satisfied. We see that this largely conforms to the description of the semantics of *toska* given by Anna Wierzbicka. Data from the parallel English–Russian subcorpus of the RNC show that another aspect may be added to this description: the subject is unable to tell anyone about what they feel. This impossibility may stem from the vague and ill-defined nature of the emotion itself or from the solitude of the subject.

In most cases, the choice of the word *toska* is not the sole possible solution. Nevertheless, its usage by translators seems indicative.

With regard to the word *toska* and its English equivalents, one should also mention V. Apresjan's incisive article (2011), which conjectures that the closest English equivalent of the Russian word *toska* is 'blues' (it even formulates a semantic invariant of *toska* and 'blues'). Nevertheless, it is notable that real translations (in particular, the translations included in the RNC) virtually never use the word 'blues' for *toska*,[13] while 'blues', even when it is an emotion rather than a shade of colour or a musical genre, is rarely translated as *toska* (Nadezhda Volpin in her translation of Galsworthy renders 'blues' by *zelenaja toska*, changing the colour, amusingly enough: '… this country will give me the blues'—… *èta strana nagonit na menja zelenuju tosku*).

As we see, the analysis of the occurrence of such words as *toska* in Russian translations helps to verify their descriptions or make the latter more precise and is thus an effective research tool. The translation of language-specific words is a problem that the translator, as a rule, reflects on, and thus the translator's individual preferences play a great role in the solution of such problems. Moreover, the translator's grounds for choosing a particular solution may be superficial understanding, the influence of bilingual dictionaries or even the desire to give the translated text a veneer of 'foreignness' to make the reader perceive the text as a translation (Mihailov 2005: 381); consider the notion of foreignisation in Venuti (2008). Thus, when the original language is Russian, the parallel corpus often gives us insufficient information about the semantic specificity of Russian

---

13 In general, its frequency with reference to an emotion is much lower than that of *toska*, and this itself reduces its serviceability as a translation.

language-specific lexical units. In contrast, the appearance of language-specific words in a translation most often results from an unconscious decision of the translator that reflects their spontaneous speech activity. By studying why a translator uses a given language-specific word, we are often able to uncover some of the latter's semantic characteristics that went unnoticed during the analysis of original texts.

References

Anderman, Gunilla and Margaret Rogers (eds) (2008). *Incorporating Corpora: The Linguist and the Translator*. Clevedon/Buffalo/Toronto: Multilingual Matters LTD.

Apresjan, Juri D. (1980). *Tipy informacii dlja poverxnostno-semantičeskogo komponenta modeli «smysl-tekst»* [*Types of Information for the Surface-Semantic Component of the 'Meaning – Text' Model*]. Wien: Wiener slawistischer Almanach, Sonderband 1. doi.org/10.3726/b12934.

Apresjan, Valentina J. (2011). Opyt klasternogo analiza: russkie i anglijskie èmocional'nye koncepty [An attempt at cluster analysis: Russian and English emotion concepts]. *Voprosy jazykoznanija* [*Topics in the Study of Language*] 2: 63–88.

Baranov, Anatolij N. (1986). 'Predpoloženie' vs. 'fakt': neuželi vs. razve ['Assumption' vs 'fact': *neuželi* vs. *razve*], *Zeitschrift für Slavistik* 1: 119–31.

Bulygina, Tatjana V. and Alexei D. Shmelev (1982). Dialogičeskie funkcii nekotoryx tipov voprositel'nyx predloženij [Dialogical functions of certain types of interrogative sentences]. *Izvestija AN SSSR: Serija literatury i jazyka* [*Proceedings of the Academy of Sciences of the USSR, Series of Language and Literature*] 41 (4): 314–26.

Bulygina, Tatjana V. and Alexei D. Shmelev (1987). O semantike častic razve i neuželi [On the semantics of the particles *razve* and *neuželi*]. *NTI* [*Science and Technical Information*] 10: 21–25.

Levontina, Irina and Alexei Shmelev (2005). The particles one cannot do without. In Juri D. Apresjan and Leonid L. Iomdin (eds), *East–West Encounter: Second International Conference on Meaning – Text Theory*. Moscow: Slavic Culture Languages Publishing House, 258–67.

Mihailov, M.N. (2005). The particle in the text: Is it possible to check correspondences of functional words in parallel corpora? *Computational Linguistics and Intellectual Technologies: Proceedings of the International Conference 'Dialog 2005'*, 377–81 [in Russian].

Nida, Eugene A. and Charles R. Taber (1969). *The Theory and Practice of Translation, With Special Reference to Bible Translating*. Leiden: Brill.

Shmelev, Alexei D. (1996). Žiznennye ustanovki i diskursnye slova [Life attitudes and discourse words]. In Natalia Baschmakoff, Arja Rosenholm and Hannu Tommola (eds), *Aspekteja*. Tampere, 311–22.

Shmelev, Alexei D. (2015). Russian language-specific lexical units in parallel corpora: Prospects of investigation and 'pitfalls', *Computational Linguistics and Intellectual Technologies: Proceedings of the International Conference 'Dialogue 2015'*, 561–70 [in Russian].

Shmelev, Alexei D. (2017). Russkie avos' i nebos' revisited [Russian words *avos'* and *nebos'* revisited]. *Die Welt der Slaven* [*The World of Slavs*] 62 (2): 276–303.

Shmelev, Alexei and Anna Zalizniak (2017). Reverse translation as a tool for analysis of discourse words. *Computational Linguistics and Intellectual Technologies: Proceedings of the International Conference 'Dialogue 2017'*, 370–80.

Venuti, Lawrence (2008). *The Translator's Invisibility: A History of Translation*. London and New York: Routledge.

Wierzbicka, Anna (1992). *Semantics, Culture, and Cognition: Universal Human Concepts in Culture-Specific Configurations*. New York: Oxford University Press.

Wierzbicka, Anna (1997). *Understanding Cultures through their Key Words: English, Russian, Polish, German, and Japanese*. New York: Oxford University Press.

Wierzbicka, Anna (1999). *Emotions across Languages and Cultures: Diversity and Universals*. Cambridge: Cambridge University Press. doi.org/10.1017/cbo9780511521256.

Wierzbicka, Anna (2002). Russkie kul'turnye skripty i ix otraženie v jazyke [Russian cultural scripts and their reflection in language]. *Russkij Jazyk v Naučnom Osveščenii* [*Russian Language and Linguistic Theory*] 2 (4): 6–34.

22
'Sense of privacy' and 'sense of elbow': English vs Russian values and communicative styles

Tatiana Larina

1. Introduction

As Anna Wierzbicka repeatedly pointed out, in different societies people not only speak different languages, they use them in different ways (Goddard and Wierzbicka 1997; Wierzbicka 2003). These differences have the potential to cause many problems in mutual comprehension, and create breaks and even conflicts in intercultural communication. To understand and explain these, it is necessary to explore the links between particular ways of speaking and culture.

There are hundreds of possible definitions of culture. Hofstede suggests a metaphorical one, defining it as 'the collective programming of the mind that distinguishes the members of one group or category of people from others' (Hofstede et al. 2010: 6). Every person carries within him/herself patterns of thinking, feeling and acting that are acquired through socialisation. These patterns are encoded in language, which is the most concrete constituent of culture, and made manifest in communication.

To see the logic of culture-specific modes of linguistic interaction and the systematic interconnectedness of language, culture, cognition and communication, it is important to look deeper at semantics, which contains rich information about culture and its values. Vocabulary is a very sensitive index of a culture. As Sapir stated, 'no two languages are ever sufficiently similar to be considered as representing the same reality' (Sapir 1929: 214). Goddard and Wierzbicka (1995) note that 'there are enormous differences in the semantic structuring of different languages and these linguistic differences greatly influence how people think' (1995: 37). They call culture-specific words 'conceptual tools which reflect a society's past experience of doing, and thinking about things in certain ways; and they help to perpetuate these ways' (ibid.: 58).

To identify, and account for, differences in cultural logic that are encoded in language, the study of words denoting social categories and types of relationships in a society is particularly important, as through them one can understand how people interact (e.g. Ye 2004, 2013; Gladkova 2013). In this chapter, the focus is on the notions of distance and closeness in Russian and English languages and cultures, and their manifestations in language and communication.

Accepting the fact that neither culture nor language represent a completely homogeneous structure, I believe that in comparative studies it is legitimate, indeed unavoidable, to speak of certain generalised characteristics of a culture, and identify dominant features of the communicative style of its representatives. Following Wierzbicka (2006a), for the English language and culture the term Anglo is used, which comprises the main varieties of English, though the data refer mostly to British English and British culture.

The aim of this chapter is to demonstrate how knowledge of cultural values, key words and cultural scripts methodology developed by Goddard and Wierzbicka (Goddard 2006; Goddard and Wierzbicka 1995, 1997, 2004; Wierzbicka 1992, 1996, 1997, 2002, 2003, 2006a, 2006b; see Gladkova and Larina 2018 for a recent discussion of the approach) enables us to observe the systematic interconnectedness of language, culture, cognition and communication, and see the logic of culture-specific modes of linguistic interaction. The focus is limited to Anglo values of distance and privacy (Paxman 1999; Fox 2003; Wierzbicka 2006a, 2006b) and Russian values of closeness and solidarity (Larina, Mustajoki et al. 2017; Wierzbicka 1997, 2002, among many others). The chapter gives a brief overview of manifestations of these values at different linguistic levels, and illustrates their impact on communicative styles. For data collection, both primary and secondary sources were used. The primary data were obtained through observations, questionnaires, interviews and the parallel corpora of the Russian National Corpus (RNC).[1]

Summing up the results of the previous comparative studies of British and Russian politeness and communicative styles (Larina 2009, 2013, 2015), as well as observations of other scholars (Wierzbicka 1997, 1999, 2002, 2006a, 2006b; Paxman 1999; Shmelev 2002; Fox 2003; Belyaeva-Standen 2004; Gladkova 2007, 2010a, 2010b, 2013; Visson 2013; Zalizniak et al. 2012; Zalizniak 2013 among others), the chapter attempts to show that the idea of closeness/unity/association is encoded in the Russian language at different levels, and forms the 'we-identity' of its speakers, while the English language, in contrast to Russian, emphasises the idea of individuality and contributes to shaping 'I-identity' (Larina and Ozyumenko 2016; Larina, Ozyumenko et al. 2017). These preferences in individual- vs group-orientation are observed in communication: they define an understanding of (im)politeness, explain a lot of features of the modes of interaction and shape communicative ethnostyles (Larina 2009, 2015).

2. Distance vs closeness in Russian and English languages

In different cultures, the notions of 'distance' and 'closeness' vary. As Wierzbicka notes, 'in Anglo-Saxon culture distance is a positive cultural value, associated with respect for autonomy of the individual. By contrast, in Polish it is associated with hostility and alienation' (Wierzbicka 1985: 156). The same could be said about Russian culture, where distance is often perceived as indifference. The value of distance in Anglo cultures, and the value of closeness in Russian culture, can be observed in English and Russian languages at all levels.

---

1   The Russian National Corpus is available at: www.ruscorpora.ru/en/.

2.1. Lexicophraseological level

At the lexical level, the English word *privacy* is a vivid example. Privacy is a quintessentially English notion that Paxman (1999) calls 'one of the defining characteristics of the English, one of the country's informing principles' (1999: 117–18). A truly comparable word for 'privacy' doesn't exist in other European languages such as French, Italian or Polish (Paxman 1999: 118; Wierzbicka 2003: 47), nor does Russian have one. Nowadays, young people have started using the expression *lichnoye prostranstvo* ('personal space'). However, what the size of this space is, who can enter it and who cannot, differ a lot in Russian and Anglo cultures.

In the Russian language and culture, where proximity, solidarity and interdependence are traditionally valued, *privacy* is a lexical and ideological lacuna that creates difficulties in translation. Depending on the context it can be translated in different ways. The adjective *private*, in many contexts, also lacks absolute equivalents. Even when there might appear to be a similar word in Russian, the words can differ in connotative meaning. Consider, for example, the phrase *private person*. While in English, this is a neutral expression that denotes a person who 'likes being alone, and does not talk much about his thoughts or feelings although he spends a lot of time in the public eye' (as per *Longman Dictionary of Contemporary English*), its Russian translation equivalents—*zamknutyy, zakrytyy, skrytnyy, nelyudimyy, neobshchitel'nyy*—carry a negative connotation, which indicates that Russians prefer openness, company, interaction and contact.

The notice *Private (No admittance)* on doors is translated into Russian as *Postoronnim vhod vospreschion* (according to the *New English–Russian Dictionary*) 'Strangers are forbidden to enter'.[2] As a cultural concept, *Privacy* can be viewed as *lichnoye prostranstvo* 'personal space'—a personal zone where nobody is allowed to intrude, but in other contexts *privacy* and *private* are translated into Russian descriptively. The fact that there is no equivalent for *privacy* in Russian and other languages is significant. As Triandis (1994) claimed:

> For important values all cultures have one word. When you see that many words are needed to express an idea in one language while only one word is used in another, you can bet that the idea is indigenous to the one-word culture. (Triandis 1994: 6)

---

2 Nowadays it has been gradually replaced by *Tol'ko dlia personala* 'Staff only'.

Wierzbicka, who in many of her works calls privacy the most important feature of modern Anglo society (Wierzbicka 2003, 2006a, 2006b, 2006c), emphasises that, in modern usage, *privacy* is not 'a descriptive but an ideological term' (2006c: 26). Indeed, it is symptomatic of an ideology, a world view, a way of life or type of relationship; it establishes norms and rules of behaviour, shows how people relate to each other and how they interact.

A memorable example, which shows that communication between members of Anglo culture is based on the observance of distance and demonstration of respect to privacy, is the expression 'sense of privacy':

(1) *He was conscious of her in every respect, yet she was not an intrusion on him or his inbred **sense of privacy**, and there was no awkwardness between them.* (B. Bradford)[3]

Russians would normally struggle to understand what *sense of privacy* might be. It is difficult to translate it into Russian, and that is not surprising as instead of *sense of privacy*, Russians have a *sense of elbow*, which means that there is always someone by your side eager to support.[4] Examples (2–3) illustrate its importance in Russian culture:

(2) ... *postoyannoye **chuvstvo loktya**—blizost' vernogo tovarishcha, krepkiy druzhnyy kollektiv.*

... *a constant **sense of elbow**—the closeness of a faithful companion, a strong friendly team.* (RNC)

(3) ... *yey nuzhno **chuvstvo loktya**, oshchushcheniye, chto ona ne odinoka, chto ryadom yest' podderzhka i pomoshch', togda ona gory svernet i nichego boyat'sya ne budet*

... *she needs **a sense of elbow**, the feeling that she is not alone, that there is support and help next, then she will turn mountains and nothing she will not be afraid of.* (RNC)

These two opposite senses—*sense of privacy* and *sense of elbow*—manifest differences in the distance characteristic of the cultures in question, different types of social relations and modes of interaction.

---

3 It is worth noting that example (1), taken from the novel by B. Bradford *To Be the Best*, describes the relations between husband and wife.
4 In English 'a sense of elbow' has a different connotation. It would refer to using one's elbows to create a space around oneself.

These expressions testify to the importance of observing distance in Anglo culture and the admissibility, even the desirability of closeness and contact in Russian culture (see section 3, below).

The idea of closeness and community in Russian can be observed in the semantics of the words *obscheniye* 'communication', *iskrennost'* 'sincerity', *sochuvstviye* 'sympathy', *sostradaniye* 'compassion', *dusha* 'soul', *gosti* 'guests' and *zastolye* and their derivatives that do not have absolute equivalents in English (Wierzbicka 1992, 2002; Shmelev 2002; Gladkova 2010a, 2010b; Zalizniak et al. 2012; Zalizniak 2013).

Gladkova (2007) gives some interesting examples, pointing out:

> Russian seems to be able to conceptualise the idea of common activity much more readily than English. One needs just one word to say how many people are doing something together as a whole. (2007: 142)

Hence, it is possible to do something *vdvoem* 'two people together', *vtroem* 'three people together', etc. On the other hand, the typical Russian expression *delat' chto-to za kompaniyu* (lit. 'to do something for the sake of the company') can be perceived by the English-speaking world as a lack of initiative and overdependence (cf. Gladkova 2007: 142).

It is interesting to note that different types of relations between friends and different expectations in Russian and Anglo cultures can be explained through the semantics of the words *friend* and *drug* and their derivatives (see e.g. Wierzbicka 1992; Richmond 2009; Zalizniak et al. 2012; Gladkova 2013; Visson 2013; Ponton 2014; Ozyumenko and Larina 2018). Evidence supports Wierzbicka's semantic model for the explication of *drug* 'friend' in the Russian language (1999: 350), which shows that *druzya* (friends) are people who know each other very well, spend (or want to spend) a lot of time together, talk a lot with each other, can say anything to each other, share their thoughts and feelings, trust and help each other if needed. In English only the phrases 'true friend' or 'best friend' carry these connotations.

Numerous proverbs also testify to differences in the conceptualisation of friendship in Russian and Anglo cultures and different levels of closeness between friends (e.g. Ozyumenko and Larina 2018).

2.2. Morphosyntactic level

The morphosyntactic level also provides numerous instances of how language can either 'associate' or 'dissociate' people. For reasons of space, these must be limited to a few examples.

The prefix so- (co-) serves for the formation of nouns and verbs, denoting a common or joint participation in something. Not many of them have English equivalents: *sozhitel'* 'room-mate', *souchastvovat'* 'participate', *sochuvstvovat'* 'sympathise', *sostradaniye* 'compassion', *sozhalet'* 'feel sorrow'. The prefix *obsche* is another example. It carries the general meaning of association and collectivity: *obshcheizvestniy fakt* 'a well-known fact', *obshcheprinyatyye normy* 'generally accepted norms' (for more details see Larina 2009: 84–85; Larina, Ozyumenko et al. 2017: 116).

The pronoun *everybody* is an example showing that the English language, in contrast to Russian, tends to emphasise individuality. In English it is singular, while in Russian *everybody* has two equivalents: *kazhdiy* (singular), while most often it is *vse,* which is plural and corresponds to the English pronoun *all*:

(4) *Everybody is here –*
    Vse zdes' (lit.: All are here)
(5) *Hello everybody*
    Vsem privet (lit.: Hello to all)

There is a number of set phrases commonly used in daily interaction that demonstrate the preference for the use of *we* in Russian phrases and *I* in their English equivalents, although this is not exclusively the case (see Larina, Ozyumenko et al. 2017).

Some examples:

(6) ***My*** *znakomy?* ('Are **we** acquainted?')
    *Do **I** know **you**?* (personal observation)
(7) *Uvidimsia* ('**We** will see each other')
    *(**I** shall) See **you**.* (personal observation)
(8) ***My*** *s drugom khodili vchera v teatr*
    (lit.: '**We** with a friend went to the theatre yesterday')

As one can see in (6–8), the Russian 'I' and the other (you or s/he) can be transformed into 'we', while the English language emphasises a person's individuality, and the 'I' and 'you' or s/he do not turn into 'we'.

The same idea of unification can be seen in the expression *u nas* (preposition u + pronoun *we* in Genitive case):

(9) **My brother and I** have similar tastes.
 U nas s bratom pokhozhiye vkusy. (RNC)

It has also the meaning of place (lit. 'at us'), and lacks a literal equivalent in English. Depending on the context, it can mean 'in our family/flat/school/university/workplace/city/country' and even 'on our planet'. The analysis of the Parallel Corpus shows that *u nas* 'at us' correlates with English *here/in this place/in this country*:

(10) Do you think you'll like it **here**?
 Vy uvereny, chto vam ponravitsya **u nas**?
(11) It was long ago, very long ago, but the tale is still remembered, and not only **in this place.**
 Eto bylo davno, ochen' davno, no istoriyu etu pomnyat, i ne tol'ko **u nas.**

Referring to what is happening in Russia, the Russians would say *u nas* 'at our place' or *v nashey strane* 'in our country' associating themselves with it. In English, in a similar situation, the expression *in this country* would be used, which construes some distance. Recently, some Russian politicians and public figures have also started using *in this country,* referring to Russia. However, this is not just a borrowing from the English language, but an ideological expression marking those who oppose themselves to their country. Wierzbicka observed an identical peculiarity in the Polish language, saying that the Polish expression *ten kraj* 'this country' used with reference to one's own country 'would mark the speaker as a psychological émigré' (Wierzbicka 2003: 49).

The examples given in this section, among many others (e.g. Larina and Ozyumenko 2016; Larina, Ozyumenko et al. 2017), show that manifestations of the values of closeness in Russian and distance in English can be observed at different linguistic levels.

3. Distance and closeness in communication

To shift the focus to communication I shall now provide some illustrations of how the values, discussed above, impact modes of interaction and shape communicative ethno-styles. Before we consider the manifestation of distance and closeness in communication, it is worth noting that there is a clear relationship between verbal and non-verbal communication; cultural values, as has been said, manifest themselves in a variety of ways. Richmond (2009), among others, observes that closeness and physical contact with other people are much more common in Russia than in the West. Russians stand very close when conversing, 'they do not hesitate to make physical contact—touching another person and invading another person's space' (Richmond 2009: 118). As argued by Brosnahan (1998), Russians are closer in all of the four parameters of distance suggested by Hall (1959)—intimate, personal, casual and public. Too much contact or proximity, typical of Russian culture, is viewed by Americans as intruding on a person's privacy or even as a threat (Visson 2013).

Given the insignificant spatial distance maintained by Russians, the absence of a zone of personal autonomy—privacy (or its minimal, in comparison with the English counterpart)—largely determines the Russian style of verbal communication. In many contexts, Russians put pressure on their interlocutor, give advice even when this is not asked for, defend their opinions, argue, ask private questions, feel free to interrupt, interfere with the conversation, and so on (cf. Larina 2009, 2013; Visson 2013). In other words, they demonstrate a significant degree of closeness in verbal contact. In many contexts, such behaviour is completely permissible and is considered not as a violation of the rules of politeness, but rather as demonstration of involvement and interest. In Anglo culture, the most influential social and communicative rules are those concerned with the maintenance of distance—that is, privacy. The value of privacy encourages people to follow strict norms to protect their right to autonomy, and demonstrate respect for the independence and personal space of every individual.

The norms involved in these processes have been described in terms of maxims (Leech 1983) and politeness strategies with the claim of their universality (Brown and Levinson 1987). Wierzbicka and Goddard propose a new methodology—cultural scripts—for articulating cultural norms, values and practices. They do so in terms which are 'clear, precise, and accessible to cultural insiders and to cultural outsiders alike' (Goddard and Wierzbicka 2004: 153). The scripts are formulated in simple language and, as my teaching experience confirms, are extremely useful in cross-cultural education and intercultural communication.

Here I will confine discussion to the script that refers to privacy and personal autonomy in English, and demonstrate its importance in explaining English vs Russian communicative differences.

> [people think like this:]
> when a person is doing something
> it is good if this person can think about it like this:
> 'I am doing this because I want to do it
> not because someone else wants me to do it'. (Goddard and Wierzbicka 1997: 156)

These four lines express the essence of Anglo communicative culture, and explain many culture-specific characteristics and dominant communicative features. The script shows that Anglo emphasis on personal autonomy prevents anyone saying, directly, what another person should do. Instead of direct imperatives, addressee-oriented whimperatives *Could you/would you/would you like*, etc. are used to avoid putting pressure on others (Wierzbicka 2006b). These restrictions not only apply to requests but to all speech acts with the meaning 'I want you to do this'. Even when the speaker urges the addressee to act in his own interest (in invitation or advice), the indirect expression of motivation is preferable in English communication.

In the next section, I provide a brief comparative analysis of the speech acts of invitation and advice based on the results of the previous study of English and Russian politeness and communicative styles using the Discourse-Completion Task (DCT) method (Larina 2009, 2013), and thus contextualise the above discussion.

3.1. Invitation

The speech act of invitation exhibits clear tendencies towards either group orientation (in a Russian context) or individuality (in Anglo) that cause serious misunderstandings in intercultural interaction. A typical invitation in the Anglo culture tends to be expressed in the form of a question focused on the willingness of the addressee to accept it. This shows respect to the addressee's personal autonomy and his/her right to make a choice independently.

Some examples (from personal observation):

(12) *Why don't **you** join **me** for lunch?*
(13) *I'm just going to the cinema. Would **you** like to come along?*
(14) *I was wondering if **you**'d like to come over for dinner next Sunday. If you have other plans, please don't worry.*

We can observe here, once more, the emphasis on the individuality of both parties in the interaction: inviter and invitee.

However, in the Russian linguacultural context such invitations would not be appreciated, for two reasons: (a) they lack any evidence that the inviter sincerely wishes the invited to accept the invitation, especially when an option is given (see example (14)); (b) there is no real evidence of the desire to 'do something together'.

The appropriate formula for (12–13) in Russian would be a direct invitation with the imperative form and an emphasis on common activity (15–16):

(15) *Davay poobedayem vmeste* ('Let's have lunch together')
(16) *Davay skhodim v kino.* ('Let's go to the cinema')

Interrogative invitations are also possible, though they may sound more like a suggestion and, in the case of rejection, another option would be suggested:

(17) *Mozhet, skhodim v kino?* (lit. 'Perhaps, we shall go to the cinema?')

In the comparative study (Larina 2009) in the situation 'inviting a friend for a birthday', none of the English informants (out of 70) used the imperative, while among Russians (of the same number), imperative statements amounted to 24 per cent:

(18) *Prikhodi ko mne na den' rozhdeniya* ('Come to my birthday party')

The results of the study showed that the most frequent conventional invitation in English (60 per cent) features the willingness of the addressee to accept the invitation:

(19) *Would you like to come to my birthday party?*
(20) *How do you fancy coming out on Saturday night for my birthday?*

Russian speakers preferred declarative utterances (56 per cent) with a performative verb *ptiglashayu* 'I invite' (21), or expression of positive attitude towards the expected acceptance of the invitation (22):

(21) *U menia v subbotu den' rozhdeniya. Ya tebia priglashayu.* ('I have a birthday on Saturday. I'm inviting you.')
(22) *U menia v subbotu den' rozhdeniya. Ya budu rad, yesli ty pridesh'.* ('I have a birthday on Saturday. I'll be glad if you come.')

Interestingly, while English speakers focus on the desire of the invitee, Russian invitees may be faced with a *fait accompli*, or pushed to come, which in Russian sounds quite normal when people are in a close relationship:

(23) *U menya v subbotu den' rozhdeniya. Zhdu. Otkazy ne prinimayutsya.* ('I have a birthday on Saturday. I expect you to come. Refusals are not accepted.')

Although some of the Russian informants (20 per cent) used the question form for an invitation, it was mostly not a question of the willingness or ability of the addressee to accept the invitation—*Ty smozhesh priyty?* ('Can you come?'), but rather whether s/he would come or not: *Ty pridiosh?* ('Are you coming?')

3.2. Advice

Advice is another speech act that demonstrates the importance of keeping distance in Anglo culture and the acceptability of contact and solidarity in Russian communication.

Despite the fact that advice is mostly aimed at the interests of the addressee, in Anglo culture generally it can be regarded as violation of the interlocutor's independence and personal autonomy, and the imposition of the speaker's will. The most 'dangerous' type of advice, in this respect, is unsolicited advice, which is given by a speaker on his/her own initiative, without any request from the listener. The old English proverbs say: *Give not counsel or salt till you are asked* and *Keep (save) your breath to cool your porridge*.

In Russian culture, advice is traditionally perceived not as an invasion of personal life, but as involvement and desire to help. It is given out of the best of motives, without fear of infringing the interests and freedom of the interlocutor, who normally understands the good intentions of the adviser. This is reflected in Russian proverbs and sayings that urge careful listening to advice and following it: *Vsyakiy sovet k razumu khorosh* ('Every piece of advice is good'), *Lyudey ne slushat' – v dobre ne zhit'* ('If one does not listen to what people say, one will not live well'), *Odin um khorosho, a dva luchshe* ('One mind is good, but two minds are better'). It should be noted that nowadays the attitude of Russians towards advice, especially on the part of young people who want to be more independent, is becoming less tolerant, yet the traditional views still prevail in many cases.

The results of the studies show that attitudes to unsolicited advice in Russian culture are quite positive. As argued by Belyaeva-Standen (2004), who studied this speech act in Russia and the USA, 75 per cent of Russian informants in her study noted that they are ready to listen to unsolicited advice if it is useful, expressed in a friendly manner and offers a convincing solution to the problem (2004: 313). By contrast, the overwhelming majority of Americans believe that 'it is not good to give unsolicited advice', 'this must be avoided under any circumstances' and that it might be acceptable only if it was necessary to warn the listener of a real danger or unpredictable mishap (ibid.: 315). The British also consider unsolicited advice unacceptable particularly when offered to a stranger, while the Russians in some situations give advice willingly and quite directly. In the situation used in our experiment ('It's very cold. A strong wind is blowing. There is a child without a hat at the bus stop.'), 90 per cent of the British informants (out of 70) replied that they would not say anything: *None of my business/It's not acceptable to advise unknown people, even a child*, while 95 per cent of Russian informants considered it permissible to advise a child to put on a hat, raise a hood, and some of them were eager to offer their scarf (Larina 2013: 203).

A few examples of these situations from personal observation:

(24) *Vy zachem sumki v rukakh derzhite. Postav'te na skameyku. Tyazhelo ved'.* (lit: 'Why are you holding the bags in your hands? Put them on the bench. It's hard to hold them.') (at the bus stop)

(25) *Zaydite pod naves. Promoknite.* (lit: 'Go under the awning. You may get wet.') (at the bus stop)

(26) *U vas shnurok razvyazalsya. Zavyazhite. Mozhete upast'* (lit: 'Your string is untied. Tie it. You could fall over.') (in the street).

It is important to note that, though all these instances of advice were given imperatively, they do not sound as imposing as their English translations do, as the speaker used a polite *vy*-form addressing the hearer.

Although unsolicited advice to strangers is not a conventional practice in Russia, especially in big cities, it is not uncommon to be a recipient of such advice in everyday situations, which demonstrates that Russians are not very vigilant in guarding personal autonomy and may very easily shorten distance, and which shows their involvement with other people's affairs and willingness to help. The perception of advice and its appropriateness greatly depend on various contextual factors including the situation, gender, age of the advice-giver and its recipient as well as intonation and other verbal and non-verbal characteristics. Nevertheless, even if they sound intrusive they are normally accepted by Russians with tolerance, if not with gratitude, as the positive motive of the speaker is obvious.

The results of the comparative analysis (Larina 2009) as well as personal observations show that, in conversation with friends and family members, giving advice is also much more typical of Russian culture in comparison with Anglo culture, where there are significant restrictions on this speech act. It is performed rarely, with numerous softeners and mostly in the form of opinions (27–28). The Russians give advice to those whom they know more willingly and in many cases quite directly (29–30).

(27) *You look tired. I think you should go to bed.*
(28) *If you're fed up with your job, perhaps you should change it.*
(29) *Ty vyglyadish' ustavshey. Idi spat'.* ('You look tired. Go to bed').
(30) *Yesli tebe nadoyela tvoya rabota, pomenyay yeyo.* ('If you're fed up with your job, change it.')

These differences are not surprising, and again it is possible to find a semantic explanation. Analysis of the definitions of the words *advice* and *sovet* 'advice' reveals their cultural specificities. In English, *advice* is 'an opinion that someone gives you about the best thing to do in a particular situation'; *advise* is 'to give your opinion to someone about the best thing to do' (as per the *Macmillan English Dictionary for Advanced Learners*). In Russian, *sovet* 'advice' is defined as '*nastavleniye, ukazaniye, kak postupit*'' ('instruction, direction of how to proceed') (in Ozhegov's *Russian Language Dictionary*). Accordingly, *sovetovat*' 'to advise' means 'to instruct, direct how to proceed' ('*ukazyvat', kak postupat*'). Thus, in English, advising means giving opinion, without inducing the interlocutor to follow it; in other words, keeping distance and showing respect to the personal autonomy of the addressee. In the Russian language, advising means giving instructions how to proceed, showing involvement and solidarity.

4. Discussion and conclusion

Through a brief analysis of some communicative differences of Anglo and Russian speakers, this chapter has attempted to give some more evidence in support of Wierzbicka's statement that in different cultures people not only speak different languages, but also use them in different ways. These differences are not random but systematic, prescribed by cultural values and corroborated by cultural logic. Cultural values that guide the communicative behaviour of the speakers and shape their communicative styles saturate language, and are manifested at all linguistic levels.

The chapter has shown that the prime Anglo values that impact communicative style—personal autonomy, privacy, independence—are based on keeping distance. They encourage speakers to keep their distance physically, psychologically and verbally. Dominant Russian values— involvement, solidarity, interdependence—in contrast, are based on closeness and make people more available. As a result, the representatives of these cultures have different understandings of politeness and appropriate modes of interaction (for details see Larina 2009, 2015). Anglo politeness (at least a part of it, called Negative politeness) (Brown and Levinson 1987) is distance-oriented. One needs to have a 'sense of privacy', not to intrude on another person's zone of autonomy and demonstrate respect for it. Russian speakers, who prefer closeness to distance, instead of 'sense of privacy' possess a 'sense of elbow' (*chuvstvo loktia*); they are less vigilant in guarding personal autonomy and tend to express their communicative intention in a more direct way, which in many cases does not interfere with politeness. The general closeness of interpersonal relations, in the

Russian context, guards against this possibility. Thus the study shows that politeness is also a culture-specific phenomenon and people interact in accordance with their understanding of politeness shaped by their values.

The chapter has demonstrated that cultural values, which guide communicative behaviour, are embedded in language, and showed that manifestations of closeness in Russian, vs distance in English, are systematic, and can be observed in lexis, phraseology, syntax and communicative styles. This confirms, once again, that language is an ideological phenomenon, which shapes different types of identity.

The chapter has also shown that knowledge of cultural values, key words and cultural scripts enables us to observe the systematic interconnectedness of language, culture, cognition and communication, and to see the logic of culture-specific modes of linguistic interaction.

Acknowledgements

I am grateful to two anonymous reviewers for their comments that helped me to improve the chapter and I am most grateful to Anna Wierzbicka for her inspiring works, personal support and encouragement.

This publication has been supported by the RUDN University Strategic Academic Leadership Program.

References

Belyaeva-Standen, E.I. (2004). Mezhkul'turnaya pragmatika soveta—russko-amerikanskii dialog: Pochemu ty menya vsegda kritikuesh'? [Intercultural pragmatics of advice – Russian-American dialogue: Why do you always criticize me?]. In N.V. Ufimtseva (ed.), *Yazykovoe soznanie: teoreticheskie i prikladnye aspekty* [*Linguistic Consciousness: Theoretical and Applied Aspects*]. Moscow, Barnaul: Altay University Publ, 305–19.

Brosnahan, Leger (1998). *Russian and English Nonverbal Communication*. Moscow: Bilingua.

Brown, Penelope and Stephen Levinson (1987). *Politeness: Some Universals in Language Usage*. Cambridge: Cambridge University Press.

Fox, Kate (2003). *Watching the English: The Hidden Rules of English Behaviour*. London: Hodder & Stoughton.

Gladkova, Anna (2007). The journey of self-discovery in another language. In Mary Besemeres and Anna Wierzbicka (eds), *Translating Lives: Living with Two Languages and Cultures*. St Lucia: University of Queensland Press, 139–49.

Gladkova, Anna (2010a). 'Sympathy', 'compassion', and 'empathy' in English and Russian: A linguistic and cultural analysis. *Culture & Psychology* 16 (2): 267–85. doi.org/10.1177/1354067x10361396.

Gladkova, Anna (2010b). *Russian Cultural Semantics: Emotions, Values, Attitudes*. Moscow: Yazyki slavyanskoi kul'tury [in Russian].

Gladkova, Anna (2013). 'Intimate' talk in Russian: Human relationships and folk psychotherapy. *Australian Journal of Linguistics* 33 (3): 322–43. doi.org/10.1080/07268602.2013.846453.

Gladkova, Anna and Tatiana Larina (2018). Anna Wierzbicka: Language, culture and communication. *Russian Journal of Linguistics* 22 (4): 717–48. doi.org/10.22363/2312-9182-2018-22-4-717-748.

Goddard, Cliff (ed.) (2006). *Ethnopragmatics: Understanding Discourse in Cultural Context*. Berlin: Mouton de Gruyter.

Goddard, Cliff and Anna Wierzbicka (1995). Key words, culture and cognition. *Philosophica* 55 (1): 37–67.

Goddard, Cliff and Anna Wierzbicka (1997). Discourse and culture. In Teun A. van Dijk (ed.), *Discourse as Social Interaction*. London: Sage Publishing, 231–57.

Goddard, Cliff and Anna Wierzbicka (2004). Cultural scripts: What are they and what are they good for? *Intercultural Pragmatics* 1 (2): 153–66. doi.org/10.1515/iprg.2004.1.2.153.

Goddard, Cliff and Anna Wierzbicka (2014). *Words and Meanings: Lexical Semantics across Domains, Languages and Cultures*. Oxford: Oxford University Press. doi.org/10.1093/acprof:oso/9780199668434.001.0001.

Hall, Edward T. (1959). *The Silent Language*. Greenwich, Connecticut: Fawcett Premier.

Hofstede, Geert, Gert Jan Hofstede and Michael Minkov (2010). *Cultures and Organizations: Software of the Mind. Intercultural Cooperation and Its Importance for Survival* (3rd edn). London: McGraw-Hill.

Larina, Tatiana (2009). *Kategoriya vezhlivosti i stil' kommunikatsii: sopostavleniye angliyskikh i russkikh lingvokul'utrnykh traditsiy* [*Politeness and Communicative Styles: Comparative Analysis of English and Russian Langua-cultural Traditions*]. Moscow: Yazyki slavyanskikh kul'tur [in Russian].

Larina, Tatiana (2013). *Anglichane i russkiye: Yazyk, kul'tura, kommunikatsiya* [*The British and the Russians: Language, Culture, and Communication*]. Moscow: Yazyki slavyanskikh kul'tur [in Russian].

Larina, Tatiana (2015). Culture-specific communicative styles as a framework for interpreting linguistic and cultural idiosyncrasies. *International Review of Pragmatics* 7 (5): 195–215. doi.org/10.1163/18773109-00702003.

Larina, Tatiana and Vladimir Ozyumenko (2016). Ethnic identity in language and communication. *Cuadernos de Rusística Española* 12: 57–68 [in Russian].

Larina, Tatiana, Arto Mustajoki and Ekaterina Protassova (2017). Dimensions of Russian culture and mind. In Katja Lehtisaari and Arto Mustajoki (eds), *Philosophical and Cultural Interpretations of Russian Modernisation*. London/ New York: Routledge, 7–19.

Larina, Tatiana, Vladimir Ozyumenko and Svetlana Kurteš (2017). I-identity vs we-identity in language and discourse: Anglo-Slavonic perspectives. *Lodz Papers in Pragmatics* 13 (1): 109–28. doi.org/10.1515/lpp-2017-0006.

Leech, Geoffrey N. (1983). *Principles of Pragmatics*. London and New York: Longman.

Macmillan English Dictionary for Advanced Learners (2006). Macmillan Publishers Limited.

New English–Russian Dictionary (1999). Edited under the supervision of Yuri Apresyan. Moscow: Russky Yazyk.

Ozyumenko, Vladimir and Tatiana Larina (2018). Cultural semantics in second language teaching: A case study of Russian *drug* and English *friend*. *INTED2018 Proceedings*, 9149–158. doi.org/10.21125/inted.2018.2235.

Paxman, Jeremy (1999). *The English: A Portrait of a People*. London: Penguin Group.

Ponton, Douglas Mark (2014). Friendship in a digital age: Aristotelian and narrative perspectives. In Garry Robson and Zachara Malgorzata (eds), *Digital Difference: Social Media and Intercultural Experience*. Cambridge: Cambridge Scholars Press, 274–95.

Richmond, Yale (2009). *From Nyet to Da: Understanding the New Russia.* Boston, London: Intercultural Press.

Russian Language Dictionary (13th edn) (1981). Edited by Sergei Ivanovich Ozhegov. Moscow.

Sapir, Edward (1929). The status of linguistics as a science, *Language* 5 (4): 207–14.

Shmelev, Alexei D. (2002). *Russkaya yazykovaya model' mira: Materialy k slovaryu* [*Russian language model of the world: Materials for the dictionary*]. Moscow: Yazyki slavyanskoi kul'tury.

The Longman Dictionary of Contemporary English (3rd edn) (1995). Pearson.

Triandis, Harry (1994). *Culture and Social Behavior.* Boston: McGraw-Hill Inc.

Visson, Lynn (2013). *Where Russians Go Wrong in Spoken English: Words and Phrases in the Context of Two Cultures.* Moscow: Valent.

Wierzbicka, Anna (1985). Different cultures, different languages, different speech acts: Polish vs. English. *Journal of Pragmatics* 9 (2–3): 145–78. doi.org/10.1016/0378-2166(85)90023-2.

Wierzbicka, Anna (1992). *Semantics, Culture, and Cognition: Universal Human Concepts in Culture-Specific Configurations.* New York: Oxford University Press.

Wierzbicka, Anna (1996). *Semantics: Primes and Universals.* Oxford: Oxford University Press.

Wierzbicka, Anna (1997). *Understanding Cultures through their Key Words: English, Russian, Polish, German, and Japanese.* New York: Oxford University Press.

Wierzbicka, Anna (1999). *Semanticheskiye universalii I opisaniye yazykov* [*Semantic Universals and Description of Languages*]. Translated from English by A. Shmelev. Moscow: Yazyki russskoi kul'tury [in Russian].

Wierzbicka, Anna (2002). Russian cultural scripts: The theory of cultural scripts and its applications. *Ethos* 30 (4): 401–32. doi.org/10.1525/eth.2002.30.4.401.

Wierzbicka, Anna (2003 [1991]). *Cross-Cultural Pragmatics: The Semantics of Human Interaction* (2nd edn). Berlin: Mouton de Gruyter.

Wierzbicka, Anna (2006a). *English: Meaning and Culture.* New York: Oxford University Press.

Wierzbicka, Anna (2006b). Anglo scripts against 'putting pressure' on other people and their linguistic manifestations. In Cliff Goddard (ed.), *Ethnopragmatics: Understanding Discourse in Cultural Context*. Berlin: Mouton de Gruyter, 31–63. doi.org/10.1515/9783110911114.31.

Wierzbicka, Anna (2006c). A conceptual basis for intercultural pragmatics and world-wide understanding. Paper presented at The 31st International LAUD Symposium, Landau, Germany.

Ye, Zhengdao (2004). Categorisation of Chinese interpersonal relationships and the cultural logic of Chinese social interaction: An indigenous perspective. *Intercultural Pragmatics* 1 (2): 211–30. doi.org/10.1515/iprg.2004.1.2.211.

Ye, Zhengdao (2013). Understanding the conceptual basis of the 'old friend' formula in Chinese social interaction and foreign diplomacy: A cultural script approach, *Australian Journal of Linguistics* 33 (3): 365–85. doi.org/10.1080/07268602.2013.846459.

Zalizniak, Andrey A. (2013). *Russkaya Semantika v Tipologicheskoi Perspektive* [*Russian Semantics in a Typological Aspect*]. Moscow: Yazyki slavyanskikh kul'tur [in Russian].

Zalizniak, Andrey A., Irina B. Levontina and Alexei D. Shmelev (2012). *Klyuchevye idei russkoi yazykovoi kartiny mira* [*Key Ideas of the Russian Language Picture of the World*]. Moscow: Yazyki slavyanskikh kul'tur [in Russian].

23

On the semantics of *cup*

Keith Allan

Like any language, a metalanguage for semantics consists of a set of symbols, a set of axioms and rules for combining them into syntactically well-formed structures, along with a set of interpretations for these structures and for the individual symbols in isolation.[1] Human languages are the objects studied in semantics, consequently, the language under investigation is known as the 'object language'. The language that a linguist uses to describe and analyse the object language is called the 'metalanguage'. The basic requirement for a metalanguage is to satisfactorily communicate the meaning of item e_{OL}—that is, any expression in the object language, whether it is a word, a phrase, a sentence, or (perhaps) a longer text—in terms of an expression 'e_M' in the metalanguage. A metalanguage is just another language, often an artificial and not a natural one. One important practical constraint on a metalanguage is that it needs to be understood by human beings who normally communicate in a natural language of which they have fluent command. If you understood neither Polish nor Swahili there is little point in my using Swahili as a metalanguage for the semantic analysis of Polish (or vice versa); for example, to say *To jest pies* means 'Ni mbwa' will not help you at all. Readers of this chapter must, perforce, know English, so we can use English as a metalanguage

---

[1] Anna Wierzbicka is an exceptionally brilliant scholar who, during the last half-century, has generated a vast quantity of excellent published work on semantics for several languages. Furthermore, as this volume demonstrates, she has inspired an impressive number of followers who are fine scholars in their own right. Although my essay is critical of some aspects of Anna's semantic theory, it is an argument for a different point of view and assuredly NOT an attack on the high esteem with which Anna Wierzbicka is very properly held.

and say *To jest pies* (in Polish) means 'It's a dog'; or we can say *To jest pies* means 'Ni mbwa' in Swahili, which means 'It's a dog'—here using English as a meta-metalanguage. As we see, the metalanguage is in effect a translation of the object language (cf. Carnap 1937: 228); in order for the metalanguage to be understood and used by human beings it must be communicable, and hence translate into a natural language. We must conclude that a metalanguage expression 'e_M' used in the semantic definition of a natural language expression e_{OL} will always be equivalent to the natural language expression through which it is interpreted.

The metalanguage is the language of a semantic theory. The principal function of the theory is to explain data (words, sentences) from natural language. The goal of the theory is to explain all the data that it was constructed to explain; therefore, limitations on its range need to be clearly stated. A theory should have predictive power insofar as it raises expectations about data that have not yet come to light. It is absolutely necessary that a theory be internally consistent. But what about its external relations? No theory of semantics can completely ignore syntax and phonology, and the ideal semantic theory will integrate with theories of both these components of a grammar. Semantic theory should also integrate with theories of pragmatics that seek to explain meaning in social and cultural contexts and with theories of discourse structure. A semantic theory should not only make useful revelations about the nature of human language but also about human cognition because meaning is often a reflex of human perception and conception. All theories, without exception, are abstractions from reality; so the relation of theory to reality 'is not analogous to that of soup to beef but rather of check number and overcoat' (Einstein 1973: 294). Like any other kind of theory, semantic theory is developed by applying the analyst's experience and intuitions to inferences drawn from occurrences of actual speech events to create a demonstrably rational account of their structures and causes.

'Semantic primitives', more recently called 'semantic primes', are the primitive symbols in a metalanguage for semantics, and their interpretations constitute the vocabulary of the semantic metalanguage. There was the search for semantic primes by Bishop John Wilkins (1668) in his *Essay Towards a Real Character and a Philosophical Language*. His contemporaries, Antoine Arnauld and Pierre Nicole in *La logique, ou l'art de penser* (1662) (Arnauld and Nicole 1965), recognised that the meanings of most words can be defined in terms of others, but that ultimately there are some undefinable semantically primitive words.

In more recent times, Uriel Weinreich (1980: 50, 161, 300, 308–09) identified a three-step discovery procedure for a semantic metalanguage built upon natural language: (a) Stratify the language into a central core of semantic primitives whose members are definable only circularly and by ostensive definition such as 'colour of the sky' in the entry for *blue*. (b) The next stratum out uses items whose definitions contain only core items without (further) circularity. (c) Each more peripheral stratum uses items from the preceding strata without circularity. This is a goal that has not yet been achieved by anyone, though it is probably worth striving for.

Since before 1972, Anna Wierzbicka (see Wierzbicka 1972), influenced by Russian semanticists such as Apresjan (1974, 2000), has been carrying out this program in a cross-language context, searching for a universal set of semantic primitives expressed principally through the vocabulary of English (though see e.g. Peeters 2006).[2] Goddard (1994: 12) (Principle VI) claims that 'any simple proposition' expressed in Natural Semantic Metalanguage (NSM) using any one natural language (e.g. English) will be expressible in NSM using any other language (e.g. Japanese). This embodies a claim that NSM is linguistically and culturally unbiased and that there is a heuristic or algorithm for translation, although in fact none has been published. The aims of NSM are consistent with what has been described above:

> all languages share a universal core, both in their lexicon and in their grammar; a core which constitutes the bedrock of human understanding, communication, and translation. This shared core is like a mini-language, which can be used as a culturally neutral semantic metalanguage for the description of all languages, for the study of cultural diversity as well as the psychological unity of humankind, and also for applied purposes, in education and cross-cultural communication. (Wierzbicka 2006: 1)

Wierzbicka's search for semantic primitives recalls the 'Swadesh list' of basic vocabulary created to plot diachronic relationships between unwritten languages in Africa, the Americas and elsewhere. The purpose of the Swadesh list was to take a pair of languages and compare 100–215 basic lexemes to see how many are cognates (see Swadesh 1955); hence, one name for the program is 'lexico-statistics'. In making the comparisons,

---

2   A reviewer has commented that s/he has heard Wierzbicka remark that her original semantic primitives were founded on her native Polish, the language in which what became Wierzbicka (1972) was first composed.

literal meanings are preferred to semantic extensions; for example, the body-part sense of English *tongue* is preferred to the sense 'language'. Assuming that two languages being compared are in fact related, the time of divergence from a common mother language is estimated from the proportion of vocabulary common to both. The scale of vocabulary differentiation derives from studies of Indo-European languages for which there are historical records. The procedure is sometimes called 'glottochronology'. Words in the Swadesh list are basic in the sense that they name things likely to be common to the experience of all human communities, hence they fall into categories such as personal pronouns, interrogatives, connectives (*and, if, because*), locatives and locations, position and movement, manipulations (*wash, hit, scratch*), time periods, numerals, quantifiers, size, natural objects and phenomena, plants, animals, persons, body parts and substances, bodily sensations and activities, colours, kin and cultural objects and activities. There is clearly some similarity with the sets of semantic primes regularly set out in most works on NSM. However, the studies of semantic and lexical universals reported in Goddard and Wierzbicka (1994), Wierzbicka (1996), Goddard (1998) and many later works are not concerned with diachronic relationships, but with the different differential values that listemes have both within and across languages (a 'listeme' is a language expression whose meaning is not determinable from the meanings (if any) of its constituent forms and which, therefore, a language user must memorise as a combination of form and meaning: cf. Di Sciullo and Williams 1987).

The number of semantic primitives identified by Wierzbicka grew from 14 in 1972 to nearly 20 in 1985, 37 in 1994, 57 in 1998 and about 65 today.[3] In addition, 'allolexes' of these primitives are permitted: for example, ME for I, WHO and WHAT for SOMEONE and SOMETHING, THING for SOMETHING, COULD for CAN, FOR for BECAUSE, PLACE for WHERE. Exactly what constrains the proliferation of allolexes remains to be defined. And although NSM is sometimes said to be 'language-neutral' (Goddard 2001: 659), it is not. There are about 65 semantic primes in every language, such that there is an English NSM, a French NSM, a Mandarin NSM, a Tamil NSM, etc. It is claimed that the primes from one language correspond to those from any other language: 'they are isomorphic and constitute, in effect, different variants of one language-

---

3   See further discussion available at: intranet.secure.griffith.edu.au/schools-departments/natural-semantic-metalanguage/what-is-nsm. This informative website is maintained by Cliff Goddard and colleagues.

independent conceptual system' (Wierzbicka 2006: 3). However, NSM primes are compositionally and often semantically different across languages. Like most translated terms, the meanings show partial overlap rather than complete identity; for example, for NSM researchers, English SOME = French IL Y A ... QUI; English THERE IS = French IL Y A. Yet French IL Y A UN X QUI is not equivalent to English THERE IS SOME X WHICH, where there is apparent translation equivalence between UN and SOME. Given that French IL Y A occurs within two primes, surely UN, the French equivalent to English prime ONE, could appear twice as well (cf. Peeters et al. 2006). Add to this that, in NSM, allolexes are not only tolerated but necessary, which makes the so-called 'semantic primes' more like meaning clusters than true primes; for example, English I and ME; DO, DOES, DID; French TU, TOI, VOUS; Italian TU, VOI, LEI, etc. Furthermore, primes are not independent of one another, there are several complementary pairs such as GOOD~BAD, BIG~SMALL, NEAR~FAR, ABOVE~BELOW, BEFORE~AFTER, LIVE~DIE. If NSM researchers were to stick rigidly to the notion of primes, such opposed pairs could each be reduced by one prime (the other being its negation) without thereby distorting natural language any more than is normal for the mini-language that is NSM.[4] Indeed, until around 1990, Wierzbicka's meaning descriptions used a lot of other items besides the primes (cf. Wierzbicka 1972: 22, 26, 106). Most recent semantic analyses stick more closely to the primes.

Today, many NSM analyses contain 'semantic molecules', marked by a subsequent [m] (see (80–120) below for instances).

> These are non-primitive meanings (hence, ultimately decomposable into semantic primes) that can function as units in the semantic structure of other, yet more complex words ... [S]emantic molecules must be meanings of lexical units in the language concerned.
>
> From a conceptual point of view, the NSM claim is that some complex concepts are semantically dependent on other less complex, but still non-primitive, concepts. For example, semantic explications for words like *sparrow* and *eagle* include 'bird' as a semantic molecule; the cognitive claim is that the concept of

---

4 A reviewer disputes this, citing objections in Wierzbicka (1996). I don't believe that there can be a restricted set of semantic primes such as those proposed in NSM; in my view, the number of semantic elements in any language is more or less the same size as its vocabulary. Furthermore, the proposed primes of NSM are rarely (if ever) monosemic. For instance, ABOVE is no more monosemic than is *over* in Brugman (1983), Dewell (1994), Lakoff (1987).

sparrow includes and depends on the concept of 'bird'. In this case, the relationship is taxonomic: *sparrows* and *eagles* are both 'birds [m] of one kind' (molecules are marked in explications with the notation [m]). (Goddard 2010: 124)

Although it is said that all semantic molecules are reducible to semantic primes, this has only been demonstrated for a few (e.g. Goddard 2010: 125–130).

How do Anna Wierzbicka's semantic analyses compare to those of scholars using other metalanguages? In this essay I limit myself to critiquing her semantics for *cup* in Wierzbicka (1984). The expressions used in a semantic representation in NSM are supposed to match those that (a) children acquire early and (b) have counterparts in all languages (Goddard 1994: 12). In her definitions, Wierzbicka is deliberately anthropocentric and subjective, referring to the natural world of sensory experience rather than intellectualised abstractions. Thus, she prefers to describe *red* as the colour of blood (Wierzbicka 1980, 1990) or fire (Wierzbicka 1990, 1992a) than as an electromagnetic wave focally around 695 nanometres in length.

> If we are trying to understand and to elucidate the intuitions of ordinary speakers, we cannot use in our definitions anything which is not independently attested to be accessible to that intuition. Translating colour terms into information about wavelength may tell us something about physiological and neurological processes but obviously it cannot tell us anything about the intuitive connections between different everyday concepts. (Wierzbicka 1984: 235)

I propose that *blue* involves more than one point of reference: not only the sky but also water—not water from the tap, but naturally occurring water, that is, the water of seas, lakes, rivers, and so on. Roughly:

X is blue
when one sees things like X
one can think of the sky
or of places (not made by people)
where there is water
(Wierzbicka 1992b: 222–23)

This is a characteristic of cognitive semantics which I fully endorse.

23. ON THE SEMANTICS OF CUP

In the remainder of this essay I discuss Anna Wierzbicka's definition of *cup* from Wierzbicka (1984: 222–24). But, because this was published some 35 years ago I shall also briefly discuss Cliff Goddard's rather similar definition from Goddard (2011: 228–29) before considering alternatives. First, Wierzbicka's semantics from 1984, to which I have added paragraph numbers for the convenience of discussion.

(1) cup
(2) A KIND OF THING MADE BY PEOPLE
(3) IMAGINING THINGS OF THIS KIND PEOPLE WOULD SAY THESE THINGS ABOUT THEM:
(4) [Purpose]
(5) they are made for people to use repeatedly for drinking hot liquids from, such as tea or coffee
(6) one person from one thing of this kind
(7) being able to put them down on something else
(8) [Material]
(9) they are made of something rigid, smooth and easy to wash
(10) which liquids can't go into or pass through
(11) and which doesn't break easily in contact with hot liquid
(12) [Appearance: top]
(13) they are rounded and open at the top
(14) so that one can drink easily from them by tipping the top part slightly towards the mouth
(15) without any of the liquid going outside, where one doesn't want it to go
(16) [Appearance: bottom]
(17) the bottom is the same shape as the top
(18) so that they are not more difficult to make than they have to be and it is flat
(19) so that things of this kind can be put down on something else that is flat
(20) [Appearance: proportions]
(21) they cannot be much wider than they are high

(22) so that the liquid inside doesn't cease to be hot before one can drink it all
(23) they cannot be much higher than they are wide
(24) so that they don't overturn easily when one puts them down somewhere
(25) [Size]
(26) they have to be big enough to be able to have not less hot liquid in
(27) than a person would be expected to want to drink of that kind of liquid at one time
(28) they cannot be too big for people to be able to raise them easily to the mouth full of liquid, with one hand
(29) IMAGINING THINGS OF THIS KIND PEOPLE COULD ALSO SAY THESE THINGS ABOUT THEM:
(30) [Use]
(31) people drink from them when sitting at a table
(32) [Use: sets]
(33) they are made and used in groups of things which look the same
(34) so that they look nice together
(35) [Use: saucers]
(36) they are made and used together with some other things
(37) made of the same stuff
(38) made for putting these things on
(39) one thing for a person to drink from, on one thing for putting such things on
(40) so that people can raise the things to drink from to the mouth to drink a little
(41) and then put them down on those other things which can be put down on the table
(42) those other things are similar to them in some ways so that they look nice together
(43) those other things are made in such a way that there can be some parts of them all around the bottom of the things that people drink from
(44) so that if any liquid goes down over the top of the things people drink from
(45) it will come onto and remain on those other things

23. ON THE SEMANTICS OF CUP

(46) and will not get elsewhere, where one doesn't want it to go
(47) [Material]
(48) things of this kind are made of something thin so that they are nice to look at and to drink from
(49) and of something that one can't see through
(50) so that things made of it can have pictures and patterns on them
(51) making them nice to look at,
(52) such as china
(53) [Appearance: sides]
(54) the sides are rounded, not flat
(55) so that all the sides look the same and one can't say where one side ends and another begins
(56) so that one can easily hold things of this kind around with a hand when they don't have any hot liquid inside
(57) the sides are not straight but roundish
(58) so that looked at from the side the opposite sides, or their upper parts, look like rounded lines
(59) whose middle parts are further away from one another than their tops or bottoms
(60) [Appearance: proportions]
(61) the bottom is smaller than the top
(62) so that if some of the liquid goes down along the outer surface of the thing one is drinking from
(63) it will come to the middle of the thing it is on
(64) and will not go outside that thing to where one doesn't want it to go
(65) [Appearance: handle]
(66) things of this kind have a thin looped part for holding
(67) which sticks out from one side
(68) which doesn't get hot
(69) because it is not in contact with the hot liquid inside
(70) this part is attached at its top and its bottom to one side
(71) so that by holding it one can prevent one part of the top from being above the others when one is not drinking

(72) and so prevent any of the liquid from getting out over the top and going where one doesn't want it to go

(73) this part has to be big enough and to stick out far enough for people to be able to raise things of this kind full of liquid for a short time

(74) holding that part with a thumb and two fingers

(75) without any parts of the hand touching the sides, which are hot

(76) it can't be much bigger or stick out much further than necessary for that. (Wierzbicka 1984: 222–24)

One of the most striking things about this definition of *cup* is its detail and consequently its length (about 830 words). A second is that it includes far more than a vocabulary of primes. I will discuss first the detail and length and turn to the exoticism after exemplifying Goddard's version, which sticks more closely to semantic primes and marks semantic molecules.

(2) identifies a cup as a manufactured, not natural, object. (3) anthropocentrically identifies the content as cognitively real. It is unclear to me why (29) is needed, but apparently characteristics (30–76) are seen as secondary elaborations on (2–28) and, in fact, many of them do seem redundant. A cup's purpose, (4–7), and the function ((30–46)) for which this artefact is manufactured will (at least partially) determine the material from which it is made, (8–11, 47–52), and its configuration, (12–28, 53–76). With respect to function: although it is true that cups are primarily for the drinking of hot liquids (which is probably why they typically have handles, (65–76)), cups are also used for cool and cold liquids and for measuring dry goods such as flour and sugar; given the amount of detail in Wierzbicka's description it is surprising that such secondary uses are disregarded.

(8–11) identify a material necessary for containing potentially hot liquid. There is no mention of semantic extensions such as single use paper and plastic cups (which typically lack handles).

Cups are very possibly modelled on a human's cupped hands. A typical cup[5] holds around 250 millilitres, which is similar to the capacity of adult male cupped hands. A single hand cupped holds around 125 mL, roughly equivalent to the amount of liquid held by an espresso coffee cup

---

5   I prefer the term *typical* to *prototypical* or *stereotypical* for reasons explained in Allan (2001: 334–36).

or a Middle Eastern tea or coffee cup—which is bowl-like (i.e. handle-less). Thus, a typical cup is a hollow oblate hemispheroid[6] container (i.e. a squashed half-sphere) with a flat base at the pole (its base or bottom) so that it can easily stand alone, open at the wide end for easy access by human lips to the liquid it contains. It is designed to be readily manipulated by the thumb and fingers of a single human hand. These matters of configuration are over-elaborated in (12–28). A rectangular cup would be atypical because impracticable, but nonetheless it could function as a cup, because the essential criterion for a cup is that it be a container for liquid with a capacity of around 250 ml.

Consequently, (31) seems to me to be irrelevant: what's criterial for a cup is that it is a container that serves as a drinking vessel which can be handled by children as well as adults, so it must be lightweight. Whether the user is sitting, standing or lying in bed, is irrelevant. It is also as irrelevant to the meaning of *cup* that cups often come in sets, (32–34), as that they come in a variety of colours and designs—and there is (correctly) nothing said about those characteristics in (1–76).

(35–46) over-elaborate the significance of saucers. Typically cups in the West are accompanied by saucers—though Middle-Eastern cups typically are not. The saucer is a practical stand for a cup, etiquette favours their use as practical protectors of clothing and furniture from hot cups and dribbled liquid; they may also be used to park a teaspoon or used tea-bag. Mugs are typically cylindrical drinking vessels that don't have saucers.[7]

(47–52) are a matter of aesthetics irrelevant to the meaning of *cup*. (53–64) are unnecessary aspects of the configuration of cups that has already been adequately covered in (12–28).

(65–76) identify a significant characteristic of (Western) cups: typically, they sport handles, (66, 67, 70, 76), to facilitate the conveyance of a cup of hot liquid to the mouth without discomforting the hand, (69, 75). Normally only the thumb and one or two fingers manipulate the handle,

---

6 Both cupped hands and a single cupped hand are similar in shape to a hollow oblate hemispheroid (if we ignore the attached arm). A tapered mug might be described as a hollow *prolate hemispheroid*, though most mugs are cylindrical.
7 Wierzbicka (1984) and Goddard (1998, 2011), written in response to Labov (1973), specifically contrast cups with mugs, which there is no space to do here, though I have done so in Allan (1986/2014, 2001).

(74). Typical Middle Eastern tea and coffee cups are small enough to be held by the thumb and first finger, often around a rim that does not overheat. Typical single-use paper or plastic cups lack handles and saucers.

Let me now introduce Cliff Goddard's semantics for *cup*. In Goddard (1998: 233) he offered a somewhat shorter version than in his revised version in 2011 to which I have, for convenience in discussion, added numbers (77–120).

(77) *a cup:*

(78)   FUNCTIONAL CATEGORY

(79) a. something of one kind

(80)   at many times people do something with something of this kind when they are drinking [m] something hot [m]

(81)   when someone is drinking [m] something like this, before it is inside this someone's mouth [m], it is for some time inside something of this kind

(82)   SIZE

(83) b. things of this kind are like this:

(84)   – they are not big

(85)   – someone can hold [m] one in one hand [m]

(86)   PART FOR HOLDING

(87) many things of this kind have a small thin [m] part on one side

(88) when someone is drinking [m], this someone can hold [m] this part with the fingers [m] of one hand [m]

(89)   OTHER PARTS

(90) the other parts are like this:

(91)   – the sides [m] are like the sides [m] of something round [m]

(92)   – they are thin [m]

(93)   – the top [m] part of the sides has a smooth [m] round [m] edge [m]

(94)   – the bottom [m] part of something of this kind is flat [m]

(95)   – someone can think that the bottom [m] part is small, if this someone thinks about the top [m] part at the same time

23. ON THE SEMANTICS OF *CUP*

(96)   MATERIAL

(97)   things of this kind are made of [m] something hard [m]

(98)   this something is smooth [m]

(99)   USE SEQUENCE

(100) c. when someone is doing something with something of this kind because this someone is drinking [m] something hot [m], it happens like this:

(101)   – at some time this something is in one place for some time, at this time the bottom [m] part is touching something flat [m]

(102)   – at this time there is something like hot [m] water [m] inside this thing

(103)   – it can be tea [m], it can be coffee [m], it can be something of another kind

(104)   – it is inside this thing because some time before someone did some things because this someone wanted it to be like this

(105)   – after this, someone picks up [m] this something with the fingers [m] of one hand [m]

(106)   – after this, this someone does something else to it with the hand [m]

(107)   – after this, because of this, part of the edge [m] at the top [m] of this thing touches one of this someone's lips [m] for a short time, as this someone wants

(108)   – during this time, this someone's fingers [m] move as this someone wants

(109)   – because of this, a little bit of something like hot [m] water [m] moves, as this someone wants

(110)   – because of this, after this it is not inside this thing anymore, it is inside this someone's mouth [m]

(111)   – after this, this someone puts [m] this thing down [m] on something flat [m]

(112)   – after this, this someone can do this a few more times

(113)   SAUCER

(114) sometimes when someone is drinking [m] something in this way, this someone wants not to hold [m] this thing for a short time

MEANING, LIFE AND CULTURE

(115) when it is like this, this someone can put [m] this thing down [m] on something of another kind, in the middle [m] of this other kind of thing

(116) these other things are made of [m] the same hard [m], smooth [m] stuff

(117) they are round [m], they are flat [m]

(118) the edge [m] of something or this kind is above the middle [m]

(119)   ARTEFACT STATUS

(120) d. many people want to drink [m] things of some kinds like this at many times because of this, some people make [m] things of this kind. (Goddard 2011: 228–29)

A few general remarks: the principal contrast with Wierzbicka's account is that Goddard's sticks much more closely to semantic primes, despite the extensive employment of 'semantic molecules' marked by a subsequent [m]. It is also a little shorter, 66 paragraphs instead of 76. In my view it is still far too long because it includes some extraneous information while omitting some criterial information. It is sectioned into four parts: (a), (78–81), identifies a cup's primary function; (b), (82–98), describes the configuration of a typical cup and the material from which it is made; (c), (99–118), describes how a cup is used and what it is used for, then brings in saucers; and (d), (119–120), says the cups are in wide use and many are manufactured.

(78–81) identify a cup as, primarily, a vessel for containing hot liquid. (82–95) identify the typical configuration: a cup can be held by the fingers of one hand, for which reason it has a handle; it is a hollow oblate hemispheroid with a flat bottom. (96–98) describe the material from which a cup is made as smooth and hard—which doesn't absolutely exclude single-use paper or plastic cups, and does recognise the character of a typical cup. (99–112) describes the use of cup for the drinking of hot liquid, mentioning that a cup is several times raised to the lips and lowered onto a flat surface; although commonly true, this is superfluous information because it has no part in defining what a cup is. (113–118) describes the configuration and constituency of a saucer but doesn't offer a satisfactory account of its function. Finally, (119–120) says that because people like drinking hot liquids, cups are manufactured to that purpose.

23. ON THE SEMANTICS OF CUP

So, the Goddard (2011) semantics for *cup* is inspired by his mentor Wierzbicka's earlier account and, as an exercise in NSM, greatly improves on it by sticking quite closely to the use of semantic primes while marking digressions into semantic molecules that stray from primes by invoking complexes of primes, though no explication of these complexes is presented. Wierzbicka (1984) was explicitly a refutation of Labov's denotation conditions for *cup* (Labov 1973: 366f), on the grounds that they 'need the help of a mathematician to understand' them and do not give the lexicographic meaning (Wierzbicka 1984: 207). She claims 'the denotation conditions can be deduced from the meaning' (1984: 209). So, let's review Labov's denotation conditions:

> The term *cup* is regularly used to denote round containers with a ratio of width to depth of $1 \pm r$ where $r \leq r_b$, and $r_b = \alpha_1 + \alpha_2 + \ldots \alpha_v$ and α_1 is a positive quantity when the feature i is present and 0 otherwise.
>
> feature 1 = with one handle
> 2 = made of opaque vitreous material
> 3 = used for consumption of food
> 4 = used for consumption of liquid food
> 5 = used for consumption of hot liquid food
> 6 = with a saucer
> 7 = tapering
> 8 = circular in cross-section
>
> *Cup* is used variably to denote such containers with ratios of width to depth of $1 \pm r$ where $r_b \leq r \leq r_t$ with a probability of $r_t - r / r_t - r_b$. The quantity $r \pm r_b$ expresses the distance from the modal value of width to height. (Labov 1973: 366f, quoted in Wierzbicka 1984: 206f)

Labov's is notably succinct by comparison with the versions of Wierzbicka (1–76) and Goddard (77–120) and I do not find it more troublesome to read through than the NSM versions. An important question arises about the playoff between the effectiveness of a definition and its accuracy. What is the purpose of the semantic analysis? Who or what is the semantic specification that results from the analysis designed for? Wierzbicka's semantic definitions are not designed to be used by machines that simulate language understanding. She intends them to be easily accessible to a non-native speaker of the language. But every such reader will already know what a cup is, so a brief description would be sufficient. In my experience, students find Wierzbicka's two-page definition of *cup* just as challenging as Labov's denotation conditions. Consider the following 'dictionary representation' of *cup* given by Jerrold J. Katz:

> Physical Object
> Inanimate
> Vertical Orientation
> Upwardly concave
> Height about equal to top diameter
> Top diameter greater than bottom diameter
> Artefact
> Made to serve as a container from which to drink liquid. (Katz 1977: 49)

Katz's description is adequate, very much simpler than Labov's 'denotation conditions', and much more succinct than Wierzbicka's 'semantic definition' of c. 830 words.

If anything, the *Oxford English Dictionary* (*OED*) is simpler still:

> 1. A small open vessel for liquids, usually of hemispherical or hemi-spheroidal shape, with or without a handle; a drinking-vessel. The common form of cup (e.g. a tea-cup or coffee-cup) has no stem; but the larger and more ornamental forms (e.g. a wine-cup or chalice) may have a stem and foot, as also a lid or cover; in such case cup is sometimes applied specifically to the concave part that receives the liquid.

But as will be seen in (121), I believe that even this august lexical entry does not fully specify what a cup is.

Wierzbicka and Goddard might object that the terms Katz and the *OED* use are more difficult than *cup* itself (which is arguably equally true for the semantics of *cup* in Wierzbicka 1984 and Goddard 1998, 2011); this however is irrelevant to proper statement of the meaning. The purpose of semantic representations is to make useful revelations about the nature of human language and/or human cognition. Wierzbicka has written:

> An adequate definition must show fully what the word in question means, not what it doesn't mean or how it differs in meaning from some other words which we happen to compare it with. ... [A]n adequate definition of a word must constitute a faithful 'portrait' of the concept encoded in it. (Wierzbicka 1984: 227)

This is inconsistent with her semantic definition of *tiger* (Wierzbicka 1985: 164), where she compared tigers with cats because we see tigers as a kind of cat. In different terms, what Wierzbicka seems to be saying is that an adequate definition of what a listeme means will capture the intension of the listeme—which is exactly my own view. And the complexity of explication is unimportant provided it is accurate and revealing—as should be obvious from perusal of entries in the *OED*.

At this point it behoves me to offer my own version of the semantics for *cup* (and, like Wierzbicka and Goddard, I restrict this to the drinking vessel, ignoring such similarly shaped objects as acorn cups and bra cups). On this occasion, I use English as an informal metalanguage.

(121) *cup*

> Hollow oblate hemispheroid vessel, flat at its pole, with a capacity ≈ 250 ml (≈ the capacity of cupped human hands) and a vertical handle to facilitate drinking when held by a human's thumb and one or two fingers in order to raise the vessel to the lips. Typically used for hot liquids. Often accompanied by a saucer to stand on. Middle Eastern cups typically have half the capacity of Western cups and, like single-use paper and plastic cups, they typically lack handles and saucers.

The prolixity of Wierzbicka's and Goddard's semantic definitions for *cup* is unjustified. Although NSM authors do not specifically create lexicon entries, such seem an appropriate application for the lexical analyses on offer—especially given that Goddard (2010: 124) writes of developing 'our picture of the overall structure of the lexicon'. As Alan Cruse (1990: 396) wrote: 'For dictionary purposes, the concept has only to be identified, not fully specified.' Nonetheless, (121) is a fuller specification than in any of the other semantics presented for *cup* that I have exemplified and discussed, and it clearly identifies the concept of a cup. Hopefully, you, the reader, will agree.

Acknowledgement

I would like to thank two anonymous referees for useful comments that led to an improved text. However, no one but me is responsible for the infelicities that remain.

References

Allan, Keith (1986/2014). *Linguistic Meaning* (2 vols). London: Routledge and Kegan Paul. [Reprint edn, (1991) Beijing: World Publishing Corporation. Reissued in one volume as Routledge Library Editions: Linguistics Volume 8 (2014).]

Allan, Keith (2001). *Natural Language Semantics*. Oxford and Malden, Massachusetts: Blackwell.

Apresjan, Juri D. (1974). Regular polysemy. *Linguistics* 142: 5–32.

Apresjan, Juri D. (2000). *Systematic Lexicography* (trans. by Kevin Windle). Oxford: Oxford University Press.

Arnauld, Antoine and Pierre Nicole (1965). *La Logique, ou L'art de Penser: contenant, outre les règles communes, plusieurs observations nouvelles propres à former le jugement* [*Logic or The Art of Thinking: Containing, Besides Common Rules, Several New Observations Appropriate for Forming Judgment*]. Éd. critique par Pierre Clair et François Girbal [critical edition by Pierre Clair and François Girbal, based on the final 1683 version]. Paris: Presses universitaires de France.

Brugman, Claudia M. (1983). *The Story of Over*. Bloomington: Indiana University Linguistics Club.

Carnap, Rudolf (1937). *Logical Syntax of Language*. London: Routledge and Kegan Paul.

Cruse, D. Alan (1990). Prototype theory and lexical semantics. In Savas L. Tsohatzidis (ed.), *Meanings and Prototypes: Studies in Linguistic Categorization*. London: Routledge, 382–402.

Dewell, Robert B. (1994). Over again: Image-schema transformations in semantic analysis. *Cognitive Linguistics* 5: 351–80. doi.org/10.1515/cogl.1994.5.4.351.

Di Sciullo, Anna-Maria and Edwin Williams (1987). *On the Definition of Word*. Cambridge, MA: MIT Press.

Einstein, Albert (1973 [1954]). *Ideas and Opinions* (Laurel edn). New York: Dell.

Goddard, Cliff (1994). Semantic theory and semantic universals. In Cliff Goddard and Anna Wierzbicka (eds), *Semantic and Lexical Universals: Theory and Empirical Findings*. Amsterdam: John Benjamins, 7–30.

Goddard, Cliff (1998). *Semantic Analysis: A Practical Introduction*. Oxford: Oxford University Press.

Goddard, Cliff (2001). *Sabar, iklas, setia—patient, sincere, loyal?* Contrastive semantics of some 'virtues' in Malay and English. *Journal of Pragmatics* 33: 653–81. doi.org/10.1016/s0378-2166(00)00028-x.

Goddard, Cliff (2010). Semantic molecules and semantic complexity (with special reference to 'environmental' molecules). *Review of Cognitive Linguistics* 8 (1): 123–55. doi.org/10.1075/ml.8.1.05god.

Goddard, Cliff (2011). *Semantic Analysis: A Practical Introduction* (2nd edn). Oxford: Oxford University Press.

Goddard, Cliff and Anna Wierzbicka (eds) (1994). *Semantic and Lexical Universals: Theory and Empirical Findings*. Amsterdam: John Benjamins.

Katz, Jerrold J. (1977). A proper theory of names. *Philosophical Studies* 31: 1–80.

Labov, William (1973). The boundaries of words and their meanings. In Charles-J. Bailey and Roger Shuy (eds), *New Ways of Analyzing Variation in English*. Washington DC: Georgetown University Press, 340–73.

Lakoff, George (1987). *Women, Fire, and Dangerous Things: What Categories Reveal About the Mind*. Chicago: University of Chicago Press.

Oxford English Dictionary (OED) (n.d.). Oxford: Oxford University Press. Available at: www.oed.com/.

Peeters, Bert (ed.) (2006). *Semantic Primes and Universal Grammar: Empirical Evidence from the Romance Languages*. Amsterdam: John Benjamins. doi.org/10.1075/slcs.81.

Peeters, Bert, Marie-Odile Junker, Patrick Farrell, Pedro Perini-Santos and Brigid Maher (2006). NSM exponents and universal grammar in Romance: Speech; actions, events and movement; existence and possession; life and death. In Bert Peeters (ed.), *Semantic Primes and Universal Grammar: Empirical Evidence from the Romance Languages*. Amsterdam: John Benjamins, 111–36. doi.org/10.1075/slcs.81.11pee.

Swadesh, Morris (1955). Towards greater accuracy in lexico-statistic dating. *International Journal of American Linguistics* 21: 121–37. doi.org/10.1086/464321.

Weinreich, Uriel (1980). *Weinreich on Semantics* (ed. by William Labov and Beatrice S. Weinreich). Philadelphia: University of Pennsylvania Press.

Wierzbicka, Anna (1972). *Semantic Primitives*. Frankfurt: Athenäm.

Wierzbicka, Anna (1980). *Lingua Mentalis: The Semantics of Natural Language*. Sydney: Academic Press.

Wierzbicka, Anna (1984). Cups and mugs: Lexicography and conceptual analysis. *Australian Journal of Linguistics* 4: 257–81. doi.org/10.1080/07268608408599326.

Wierzbicka, Anna (1985). *Lexicography and Conceptual Analysis*. Ann Arbor: Karoma.

Wierzbicka, Anna (1990). The meaning of color terms: Semantics, culture, and cognition. *Cognitive Linguistics* 1: 99–150. doi.org/10.1515/cogl.1990.1.1.99.

Wierzbicka, Anna (1992a). Semantic primitives and semantic fields. In Eva Kittay and Adrienne Lehrer (eds), *Frames, Fields, and Contrasts*. Norwood, NJ: Lawrence Erlbaum, 209–27.

Wierzbicka, Anna (1992b). Personal names and expressive derivation. In *Semantics, Culture, and Cognition: Universal Human Concepts in Culture-specific Configurations*. New York: Oxford University Press, 225–307.

Wierzbicka, Anna (1996). *Semantics: Primes and Universals*. Oxford: Oxford University Press.

Wierzbicka, Anna (2006). Preface. In Bert Peeters (ed.) *Semantic Primes and Universal Grammar: Empirical Evidence from the Romance Languages*. Amsterdam: John Benjamins, 1–6. doi.org/10.1075/slcs.81.05wie.

Wilkins, John (1668). *Essay Towards a Real Character and a Philosophical Language*. London: S. Gellibrand and John Martin for the Royal Society [Menston: Scolar Press Facsimile. 1968].

24

Where we PART from NSM: Understanding Warlpiri *yangka* and the Warlpiri expression of part-hood

David Nash and David P. Wilkins

1. Introduction

As Wierzbicka and Goddard (2018: 31) (W&G) observe, 'NSM researchers have long maintained that PART(s) is a universal semantic prime, i.e. an indefinable meaning expressible by words or phrases in all human languages'. In fact, 'be a part of' was among the original list of fourteen semantic primes published in Wierzbicka's seminal work *Semantic Primitives* (1972), and it remains among the current list of 65 primes as a 'relational substantive' represented as PART ~ HAVE PARTS. NSM (Natural Semantic Metalanguage) has a strong position that all conceptual semantic primes of the *lingua mentalis* must have a corresponding lexical exponent in every natural language. If there were a natural language where PART was not one of the senses of at least one word, morpheme or phrase of the language, then PART would need to be removed from the set of universal semantic primes. Alternatively, NSM would need to allow that some conceptual primes do not have basic lexical expression in *all* languages, but are still part of the *lingua mentalis*.

W&G's search for lexification in the Australian language Warlpiri of the concept PART has led them to the controversial conclusion that it is one of the senses of the non-spatial (evocative/recognitional) demonstrative *yangka* 'that one, you know the one, the one in question', the most common form in the Warlpiri corpus. W&G started from the English translations of Warlpiri examples relating to body parts in resources produced by the Warlpiri Dictionary project. They believed they could uncover the Warlpiri exponent of PART by matching the English translations—particularly those that included the word 'part'—with the Warlpiri originals. We present our objections to their method and analysis, situated in a discussion of how *yangka* is used in vernacular definitions in the Warlpiri Dictionary, the meaning of *yangka* and how Warlpiri does express the concept PART.

W&G's general point is this:

> We seek to interrogate the material included in the Warlpiri Dictionary (both Warlpiri sentences and their English translations) to make the case that Warlpiri speakers can and do talk about 'parts of the body'. (W&G 2018: 32)

We agree: it hardly needs stating that Warlpiri speakers can and do talk about parts of the body. Our divergent view is that this obtains without the language having a word-for-word equivalent of 'part of someone's body', and that the meaning PART is not expressed by a Warlpiri lexeme. We further hold that *yangka* is basically monosemous, and that the cooperative interactional expectation encoded in its meaning licenses context-dependent pragmatic inferences that convey all manner of variously translatable concepts, of which PART is just one.

W&G (2018: 32–37) provide the background to the treatment of the concept PART within NSM studies, including previous disagreement concerning Warlpiri (Nash 2014). It is fair to state, however, that their and our joint inquiry is of wider import and does not depend on particulars of the NSM approach.[1]

---

1   At least since the publication of her seminal *Semantic Primitives* in 1972, Anna Wierzbicka has been indefatigable in the development and promulgation of what has become known as the NSM approach to semantics. We each recall fondly our encounter with Anna in her semantics classes when we were students at ANU, in 1974 and 1978 respectively, and share her interest in comparative semantics. Anyone who knows Anna knows she is up for an argument and would rather have people engage critically and seriously with NSM rather than ignore it. We choose to honour her and her achievements through just such a critical engagement.

2. Methodological flaws in W&G's approach

As already noted, W&G's study is based on a correlation they noticed in the Warlpiri Dictionary between illustrative Warlpiri sentences about body parts (especially the occurrence of 'part' in their English free translation) and the word *yangka*. (W&G apparently did not study the other Warlpiri sentences whose English free translation also contains 'part'.) Note that, in general, the English translations were not provided by the Warlpiri speakers, so 'part' was introduced by native English speakers in their best effort translation of the sense of a Warlpiri example, not as an attempt to reflect Warlpiri semantics.

2.1. Problems with purported examples of 'part' sense of *yangka*

Consider (1), W&G's (2018: 12) prime example of the supposed PART sense of *yangka*:[2]

(1) *Kantumi, ngula kuyu yangka marlu. Kantumi manu yardipi*
    hip   that animal part   kangaroo hip   or   hip
    yi-ka-rlipa   ngarri-rni
    AUX.COMP-PRS-1PL.INCL.SBJ call-NPST
   '*Kantumi* is what we call that part of the kangaroo which is its hip.'
   (W&G's glosses)

This example and free translation has been taken from the dictionary entry for *yardipi* 'hip', with interlinear supplied by W&G. The dictionary took the illustration lightly edited from Hale's (1966–67: 0215) original transcription shown in (2) (and note our closer translation). The speaker uses equivalents of the word he is explaining:[3]

---

2 Abbreviations: 1 first person, 12 first person inclusive, 2 second person, 3 third person, AUX auxiliary, COMP complementiser, DU dual, ERG ergative, EVOC evocative, INCL inclusive, LOC locative, NOMIC nomic, NPST non-past, OBJ object, PL plural, POSS possessive, PRS present, REL relative, SBJ subject, TOP topic.
3 See Appendix 24.1 for source and context.

(2) *Kantumu, kantumu ngula   kuyu   yangka marlu. Wawirri.*
    rump   rump   that   animal/meat EVOC kangaroo kangaroo
    Kantumi manu   yardipi yi-ka-rlipa   ngarri-rni
    rump   or   hip   AUX.COMP-PRS-1PL.INCL.SBJ call-NPST

Kantumu, kantumu that is [used for] game animals, say, kangaroos.
'Kangaroo. We call it *kantumu* ('rump') or *yardipi* ('hip').'

W&G comment that '[c]learly, this vernacular definition does not refer to "that kangaroo" but to "part of a kangaroo" (i.e. the hip)' (2018: 42–43). But it is not clear, for two reasons: (a) *kuyu yangka marlu* is a prosodic and syntactic unit (as apparent in the audio recording), and semantically *yangka* can be construed with *kuyu* 'game animal, meat'; (b) if *yangka* is construed with *marlu*, it can indeed mean 'that (EVOC) kangaroo', and *kuyu* 'meat' could be in a part–whole apposition with *marlu*, so it either means 'meat of the/that kangaroo' or 'game animals, say, kangaroos' (similar to the Arrernte construction discussed by Wilkins 2000). As part of understanding this passage, it helps to realise that it appears that *kantumu* only applies to (game) animals and is better glossed 'hind quarter' or 'rump', and that the speaker isn't defining *kantumu* but rather is distinguishing it from *yardipi* (and *yarlipiri*) as used for the analogous part on humans; he apparently intuits the less-common word *kantumu* is new to the interviewer (Hale). One clearly needs to understand the broader context of dictionary examples (and their interpretation and unedited origin) if they are to be used as data for other analysis.

2.2. PPJ's definitional style not allowed for

With regard to the Warlpiri vernacular definitions of body parts that they are working with, W&G (2018: 38) acknowledge 'that almost all these vernacular definitions are the work of a single indigenous Warlpiri lexicographer, the late Paddy Patrick Jangala (henceforth: PPJ)'. A key point is what to make of the expression *ngulaji yangka*, of which W&G claim: (i) it is not simply a definitional formula commonly used by indigenous Warlpiri lexicographers; (ii) though used extensively in body part definitions, it is not widely used in definitions of nouns of all kinds, being largely absent from fauna and artefact definitions; and (iii) 'its use in the definitions of body-parts is *sui generis*, and supports the hypothesis of "part" as a distinct meaning of yangka' (2018: 49).

24. WHERE WE PART FROM NSM

One of us (Wilkins) has made a close inspection of a corpus of more than 1,500 of PPJ's vernacular definitions, which undermines the position W&G take with respect to the significance of the sequence *ngulaji yangka* in PPJ's definitions. The study reveals that it is part of an opening definitional formula heavily favoured by PPJ, occurring in nearly 80 per cent of PPJ's 943 nominal definitions.

Two different (non-overlapping) corpora were taken from the total set of PPJ's vernacular definitions for the variety of Warlpiri spoken at Lajamanu. The first is a corpus of 943 vernacular definitions of Warlpiri nominals, and the second is a corpus of 581 definitions of verbs (including basic verbs, preverb–verb combinations, verbs derived from nominals, etc).

PPJ's definitions have a discernible format. To begin with, 99.5 per cent of all PPJ's vernacular definitions begin:

[Definiendum]   (,) *ngula=ji* ...
[definiendum]   (,) that (discourse topic)=TOP

So, almost all definitions begin with something translatable as '[Definiendum], that's ...', where the word being defined is clearly in mention function and is being treated as the topic of the definitional textlet that follows.

By far the most common word to follow *ngulaji* in the definitional opener is *yangka*. The string '[Definiendum](,) *ngulaji yangka* ...' opens 749 (79 per cent) of PPJ's nominal definitions and 567 (98 per cent) of PPJ's verb definitions. (*Yangka* is the most frequently occurring word in PPJ's corpus of vernacular definitions, occurring 3,044 times.)

Clearly, *ngulaji yangka* is very widely used in nominal definitions, and body part definitions with *ngulaji yangka* are simply among the roughly 80 per cent of PPJ's nominal definitions that contain it. It is the roughly 20 per cent of nominal definitions which don't include *yangka* in the opening that may need explanation.

2.2.1. PPJ Definitions without *yangka*

There are two relevant factors which are highly predictive of the non-occurrence of *yangka* in the opening of PPJ's nominal definitions.

First, PPJ's earliest definitions, particularly those from 1985, are generally briefer relative to later definitions and have relatively fewer instances of *ngulaji yangka* in the opening. Two body part examples are his definitions of *rdaka* 'hand; forepaw of bipedal' and of *lampurnu* 'breasts', both from October 1985.

(3) *Rdaka   ngula=ji   ka-rlipa   marda-rni   kardiya-rlu,*
    Rdaka   that=TOP   PRS-1PL.INCL.S   have-NPST   whitefella-ERG
    yapa-ngku,   marlu-ngku,   rdaka-jarra=ji.
    person-ERG   kangaroo-ERG   rdaka-DU=TOP

'*Rdaka*, that's what we all (inclusive) have—White people, Aboriginal people, kangaroos—a pair of *rdaka*.'

(4) *Lampurnu ngula=ji ka=lu marda-rni karnta-ngku jirrama kamparru rdukurduku. Kuja-ka=lu=jana yi-nyi kurdu-ku wita-wita-ku lampurnu=ju. Ngapurlu waja.*

'*Lampurnu* are the two things that women have in front on their chests. That they feed babies milk with breasts. (Literally, *Lampurnu*, that's what they have, women, two on (their) chest front. They give them to babies—that's *lampurnu*, it's the same as *ngapurlu*.)[4]'

Second, and consistent with W&G's observation of fewer instances of *ngulaji yangka* in vernacular definitions of fauna terms (see section 2.3), is the fact that nominals that are hyponyms of a labelled superordinate are relatively more likely to have definitions in which the superordinate nominal appears immediately after *ngulaji*. For example, the 26 nominal definitions that begin '[Definiendum](,) *ngulaji jurlpu* …' all define kinds of *jurlpu* 'birds' (24 species terms and 2 bird life stage terms). Similarly, the 18 definitions that begin '[Definiendum](,) *ngulaji watiya* …' overwhelmingly define terms for kinds of *watiya* 'tree, bush, shrub' (15 species of wooded plant; 2 descriptor or part of wooded plant; 1 artefact made of wood). All such cases are definitions of Warlpiri nominals that are concrete, non-relational, non-descriptive/predicative. As a corollary, nominals that are relational or non-descriptive/predicative or non-concrete or for which there is no obvious genus level superordinate terms are more likely to have definitions that include *ngulaji yangka*. So,

---

4   Compare with PPJ's later, parallel definition of the synonym *ngapurlu*, which appears as example (17) in W&G and opens *Ngapurlu ngula-ji yangka kuja-ka-lu marda-rni karnta-ngku* …

as relational terms, it is not surprising that 'body part terms' are more likely to include *yangka* after *ngulaji*, but, as we see below, they are also more likely to include *kujaka* after *yangka*.

The non-occurrence of *yangka* after *ngulaji* in the opening of such 'taxonomic' definitions is merely a tendency in PPJ's corpus. For example, there are 15 nominal definitions that open with '[Definiendum](,) *ngulaji yangka watiya* …' and 8 of these define species or types of wooded plant, 4 define parts of a wooded plant and 3 define artefacts made from wood. The following examples show parallel openings for definitions of fauna and flora terms without and with *yangka*.

(5) *Rdukurduku-tiri-tiri* **ngulaji jurlpu** *wita manangkarra-ngawurrpa*. …
'*Rdukurduku-tiri-tiri* are little birds that are found in the open grass lands. …[PPJ 10/85]'

(6) *Lirra-lirra,* **ngulaji yangka jurlpu** *wita ngapa-ngawurrpa,* …
'*Lirra-lirra* is a small water bird … [PPJ 6/87]'

(7) *Ngarlurrpu* **ngulaji watiya** *wita,* …
'*Ngarlurrpu* is a small bush … [PPJ <9/86>]'

(8) *Pinamparli* **ngulaji yangka watiya** *wita* …
'Sturt's Desert Rose is a small bush … [PPJ <9/86>]'

In the above examples, the translations do not show any distinction between definitions with and without *yangka*. We might propose that those with *yangka* could instead be rendered as a something like 'X is that little bird which …' or 'X is the small bush which …'. More literally, examples without *yangka* might be rendered as 'X, that's a Y that …', and those with *yangka* might be rendered as 'X, that's that Y which …' (or, perhaps even 'X, that's the Y which …' or 'X, that's that one, a Y which …'). The critical thing is that the propositional meaning is not different.

2.2.2. Aside on Arrernte

It is useful to here compare vernacular definitions by Arrernte native speakers. These often begin '[Definiendum] *apele nhenge* …' The first element of the Arrernte opening, the particle *apele*, is 'commonly used in identifying something or explaining what a word means' and '[s]hows that the speaker wants to make a point of something so that the listener will take special note of it' (Henderson and Dobson 1994: 179). The second element of the opening is the non-spatial demonstrative *nhenge*.

This demonstrative overlaps with many of the functions of Warlpiri *yangka*, including having an 'evocative' function. In describing the use of *nhenge* as it appears in the definitional opener Henderson and Dobson (1994: 501) write that it:

> 5a. Introduces some more information about something; (the one) that ..., (those ones) which ..., (the time) when ..., (the place) where ...
>
> *Akaperte aheye-aheye* **apele nhenge** *akaperte mepepele* **nhenge** *atyetele aneme re.*
>
> The fontanelle is that (thing) which is in the middle of the head, that (thing) which is soft.
>
> *Perlape* **apele nhenge** *annge urrperle akweke mape akeme arleke-arleke.*
>
> Conkerberries are those small dark fruit which you get from a bush.

In definitional openings, Warlpiri *yangka* could be interpreted as functioning in a way very similar to that described for Arrernte *nhenge*. As with *nhenge*, whether *yangka* is taken to be referring to a person, place, thing, time or event is dependent upon context (in this case, provided by the co-text of the definition). Ennever (pers. comm.) notes a similar formulaic use of the Ngardi recognitional/evocative demonstrative *jangu* in the openings of vernacular definitions.

2.2.3. Further properties of PPJ definitions

Of the 52 vernacular definitions PPJ provided for human and animal body parts, 34 (65 per cent) contain *ngulaji yangka* and 13 (25 per cent) contain no *yangka* at all. However, this does not fully represent the relevant opening formula. W&G neglect the fact that the openings of many definitions, including body part definitions, tend to include the auxiliary complex *kuja-ka-* 'REL-PRS' after *ngulaji*, and following *yangka* if it occurs. In the Warlpiri Dictionary, *kuja*, the first element of the auxiliary complex, is identified as a 'sentential complementiser' and given the English glossing of 'that, when, where, which, who, what'.

This fuller definitional opener—'[Definiendum](,) *ngula-ji yangka kuja-ka* (-pronominal enclitics) ...'—occurs in 586 (62 per cent) of PPJ's nominal definitions and 555 (96 per cent) of verb definitions. It is this fuller construction that may more closely parallel the Arrernte opener discussed above. It introduces the definitional information that will allow the addressee to identify the unique concept/sense that PPJ is defining. We see *ngula* as referring to the word form (definiendum), *yangka* as referring to the specific concept associated with the word form and *kuja-ka-* marking a kind of 'relative clause' that introduces the critical elements for narrowing in on that concept. This opening construction basically says 'attend to the following information and you'll know the one I mean'. Close translations of the opener would include 'X, that's that one which ...'; 'that's that thing that'; 'that's that time when'; 'that's that person who'; 'that's that action which'; 'that's the place where'; 'that's the way (it is) when'; etc. (The exact construal is not coded in the opener but is dependent on the following co-text and context.)

Of PPJ's 52 body part definitions, 30 (58 per cent) include *kuja-ka* (-pronominal enclitics) in the definitional opener, and, of these, 25 (48 per cent) include the full definitional opener '[Definiendum](,) *ngula-ji yangka kuja-ka* (-pronominal enclitics)'. As noted for *yangka*, *kuja-* in definitional openers occurs less in the earliest definitions. Note that the body part definitions of *rdaka* and *lampurnu* above don't have *kuja-* but simply have the auxiliary base *ka-* in the definitional opener.

Again, the more predicative or relational a nominal is, the more likely a nominal will contain this full opener. More than 50 per cent of PPJ's definitions of kin term nominals contain this full construction, and the vast majority of Warlpiri adjectival nominals contain this construction. Nominals that tend to have a default adjectival function (or a more predicational focus) typically have a stance verb in non-past tense immediately following *kuja-ka-ø*. In fact, 251 (27 per cent) of PPJ's nominal definitions begin: '[definiendum], *ngula=ji yangka kuja-ka-ø* stance.verb-NPST ...' ('[definiendum], that=TOP EVOC REL-PRS-3SG.S stance.verb-NPST') and more than 80 per cent of these definitions are of nominals with adjectival function. Thus, the more predicative a nominal is, the more it has the same kind of definitional opener as verbs.

One of PPJ's body part definitions deviates from the standard definitional opening in an instructive way—it substitutes the demonstrative *nyampu* 'this; here' where the demonstrative *yangka* would be expected.

(9) *Pirlkiri ngula=ji nyampu kuja-ka=rlipa mardarni jimanta-rla kankarlu yapa-ngku manu kardiya-rlu, pirlkiri=ji.* [Source: PPJ 6/87]

'*Pirlkiri* is the upper part of our shoulders, what we have on top—both Aboriginal people and whites. [Literally, *Pirlkiri* that's this (one) that we all have at the top of our shoulder(s), Aboriginal and white people, that's *pirlkiri*.]'

W&G don't discuss this example, but presumably they don't attribute the 'part' reading to the use of *nyampu*, which they already include among their Warlpiri exponents of NSM. While 'part' makes sense in the translation, it is merely deducible from the deployment of the demonstrative in context. Here we might expect that PPJ touched the top of his shoulder when dictating the definition. We have no doubt that *yangka* could sit in place of *nyampu* in this definition and it would literally mean something like '*Pirlkiri* that's that one that we all (inclusive) have at the top of our shoulder(s), Aboriginal and white people, that's *pirlkiri*'. Its construal as a 'part' is part of the mental deictic work which *yangka* contributes to.

For now, we are working on the assumption that the meaning of the definitional opener that includes *yangka* is compositional, rather than being an idiomatic construction. Only work with native speakers can fully clarify the situation.

While variations in the typical deployment of definitional openings:

from [Definiendum], *ngula=ji* ...;
through [Definiendum], *ngula=ji yangka* ...;
to [Definiendum], ngula=ji yangka kuja-ka ...

are broadly indicative of a cline from more concrete object concepts through to more relational and predicative concepts, they are not diagnostic of semantic classes at the level of 'body parts' or 'birds'. It is the elements that follow these formulas that get us into the territory of semantic fields.

Looking at PPJ's corpus of vernacular definitions, we undertook an examination of statistically significant collocation relations at the sentence level of all the morphemes which jointly occur in at least 5 definitions, within at least 8 positions in either direction of one another. This allows us to determine any significant patterns of co-occurrence that could be diagnostic of semantic classes. Not surprisingly, given its high frequency, the occurrence of *yangka* does not significantly predict the occurrence of any other morphemes within the same sentence in PPJ's definitions (not even *ngula-ji* or *kuja-ka-*).

However, there are two significant collocations that are uniquely associated with body part definitions in PPJ's corpus, both involving *marda-rni* 'have-NPST'. In the first, the elements *ka-rlipa* 'PRS-1PL.INCL.S' and *marda-rni* 'have-NPST' occur jointly 27 times (*ka-rlipa* always preceding *marda-rni*, typically with nothing occurring in between). These 27 co-occurrences appear in 23 different definitions, all of which define body part terms. So, PPJ's use of these two elements together is unambiguously linked to a single semantic class: 'parts that we all (inclusive) have'.

In the second, *ka-lu* 'PRS-3PL.S' and *marda-rni* 'have-NPST' occur jointly 16 times (*ka-lu* always preceding *marda-rni*, typically with nothing occurring in between). These 16 co-occurrences appear in 15 different definitions, 12 of which are definitions of either gender-specific or animal-specific body part terms—parts that they have.

Recognising the importance of *marda-rni* 'have' in the Warlpiri definitions of body parts, W&G (2018: 46) propose two similar exponents of PART for Warlpiri NSM: YANGKA ~ YANGKA MARDARNI 'PART ~ HAVE PARTS'. They argue that *mardarni* 'to have' 'is one of the formal features which can help distinguish *yangka* "part" from *yangka* "that, the one"' (2018: 46). However, we take it as instructive that PPJ's earliest definitions of body parts did not use *yangka* or *kuja-*, but did use the pronominal clitics *-rlipa* '1PL.INCL.SUBJ' or *-lu* '3PL.SUBJ' on the auxiliary base *ka-* along with the verb *marda-rni* 'to have'. He had not fully developed his opening formula, but he had identified his criterial features for the genus-level statement of the class: 'that which we all (inclusive) have' and 'that which they have'. It is these collocations that are truly *sui generis* for body part terms. Nearly one-third of PPJ's body part definitions that include *marda-rni* do not include *yangka*, and since PPJ did not define body parts one after another (unlike W&G's false suggestion), there is no reason to believe there was any particular local discourse factors that would predict omission.

We can summarise our observations regarding PPJ's dominant pattern for starting definitions for the body part domain in the diagram in Figure 24.1.

```
Opening formula:
    [Definiendum](,) ngula=ji (yangka) (kuja-) ka-
    [Definiendum](,) that=TOP (EVOC) (REL-) AUX.PRS-
Class identifier:
                                    P ( ... ) marda-rni ...
                                              have-NPST
```

where **P** is one of

=rlipa	=lu
=1PL.INCL.SUBJ	=3PL.SUBJ
e.g.	e.g.
palka 'body, torso'	*ngurrurnpa* 'pubic hair'
pirlirrpa 'spirit; life force'	*ngirnti* '1. tail; 2. penis'
rdaka 'hand'	
'that's (that one) (which) we all have' [identifies parts all we human beings have]	'that's (that one) (which) they have' [identifies gender-, age-, and animal-specific parts]

Figure 24.1. Dominant pattern for starting body part definitions in PPJ.
Source: Authors' summary.

The diagram only accounts for the beginning of body part definitions: the definitional opening formula followed by the semantic field identifier. Following this are the statements of differentiae that identify individual parts. These may include specifying particular possessors, localising the part with respect to other parts, identifying the function of the part and/or quantifying and describing the size of the part. Our main purpose, however, has been to show that W&G's claims regarding *yangka* (more specifically *ngulaji yangka*) do not hold for the extensive corpus of PPJ's vernacular definitions. Our claim, therefore, is that PPJ does not use anything that immediately translates as 'part'; instead he makes a possession statement using *ka-rlipa* or *ka-lu* with *mardarni* 'have' which, along with specific spatial location and/or function statements, define referents in the so-called 'body part' domain. More precisely, PPJ uses *mardarni* to indicate the possessive relation between humans and/or animals and any of their immediate subparts.

2.3. Flaw when comparing definitions across semantic domains

W&G (2018: 46, note 9) do recognise that definitions have been contributed by Warlpiri people other than PPJ:

Since so many of the vernacular definitions originate with PPJ, it is possible that other Warlpiri speakers may have alternative definitional strategies, or different preferences so far as the balance between the two *yangka* constructions described in Sections 6 and 7 are concerned.

W&G could have applied this cautionary note later when considering how the use of *yangka* in definitions varies across semantic domains:

> the sequence *ngulaji yangka* is not widely used in the definitions of nouns of all kinds. When we inspected 50 randomly selected entries in the Warlpiri Dictionary's 'fauna domain' we found that only two of them used *ngulaji yangka*. Of these, one was clearly used in the sense of 'like' and the other in the sense of 'that, the one'. By contrast, in our collection of 64 body-part entries as many as 19 include the sequence *ngulaji yangka*, with *yangka* almost always indicating a particular part of the body. A similar sampling exercise with words from the 'manufacture domain' produced parallel results, i.e. in most of these definitions an opening *yangka* had the sense either of 'like (when)' or 'that, the one'. (W&G 2018: 48)

The correlation is more with PPJ as definition author: definitions in the fauna and manufacture domains were mostly created by other Warlpiri speakers. Hence we disagree with W&G's (2018: 49) inference that

> while the sequence *ngulaji yangka* can indeed be found in many parts of the Warlpiri Dictionary, its use in the definitions of body-parts is sui generis, and supports the hypothesis of 'part' as a distinct meaning of *yangka*.

As shown above (section 2.2), the sequence *ngulaji yangka* is part of an opening definitional formula heavily favoured by PPJ and its use in body part definitions is not *sui generis*.

In the version of the dictionary consulted by W&G, there are 385 entries in the 'Fauna: kuyu' domain. Of these, 205 entries contain one or more vernacular definitions which define a species or kind (of 'fleshy fauna'). Of these 205, PPJ provides vernacular definitions for 46 (22 per cent), a much smaller proportion than in the domain of body parts, and his definitions all begin, '[Definiendum], *ngulaji* …' and 9 of these include *yangka* after *ngulaji*. That is, 20 per cent of PPJ's fauna definitions begin '[Definiendum], *ngulaji yangka* …'. Only one other definition of a species or kind in this domain contains *ngulaji yangka* [*yilyinkarri*, HN0279]. Only two further vernacular definitions for species or kind in this domain contain *ngulaju yangka*, unsourced. So, of definitions not sourced to PPJ, only about 2 per cent contain *ngulaji yangka* or *ngulaju yangka*. Thus, while PPJ does (for reasons explained) use *ngulaji yangka* less in vernacular definitions for 'Fauna: kuyu', he still uses it much more than the other contributors to the domain. W&G's methodological error in their fauna study was to not distinguish PPJ's definitions and to presume that other definers use the same locution. In non-PPJ fauna definitions, the most common opener includes *karnalu ngarrirni* (PRS-1PL.EXCL.SBJ tell-NPAST 'we call it') (49 examples, with the most common being '[Definiendum], *karnalu ngarrirni ...*').

Another misapprehension is about the order in which PPJ chose words to define:

> The word *palka* 'body' occurs in some definitions, but it is mostly omitted since the indigenous lexicographer is, presumably, composing several definitions one after another so it is understood that the context is about parts of the body. (W&G 2018: 46)

Actually, PPJ usually proceeded with groups of phonologically similar words, often from alphabetical lists of words beginning with a particular sound; and even when defining words from the same semantic domain he would repeat the parts of the definition in common, so that each definition could stand alone.

2.4. Spurious correlation

As Wierzbicka (2008) has observed, the concept COLOUR is not lexicalised in Warlpiri. Inspection of the vernacular definitions of particular Warlpiri colour terms often include *yangka*, and their English translation of the definition uses the word *colour*, as in these examples:

(10) *Tiri-tiri   ngulaji   yangka   yalyu-yalyu,   kujaka   ngunami   yurlpu*
     red   that   EVOC   red   which   lies   red.ochre
     manu   karrku   yalyu-yalyuju,   tiri-tiriji. [PPJ 10/85]
     and   red.ochre   red   red

'*Tiri-tiri* is like red, like the colour of red ochres. (or, *Tiri-tiri* that's that red, how *yurlpu* and *karrku* ochres are red, (that's) *tiri-tiri*.)'

and

(11) *Puyurr-puyurrpa,   ngulaji   yangka kujaka nyinami   warna*
     grey   that   EVOC   which sits   snake
     kunjuru-kunjuru,   yangka   kunjuru-piya. [PPJ 6/87]
     smoke-smoke(grey)   EVOC   smoke-like

'*Puyurr-puyurrpa* is like a grey snake, one that is (coloured) like smoke.'

By a reasoning parallel to that used by W&G to infer that *yangka* has a sense PART, one could also infer that *yangka* has a sense COLOUR. Instead W&G (2018: 41–43) use such examples to claim that *yangka* has yet another sense, 'like', and so take *yangka* to also be a Warlpiri exponent of NSM's prime LIKE.

2.5. Poor fit with NSM theory

The NSM framework includes these standard combinatorial possibilities of PART:[5]

> part of someone's body; this part, the same part, another part, this other part; this something has two/many parts

Apart from the first of these, W&G do not show how *yangka* could be used to express these phrases. If they had been right about *yangka*, then it would only have been in one context of use, and until a demonstration is made about the exponents (allolexes) that are used for the other combinatorial contexts, Warlpiri stands as a language for which the NSM equivalent of PART ~ HAVE PARTS is to be discovered. One allolex in one context does not make an NSM prime.

The wide range in Warlpiri of contextual translation equivalents for the PART meaning is to be measured against NSM's Strong Lexicalization Hypothesis (Goddard 1994a: 13), which has from its inception been compromised in its application by allolexy and purported polysemy.

---

5   Chart of NSM semantic primes, version 19 (12 April 2017). Available at: intranet.secure.griffith. edu.au/__data/assets/pdf_file/0019/346033/NSM_Chart_ENGLISH_v19_April_12_2017_Greyscale.pdf.

W&G postulate polysemy of *yangka* in particular to meet the requirement for lexical expression of PART. We prefer the monosemic bias (until forced to polysemy), following Ruhl (1989), and indeed another NSM tradition:

> One assumes to begin with that there is but a single meaning, and attempts to state it in a clear and predictive fashion, in the form of a translatable reductive paraphrase. Only if persistent efforts to do this fail is polysemy posited. (Goddard 2000: 132)

3. Other difficulties for W&G's account

This section describes some hurdles for W&G's account; these are not complete obstacles, but rather are considerations which should give pause.

First, it is significant that a PART sense has remained unnoticed by lexicographers and translators. No Warlpiri wordlist or dictionary has associated *yangka* with a sense of PART, including the two lexicons compiled independently of the main dictionary used by W&G.[6] Further, *yangka* has not been used to express PART in published translations (see section 5).

Next, consider the equivalent of *yangka* in related languages. Ennever (2018: 177) discusses recognitional/evocative demonstrative *jangu* (and *yangka*) in Ngardi, a western neighbour of Warlpiri. McConvell (2006: 112, 117) mentioned Warlpiri *yangka* in his comparative discussion of demonstratives as complementisers. He pointed out parallels in other central Australian languages: Arrernte *nhenge* (Henderson and Dobson 1994) and Pitjantjatjara/Yankunytjatjara *panya* (Goddard 1996: 124–25);[7] there is also Anmatyerr *nheng* (Green 2010: 447–48) and Kaytetye *wenhe* (Turpin and Ross 2011: 633). Their detailed dictionary entries of these equivalents

---

6 The Swartz lexicon (available at: ausil.org/Dictionary/Warlpiri/lexicon/index.htm) has *yangka* 'aforementioned one, same one mentioned before'; Reece (1975) has *yangkaṟi* 'another time, another, other one', *yangkakurra* 'to the same place'.

7 '1. that, "you know the one". Calls the listener's attention to the fact that he or she is already familiar with the thing being referred to (generally something not explicitly referred to so far) … 2. Used as an introductory particle to present the following clause as an explanatory comment; can often be translated as "because" … 3. Used as a hesitation particle while groping for something to say'; and Goddard (1983; quoted by Himmelmann 1996): 'It is not usually used about things which are fully topical— ie already being talked about, but rather to re-introduce something into the conversation … Actually, *panya* ANAPH does not presuppose an explicit mention in previous discourse, but simply that the addressee be able to call to mind the intended referent'.

give no hint of a PART sense, nor a plausible bridging context that would semantically link PART and a non-spatial recognitional demonstrative sense. McConvell (2006: 116) observed a parallel with Walmajarri *yangka*:

> GMSCs [general modifying subordinate clauses] appear to be formed mainly with the complementizers *yangka* in Eastern Walmajarri and with *yangkakaji* in other dialects. *Yangka* is also a demonstrative which is both evocative and anaphoric—'that one known to both speaker and hearer or previously referred to' and the related complementizer also retains at least part of that meaning according to the Walmajarri dictionary—'when (something we both know about happens)' (Richards & Hudson 1990: 307). … The meaning of the demonstrative *yangka* is similar to Nash's 'evocative' and Himmelmann's 'recognitional' previously referred to.

More broadly, consider that a lexical gap for PART has been noted in some other languages. Generally, Enfield et al. (2006) observe that an equivalent to PART was not immediately available in several of the 10 languages they examined, and that instead various kinds of possession and location constructions were used in place of partonomy statements. Significantly, in Casagrande and Hale's (1967) seminal work on Papago folk definitions, not one of the 800 definitions specifically encoded a part–whole relation and the authors merely suggested it as a potential semantic relation despite its absence from their data.

W&G cite two languages that seem at first to lack a word with the sense PART, but in which, on a closer look, PART has been found as a sense of a word with other senses. First, Goddard (1994b: 255–56) discerned HAVE PARTS as a sense of the Yankunytjatjara nominal suffix *-tjara* 'having'[8] (and made no suggestion of the *panya* mentioned above). Second, W&G (2018: 50–51) claim a precedent in the Papuan language Koromu, citing Priestley (2017):

---

8   Goddard (1994b: 256) associates the suffix with the nominal stem *tjara,* which he also glosses as 'part (of)', but it is not clear that *tjara* has the sense PART required to be an exponent of the NSM prime. The entries in his dictionary (Goddard 1992: 147) have the stem *tjara* with a somewhat different meaning 'divided, apart, spatially separated'. In Pintupi/Luritja, another dialect of the Western Desert Language, Hansen and Hansen (1991: 141) define *tjarra* as 'forked stick; divided; the fork where branches protrude from the trunk or other branches', and the combination *tjarra kutjupa* 'branch; another subject; lit. "another fork"; can be used literally to refer to the fork of a tree branch or creek tributary; can be used figuratively of a change in subject matter under discussion'.

> What is particularly interesting in the present context is that one of the main exponents of PART in Koromu is a demonstrative, somewhat like the situation in Warlpiri. (W&G 2018: 51)

We would agree with the parallel with Warlpiri, but for a different reason: in our view the demonstrative does not have a second sense but rather it can function pragmatically to convey the PART concept. Note that earlier, Priestley (2008: 173, 149) had described the demonstrative *mo* 'this/here' and the quantifier *asao* 'some (some others) [also 'part']' without polysemy.

4. The meaning of *yangka*

Warlpiri *yangka* has been taken to be a recognitional demonstrative, of the type described by Himmelmann (1996: 230), though as we elaborate below, this does not capture the range of uses. *Yangka*, the most common word in the Warlpiri corpus, mostly occurs absolutely; the next most common occurrence is with some enclitic (notably focal *-ju*) or suffix, and there are relatively few occurrences with a nominal suffix. It seems that (absolute) *yangka* can be omitted from (most?) utterances without a change in the 'coded' or 'propositional' meaning, as exemplified in section 2.2.1. Also, note the various paradigmatic/non-co-occurring sets that involve *yangka*: it rarely occurs in the same noun phrase as *nyampu* 'this', *yali* 'that', or other demonstratives (see example (9), in section 2.2.3).

The recognitional component of the meaning of *yangka* is well-suited for use in interaction. However, *yangka* is also not uncommon in written Warlpiri, as witness its occurrence in nearly a hundred of the Warlpiri booklets in the Living Archive of Aboriginal Languages (LAAL).[9] Here is one example in the middle of a written story (Napaljarri and Jakamarra 1976: 5):

(12a) *Yuka-ja   karnta   yangka=ju   janganpa-jangka=ju.*
       enter-PST   woman   EVOC=TOP   possum-from=TOP
(12b) *Karnta   nyanungu=ju   yuntardi nyayirni.*
       woman   he/she/it=TOP   beautiful very

---

9   Available at: laal.cdu.edu.au/search/?q=all:yangka&f[]=language:450808&o=dd&mode=.

The first sentence refers to a woman who has been mentioned in preceding sentences. In (12b), the referent of *yangka* is taken up (after a direct speech clause) by the determiner *nyanungu*, pronominally definite and translated by 'the'.

In interactional contexts, *yangka* could colloquially be glossed 'you know', as when the speaker is searching for a word or talking about something for which there is not an easy expression. Bromhead (2009: 217–19) shows how this English expression has arisen in the last few centuries. The meaning of the English near-equivalent *you-know*-WHAT has been explicated by Enfield (2003: 107) as:[10]

you-know-WHAT
something
I don't want to say the word for this thing now
I don't say it now because I know I don't have to
by saying *you-know*-WHAT I think you'll know what I'm thinking of

An explication of Warlpiri *yangka* can be based on the last line of Enfield's explication. We can allow that, depending on further contextualising information, the concept that would be called up by *yangka* could be PART, with the conceptual primitive nevertheless still not lexicalised. There is a close equivalence also with Cutfield's (2012: 383) analysis of Dalabon *kanh*: 'what the speaker is appealing to is not a prior mention or shared knowledge per se, but the addressee's deductive capacity … the speaker is not merely saying "you know what I'm talking about", but rather "you can work out what I'm talking about".'

5. Expressing 'part' in Warlpiri

Warlpiri has various ways of expressing the PART concept or translating English *part (of)*, including: the part–whole construction (Hale 1981), the use of coverb quantifier *puta* 'incompletely' and nominals such as

---

10   Note the Lao near-equivalent (Enfield 2003: 110) shares with Warlpiri *yangka* the possible lack of an expression for the relevant notion:

qan0-nan4 'that thing'
something (happens/is the case)
I don't know how to say what I'm thinking of
by saying *qan0-nan4* ('that thing') I think you'll know what I'm thinking of

ngalya-kari (which W&G 2018: 21 mention in relation to SOME), and in some contexts *rdilyki-kari* 'a broken-off bit', or *larrakari* 'piece, split off bit' ('part, half', Reece 1979: 120). The verb *marda-rni* 'to have, hold' has a wide range, which can translate 'have as a part' and many other concepts, but not as a distinguishable sense as far as we can discern (see section 2.2.3 and footnote 11). And, as for Yankunytjatjara *-tjara*, it would have to be demonstrated as a polysemous sense of the form, since expressions for 'with' (comitatives) could be proposed to have HAVE PARTS as a sense, although, (for example) a person with brothers or sisters is 'with something' but a sibling is not a part of a person. Nash (2014: 84–85) discusses *part* and *side* in defining certain Warlpiri kinship meanings.

It is instructive to consider how English *part* has been translated into Warlpiri. Several substantial texts have been translated into Warlpiri in collaboration with trained Warlpiri translators. The largest of these is the Warlpiri Bible, two key passages of which are presented in Appendix 24.2, to which the reader is referred for the circumlocutions around *part*, and also the absence of *yangka* as its translation. Two other translations we have checked are that of the short children's novel *Storm Boy* (Thiele 1963) and of a manual on troubleshooting ignition systems (Granites and Shopen 1987). The former has no instance of *part* but has a few instances of *bit* in a sense like PART. The only one clearly translated is

(13) It had a dirt floor, two blurry bits of glass for windows
(Kindle Location 31)

Kaninjarniji kala ngunaja walyajuku kanunjuju purluwu-wangu. Wintawu-kuju ngulaju kirlajijarra 'Inside there was no floor just dirt on the bottom. For windows two bits of glass' (our back-translation)

The addition of *-jarra* 'two' on *kirlaji* 'glass' favours the countable entity reading, whereas the unmarked sense of Warlpiri nouns covers mass or property readings, consistent with their ability to be predicates as well as forming individual referring expressions.[11]

---

11 We thank Mary Laughren for helpful discussion of this point.

The English original of the troubleshooting manual has several instances of *part*, as one would expect in instructions about mechanisms. A couple do show a potential translation equivalent of *part*, notably *jintakari jintakari* 'one by one' construed with the plural pronominal enclitic *=jana* object of *mardarni* 'have' in:[12]

(14) 24. The primary circuit has the following parts, starting with the battery:

24. *Wirlinyi*	*parnka-ngu*	*jinta-ngku*	*ka=jana*
24. day.trip	run-NOMIC	one-ERG	AUX.PRS=3.PL.OBJ
marda-rni	*jinta-kari*	*jinta-kari,*	*pirilyi-ngirli:*
have-NPST	one-other	one-other	charcoal-from

6. Conclusion

W&G went looking for 'part' quite literally, presuming that the uses of the English word *part* in translations of Warlpiri sentences in the Warlpiri Dictionary would yield a Warlpiri counterpart of the NSM prime PART. They thought they had found it in the form of the demonstrative *yangka*, used primarily in the vernacular definitions of the native Warlpiri lexicographer, Paddy Patrick Jangala. We have shown that a close look at PPJ's definitions and definitional style doesn't support their hypothesis. Keeping to a monosemic bias (until forced to polysemy), we argue that uses of *yangka* in definitions is consistent with its use as a demonstrative elsewhere—directing the addressee to use context and co-text to bring the speaker's intended referent to mind. In section 4, we suggested directions an NSM-style definition of *yangka* might take, indicating that a 'part' interpretation is a consistent pragmatic deduction by the addressee in certain contexts, but is not what *yangka* is coding. However, we also

---

12 This use of *mardarni* 'have' to predicate an entity's possession of an inherent corporeal or non-corporeal part also occurs in definitions of terms for birds and for meat animals and elsewhere. In fact, more than half of the 91 occurrences of *mardarni* across PPJ's 943 nominal definitions are in this function, despite it being listed as the fifth, and last, sense of the verb in the Warlpiri Dictionary. Though still glossing this function as 'have', the dictionary states for this sense: 'Definition: Y is part of X'. However, it appears that X can only be a term for the complete being of which Y is a part, it cannot itself be a part. This is consistent with the dictionary's example sentences for this sense. It is not that *mardarni* 'have' is the Warlpiri reflex of PART; possession is clearly the relevant notion.

identified the more widespread and consistent resources Warlpiri speakers use when discussing part-relations. In the process, we hope we have helped NSM refine some of its methodological assumptions and approaches.

Acknowledgements

We have benefited from discussion of the topic with Mary Laughren, and the comments of two reviewers.

References

Australian Society for Indigenous Languages (2001). *The Bible in Walpiri*. Available at: aboriginalbibles.org.au/Warlpiri/.

Bromhead, Helen (2009). *The Reign of Truth and Faith: Epistemic Expressions in 16th and 17th Century English*. Berlin: Mouton de Gruyter. doi.org/10.1515/9783110216028.

Casagrande, Joseph P. and Kenneth L. Hale (1967). Semantic relationships in Papago folk definitions. In Dell H. Hymes and William E. Bittle (eds), *Studies in Southwestern Ethnolinguistics*. The Hague: Mouton, 165–93.

Cutfield, Sarah (2012). Demonstratives in Dalabon: A Language of Southwestern Arnhem Land. Unpublished PhD dissertation, Monash University. Available at: hdl.handle.net/11858/00-001M-0000-0013-AAB9-A.

Enfield, Nick J. (2003). The definition of *what-d'you-call-it*: Semantics and pragmatics of recognitional deixis. *Journal of Pragmatics* 35 (1): 101–17. doi.org/10.1016/S0378-2166(02)00066-8.

Enfield, N.J., Asifa Majid and Miriam van Staden (2006). Cross-linguistic categorisation of the body: Introduction. *Language Sciences* 28 (2–3): 137–47. doi.org/10.1016/j.langsci.2005.11.001.

Ennever, Tom (2018). Nominal and Pronominal Morphology of Ngardi: A Ngumpin-Yapa Language of Western Australia. Unpublished MPhil thesis, University of Queensland. doi.org/10.14264/uql.2018.560.

Goddard, Cliff (1983). A Semantically-Oriented Grammar of the Yankunytjatjara Dialect of the Western Desert Language. Unpublished PhD dissertation, The Australian National University. Available at: hdl.handle.net/1885/132711.

Goddard, Cliff (1992). *Pitjantjatjara/Yankunytjatjara to English Dictionary*. Alice Springs: IAD Press.

Goddard, Cliff (1994a). Semantic theory and semantic universals. In Cliff Goddard and Anna Wierzbicka (eds), *Semantic and Lexical Universals: Theory and Empirical Findings*. Amsterdam: John Benjamins, 7–30.

Goddard, Cliff (1994b). Lexical primitives in Yankunytjatjara. In Cliff Goddard and Anna Wierzbicka (eds), *Semantic and Lexical Universals: Theory and Empirical Findings*. Amsterdam: John Benjamins, 229–62. doi.org/10.1075/slcs.25.13god.

Goddard, Cliff (1996). *Pitjantjatjara/Yankunytjatjara to English Dictionary* (revised 2nd edn). Alice Springs: IAD Press.

Goddard, Cliff (2000). Polysemy: A problem of definition. In Yael Ravin and Claudia Leacock (eds), *Polysemy: Theoretical and Computational Approaches*. Oxford: Oxford University Press, 129–51.

Granites, Kurt Japanangka and Tim Shopen (trans.) (1987). *Jitirninjakurlangupinki pina-jarrinjakurlangu. Lajamanu* [*Simple Method of Locating Faults in the Ignition System: Sections 1–34*]. Lajamanu: Vocational Training Branch, International Labour Office. Available at: laal.cdu.edu.au/record/cdu:59936/info/.

Green, Jennifer Anne (2010). *Central & Eastern Anmatyerr to English dictionary*. Alice Springs: IAD Press.

Hale, Ken (1981). Preliminary remarks on the grammar of part–whole relations in Warlpiri. In Jim Hollyman and Andrew Pawley (eds), *Studies in Pacific Languages and Cultures in Honour of Bruce Biggs*. Auckland: Linguistic Society of New Zealand, 333–44.

Hale, Kenneth L. (1966–67). [Warlpiri transcripts]. AIATSIS Library, call number MS 3171, etc.

Hansen, Kenneth C. and Lesley E. Hansen (1991). *Pintupi/Luritja Dictionary* (3rd edn). Alice Springs: IAD Press.

Henderson, John Keith and Veronica Dobson (1994). *Eastern and Central Arrernte to English Dictionary*. Alice Springs: IAD Press.

Himmelmann, Nikolaus P. (1996). Demonstratives in narrative discourse: A taxonomy of universal uses. In Barbara A. Fox (ed.), *Studies in Anaphora*. Amsterdam: John Benjamins, 205–54. doi.org/10.1075/tsl.33.08him.

McConvell, Patrick (2006). Grammaticalization of demonstratives as subordinate complementizers in Ngumpin-Yapa. *Australian Journal of Linguistics* 26 (1): 107–37. doi.org/10.1080/07268600500531669.

Napaljarri, Tess and J. Jakamarra (1976). *Yarlpurru-rlangu-kurlu*. Yuendumu, Northern Territory: Bilingual Resource Development Unit. Available at: laal.cdu.edu.au/record/cdu:36461/info/.

Nash, David (2014). Alternating generations again again: A response to Wierzbicka on generation moieties. In Lauren Gawne and Jill Vaughan (eds), *Selected Papers from the 44th Conference of the Australian Linguistic Society (2013)*. Melbourne: University of Melbourne, 77–101. Available at: hdl.handle.net/11343/40958.

Priestley, Carol (2008). A Grammar of Koromu (Kesawai): A Trans New Guinea Language of Papua New Guinea. Unpublished PhD dissertation, The Australian National University. Available at: hdl.handle.net/1885/150382.

Priestley, Carol (2017). Some key body parts and polysemy: A case study from Koromu (Kesawai). In Zhengdao Ye (ed.), *The Semantics of Nouns*. Oxford: Oxford University Press, 147–79. doi.org/10.1093/oso/9780198736721.003.0006.

Reece, Laurie (1975). *Dictionary of the Wailbri (Walpiri) Language of Central Australia. Part I: Wailbri–English*. (Oceania Linguistic Monographs 19). Sydney: University of Sydney.

Reece, Laurie (1979). *Dictionary of the Wailbri (Walpiri) Language of Central Australia. Part II: English–Wailbri*. (Oceania Linguistic Monographs 22). Sydney: University of Sydney.

Ruhl, Charles (1989). *On Monosemy: A Study in Linguistic Semantics*. New York: SUNY Press.

Thiele, Colin (1963). *Storm Boy*. London: New Holland.

Turpin, Myfany and Alison Ross (2011). *Kaytetye to English Dictionary*. Alice Springs: IAD Press.

Wierzbicka, Anna (1972). *Semantic Primitives*. Frankfurt: Athenäum.

Wierzbicka, Anna (2008). Why there are no 'colour universals' in language and thought. *Journal of the Royal Anthropological Institute* 14 (2): 407–25. doi.org/10.1111/j.1467-9655.2008.00509.x

Wierzbicka, Anna and Cliff Goddard (2018). Talking about our bodies and their parts in Warlpiri. *Australian Journal of Linguistics* 38 (1): 31–62. doi.org/10.1080/07268602.2018.1393862.

Wilkins, David P. (2000). Ants, ancestors and medicine: A semantic and pragmatic account of classifier constructions in Arrernte (Central Australia). In Gunter Senft (ed.), *Systems of Nominal Classification. Vol. 4: Language, Culture and Cognition.* Cambridge: Cambridge University Press, 147–216.

Appendix 24.1

The source of W&G's example in (1), equivalent to our (2), derives from Hale (1966–67: 0215) in a 'Check on Lander River vocabulary vis à vis Yurntumu'; field tape 2.32, 1:00:57 to 1:01:29 of AIATSIS (Australian Institute of Aboriginal and Torres Strait Islander Studies) archive recording Hale_K01 499A. The corresponding audio excerpt (SJJ-kantumu.wav) is available at: cloudstor.aarnet.edu.au/plus/s/BemyHVBPfXvuwk3/ download. The speaker, Sam Johnson Japangardi, has used *kantumu* in the immediately preceding part of the interview (defining *palkarni* 'scarce, last supplies of, precious, indispensable'), in this context:

> *Kuyu yalumpu—wanarri jinta, ngulalu panungku muurlpa pajika—palkarni. Yapangka panungka yangka. Panupuru yapapuru. Kultu kajilpajana panukariki yungkarla, manu yangka wanarrikari jintakari, o jurrurlangu, ngurljurlangu, manu kantumu, yardipi yangka kantumu karlipa ngarrini, muurlparlulu nganja palkarni. Panukurnajana muku-yungu, kala yalumpu wanarri jinta, ngulalu nyurrurlapaturlu palkarni nganja. Wiyarrparlu. Jintajuku. Jipirri yangka panungku. Ngulajuku.*

> 'That meat—one upper leg, you lot cut it carefully—it's the last one. That's for many people. (Shared) among many people. He would give the ribs to many others, and that other upper leg, or the head for example, the ribs too, and the rump, the hip we call *kantumu*, you lot eat the last one carefully. I gave it to all of them, but that one upper leg, you lot eat that one, it's the last. Poor things. Just one. Many (people) jointly. That's it.'

Sam continues his explanation of *kantumu*:

> *Jirrimaja. Kala yapa yardipi, ngulaji yardipi. Yarlipiri. Jirrima. Karlipanyanu ngarrini jirrimayijala. Yardipi, yarlipiri. Ngulajuku.*

> 'We have two names for it. As for people, it (hip) is (called) *yardipi* or *yarlipiri*. We call that part of ourselves by two names as well: *yardipi* and *yarlipiri*.' (translation in dictionary)

MEANING, LIFE AND CULTURE

Appendix 24.2. 'PART' in the Warlpiri Bible

There are two passages in the Warlpiri Bible where the concept of PART is central to the message. Consider how the Warlpiri Bible translation expresses these two passages (Matthew 5:28–30 and 1 Corinthians 12:12–27; from *The Bible in Warlpiri*, with our back-translation).[13] In short, there is no particular lexeme expressing the notion of BODY PART, but rather it is evoked in context by listing a few. *Yangka* doesn't appear in these Warlpiri translations, but the comitative *-kurlu* and the verb *mardarni* variously predicate the relation between the body and its parts (and the privative is used to predicate part absence).

Matthew 5:28

> (King James version) But I say unto you, That whosoever looketh on a woman to lust after her hath committed adultery with her already in his heart. 29. And if thy right eye offend thee, pluck it out, and cast it from thee: for it is profitable for thee that one of thy members should perish, and not that thy whole body should be cast into hell. 30. And if thy right hand offend thee, cut if off, and cast it from thee: for it is profitable for thee that one of thy members should perish, and not that thy whole body should be cast into hell.[14]

29 *Yuwayi, ngaka kajikanpa marda karnta-kari lirlki-nyanyi milpa-jarrarlu. Kuja-kujakuju-nyanu milpa-jarra wilypi-manta jurnta, kajikangku Kaaturlu kijirni milpa-jarra-kurlu-juku warlu wiri-kirra kuja-ka jankami tarnnga-juku.*

Yes, if you might look lustfully at another woman with both eyes. To avoid that, pluck away your eyes, or God will throw you still with both eyes into the big fire which burns forever.

---

13 The Walpiri Bible is a project of the Australian Society for Indigenous Languages (2001), available at: aboriginalbibles.org.au/Warlpiri/.
14 Matthew 5:28 available at: ebible.org/study/?w1=bible&t1=local:wbp&v1=JN1_1.

30 *Ngaka kajikanpa marda majungka-jarrimi, kajikanpa marda nyiyarlangu purungku-mani rdaka-jarrarlu. Kuja-kujakuju-nyanu rdaka-jarra mururl-pajika jurnta, kajikangku Kaaturlu kijirni rdaka-jarra-kurlu-juku warlu wiri-kirra kuja-ka jankami tarnnga-juku.*

Yes, if you might do bad, you might steal something with both hands. To avoid that, chop off both hands, or God will throw you still with both hands into the big fire which burns forever.

Kajilpangku Kaaturlu kijikarla nguru yali-kirra palka wanapi-jiki, ngulaju maju-nyayirni nyuntukuju. Kala kajinpa yukamirra Kaatu-kurlangu-kurra nguru-nyayirni-wangu-kurra rdaka-jarra-wangu manu marda milpa-jarra-wangu, ngulaju ngulajuku. Kapunpa nyanungu-kurlu nyina tarnnga-juku.

If God were to throw your whole body into that region, that is very bad for you. But when you enter God's special area without both hands and maybe without both eyes, then alright. You will be with him forever.

1 Corinthians 12:12–27

(King James version) 12 For as the body is one and has many members, but all the members of that one body, being many, are one body, so also is Christ. ... 14 For the body is not one member but many. 15 If the foot should say, 'Because I am not hand, I am not of the body,' is it therefore not of the body? ... 18 But now hath God set the members every one of them in the body, as it hath pleased him ... 23 And those members of the body, which we think to be less honourable, upon these we bestow more abundant honour; and our uncomely parts have more abundant comeliness. 24 For our comely parts have no need: but God hath tempered the body together, having given more abundant honour to that part which lacked:[15]

---

15 Available at: ebible.org/study/?w1=bible&t1=local:wbp&v1=JN1_1.

12

Yapa-kurlangu-rlu	palka-ngku	ka	marda-rni	jurru	rdaka-jarra,
person-POSS-ERG	body-ERG	AUX.PRS	have-NPST	head	hand-DU
wirliya-jarra	manu	panu-kari.	Panu=juku	ka-lu	jinta-jarri-mi
foot-DU	and	many-other	many=still	AUX.PRS-they	one-become-NPST
yapa-ngka	palka-ngka	jinta-ngka=juku.	Ngula-piya-yijala		Jesus Christ=ji
person-LOC	body-LOC	one-LOC=still	that-like-too		JC=TOP
manu	ngalipa	yapa	nyanungu-nyangu.		
and	1.PL.INCL	person	he-POSS		

Literally: 'A person's body has a head, two hands, two feet and many other (things). While they are many they are one in a person's one body. So like that too is Jesus Christ and we his people.' (our interlinearisation and back-translation)

14 *Yapa-kurlangurlu palkangku-ka mardarni jurru, rdaka-jarra, wirliya-jarra manu panu-kari. Panu-juku kalu jinta-jarrimi yapangka palkangka jintangka-juku.*

Literally: 'A person's body has a head, two hands, two feet and many others. The many are united in a person's single body.'

18 *God-rlu-ngalpa palka kardu-manu jurru-kurlu, rdaka-jarra-kurlu, wirliya-jarra-kurlu manu panu-kari-kirli, ngulaku-ngarntiji kamparru-juku jirringi-yirrarnu-wiyi nyarrparlu yungu-ngalpa jinta-maninjarla yirrarni palkangka jintangka ngalipa-nyangurla jurru, rdaka-jarra, wirliya-jarra manu panu-karirlangu.*

Literally: 'God made our body(/bodies) with a head, with two hands/arms, with two feet and with many others, ready for that he first decided how, having made us one, to put us in our one body a head, two hands/arms, two feet and many others too.'

23 *Yapangku marda kajika manngu-nyanyi pinti ngulaju nganta nyirntinyirnti nganta. Kujarlaju kajika-nyanu maparni jarangku karalypa-kardalku. Manu kajika-nyanu marda ngarntapiri nyanjarla kurntaku ngurrju-mani. Ngula-kujaku kanyanu parnta-yirrarni wawarda kurntangka yapa-patu-kari-kijakurlangu.* **24** *Yinngirri manu jurru wakurlu, ngulaju marda kajika-nyanu miimii-nyanyi yuntardi nganta. Kujarlaju, kula kanyanu parnta-yirrarni. Jijaji Kiraji-kirlangu yapa, ngulaju karlipa nyina turnu jintangka-juku. Kujarlaju kajilpa-nyanu nganangku-puka Kirijinirli ngurrju-pajikarla Kirijini-kari-piya-wangu nganta, ngulaju jarrwara-nyayirni! Kaaturlu kangalpa turnu-maninjarla jinta-kurra-mani, ngula-jangkarluju yungurlipa-jana warrawarra-kanyi Kirijini-kariyi-nyanu yangka rampaku.*

Literally: **23** 'A person might perceive skin as rough. So he might rub himself smooth with fat. And on seeing his groin he might perhaps make himself ashamed. To avoid that he covers himself with clothes out of shame so that others can't (see it) either.' **24** 'His face and head hair, he might take a long look at thinking how good-looking he is. So he doesn't cover (that part of) himself. Jesus Christ's people, we are together in one. Thus whatever Christian calls himself "good" thinking he's not like other Christians, that is very wrong! God gathers and unites us, so that we look after other Christians—those weak (ones).'

ENVOI

Anna Wierzbicka's life

Kevin Windle and Mary Besemeres

Anna Wierzbicka's early life, like that of most of her generation in Poland, was dominated by war and Nazi occupation, with all that that entailed. Born Anna Smoleńska in Warsaw in 1938, she was one year old when Poland was invaded, and the family would spend the next five years in the occupied city, which meant that her childhood vocabulary was enriched by terms such as *łapać* (to catch, round up) and the related noun *łapanka* (round-up, mass arrest). After the failure of the Warsaw Rising in the autumn of 1944, the Germans razed most of the remaining buildings and deported the surviving non-combatants to forced labour in Germany. Anna's father Tadeusz and mother Maria were separated, and Maria, Anna and her elder sister Marta taken to Hamelin, where the women were put to work sewing blankets for the Wehrmacht at a local factory. The children spent their time chasing the rats that abounded along the Weser and in the barrack huts in which they lived—this being the home town of the Pied Piper—and (in some cases) roasting their captives on bonfires. The labour camp food was turnip soup, which Anna liked.

On 14 March 1945 an allied daylight bombing raid destroyed much of the city and caused many casualties. As Anna recalled: 'Everything was on fire and the roofs were falling in.' She sought refuge under the doubtful protection of a bush, but was soon found unharmed by her very relieved mother. A few hours later, soldiers of the US Army reached Hamelin. 'They gave chewing gum and chocolate to us children,' Anna remembers.[1]

The war over, the Smoleński family was reunited and returned to Poland, first to Bytom in Silesia, then to the ruined capital in 1947.

---

1 Anna Goc, 'Przekładanie siebie' [Translating oneself], *Tygodnik powszechny*, 31 August, 2015. Available at: www.tygodnikpowszechny.pl/przekladanie-siebie-29914.

From an early age, Anna was fascinated by dictionaries and the Polish language, encouraged by her father, an engineer by training, with a great interest in language. With her father's help she composed humorous poems about their family.

Poland was now firmly under Soviet control and Marxist ideology increasingly dominated every sphere of life. Popular resistance could only be of the passive and sullen variety.

In 1954, at the age of only 16, on the strength of an outstanding school record, Anna was admitted to Warsaw University to study Polish philology, although she had refused to join the regime-run League of Polish Youth—a requirement for university entry. Stalin had died in March 1953, but remained the object of compulsory posthumous reverence as 'the coryphaeus of all the sciences', in the words of a satirical song. Linguistics was not exempt: he had published his views on the subject in *Pravda* under the title 'Marxism and problems of linguistics' (*Pravda*, 2 August, 1950). However, Marxism had made only limited inroads into the field of Anna's interest at the time: historical linguistics, the history of Polish grammar, the Slavonic languages and Polish literature, in particular poetry. These were taught by distinguished scholars who managed to protect the integrity of their disciplines and resist ideological contamination. She recalls them with much affection and gratitude, in particular Maria Renata Mayenowa, a specialist in poetry, and Zofia Szmydtowa, who introduced her to classics of world literature, from Homer to Cervantes.

Anna was never one to fear speaking her mind. Friends recall that she took the part of students who were being harassed by the authorities, and openly opposed the anti-Semitic campaigns that characterised the period. Always uncompromising in matters of conviction, she did not hide her devotion to Catholicism, even at times when discretion made it advisable.

During her studies she met Piotr Wierzbicki, a budding writer and scholar, whom she would marry immediately after graduation.

Anna was in her third year of university when the country was shaken by something resembling a revolution, later to be known as the Polish October, in 1956. This was a direct consequence of Khrushchev's exposure of Stalin's crimes in the Soviet Union, and the onset of the ensuing cultural 'Thaw'. The result in Poland, to an even greater extent than in the USSR, was a period of increased intellectual ferment and relative freedom. In the universities, the official ideology seemed to be in retreat, and scholars who had been banished from Academe were permitted to return.

After graduating from the university, Anna took up an offer of academic work in the Institute of Literary Studies, in the section headed by Professor Mayenowa, studying language and literary genres. Under Professor Mayenowa's supervision, she defended a doctoral thesis that drew together literary study and linguistics in a study of the syntactic and stylistic system of Polish Renaissance prose. She would go on to a higher doctorate, known in Poland as *habilitacja*, awarded on the basis of her book *Dociekania semantyczne* (*Semantic Investigations*), which laid out her new linguistic interest. Some of her colleagues and lifelong friends from this period were Lucylla Pszczołowska, Elżbieta Janus, Teresa Dobrzyńska, Jadwiga Wajszczuk and Zofia Zaron.

It was Professor Mayenowa who introduced Anna to academic life and the intellectual and scholarly environment of Warsaw and other centres, and arranged for her to spend six months in Moscow in 1964–65. There she met some of the pioneers of a new school of Russian linguistics, in particular Igor Melčuk and Juri Apresjan, who were then becoming known for their work in the field of semantics. Their friendship and companionship in linguistic research she sees as one of the greatest gifts life has given her. A fluent speaker of Russian, she would later say of this period: 'My time in Moscow also awakened an interest in Russian culture and language, which has stayed with me all my life.'

The friendships from her time in Moscow also endured throughout her life. Igor Melčuk recalls her preparing to fly to Moscow in 1977, laden with gifts of food, books and presents for children:

> The suitcases were already full, and she went on hanging all kinds of bags on her shoulders, round her neck, on her arms—that left only her teeth free—and she ran to the plane weighed down by an extra 15 kilograms.

A pivotal moment in Anna's development as a linguist came in 1964 when Andrzej Bogusławski, whom she described as 'the most original thinker I had ever met', delivered a lecture at Warsaw University with the title 'On the foundations of semantics'. His central idea came as a revelation, contained in the word 'indefinibilia', the hypothesis of the existence of a few dozen basic concepts, innate and universal, on which the meanings of all words in all languages and all human thought are built. This idea was to become the principal focus of her subsequent scholarly work. As she related:

> Bogusławski's hypothesis was in tune with an idea of Leibniz's, the idea of an 'alphabet of human thoughts' (*alphabetum cogitationum humanorum*). To Leibniz, however, this was a purely theoretical and speculative idea. Bogusławski, on the other hand, was proposing to make it the basis of modern semantics.

From these ideas sprang the current of thought that would define Anna's future research. As she has said: 'Everything I've done since has been based on the key idea of that lecture.' Her aim would be to reconstruct Leibniz's 'alphabet of human thought'. Her aim in doing so reached beyond philosophy and scholarship: the understanding to be obtained held potential benefits for human society as a whole. As she puts it:

> Simple indefinable concepts form the basis of simple, broadly comprehensible explanations in every sphere of life, as well as a basis for improved communication among people from different cultures. In my view, an innate and universal alphabet of human thought also gives us a tool with which to understand, and above all to think in any field, be it ethics, discussion of values, law, psychology, cultural research, international relations etc.

In 1966, Anna secured a post-doctoral stipend to spend a year at the Massachusetts Institute of Technology (MIT), with the support of the Russian linguist and literary theorist Roman Jakobson. At MIT she familiarised herself with the work of Noam Chomsky, whose generative grammar was then causing much excitement in the world of linguistics. As she tells it, this gave her

> a year in which to confirm to myself that I did not want to do what the Chomskyans proposed … The generativists focused on linguistic form, whereas I was also interested in the people who use language, and the meanings they impart to the words they utter.

She was confirmed in her intention of engaging with semantics and seeking fundamental human concepts.

On her way home to Poland, she was able to spend a few weeks in Oxford, thanks to the support of the renowned philosopher and historian Isaiah Berlin, and there she met John Besemeres, an Australian postgraduate working in Slavonic studies, with whom she remained in touch, despite obstacles imposed by censorship and what Anna would remember as 'the political events of the terrible year 1968'. That was the year of student demonstrations in Poland, a virulent anti-Semitic campaign in response, and the Warsaw Pact invasion of Czechoslovakia. At the end of August, while 'fraternal assistance' was suppressing opposition in Prague, the International Semiotic Symposium was held in Warsaw. Anna delivered her paper wearing a red blouse, white skirt and blue stockings, the colours of the state flag of Czechoslovakia, and in her paper examined alternative terms that define a speaker's point of view, such as 'spy' vs 'intelligence agent', and 'fraternal assistance' vs 'invasion'.

In 1970, by which time Anna was divorced from Piotr Wierzbicki, she and John Besemeres were able to marry in a civil ceremony in Belgrade, where John was then working as a translator. They returned to Poland together, and a church wedding was held in the Franciscan chapel in Laski, a unique centre of Catholic intellectual and spiritual life known in communist times as a refuge for dissidents. Two years later, their daughter Mary was born in Warsaw, and in December 1972 all three moved to Canberra, where Anna and John's second daughter Clare was born in 1975.

As Anna herself puts it in a piece for the Polish Science Foundation that awarded her a prize in 2010, she identifies Warsaw with the first half of her life and Canberra with the second. In 1973 she was appointed lecturer at The Australian National University (ANU) in Canberra, where she would soon become a pillar of the very strong linguistics team and remain until her retirement in 2016, maintaining a steady output of scholarly work throughout those years and not ceasing in retirement. The position opened up to her a whole new world of unfamiliar languages—Indigenous Australian languages through the work of her colleagues, such as Jane Simpson and Harold Koch, as well as Chinese, Japanese, Korean and Malay among others—the mother tongues of many of her international students. Some of those students, over the years, have included Rie Hasada, Yuko Asano, Ryo Stanwood, Kyung-Joo Yoon, Adrian Tien, Gian Marco Farese and Rui Shen.

In Canberra, Anna and John made close friends among the local Polish community, including Ola and Jerzy Zubrzycki, Irena Żywczak, Nina and Krzysztof Zagórski, Grażyna Żurkowska, Maciej Ciołek and Irena Golc, Marysia and Krzysztof Tarłowski and Maria Sikorska. In 1982, with Peter Hill, John co-founded the department of Slavonic Studies at Macquarie

University, and taught Polish Studies there until 1985, commuting between Sydney and Canberra. In 1983, Anna, Mary and Clare joined him in Sydney for six months. In 1996, Anna was appointed a Humboldt Fellow at Cologne in Germany, and John, Mary and Clare accompanied her there for six months.

Perhaps the most significant element of Anna's professional life in Australia has been her collaborative work with Cliff Goddard, who, as she writes in her piece for the Polish Science Foundation, was her student and, initially, an 'opponent' in the 1970s but from the 1980s her frequent co-author and the co-founder of the Natural Semantic Metalanguage (NSM) approach, which posits a core set of basic, indefinable and universal human concepts. Together with Cliff and other colleagues (many of them also former students) such as Deborah Hill, Felix Ameka, Jean Harkins, Carol Priestley, Bert Peeters, Jock Onn Wong, Anna Gladkova, Zhengdao Ye, Helen Bromhead, Zuzanna Bułat Silva and Sandy Habib, Anna has conducted research across a wide range of languages into the cross-translatability of NSM, continually updating and refining it accordingly.

In 2004, with her daughter Mary, Anna convened a symposium at Curtin University, which led to the publication of their co-edited volume *Translating Lives: Living with Two Languages and Cultures* (University of Queensland Press, 2007), a collection of personal essays by bilingual Australian authors, including the writers Kim Scott and Eva Sallis, and the linguists Michael Clyne and Zhengdao Ye. Anna's own contribution, entitled 'Two languages, two cultures, one (?) self: Between Polish and English', reports on her experience of struggling to translate her Polish emotional world into English. She gives the example of being asked by Australian friends about her baby granddaughter Elżbietka (who at that time lived in Perth), and being lost for words: English terms like 'cute' and 'adorable' had no emotional resonance for her and felt fake, while the diminutives she would naturally use in Polish (e.g. 'loczki', little curls) were unavailable in English.

Two of Anna's particular passions over the past two decades have been the English language in cultural and historical perspective, and theology and biblical studies.

Her work on English probes the cultural assumptions that (she argues) underpin key concepts like 'evidence', and the dangers of ethnocentrism, given the global status of English. To date, she has published, in addition to numerous articles, three major works in this field: *English: Meaning and Culture* (2006); *Experience, Evidence, and Sense: The Hidden Cultural Legacy of English* (2010) and *Imprisoned in English: The Hazards of English as a Default Language* (2014).

Anna's work in theology combines her love of semantics with her Christian faith. In 2001, she published *What did Jesus Mean? Explaining the Sermon on the Mount and the Parables in Simple and Universal Human Concepts* (Oxford University Press). Drawing on biblical studies, including the work of Jewish scholars, the book interprets Jesus's sayings in the Sermon on the Mount and the parables, and translates them from the original Greek of the Gospels into NSM. Anna's latest book is *What Christians Believe: A Story of God and People* (Oxford University Press, 2019; Polish edition: Znak, 2017). It consists of a retelling—using 'Minimal English'—of key episodes in the Hebrew Scriptures and the New Testament, which together, Anna argues, convey the central meanings of Christianity.

Throughout the 1980s and 1990s, Anna returned every couple of years to Poland to visit her mother Maria and sister Marta, and Marta's family (husband Adam and children Ania, Michał, and Asia), in Miedzeszyn, outside Warsaw. On two occasions, Anna's mother ('Babcia Marysia' to her grandchildren) came out to Australia to stay with her for several months. If home alone, Babcia Marysia would invariably answer the phone in French, as she spoke no English. She died in 1999, aged 100.

Anna is herself a loving and intensely devoted grandmother to six grandchildren: (in chronological order) Elizabeth (born in 2002, and named for Anna's childhood friend Elżbieta Galewska), Nicholas (2005), Catherine (2008), Therese (2010) and twins John and Benedict (2015). While Mary was living with her husband Nigel in Perth, Anna visited frequently for weeks at a time to help look after their children Lizzie and Nick. She taught both of them to read, using the Bible, and has read countless books with them and Clare and Phil's daughters Catherine and Therese, most recently, with Nick, *Uncle Tom's Cabin*. Drawing on sayings of Clare and Phil's toddlers John and Ben, she has provisionally outlined five stages of how young children think, in NSM. For example: 'I can be there, I want this'—would be John or Ben gazing purposefully through the baby-gate blocking their entrance to the kitchen.

Since 2016, Anna has been a Professor Emerita in the School of Literature, Languages and Linguistics at ANU. Although formally retired, she continues to research and publish, to supervise graduate students and give guest lectures in undergraduate linguistics courses, and leads a weekly open seminar in semantics and theology.

Index

Note: Numbers in italics indicate tables or illustrations; footnotes are indicted by 'n'.

Adams, Douglas, 293
address studies, 85–88
    cultural meaning, 88, 95–96
    royalty, 89–90, 91, 94, 95
    T-V pronouns, 85, 86, 87
adjectives
    absence of, 341–342
    classes of, 343–345
    defining, 341–346
    degree modification, 345
    positioning, 343–345
    semantic cores, 341, 345
    stative verbs, 342–343
    universality, 341, 345–346, 350
advice, 432–435
aesthetics
    cultural scripts, 165–167
    visual terms, 155–156, 158–159, 161, 164, 165, 167
African languages. *see* Ewe
alphabet of human thoughts, 1, 496
altercentric reference usage, 284–285
Amele, 323
American Sign Language (ASL), 292, 296
Arrente, 467–468, 476
Asian languages. *see* Chinese; Japanese
aspect (grammatical), 18, 324, 349
Asperger's syndrome, 297

Australian English. *see also bushfire* analysis; *migrant* analysis
    corpus for study, 139
    migrant education, 150–152
    use of *migrant,* 141–147, 148–150
    weather and climate events, 115, 116–119, 125–127, 128–130
Austronesian languages. *see* Chamorro
avos' analysis, 406, 413

Basque. *see also chirrinta* analysis; *ciriquiar* analysis
    culture-specific terms, 196
    geographic distribution, 197n
    loanwords into Spanish, 193, 195–196, 207
    residual lexicon, 195
biculturalism, 251n5
bilingualism, 196, 495
birrimbirr analysis, 266–268. *see also mind* analysis
    connotations of 'goodness', 266–267
    explication, 267
    usage, 265
    Yolngu spirituality, 267–268
bojio analysis. *see also kiasu* analysis
    cultural keyword, 103–104
    cultural scripts, 108–109
    cultural values, 111–112

etymology, 104
examples, 104–107
explications, 107, 109
jio comparison, 106–107
jio explications, 108
meaning, 102–103
relationship with *kiasu,* 107
usage, 103–106, 110
Borges, Jorge Luis, 294–295
borrowings in language, 193, 195–196, 207. *see also chirrinta* analysis; *ciriquiar* analysis
British Sign Language (BSL), 292
buku analysis, 258–260
Bulgakov, Mikhail, 410
bushfire analysis
    Australian responses, 125–127
    bush analysis, 120, 124
    climate event terms, 117
    compared with *wildfire,* 115, 127
    cultural keyword, 118–119
    cultural scripts, 116, 125–128
    definition, 115, 118
    examples, 120–122
    explications, 123–124, 126–127
    geographic distribution, 129
    Indigenous Australians, 116–117
    role in Australian history, 116–118
    role in Australian identity, 125, 128–129
    semantic encoding, 127
    usage, 119–123

calques, 409
Cape York languages, 280–283
capitalism
    austerity, 314–315
    Chicago Board of Trade (CBOT), 312–313
    definition, 308
    as discourse, 309
    gambling, 308, 310, 312
    and identity, 313–314
    metaphors, 310–312
    participation in, 316
    and reality, 313, 316
    role of luck, 310–311
    role of risk, 312–314
    role of rules, 309–310
carità analysis
    Christian meaning, 175–180, 189
    cultural values, 189–190
    examples, 176–177, 178, 180, 182, 184, 185–186, 187, 188
    explications, 179–180, 183, 185, 186, 187, 188
    idiomatic usage, 180–188
    phraseological meanings, 181–188, 189–190
    polysemy, 174, 180, 189
    values, 177–178
Chamorro, 343
Chinese, 110, 222–223
chirrinta analysis, 197–202
    culturally specific, 207
    definition, 197–198
    examples, 198, 199
    explications, 201–202
    prototypical use, 200–201
    usage, 198, 199–200
Chomsky, Noam, 496
chou analysis
    compared with *saudade,* 222–223
    explication, 222
Christianity, 499
    influence on Italian culture, 173, 189–190
    in Italian idiom, 173–174
    meaning of *carità,* 175–180
    translation, 175n
ciriquiar analysis, 202–206
    culturally specific, 203, 207
    definition, 202–203, 204
    examples, 204
    explication, 206
    geographic distribution, 202
    prototypical use, 203–206
    usage, 204–205

classifiers, 340
climb analysis, 14–16
   covert alternation, 28–29
   examples, 20–22, 26, 27–28
   explications, 19, 20, 21, 23–25, 27, 29
   frequency in English, 20
   non-human actors, 21
   numbers, 22
   prototypical scenario, 25–26
   semantic base meaning, 22–26
   usage, 19–23, 25–29
   variations in meaning, 19–30
closeness (social)
   advice, 432–435
   communication style, 429–435
   cultural scripts, 430
   examples, 425, 427–428, 431–432, 433–434
   friendship, 426
   individuality, 427, 431, 432–433
   invitations, 430–432
   perceptions of, 423
   phrases, 424–426
   physical closeness, 429
   sense of elbow, 425–426, 435–436
   sense of privacy, 424–425, 435
   shared identity, 427–428, 431–432, 433–434
   systemic nature of, 436
   value of, 425–426
collocation analysis
   bushfire, 121–122, 125–126
   carità, 176, 177
   chirrinta, 199
   climb, 27
   migrant, 142, 147
   nagljadest'sja, 157
   saudade, 217
   yangka, 470–471
colour, 474–475
comparative semantics
   cultural differences, 34–35
   forms of address, 93–95
   open verb analysis, 51–57

constructional semantics, 14, 17–18
   process of, 30
CORIS/CORDIS corpus, 174
corpus-based linguistics, 119–120, 139–149, 326–327, 375–377, 403–405, 465. *see also* Russian National Corpus (RNC)
cross-cultural communication, 251n5, 421, 430. *see also* translation
cross-cultural metacategories, 250, 253–255, 268–269
   soul, 266–268
cross-cultural psychology, 211
cross-cultural verb analysis, 323–325
cross-linguistic analysis. *see* comparative semantics
cultural keywords, 61–64, 78, 116–117. *see also* culture-specific words; language-specific terms
   address studies, 87, 88, 95–96
   aesthetics, 166–167
   bojio, 103–104
   bushfire, 118–119
   changes in use, 100, 111–112
   Christianity, 175
   emotion, 165–166, 215, 219, 223–224
   gezellig, 62–64, 78
   kiasu, 101
   ljubovat'sja, 165–167
   nagljadest'sja, 165–167
   privacy, 424–425, 435
   saudade, 217
   Singapore English, 99–102, 109–110
   translations, 403–404
cultural scripts
   aesthetics, 165–167
   bojio usage, 108–109
   bushfire usage, 125–128
   De usage, 94–95
   distance/closeness (social), 430

503

nagljadest'sja usage, 165
  as research methodology, 116, 422, 429–430
culture
  culture-specific communication, 422
  definition, 421–422
  impact on language, 100, 422, 429, 435
  values encoded in language, 429, 435–436
culture-specific words, 422, 436. *see also* cultural keywords; keywords
  borrowings, 196
  translation, 403
cup analysis
  definition (Oxford English Dictionary), 456
  denotation (Labov), 455
  dictionary representation (Katz), 456
  explication (Allan), 457
  explication (Goddard), 452–454
  explication (Wierzbicka), 447–450
  critique of, 450–452
cut analysis
  context, 362–365, 369, 370, 374–375, 376
  defining, 362–365
  distinctions concealed by English translation, 365–377
  examples, 358, 361, 363, 365, 368–369, 370–374
  general *cut* verbs, 370–372, 373–374, 375–376
  lack of correspondence to English, 356
  specific *cut* verbs, 363–365, 376
  transitivity, 360–362
  types of *cut,* 364
  usage, 366–367, 369, 374–375
  verbs used, *358–359*

Danish. *see also De* analysis
  address studies, 88–91
  contrasted with German, 93–94
  egalitarianism, 89, 95
  politeness, 92
  royal family, 89–90, 91, 94, 95
  sarcasm, 94–95
De analysis
  address categories, 88–89
  comparison with *Sie,* 93–95
  cultural scripts, 94–95
  examples, 90–91
  explications, 93, 94, 95
  reactions to, 92
  usage, 89–92
derivational bases, 17–18
Dharumba, 275–276
diminutives, 66, 74
direct speech
  definition, 291
  in signed languages, 295–296, 298
discourses, 309
distance (social)
  advice, 432–435
  communication style, 429–435
  cultural scripts, 430
  examples, 425, 427–428, 431–432, 433–434
  friendship, 426
  individuality, 427, 431, 432–433
  invitations, 430–432
  perceptions of, 423
  phrases, 424–426
  physical closeness, 429
  sense of elbow, 425–426, 435–436
  sense of privacy, 424–425, 435
  shared identity, 427–428, 431–432, 433–434
  systemic nature of, 436
  value of, 425–426
djambatj analysis, 257
Dostoyesvky, Fyodor, 407–408

Dowty, David, 16
Dutch. *see also gezellig* analysis
    cultural keywords, 62–64, 78
    linguaculture, 78
    Natural Semantic Metalanguage (NSM) analysis, 62, 81–94
    semantic primes, 80–81

embodiment, 321
emotions
    duration, 215–216, 223
    intensity, 215, 217
    time and, 211, 219, 220
endangered languages, 355
English. *see also* Australian English; *climb* analysis; *cup* analysis; distance (social); *game* analysis; *privacy* analysis; sensing (physiological); Singapore English
    adjectives, 341, 345
    bias of, 86, 109, 216, 355
    as culture-free medium, 78
    grammar, 22–23
    as metalanguage, 441–442
    politeness studies, 429–430, 436
ešče analysis, 411–412
European languages. *see also under* individual languages
    adjectives, 341
    diversity of, 87
    German, 93–94
    Greek, 342, 344–345
    Polish, 219–220
    T-V pronouns, 85, 86, 87
Event Stage, 293–294, 295
Ewe. *see also open* analysis
    comparison with Longgu, 51–57
    constituent ordering, 34
    ke analysis, 37–39, 51–53
    open verbs, 36–44
    serial verb construction (SVC), 34
    vu analysis, 39–44, 53–54
explications
    analysis of, 25–26
    birrimbirr, 267

bojio, 107, 109
bushfire, 123–124, 126–127
carità, 179–180, 183, 185, 186, 187, 188
chirrinta, 201–202
chou, 222
ciriquiar, 206
climb, 19, 20, 21, 23–25, 27, 29
    for comparison, 51–57
    construction, 17
    critiques of, 450–452, 454–455
cup, 447–454, 457
De, 93, 94, 95
game, 307
gezellig
    activity attribute, 73
    atmosphere attribute, 69
    in Dutch, 81–83, 84
    event attribute, 75
    human attribute, 77
    period of time attribute, 76
    place attribute, 67, 84
    reference to bustle, 71
jio, 108
kiasu, 101
ljubovat'sja, 164
migrant, 146, 148–149
mind, 251, 252
morriña, 221
nagljadest'sja, 160
no da (のだ), 240, 242, 243
nouns, 338
open
    avure, 47–48
    comparison, 51–52, 53–54
    ke, 38
    tavangia, 50–51
    vu, 43–44
pragmatically necessary particles, 413
saudade, 218
tęsknota, 220
toska, 407n4
extended meanings, 19–22

false friends, 250
Fillmore, Charles, 14–15
first language acquisition, 327
folk aesthetics, 155, 157, 167
FOMO (fear of missing out), 102

game analysis
    and capitalism, 308, 313, 314–316
    definition, 305–306, 315
    explication, 307
    Manser typology, 306
    and reality, 305–306, 315
    relationship to capitalism, 308–315
    role of luck, 307
    role of rules, 307, 308, 309–312
    Rowe typology, 304–305
    Wittgenstein, Ludwig, 304
generative grammar, 496
    generative syntax, 334–335
German, 93–94
German Sign Language (SL), 292, 296
gestures, 297
gezellig analysis
    comparison with *hygge*, 67
    cultural keyword, 62–64, 78
    difficulty in translating, 62–63
    etymology, 63
    examples, 65–67, 68, 69–71, 72–73, 74–77
    explications
        activity attribute, 73
        atmosphere attribute, 69
        in Dutch, 81–83, 84
        event attribute, 75
        human attribute, 77
        period of time attribute, 76
        place attribute, 67, 84
        reference to bustle, 71
    geographic distribution, 64
    iconic status, 64
    usage, 62, 67, 69, 71–72, 73–74, 75–77
    variations in meaning, 65–77, 78

globalisation, 195
glottochronology, 444
grammatical ordering, 22–23
grammaticalisation, 324
Greek, 342, 344–345

head marking languages, 34
How it Happens. *see* Manner (semantic template)
hypernymy, 370

idioms, 349
Indigenous Australian languages. *see also* Warlpiri; Yolngu Matha
    Arrernte, 467–468, 476
    Cape York languages, 280–283
    Dharumba, 275–276
    Jaminjung, 347, 348, 349
    Linngithigh, 283, 286, 287
    Ngangaruku, 279–280, 286
    Ngarrindjeri, 277–279, 286
    Tjungundji, 283
    Wik Mungkan, 280–283, 286, 287
indirect speech
    definition, 291
    in signed languages, 295–296
inflection, 108n, 336–337
intercultural communication, 251n5, 421, 430. *see also* translation
interjection, 102–103, 104, 181, 189
interpretation of signs and speech, 35–36
interrogation, 298
invitations, 430–432
Italian. *see also carità* analysis
    acquisition of, 328
    CORIS/CORDIS corpus, 174
    idioms, 174
    influence of Christianity on, 173–174, 189
    role of Christian values, 189–190
Italian Sign Language (SL), 292, 295

Jackendoff, Ray, 15
Jaminjung, 347, 348, 349
Japanese. *see also no da (のだ)* analysis
　adjectives, 343
　learning, 230
　particles, 230, 234–235, 236n, 239–240, 243

Kalam. *see also* sensing (physiological)
　compared with English, 399–400
　grammatical structure, 389, 398–399
　nŋ (verb of perception), 390–391
　orthography, 389n7
　senses (physiological), 390–400
　speakers, 389
Kanjobolan, 340
keywords, 61–64, 78, 116–117. *see also* culture-specific words; language-specific terms
　address studies, 87, 88, 95–96
　aesthetics, 166–167
　bojio, 103–104
　bushfire, 118–119
　changes in use, 100, 111–112
　Christianity, 175
　emotion, 165–166, 215, 219, 223–224
　gezellig, 62–64, 78
　kiasu, 101
　ljubovat'sja, 165–167
　nagljadest'sja, 165–167
　privacy, 424–425, 435
　saudade, 217
　Singapore English, 99–102, 109–110
　translations, 403–404
kiasu analysis, 101–102. *see also bojio* analysis
　cultural keyword, 101
　cultural values, 110–112
　explication, 101
kinship terminology
　affinal terms, 274–280, 281n16, 282–283, 284–285, 287
　consanguineal, 274, *282,* 283, 285, 287
　Dharumba, 275–276
　educating children, 284
　etiquette, 285
　etymology, 287
　geographic distribution, 283
　grandkin terms, 276, 277–280, 281
　in-law terms, 274–280, 281n16, 282–283, 284–285, 287
　Indigenous Australian characteristics of, 273–275, 287
　as insight into communication strategies, 284–286, 287
　Linngithigh, 283, 286, 287
　Natural Semantic Metalanguage (NSM), 286
　Ngangaruku, 279–280, 286
　Ngarrindjeri, 275, 277–279, 280, 286
　polysemy, 285
　pragmatic explanation, 284–285
　relationship abbreviations, *274*
　semantic analysis, 285–286
　subjects of, 274–275
　taboo avoidance, 285
　Tjungundji, 283
　Wik Mungkan, 280–283, 286, 287

Lahiri, Jhumpa, 328
language
　as abstract system, 320, 329
　conventionalisation, 296, 298–299
　endangered languages, 355
　grammaticalisation, 324
　iconicity, 296, 298
　individual changes in use, 327–328
　influence of life circumstances, 328
　origins, 292, 296 (*see also* paralanguage)

language acquisition, 327, 328
language-specific terms, 403–405.
   see also culture-specific words;
   keywords
   autosemantic units, 411, 414–417
      (*see also toska* analysis)
   challenges in translation, 405,
      417–418
   discourse markers, 411–414
   translation of, 405–411
Leibniz, Gottfried Wilhelm, 1, 496
Leopold, Werner F., 327
Levin, Beth, 15
Lexical Functional Grammar, 334
lexicalisation, 45, 266, 287, 390, 474,
   479
lexicogrammar, 14
Lexicosyntactic Frame (semantic
   template), *17*, 18, 260
   used for comparison, 51–52
linguistic artefacts, 215, 223
linguistics
   aggregate data, 326
   cognitive linguistics, 321, 322
   comparative studies, 422
   corpus-based analysis, 119–120,
      139–149, 326–327, 375–377,
      403–405, 465 (*see also* Russian
      National Corpus (RNC))
   data gathering, 356–359
   embodiment, 321
   experientialist approach, 320–
      325, 321n
   first language acquisition, 327
   glottochronology, 444
   human-oriented research, 123,
      322–325, 369, 375
   identifying parts of speech,
      333–337
   individual-oriented research,
      325–329
   language acquisition, 328
   metalanguage, 441
   natural languages, 461
   observations of usage, 369
   research approaches, 320, 375–
      377, 422, 429–430
   role of speakers and writers,
      319–320
   semantic theory, 442
   Swadesh list, 443–444
Linngithigh, 283, 286, 287
liya analysis, 257
ljubovat'sja analysis
   compared with *krasivyj,* 164
   cultural keywords, 165–167
   definition, 161
   difficulty in translating, 155, 161
   examples, 161–163
   explication, 164
   semantic analysis, 161–164
   usage, 161–163
loanwords, 193, 195–196, 207.
   see also chirrinta analysis; *ciriquiar*
   analysis
Longgu. *see also open* analysis
   avure analysis, 45–48, 51–53
   comparison with Ewe, 51–57
   constituent ordering, 34
   open verbs, 45–51
   serial verb construction (SVC), 34
   tavangia analysis, 48–51, 53–54
   vuresia analysis, 45–48

Manam, 324
Manner (semantic template), 15, *17,*
   18, 23, 25n
Marxism, 494
Mayan languages. *see* Kanjobolan
meaning
   context-dependence, 294–295
   interpretation, 35–36
   as tool to understanding, 4
metalanguage, 441–442
metalinguistics, 296
metaphor, 129, 258–260, 316
   as barrier to analysis, 175
   game, 310–312

metonymy, 41
migrant analysis
　compared with *immigrant,* 141, 147–148
　corpus used, 139–141
　countries of origin, 142–143
　definition, 136, 141, 148
　English-speaking, 151–152
　examples, 142, 143–144, 145, 148
　explications, 146, 148–149
　Heritage Museum of the Bonegilla Migrant Experience, 150–151
　institutional usage, 149–150
　marked and unmarked, 152
　modifiers used, 143, 144–145
　positive portrayal of, 143–144, 152
　rates of migration in Australia, 135–136
　role in Australia, 150–151
　usage, 141–145, 148, 152n20–21
mimetic performance, 291
mind analysis. *see also birrimbirr* analysis
　conceptualisation of, 250–253
　cross-cultural analysis, 251, 264–266, 268–269
　definition, 249–250
　European theory, 250
　explications, 251, 252
　knowledge, 261, 265–266
　mind–soul complex, 253
　relationship to body, 250–251, 256
　relationship to soul, 253, 261–262, 264, 265, 266–268, 269
　usage among Yolngu, 262–264
　Yolngu conceptions of, 251–253
　in Yolngu Matha, 255, 256–260, 265
minimal pairs, 256
modifiers, 343
morriña analysis
　compared with *saudade,* 220–221
　explication, 221

*mu*ḻ*kurr* analysis, 257
multilingualism, 196

nagljadest'sja analysis
　adjectival form, 159
　aesthetic appreciation, 158–159
　cultural keywords, 165–167
　cultural scripts, 165
　definition, 156, 157
　difficulty in translating, 155, 156
　examples, 157–159
　explications, 160
　negative use, 157–158
　polysemy, 159
　semantic analysis, 156–160
　usage, 156–159
Natural Semantic Metalanguage (NSM), 1. *see also* culture-specific words; explications; keywords; language-specific terms; semantic primes
　address studies, 87, 95
　allolexes, 445, 475
　approach to linguistics, 322
　bias avoidance, 61, 78, 211–212
　childhood development, 499–500
　and Christianity, 189
　culture-specific words, 207
　emotions, 215
　keywords, 61–62
　and nouns, 138
　origins of, 498
　prolixity, 457
　purpose of, 14, 443, 455–456
　Strong Lexicalisation Hypothesis, 475
　time, 212–214
　verb semantics, 17–18
　word classes, 333–334
nebos' analysis, 413–414
neoliberalism, 308, 314
neuželi analysis, 413
Ngangaruku, 279–280, 286
Ngarrindjeri, 277–279, 286

no da (のだ) analysis
    difficulty in translating, 229–230
    as evidence, 232
    examples, 229, 230, 231–240, 241–242
    as explanation, 231, 234
    explications, 240, 242, 243
    listener role, 232–233, 236–240, 241–242, 243
    meaning, 230–231, 236–242
    as proposition, 233–234, 235
    role of information, 238–240
    understanding, 241–242
    usage, 236–240, 241–242
nouns
    abstract nouns, 202
    categorisation, 136–138, 336, 339
    and classifiers, 340
    defining, 338–340
    explication, 338
    and semantic primes, 138
    as universal word class, 137
    and verbs, 335, 349

object–subject–verb (OSV) structure, 393
Oceanic languages. *see* Longgu; Manam; Teop
open analysis
    avure, 45–48
    categorisation, 33–35
    comparison, 51–57
    Ewe, 36–44, 55–57
    examples, 39–43, 46, 48–50
    explications
        avure, 47–48
        comparison, 51–52, 53–54
        ke, 38
        tavangia, 50–51
        vu, 43–44
    ke, 37–39, 56–57
    Longgu, 45–51, 55–57
    semantic properties, 34–36

tavangia, 48–51, 55–56
    transitivity, 37–39, 45–48
    vuresia, 45–48, 55–56
    vu, 39–44, 56–57
Outcome (semantic template), *17*, 18, 23, 55
    used for comparison, 53

paralanguage, 296–298
    definition, 297
part (semantic prime)
    in Natural Semantic Metalanguage (NSM), 475–476
    universality of, 461, 477
    in Warlpiri, 479–481
particles, 230, 234, 243
parts of speech
    classing, 334–335
    complex words, 347–348
    defining, 333, 336–337, 350
    function, 334
    identifying, 335, 343
    meaning-based approach, 335
    Natural Semantic Metalanguage (NSM), 333–334
    structural approach, 334, 335
    universality, 351
person-oriented research, 322–329
phrasal structures
    object–subject–verb (OSV) structure, 393
    subject–object–verb (SOV) structure, 389, 393
    subject–verb–adjective (SVAdj) structure, 387
    subject–verb–object (SVO) structure, 34, 386–387, 388
    subject–verb/transitive subject–verb–object (SV/AVO) structure, 34
    verb–subject/verb–object–transitive subject (VS/VOA) structure, 34
poker, 310

Poland
    cultural keywords, 219
    Second World War, 494
    Warsaw Pact invasion of
        Czechoslovakia, 497
Polish, 219–220
politeness studies, 429–430
    cultural influence, 436
politeness theory, 85
polysemy, 475–476
    ke, 37
    necessity for understanding, 13
    vu, 39–43
Portuguese. *see also saudade* analysis
    cultural keywords, 215, 217–219
    Great Portuguese Discoveries, 223
Potential Outcome (semantic
    template), *17*, 18, 23, 55
    used for comparison, 53
pragmatically necessary particles
    definition, 411
    ešče analysis, 411–412
    explications, 413
    že analysis, 412–413
privacy analysis, 424–425, 435
pronouns, 393
propositus, 277, 282, 284, 286
prototypes, 13
Prototypical Scenario (semantic
    template), *17*, 23, 25
    emotions, 215

quotative frames, 292

Rappaport Hovav, Malka, 15
razve analysis, 413
Received Pronunciation, 327
recognitional demonstratives, 478–479
reduplication, 34, 43, 49, 347
regional variation, 129, 193–194,
    197, 197n, 202
regular expressions, 356
relational grammar, 96. *see also*
    address studies

Relevance Theory, 233
religion. *see also* Christianity
    cross-cultural definition, 254
    Yolngu spirituality, 260–262, 264,
        265–266, 267–268
rising intonation, 298
Russian. *see also* closeness (social);
    ljubovat'sja analysis; *nagljadest'sja*
    analysis
    attitude towards pleasure, 163
    autosemantic units, 414–418
    avos' analysis, 406, 413
    communication style, 429–435
    in comparison with English,
        166–167
    cultural keywords, 403, 405–418
    cultural themes, 165–167, 424,
        425–428, 435–436
    discourse makers, 403–404,
        411–414
    ešče analysis, 411–412
    language-specific expressions,
        405–418
    nebos' analysis, 413–414
    neuželi analysis, 413
    razve analysis, 413
    Russian National Corpus (RNC),
        156, 407, 410, 414, 423
    sense of elbow, 425–426, 435–436
    senses, 161
    toska analysis, 406–410, 414–417
    translated texts, 404
    verb structure, 156
    verbs of satisfaction, 156–159
    že analysis, 412–413
Russian National Corpus (RNC),
    156, 407, 410, 414, 423

sarcasm, 90, 94, 95
saudade analysis, 217–224
    collocation, 217
    compared with other emotions,
        219–223
    definition, 217

duration, 223–224
explications, 218
national identity, 217
translation, 217
semantic change, 286–287
semantic cores, 333, 350
adjectives, 341, 345
nouns, 338, 339
semantic domain, 116–117, 360
semantic extension, 374–375
semantic molecules, 17–18, 124, 201, 454–455
definition, 445–446
and meaning of nouns, 138
semantic primes
complexes, 455
definition, 442–443, 461
development of, 443–446
in different languages, 444–445
Dutch, *80–81*
list of, 9, 444–445
and meaning of nouns, 138
nouns, 339
overview, *9,* 441–446
part, 461, 475–476, 477, 479–481
polysemy, 9
pursuit of, 14
senses, 383
time, 212–214
verbs, 347, 349
Wierzbicka's pursuit of, 443–446
words, 336
semantic schematics, 14, 15–16
semantic templates, *17,* 17–18, 146
used for comparison, 51–57
semantics
cognitive semantics, 446
semantic theory, 442
study of, 441
sense of elbow, 425–426, 435–436
sense of privacy, 424–425, 435
sensing (physiological), 382
active verbs, 387–388, 394, 395, 396, 399
affective verbs, 388, 398, 399
categorising, 383
cognitive verbs, 385–387, 399
definition, 382, 386
differences in language, 399–400
in English, 385–388, 399–400
examples, 386, 387, 388, 390, 391–399
feeling, 386, 395–396
hearing, 384, 386, 392
in Kalam, 389–400
language of, 382–385, 399–400
phrase construction, 385–388, 390–399, 400
seeing, 383–384, 386, 391–392
semantic primes, 383
smelling, 384, 386, 393–394
tasting, 394–395
transitivity, 386, 390, 400
visceral senses, 382, 387, 396–398
sentence order
object–subject–verb (OSV) structure, 393
subject–object–verb (SOV) structure, 389, 393
subject–verb–adjective (SVAdj) structure, 387
subject–verb–object (SVO) structure, 34, 386–387, 388
subject–verb/transitive subject–verb–object (SV/AVO) structure, 34
verb–subject/verb–object–transitive subject (VS/VOA) structure, 34
separation verbs, 33–34
serial verb construction (SVC), 34, *371,* 373–374
signed languages
direct speech, 295–296, 298
eye contact, 292–293, 295–296, 298
indirect speech, 295–296
natural model, 296
origins, 292

Singapore English. *see also bojio*
analysis; *kiasu* analysis
cultural keywords, 101–102, 103
cultural values, 109–112
evolution of, 99–102
mianzi analysis, 110
Singlish. *see* Singapore English
social logics, 309–310
Spanish. *see also chirrinta* analysis;
ciriquiar analysis
adjectives, 344, 345
añoranza analysis, 220–221
borrowings from Basque, 193, 195–196, 207
geographic distribution, 197, 202
morriña analysis, 220–221
speech markers, 292–293
Speech Stage, 293–294, 295
Stalin, Joseph, 494
subject–object–verb (SOV) structure, 389, 393
subject–verb–adjective (SVAdj) structure, 387
subject–verb–object (SVO) structure, 34, 386–387, 388
subject–verb/transitive subject–verb–object (SV/AVO) structure, 34
subsequent language acquisition, 328
suffix marking, 277–278, 281, 389
Swadesh list, 443–444
syntactic analysis, 334–337
adjectives, 341–346
nouns, 338–340
verbs, 346–349
syntactical alterations, 16

T-V pronouns, 85, 86, 87
teknocentricity, 275, 283–287
teknonymy, 285n
Teop. *see also cut* analysis
colexification, 374
cut verbs, 358–359
description, 355
Teop Language Corpus, 355, 356–357, 375

tęsknota analysis
compared with *saudade,* 219–220
explication, 220
time
in defining emotions, 211, 214–216, 219, 220, 223–224
perception of, 216, 224
polysemy in, 214
Tjungundji, 283
tone languages, 34
toska analysis, 223n, 406–410
examples, 408, 415–416
explication, 407n4
translation, 407–410, 414–417
usage, 415–416
Trans New Guinea languages. *see* Amele; Kalam
Transformational Grammar, 334
translation
approaches, 405–406
Bible, 175n
calques, 409
cross-cultural metacategories, 268–269
cultural translation, 254–255
in data mining, 357–358
dictionary examples, 463–464
difficulties in, 254, 268, 405, 421, 463
encoded meanings lost, 369, 375–377
fiction, 407
importance of context, 464
as information source, 403–405, 418
and language-specific terms, 404, 409, 411, 417–418
pragmatic necessity, 411–413
shortcomings, 369, 404
style, 410, 417
use of metalanguage, 442
vernacular definitions, 464, 467–468, 473–474

Universal Grammar, 351
universal semantic primes. *see* semantic primes
universality, 350, 429
untranslatable, 254, 321n, 405
   gezellig, 62–64
   lexicon of bilinguals, 196
   ljubovat'sja, 155, 161
   nagljadet'sja, 155, 156–157
   no da (のだ), 229–230
   saudade, 217

verb–subject/verb–object–transitive subject (VS/VOA) structure, 34
verbs, 350. *see also climb* analysis
   active verbs, 387–388
   adverbial modifiers, 20
   affective, 385, 388, 398
   basic verbs of human life, 322–325
   cognitive, 385
   copulas, 66, 68, 342, 387, 388
   coverbs, 346–347, 348, 350, 479
   cross-linguistic examination, 55–57
   defining, 346–349
   frequency in English, 20
   grammaticalisation, 324–325
   grouping of, 360
   idiomatic prepositions, 349
   of the mind, 256
   and nouns, 335, 349
   perception, 383, 390–391
   phrasal verbs, 389
   physical activity verbs, 206
   semantic classes, 17
   semantic extension, 374–375
   semantic primes, 349
   sensing, 385–388
   separation verbs, 33–34
   serial verb construction (SVC), 34, *371*, 373–374
   stative verbs, 342–343
   transitivity, 37–39, 45–48, 360–362, 386, 390, 400

valency, 360–362
verb adjuncts, 389
verbs of satiety, 156–157, 160
vernacular definitions, 464–465, 468–474, *472*
visual semantics, 156
vocabulary, 422

Warlpiri. *see also* part (semantic prime); *yangka* analysis
   adjectives, 341–342
   colour, 474–475
   comparison of semantic domains, 472–474
   definitions in, 472–474
   Natural Semantic Metalanguage (NSM), 475–476
   and other languages, 476–478
   Paddy Patrick Jangala (PPJ), 464–467, 468–473, 481
   part (semantic prime), 479–481
   translations, 463, 480–481, 485–489
   Warlpiri Dictionary, 462
Wierzbicka, Anna
   academia, 495–496, 497–498, 500
   birth, 493
   childhood, 493
   children, 497
   collaboration with Cliff Goddard, 498
   controversy, appreciation of, 4
   divorce, 497
   doctorates, 495
   early university studies, 494–495
   faith, 494, 499
   family, 499
   grandchildren, 499
   interest in Russia, 495
   labour camp, 493
   marriage, 494, 497
   move to Australia, 497
   multilingualism, 495, 498
   political resistance, 494, 497

scope of work, 303–304
Second World War, 493
select bibliography, 5–9
semantics, 495–496
studies in English language culture, 498–499
theology, 499
travel, 495, 496–497, 499
Wik Mungkan, 280–283, 286, 287
Wittgenstein, Ludwig, 304
word classes. *see* parts of speech

yangka analysis. *see also* part (semantic prime)
collocation prediction, 470–471
colour, 474–475
compared with *nhenge,* 467–468
equivalents in related languages, 476–477, 478
examples, 463–464, 466, 467
meaning, 478–479, 481–482
monosemy, 462, 476, 481
Paddy Patrick Jangala (PPJ), 464–467, 468–473, 481
sampled texts, 485
as semantic prime part, 462
translation of, 467, 469, 471, 479
use in definitions, 465–467
use in written Warlpiri, 478–479
vernacular definitions, 464–465, 468–474, *472*
Yolngu Matha. *see also birrimbirr* analysis; *mind* analysis
art, 262–263
buku analysis, 258–260
discussion of mind, 255, 256–260, 264–266
djambatj analysis, 257
idioms, 256–260
liya analysis, 257
muḻkurr analysis, 257
role of Wangarr beings, 260–262, 264, 265–266, 267–268

že analysis, 412–413

www.ingramcontent.com/pod-product-compliance
Lightning Source LLC
Chambersburg PA
CBHW040332300426
44113CB00021B/2730